ERNEST TUBB

ERNEST TUBB

· · THE TEXAS TROUBADOUR · ·

RONNIE PUGH

DUKE UNIVERSITY PRESS   Durham   London   1996

© 1996 Duke University Press
All rights reserved
Printed in the United States of America on acid-free paper ∞
Typeset in Cheltenham by Keystone Typesetting, Inc.
Library of Congress Cataloging-in-Publication Data appear
on the last printed page of this book.

CONTENTS

PREFACE

THE APPEAL OF ERNEST TUBB

Why did I become an Ernest Tubb fan? Why does anyone? Delving into my psyche and my past for a subjective look at the great Tubb career, maybe I can answer the second question alongside the first.

My Tubb fandom was in many ways against the grain, a leap I had to make across generational and cultural barriers. I grew up in a comfortable, middle-class, East Texas home, one of three grocer's sons. A mid-baby-boomer (born 1953), I was seriously out of step with more publicized members of my generation; but then, if I hadn't been, I might never have loved Ernest Tubb. From my parents I first learned certain values that I have never seriously questioned. We were Republicans well before most Texans were, liking Ike (and Richard Nixon), at odds with our "Yellow Dog Democrat" surroundings, which had been Ernest Tubb's East Texas a generation before. Even more antithetical, perhaps, to any appreciation of Ernest Tubb was a belief instilled by my old-school Methodist parents, that decent people do not smoke or drink. It pains me to go into a nightclub to hear a country singer, though on rare occasions I have done it.

The lifestyle chronicled in so many country songs may have been worlds away from mine, but the music was always acceptable, to my parents and to me, and I warmly embraced it. It was my first and only favorite popular music, the choice of my adolescent years, and I never once wavered in the face of peer pressure from my rock-loving contemporaries. Mom loved and taught us the music of her youth—gospel that ranged from Stamps-Baxter to the Cokesbury (Methodist) Hymnal—and Dad, though not musical himself, was a big country music fan. He had actually seen Jimmie Rodgers perform in Marshall in 1932, an admirable accomplishment that I rated right up there with his attending the first All-Star game in Chicago the next year.

In the spring of 1966, I first saw Ernest Tubb on television, and Tubb's TV show soon became my hands-down favorite. I agonized when Saturday afternoon NBC baseball games of unplanned length preempted *The Ernest Tubb Show,* though I've always loved and still love baseball. Just a few weeks after meeting Tubb through television I bought my very first album, at the Famous Discount Center in my hometown of Marshall, Texas: Ernest Tubb's debut LP with Loretta Lynn. In the next few months I purchased every Tubb LP that Marshall stores carried; a few more years passed before I knew about mailorder from the Ernest Tubb Record Shop.

For years Tubb records topped my want lists, and during high school years I started tuning in the Grand Ole Opry on Saturday nights. If Ernest was on the Luzianne Coffee show at 8:30, then I'd do my best to stay up right on through the *Midnite Jamboree,* to hear his songs and to learn where he and the Texas Troubadours would be playing in coming weeks. I gladly forsook a high school band trip to Galveston, Texas, to see Tubb in person for the first time on Shreveport's *Louisiana Hayride,* March 22, 1969. Concerts that I attended were so rare as to be memorable. I guess most of his East Texas–area dates were at nightclubs like Longview's Reo Palm Isle, where I wouldn't dream of going, even if I'd been old enough—but there were always fan club publications, infrequent new records, and best of all, new *old* records.

What struck me from the beginning was Tubb's sheer staying power. At the time Tubb was still a major star and a force to be reckoned with, a full twenty-five years after his first hits. Thinking back now on those impressionable days, I recall that veterans in all walks of life fascinated me. A favorite TV show was David Wolper's *Biography;* my favorite baseball player just before his retirement was Warren Spahn, who pitched his last in 1965, the year before I discovered the great country music veteran Ernest Tubb via syndicated television. Small wonder that history later became my academic major. I could not have said just why longevity as such impressed me; I did not then infer from it such admirable qualities as perseverance, flexibility, or determination. One new Tubb record I particularly enjoyed from those days even spoke (tongue in cheek, perhaps) of his own staying power—looking ahead to the day "When My Getup Has Got Up and Gone."

It never occurred to me then that Ernest Tubb was not a "good" (i.e., "trained," "smooth," "melodious") singer; unlike the drunks hanging around the jukeboxes, I never imagined I could do as well or better. I only knew that he was fun to listen to, even on the sad songs. He enjoyed singing, and he made me enjoy his singing. I discovered him through television, and there I could plainly see a man singing right through a smile. Tubb had fun teasing his band during instrumental breaks, and he faced the camera with a succession of smiles and winks.

Only years later could I divorce that visual image from his sound sufficiently to realize a truth that his radio audience of a previous generation had perceived: Ernest Tubb sang with an audible smile. You didn't have to see him: something in that warm, drawling baritone told you he was happy.

The songs themselves had a directness, simplicity, and clarity that made them easy to understand and easy to remember. "Waltz across Texas" and "There's a Little Bit of Everything in Texas" naturally appealed to a fellow Texan. While our shared Texas origins went some distance toward cementing my admiration of Tubb, the same factor didn't help his TV show co-star Willie Nelson; I couldn't wait for the idiosyncratic Willie to quit so I could hear more of Tubb.

Ernest Tubb matched each song to the appropriate emotion. I sympathized when he sang "Our Baby's Book," and while I certainly didn't know what "I've been untrue" meant, it was as though he felt and made me feel the narrator's anguish for wrongdoings in another early favorite, "Try Me One More Time."

When I later saw Ernest Tubb on stage—several times ultimately—my admiration increased. Here was a man who'd go to almost any lengths to please his fans. He certainly pleased me, and I could tell he pleased the others who came. At his best on stage before a live audience, Tubb seemed genuinely glad that you cared enough to come; you left a concert feeling almost that you had done him a favor. That kind of favor you wanted to do more often.

Reading about Ernest Tubb in country music's periodical literature—the record of his many accomplishments and the words of praise from his peers—learning, in short, what he meant to country music certainly enhanced his appeal for me. That's still true, even after the years of research that went into this book (including those years of fandom only, which I didn't know at the time were research years). I have tried to be objective, to rise above mere fandom, in this book; but I can truthfully say that learning of Ernest Tubb's darker side, his human failings, has not lessened my esteem for him or my love for his music.

PURPOSE AND PITFALLS OF BIOGRAPHY

Biography for me was a daunting genre. Before I could attempt such an approach with Ernest Tubb (or anybody else), there were several hurdles in my own mind to jump. I agree with Albert Jay Nock's view that the only legitimate purpose of biography is to help the historian, and that too many biographies are written nowadays simply to "acquaint the public, often with great overemphasis, with a variety of matters which not only are void of historical significance, but also are preeminently none of the public's business."[1] Another reason to pause: there are great artists and writers (and surely great country singers also) whose lives apart from their work do not justify full biographies. Is it not possible to know

Ernest Tubb better from his recorded works than from anything I or anyone else might write about him? Might not a biography impede full appreciation of Tubb's work by fostering the illusion that "knowing something about a subject, even knowing a great deal about him, is the same thing, or just as good, as knowing the subject himself"?[2] So, by all means listen to Ernest Tubb's records, watch him on video before you judge any of my assessments or formulate your own from this book.

Writing about the dead has advantages too obvious to mention here. But it has many pitfalls also. When the available factual record is incomplete (as it always is)—when Tubb, let's say, has taken to his grave a crucial fact about a certain song—how do biographers resist the temptation to make constructions, guesses, surmises? They seldom do. C. S. Lewis noticed this about the criticism of his own work: that most critics, instead of imparting factual information about his books and passing judgment upon them, preferred guessing about their history, when and why they were written. And Lewis adds that they were *always wrong*. "The imaginary histories about my books are by no means always offensive. Sometimes they are even complimentary. There is nothing against them except that they're not true, and would be rather irrelevant if they were."[3] I have tried to make this biography lean heavily in the direction of career study, imparting factual information and passing sound judgment upon those facts.

OBJECTIVITY

I warned you in advance of my Tubb fandom because, try as I might to hide it or balance it out by clinging to a fact-based objectivity, it will come out in these pages, in or at least between many of my lines. If I therefore fail to achieve a proper objectivity, either with too great praise when I let my guard down or with too great dispraise as I strive for objectivity, please understand and forgive. This book will not satisfy readers at the two extremes: fans, on the one hand, who can't bear to read or hear anything negative about their star or to know that he or she possessed common human frailties; or, on the other hand, prurient scandalmongers who expect the biographer to be a full-time iconoclast. Only if I fail wholly to please either side will I have succeeded.

I covet approval from the readers who fall anywhere between these extremes. My hope for this book is that it will enhance their appreciation and understanding of a truly seminal figure in the long history of country music in America.

Nashville, Tennessee

ACKNOWLEDGMENTS

No one would undertake a work of this magnitude, let alone complete it, without the encouragement and active assistance of a great many people. I have not the space to mention every name and every contribution, but I must here thank a very special few who in different ways made this book possible.

From the long ago days of college research into the Tubb career (1977–1978), Dr. Tom Nall, Dr. Bobby Johnson, and Dr. Archie MacDonald of the Stephen F. Austin State University faculty deserve my thanks. Mrs. Evelyn Stallings at that time provided financial support for the research and publicity for the completed thesis.

Twenty-seven persons then were contacted for information, among whom were some who died before my 1990s' round of intensive book research: Ernest Tubb himself, Jimmie Skinner, Townsend Miller, Merwyn Buffington, Mrs. Lucille West, and Mrs. J. L. Frank among them.

The most helpful of my Country Music Foundation colleagues were Bob Pinson, an unfailing resource for all country music scholars and a personal friend, and the successive editors of the *Journal of Country Music,* Kyle Young and Paul Kingsbury, who encouraged and published three of my Ernest Tubb articles in the 1980s. Use of the unparalleled CMF library collection was absolutely invaluable for my research.

Outside the CMF, Joe Specht of Abilene Christian University, Eddie Stubbs, and Geoff Hayes in Australia have made the most and best corrections to my Tubb discography. Encouragers have been legion: my wedding's best man David Martin; a good friend and terrific Tubb collector, Charles Beck of Newark, Ohio; the dean of country scholars, Bill C. Malone, who was the first to call me Ernest Tubb's biographer at a public gathering; my Maryland and Tennessee gadfly, the aforementioned Eddie Stubbs, who not only encouraged me but actually conducted several interviews for this book; my editor, Ken Wissoker; and Bear Family Records guru Richard Weize.

The late Mrs. Floy Case deserves special mention. The letters and photos she kept, the articles she wrote, even the home recordings she had were simply invaluable. We were friends and correspondents between 1981 and her death in 1988, during which time there were no real plans for this book. God bless you, Mrs. Case; you've helped me more than I ever let you know.

To all my interview subjects I express my thanks, but most of all to those members of the Tubb family who gave unstintingly of their time, their memorabilia, and their memories. Justin Tubb gave me a five-hour interview, as did his cousin, Douglas Glenn Tubb. But none spent more time with me, shared more of her personal papers, or opened more doors for me than Mrs. Ruth Husky of Lubbock, Texas, niece of Ernest Tubb. She and her kind husband Mr. G. A. Husky made two long trips to meet me and share their belongings and then opened their home to me for one glorious weekend. Joining the perspectives of fan and family member in one unforgettable personality, Mrs. Husky probably knows Ernest Tubb better than any living person.

Speaking of fellow Texans, two young men I've come to know and love for their help on this project, their wonderful spirits, and their dedication to historical country music are Tracy Pitcox of Brady, Texas, and Kevin Reed Coffey of Fort Worth. Tracy, a much loved country disc jockey and concert promoter, patiently dug into Ernest Tubb's San Angelo past for me, and Kevin is unmatched for the vigor and quality of his research into early-days Texas music. The world of country music has already benefited from their work, and both young men have wonderful futures ahead of them.

A book should not be undertaken without advice, direction, and encouragement. It couldn't be written without the cooperation and assistance of knowledgeable persons and firsthand sources. But it would never be finished without the patience of those closest to the writer and the writer's day-by-day work. My wife, the lovely Julie, has shown the patience of a saint through all of this, looking after me and our little son John Milton Pugh, born during my work on this book.

ERNEST TUBB

1

Family and Early Life

To tell the whole story of the Tubb family and its many branches would require several books. From its ample ranks came colorful characters in at least the last five generations. Ernest Tubb grew up knowing one grandmother; parents who lived long (though largely separate) lives, each of whom remarried (his father twice); four aunts and one uncle from his father's side; and four older siblings. Later came numerous nieces and nephews, Ernest's own two wives and eight children, and the grandchildren and great-grandchildren whom he lived to see. Family was, of course, not the only formative influence on Ernest Tubb, and it wasn't always a "good" one in terms of character building, support, or encouragement. "Ernest Tubb did a lot more for his family than his family ever did for him," his nephew Talmadge admitted.[1] But of his formative influences, family was the first in point of time and always near the top in terms of importance, for good or ill. Ernest Tubb and his rise to prominence in the world of country music begin here, in a large family rooted in the Texas soil.

PARENTS

Ernest Tubb's father, Calvin Robert Tubb, was the first of six children born to a Baptist preacher, John Brown Tubb (named for the abolitionist), and his second wife. John Brown Tubb had two sons by a previous wife, then two boys (J. B. and Calvin) and four girls by his second, a dark-haired, dark-eyed lady who would survive him by many years. Remarried and known as Grandma Dixon, she would be the only grandparent that Ernest Tubb knew.

A history of Pine Grove Baptist Church in Bernice, Louisiana, where Calvin Robert Tubb was born, lists John B. Tubbs as one of that church's twenty-four charter members at its founding on June 21, 1890. Born on October 2, 1886,

Calvin was almost four years old by then. Sometime after that, when Calvin Robert was still a "small boy" (his obituaries say), preacher Tubb moved from Louisiana to Comanche County, Texas, in hopes that the drier air would speed his recovery from a lung ailment. Of Calvin's five younger siblings, one was a boy, John Brown Tubb Jr., "Uncle J. B." in later years to Ernest. Together the two boys were the classic hell-raising "preacher's kids." No prank, no meanness, was beneath them. The one that family members still tell involved baby-switching at their Dad's brush arbor revivals. With the worshipers intent upon the proceedings, the two Tubb boys slipped off into the darkness—fit setting for their deed—climbed into the buggies where sleeping babies lay, and swapped them around. Families leaving the meeting got home before they discovered they had somebody else's baby.[2] Imagine the alarm, delay, and confusion thus occasioned in those pre-telephone days. Likewise imagine the whipping that the Tubb boys got when their deed came to light.

A hell-raiser for most of his life, Calvin Robert Tubb grew to be a tall, handsome, rugged, big-boned farmer. Uneducated even by the standards of his time and place, he was nevertheless shrewd and ambitious, always looking out for a chance at a better life, for himself if not always for his family. Over the course of his long life, he tried his hand at several kinds of work. Not only did he own or sharecrop cotton and livestock farms in East and West Texas (the work he always seemed to come back to), but he once owned a gas station in Brownwood and for a time worked as foreman on the Con Can ranch near Uvalde. Some say he ran bootleg liquor during the days of Prohibition, maybe even with the help of sons C. R. Jr. and Ernest. All agree that he was stern with his children, sparing not the rod to enforce his commands. When he was around his wife and children—by no means all the time, even before the divorce—no one doubted who was in charge. "His dad ruled the roost . . . He'd just as soon knock you with a two-by-four, you didn't backtalk him." A fondness for drink, smoke, and gambling was a character trait that his youngest son Ernest picked up. "He was not the best security in their lives. He'd take off, drinking, and wouldn't come back for weeks. If he didn't take off, he'd get in a poker game and hock their farm . . . [His children] loved him, but he treated them pretty badly," says great-grandchild Debbie Tubb.[3] Poker alone did not satisfy his gaming lust: grandchild Douglas Glenn Tubb recalls that he once bet a companion which way a bird in a tree would fly when it took to flight.[4]

The first woman he married was Sarah Ellen Baker, usually called Ellen, three years his senior and in many ways his opposite. Born November 25, 1883, she never knew mother or father. Newton Baker, a full-blooded Cherokee, was her father, but according to great-grandson Talmadge Tubb, "When he was nineteen he rode away on his mule before my grandmother was born, and no one ever saw him again."[5] To make matters worse, Ellen's mother died from childbirth complications, leaving Ellen to be raised by her mother's mother, Mrs. Tidwell. By all accounts, Grandmother Tidwell did a tough job well: Ellen Baker was not only hard-working like most women of that time and place, but religious, and was considerably more well-mannered, cultivated, and dependable than the man she married. They were wed in Comanche County, Texas, probably in 1904, and their first three children were born there. What the two had in common—strong-willed, determined personalities—was a factor in their breakup after twenty years of marriage and the birth of five children. To his mother, Ernest Tubb was always close; she loved all of her children, but he was her "baby," and when his years of stardom came he consistently provided much of her support.

SIBLINGS

Ernest Tubb was the youngest of five children. Given the breakup of his parents' marriage when he was only ten, it is understandable that in many ways he was closer to his siblings than to either parent. Between the ages of sixteen and twenty, Ernest lived with or was neighbor to one or the other of his married siblings.

Calvin Robert Tubb Jr., "C. R." to those who knew him but "Bud" to little brother Ernest,[6] was the only other boy in the family and more than a big brother to Ernest: he was a friend, counselor, and almost a surrogate father. Born August 22, 1906, C. R. had passed seven when Ernest was born. By the time his parents divorced, C. R. himself was married, to Annie Lonsford: their son Quanah Talmadge Tubb was born December 21, 1925. Soon afterward, Annie took the boy back to her home country around Corsicana, and C. R. started a new life in the gasoline business with his father out in Brownwood. There he met and married the woman who would be his wife for sixty-five years, Margie Estes; together they would have eight children. In San Antonio in the 1930s, Fort Worth in the early 1940s, and in Nashville between 1947 and 1955, even with all the cares of his own large family, Bud was close by when Ernest needed him, exerting a calming, guiding, trusted influence. C. R. Tubb gave nicknames to all five of his children, and C. R. Jr. he dubbed "Pat," borrowed from a particularly slow-moving family mule. The name was apt. "One thing's for sure," Ernest said in 1950 when calling his brother up to the *Midnite Jamboree* microphone for a song, "he doesn't get in a hurry for anybody."

The next three children born to C. R. and Ellen Tubb were girls, each one special in her own way to baby brother Ernest. Jewell May Tubb (nicknamed Jude or Jew Jew), born May 26, 1908, did her best to spoil young Ernest with kindness and consequently became a favorite. She first described to Ernest the music of Jimmie Rodgers, as we shall see; at her San Antonio home on her twenty-sixth birthday, Ernest married his first wife, Elaine. Jewell's own home life was unsettled from start to finish: she married seven times and moved all over Texas and for a while to Tennessee. Ernest returned her early kindness toward him with financial support for much of her life, buying homes for her in both states. An emphysema sufferer like Ernest, she was the only sibling that he outlived.

Thelma Lucille Tubb ("Fatty," her dad called her, which she fortunately outgrew), known as Lucille, came into the world April 13, 1910. Her long and stable marriage to Ike West was a godsend to young Ernest, who worked for board with them on their West Texas farm in the early 1930s. The Wests were very religious people; their three sons all became Baptist preachers, following in the footsteps of great-grandad John Brown Tubb. Sometimes this drove a wedge between them and Ernest in later years: longtime San Antonio residents, they would not attend his club dates in that area because of the drinking and dancing. Then too, in the early days on the farm in West Texas, they had not encouraged Ernest in his musical ambitions, seeing no way that it could lead to a livelihood. During such tough times, though, they were not the only ones offering that wise caution.

Two years and two days elapsed between Lucille's birth and the coming of Opal Marie "Blondie" Tubb (April 15, 1912), whose nickname followed her for life. Closest to baby Ernest in age, she was his natural confederate growing up, and they remained extremely fond of each other throughout their lives. She remembered that Ernest as a boy of three or four years would walk to a nearby store, buy a peanut patty, and, instead of eating any of it then, right away brought it home and divided it with her. Sharing his later financial bounty with Opal and her large East Texas tenant-farm family, the Colliers, Ernest repeated this childhood pattern. Hillary Orran Collier, Opal's husband for sixty years, got from brother-in-law Ernest a new tractor and a Ford station wagon during World War II, when such vehicles were hard to come by. Word got back to Ernest after this that Orran was taking undue advantage of this largesse, so Ernest at the next opportunity reproved him. "Orran, I'm trying to help you, and you're spending all your time in the Dallas honky-tonks drinking beer while Blondie and the kids are out in the fields working all day." "Well, Ernest, you drink beer." "Yeah, but I can afford it, Orran, and you can't."[7]

BIRTH AND UPBRINGING

Ernest Dale Tubb joined this family as its fifth and final child on February 9, 1914, born in the little community of Crisp, Texas, five miles or so west of Ennis in Ellis

County. Crisp now consists of scattered farmhouses and neatly fenced pasture land; a single sign bears the simple name Crisp, citing for reasons obvious to any bystander no population figure. A marker placed by the Ernest Tubb Fan Club on the opposite side of the small farm-to-market road proclaims the defunct community's great distinction as Ernest Tubb's birthplace. It stands where the general store and cotton mills were in the days when Crisp was a real place. A photo in his *Ernest Tubb Folio of Recorded Hits No. 1* purports to be of his birthplace,[8] but much later fan club president Norma Barthel reported that it was what remained of one of his boyhood homes in the area, none of which has stood now for many years. Ernest laughed in later years to think that he was "the only entertainer in the United States whose birthplace actually disappeared."[9]

At the time, his father was overseer for the three-hundred-acre cotton farm on which they lived. Soon after Ernest's birth, the family moved five miles out of Crisp, but stayed in East Texas until Ernest was six. The Great War in Europe meant good times and high prices for America's cotton growers; when the postwar bust came, it came down hard and lasted long. That's when the Tubb family pulled up stakes and headed for West Texas in a covered wagon.

Brother and sisters remembered young Ernest as "a happy child who loved to listen to stories."[10] They were not above using this fondness to coax extra work out of him: "We could always get Ernest to wash the dishes if we would tell stories to him." The nickname his father gave him was "Slick," as good a name as any for the combination of smarts, ambition, and drive that the boy had. Family members cite two favorite examples. When one of the kids had disobeyed an order or otherwise offended, and none would name the guilty party, all of the children got whippings, by order of age. Ernest, knowing that he'd be last, used the extra time to line his pants with padding of whatever sort he could get. The other story deals with cotton picking. At the beginning of the picking season, Father Tubb would sometimes bribe his children to greater efforts by promising payments gauged to the amount that they picked. The trouble was that invariably the bribes didn't last long, though Dad came to expect the same amount of work each day: "You did it once; just keep doing it." Young Ernest invariably would take it easy on payment day, willing to make less money that one day so that less work would be expected of him in the weeks to come.[11]

Ernest came through his one childhood health crisis with the help of what became a favorite food: red beans. A 1962 issue of Tubb's fan club journal says that "once when very small, he was quite ill. Suddenly he wanted beans to eat. His mother didn't want to let him eat them, but the Doctor said, 'He's gonna die anyway, so let him have 'em.' He ate all the beans he wanted and was soon well."[12]

Young Ernest, siblings remember, was "very imaginative" and wrote poems when still a small boy, "which later led to his songwriting."[13] A niece remembers stories about his habit of writing his full name, Ernest Dale Tubb, on everything he made or wrote, part of a creative drive that exhibited itself early, she believes.[14] On the musical side, their mother played piano and organ, brother C. R. remembered, and "encouraged Ernest's early interest in music."[15] But no serious musical interest surfaced before his early teens, when he first heard the music of Jimmie Rodgers.

Ernest's mother, a very religious woman, worked hard to shape her younger son's character. The practical essence of her code was "Treat other people right, and you'll come out well in the end." No one could miss the similarity of this to Ernest's famous parting advice to each audience: "Be better to your neighbors, and you're gonna have better neighbors, doggone ya." It was his mother who forcibly brought home to him the lesson "Thou shalt not steal" when Ernest, at age eight, buying a cap gun, served as the diversion while a friend stole six rolls of caps. Proudly telling his mother of their caper, Ernest, protesting "I didn't steal anything—he did," got what Norma Barthel called "a whale of a paddling";[16] he probably didn't need the accompanying lecture on guilt by facilitation to learn indelibly that the way of the transgressor is hard. This prohibition against theft, along with "Thou shalt not bear false witness," became the twin pillars of his business code, said friend and bus driver James Garland "Hoot" Borden. "Just don't ever lie to him, no matter how much it hurts, or steal from him. He'll forgive almost anything else. Ernest really has never understood dishonesty."[17] C. R. Tubb Jr. recalled that Ernest joined the Baptist church at age fourteen, unprompted by his mother,[18] though surely not without her blessings. If his recollection of Ernest's age was right, and if Ernest was literally recounting a salvation experience in his early song "The Right Train to Heaven," that would date the event September 7, 1928.

About 1921, at the time of the cotton bust, the whole Tubb family piled into a covered wagon and headed west, taking several days to reach the little community of Benjamin, Texas, in Knox County. Formal schooling was a low priority for the Tubb children, since the farmwork had to come first, but it was in Benjamin that Ernest Tubb, already nine years old, first sat behind a school desk. On a biographical form he filled out for author Linnell Gentry in 1959, Tubb listed two separate years as the extent of his schooling: "Grade School" (no mention of the level), "Benjamin, Texas, 1923 to 1924," and "Phoenix School, Kemp, Texas, 1925 to 1926."[19] In Benjamin, young Ernest had a four-mile walk to the school in town from the farm where they lived. The year at the Phoenix School in Kemp followed the family's move back to East Texas.

Tubb later explained that in seventeen months of school, he got credit for four years; that is, he left school with a fourth-grade proficiency at age twelve.

But these seventeen months, plus whatever he could do at home or on his own time, sufficed to teach him reading (he became a voracious and wide-ranging reader in later life), writing (some of his letters border on eloquence, to say nothing of his eventual mastery of the songwriter's craft), and arithmetic. "When I realized what I had missed, I began educating myself," Tubb remembered; in later life his lack of formal education was imperceptible to most observers.[20]

Besides the three Rs, Tubb learned at school a rough and ready sort of egalitarianism that never left him. He befriended two brothers there who were shunned by most of the other kids because their father was a garbage collector. To young Ernest, occupation didn't determine a person's worth: "Some of the kids probably looked down on what my parents did."[21] Skin color didn't matter, as he proved by befriending a black fan in the Deep South early in his years of stardom. Only the inside of a person, so far as that could be determined by actions and attitudes, mattered to Ernest Tubb. The underdog, the worthy person or cause laboring under unfair disadvantages, would always claim his sympathy. That's part of the reason he did so much to help deserving new country music performers for so many years.

About the time that the family moved back to East Texas and settled in Kemp in Kaufman County—some sources say "the next year"—Ellen and Calvin Robert Tubb separated. Family members now don't say much about it; none now living were alive then. Divorce was uncommon then, and this particular marriage had endured for two decades when it finally collapsed. But Calvin Tubb's rowdy ways, frequent departures, and financial instability proved to be more than Ellen Tubb could endure. With her youngest child Ernest now past ten years of age and to some degree able to take care of the two of them, she had had enough. Whatever its effect on the children, family members agree that the divorce was more of an emotional blow to the husband than to the wife. Children or grandchildren visiting him in later years say he always asked about her; she never asked about him. After the divorce, they did not lay eyes on one another again until January 1944, at an all-family reunion for C. R. Jr.'s imminent military induction; when she saw him again after nearly twenty years, passing him silently in the kitchen, he had changed so much that she didn't recognize him.[22]

If losing his father through divorce was tough on young Ernest, he never let it show. Clearly his mother's remarriage in 1930 was a bigger blow to him. For the time being, he may have been pleased to have an unreliable father out of the picture and his mother all to himself. The divorce was a factor in bringing his formal education to such an early close; without a father-provider in the picture, it became even more imperative that young Ernest handle farm chores full time. With the new responsibilities he doubtless matured faster than he otherwise would have. Ernest appears to be well beyond his actual age of fourteen in his earliest surviving photo—taken November 28, 1928—kneeling in a snowy Texas field.

Brother C. R. was married and gone; Jewell, the next oldest sibling, was living and working in Dallas. Opal lived for a time with her Aunt Allie Tubb Cooper in the vicinity of Kemp, and Lucille moved in with a cousin not far away. So for some five years, Ernest and his mother shared a shack on the farm of Ted and Stella Barrow. Stella was one of Ernest's paternal aunts, sister-in-law to Ellen, and Ted was a cousin, Ernest thought, to outlaw Clyde Barrow.[23] He told fan club president Norma Barthel years later that Clyde may have come by to see his cousin a time or two, but he didn't remember much about it. The farm was between the tiny communities of Lively and Stykes, Texas, not far from Kemp and within fifty miles of Dallas. Mother and son had visits from and made visits to family members, though the number of immediate family members living close by dwindled in 1928, when children already out of the nest married and moved further away. Lucille married Ike West and removed to Haskell, Texas, while Opal married Orran Collier on December 22, 1928, out in Munday, Texas.

Jewell Tubb stayed on in the Dallas area a while longer, and a visit she paid to her mother and baby brother Ernest sometime in the summer or fall of 1928 opens a new chapter in this story. To that little corner of the Barrow farm, and to the very soul of Ernest Tubb, she brought word from the big city of a new singing sensation, a recording artist like none before him: Jimmie Rodgers.

2

Jimmie Rodgers

Ernest Tubb had favorite performers before Jimmie Rodgers. From the time he first saw cowboy movies, he loved them. The earliest he saw, from the days of his boyhood, were the silent films of Tom Mix and Buck Jones. Cowboy music became another early love; Tubb said in 1977 that he "particularly admired the cowboy songs of . . . Jules Verne Allen."[1] Tubb remembered singing in his early days on San Antonio radio "The Big Rock Candy Mountain" by Harry "Haywire Mac" McClintock.[2] His familiarity with that and a few other songs predate his awareness of Jimmie Rodgers.

Tubb was aware of one music that influenced Jimmie Rodgers: the blues. "He grew up working with blacks in the field, listening to phonograph records of Ethel Waters and Bessie Smith . . ."[3] Jim Jackson's "Kansas City Blues," released on records the same year that Tubb first heard of Jimmie Rodgers (1928), became a longtime favorite, though he probably learned it from subsequent country versions. In all likelihood, the few blues song structures and speech idioms that found their way into Ernest Tubb's music got there via Jimmie Rodgers, the first performer to make an overwhelming impact on him.

THE FIRST EXPOSURE

If you had grown up in Texas during the late 1920s it would have been difficult to avoid hearing Jimmie Rodgers's music. Floyd Tillman, Tubb's great contemporary (born the same year), shares a vivid recollection from his boyhood days in Post, Texas, not awfully far from Benjamin, where Ernest did much of his growing up. "I was just a kid, delivering telegrams for Western Union; and you could hear Jimmie Rodgers records being played in every house up and down the street, on those $5 Victrolas in the days before radio got so popular. I'd be pedaling along, and hear part of 'In the Jailhouse Now' coming out of one house, then hear the rest of it coming out of the others."[4]

The Victor Records artist first came to national prominence in 1928, with the huge success of "Blue Yodel," "Away out on the Mountain," "In the Jailhouse Now" and "Ben Dewberry's Final Run." That same "In the Jailhouse Now," so popular in Post, Texas, was the song that Tubb's sister Jewell sang for Ernest when she came for a visit to the Barrow place from Dallas in the summer or fall of 1928. "My oldest sister . . . came home, she'd been working in Dallas, she was singing one of his songs, and told me about Jimmie Rodgers before I'd ever heard him, and said she thought I'd enjoy him."[5] Jewell hadn't mastered Jimmie's yodel break—she didn't even know it was a yodel: "He does a little hollering or something in there." Ernest was impressed, enough to want to learn the song himself; he got Jewell to write down the words and go over the melody enough times that he might commit it to memory. Fifty years later he was opening concerts with "In the Jailhouse Now."

Ernest spent the summer of the next year, 1929, in Brownwood, Texas, visiting his father and brother at their invitation. C. R. Tubb Sr. had married a Brownwood woman named Myrtle who had two sons by a previous marriage, and when C. R. Jr.'s first marriage ended, he went out there to work with his dad; father and son were soon operating filling stations in Brownwood. C. R. Jr. met and married another Brownwood woman, Margie, who among other things worked at hand-tinting photographs in those days before color photography. C. R. Jr. also owned one of those popular Victrolas. There Ernest actually heard Jimmie Rodgers's recorded voice for the first time. Bud, whose record collection also included the popular Gene Austin, first played "The Brakeman's Blues" and its flip, "Blue Yodel No. 2," but according to Norma Barthel, "he had all of the other Jimmie Rodgers records, too, and Ernest loved playing them over and over on the Victrola."[6] Word for word, note for note, even yodel for yodel, Ernest Tubb learned the songs of Jimmie Rodgers. He'd slip out behind his dad's gas station on the two or three adjoining acres and practice his vocalizing (he had no guitar at this point, a serious shortcoming), seeing how much he had committed to memory, away from the safety of the Victrola. Back at the gas station, his dad would greet him with good-natured encouragement: "You know, I could have swore I heard Jimmie Rodgers down there in the pasture a while ago, but I guess not."[7]

Collecting Jimmie Rodgers's new records became more a passion than a hobby for the teenager. Very late in his career (1981), Tubb told the *Miami Herald:* "Immediately after I heard that first record, I decided I had to try and sing, not as a profession so much but just try to sing like him. I bought every record he put out. One time—this was way back in the Depression—my parents were going away for a couple of days, and they left me $1 to eat on. You could do that back then. But a Jimmie Rodgers record came out, and I paid 75 cents for it. I used the quarter to eat on for two days."[8]

ON THE PERSONAL SIDE

Tubb's love for the music of Jimmie Rodgers was the constant in his life those next few years, as he grew to adulthood amid economic hardship and family upheaval. What became the Great Depression began to settle over the nation that winter of 1929–1930; nobody could have guessed then that it would be so bad or last so long. Its extended privations did as much as anything else to shape the man that Ernest Tubb became, inuring him to hardship (though he was certainly no stranger to hard times when the Depression came) and endearing to him "the underdog," the man who was down and out—in part because he was for so long in that class himself. Hard times may have made Ernest Tubb's path to the top a long, tough climb, but if so they also made him eternally grateful for the success that finally did come to him.

On the home front, his mother remarried in 1930. Her marriage to Sam Ashton was a severe blow to Ernest, much worse to him than his parents' divorce. For some four years he had been his mother's mainstay and support, the man in her life. Norma Barthel got it firsthand from Tubb that when his mother married Sam "It almost killed him . . . he really didn't understand."[9] Clearly there was no love lost between stepson and stepfather. Family members looking back today don't think they ever lived under the same roof,[10] and at least one thinks that a fistfight marked their parting.[11] When Sam Ashton came into his mother's life, it was time for Ernest to leave the nest, though a comfortable one it had never been. For the next four years, this meant living with one married sibling after another, always working for his keep—but always working on his music, too.

First he lived for a time with sister Lucille and her husband Ike West out in Haskell, Texas, near Benjamin, helping out on their cotton farm for his room and board and earning a little money from work for neighbors and his sister's in-laws. In the fall of 1931, he moved in with his paternal grandmother, Grandma Dixon (J. B. Tubb Jr. was long dead, and she had remarried), in Anson, Texas, picking cotton in that area for a while. Eager to find better work in the city, he jumped at the chance to move to San Antonio on the invitation of sister Jewell, by then Mrs. Till Adams. There were no guarantees of a job, of course, but she welcomed him while he looked for one. Hitchhiking to San Antonio on a three-day trip, going largely without food and sleeping in ditches along the way, he alighted in the Alamo City from the back of a chicken truck on a rainy day in the winter of 1931–1932. The driver let him off some seven miles from his sister's house, and Ernest, not knowing this, covered the whole distance on foot and was famished when he finally made it. His stomach, trim in the best of times, had shrunk to the point that he could hardly eat the meal that the Adamses laid out before him.[12]

Till Adams was looking for work too, so the brothers-in-law set out together to Kelly Field every morning for two weeks, only to be told "Sorry, not today." Ex-servicemen got first crack at the available jobs, then men with families to support, so Till as a married man had a real advantage. Finally a day came when young Ernest's perseverance paid off, and he was put to work with pick and shovel digging ditches for sewer lines. The pay was 30 cents an hour and the work was hard, but Ernest was glad to have it and did his best. In this case, "his best" might have been too good for one particularly self-important, fault-finding foreman, who saw the young man's smooth ditch section and said, "Tubb, we're not digging this ditch to put on exhibition. We're trying to lay a sewer line, so quit trying to make it look so pretty and get to work." Stung by criticism where he expected praise, Tubb resisted his first inclination to strike the foreman with his shovel and let his hair-trigger temper cool off. Luckily for him, a different foreman took pity on the young man and switched Tubb's work to truck driving and errand running over at Fort Sam Houston, which involved a raise in pay to 40 cents an hour.[13] To make this switch, Ernest had to claim more truck driving experience than he actually had; his inexperience surfaced one morning when he came within three feet of ramming a crossing train.

As the young single men were the last to be hired, they were likewise the first to be let go, and Ernest was an eventual casualty. The Kelly Field and Fort Sam Houston job had been civic make-work from the start: the mechanical equipment existed that could have dug the ditches, but the city wanted to put some of the huge number of unemployed men to work, so they opted to hire it out by hand.[14] Ernest was there long enough to get a generous sample of city life, and though the work he found wasn't any easier than the cotton picking he had left behind, other aspects of San Antonio were much to his liking.

JIMMIE RODGERS AGAIN: SOME NEAR MISSES

For one thing, he was in the same city as his idol, Jimmie Rodgers. Racked by tuberculosis and facing declining record sales caused by the Depression, Jimmie Rodgers may have passed his peak as a recording star: but not in the eyes of Ernest Tubb. By the end of 1931, Jimmie, a Texas resident since 1929, had moved his family from Kerrville and his Blue Yodeler's Paradise to a duplex bungalow at 142 Montclair in the Alamo Heights section of San Antonio. In January 1932, radio station KMAC began carrying *Jimmie Rodgers,* a weekly program of his recorded music that featured Jimmie live and in-studio when his health and breaks in his touring schedule permitted.[15] Work probably made it impossible for Ernest to listen to the program with any regularity: it aired at 4:00 P.M. on Tuesdays. Once he did hear Jimmie Rodgers talking over the airwaves, though: "He was at a big affair at some hotel, being interviewed."[16]

Tubb and Rodgers had a mutual friend in San Antonio, a record store dealer on the Plaza near the Alamo. Tubb recalled:

> I was there [in San Antonio] part of 1931 and part of 1932 . . . [This] was probably about a year before he died. Jimmie had a record come out just almost exactly every three months—he'd have a release. And so back in those days they did not have salesmen like now; I have record stores you know, and you've got salesmen come around every so often to take your orders. Back then they'd send samples—you'd play the samples and then fill out an order blank on how many you wanted. And so they'd get the samples two weeks before the record would really be available, see. So I made a deal with this store—that's how come he knew that I was such a big fan—I asked him [the store owner] would he save me the sample every three months. Let me buy the sample. He would call me, he had my phone number . . . Cause he knew what he was going to order anyhow . . . So he'd just sell me the samples.
>
> So one day . . . there was a lady, his [the store owner's] wife I guess it was, who said, "Jimmie was in here yesterday." And I couldn't hardly believe that, you know. "Yeah, he comes in my store. We were telling him about what a big fan you were, and he said to tell you to come out and see him in Alamo Heights." But I didn't. You know, I thought, well, I took that with a grain of salt. I said, "Well, thank you," you know, and I never did ask them the address.[17]

So close, and yet so far.

Passing up this chance to meet Rodgers, Tubb later passed up a chance to see him perform. "I was afraid to meet him. I worshipped him so much, I was afraid he would say or do something that would upset the image I had of him . . . So I was baby-sitting for my brother and his wife while they went to see Jimmie in a tent show there in San Antonio, and I said I'd go the next night, but I didn't. That was in 1932, about a year before he died. I was just afraid to go . . . Now I could kick myself of course. I was just a kid, but I'm sure he would have been nice to me."[18] Rodgers biographer Nolan Porterfield lists a probable stand of appearances that Jimmie made in San Antonio sporadically between February 1 and March 5, 1932, with Skeeter Kell and His Gang,[19] as close as we'll come to dating this second and final near miss between star and fan, hero and hero-worshiper.

THE PASSING OF JIMMIE RODGERS

As that last anecdote recounted, yet another branch of the Tubb family had migrated to San Antonio by that time: C. R. Tubb Jr., his wife Margie, and their young son Tommy Gene, joining Jewell and Ernest. The Tubb who would eventually live in San Antonio the longest, Lucille West, was still farming with husband Ike up in Ike's home country near Benjamin. When Ernest's make-work job ended, before 1932 had passed into history, he went back up to join them, leaving the big city for a time.

Back in Benjamin, and still only in his late teens, Ernest Tubb for the first time sang in public, at parties and dances. His days were spent with farmwork, either for Ike West or for Ike's brother Tom West (later the postmaster of Benjamin, Texas). At night he could listen to his Jimmie Rodgers records and sing along with them, if he wasn't singing himself at a social gathering or otherwise occupied. Then one peaceful day in the late spring of 1933 came news that shocked him.

> I was out there farming with Ike's brother, Tom West, . . . the week Jimmie passed away. I won't ever forget it. I'm not positive how late we got the news, but I went to the post office to get the mail—in fact, I rode in on a horse to pick up the mail and get the weekly paper, the *Knox City News*—I don't think Benjamin even had a paper then. But I got the paper and it was on the front page, "Jimmie Rodgers Is Dead." And this was one of the saddest days of my life . . . The paper might have been two or three days old, I don't know. But I do know that that's where I got the news.[20]

The memory makes plain Tubb's distress. But his fidelity to Rodgers and his music was undiminished; in fact, it took on a new intensity. Jimmie Rodgers's music assumed an almost sanctified aura, as the man's brief and tragic life grew to legendary proportions. "I know you shouldn't worship anyone in this life, but I have to admit I worshiped Jimmie Rodgers. It was that bad. I worshiped him so much that for a time I was convinced that I wouldn't live past age thirty-five either."[21] He did live past thirty-five, but decades later, his idolatry of Rodgers had not lessened, as these verses from a recitation that Tubb tacked onto the old hymn "When I Take My Vacation in Heaven" make clear.

> Once inside the pearly gates I heard a familiar sound
> The voice of Jimmie Rodgers echoed all around.
> Memories that have stayed with me for many and many years
> Now had come to life again, I saw through happy tears.

There he was, resplendent, with a guitar of solid gold
Singing as he only could, in the land where we never grow old
"T for Texas" yodel blues, just as true as ever,
So happy up on heaven's stage, where he can sing forever.

In this imagined meeting, Tubb's dream takes him to heaven incognito—still afraid to meet his idol face-to-face?—as we see from Jimmie's words in the final stanza.

"Howdy, friend," he said to me, and warmly shook my hand,
"Please take a message for me back to the other land.
Tell my good friend Ernest Tubb that I've heard all his songs
He's sung with my old guitar, through all these years so long.
Some great day I know that he will enter yonder door,
Then I'll really harmonize with the Texas Troubadour."[22]

Tubb's own musical aspirations also assumed a new urgency. Was there not now a void to be filled? A musical legacy to carry on? That other young men about this time felt exactly the same way (Gene Autry, Tommy Duncan, Rex Griffin, Dwight Butcher, Bill Bruner, and many others) did not deter Ernest Tubb, assuming that he was aware of their efforts this early. Tubb approached singing from this point on with a determination he'd not shown before. Making his own mark as a singer in the Rodgers style became a consuming passion.

GUITARS AND LESSONS

Encouraged to sing by some family members, he found his strongest support from some friends he made once he was back in the Benjamin area, men who happened to know more about music than he did. Tubb took a job sponsored by the brand new WPA (Works Progress Administration) on a road-building crew, making the area's first paved highway. Tubb worked in what was called "the curing gang"; his task was to help put down a tarpaulin over the first layer of concrete, wet that down, and then shovel dirt over it. Calling this "the hardest job I ever had" (and he'd already had some hard ones in his nineteen years), Tubb scooped dirt for eight hours a day, more if the job required it. He may not have stayed with it but for sister Lucille applying liniment "to get him out of bed every morning."

Merwyn J. "Buff" Buffington, who worked on the same crew, remembered their meeting: "He [Ernest] was on one side of the highway throwing dirt on the wet burlap, the same work I was doing, and I heard him singing. He sang nearly all the time, and all he would sing would be Jimmie Rodgers records, which I was very familiar with them. I was impressed by his singing . . ." Buffington encouraged Ernest to learn to play guitar: "I approached him out on the highway work out there and asked him why he didn't get him a guitar, and I'd teach him how to play enough chords to sing all of Jimmie Rodgers's numbers. So he took off from there and was going to San Antonio and got as far as Abilene and found the guitar, then he turned around and came back."[23] And thereby hangs a tale.

The different (though similar) stories of how Tubb bought his first guitar are pieced together in the following account. It seems that he had borrowed $12 from brother-in-law Ike West to keep body and soul together as he hitchhiked back to San Antonio. He'd made it to Abilene, about a hundred miles down the road, when he spotted an appealing mahogany guitar in a pawnshop window. "He had never owned a guitar, and didn't know how to play one, but had been singing with some guys he worked with on the highway [Buffington and his friends Jim and Joe Castleman] and wanted one so bad."[24] The listed price was $5.95, nearly half of his pocket money; he couldn't buy the guitar and still make it to San Antonio. So he made the plunge. Talking the pawnshop owner into taking $5.50, he bought the guitar, had it wrapped in a paper sack, and headed back to Benjamin on foot and with raised thumb, confident he could find some sort of work there while his friends taught him what they knew about guitar playing. All the way back, people passing him on the highway (those not giving him rides, apparently) would yell out, "Hey, cowboy, why don't you play that guitar?"[25] Young Tubb brushed it all aside good naturedly and kept walking.

Ike West may not have been as good-natured when he saw Ernest heading back so soon, guitar in hand. It wasn't the money, surely—Ernest could work off his loan in short order—as much as the aggravation of Ernest's constant practicing between suppertime and bedtime. Merwyn Buffington and two other co-workers, Alvin Connors and J. W. Smith, all spent time with Ernest, showing him on work breaks the chords they knew.[26] The biographer of Tubb's early days, Norma Barthel, says, "it took him forever to learn a few simple chords, and it was probably a year before he could tune the guitar even halfway right"; but, she adds, "he now knew what he wanted to be and he was a very determined young man."[27] He had to be determined, as he nearly drove his sister and brother-in-law to distraction with his constant practicing, fictionalized in the first song he ever wrote, which was titled, appropriately enough, "When I First Began to Sing." Truest to life are the words that open the second of the song's ten verses: "I'd sing out in the field all day, I'd sing around the barn, / but when I sang right in the house that's where I did most harm."[28] Or the opening to "Ernest Tubb's Talking Blues": "Now if you want to get into trouble, I'll tell you how to do it; / get a guitar, and then you're into it. / You play all day, you play all night, / and your folks say you'll never learn to play the thing right; / always fussing you, griping—won't let you practice."[29] Both songs emphasize how hard he found it to master the chords: "weeks and weeks" in "Ernest Tubb's Talking Blues," and the same "weeks and weeks to learn what was a key" in "When I First Began to Sing." Merwyn Buffington remembered that "his brother-in-law would beg him to give it up many, many times and go to work."[30]

Tubb, who always played and sang strictly by ear as he was taught, still hadn't learned guitar chords well enough to accompany himself when he began singing professionally in San Antonio with these same Castleman brothers and Merwyn Buffington later that year (1933), from which fact I surmise that this latest (and last) stay in Benjamin with the West family was short-lived.

A LOVE THAT NEVER FADED

Jimmie Rodgers was dead when Ernest Tubb returned to San Antonio in the latter half of 1933. But the memory of the Blue Yodeler and the inspiration he provided would never leave him. After decades of touring, long since a star in his own right, Tubb's love for Jimmie Rodgers's music was eloquently captured in this poignant account of an episode in Borger, Texas.

> Time after time, throughout the busy night, Tubb was asked to pose for a photo, never showing a sign of antagonism. "Can we get another shot, Mr. Tubb?" . . . "Say when, and I'll grin." . . . Later, Tubb was sitting alone in a small dressing room on the bus, away from the crowd and noise . . . Beside him was a portable phonograph. Thinking himself alone, he was sitting there in the dark, sad-eyed, and the spinning record emitted lonesome yodels of that great singing trainman . . . the late, great Jimmie Rodgers. For two minutes of the twenty-four hours, the Texas Troubadour chose his own company.[31]

Tubb never wanted even his most ardent fan to call him "the greatest country star," because in his own mind neither he nor anyone else could even come close to Jimmie Rodgers. "Ernest remembered [that] one of the nicest letters he ever received . . . said in part, 'I just bought your new record and I listen to you on the radio regularly. To me, you are next to Jimmie Rodgers . . .' To Ernest, being next to Jimmie Rodgers was just about the biggest compliment he could receive . . . He appreciated these fans perhaps more than any others because he feels that they understand him more than some of those who have said that he is the greatest."[32]

In 1977 I asked him to talk about his favorite Rodgers song, and he couldn't do it. "I have maybe a few that I favor over some of them, but actually he never did anything that I didn't like, you know . . . He did all types of things. In fact, any subject you could think of: he did it all in six years. Mother songs, the father songs, the kid songs, the baby songs . . . One of my favorites . . . was 'Lullaby Yodel,' which was about the babies, a baby song. And another of course was 'I'm Sorry We Met,' which was a love song. 'Hobo Bill's Last Ride' . . . He didn't do any bad songs. I loved them all."[33]

The next chapter in this story finds Ernest Tubb, only three years after Jimmie Rodgers's death, handed the Rodgers mantle by his widow—an honor beyond his wildest teenage dreams, but a daunting task at the same time. The final stanza of Elsie McWilliams's lyrics to the first song Tubb recorded, "The Passing of Jimmie Rodgers," clearly states the honor and his predicament, describing Rodgers's passing in a double sense: his death, yes, but also the "passing" of his musical torch to this one member of the next generation.

> With his memory as my inspiration
> I'll pick up the torch he laid down.
> I'll enter the race, to record in his place
> To banish your sighs and your frowns.
> I'll sing all the songs he has written,
> I'll follow his steps day-by-day,
> So dry up your tears, as I strive through the years
> To yodel your blues away.[34]

3

San Antonio Days: "Blue-Eyed Elaine" and "Jimmie's Wife"

Nineteen-year-old Ernest Dale Tubb had indeed been bitten by the entertainment bug, and so had his friends the Castlemans and "Buff" Buffington. All migrated to San Antonio about the same time in late 1933.

Jim and Joe Castleman formed a western-style trio by adding Merwyn Buffington to a group they called The Castleman Brothers, and preceded Tubb into San Antonio radio work. Jim played fiddle, Joe played mandolin, and Buffington was their guitarist. Later a third brother, Barney Castleman, joined the act as bass violinist. Merwyn Buffington's recollection in 1977 was that their early morning show (Tubb said it was on KMAC) was "mostly western; plus something on the order of Jimmie Rodgers."[1] All group members had day jobs—not as strenuous, one hopes, as those they left in Benjamin—that followed their radio work. At night they played drive-ins. Once in San Antonio, their friend Ernest Tubb was willingly drawn into this routine: "The first time he sang over the radio was with us as a guest singer."[2] They had liked his singing in Benjamin, and they still liked it in San Antonio.

For his day job, Ernest Tubb and his brother C. R. (with whom he was living) turned again to government relief work, in an almost exact replay of what he had done before. For a week he walked the four or five miles down to the San Antonio courthouse to find a line of 100 to 150 men already there, waiting for the available jobs. Preference again was for ex-servicemen with large families, and Ernest once more was at the opposite end of the spectrum. He may never have gotten an interview but for a stranger who asked him for a match (at nineteen, Ernest was already rolling Bull Durham tobacco for smoking), thereby pulling him from the back of the line. The stranger struck up a conversation with Tubb, and suggested that they head up the line together, as though they were friends. Citing this in later years as the answer to a prayer ("I prayed all the way down there that this morning I would get inside the door some way"), Tubb got an interview and was asked if he was married. "No. I'd like to get married, but how can I if I don't have a job?" The head of the department asked him, "How did you get in here anyway?" but instead of giving him the divine explanation, Tubb said that it didn't matter and made clear his willingness to work. He got a job, for the same 30 cents an hour as before. And again his work took him to the area's growing military establishments, this time to Randolph Field (now Randolph Air Force Base) east of town, and later back to Fort Sam Houston.[3] C. R. was hired too, though he would ultimately find work in the private sector as one of San Antonio's best Yellow Cab drivers.[4]

Ernest's private-sector ambitions for the time being were both musical and romantic. He became a regular on the Castleman Brothers' program, though sometimes he had to miss their show because of his job. At night he tagged along as they played drive-in restaurants on New Braunfels Avenue or on Broadway, all the time improving his singing and his guitar work. Before leaving Benjamin for the last time, Tubb had swapped his mahogany pawnshop guitar for a Sears Roebuck model from J. W. Smith, the man who, along with Alvin Connors, taught him his very first chords. It was a lighter colored model with a flowery trim design.[5]

Tubb increased his skill on the guitar to the point where he felt confident playing on radio and at the drive-ins. The whole group branched out into additional broadcasts, and it was Ernest Tubb, acting as their savvy young manager, who swung this deal. Under his own name, and with a different sponsor, they added a new show on KONO while keeping their KMAC show. The problem was that the competing sponsors for the group were in the same business: both were cab companies. Tubb recalled, "I got them over at KONO, and I sold another cab company, and we were playing as 'Ernest Tubb.' Somebody said, 'These cab companies are gonna catch up with y'all and kill all of you.' "[6] Their KMAC spot by this time had moved to noon three days a week. To make the show, Ernest had to eat lunch during his bus ride from Randolph Field, play the fifteen-minute show downtown, and grab a return bus.

As group manager, Tubb also had the responsibility of lining up the night jobs. After work, he'd book their advance dates; "a dollar apiece per night was just about the best he could get for them"[7] as the set fee. Tips were extra: on a good night, these could exceed what management was paying.

In cool weather, since most of their gigs were outdoors, the boys sometimes played their drive-in dates from inside their car. They rigged up a P.A. system in their large seven-passenger car, with the speakers on top. The boys were comfortable, if a bit crowded, picking and singing while carhops brought the written requests to their window. They lost one particular drive-in job on Hackberry Street, though, when Jim Castleman happened to let loose with a stream of chewing tobacco just as the manager came up to hand them a request. Ernest was fit to be tied, as that job went out the window just as surely as Jim's tobacco had.[8] A later and more fundamental difference with Jim Castleman would bring an end to Tubb's association with the group.

"BLUE-EYED ELAINE"

Whatever the young man's love life may have been to this point, the tempo picked up in the big city once his musical career commenced. When he told the job interviewer that he'd like to get married, he may already have had someone in mind. He had dated a San Antonio girl, Lois Elaine Cook, even before spending those last few months in Benjamin, and renewed his acquaintance now that he was back and living with his brother. Elaine, as she was called, lived with her mother and stepfather, the Webbers, in the same house where the Tubb boys lived. "I was about sixteen when I met him, and then he left and went to Benjamin, and then he came back, and I was eighteen when we married . . . I didn't meet Ernest until we moved over next to them . . . It was the same house."[9]

Tubb fan club president Norma Barthel surmised in her book that this pretty, blue-eyed girl also knew Ernest when she was a waitress in one of the drive-ins that he played with the Castlemans, and that "she was a pretty good little singer," adding that "she didn't get to sing much after they married as Ernest didn't feel that a singing career was very good for a woman, then."[10] What clearly emerges in conversation with Elaine today is that Ernest indeed did not involve her in career decisions or developments very much once they were married, given the children she had to raise and the unsavory atmosphere of so many of the "joints" he played.

Their marriage, which was announced by one brief line after the fact in the San Antonio newspapers, took place May 26, 1934, at the home of Ernest's eldest sister Jewell Adams. The date was important as Jewell's birthday (her twenty-sixth); only later did Tubb realize that it was the first anniversary of Jimmie Rodgers's death, which by hindsight made the day extra special. Norma Barthel relates the storybook difficulties that Ernest had making it to his own wedding because of a singing date, a borrowed car, and a police officer. I paraphrase.

On his wedding day, Ernest and the Castlemans were scheduled to play a drive-in on New Braunfels Avenue, and the owner wouldn't let Ernest off even to get married. She didn't want the group at all if Ernest wasn't there to sing, but after consultation, she agreed that if Ernest would open and close the show at least, what he did in between was his own business. And what he did was to borrow the Castlemans' Model-A Ford to drive over to Jewell's house for the evening wedding. Ernest had no car of his own yet, so he had to take what he could get, even though he knew the old Ford had problems. Sure enough, the headlights went out while en route, and rather than stop to get under the hood to fix them, he took his chances driving by streetlight. As luck would have it, a police officer pulled him over and then heard the whole incredible story. More incredibly, he believed Ernest and had mercy, allowing him to drive on sans headlights. So even though the groom came a little late to the wedding, all went fine.

The newlyweds' first love nest was the apartment formerly occupied by the Buffington group (and Ernest too for a time, having left his brother's place). Jim, Joe, and Merwyn simply moved out to separate digs and turned it over as a wedding gift of sorts, since they couldn't attend the ceremony. Norma Barthel finished her detailed account of the story by saying that the next rent check exhausted Ernest's money; he had to charge their first grocery bill, which came to the princely sum of $4.60.[11]

SOLO ACT

At the time of his marriage, Tubb's relationship to the Castlemans was still close, but not long afterward a rupture came. The informal agreement, whether or not his job could be called "managing," called for Tubb to do the bookings for the group. Jim Castleman—he of the ill-timed spittle—was approached for a booking that he found irresistible: $1.50 per night for each man at a drive-in that wanted them every night. He took it, without first talking it over with Ernest or seeking his advice. Ernest was not only dubious of the offer—half-again the pay? every night of the week, for a group barely known?—but was furious that his role as booker had been undermined. According to Barthel, Ernest sang one final Saturday night with the Castlemans and then struck out on his own. The Castlemans stayed in music around San Antonio for awhile, then headed back to Benjamin, their home country.[12] Merwyn Buffington, a Seymour, Texas, native, joined the Army about this time, but was fortunate to serve his entire three-year hitch at Fort Sam Houston there in San Antonio. He continued to play drive-in dates with Ernest around town when he could get off-duty time, especially after the Castlemans disbanded and went home.[13]

Though San Antonio newspapers of those years never listed KONO in their daily radio logs, Ernest Tubb made his first impact as a solo artist over its airwaves, beginning in 1934. The 100-watt station, which broadcast at 1370 khz, first from the city's St. Anthony Hotel and as of 1936 in the Milam Building, hired Tubb even before he split off from the Castlemans. Program Director Jerry Morgan auditioned him, according to engineer George W. Ing, who both engineered and announced all of Tubb's programs. Tubb by then was a fairly proficient guitarist, with a new, dark Kalamazoo guitar in hand, singing the hillbilly hits of the day plus a generous sampling of Jimmie Rodgers songs, performed as close to the Rodgers style as possible. His quarter-hour program aired three mornings a week at 6:00 A.M., and according to Ing, Tubb, "with guitar slung over his shoulder, rode his bicycle to the station every [sic] morning."[14] The pay was minimal, but he could at least plug his drive-in dates. After doing his programs, he biked off to his first steady paying job, at Mr. Henry Hein's new drugstore on Hackberry Street.

Hein had been in the drugstore business for years with the Goliad Street Pharmacy when he bought the former Taylor Drug Store on Hackberry Street. Looking for someone to manage the place, Hein was convinced by some favorite customers to hire their new husband/son-in-law, Ernest Tubb. "Mother and I got him the job at the drugstore," Elaine recalls. "I was raised on that drugstore, Mr. Hein's, and that's where we'd always go. And my school was right across the street from Mr. Hein's drugstore . . . Ernest and I were dating, and so Mother suggested that, she talked to Mr. Hein, and I talked to him . . ."[15] Tubb got the job, which meant he kept the store clean, stocked the shelves, made ice cream sodas, handled the counter business, took phone calls, and even made drug deliveries on the same bicycle that took him to the radio station and to work in the mornings.

This new day job brought him $10 per week: not as much as his last government pay, but far more steady and reliable. Tubb worked there almost three years as he pursued his musical career in various ways. With three early mornings each week devoted to KONO broadcasts, he had the lunch hours he'd formerly given to the Castleman Brothers free to sing at meetings of the various civic clubs to which Mr. Hein belonged. Mr. Hein knew economical entertainment when he saw it; added exposure and a free lunch, plus the joy of singing, was all that Ernest got from these junkets.

Charlie Walker, in later years San Antonio's top country disc jockey and a country star, relates what songwriter Lou Wayne told him of Ernest Tubb and some early amateur contests in San Antonio.

Lou and Ernest used to enter amateur contests down in San Antone when Ernest was about nineteen years old. And Ernest didn't like the name "Ernest"; he called himself "Dale Tubb." His real name was "Ernest Dale Tubb" . . . He was writing [songs] then, this was early '30s, [as] "Dale Tubb." [Lou Wayne said to Walker] "You know what I've got? I'm gonna give them to you." They were written on regular loose-leaf note-book paper, must have been ten or fifteen songs that Ernest wrote. Can you imagine the value of those songs right now? And he signed them "Dale Tubb," he never used Ernest at all at that point, until he made records . . . Just lyrics on loose-leaf notebook paper. I don't know if the songs were any good or not . . . [Lou] said they sang on two or three, or maybe more, amateur shows. I guess they sat around and wrote songs, picked and sang together and stuff . . . Course I'm sure his wife [Olene] has got them now.[16]

Wayne was a local boy trying hard to make it then, more as a songwriter than a singer. Lou got nowhere on New York's Tin Pan Alley: the only man who saw him said, "Go back down to Texas, write me a song and then come back to see me." To show Lou the kind of song he wanted, he did a little dance and sang "When the red, red robin comes bob, bob, bobbin' along," and wouldn't listen to any of Lou's songs. Lou had a temper, his friend Charlie Walker remembers, and vowed, "I'm gonna go back and I'm gonna show them New York so-and-so's what about that."[17] Wayne certainly went on to do just that, once he got a foot in the door with San Antonio's great western swing band, the Tune Wranglers, and later with Cliff Bruner, Jimmie Davis, the Shelton Brothers, Moon Mullican, Bob Wills,[18] and, eventually, Ernest Tubb. Wayne co-wrote "Careless Darling" (1945 release) and "Fortunes in Memories" (1952, co-written with Charlie Walker).

Looking back on those years from a distance of several decades, Ernest Tubb considered them the happiest of his life. He was newly married, still just twenty years old, on his own as a breadwinner with his first steady job, answerable to no one else now in his musical career (though Buff when on leave from the Army would work for Tubb occasionally). Soon he had cause for even more joy. A few months into their marriage, Ernest and Elaine moved from the former Castleman apartment on Porter Street to a duplex on the same street with C. R. Tubb Jr.'s family on the other side. Ernest was happy being close to Bud again, and Elaine was always happiest in her home town, near her parents. C. R.'s growing family welcomed its third son (his fourth), Douglas Glenn Tubb, to the Porter Street duplex on June 29, 1935. Then seven weeks later, on August 20, the stork came back to the duplex bringing Ernest and Elaine's first child, a son they named Justin Wayne Tubb. Elaine favored "Ernest Dale Tubb Jr." for the name, but Ernest, no great fan of his own name, as we have seen (and as his first published letter in 1940 to the *Mountain Broadcast and Prairie Recorder* confirms), picked "Justin" out of a book, a name meaning "true, right, just." The new baby brought Ernest a 25 percent raise from Mr. Hein, to the grand sum of $12.50 per week.

"JIMMIE'S WIFE"

Not long after Justin's birth—probably in the spring of 1936—on a mere chance call, a whim, Ernest Tubb met the lady he would later describe as his guiding light: Mrs. Carrie Rodgers, the widow of his idol. Her faith and belief in him would soon open some very important career doors, and her advice would make the bumps in his long road to stardom easier to take. They forged a mutually beneficial relationship, cemented by trust and affection, which held for the rest of her life—twenty-five years, almost twice the length of her thirteen-year marriage to Jimmie.

The story of their meeting is one of the best-known anecdotes from previous accounts of Tubb's career; only its date remains problematic. Mildred Williamson, youngest sister of Mrs. Rodgers, who was finishing her studies at San Antonio's Incarnate Word College and living with Carrie and her daughter Anita Rodgers in an upstairs apartment in the duplex, remembers that when Ernest paid his visit, Elaine and baby Justin came along. This places the meeting sometime between August 1935, and October 27, 1936, the date of the Tubb-Rodgers Bluebird recording sessions. A chance circumstance that Tubb recalled from their meeting—that Mrs. Rodgers, to his surprise, was planting in her flower garden as he walked toward her door—makes the springtime of 1936 their probable meeting date, which allows the necessary several months for the relationship to build and the wheels to spin prior to the recording session.

The meeting itself took place because the only photograph of Jimmie Rodgers that Ernest had was a tattered, wallet-sized shot. Longing for a better, bigger one, perhaps an autographed print suitable for framing, he looked up Mrs. Rodgers's number in the phone book and prepared nervously to place a call. He had no idea what sort of person she was or how receptive she might be to such random fan phone calls. Assuming that many of Jimmie's songs had been autobiographical, he wondered whether she was more like the affectionate housewife of "Home Call" or the more numerous examples of dreadful women, from Thelma in "Blue Yodel" down through Jimmie's various mean, night-lifing "High Powered Mama[s]." Somehow he got the nerve, made the call, and once reassured that he was indeed talking to *the* Mrs. Jimmie Rodgers, asked about a photo. She couldn't have been nicer, assuring him that she probably had a picture that would be just right, and that he might want to drop by the house and pick it up. The date was set for the next Sunday afternoon that Tubb did not work.

Another thing Tubb could not have known and would never have guessed was that the widow of the great Jimmie Rodgers had fallen on (comparatively) hard times, not unlike just about everyone else. In later years, Charlie Walker got the story from Mrs. Rodgers firsthand.

She told me she and Jimmie had borrowed against future royalties to have money to put into it, so they put everything they had just about to build this dream home of theirs in Kerrville, Texas . . . I think they sold it for nearly nothing, less than half of what they had put into it. So she told me that after he died and the royalties were just nothing because there weren't any sales . . . she was almost ashamed to go to the grocery store, cause where she had gone in there and cashed checks for $1,000, they'd [now] be $2.98, $5.00 . . . "Well, I don't have it now, but I can always say I had it." . . . They drove Cadillacs that cost as much in those days—I mean, custom-made Cadillacs . . . $10,000 back in the early thirties . . . and I only paid $6,500 for my first Cadillac, a 1977 model.[19]

Floyd Tillman met her at or shortly after Jimmie Rodgers's prime, and fan that he was, Floyd was ready to be impressed; he now says that he thought she was "a real-life Sears Roebuck fashion model."[20] One sister affectionately recalls her manner by dubbing her "the aristocrat of the family."[21] Norma Barthel called her "one of the daintiest and best-groomed ladies that I ever knew."[22] No wonder Tubb was surprised to see her working the flower beds rather than having servants do it, when he and his young family strolled up to her door on Montclair Avenue in Alamo Heights that fateful Sunday afternoon. She did, of course, have on a nice apron to keep from unduly soiling her Sunday clothes.

The lovely aristocrat proved to be the soul of kindness to the visiting Tubb family. What the Tubbs had planned as a ten-minute stay stretched to more than two hours. Mrs. Rodgers showed Ernest pictures, costumes, guitars—most of which he never dreamed existed. He even got to hold Jimmie's guitar, the legendary Martin D-45 that he would eventually use for far more years than Jimmie ever did. Of course he got the photo he came for, and left on cloud nine. And he somehow remembered to say in passing as they left that he had a program on KONO three mornings each week and that he often sang Jimmie Rodgers songs on his shows. Not dreaming she'd actually get up that early to listen, he left, figuring that delightful afternoon would be the extent of his contact with Jimmie's wife.

It wasn't. A few months passed and, much to his surprise, he got a call from Mrs. Rodgers with "good news and bad news." The bad news (to Tubb) was her opinion, after listening to some of his KONO shows, that he didn't sound at all like her late husband. Tubb's earliest recordings, made within the next two years, indicate that she was right, though workmates, family, and friends had always told him otherwise. To Mrs. Rodgers, his phrasing was comparable to Jimmie's, and his heartfelt, convincing delivery of a song was very much the same. Her belief that he sang from the heart in such a convincing manner led to the good news: because of this, she thought he had possibilities and would, with his permission, try to open a few doors to help his career. Naturally Tubb was elated to accept whatever help she might offer; he probably would have taken anyone's help at this point, but from the widow of his idol, there was no way he'd refuse. Weeks passed, and she would call him with ideas and ask him to come out to her house and talk them over. Carrie's sister Mildred Williamson remembers keeping baby Justin on more than one occasion while Ernest, Elaine, and Carrie went out to make useful contacts. Sometimes Mildred went along with Carrie to watch Ernest and Merwyn Buffington work the drive-ins from makeshift platform stages.

Their growing professional association seemed to slow over the summer of 1936, when Carrie, Anita, and Mildred, just after Mildred's college graduation, went back to their home country in Mississippi to spend a few weeks there as they always did. But even then, Carrie Rodgers was not idle on Ernest's behalf. She was talking to one of her Meridian sisters, the famous Mrs. Elsie McWilliams, composer of several of Jimmie Rodgers's best songs, about song material that Ernest might use. According to Norma Barthel, Elsie had largely lost interest in songwriting after Jimmie Rodgers's death, although Jimmie Davis, singer of "Nobody's Darlin' But Mine," may have obtained a few songs from her in the intervening three years. There were a couple of songs she had written about Jimmie Rodgers, though, that Carrie felt might work for Ernest Tubb, since he was such a dedicated disciple: "My Blue Bonnet Dream" and "The Passing of Jimmie Rodgers." Elsie had written the first song from conversations she'd had with Jimmie's nurse about what was on Jimmie's mind at the time of his last trip to New York in May 1933 to make records. His Texas home, bluebonnet flowers, wife, daughter: these themes Elsie wove into a musical picture of Jimmie Rodgers's final thoughts. In fact, the title Ernest used years later for his Decca recording of the song was "Jimmie Rodgers's Last Thoughts," although, as we shall see, RCA chose "The Last Thoughts of Jimmie Rodgers" when he first recorded it, to link the title as closely as possible with its companion, "The Passing of Jimmie Rodgers."

This song Elsie wrote for a kinsman of Jimmie's, Doug Rodgers, who had planned to step into the show business void left by Jimmie's passing. Doug remains a mystery figure, since he too very soon died and never got to sing that (or any other) song on record. Tubb told Norma Barthel that he never heard Doug Rodgers or even heard of him before talking to Carrie Rodgers about this song. But the lyrics really do describe what Ernest Tubb was trying to do at that time:

> Though unworthy am I, yet I'm happy to try
> To finish the task he begun.

Lyrics are, of course, one thing and melody another; even when Carrie brought back sheet music of these two songs, Tubb couldn't learn them that way. He couldn't read music, and Carrie couldn't play piano. Elsie had no way to make or send home recordings in those faraway days, so at Carrie's insistence, Elsie made a trip to San Antonio early that fall to teach Ernest Tubb those two songs, singing them to her own piano accompaniment while Ernest worked it out with voice and guitar as best he could. This was the same way she'd written for and with Jimmie Rodgers, and the similarity of these sessions doesn't end there. She's been quoted saying that Ernest was "hard-headed like Jimmie Rodgers."[23] One wonders now if that means "slow learner" or simply "determined to do the songs his way." In any event, she had the patience to see it through, and Ernest Tubb had his first two custom-made songs from another writer.

4

Bluebird Records and a Tour

THE BLUEBIRD RECORDINGS

Why the urgency to learn "The Last Thoughts of Jimmie Rodgers" and "The Passing of Jimmie Rodgers"? Sometime in the late summer or early fall, Carrie Rodgers had pulled her first successful string for Ernest Tubb: she had convinced Eli Oberstein of RCA, the man who had produced Jimmie Rodgers late in his life, to record Tubb (and herself) for the label when he came to San Antonio for sessions in October.

Bluebird Records was RCA Victor's 35-cent, budget-line label, a Depression-era necessity, home by this time to the company's hillbilly and race musicians, who were no longer accorded releases on the main company label (and would not be until the end of World War II). To cut costs, Oberstein hit the road from his New York offices and, with portable equipment in tow, recorded his Bluebird artists "on location" in such Southern cities as Atlanta, Dallas, and San Antonio. Tubb was then largely unknown around San Antonio and completely unknown outside of it, but Oberstein agreed to record him as a favor to the widow of a man he had known, a man who had once made his company a lot of money.

Oberstein set up shop where he always did on San Antonio trips, in the Texas Hotel. He had been on the road much of the month, on a Southern swing that had already included recording stops in Charlotte and New Orleans. The two most prolifically recorded acts that week in San Antonio from the country field were the Tune Wranglers of San Antonio and Bill Boyd's Cowboy Ramblers, down from Dallas. Each band, pioneers in the burgeoning western swing genre, cut multiple sides for Oberstein: the Tune Wranglers on October 24 and Boyd's group on the 27th.

Mrs. Rodgers's lone recording of the sessions was made October 26, the day before Ernest made his six. It was an Elsie McWilliams song, written from the family's viewpoint: "We Miss Him When the Evening Shadows Fall." Carrie always said she was no singer, and proved it here, while Ernest provided the chords and simple runs on Jimmie's famous Martin. The irony is striking: Tubb sang long before he played the guitar, and had certainly not mastered the instrument by this time, but his first recorded performance is as guitarist. RCA company ledgers make much of the guitar, and nothing of the guitarist: "Accompaniment played on Jimmie Rodgers' own guitar." It may seem odd that only one song was done, causing Mrs. Rodgers to be paired on 78s with other artists; but in three of its four releases, the other artist was her late husband (Bluebird B-6698, Regal Zonophone ME33, and MR 2429). The Montgomery Ward issue of "We Miss Him When the Evening Shadows Fall," M-7085, had the Blue Sky Boys on the flip. In 1968, RCA Victor issued an LP of Jimmie Rodgers tributes and used this as the title cut (RCA Victor LSP-4073).

Ernest Tubb got his big chance the next day, Tuesday, October 27, from 1:00 to 2:15 in the afternoon. Bill Boyd and his Cowboy Ramblers were on a lunch break, resting between the first six and last twelve recordings in their eighteen-song marathon, when Oberstein put Tubb before the microphone. Somehow the nervous rookie, alone with the famous guitar, laid down six cuts in the space of that hour and a quarter, three in two takes and three in only a single take. He began with credible performances of the two McWilliams songs, "The Passing of Jimmie Rodgers" and "The Last Thoughts of Jimmie Rodgers," which would constitute his first release (Bluebird B-6693) that December. Quickly he moved on to four of his own compositions, about which he said in a 1960s questionnaire from collectors Bill French and Gene Earle, "The blues numbers was [sic] inspired by his [Rodgers's] blue yodels . . . 'My Mother Is Lonely' by 'Mother the Queen of My Heart.' All [were inspired by Rodgers] except 'The Right Train to Heaven,' which was my own inspiration."[1] His blues numbers were "Married Man Blues," a lament for the loss of freedom within the marital bonds, and "Mean Old Bed Bug Blues," a jailhouse blues with affinities to several Rodgers songs and identical melodically to Tubb's own later "Mean Mama Blues." RCA chose the Rodgers tributes for first release and may never have issued the four Tubb originals but for his later success with Decca. "Married Man Blues"/"Mean Old Bed Bug Blues" was issued as Bluebird B-8899 in early 1942, and "My Mother Is Lonely"/"The Right Train to Heaven" as Bluebird B-8966 later that same year, by which time Tubb was a national jukebox favorite.

Years later, Ernest Tubb still talked about the thrill of hearing his own voice on records for the first time as a career landmark. And as he explained, he had to wait until the record came out to have that privilege: there was no tape in 1936, and an in-studio playback was out of the question. During the hurried session, he had no sense of the quality of his performances. And though he thought little of their professional quality in later years ("They were very amateurish"), clearly at the time he was thrilled to have anything out on records. At least twice he posed for family snapshots holding his first record. Tubb sent copies to family members, including one to sister Blondie Collier up in Kaufman, Texas. They had no phonograph, but could play it at neighbors' homes. The Colliers' six-year-old daughter, Anna Ruth, wondered at first who the "Ernest Tubb" on that label was: she'd only known him as Uncle Slick to that point.

Disappointment only began to set in with the sales figures. Maybe his release's coming so late in the fiscal year made this amount unrealistically low, or perhaps it reflects deducted session costs; in any event, Tubb never forgot that his first RCA royalty check was for $1.27.[2] Presumably this was in addition to a flat fee at the time of recording, since Tubb was his own session musician. But sales are what the company considers when it ponders an artist's future, so it was probably fortunate for Tubb and Mrs. Rodgers that so little time elapsed between their first record releases and Mr. Oberstein's next trip to San Antonio for recordings. A follow-up session may have been part of Mrs. Rodgers's original agreement with Oberstein. In any event, Oberstein, by now the top dog at RCA,[3] returned to San Antonio's Texas Hotel for late February and early March 1937 sessions.

Tubb and Carrie Rodgers, his manager, were ready when Oberstein recorded them March 2, with songs from a familiar source: Mrs. Elsie McWilliams. First up (1:45 to 2:15 P.M.) once again, Carrie Rodgers made a single recording, Elsie's "My Rainbow Trail Keeps Winding On," a dreamy, sentimental song that Ernest would record in 1940 as simply "My Rainbow Trail." This time, in addition to Ernest's playing on the D-45 Martin guitar, there was a second former Jimmie Rodgers Martin, a smaller model, played by Merwyn Buffington. Buff's Army duties had apparently kept him away from the first session, but his subdued and tasteful licks add a lot to these later recordings. Mrs. Rodgers's vocal, as before, needs all the help it can get. Her recording, issued considerably later in Bluebird's numerical sequence than Ernest's two songs of the day, was buried on the flip side of its only Bluebird release (B-7339) with the scarcely known McClendon Brothers & Georgia Dell.

One of Ernest's two selections that day was also an Elsie McWilliams composition, "Since That Black Cat Crossed My Path," and likewise features the capable second guitar assistance of his friend Buff Buffington. Buffington takes solo breaks in the song—"Play it, brother"—but he doesn't really play the straight melody lead guitar work that Jimmie Short and Billy Byrd would immortalize on later Tubb records. "Merwyn did not play lead guitar. He played runs, what we call bass runs, like they still do, the old-fashioned fiddle players [when] they have a guitar in there . . . But Merwyn, instead of playing mainly just chords, played a lot of runs behind you, especially if you were singing something. But he did not play melody."[4] Their two takes on "Since That Black Cat Crossed My Path" ate up most of the miserly quarter hour (2:15 to 2:30 P.M.) they were allotted.

Tubb's first recording that day, made in only one take, was his own answer to a Jimmie Rodgers classic. Jimmie had optimistically sung of "Whipping That Old T.B." a couple of years before the dreaded disease took his life. Ernest's less cheerful adaptation—a song that only a man not suffering from the disease could sing—he called "The T.B. Is Whipping Me" and recorded it in classic Rodgers style with the one guitar. Later, after decades of cigarette smoking, Tubb could truthfully say, "My lungs are rattling, and you oughta hear this cough of mine," but at the time he had little to worry about. Even if his Rodgers idolatry had convinced him he too would die at age thirty-five, he still had twelve years to go at that point.

Record sales rather than health were his real concern now, and his worst fears were justified when the sales of this next coupling, Bluebird B-7000, proved virtually nonexistent. Since the two wartime Bluebirds sold considerably better, B-7000 is now the most rare Tubb recording, with B-6693 a close second. Either of these first two Bluebirds will fetch at least $100 when sold by knowledge-able collectors. Anyone who pays less for them has profited from some poor soul's ignorance.

THE TOUR

Come what may, Ernest Tubb and Carrie Rodgers could truthfully call them-selves "Exclusive Victor Recording Artists," at least for the time being. And that's just what they did, on a famous tour of South Texas towns they embarked on for part of May and June 1937.

Mrs. Rodgers figured that her name would pull some good crowds for both of them on a theater tour. It would be a good way to give Ernest much-needed stage experience and promote the record at the same time. She planned to do little more than introduce Ernest with the famous guitar; his singing would take up nearly all of the twenty-minute program they'd do between movie features. Mrs. Rodgers scheduled the theater dates, worked out the deals with the theater managers, arranged the hotel accommodations, supplied the transportation, and even paid for promotion. One long banner and two large stand-up marquees were used on each stop of the tour. A handbill for their performance on June 5, at Comfort, Texas's Community Theatre is shown in the photo section.

Another up-front cost for Mrs. Rodgers was Ernest's salary. To make a two-week tour, he had to leave his job at Mr. Hein's drugstore, so she paid him his full monthly salary of $50. Ernest had his money even if the tour proved disastrous; the risk was all hers. Carrie's sister Mildred (Mrs. George Pollard as of Christmas Eve 1936), who still lived with Carrie and Anita Rodgers in their Alamo Heights duplex, went along on the tour primarily "to stop wagging tongues," as she puts it now. She helped with the driving and was Carrie's roommate each night out.[5] Elaine Tubb had young Justin to care for and could not go. And for whatever reason, probably his continued Army service, guitarist Merwyn Buffington did not go along either.

Posted on the marquees were brand-new publicity shots of Mrs. Rodgers and Ernest—in his case, the famous tuxedo photos. A handwritten note to my 1977 Ernest Tubb interview transcript, at the point I asked about the tuxedo, reads "Mr. Tubb moans."

> That was a case of economics. I didn't have any money—I was making $12.50 a week. I didn't own a coat. She wanted to take some professional pictures and she said, "I'll make the appointment. You put on a suit." I said, "I don't own a suit." . . . She was gonna pay for the pictures; I didn't want her to spend a lot of money. So I said, "How about Jimmie's tux?" 'cause she'd shown me the tux . . . The pants were too small, but the coat I could wear. She said, "Well, have you got a dark pair of pants. Put them on, and we'll just shoot from the waist up." . . . So she did buy me a new pair of pants to go with the tux, that would fit me . . . and so this was the most economical way she could dress me to start to do those shows . . .[6]

The best-known photo from this session adorned the cover of Tubb's first *American Music Song Folio* (1941).[7] In one of the other shots, Tubb sports Jimmie Rodgers's jaunty black derby hat.[8] Apparently, with such photos on the tour marquee, it was decided that that's what he must wear on stage: in hindsight a big mistake, given the type of audience.

> I shouldn't have been in a tux to start with. She later realized that . . . And what I discovered then which I really didn't think about—I was too scared to even think anything—but the fact was we played the little towns out in South Texas and the fans, they'd come to see because it was advertised: she's the one that brought the people, no one had ever heard of Ernest Tubb. I had the one record out, you know, "The Passing of Jimmie Rodgers." . . . So a few people came. Let's say we didn't make any money but she didn't lose any money, we paid for the promotion . . . But the fact is I learned one thing: that people, by my wearing this tux, they were even afraid to come back and say hello. I mean, they came to

see the guitar and they did seem to like my singing. But I had put myself above 'em, follow me? They came in there in overalls and blue jeans, and here I was up there singing Jimmie Rodgers songs in a tuxedo, so they didn't think I was very friendly.[9]

Around Ernest Tubb, then, the people were afraid to speak. But it seems that a few of them weren't shy to vent their opinions in private. Norma Barthel relates this heartbreaking conversation Tubb overheard through the thin walls of one of the small-town hotels on their tour: "Who in the world does he think he is, that he can sing like Jimmie Rodgers? . . . And she lets him have Jimmie's guitar . . . and my goodness alive, the man can't sing at all . . ."[10] Words like that a rookie entertainer never forgets; not only did they not like his singing, but these particular listeners (and surely most of the rest of them) misunderstood his whole purpose, taking it to be practically the opposite of what it was. If ever soul lived who believed Jimmie Rodgers to be irreplaceable, it was Ernest Tubb. Barthel says, surely paraphrasing Tubb's own explanation, "What he was trying to do was carry on Jimmie's work, his type of singing, and not to try to replace him in any way. Mrs. Rodgers understood what he wanted to do, but he could see now that the public did not."[11]

Nonetheless, this famous tuxedo tour, with shows in San Antonio, Seguin, Uvalde, Del Rio, Comfort, and elsewhere, was not without its light moments and good times. Mildred Pollard, whose working life would be spent as a librarian, tells a wonderful story about this trip's being the one on which she discovered the joys of Margaret Mitchell's *Gone With the Wind*. Carrie Rodgers had been totally captivated the previous year by the brand-new book and ever since had urged sister Mildred to read it; on this tour, she finally found the time to do just that.

> I started reading it, and I'd read about a hundred pages, when Ernest knocked on our hotel door to see if we wanted to go for breakfast. I told them to go right ahead, I wasn't much of a breakfast eater . . . and I would keep on reading and see them later. So Carrie asked me, "What do you think of it?" And I, being very scholarly, said, "Well, there's no question about the fact that it's well-written, and definitely well-researched . . . but I just don't get it, this business of being so absorbed in it." Not like she was! And so she laughed and said, "Don't worry. You will!" So they went, and they had their breakfast, and when they came back I looked up and said, "Where have you been?" So that called forth a laugh from both of them, because it had really gotten me by that time.[12]

The story only gets better with the final episode.

We went on down to Del Rio, [to] that big station you can hear all over the United States. Carrie was a friend of Mrs. Brinkley [wife of the station owner], and so through that association they got on that radio station during that particular tour. And I was to stay back at the hotel where we were, and tune in to critique their performance over the radio. And when they came back, I had forgotten to turn on the radio because I was reading *Gone With the Wind* . . . And Carrie, I can still see her, standing there and looking at me, she was the aristocrat of the family . . . She stamped her foot, and she says, "Honey, if it were anything but *Gone With the Wind,* I would be so provoked with you I would not know what to do! But since it is, I so completely understand that you're forgiven."[13]

What would an Ernest Tubb fan today give for a recording of that broadcast? Or of any of their theater shows, for that matter? Norma Barthel, describing Tubb's own memories of the shows, says they consisted of Mrs. Rodgers's spoken introduction, about seventeen minutes of Tubb singing Jimmie Rodgers songs and his own "The Passing of Jimmie Rodgers," and a closing unison duet on "When It's Peach Picking Time in Georgia." Tubb's own realistic appraisal of the finale, in Norma's words, is "It didn't turn out too well, as Ernest couldn't sing harmony at all and Mrs. Rodgers had never tried to sing . . . , except maybe in church, and she certainly didn't claim to be a singer. She agreed to do these things only to help Ernest."[14] If they learned from their mistakes, Carrie Rodgers and Ernest Tubb finished this tour much wiser, if no richer. But there was yet more embarrassment for the first-time trouper on this tour. In the "life's most embarrassing moment" department, Tubb never forgot being blinded by the spotlight in the theater in Burnet, Texas, throughout his set of five or six songs. When he rose to go down the front steps into the audience (his only exit from the stage), he missed a step and stumbled right over the edge into the pit. A stunned audience watched in silence as he rose sheepishly from his pratfall; Tubb, and more importantly the tour's real star, the well-advertised "$1,500 guitar," were unhurt.[15]

AN ENDURING FRIENDSHIP

A year's tutelage from Mrs. Rodgers, from the spring of 1936 through the spring of 1937, had really not taken young Ernest Tubb very far in the music profession. He'd made eight recordings, though only half of these had been released, and they weren't selling. He'd seen South Texas at no personal expense. When the tour wrapped up with so little fanfare and profit, Mrs. Rodgers really didn't know what more she could do. She'd found songs and she'd gotten him on records; but as yet she'd had no luck getting Tubb's own songs published or finding him more lucrative radio work. Ernest could not go back to his drugstore job, so with a family to support he had to look for work elsewhere: outside of San Antonio, as it turned out, to places Mrs. Rodgers and her own young daughter could not possibly go. But she could and did lend him the finest guitar around. Forever after his first recording session, Ernest Tubb had the use of the D-45 Martin, with "Jimmie Rodgers" down the neck in mother-of-pearl, and "Blue Yodeler" across the tuning keys.

What, after all, had she seen in this young man that had made her place such faith in his ability? In her own words, just this:

> When I first met Ernest . . . I was impressed not only by the similarity of his voice to that of Jimmie Rodgers, but by the man himself and his devotion to "America's Blue Yodeler." His personality and character, plus his ability both as a singer and songwriter, made it quite evident that here was a man who would succeed. I decided to help him attain that goal, in whatever way I could. And I gave him Jimmie's beloved Martin guitar to use . . .[16]

In the earliest description of her reasons for helping Tubb, Mrs. Rodgers alludes to the fact that others before him sought her help, though her use of the word "auditioned" makes it sound like she was actively seeking a Jimmie Rodgers successor to promote, a highly dubious construction of the facts, given her limited funds.

> Of all the artists I've auditioned since the passing of my husband, Ernest Tubb is my choice. I think America's Blue Yodeler would have been proud of my having selected Ernest Tubb to sponsor as he has proven worthy in every respect. He has the voice, personality, and ability to put the feeling into his songs that have won him many admirers among Jimmie's fans and Ernest is very grateful, as Jimmie Rodgers has been his inspiration since his youth. For radio work and personal appearances, as well as recordings, I am proud to extend to Ernest the privilege of using Jimmie's famous guitar, for which privilege he has expressed his gratitude.[17]

Obscured by the somewhat condescending tone of this statement (perfectly in keeping with the adjacent unsmiling photo of Mrs. Rodgers in the songbook) is a real bond of personal and professional association that would ultimately bear much fruit for both parties. No one could blame Mrs. Rodgers for wanting some return on her considerable invested capital in Ernest Tubb: money for clothes, for pictures, for the tour expenses, the use of a $1,500 guitar, and the continued hunt for contacts. Ernest's nephew Talmadge Tubb says that their agreement for her sponsorship and managerial services was 50-50 on future proceeds, though he admits that she was a long time making *anything* on Ernest Tubb.[18] In fact, so much time passed between her initial investment and his stardom—four years, with very little active involvement on her part beyond letters and calls to record company and publishing contacts—that she couldn't possibly have held him to that agreement. Mildred Pollard believes "that they had an understanding. Ernest used his influence after he became the star to boost her income as well as his own: it was kind of tit-for-tat there for awhile . . . I do know that Ernest made his own contacts finally, and started off on his own." In the 1940s Tubb used lawsuits and the threat of lawsuits against Jimmie's old publisher, Peer, to boost her royalty income.[19] Later, Ernest Tubb the star pushed RCA to reissue more Jimmie Rodgers records, then plugged the records incessantly on his *Midnite Jamboree* broadcasts. He even recorded Jimmie Rodgers songs himself on tribute records, long after he'd lost the "obligatory" yodel technique. Tubb took Mrs. Rodgers to Hollywood with him on moviemaking trips, and in 1952 he bought her a Cadillac,[20] to say nothing here of his financial assistance during her final illness. Clearly, she was well repaid personally for the early capital she invested in Ernest Tubb: it wasn't simply that he followed her advice, "Ernest, if you want to repay me, just help others." And that he did, without leaving these other things undone.

Mrs. Carrie Rodgers was present, either at the hospital or at the Tubb home just afterward, for the birth of all five of Ernest Tubb's Nashville children by his second wife, Olene (in 1951, 1952, 1956, 1958, and 1960). She was a frequent visitor in the Tubb home, a tagalong on his Texas tours, and a favored though infrequent guest of his *Midnite Jamboree* radio show between 1948 and 1960: as close to Ernest Tubb, in other words, as she could possibly be, bridging the miles between San Antonio and wherever Ernest was—San Angelo, Fort Worth, or Nashville.

Mrs. Rodgers will reappear in this story at important strategic junctures, but for now, I close the subject with a poem, "Jimmie's Wife," that Ernest Tubb published in the June 1941 *Mountain Broadcast and Prairie Recorder*.

> There's an old guitar that's lonely
> For it's [*sic*] master's hand today,
> But he has gone on to heaven,
> Up where the angels stay.
>
> Many songs he left here behind him.
> In memory he is with us yet.
> His records just keep on playing,
> So how could we ever forget.

We have heard songs about his passing,
And songs about his life,
But I am writing this little poem
To tell you about his wife.

Of course we all loved Jimmie
He was the greatest of them all.
Yodelers will come and go
But his fame will never fall.

But let us not forget the one
Who took the hardest blow.
When the Lord called Jimmie from her,
I know it grieved her so.

She was the one who shared his life,
When he was gay or sad,
She never grumbled, I am sure,
When things seemed kinda bad.

She smiled and pushed him on his way
To better things in life,
She was the one who loved him best.
Yes, I mean Jimmie's wife.

And since he has gone and left her
Alone with memories,
I wonder if she's lonesome
For days that used to be.

And when she looks at his picture
Hanging there on the wall,
I wonder if the times turn back,
And sweet days she recalls.

And when she heard that familiar voice,
Upon that round black disc,
I know her heart is bound to throb
With pains of loneliness.

For her I say a little prayer,
Who gave up all in life,
To tread a road that was sometimes hard,
To be our Jimmie's wife.[21]

5

Detours

For Ernest Tubb, the South Texas tour, itself no great triumph, was followed by a series of detours. He couldn't have known it at the time, of course; nothing necessarily prevented the success of his next few entertainment ventures. Some of them even started out well, as we shall see. But in the months between May 1937 and January 1938, Ernest Tubb was practically an itinerant musician—or at least as close to one as family responsibilities would permit.

MIDLAND

Shortly after the tour, Tubb's guitar playing buddy Merwyn Buffington received his Army discharge. With the cash that was customarily given to a discharged soldier, Buffington bought a big car, a seven-passenger Buick. Why he wanted or needed a car that size is anyone's guess, but it certainly came in handy for the scheme that he and Ernest soon hatched.

Buffington wanted to get back into music with Ernest; he had never really left it, in fact, playing San Antonio drive-ins with Tubb and one recording session during his three Army years. Ernest was out of a day job and with no real musical prospects in San Antonio, so he was game for a ride to West Texas with Buffington in his big car to test the musical waters out there. Merwyn had a brother in Monahans, Texas: "We visited him and stayed overnight and then we left and went on as far as Midland, and that's of course where we did land a contract with Blatz-Old Heidelberg."[1] I wish I had more details, but at this same point in my Tubb interview, a similar elision occurs: "We wound up . . . in Monahans. He had a brother living in Monahans. We went out there, and to make a long story short, we finally got on the radio in Midland, Texas."[2] Without relating any of that story, long or short, Tubb added, "There was a beer distributor there [who] heard us, liked us, and called and got the Blatz Brewing Company to sponsor us."[3]

Mr. Russell was the Blatz distributor in Midland, and soon that town's only radio station, KRLH, 250 watts at 1450 on the dial, could boast a program featuring Blatz's Western Melody Boys. Besides Tubb and Buffington (Buff providing a second guitar sound and occasional harmony vocals), there were one or two female singers in the group. Tubb later only remembered one, Kathleen "Kitty" Hewitt, and said it was Buff's idea to hire her. "He wanted the little girl singer there in town that he'd heard, Kitty Hewitt, and he wanted us to hire her, take her and let her sing with us for color. She was a pretty girl and from a real fine family. Her daddy used to be a religious singer; used to be in the Stamps Quartet, in fact. This is how we had the three of us. She sang, I sang solo, and then Buff and I would sing duets together—he also sang harmony, you see. That was in Midland, and we were there I guess for about a year."[4] Buffington too remembered their Midland stay lasting about a year,[5] so it could well be that they had started work in Midland even before the final San Antonio session and the South Texas tour. Norma Barthel's book is probably accurate when it says they stayed in Midland only about three months before heading back to San Antonio.[6] The only significant difference in their accounts involves a second female singer whom Buffington believes they used: a dark-haired woman whose name he could not recall. "They were real good . . . I oftentimes wondered [why] they didn't go up. They could have, very easily . . . The dark-haired girl finally got a job with an orchestra that came through there."[7]

Elaine Tubb remembers that the family moved to Midland with Ernest, though in 1977 he was not so sure. "Yeah, well, no, actually, we wound up living, moving to San Angelo. His [Mr. Russell's] father was a distributor in San Angelo, and he was a distributor in Midland, so we finally wound up working for both of them eventually: so we settled in San Angelo."[8] Buffington's recollection about the living accommodations was: "We [Tubb and Buffington] stayed there ourselves about a month, or month and a half, until we made enough money to rent a place, and then we sent for Elaine and Justin . . . and she lived there in Midland about a year."[9] Buff was still a single man at the time, with his eye on one of the two singers, unless I misread Mr. Tubb's comment. Wherever the Tubb family was settled the latter half of 1937, by January 1938 they had moved to San Angelo, as we'll see shortly. But before that, Tubb and Buffington took yet another detour.

BEAUMONT

About the Beaumont detour even less is known, and that little is contradictory. It seems to have been almost a lark, the sort of crazy idea that young men sometimes get and sometimes act upon. Probably the Midland broadcasts had played out, and, still hoping to make it somewhere as a twosome, Tubb and Buffington got the idea to hitchhike to Nashville from San Antonio.

What follows is my 1977 dialogue on the subject with Merwyn Buffington, with his comments in quotes.

What had happened to the seven-passenger Buick? "Well, I sold that car. I don't remember just where I sold it—seems like in San Antonio . . . It started giving me quite a bit of trouble, so I sold it." Where were Ernest's folks at this time? "They stayed with her folks [the Webbers, in San Antonio]." Elaine did know that you were going? "Oh yes . . . She had faith that we's gonna make it." Nashville was your destination? "And we got stopped in Beaumont . . . one of us suggested that we just go in the station there [KRMD, the big one in town, if Edward Linn is right in his 1957 *Saga* article on Tubb],[10] it was real handy, close by, and so we went in there, and they wanted us to play some. And then they just prevailed upon us to stay. They said they'd practically guarantee us a sponsor within a week. So that sounded pretty good to us . . . no sponsor came and so we ran out of money, just about, and we had to go back."

Did you play any night spots, drive-ins, the week that you were there? "Yeah; we couldn't get hardly but one night spot. We were taking the money away from their nickelodeons, then. They didn't like that. We couldn't get over one night at each place . . . I was using Jimmie Rodgers's small Martin guitar; I had had my large Martin guitar stolen from me in the meantime in San Antonio. And Mrs. Rodgers loaned me the small guitar that Jimmie made his first recordings on . . . Ernest had the Jimmie Rodgers guitar with Jimmie's name written in mother-of-pearl down the neck. So we were going to Nashville with two famous guitars, anyway!"[11]

In Edward Linn's 1957 version of the story, based on interviews with Tubb at the time, Tubb and Buffington (whom he does not mention) actually did broadcast on KRMD, gratis, having been promised the sponsor that never came.[12] KRMD may have kept them on a good while at no pay, as San Antonio's KONO had with Ernest. But as Buffington said, the money ran out, so it was back to San Antonio.

Trying to place his Ernest Tubb adventures in chronological sequence, in 1977 Mr. Buffington was unclear about several things, but sure of this: the Beaumont mishap was the end of the line. "After we came back from Beaumont, I quit the music business . . . I stayed in San Antonio then . . . until I went to traveling. It wasn't too long [after that] . . . I traveled in the evangelistic work thirty-six years [for] the Church of Christ . . . I was getting just a little bit sick of the music business." His fondest memories were of Midland: "We made personal appearances every night in Midland. We had it good there, if we'd a saved our money, but we spent it 'bout as fast as we made it."

And his least fond memory? Not counting the time he said that he had to pull a jealous husband off Ernest before he was choked to death,[13] it would have to be this:

> I could tell you that we slept under several bridges during our time. Well, I remember one time—I think it was Fredericksburg, Texas—we was hitchhiking, and we hadn't had anything to eat for three days. And he had too much pride to ask—he was just like I was—to ask anybody for anything, you know, so I said, "Well, I'm going down to this bakery down here and tell him to give us some day-old bread, something they're gonna throw away anyhow. I got that much pride." Well, the old baker, he just pulled the glass back, and filled our sack full of goodies, and I told him, "I didn't ask for that." He said, "That's all right." We went on down to the bridge where we're gonna make our bed that night and we filled up and had a good night's rest. We saw some hard times, but Ernest has come up; he's made his the hard way, I can say that.[14]

Besides his four years of good guitar work at drive-ins, radio stations, and on Bluebird records, not to mention providing the car and the contacts on the Midland adventure and tramping with Ernest literally across the state of Texas (it's a long way from Monahans to Beaumont, friends), Merwyn Buffington told me that before leaving Ernest to go into preaching (and Elaine Tubb says "He needed to do that; he was a good preacher"),[15] he lent a hand on what became some three years later Ernest's first Decca Records hit. "Now, the first record that he got a hit on was 'I'll Get Along Somehow.' He threw that song away and I picked it up and rewrote the chorus . . . I remember him writing me and asking me about recording it. He knew that I had something to do with it, you know. And I told him I didn't care what he did with it, he could do whatever he wanted to. And it wasn't long until I heard them playing it over the radio . . ."[16]

Merwyn Buffington visited Tubb in his Fort Worth days, on his way to visit relatives at Seymour, Texas, and was the second person to hear "Walking the Floor over You." The first person, Buffington says, was Jimmie Davis, who offered to buy it for $100. As badly as Tubb needed the money, Buffington said, he turned it down, figuring that if it was worth that much to Davis, it might be worth more to him. A fortunate intuition, indeed.

Though their contacts in later years were infrequent—a few letters, and phone calls when Tubb came to Austin, Buffington's long-time residence—the two men maintained a mutual love and respect. Tubb always acknowledged the great help that Buffington had been to him during some mighty lean years. When I talked to Buffington, he had retired from preaching after those thirty-six years of evangelistic travels and was confined to home and church by heart trouble.

Merwyn Jesse Buffington, born September 19, 1914 (seven months younger than Ernest), died October 3, 1987, having survived Tubb in spite of his heart trouble by just over three years.

BEER SALESMAN IN SAN ANGELO

In Midland, Tubb had worked for the Russell Distributing Company as a radio singer. After the Beaumont adventure, desperately seeking steady work, Tubb headed west again, to see if the Russells had another job for him. Mr. Russell's father had a beer distributorship in San Angelo, and he put Ernest Tubb to work in very late 1937 or very early 1938 in a new sort of day work, which was a considerable departure from cotton picking, ditch digging, or store tending: Tubb became a beer salesman.

Yes, there was a musical component to his job. The Russells knew from the Midland experience that Tubb loved to sing, so Russell senior hired him in San Angelo to sell a Texas beer, sing on the radio, then hit the road at night to sing in the beer joints selling an out-of-state brand. The Texas-brewed beer was Travis (from the Salinas Brewing Company; it's now Lone Star Beer); his old Midland sponsor, Blatz, was Tubb's nighttime beer, for which Russell had the distributorship in a four- or five-county area outside of San Angelo's Tom Green County. Tubb got $2 per night to plug Blatz at honky-tonks and nightclubs with his singing, plus 8 cents for each case sold. The singing was only supposed to last two hours, but with folks hollering for more, he'd often sing beyond three hours, effectively lowering his wage with each additional song.[17] Russell also lined up radio sponsors that paid Tubb $2.50 a day for a fifteen-minute program on San Angelo's KGKL, airing six afternoons per week at 5:30 P.M. So Tubb would sell Travis beer all day in San Angelo, clean up, do his radio show at KGKL's studios in the St. Angelus Hotel, then truck on out to the surrounding counties and sing for Blatz beer. San Angelo newspapers first list Tubb's program (*Ernest Tubbs,* a mistake lots of people have made since) on January 20, 1938. Home for Elaine and Justin (by New Year's 1938 Elaine was expecting their second child), and of course for Ernest when he wasn't working, was in a small place at 21 North Koenigheim in San Angelo.[18]

Learning "how to talk to people" was the main thing Tubb took from his few years in the beer business. Hard to believe as it may be, Ernest Tubb at that time had trouble talking to strangers, but beer selling cured him of it.

> I learned to talk. I didn't know a thing about beer when I first started selling it . . . I'd go in those places to sing, and they wondered what I was doing there. They figured I was advertising something, but I couldn't

talk. The distributor said, "You better learn to talk, or you ain't gonna have a job." So I said, "Write me out something." . . . In a short time, I finally learned to say, "Well, I'm selling Blatz Beer. Try some Blatz Beer."

From that modest beginning, Tubb soon branched out into a very effective spiel.

I learned that Budweiser put rice in their beer, and I hate rice, you know. From childhood I've never liked rice. And I would use that against Budweiser, my biggest competition [of the out of state beers]. And I would tell the old guys, the cowboys that come in there, "You don't even know what you're drinking." I'd kid 'em. I learned to talk. I said, "You're drinking beer that's got rice in there. Blatz would never put rice in beer." And they would say, "Aw, you're kidding." I'd say, "Naw, look on the label— they even print it on the label." . . . Course I didn't tell them that, they thought just because I said it had rice in it it wasn't good—probably was good for the beer, I don't know! They'd read on there, "Well, it sure has got rice. Give me some Blatz." So I did sell quite a bit of beer. I learned a lot. I learned how to talk. It helped me out in later years.[19]

In San Angelo, for the first time, Ernest Tubb got the gift of gab; he learned how to talk. He already knew how to sing, at least in the Jimmie Rodgers style, and by his own estimation was doing rather well at that on his KGKL program. "During those years when I wasn't recording at all, that's when I did my best singing and yodeling: 1937 or 1938. I have no records of my voice then."[20] "Between those [Bluebird] records and Decca there were about four years when I did not record anything. And about two years after I did those [Bluebird] records, I think I did my best singing and yodeling. I was real amateurish on those records, but I finally developed to where I could yodel pretty well. People would hear me on the radio and friends would bet one another as to whether it was me or a Jimmie Rodgers record."[21]

Things were going well in San Angelo up to and including the birth of a second son, Rodger Dale Tubb, on July 19, 1938. Named for Jimmie Rodgers (spelled with a "d") and Ernest Dale Tubb (he always liked the Dale part best), blue-eyed Rodger Dale, the image of his dad, was tragically killed in an auto wreck at just seven weeks. Here is the San Angelo newspaper account:

San Angelo Babe Car Wreck Victim
The two-months old baby of Mr. and Mrs. Ernest Tubb, 21 North Koenigheim, was killed in an automobile wreck near Fredericksburg early Friday morning, it was reported here Saturday. Mrs. Tubb, accompanied by the baby and a nurse, was enroute to San Antonio to visit her mother. They were reported to have left San Angelo late Thursday night or early

Friday morning. Word was received here about 8:30 o'clock Friday morning of the crash, and the baby was reported dead about 10 o'clock. Mr. Tubb left immediately for Fredericksburg. Burial was Saturday in a San Antonio cemetery. Mrs. Tubb and the nurse were not reported injured. Tubb, who has lived in San Angelo for about nine months, is employed by the Russell Distributing Company of San Angelo.[22]

The late-night departure of Mrs. Tubb, nurse, and baby—three-year-old Justin was already with Elaine's mother in San Antonio—supports the opinion that she was leaving home after a marital row.[23] The account makes no mention of a second car in the accident; this too lends credence to the source offering the detail that Rodger Dale was killed by a beer case that came loose on a sudden turn or stop.[24]

In any event, the young couple was devastated by the tragedy; if there was a marital rift, the shared tragedy healed it for the time being. Nothing could make up for Rodger Dale's loss, but the grieving father turned tragedy to eventual artistic triumph by writing the song "Our Baby's Book," what Ernest Tubb always called "the only 100% true song I ever wrote." By this he meant that every single detail in the lyrics was true to life: the baby's physical description, the parents' joy, even the song's composition on the pages of a pink baby book. "We just knew we's gonna have a daughter. See we had Justin, so we had already bought a pink baby book . . . I wrote the words of this song—actually, I wrote the words in my beer truck first, on the back of a scratch pad, I started it. But I wrote it off in our baby's book."[25] Rodger Dale Tubb lives on, not only in the song, but in the hundreds of baby boys named Rodger Dale after the hit record appeared in 1942.

The personal tragedy of Rodger Dale's death was almost immediately matched by a setback on the professional side. Tubb lost his KGKL program the next week. Wednesday, September 14, 1938, was the last listed airdate for the program. The very next evening, *Hillbilly Tunes* replaced the usual 5:30 listing for *Ernest Tubb,* and that night KGKL carried an entire evening of Texas State Network programming, a local spinoff of the Mutual Network. An accompanying article explained that "local talent will be affected by the shakeup." Tubb seems to have been one of the casualties. In view of the family tragedy, Tubb may already have determined on a temporary change of scenery. KGKL's programming change may only have hastened the move.

CORPUS CHRISTI

For the next eight months, roughly October 1938 to May 1939, the Tubbs lived in Corpus Christi. Ernest stayed in the beer business, changing only his distributor and his brands. In Corpus he sold Alamo beer, brewed in Houston by the Southern Brewing Company, a Howard Hughes venture. The rest of his life, Tubb could tell interviewers with some pride that he had once worked for the famous billionaire, though at the time things must not have been going very well for Mr. Hughes. Hard as it may be to believe about a Hughes company, the Southern Brewing Company went bankrupt, just as the makers of Travis beer—Salinas Brewing Company—had. A pattern emerges. "I used to kid about it; I said, 'Boys, don't give me a job. Everybody I go to work for goes bankrupt.'"[26] I have not yet determined if Southern's bankruptcy is what ended the Corpus Christi stay after eight months, but end it did. Similarly, there is no indication I have seen or heard that Ernest Tubb ever did any radio work in Corpus Christi, a shame if Tubb was in fact doing his "best singing" in those years. Truly this proved to be one more detour, though it would be just about his last.

Elaine Tubb remembers the work in Corpus rather clearly. "Well, we drove to Houston in a big truck. You'd slide your beer in like this, on both sides, and they just kinda slanted all the way up . . . In Houston we'd unload empties and bring back beer. And let me tell you: I drove for Ernest! Yeah, he'd lay down and put his head in my lap and go to sleep. He'd be so tired and everything." For living accommodations, she recalls that they rented rooms in a tourist-court type of establishment near Corpus Christi's great causeway. "The middle room was our beer, and Ernest would get up on the truck, open the window, and he'd slide it down a thing [slide] and I'd stack them as high [in the room] as I could. And then I'd start another one [stack], and then I'd walk up and finish filling it. . . . Oh, we had a time! It was fun."[27]

Maybe that sort of "fun" was what the Tubb family needed after the Rodger Dale tragedy. But Ernest Tubb had tasted enough success in music that he hankered for more. After eight months in Corpus Christi, Tubb could hear San Angelo calling again, and in the spring of 1939, the family headed back to "Swell San Angelo."

6

"Swell San Angelo"

On Thursday, May 25, 1939, the San Angelo *Standard-Times* newspaper carried the following news item:

> Cowboy Singer Returns to KGKL
>
> Ernest Tubb, whose program of cowboy and yodel songs won hundreds of friends in this section last year, is now broadcasting over radio station KGKL for an unlimited time. The program is on the air from 5:30 to 5:45 o'clock each day except Sunday.

Ernest Tubb came back to the city on the Concho River, the seat of Tom Green County, and back to KGKL in his old time slot. The Tubb family must have felt the sensation of déjà vu: moving to San Angelo again, and Elaine Tubb pregnant. Their next child, a daughter they named Violet Elaine, came December 3, 1939.

KGKL seems to have taken Ernest Tubb more seriously this time around. Another future Country Music Hall of Fame member, Jesse Granderson "Grant" Turner, remembers how hard the station management was grooming Tubb.

> I had gone there [San Angelo] to ask for a job, try to get a job as an announcer, and I was just a kid. And the station manager told me . . . "I've got this fellow here that we're trying to build into a star. We're trying to get him up to the point where we can promote him; we think we've got a diamond in the rough." And it was Ernest, and he was in the studio—again I didn't meet him—but he was working out. This man had him rehearsing in there, he had him up in front of a microphone, hour after hour, to try to learn something about radio.[1]

As before, Tubb could not make his living solely through a quarter-hour radio show, but it's unclear just which of two or three San Angelo day jobs he undertook first. Charlie Walker believes that for a time he was back in the beer business, selling a different Texas brand, Shiner beer.[2] Certainly that's what he had the most experience doing, and if Travis beer had vanished by this point, Mr. Russell may well have hired Tubb to peddle their new Texas beer around San Angelo. At nights he was for a time on the prowl for singing engagements. Cliff Kendrick of Bob Skyles and His Skyrockets, the popular Bluebird Records novelty band, recalled playing a swank San Angelo night spot ("so swanky they had checked tablecloths"), the Goodwin Tavern, in 1939, when a certain cowboy singer approached the snuff-dipping owner, Ma Goody, about work.

> We were playing there one time and some old boy came up; came in the front door and had this guitar strapped over his shoulder, his big old cowboy hat on, his boots on. And he came in there and says to old Ma Goody, "I'd like to get up there and sing some tunes." And old Ma says, "Well, Ernest, you ain't got no business coming out here in this place. You just get your ass out of here." She run him out, see? . . . He was making all these beer joints and playing for his kitty, his tips . . . And he came back [at another date] . . . so she let him get up there and sing during intermission . . . Nobody paid any attention to him . . . But a year or two later![3]

Old-timers in San Angelo recall Tubb also playing at the Wayside Inn and the Hangar Club. But before long, Tubb had had enough of singing for his kitty at other people's establishments. He bought his own beer joint.

THE E&E TAVERN

At some point before the end of 1939, Tubb became an entrepreneur. After wholesaling beer for years and collecting what tips he could for singing, he turned to the retail side of things and purchased the E&E Tavern on West Beauregard Street. Apparently the owner was eager to get rid of it: "I had $1.45 in my pocket when I bought it."[4] He took the name E&E to be a good omen, for Ernest and Elaine. He couldn't have given it a better name himself. Senior San Angelans remember Ernest Tubb's "little bitty beer joint"; one recalls, "The first time I ever knew him, he was sitting up on top of that beer joint [on an outside roof] a-playing for his tips. He was trying to make a living. He wasn't making any money."[5] Tubb recalled in 1959 that he owned the tavern for about eight months.[6]

When I asked Elaine Tubb her memories of this nightclub, fifty-five years after the fact, she was quick to correct my word choice: "He owned a *beer joint!*"

> Out [on] Chadbourne, we had a little house out behind, it's what I call a shotgun house—bedroom, dining room/office; the kitchen was small,

you could just barely get into it . . . That was out Chadbourne; and it was on the righthand side, and it was on a corner. Go around the corner, and then our house was right behind it . . . [The club came before the Western Mattress job?] Yes, before that. See . . . Elaine Jr. was born while we had that down back there, at the club.[7]

Mother Elaine remembered more about their "shotgun house" than she did about the "beer joint," for a simple reason: "Ernest wouldn't let me go in [to the tavern at night]! Every morning, he'd let me go in, and clean up. He had it all worked out."[8] The demands that the E&E Tavern made upon its singing proprietor turned what should have been a minor operation into a career watershed, when Ernest's inflamed tonsils had to come out. "I did ask the doctor if it would affect my voice and my yodeling. And he said, 'No.' They were so infected that they had to come out. They were swollen—in fact I had to let the swelling go down before he could even take them out. But he said, 'If it does anything, it will improve your voice.'"[9]

Had the doctor heard Tubb's two Bluebird releases? Was he a regular listener to Tubb's KGKL program? Was this a musical, as well as a medical opinion? In any event, Tubb continued the story:

> Well, of course I blamed him for a long time after this. But what really happened, it may have improved my voice had I given my throat a chance to heal up, but I didn't. I went back to singing, against his wishes, before I was supposed to . . . in about three days. I had a little club by this time, in late '39, I had a little club in San Angelo. And my singing's what brought business in, and when I had my tonsil operation I couldn't sing, and so to save my business I rushed back into singing before I should have—started yodeling and everything. And I tore my throat loose again. It started bleeding and so then I had to quit another three or four days, see. After that, my yodeling never was the same anymore, but part of that was my fault.[10]

The yodeling, for all practical purposes, was gone,[11] making of this simple tonsillectomy a career watershed. Angry and frustrated at the time, he not only didn't pay the doctor his $50 fee, but considered suing him. But as the quotation makes clear, Tubb gradually realized how much of the problem had been of his own making. Besides, the long-term effects of this tonsillectomy were only good. Without the yodel, he never again felt comfortable singing Jimmie Rodgers songs; hence he would have to find and develop his own singing style. And without the Jimmie Rodgers songs, he had to begin writing more of his own. "Jimmie's songs, most of them, didn't sound right at all to me without the yodel— they still don't—I still think the yodeling belongs in there. A few of them you can get by with, but normally, the yodel belongs with the song . . . When this happened, that's when I started writing: I wrote 'Blue-Eyed Elaine,' 'I'll Get Along Somehow,' 'Try Me One More Time.' I had to start writing my own songs without yodels."[12]

The subject of "Blue-Eyed Elaine" remembers of this song that "he wrote it coming in from a show date, and I was with him. But that's the only one [song history] I know."[13] Maybe it's best that she didn't know how or why "I'll Get Along Somehow" and "Try Me One More Time" were written. The former takes a cheerful, I-don't-care attitude toward a separation of "many months," and the latter is a frank confession of infidelity and a plea for forgiveness. If they have real-life roots at all, perhaps they are best not known.

Another new Ernest Tubb composition in the immediate aftermath of the tonsillectomy draws on real life beyond any doubt. He described the operation's effects and his frustration in a song he never recorded or published: "He Took Fifty Bucks and My Yodeling Too When He Took My Tonsils Out." Tubb never actually parted with the $50, but the rest of the song, written in 1941 or 1942, rings true and is interesting for its list of Tubb's post-Rodgers favorites.

He Took Fifty Bucks and My Yodeling Too . . .

The late Jimmie Rodgers, the yodeling king, was the greatest of all time,
My friend Rex Griffin can yodel too, and really does it fine.
Tommy Duncan can yodel so smooth, boy I think he's good.
I'd like to yodel for you right now, Lawd, if I only could!

CHORUS
I used to be a yodeling man, and I yodeled all about.
Till that doctor looked right down my throat, said "Those tonsils must
    come out."
After he got through with me, brother, I'm here to shout,
He took fifty bucks and my yodeling too when he took my tonsils out.

Now of course I like to sing, I've done it all my life.
But my yodeling was my greatest pride, why it even won my wife.
Now when I sing a yodeling song, where a yodel should come in,
I twist and squirm and grit my teeth as the next verse I begin.

REPEAT CHORUS[14]

Looking back on the operation and its results from the vantage point of a long and successful country music career, Tubb could laugh with friends about ever being angry because of it. "Sue the doctor?" asked his deejay friend of later years, Smilin' Eddie Hill. "You oughta put him on a pension, because you never made any money as long as you tried to yodel like Jimmie Rodgers. Now you're making money."[15]

In the months he owned the E&E Tavern, not only did Tubb start singing new songs in a new style, but he found a couple of musicians who played a new type of accompaniment for him. The Short brothers were two tall Texans who'd grown up in the panhandle town of Borger. The elder was Erwin Short, who sang and played melody parts on guitar; his taller, thinner, younger brother was Melvin Short, rhythm guitarist and vocalist. Erwin was in his early twenties (born Valentine's Day 1916 in Ardmore, Oklahoma) and Melvin barely eighteen (born December 28, 1921, in Ranger, Texas), but they were already veterans of Texas radio stations KBST (Big Spring, only about eighty miles from San Angelo) and KPDN (Pampa, up in the panhandle above Amarillo),[16] when they went to work for Tubb in San Angelo. Their more famous names, Jimmie and Leon, they adopted professionally later. At that time they were Smoky and Bashful. Tubb recalled: "Smoky was the talker. He had the personality: he was always talking. He did the emceeing, did the talking for both of them. Oh, they'd tell little jokes, like we still do nowadays. But Leon was so timid: they called him that since he was a little kid. That was his nickname. And "Smoky," that was his nickname . . . In fact on my first record I called him Smoky."[17]

Elaine Tubb thinks they may actually have met the Short brothers first in San Antonio, and that's possible, since a 1946 magazine profile has them on San Antonio radio in 1936, well before Tubb had left the Alamo City,[18] although the call letters mentioned in an earlier article by the same writer don't match up with San Antonio. Mrs. Floy Case, the writer in question (about whom much more in due course), makes no mention in either article of their work with Tubb in San Angelo, but that's well established from Tubb's firsthand recollection, plus aural evidence from the first Decca session ("Aw, pick it out, Smoky"), dated April 4, 1940, months before Tubb left San Angelo as his base. Tubb recalled in 1977 that the boys were often featured at his tavern; there it was that they worked out a new sound behind Tubb's new songs. Unlike Merwyn Buffington with his simple runs and fills, Jimmie played melody. Lead guitar became the key instrument in the Tubb sound, and the style of melody that Smoky Short played would set the standard for all of Tubb's subsequent guitarists. Mrs. Case's 1946 account says, "At an early age, they became the proud possessors of guitars, and Jimmie learned by hard practice to 'take off' on a lead guitar, with Leon playing rhythm guitar . . . It's really a treat to watch him stand and play that guitar, with that half-grin on his face. And it looks easy too!"[19]

WESTERN MATTRESS COMPANY

January 17, 1940, marked Ernest Tubb's final listed KGKL broadcast. Perhaps the tonsillectomy just about this time had something to do with his losing that job after eight months. Not long afterward Tubb took a job that necessitated his selling the E&E Tavern. One of San Angelo's biggest employers, Jim Patterson's Western Mattress Company (founded in 1925), hired Tubb as their main roving musical ambassador, a task akin to what he had done before for Blatz beer, but at much better pay (salary plus commissions) and working conditions, singing from an open-air trailer in broad daylight instead of in the loud, smoky, and sometimes dangerous atmosphere of the beer joint.

Tubb was joined by two other musicians, a fiddler and guitarist—*not* the Short brothers, who left San Angelo shortly after Tubb's April 1940 recording session to work on KFAB way up in Lincoln, Nebraska. Tubb and his twosome are pictured along with an announcer standing in "the Chariot," the Western Mattress Co. Advertising Trailer, pulled behind a long-bed pickup truck to parking lots and town squares, where the boys did their thing. Tubb recalled a once-a-week, Monday morning broadcast for Western Mattress. "I used to do the program, then rush to work."[20] Shows were free to the public, and, besides the music, crowds were attracted by amplified pitches for free balloons and, yes, even a free mattress, which normally sold for $19.75. Company headquarters often hosted an open house, where spectators were given the chance on an amateur hour to sing their favorite songs, with Tubb and the other two boys providing the backup.[21] "The big thing then was to get the farmers out in Texas and the folks in the small towns to convert their old cotton mattresses to innersprings. That was big business; I did that for about a year. I'd sing on the courthouse lawn, and have a drawing to give away a mattress to the winner, and then during the week I'd knock on doors soliciting business."[22]

Tubb's quarter-hour Monday morning show for Western Mattress went out to several stations from KGKL over the Texas State Network chain, which marked the birth of the name "The Texas Troubadour." Actually, at that time, it was usually rendered "Texas' Smiling Troubadour."[23] "When I started singing, everybody had a title. Jimmie Rodgers was 'The Singing Brakeman.' And I remember 'The Street Singer' . . . So I looked in the dictionary, and found the word 'Troubadour.' I liked the word, and the definition fit what I wanted to do very well: 'Strolling, traveling musician.' "[24]

On Tubb's Monday morning program, Justin Wayne Tubb was first introduced to the listening public: "When Justin was about four years old, we'd go up to the radio station in San Angelo, and I'd try to get him to sing. Sometimes he would, and sometimes he wouldn't. One day I said, 'Will you sing a song for the folks?' He said, 'If you'll go by the Piggly Wiggly Store on the way home and get me three candy bars: a Milky Way, a Baby Ruth,' and I don't know what else. You could get three for a dime then."[25]

Economically at least, things were looking up for Ernest Tubb in 1940. Though a baby daughter was an additional mouth to feed, his job with Western

Mattress Company was his most lucrative yet. In a good week, he earned as much as $168 in commissions,[26] a far cry from the $12.50 per week at Henry Hein's drugstore in San Antonio. He was writing new songs and singing (sans yodel) in a deeper, warmer, more mature-sounding voice. Best of all, he was finally recording again, with April and October 1940 sessions for Decca Records—the story of the next chapter.

Small wonder that Ernest Tubb loved San Angelo, and always looked back on the city and his days there fondly. Not once but twice it had proven a haven for Tubb. Coming back for a concert there in October 1959, Tubb could say, "I've always liked San Angelo. I remember seeing millionaire ranchers in the lobby of the hotel that looked like just ordinary $30-a-month cowboys. That's just the kind of nice people who lived here . . . I even wrote a song called 'Swell San Angelo' because I liked the place so much."[27]

Recorded at his October 1940 Decca session and later featured in his 1947 film, *Hollywood Barn Dance,* "Swell San Angelo" put to music his warm feelings about a place that was very good to him. The chorus concludes, "Now I have roamed this wide world o'er, but I'll never move no more, / for I love you, swell San Angelo."[28] His love for San Angelo was real and lasting; but this was a promise he would not keep. The desire to work full-time in music, to be closer to extended family members, and to be in a place with more musical activity all led him out of San Angelo in the early fall of 1940. By then, he was once again a recording artist, and he needed and wanted a bigger radio market if he was ever to make it as a full-time musician.

7

Decca Records: The First Two Sessions

When the spring of 1940 came, Ernest Tubb had not recorded in three full years, not since the second Bluebird session with Merwyn Buffington of March 2, 1937. Eli Oberstein at Bluebird had only recorded him as a favor to Mrs. Rodgers anyway, and when the two releases didn't sell, Tubb was dropped with half of his eight masters still in the can.

It wasn't as if Tubb, with some help from Mrs. Rodgers, wasn't trying to get back on records. Bob Kendrick of the group Bob Skyles and His Skyrockets remembers being asked by Tubb out in San Angelo how to get a record contract. Kendrick's advice was to "get your songs together, rehearse up on 'em and get 'em down real good and find out where they're recording . . . and go right up there and introduce yourself. And they'll listen close to you and if they like you, they'll record you."[1] Presumably this was the approach Tubb tried with Art Satherley and Don Law of the American Record Corporation, a big player in the country field, the label of Bob Wills, Roy Acuff, Bob Atcher, and others. It didn't work. Law would long regret not signing Tubb when he had the chance. That's the reason he so quickly signed Stonewall Jackson on Tubb's recommendation in the mid-1950s: "I remember one time I turned you down, and I always said then, after you became so big, that if you ever recommended anybody to me, I was gonna record them."[2]

Tubb and Mrs. Rodgers were also intrigued by a much newer company, Decca Records, which had had the audacity to open its American operations in 1934—right in the midst of the Depression—and almost immediately sign some of the top names in the pop (Crosby, Lombardo, Mills Brothers) and hillbilly (Jimmie Davis, Stuart Hamblen, Frank Luther, Sons of the Pioneers) fields. Jack Kapp, a former Brunswick Records executive, brought most of their pop talent with him when he started Decca, and marketed a 35-cent record (down from the customary 75 cents) to lure back the hard-hit Depression record buyer. He hired his younger brother David to build up Decca's hillbilly roster. The earliest rural talent was brought into New York, Chicago, or Los Angeles studios to record; but starting in 1936, Dave Kapp and one engineer began making rounds of select southern locations—Charlotte, New Orleans, Dallas, San Antonio, and Houston— to record their acts closer to home.

In short order, Dave Kapp's country division of Decca, on a smaller scale, began matching the success of the pop division, largely because of Decca's foresight in seeking the new jukebox market. In 1936, the nation's 150,000 jukeboxes—the coin-operated phonographs so popular in night spots—bought some 40 percent of all records sold, and Decca took the lead in this field by selling their product to coin machines at 21 cents each, lower than Victor or Brunswick could do with their budget lines.[3] Kapp was on the prowl for acts that might appeal in the juke joint milieu and signed country talent of all stripes: cowboys, swing bands, Cajuns, mountaineers, novelty. By 1940, Decca catalogues and catalogue supplements describing the company's "Hill Billy" releases in the blue-labeled 5000 series listed such diverse styles as "Sacred," "Old Time Singing," "String Bands," "Fiddlin," and "Old Time Dance."[4]

Certainly there were affinities between Tubb and Decca Records that he felt immediately, though it seems he and Mrs. Rodgers were a good while convincing Dave Kapp and Decca of these. Tubb was a newcomer, an underdog; among the record labels, Decca was too. Tubb sang in nightclubs, had even recently owned one; Decca, already the nation's top jukebox label, was looking for talent that might appeal to a nightclub crowd. Repeated letters from Mrs. Rodgers brought no response; Tubb even wrote to Kapp, not necessarily with Mrs. Rodgers's knowledge or permission, but still no audition.

Cliff Bruner, fiddle virtuoso and leader of Decca's popular Texas Wanderers band, claims to have introduced Tubb and Mrs. Rodgers to Dave Kapp—"They had never seen him before; I had to tell them which one Kapp was"—though his details are a bit fuzzy. However and whenever the Bruner introduction took place, when Kapp finally agreed to record Ernest Tubb, it was in all likelihood to stop the letters and get Tubb (and Mrs. Rodgers) off his back. As Tubb remembered, "It had gone on for about three years before I ever got an audition—she'd been writing to him and I had too. I don't think he even told her that I was writing him also. Maybe I should have left it up to her."[5]

In February or March of 1940, Tubb got word of Kapp's plans to come to Houston for recordings the first week of April and sent a telegram to Kapp's office seeking an audition. A letter came back promising nothing, only confirming Kapp's Houston trip.[6] For Tubb, the young Western Mattress salesman, this was encouragement enough. As Charlie Walker heard the story later from Mrs. Rodgers, "He called her one day and told her, 'Decca Records representative Mr. Kapp is gonna be at the Rice Hotel in Houston, he's recording a bunch of guys. I feel like he might take a couple of things [songs] I've got, if I could get over there.'"[7] Mrs. Rodgers offered (perhaps even sent) bus fare to get Ernest from San Angelo to San Antonio, but he wanted to bring the Short brothers along to back him on the session—they knew his new songs, "I'll Get Along Somehow" and "Blue-Eyed Elaine"—so the three of them hitchhiked. Decca could only record union musicians, so they stopped in Waco long enough to join the American Federation of Musicians. As Tubb recalled, "We hocked Leon's guitar in order to join the union in Waco. Back then it cost you $10—$5 to join the union and a $5 fee for a year . . . So we all three had to join the union, cause we're hoping that Leon would get to play rhythm guitar on the record . . ."[8]

As things turned out, Kapp wouldn't use Leon on the session. How could he? Leon didn't have a guitar! But the boys pressed on to San Antonio, and there they were given not only Mrs. Rodgers's best letter of recommendation addressed to Dave Kapp, but the use of her car for the rest of the trip to Houston. Since her first call from Tubb, she had written to Mr. Kapp on Tubb's behalf, and his answer came just after the boys pulled out in her car. Tubb never knew it, but it was a yes: he could have an audition at the Rice Hotel.

THE FIRST SESSION

With or without Cliff Bruner's intervention (his Texas Wanderers were a star attraction of the April 3 sessions), Tubb and the Short brothers finally arranged their meeting with Dave Kapp. The Rice Hotel lobby was filled with some five hundred musicians, as the story was later told to Charlie Walker, but somehow Tubb got his letter of recommendation up to Dave Kapp's room. "Son, this is a pretty good recommendation you got here; I guess I'll listen to your singing." He did listen, and especially liked "I'll Get Along Somehow." "Yeah, that's pretty good, I believe that one there, I believe we could put that out, plus 'Blue-Eyed Elaine.' I'll give you $25 a song, and we'll get you out there on them jukeboxes and radio stations."[9] Besides not wanting to use Melvin "Leon" Short, another hitch developed: following Mrs. Rodgers's advice, Tubb wanted a royalty contract rather than flat payment per song. Mr. Kapp lost his temper, and Ernest Tubb nearly lost the whole deal.

What follows is a composite picture that Ernest Tubb in 1977 and Charlie Walker in 1994 painted of Kapp's reaction.

He like to have blown up . . . "You mean to tell me that you have been bugging me, writing to me, having Mrs. Rodgers write to me, and bugging me for two or three years . . . I've gone through all this, I finally tell Mrs. Rodgers that I will listen to you, and then you come down here and tell me you're gonna have to have a royalty contract?[10] What kinda guy are you? There are five hundred musicians down there wanting me to record them, and they'd record under any circumstance I'd want to do it, and here I'm offering to record you . . . and you're telling me you've got to have a royalty?[11] Well, I don't have time to fool with you right now. Call me at nine o'clock in the morning."

Tubb was frightened that the whole thing was off. He and the Shorts hadn't planned on spending the night of April 3 in Houston; to do it, they'd have to skimp on meals the next day. "But we stayed, and I don't think I slept thirty minutes . . ."[12] Tubb anxiously placed the call at nine o'clock sharp on the fateful morning of April 4, 1940: 4-4-40, a date that would forever be etched in Tubb's memory. Tubb's career hung in the balance, but to his relief, Dave Kapp relented once more: "Be up here at 2 o'clock this afternoon. I'm gonna give you that royalty contract you wanted." Ernest Tubb and Smoky Short came up at two for Kapp's first session of the day (the Texas Wanderers recorded that night) and waxed four songs, all new Tubb compositions: "Blue-Eyed Elaine," "I'll Never Cry over You," "I'll Get Along Somehow," and "You Broke a Heart (That Was Breaking for You)."

Tubb later recalled:

I had written the songs, so I had to sign three contracts on each song, and three or four on the royalty thing, which was one-half cent a side. Course it was a duplication, you know, but I said, "Gosh, you gotta sign all these?" He said, "Don't worry about it. Every time you sign one it's gonna make you some money." And that made me feel pretty good . . . So it wound up with me as the leader and Jimmie as the side man, which gets scale [leader gets double scale] . . . Union scale was $30 for the side man and $60 for the leader, so when I got through, he says "Come by my room, I've got a check for you." Well, he wasn't supposed to pay us but $90, but he says, "I'm gonna give you the $100 I offered you anyhow." . . . He'd already had the check made out, he was so sure I was gonna take the $25 [per song].[13]

After this favorable settlement of the payment question, Tubb asked Kapp what he thought of the records and what would happen on the promotion front. "Ernest, I'm gonna do for you what I do for anybody else we record. I'm gonna give you every chance in the world; I ain't gonna do nothing special for you, no more than I would for anybody else. But I don't think you have anything to worry about." Comforting words indeed, and as Ernest concluded the story of his first Decca session, "the first record did sell well enough to keep me."[14] "Blue-Eyed Elaine," in fact, made enough of an impression to be covered by no less a star than Gene Autry,[15] which brought the twenty-six-year-old mattress salesman some welcome additional royalties.

HOLLYWOOD AND A SECOND SESSION

The success of "Blue-Eyed Elaine" and "I'll Get Along Somehow" was such that Ernest Tubb felt he could quit his Western Mattress job and seek new work, in cities maybe a little closer to the beaten path than San Angelo. In a letter he wrote (the earliest surviving Ernest Tubb prose), published in the November 1940 *Mountain Broadcast and Prairie Recorder,* Tubb, who may have written it as early as September, has clearly left San Angelo and Western Mattress for a visit to his old stomping grounds, KONO in San Antonio.

> Well, well, well, and I thought I half way kept up with Hillbilly Music! But when I drifted into the studios of KONO yesterday after spending three years at KGKL, I found out I was far behind. With all due respects to KGKL, I didn't realize that I was so far out of the world, out there in the western part of this great state of Texas, of which I call home. Of course we have lots of Cowboys out there, but really they know more about cattle than music. (Perhaps they're wise at that) . . . I'm known to my listeners at KGKL as Ernest Tubb, Texas' OWN Cowboy Singer. For the past few months I have been on the air for the Western Mattress Co., the program originating at KGKL, and heard over part of the Texas State Network. I also made personal appearances in connection with the program. Not trying to pat myself on the back, but we really got results. So when you can sell beds with this type program, there's no need for us to worry about our Hillbilly Music being banned from schools. But we should be on our toes at all times to stand up for our rights. I would like to call the attention of my Hillbilly friends to my number "I'll Get Along Somehow," which has proved very popular . . .[16]

Besides the usual lead time necessary to get a letter into print, another reason for believing this very revealing letter was written in September (or at the latest, early October) 1940 is that it makes no mention of his second Decca session. Held in Los Angeles over a three-day period—October 28–30, 1940—

Tubb cut twelve masters, four each day: a marathon compared to the Houston session, with three times the output.

Tubb had been busy writing songs since the spring. Though of course some of these could have been older compositions, nine of the twelve new recordings came from his own pen, including "Swell San Angelo." None, though, were really standout songs. He would rerecord them all in 1944–1945 for World transcriptions, and one of them ("Last Night I Dreamed") many years later for *The Ernest Tubb Story* double LP. Two were credited to Mrs. Rodgers: "I Cared for You More Than I Knew" and "I'm Missing You" (which had the good fortune later to be the flip side of "Walking the Floor over You"). She even received co-composer credit with her sister, Elsie McWilliams, on "My Rainbow Trail," which Tubb recorded, shortening the original title.

The problem with these twelve recordings wasn't so much the songs or Tubb's singing; it was the instrumental accompaniment. Smoky and Bashful by this time had left San Angelo for work on KFAB in Lincoln, Nebraska, so he couldn't take them to the West Coast. Instead he drove out in Mrs. Rodgers's car with Dick Ketner, a San Antonio guitarist who still played in Alamo City bands twenty-five years later.[17]

We don't know how Decca felt about these Hollywood recordings. Ernest Tubb said years later, "I didn't like how any of them turned out . . . What happened, he [Dick Ketner] played electric guitar but we didn't have room to put his amp in the car going to California—Mrs. Rodgers's car—we thought they would rent us one, the people there. Wasn't Dave Kapp, but he let the people in Hollywood record me, but they wouldn't get us an amp. So Dick had to play electric guitar—it was supposed to be electric—without the electric. It wasn't a Martin, it was a Gibson, see what I mean? And it doesn't have the carrying tone. So those records were pretty bad. Had he had his amplifier, those records would have been much better, and he would have done better, 'cause he was used to playing electric guitar."[18]

What the Hollywood sessions had in quantity they lacked in quality, by Tubb's own admission. Knowing how critically important good follow-up records are, Tubb must have been especially disappointed. Record companies don't always display lots of patience with artists whose second batch of records aren't as good as their first. Two sessions, remember, had been the extent of his association with RCA-Bluebird.

Knocking about San Antonio upon his return, hoping to stay close to Mrs. Rodgers and to family there on both sides (his and Elaine's), Tubb was unable to find employment at KONO or anywhere else in the Alamo City and decided to take his chances up in Fort Worth. Though two of his married sisters were in San

Antonio, brother C. R. had moved up to Cowtown where he held as many as three jobs at a time to support his family of four boys: iceman in the summer, cab driver, and trucker for a petroleum company.[19] Ernest could leave his family with Elaine's folks in San Antonio and see about finding musical work in Fort Worth, where a lot of things were happening. Mrs. Rodgers advised him to give it a try; in his own mind, Ernest was determined to give it a year. If nothing really broke by then, he'd take the advice of those in-laws who begged him to stick to a regular job. As Norma Barthel put it in her book, "He was either going to be a singer or he wasn't going to be one. He was tired of almost making it."[20] In Fort Worth, he made it.

8

Fort Worth Days

COMING TO COWTOWN

Ernest Tubb's move to Fort Worth began with an exploratory trip: a brief stay with his brother's family to hunt up some radio work well before he moved himself or his wife and kids. Nephew Quanah Talmadge Tubb, fifteen at the time, remembers that "When Uncle Ernest first came to Fort Worth, he hitchhiked from San Angelo to Fort Worth and came to my dad's house . . ."[1] Talmadge's half-brother, Douglas Glenn Tubb, though only five, recalls his uncle's earliest days in town: "The first memory I have of him is looking out the bedroom window in a little house we were renting in Fort Worth, and seeing him walk across the front yard, and step over this short picket fence there. He had his guitar; it was about five o'clock in the morning; he was going to work at a radio station, probably KGKO . . . He was staying with us for a while, I don't remember how long, but a short while. Evidently Elaine and Justin [and Violet Elaine, or 'Scooter Bill'] were still in San Antonio or San Angelo and hadn't got to come up that far yet."[2]

Floy Case, a friend he would soon make in Fort Worth, adds the detail from her published account, "My Friend—Ernest Tubb," that "he arrived in our city all alone and with only $5.00 in his pocket. He also had an album of favorable press clippings . . ."[3]

Talmadge tells the story of his uncle's KGKO audition:

> He rode the city bus downtown the next day [after his arrival] and went up to KGKO there in Fort Worth, the radio station there, and talked to the program director about getting a program. Of course the guy gave him the usual, you know, "Leave your number and we'll call you." And so Uncle Ernest was leaving, and the station manager had overheard the conversation, and he asked the program director, "Did that guy say his

name was Ernest Tubb?" Uncle Ernest had a record out at the time, "I'll Get Along Somehow," that was getting a lot of airplay. So the station manager caught Uncle Ernest before he got on the elevator and brought him back and told him that he didn't have a sponsor for him at the time, but he thought he could get one, and that the station would pay him $25 a week to do an early morning, fifteen-minute radio program, so that's what Uncle Ernest did there for awhile.[4]

Pieced together, the various accounts of his coming to Fort Worth indicate that this is the point at which Ernest talked over the offer with his family and with Mrs. Rodgers and decided to take it, low though the initial pay was. Dallas–Fort Worth newspapers first list *Ernest Tubb* on KGKO Monday morning, December 2, 1940, from 7:15 A.M. to 7:30, six days a week, plus an 11:45-to-noon show on Tuesdays and Thursdays for the first month.

KGKO

KGKO, 570 on the dial, had the power of 5,000 watts during the day (Tubb's only airtime) and 1,000 watts at night. KGKO had originated in Wichita Falls in September 1928 but had been purchased by Amon G. Carter, magnate of the Fort Worth *Star-Telegram* newspaper, in 1935, to bring NBC programming into Dallas–Fort Worth, which until then had only WFAA and WBAP. Carter moved KGKO to new facilities in Fort Worth's Medical Arts Building and built a new transmitter just north of Arlington (midway between Dallas and Fort Worth), which first boomed its stronger signal May 1, 1938—reaching "listeners as far north as Amarillo, as far south as Corpus Christi, as far east as Texarkana, and as far west as Sweetwater." In July 1940, Carter formed the KGKO Corporation with his Dallas newspaper-radio counterpart, G. B. Dealey, in which each man held half-interest in the station. Starting September 1, 1940, KGKO became a sort of third partner with WBAP (Fort Worth) and WFAA (Dallas). "Dallas controls KGKO's time on the air when WFAA is silent and WBAP transmitting. Similarly, Fort Worth's periods on KGKO are timed with WFAA's operations . . ."[5] Ernest Tubb had never worked for a station with this sort of coverage. Even at a $25 opening salary, he knew he was in radio's big leagues.

Within two months, his mail pull was proving it. On February 11, 1941, he wrote his first letter to Fort Worth music journalist and future friend, Mrs. Floy Case. She wrote the "Down Blue Bonnet Way" column for Dixie Music's *Mountain Broadcast and Prairie Recorder,* a two-year-old New York–based publication that was virtually alone in its exclusive interest in "hillbilly" music. Addressed to "Mr." Floy Case (how was he to know that she was the wife of J. C. Case, daytime jeweller and fiddler for the Royal Ramblers, a Fort Worth radio band?), Tubb opens with an apology for his delay: "I'm so sorry that your letter of Jan. 4th got mixed in the [fan mail] requests for pictures, and I've just now read your letter. But when you stop and think that I received over 10,000 cards and letters from Jan. 2nd to Jan. 7th, I'm sure you will just feel like forgiving me for the delay. At least I hope so."[6] His only program between January and May 1941, still on a sustaining, no-sponsor basis, aired in the 11:45-to-noon time slot.

At the close of that letter (to which I shall return presently), Tubb gives as his address 518 Carlock Street. From Mrs. Case's recollections published in Norma Barthel's book we learn that this was a rented "garage apartment," and that Elaine and the kids were there by this time. He mentions them in his next letter to Floy, a week later: "I wish to say that my wife and I are regular listeners to your husband's programs, or I might say the Royal Ramblers . . . I think she sent in a request for 'Blue-Eyed Elaine,' a song I wrote in her honor. We would especially like for you all to visit us, just any time you find it convenient. We don't get out very often as we don't have a car at present. But I will try to visit the studios of KFJZ sometime in the near future, long about 7:30 P.M."[7] Ernest did indeed show up at one of the Royal Ramblers' broadcasts shortly after this, introduced to the rest of the group by bass player Vernon Young, whom Tubb had already met. Vernon tells of their meeting this way:

> When Ernest Tubb first came to Fort Worth, Elaine and my sister-in-law worked in the same beer joint as car hops. She said her husband made a little bit of music, so I met him. He didn't have a car, so we rode around a little together. I'd take him to places I'd go . . . He wanted to play with our dance band some, but we didn't think he was good enough for that! See, I was also with a western swing band: we called it The Rhythm Wranglers. . . . We went around and played the honky-tonks and beer joints, but we didn't think Ernest was good enough to play with us. We were hotshots. We just didn't realize what a crowd appeal he had. There was just something about that man that would take over a crowd of people.[8]

Vernon Young introduced Ernest to the members of the Case band (Bill Case and the Melody Boys for morning broadcasts; the Royal Ramblers for Royal Credit Clothiers at night) soon after Tubb's letter of February 18. Young remembers that Ernest later sang on their program sometimes, even though he sang regularly for KGKO, a competing station. The night of their first meeting ended with the whole gang adjourning to the Tubb apartment, where they all met Elaine; they "listened to some records, he sang some of the new songs he was writing," and J. C. Case and Homer Hargrove (vocalist and guitarist for the group) got to play the famous Jimmie Rodgers guitar.

That wasn't the only benefit of knowing Ernest Tubb. Just about this time, Tubb signed a letter of permission for them to broadcast songs that he had copyrighted. Ten song titles—all tunes that he had recorded for Decca at his first two sessions—follow this simple statement: "I hereby grant the right to Bill Case and his band to broadcast for profit or otherwise the following songs which I own the copyright. Titled as follows . . . [1–10] Signed, Ernest Tubb [dated March 14, 1941]."[9] This was a boon in light of the broadcasters' war with ASCAP about that time, which eventually resulted in the formation of BMI.

J. C. and Floy Case lived at 3413 Townsend Drive in Fort Worth then. Before long, Ernest and Elaine became their near neighbors, moving to 3404 Frazier Street. Ernest by then had Gold Chain Flour as sponsor, and Floy from her front window "could see whether Ernest was at home or not, as the truck was very conspicuous." The Tubbs and the Cases visited often from that point forward; Tubb even "recorded several of his new songs on our little disc home recorder which was a new invention at the time." Once he called her with an immediate need for a disc on a song he was writing at the moment, fearful of forgetting the tune (he could always save the words). She hung up the phone, "turned on the machine, opened the door, and he literally came in singing." Soon, she says, he had his own disc recorder; with it he recorded those few examples of his Fort Worth broadcasts that survive.[10]

New friend Floy Case first wrote about Tubb in the April 1941 issue of *Mountain Broadcast and Prairie Recorder*. This is her revealing paragraph: "Ernest Tubb, Texas' Smiling Troubadour, is still a headline attraction at the same station where he warbles cowboy songs in the manner of the late and still beloved Jimmie Rodgers. He is using an old guitar of Jimmie's, with the famous singer's name all across it. He has several original compositions recorded on Decca which are definitely 'hits' in this section of the country."[11] No longer was he "Texas' OWN Cowboy Singer." Though still a singer of cowboy songs, he had become "Texas' Smiling Troubadour." Those autographed photos Tubb was mailing out a few months later, standing so happily at the KGKO microphone and holding the Rodgers guitar, were signed "Smilingly Yours."

The very month that Case's description was published, Ernest Tubb got a third chance to stand before the Decca microphones. His list of "hits" would very soon lengthen, and no longer would they be confined to his "section of the country."

"WALKING THE FLOOR OVER YOU"

Ernest Tubb wrote this about his recording past and future in that first letter to "Mr." Floy Case, February 11, 1941: "I went to Hollywood to make my last recordings for Decca, instead of New York as the plans were at first. I recorded twelve sides. Two records have been released to date. I plan to record some more this month, in Houston."[12] Once again, though, Decca changed plans. Dave Kapp did not go to Houston in February, but instead went to Dallas in late April. Though Tubb had to wait a few additional weeks, the location was of course much more convenient, only about thirty miles to the east. And with the two months' reprieve, Tubb had more time to get his song material in order and to develop a very new wrinkle in his accompaniment. The six songs he recorded were all first-rate, each one better than any of the twelve he'd recorded in Hollywood.

"Our Baby's Book," the true and tragic tale of Rodger Dale Tubb's short life, was finally ready for the recording studio as Tubb looked ahead to this third and crucial session. Completely true to life as we have seen, it stands as the only song of the six recorded in Dallas that does not deal with sundered love. This could hardly be coincidental and must reflect some more bumps in the road for the Ernest-Elaine marriage. Lonely in their new city, with few friends and only Ernest's brother for family, Elaine seems to have headed back to San Antonio with the two children sometime after the winter or late spring meeting with members of the Case band. Maybe she got tired of car-hopping to supplement Ernest's $25 weekly pay; surely she missed her parents and San Antonio friends. Some people say the more humid heat of Fort Worth's spring weather, certainly more oppressive than the climate in San Antonio or San Angelo, afflicted her. One very reliable account has it that she had troubled Ernest by running up installment debts with certain Fort Worth merchants.[13] In any event, the woes he poured into song all deal in one way or another with the agony of parting.

Tubb himself gave conflicting accounts of the inspiration for his greatest song. What never changes is the fact that he was literally pacing his apartment floor, as the song describes, in a fit of anxious inspiration as he dashed off the song in about twenty minutes, so fast he "could hardly get the words down on paper." Tubb's opinion of the finished song was justifiably high. "I thought there was something about 'Walking the Floor,' it had a little bouncy thing. I thought it was catchy and I thought it would sell."[14] Small wonder that Tubb cut the song first out of the six done in Dallas. But before he could record any of them, he had to find a substitute guitarist and teach him the songs.

FAY "SMITTY" SMITH AND THE ELECTRIC GUITAR

In the short months between Ernest Tubb's move to Fort Worth and the Dallas session—November to April—he chanced to hear some advice that, acted upon, helped give him the unique and commercial sound he'd been seeking. Tubb met a Fort Worth jukebox operator on the city's streets who happened to recognize him, and the two men struck up a conversation. This is Tubb's account of the man's comments: "Ernest, I own 150 and some odd jukeboxes, and you're making me a lot of money, but I wish you would do something. I don't know what to tell you to do, but in the afternoons, when just a few people are sitting around drinking beer in these joints where my boxes are, they'll play your records all afternoon. But as soon as the crowd gets in there and gets noisy, they start dancing, they can't hear your records, they start playing Bob Wills. They're not playing your records: you need to make them louder."[15]

One solution, since on $25 a week he couldn't hire a Wills-sized orchestra, was to electrify his guitarist: the very thing he had tried to do with Dick Ketner at the Hollywood session. Tubb bought a D'Armand electric pickup ("back then they went right across the sound hole in your guitar") at a Fort Worth pawnshop for about $20 and promptly shipped it off to Jimmie Short in Lincoln, Nebraska. "Learn to play electric: we gotta make 'em louder."[16] He still wanted Jimmie as his guitarist, in view of their success on "I'll Get Along Somehow" and "Blue-Eyed Elaine," and hoped that when Dave Kapp next came to Texas, Jimmie could get away from his radio work long enough to come down and play the session. When April rolled around, Kapp went to Dallas and called Tubb about coming over; Tubb then phoned Jimmie Short in Lincoln, but Short's bosses at KFAB wouldn't let him off. Fearing that might happen, Tubb had a contingency plan: an emergency guitarist named Fay "Smitty" Smith. Fay was the electric guitarist for a WBAP staff orchestra called the Red Hawks.[17] Tubb recalls that Smith had traveled with Glen Gray's orchestra before settling in Fort Worth at the behest of his wife, who wanted him home more.

> I'd already talked to Fay just in case Jimmie couldn't make it. I asked Fay—"I see you play electric guitar. Can you play lead guitar?" He said, "Well, I can but they won't let me . . . I can't do it by ear. I'll have to write the notes out." So I'd have to sing all the songs to him, and he'd write out the lead notes; then he could play it . . . So this is one reason that I didn't keep him with me, because it was too much of a job trying to write out everything, and Jimmie played everything by ear.[18]

Necessity was the mother of that particular invention, though, and by the scheduled April 26 date, Fay was ready to head to Dallas with Ernest. He was even equipped with a steel guitar, on which he played nice octave-length fills on "Our Baby's Book." Smith's lead guitar work on the other five is more than passable: if Smitty was not playing by ear, then at least he seems to have memorized his parts, playing them with an ease that actually gave his style a jazzy, improvisational feel.

The studio for the Tubb session (Kapp used a different, larger building on

Industrial Boulevard for at least some of the other sessions) was a small one owned by Bunny Biggs, veteran of the Salt & Peanuts duo and a future "Jamup" in the blackface Jamup & Honey team. "He had the recording studio in Dallas, right up the street on the right from the White Plaza Hotel . . . I recorded 'Walking the Floor' in his studio and later he asked me to autograph all the songs I recorded in his studio."[19]

With their day's work done and the session completed, Tubb and Kapp discussed the coming sequence of Ernest Tubb record releases, and an argument ensued. Tubb was high on "Walking the Floor over You" and wanted that issued next, whatever song Kapp chose to put on its flip side. Kapp, on the other hand, was most impressed by the session's final song, "I Wonder Why You Said Good-bye," but finally gave in and agreed to do it Tubb's way when he pleaded, "Just do this for me and I'll never ask you another favor. I think it'll sell."[20]

"To make a long story short," Tubb explained, "the record was released. It did sell. I didn't know how great it was selling, but I knew it was selling in Texas, it was on all the jukeboxes. So I waited. Three months and I still hadn't heard; usually they would write me and say they were gonna release another record. Finally the phone rang, and this was the first time I can remember him [Kapp] calling me about a record. Of course I was excited, and he said, 'This is Dave Kapp, Ernest. All right, you win! What do you want released next?' Because I had picked that one. That was the situation. [After that] he'd always ask me before every release."[21]

THE GOLD CHAIN TROUBADOUR

The second regular installment of Ernest Tubb news that Floy Case submitted to her magazine—published June 1941, though probably written sometime in May—says this:

> Ernest Tubb, Texas' Smiling Troubadour, a popular Decca recording artist, has been steadily gaining in popularity since coming to KGKO from KGKL in San Angelo a few months ago. Ernest has a good voice, a pleasing personality, is tall, slender, has dark hair and blue eyes, and always has a large studio audience (mostly women). He is one of the nation's heaviest mail-pullers . . . Ernest recently made several new Decca recordings over in Dallas. At present he is making theatre appearances. Keep your eye on this Tubb fellow. Sooner or later he'll be heading for Hollywood—or I miss my guess.[22]

For her next column, published three moths later, Mrs. Case could report some very good news for Ernest Tubb at KGKO.

Ernest Tubb, who had been heard on a sustaining program from KGKO for the past few months, now has a good contract with Universal Mills. This series of programs which began June 9th, may be heard Monday through Friday at 10:45 A.M. and is scheduled for the Lone Star Chain this fall. Known as the Gold Chain Troubadour, Ernest is doing a swell job of singing as well as telling the folks about "That good Gold Chain Flour." He will be making personal appearances throughout the southwest, so watch out for him and that famous guitar of the late Jimmie Rodgers, for we know you'll enjoy seeing him in person.[23]

The Case band's bass player, Vernon Young, friend and sometime "chauffeur" for the Tubb family, tells the story of how the Gold Chain sponsorship came about: "A man called the station and said he had a job for a band or something, so Ernie called me, and he and I went out there to Saginaw to a mill, and we went in there, played around a little bit, then he came out later just as happy as he could be. He'd just got the job to be the Gold Chain Troubadour. And they got him an old Plymouth car, and put a platform on top, and he'd go around to stores and play from that platform. That was his first commercial sponsor."[24]

Tubb's new series of radio broadcasts was indeed popular. Besides the enthusiastic women in the studio, thousands of persons all over Texas were hearing Ernest Tubb for the first time, and liking what they heard. Ernest, helped by a single announcer, filled his broadcasts with songs and upcoming show dates. Country music legend Hank Thompson remembers listening as a schoolboy in Waco: "I listened to his 7:15 morning show on KGKO out of Fort Worth before I'd go to school. Ernest's theme was a talking blues which was autobiographical; things like how sore his fingers were, how tough it was for him in the early years . . . The show consisted of Ernest and his guitar. But for me, Ernest was right up there with Jimmie Rodgers, Gene Autry, and Roy Acuff as an inspiration."[25]

Floy Case, using her home disc recorder, saved small portions of a few of Tubb's "Gold Chain Troubadour" broadcasts, with the announcer listing stores that sold Gold Chain Flour and occasionally helping Ernest out with the description of a song. One program she saved has Ernest, who had surely told her that this was coming, singing a song written by the Case band's guitarist, Homer Hargrove, "I Hate to See You Go." That fall, Tubb recorded the song for Decca. Another early broadcast gives Tubb's complete closing theme, also in his "talking blues" style.

> Now goodbye, folks, I've got to go
> I hope you've liked my little show

I'll be back tomorrow at this same hour
So keep on calling for Gold Chain Flour.
   'Cause how in the world you think I'm gonna get along,
   If you folks don't use Gold Chain Flour?
   Let me hear from you, would you?
   So long, folks.

Tubb's affinity in KGKO days for talking blues and cowboy songs he later dropped as his own catalogue of original love songs and honky-tonk songs swelled; but for the time being, they were a big part of his performances. As to cowboy songs, niece Anna Ruth Collier remembers that her favorite songs of those he did was "Ridin' Old Paint and Leading Old Ball"; a recording survives of Tubb singing "It's Hard to Ride after the Fall"; he featured at least two Sons of the Pioneers songs, "At the Rainbow's End" and "Happy Roving Cowboy" (the latter he sang in his first movie, 1942). He even published an original cowboy song, which he also sang in his first film, "Riding That Dusty Trail." The lure of Tom Mix, Buck Jones, and their musical counterparts was still strong.

Texans were especially privileged in 1941–1942: they could now not only listen to Ernest Tubb daily, but often see him in their towns, singing from the platform atop his painted Plymouth. Nephew Talmadge Tubb, later one of Ernest Tubb's key songwriters, says that he first saw his uncle singing as "the Gold Chain Troubadour."

> He did these personal appearances on Saturdays, and so I was out of school, so he took me with him a couple of times—once down at Cleburne and once we went up to Jacksboro. KGKO was a strong radio station and it covered Texas pretty well, and so Uncle Ernest would announce on his radio program where he was gonna be Saturday. I think he usually did his show about 12 or 1 o'clock on Saturdays on the courthouse squares and the people would be there, and Uncle Ernest would pull in on the park there and find a place to plug in. He had a couple of speakers on top of his paneled truck, and a platform up there, and he'd get up there with his mic and his guitar and he'd entertain those people for about an hour, and he'd really put on a show for them.[26]

Charlie Walker remembers:

> I was just a kid, one of my aunts said, "Hey, there's a guy you oughta listen to on the radio. He's out of Fort Worth, he's playing on the Jimmie Rodgers guitar, and his name is Ernest Tubb." I thought that was the silliest name I'd ever heard, "Tubb." I was a country boy, a tub is what

you took a bath in . . . I got to listening to him, and I liked the little lick he hit on the guitar. He'd sing out to the end of a line, then he'd hit a little quick thing, and come back and play it soft while he was singing, so I liked that. Anyway, he came to our little town. I grew up in the little town of Lavada, which is just north of Dallas County . . . they put up a few posters in this little town, and said, "Ernest Tubb the Gold Chain Troubadour will sing on the city square at two o'clock Saturday afternoon." What he was doing then, he'd make all these little bitty towns and he had a, looked like an old bread truck, old van-looking thing, like they used to have candy trucks and bread trucks, and he had a microphone, and a guy riding along with him, I guess this guy helped drive. And they'd hit Saturday afternoon half-a-dozen of these little towns and sing for maybe fifteen minutes, then move on to the next town . . . There was maybe fifteen or twenty people stood around on the square while he sang his songs, and I liked the way he handled himself. I thought the way he was dressed—all of us dressed in bib overalls, cotton pickers where I was—and I thought, "Boy, I'd sure like to be doing what he's doing, wear them nice Western clothes and a big hat and boots." I went up and got his autograph, first time I'd ever gotten an autograph from anybody, first country star I ever saw . . . He had a little notebook about this size and about that wide, and he scribbled, "Sincerely yours, Ernest Tubb."[27]

A fan named Marie White told this story about seeing the Gold Chain Troubadour on one of his weekend tours: "We drove up to Waller and Hempstead to see him one Saturday . . . He passed us on the road between Cypress and Waller . . . and he waved at us and flashed that special smile of his . . . He was appearing in front of grocery stores and he would sing all kinds of nonsense to the storekeepers, like his version of 'I Saw Your Face in the Moon,' which went 'I saw your feet in the moon, honey, you wiggled your toes at me, etc.' "[28]

Tubb was always proud of the fact that his KGKO mail response exceeded that of more established artists on bigger stations in the same basic market: the Chuck Wagon Gang, the Light Crust Doughboys. He had once envied them: "God love 'em, the Doughboys, I used to listen to them and thought, 'They've got it made.' I discovered they were making—the vocalist, Leon Huff, was getting $25 a week, the other boys was getting $20 a week, and the leader was only getting $27.50 a week, and they went out and did the broadcast every day plus the weekend. Course, they got their hotel bills paid, but that was it . . . I wound up making $75 a week by myself: just me and Jimmie Rodgers's guitar."[29] No wonder that fellow entertainers in the Dallas–Fort Worth area folk music field were soon growing just a tad jealous of the young singer's rising popularity. About this time the

Doughboys changed sponsors, reorganized, and became the Coffee Grinders. They toured through much of the same North Texas territory as Tubb in a fine bus, carrying a complete, state-of-the-art sound system too. Along came Ernest in his small Plymouth, with a much less sophisticated sound system, drawing larger, more enthusiastic crowds.[30] Joe Frank Ferguson, the Coffee Grinders bass player about this time, thinks that Tubb occasionally played to crowds that *they* had drawn.[31]

Soon the Gold Chain Troubadour was ranging farther afield to peddle flour and showcase his songs. As "Walking the Floor over You" grew to the proportions of a national hit that fall, Ernest Tubb was getting notices like this one, in advance of playing the Gilmer, Texas "Yamboree":

Popular Radio, Recording Artist Entertains Here

Ernest Tubb, the "Gold Chain Troubadour," will be here in person Saturday, October 25, at 11:00 a.m., to friends of Nelson Grain & Grocery Co., and visitors to the Yamboree.

"Smiling Ernest," as he is known throughout the Southwest, is heard daily (Monday through Friday) at 7:15 a.m. over Station KGKO out of Fort Worth, and his recordings of popular tunes are a big hit throughout the nation.

In Ernest Tubb, the State of Texas has given America another great writer of native American songs, songs whose simple charm and deep heart appeal are winning a sensational popularity on records, radio, and wherever songs are sung.

Come and hear him; bring your friends and neighbors—there is no admission charge to see and hear this popular radio and recording artist. He is being brought to Gilmer through the courtesy of Universal Mills of Fort Worth—the millers of Gold Chain Flour.[32]

And Gilmer, Texas, Tubb recalled, was only a stop on the way to Shreveport, Louisiana, and a big Sunday package show with the great Bob Wills, whom he met for the first time.

I played Gilmer, Texas, that Saturday afternoon advertising flour and I drove from there to Shreveport. I was getting . . . $50 a week, but it increased every three months, I'd get a little raise. So I went to Shreveport and got $50 for the one show, and it was pouring down rain. But he had also booked Bob Wills to fly in, and not to bring his band: I remember Bob was kinda irritated because it looked like he was supposed to have all his Texas Playboys. He brought Eldon Shamblin and Tommy Duncan. The three of them flew down to Shreveport Sunday morning, see, 'cause they played in Cain's Ballroom on Saturday night . . . Bob said, "I told you not to advertise nothing except Bob Wills: I didn't tell you I was gonna bring anybody." Anyhow, even though it was raining, the auditorium was packed, and I'm sure that Bob Wills was the one that packed them.[33]

A Shreveport auditorium show for $50, his whole week's pay: but this was only the beginning. Tubb may have been overly modest to attribute the main drawing power that day to Wills: "Walking the Floor over You" was beginning to rival "New San Antonio Rose" for jukebox plays nationwide. Those nighttime juke joint crowds could hear Ernest's records now and were calling his number almost as often as Wills's. Tubb once mentioned that it was at this Shreveport show where he got a tumultuous response to a brand-new blues number that he hadn't even recorded yet, a little ditty called "You Nearly Lose Your Mind." "I wrote that back in Fort Worth, Texas, in 1941. I remember I played a show with Bob Wills in Shreveport, and I only had [a few] records out at the time—this one hadn't even been released yet—but they wanted me to sing three or four songs. But it was a good stage song, so I sang it anyway, and it actually got the best hand—better than the ones they were familiar with."[34]

Prospects were bright, and getting brighter all the time, for the Gold Chain Troubadour. A second year in Fort Worth held for him more hit records, bigger package shows, and the chance to be in movies, just as Floy Case had predicted.

An early Tubb home in Crisp, Texas. Although not his actual birthplace, it was the only former home standing when an Ennis, Texas photographer took this shot for a songbook in the mid-1940s.

Earliest known Ernest Tubb photo, showing him as a fourteen-year-old farmboy in a cotton field on a snowy day (November 28, 1928). (Courtesy Mrs. Ruth Husky)

The last days of young farmer Tubb, holding the pawnshop guitar in West Texas. (Courtesy Mrs. Ruth Husky)

Elaine and Ernest with baby Justin, San Antonio. (Courtesy Mrs. Elaine Tubb Lemieux)

From the first publicity photos: Tubb with the ill-advised Jimmie Rodgers tuxedo jacket. Marquees of the South Texas tour. (Courtesy Mr. Jimmie Dale Court)

Newspaper playbill for the one verified tour date: June 5, 1937, Comfort, Texas. (Courtesy Mrs. Ruth Husky)

Tubb, holding his first record release. (Courtesy Mrs. Elaine Tubb Lemieux)

Little Justin at the microphone, San Angelo days. (Courtesy Mrs. Merwyn J. Buffington)

Keeping a Jimmie Rodgers tradition: a grateful troubadour flashes his thanks from his Porter Street home. (Courtesy Mrs. Elaine Tubb Lemieux)

Where did the tux go? Ernest-as-cowboy in his early days. (Courtesy Mrs. Ruth Husky)

With brother C. R. at the Travis Beer
truck, San Angelo. (Courtesy Mrs. Elaine
Tubb Lemieux)

By the lazy Concho River in San Angelo.
(Courtesy Mrs. Elaine Tubb Lemieux)

Selling Western-Bilt mattresses with song:
Tubb on far left, others unknown.
(Courtesy Mr. Tracy Pitcox)

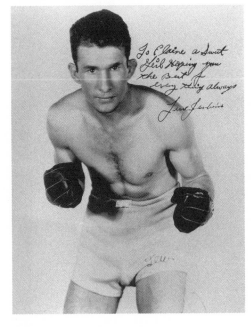

Ernest with the Short Brothers in Fort Worth:
Jimmie (left) and Leon.

Lew Jenkins. (Courtesy Mrs. Elaine Tubb
Lemieux)

Tubb with his first Decca producer, Dave Kapp.

The Fort Worth cowboy singer, 1942. (Courtesy Mrs. Elaine Tubb Lemieux)

"Your Gold Chain Troubadour" and his equipment, Fort Worth. (Courtesy Mr. Johnny Case)

The Short Brothers sub for Tubb, summer of 1942. (Courtesy Mr. Johnny Case)

In his Fort Worth home, Tubb readies one of his new Decca discs for play. (Courtesy Mrs. Elaine Tubb Lemieux)

ERNEST TUBB'S RANCH BUDDIES

JIMMIE AND LEON

PINCH HITTING FOR ERNEST
WHILE HE'S IN HOLLYWOOD

Presented by the Millers of

Gold Chain
FLOUR

KGKO 7:15 A. M. MON. THRU FRI.
570 ON YOUR DIAL

UNIVERSAL MILLS - FORT WORTH

ENRICHED
Vitamin B.
WITH NIACIN AND IRON

Gold Chain
ENRICHED FLOUR

VALUABLE FREE COUPON

The "Riding West" cast on the Columbia Pictures lot, late 1942: (from left) Johnny Bond, Ernest Tubb, Wesley Tuttle, Shirley Patterson, Charles Starrett, Cal Shrum, Art Wenzel, two unknowns. (Courtesy Mr. Bob Pinson)

Backstage in Birmingham: (from left) Bill Boyd, Constance Keith, Texas Ruby, and Ernest Tubb. (Country Music Foundation)

In the WSM studios, 1943, with Harold Bradley (left) and Vernon "Toby" Reese. (Courtesy Mrs. Elaine Tubb Lemieux)

Early Texas Troubadours: Ray "Kemo" Head, Herbert "Tommy" "Butterball" Paige (pulling boots), Tubb, fiddler Johnny Sapp (seated), Chester Studdard, Vernon "Toby" Reese. (Courtesy Mrs. Elaine Tubb Lemieux)

The Short Brothers rejoin the early band: (from left) "Butterball" as rube, plus Jimmie Short, Tubb, Johnny Sapp, Leon Short. (Courtesy Mrs. Elaine Tubb Lemieux)

Tubb serenades his Nashville radio audience, circa 1943. (Courtesy Mrs. Elaine Tubb Lemieux)

Judge Hay flanked by Pee Wee King and Ernest Tubb hawking their early Opry sponsor, Royal Crown Cola. (Courtesy Mrs. Dollie Denny)

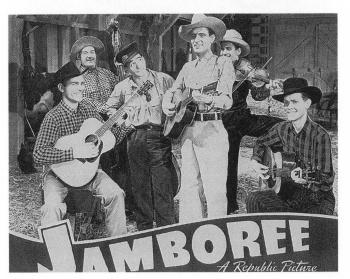

From *Jamboree*, 1944: (from left) Jimmie Short, Butterball, Shug Fisher, Ernest Tubb, Johnny Sapp, Leon Short.

Faye Flanagan, founder of first fan club. (Country Music Foundation)

Tubb family reunion near Fort Worth, early 1944, just before C. R. Jr.'s military induction: (standing) C. R. Tubb Jr., C. R. Tubb, Ernest Tubb; (seated) Opal Tubb Collier, Ellen Tubb Ashton, Lucille Tubb West, Jewell Tubb Adams. (Courtesy Mrs. Ruth Husky)

Father and sons from the Tubb family reunion in early 1944. (Courtesy Mrs. Ruth Husky)

"You're In the Navy Now": wartime stateside meeting between Ernest and his "Bud," C. R. Jr.

1944 war-bond rally in downtown Nashville. The Duke of Paducah clowns out front, while Bill Monroe's Blue Grass Boys wait to come on behind the Texas Troubadours. (Courtesy of Mr. Jerry Strobel, Grand Ole Opry Archives)

Jack (left) and Bill Drake in St. Louis, well before both men joined Tubb's band in October, 1944. (Courtesy Mr. Buddy Griffin)

Tubb, Curley Bradley (Mutual Radio's "Tom Mix" at the time), and Eddy Arnold, on debut date of *Checkerboard Jamboree*, November 17, 1945. (Courtesy Mr. Richard Weize)

The seaman of "Seaman's Blues," writer Talmadge Tubb, poses in uniform with his famous uncle about the time of the song. He later wrote "Waltz Across Texas." (Courtesy Mrs. Loretta Jordan)

Snowy day at the Madison homeplace, December 5, 1945.

Cover of the cutout book sold with "Ernest Tubb Radio Song
Book No. 4," 1946. (Courtesy Mr. David McCormick)

9

Movies and Package Shows

THE CHICAGO SESSION

Given Tubb's growing national popularity that fall of 1941, it was time for another Decca recording session. Not only was "Walking the Floor over You" a national smash, but subsequent releases of "I Wonder Why You Said Goodbye," "Mean Mama Blues," and "I'll Always Be Glad to Take You Back" were going great.

Kapp placed another phone call to Tubb in Fort Worth and asked him when he could come up to Chicago to record twelve new songs. Of course Tubb had been busy writing new material, but even at that, twelve songs were more than he had ready; Kapp would have to be content with eight. Besides, KGKO and Gold Chain Flour would only give him one day off from his program, which meant driving furiously out of Fort Worth after his program of Friday, November 14, 1941, and reaching Chicago late the next day. Sunday he spent resting and re-hearsing the songs (almost to the point of laryngitis) with second-time electric guitarist Fay "Smitty" Smith, who would go with him against Dave Kapp's wishes. "They wouldn't pay for his transportation: they would hire me a guitar player [there in Chicago]. Well, I didn't want that, so I said, 'I'll bring him anyhow.'"[1] Maybe it wasn't simply Kapp's demand for twelve songs, but the fact that Tubb once again had to sing the songs until Smith learned them, that accounted for his voice strain. But by Monday, November 17, they were ready with eight songs. Six were new Tubb creations, one was Homer Hargrove's "I Hate to See You Go," and then there was the Short Brothers' "Time after Time." Again the Shorts couldn't make it over from Lincoln, but at least they were represented by a song.

FRIENDS AND FAMILY

When Tubb returned to Fort Worth and his regular Gold Chain duties, Universal Mills gave him a new time slot. The 10:45 quarter-hour, his since May, was switched to 7:15 A.M. at the beginning of December 1941: this is the time slot his younger fans best remember, since they could now hear him before school. The company gave him a new sound truck, according to Floy Case's third mention in *Mountain Broadcast and Prairie Recorder:* "It is white and has his name in large letters in the most conspicuous places." She also disclosed that one of Ernest Tubb's biggest fans was the lightweight boxing champion of the world, a Sweetwater, Texas, boy who had known Ernest since his San Angelo days: Lew Jenkins. "Jenkins . . . is also learning to strum the guitar, and Ernest is proud to number him among his most ardent fans. Lew recently called Ernest long distance from Minneapolis, Minnesota, to ask for a large autographed picture, and the conversation lengthened into a fifteen minute chat."[2] Ernest would later put Jenkins's name as co-writer on a 1944 transcription, "This Time We're Really Through." Jenkins remained Tubb's friend for many years. He was one of many colorful characters on the contemporary sports scene; he loved motorcycles, women, and whiskey, in addition to prize fights and country music. Jenkins went overseas in World War II, and on one of his wartime drunks, according to Douglas Glenn Tubb, Jenkins tried to place an angry phone call to Adolf Hitler. Failing in his bid for a boxing comeback after the war, he bounced from one branch of the armed services to another, usually lying about his fight-impaired senses to pass entrance. Jenkins was in the Army at Fort Benning, Georgia, in 1951 when he had a publicized "reunion" with Ernest Tubb, who came to Columbus to play a show. The press account of that meeting says that Jenkins went to Hollywood with Tubb when he made one of his early films.

Ernest and Elaine Tubb were making other friends as the weeks and months passed in Fort Worth, usually from the music world, of course. Tommy Duncan he'd gotten to know in a long conversation backstage at the Shreveport show in the fall of 1941; until then, Tubb had not realized what a Jimmie Rodgers fan the great Bob Wills vocalist was. At about this time he came to know Rex Griffin, the Alabama singer who was another Rodgers disciple. Griffin was then on KRLD in Dallas; the same Floy Case article that mentions Lew Jenkins also mentions Rex Griffin, looking ahead optimistically to a coming Bluebird session that seems never to have happened. Tubb learned and performed many of Griffin's great earlier songs that he'd recorded for Decca in his 1930s heyday: "The Last Letter," "Beyond the Last Mile," "Over the River," "My Hillbilly Baby," "I Loved You Once," "I Told You So," "I'll Never Tell You I Love You." Most of these he recorded for World transcriptions in 1944–1945, one in his very first twelve-inch album (1956) and all the rest in a 1960s Rex Griffin tribute album, titled for Griffin's last great song, "Just Call Me Lonesome." They toured together for a while in the mid-1940s and co-wrote "How Can I Be Sure," which both men recorded. Griffin and Tubb remained good friends the rest of Griffin's life (he died in 1958), at least to the extent that Griffin's itinerant lifestyle and poor health (diabetes, among other problems) allowed. Griffin and Duncan, as we have seen, are praised in Tubb's unrecorded lament, "He Took Fifty Bucks and My Yodeling Too When He Took My Tonsils Out."

Over the Christmas holidays of 1941 the Tubb and Case families were graced with a visit from Mrs. Carrie Rodgers and her daughter, Anita, stopping in Fort Worth on their way from San Antonio to Meridian. Ernest had loaned Floy Case a copy of Mrs. Rodgers's book, *My Husband Jimmie Rodgers,* on the occasion of their first meeting at the KFJZ studios nearly a year earlier. Reading it, she published her own tribute to Mrs. Rodgers in the June 1941 *Mountain Broadcast and Prairie Recorder,* the same issue in which she prevailed upon the editors to publish Ernest's poem, "Jimmie's Wife."[3] So when Mrs. Rodgers came through Fort Worth to see the Tubbs, she was glad to meet the Cases; Mrs. Case and Mrs. Rodgers carried on a voluminous correspondence for the last twenty years of Carrie Rodgers's life. Her baby sister, Mrs. Mildred Pollard, rounded out the Fort Worth gathering that Christmas of 1941; her husband of five years, George Pollard, a career Army officer, was being shuttled off to Colorado in the wake of the Pearl Harbor attack only days before, and she recalls that her sister and Ernest came to see them at their motel.[4] Mrs. Rodgers was no doubt pleased with the progress her protégé had made that year. Ernest had promised her that if he couldn't make it as a full-time musician in the course of that year, after five years of being more or less under her tutelage and guidance, he'd give it up.

JUKEBOX STAR

He wouldn't have to give it up, then or ever. Just after her account of meeting Mrs. Rodgers that Christmas, Floy Case wrote this about Ernest Tubb's recent past and bright future.

> Ernest Tubb, Universal Mills' popular Gold Chain Troubadour, and Fay (Smitty) Smith, had a pleasant trip to Chicago some time back, where they cut eight new sides for Decca. Fay Smith plays the electric guitar on Ernest's recordings, and take it from me he really takes off and goes to town on them. These records are being well received in every section of the country, and seem to be steadily increasing in popularity. In fact, you don't run into many "Juke boxes" without at least one of his numbers on it. Mrs. Conn, of the Conn Music Co. here, told me that she had people standing in line waiting for one of his more popular numbers when it became known that she had a new supply. A major studio has been dickering with him in regard to a movie contract, so it probably

won't be long before he's Hollywood bound. In the meantime, he continues to sing those sweet love songs, that the fairer sex seem to like so well, from KGKO, 7:15 A.M. Monday through Friday, and the fans continue to bombard him with cards and letters.[5]

The "dickering" for Tubb's movie roles took nearly six months to come to fruition. Meantime, the first half of 1942 saw mounting accolades for Tubb's work from the jukebox press, which paid more and more attention to the lucrative hillbilly field as America's war involvement deepened. Typical is this from *Billboard*'s March 7, 1942, "American Folk Records" column: "W. N. Klein of Klein Distributing Company, Elkton, Ky., says at present his best numbers are 'Corinne Corinna,' 'I Ain't Going Honky Tonkin' Anymore,' 'I'll Always Be Glad to Take You Back,' 'I Wonder Why You Said Goodbye,' 'You're in the Army Now.'"[6] Three of the five top records: Ernest Tubb hits. Mrs. Conn and Mr. Klein were not alone; Tubb was becoming a national phenomenon. From the same column, dated April 18, 1942: "Probably the top folk tune, taken on a nationwide basis, is Ernest Tubb's 'Walking the Floor over You.' It is placing high on lists from the Midwest, South, and particularly from the West Coast."[7] In Richmond by late June, operators there said "When the World Has Turned You Down" should rank at the top of all lists, since it was getting more plays than any pop band disc.[8] By late July, three areas not known as country music hotbeds had joined the crowd: "'Walking the Floor over You' tops reports from Des Moines and Philadelphia, while 'When the World Has Turned You Down' leads in Milwaukee and 'Our Baby's Book' is going strong, particularly through the Midwest."[9] Small wonder that on May 27, 1942, pop titan Bing Crosby cut "Walking the Floor over You."

Clearly, if *Billboard* had had country record charts then, instead of waiting until the beginning of 1944, Ernest Tubb would have cleaned up, showing a dominance comparable to Eddy Arnold's of 1948 or Lefty Frizzell's of 1951.

FIGHTING BUCKAROO

The man who "dickered" successfully with Columbia Studios on Ernest Tubb's behalf was Elbert Haling, who worked in the continuity department of station KGKO. Haling received questionnaires from the studio, forms that went around to many stations, seeking the most suitable western or hillbilly talent to put in films alongside Charles Starrett, their handsome, rugged cowboy star who couldn't sing. Haling answered the questionnaire, drafted letters on Tubb's behalf, mailed in publicity photos, recordings, press clippings like the early ones quoted above, probably even sent samples of Tubb's heavy fan mail: all to prove that Ernest was their man. Columbia Studios ultimately agreed, but they wanted

Tubb to put on just a little extra weight. A diet of malts, eggs, and other fattening foods managed to add just a few pounds, but the first picture went ahead as scheduled.

The Short Brothers, Jimmie and Leon, came back to Texas that spring, and they got a show on KGKO at 7:00 A.M., first broadcast on June 1, 1942. Exactly a month later, when Ernest began a one-month leave of absence to head to Hollywood, the Shorts took over his slot at 7:15. Ernest (Mrs. Rodgers may have gone along too—Elaine Tubb remembers it that way—and possibly boxer Lew Jenkins) stayed at Hollywood's Chateau Marmont Hotel and apartments, 8221 Sunset Boulevard, the very place that songwriter and expatriate Texan Cindy Walker lived with her parents.[10] Filming began for *Fighting Buckaroo* on July 7 and lasted some nine days.

On the third day of shooting, July 9, Tubb sent a letter to the Case family back in Fort Worth that describes how much fun moviemaking was, gives some news from Bob Wills and his new group of Texas Playboys, and tells how friendly Charles Starrett and the rest of the cast were—a cast that included Norma Jean Lee, little "Buckshot" in the film; Kay Harris, the female lead; Stan Brown, the young man wrongly accused who finally "gets the girl"; and Arthur "Arkansas" Hunnicutt. Tubb played "Ernie" (the name he never wanted in real life), Starrett's singing sidekick. With the help of a trio (Johnny Luther's Ranch Boys) on two songs and from "Buckshot" on the finale, Tubb sang "Happy Roving Cowboy," "Walking the Floor over You," "Blue-Eyed Elaine," and, as the finale, "Ridin' That Dusty Trail." For his film work, Tubb was paid $1,000, plus $50 each for the four songs.

Another important note surfaces in his letter: "I'll record for Decca as soon as the picture is finished." The session took place at Decca's Melrose Avenue studios between 11 A.M. and 1:30 P.M. on July 17, 1942. In view of the looming American Federation of Musicians strike (effective August 1), it's surprising that Tubb cut only six masters at this session, which would be his last for a year and a half. After all, he'd cut twelve on his previous Hollywood trip, six in Dallas, and eight in Chicago (when Dave Kapp had wanted twelve). But two of the six recordings, "You Nearly Lose Your Mind" and "Try Me One More Time," stand among the very best he ever made, thanks in no small part to the fine trio of musicians that Decca put around him.

Rhythm guitarist was Charles Quirk, a veteran from the old Beverly Hillbillies days, when country music first came to the southern California airwaves. Bassist was Wesley Tuttle, back in California after three years at WLW. A future Capitol Records star, this busy West Coast session player had bit parts in eight different Charles Starrett Westerns himself—not *Fighting Buckaroo,* though he would be in Tubb's next one with Starrett, *Riding West.* Tuttle's recollections are my source of information about the third musician, session leader and electric lead guitarist Oliver Edward "Eddie" Tudor. Tudor was lead guitarist on Gene Autry's *Melody Ranch* radio program (on this very trip to Hollywood, Tubb attended Autry's last program before Army induction) and worked in at least one of Starrett's Westerns himself. Whether from earlier records or just through his native ability, Tudor mastered the Tubb lead guitar style for these six songs— indeed, he helped set the standard for all who would later fill his shoes. On "Try Me One More Time," second cut of the session, Tudor's four-note upward fill at the end of the intro became the favorite lick of Tubb's later lead guitarists, particularly Billy Byrd and Leon Rhodes, though the latter would often embellish the basic lick with extra eighth and sixteenth notes. "You Nearly Lose Your Mind," the Shreveport crowd pleaser, was finally recorded at this session. Tudor sparkles again on that one; Quirk (or Tubb himself) playing the seconding acoustic guitar part gets behind on the instrumental break, but catches up nicely before it ends.

Eddie Tudor did such a fine job on this session that it's a shame he never got the chance to do another one. Wesley Tuttle recently confirmed what Tubb himself long suspected (but never knew) when frequent attempts to track him down in after years proved fruitless: Tudor perished in the Second World War. "He was killed late in the war. He was piloting a two-engine bomber for the Army Air Corps out of, or over, England when the prop from one of the engines came off, came back in the cabin, and killed him."[11]

Tubb was in no hurry to get back to Fort Worth after the session. His July 9 letter to the Cases closed, "Guess I will be back home by August the 1st."[12] Besides attending Gene Autry's last premilitary radio show, he met Roy Rogers and the Sons of the Pioneers on the set of their latest Republic film: "spent half a day on the set with Roy," Floy Case reported in the November 1942 *Mountain Broadcast and Prairie Recorder*.[13] Tubb got back to Fort Worth and his regular broadcasts even later than he had guessed: newspaper logs don't show *Ernest Tubb* back in that 7:15 slot until Monday, August 17. Jimmie and Leon Short were then relegated by KGKO to 7:45, cut back to Tuesdays and Thursdays.

THE OSCAR DAVIS SHOWS

The two men who had promoted the Shreveport show in October 1941 were Rhode Island native Oscar Davis and one of the performers, Alabamian "Happy" Hal Burns of WMC Memphis, star of the Garrett Snuff Varieties. Davis had met Burns in Birmingham in 1937, since which time he had taken to promoting country music shows. His big productions were Sunday afternoon National Hillbilly Jamborees. Burns and his whole Garrett Snuff Varieties gang played each of the shows, but the headline and guest acts varied somewhat from city to city. The shows were tremendous successes, drawing multiple thousands to double performances on Sundays across the nation. Sometimes, varying the talent only a little, they would play the same city two or three Sundays in a row. *The Billboard 1943 Music Year Book* took note of their great regional success: "The personal appearance field, highly developed only in the last few years, has proved a gold mine to many artists, as well as to the promoters handling the shows . . . In the South the leaders have been Oscar Davis and Hal Burns, whose units, built with two or three widely known radio artists surrounded by lesser known people, often from stations in the territory played, have played to phenomenal business. One of the Davis-Burns shows in Dallas grossed $2,970 the first day and $3,780 the second. At Nashville the unit drew 20,000 to four shows in one day. A Davis jamboree in the Auditorium at Little Rock, Ark., last fall played to $8,200 in one day, giving three shows."[14]

Davis, Chicago-based at this time, had won his big gamble and with it a reputation as country music's first great show promoter. Soon he was "the Baron," famous for drawing big crowds everywhere with expensive advance campaigns on radio and in the newspapers: "Don't You Dare Miss It!" became his signature slogan.

"Happy" Hal Burns first met Ernest Tubb back in his San Antonio days, when both were trying to break into the business. In Memphis, Burns found radio fame via his Garrett Snuff shows. But he remembered Ernest, and once Tubb's Decca records began to hit nationwide, Burns wanted him on as many of the National Hillbilly Jamborees as Tubb's broadcast work and travel time allowed. One week after Tubb got back to Fort Worth from Hollywood and the filming of *Fighting Buckaroo* he was on his way to Memphis, his most distant tour date yet, to work another big Burns-Davis promotion: the second of three Sunday shows at the Fairgrounds. Looking back on all three shows—August 16, 23, and September 6— Floy Case in *Mountain Broadcast and Prairie Recorder* said, "Hal Burns of Memphis, Tenn., and Oscar Davis of Chicago, those two outstanding promoters of Hillbilly Jamborees, really out did themselves sometime ago, when they held these popular shows on three separate Sundays . . . at the Fairgrounds in Memphis. The six performances played to a grand total of 47,000 people, who were seated in the grand stand at the race track. There was a special stage built upon a high platform and special lighting effects. The elaborate sound system included 24 loud speakers. Part of the program was broadcast by remote control from WMC."[15] Tubb appeared on the second date, August 23, at each of the two shows (2:30 and 8:00 P.M.), billed just beneath the headlining acts, the Hoosier Hot Shots and Roy Acuff. Lew Childre, Hal Burns, the Loden Family (which included fiddling Jimmie Loden, the future "Sonny James"), Rachel and Oswald (from Acuff's group), and a bevy of Memphis favorites rounded out the bill, which customers paid 45 cents to see. An ad two days earlier, in the Friday, August 21, Memphis *Commercial Appeal,* spotlighted the coming attraction, "Balladeer" Ernest Tubb, with a nice photo. Even though he'd just finished making his first film and it wouldn't be released until early 1943, the caption reads, "Ernest Tubb, rural rhythm balladeer of radio and the movies, is one of the headline attractions of the National Hillbilly Jamboree at the Fairgrounds Sunday afternoon and night."[16]

The kind of money Ernest Tubb was making for these Oscar Davis–Hal Burns Sunday afternoon promotions was as much or more than his weekly Gold Chain Flour salary ($75), so these shows, plus the movie money, perhaps even more than his record royalties or *Billboard* clippings, convinced him that he should get a sizable raise from his sponsor or move on to something else. He fulfilled his obligations right on into the fall of 1942, but moviemaking and package shows were now in his blood, and it was time for a talk with the boss. So sometime during October 1942 he sat down with Universal Mills' Mr. Stone. "I didn't know what I was gonna do, but I can thank God Mr. Stone was a gentleman. I said, 'I've got another year to go on my contract. I'll fulfill it, but I won't be happy. I think I can do better.' He just tore my contract up and said, 'I know you can. I wish we could keep you, but we can't. We can't pay you what you're worth. I just want you to know that you've doubled our business in eighteen months selling flour . . . If you ever need anything, if we can help you, remember we'll be behind you.' "[17]

Elbert Haling had helped promote Ernest Tubb right off KGKO by sending him to Hollywood the first time. In November 1942, Tubb relinquished all but one morning (Mondays at 7:15 A.M.) of his former six-day-per-week show, with the Short Brothers taking over the Tuesday, Wednesday, and Friday slots. Tubb had places to go and shows to do. He played a big Radio Jamboree and Fiddler's Contest in Dallas on November 15, 1942, just days before he was off to Hollywood for a second film.

RIDING WEST

Traveling alone this time, he arrived in the film capital on Thanksgiving Day, November 26, and checked into the St. Moritz Hotel at 5849 Sunset Boulevard. Shooting began on Monday, November 30, with Tubb riding to the set each day with one of his movie musicians, an Oklahoman named Cyrus Whitfield "Johnny" Bond.[18] Bond, a favorite bit part actor of the B Westerns because of his fine musical ability and horsemanship, had been a regular on Gene Autry's *Melody Ranch* prior to Autry's Army induction and had returned to weekly radio work with the Oklahoman he'd come to Hollywood with, Tubb's Decca labelmate Jimmy Wakely. Though Tubb had ridden a horse and worn hats most of his life, he credited Bond with teaching him a simple trick of the cowboy movie trade: how to keep your hat on during a high-speed dash on horseback. "Out on the farm it didn't matter. But in a film, they don't want it to blow off. He showed me how to duck my head and keep it on."[19]

Johnny was the rhythm guitarist on the soundtrack recordings in a group simply dubbed Ernest Tubb and his Singing Cowboys, which also had Wesley Tuttle (bass), Cal Shrum (fiddle), and Art Wenzel (accordion). Tubb, in his letter to the Case family about this film, mentions a steel guitarist on the soundtrack recordings without naming him. But he does name the songs, and it's a good thing, since no copy of the final film *Riding West* (original plans were to call it *Code of the Pony Express*) seems to be in anyone's possession. They were "Skyball Paint" (like "Happy Roving Cowboy," a Bob Nolan favorite), "Swell San Angelo," "I'll Get Along Somehow," and "When the World Has Turned You Down." The commercial recording ban by then was three months old with no agreement in sight, but it obviously did not affect making movie soundtrack recordings; these would be Tubb's only "recordings" between July 1942 and January 1944. Wesley Tuttle remembers that all the songs were prerecorded at the movie lot's soundstage and that learning the songs was fairly easy, even though he'd not heard them before. They were, of course, lip-synched on the screen.[20]

Besides Tubb and Starrett, the only other holdover from his first film was the comic star, Arthur "Arkansas" Hunnicutt. Shirley Patterson played the female lead, and a relative unknown named Lloyd Bridges played the tough bad guy. Besides the Johnny Bond hat story, the only thing resembling a blooper that Tubb recalled from his moviemaking came in a scene in which Bridges pulls a hunting knife on Starrett and has him pinned up against a fireplace. "I was supposed to come in and say, 'Drop it,' and he doesn't, and I shoot the knife out of his hand. But the mic for me to speak was too close; I couldn't shoot the gun, someone else had to shoot a gun. I had to hold it, but it was too close to my speaking mic for me to shoot it. But I came in, and before I could say 'Drop it,' the prop man shot the gun, and it scared me and Charlie [Starrett] both. That was quite a mixup. [The director said,] 'Look it, as soon as you come in the door, say, 'Drop it.'"[21]

This trip to Hollywood, as before, found Tubb busy in his time off the set. He was a guest on Jimmy Wakely's local radio show on Friday, December 4, and appeared the night before that at a military service benefit at the Hollywood Canteen, where he met Claire Trevor, Rudy Vallee, and the Ritz Brothers. At this point in his letter to the Cases, a little of the glitz and romance surrounding Hollywood begins to fade. Pleased that Tex Ritter, Bob Wills, and Tommy Duncan had been out to see him on the set, he admitted that he hadn't yet seen Roy Rogers or the Sons of the Pioneers on this visit as before. "But I heard that Republic has planned to spend $100,000 on publicity for Roy next year. Not bad, eh?"[22] In my 1977 interview, Tubb looking back described this as "the politics" of Hollywood, against which a newcomer's chances were "pretty small."[23] But at the time he was still upbeat about wanting to stay in Hollywood, free of his Gold Chain contract as he was: "I have an appointment with my agent today, to discuss my staying in Hollywood for radio work. If I don't land something worthwhile, I plan to return to Fort Worth about next Monday (Dec. 14). We finish the picture this coming Tuesday, Dec. 8th. Sure hope I get something to hold me here, as I'll have a better chance to get picture work if I am here."[24] This was a pivotal time in Ernest Tubb's career and, as his letter indicates, he knew it.

To Tubb's disappointment, nothing turned up to hold him in Hollywood, so for the Christmas holidays it was back to Fort Worth. But with Gold Chain only a memory, there was nothing to hold him there either. Arriving on December 19, he stayed in Fort Worth exactly one week, just through Christmas and visits from his father and stepmother Maudie up from the Con Can ranch and sister Blondie's big family over from Kemp, and then he was off again, bound this time for Birmingham, Alabama. On Sunday, December 27, 1942, he played an auditorium show there for the same man that had found him lucrative bookings for much of that year, Oscar Davis. Bill Boyd, Curly Fox and Texas Ruby, and the Milo Twins were on the same bill with Ernest; he got $100 for his part. More important, though, than the initial $100 job was the fact that he kept getting calls from people wanting to book him in the Southeast. Chester Studdard, over from Gadsden, Alabama, brought a message from a Nashville promoter named Joseph Lee "J. L." Frank (who subsequently phoned Tubb directly at Birmingham's Bankhead Hotel). Studdard, a future Texas Troubadour, remembers it this way: "J. L. Frank called me here in Gadsden, and said that Tubb was going to be in Birmingham on a Sunday evening. And he asked me if I would go down there, and meet him, and ask him if he would come be on the show we were going to have in Gadsden on the next Sunday."[25]

Tubb, while omitting the detail of Chester as the messenger, remembered the call and the offer: "So when I was in Birmingham, I was free, so when Joe said, 'Could you stay?' I said, 'Yes, I can stay.' He said, 'I'll give you $150 to play Gadsden, Alabama.' That was on a Friday. I hung up from him and somebody else called me, wanting me to play a date in Atlanta, Georgia, the next weekend. So as it happened, I never got back to Fort Worth. That was it. I got there, and worked two or three dates that week . . . I was there two weeks. Atlanta, then some local groups hired me to play Montgomery, Alabama, and play some schoolhouses. But Joe's the one that took me to the Opry . . ."[26] With Birmingham as his base for a few weeks, wife Elaine joined him at the Bankhead after the New Year—between January 8 and 13—leaving Justin with Jimmie and Cherry Short (a nurse Jimmie had married a year earlier in Lincoln, Nebraska) and Violet Elaine ("Scooter Bill") with C. R. and Margie Tubb, both in Fort Worth.[27]

JOE L. FRANK

Who was Joe L. Frank? How and why did he latch on to Ernest Tubb? Both answers make interesting stories and bear heavily on Tubb's immediate future.

Mr. Frank was a Birmingham native who'd won the respect of many of country music's pioneer performers for his fair dealings, his generosity with the artists, and a great track record for success. Alton Delmore of the Opry's Delmore Brothers gives this description of Mr. Frank, the best firsthand account from a country artist: "a great man in the entertainment field who goes, I think, as one of the most neglected persons in the entire field of country and western music. Joe was an understanding person who could prod out real talent when he saw it. He was not a 'high hat' person but just a down-to-earth businessman who knew what would seem to go in the game. He was . . . just an ordinary person, who talked and acted like a plow boy but had a tremendous knowledge of the entertainment world, hard to beat."[28] As Delmore then points out, J. L. Frank had managed Gene Autry in his very early days at WLS in Chicago, as well as the popular radio comedy team Fibber McGee and Molly. From Louisville in 1937 he brought the Golden West Cowboys to Nashville and the Grand Ole Opry, about which Delmore says, "When he first came to the Opry, he brought Pee Wee King (his son-in-law) and the Golden West Cowboys, and he made a good go of it from the very first. They had a good band, but nothing spectacular, but Old Joe knew the score and he drained every drop of goodness out of them. He wanted, and demanded, the best they had and he got it. They were soon one of the most popular acts on the Opry."[29]

Delmore goes on. "Joe was a clean-cut, neat fellow, handsome, with a little moustache and a big Texas hat . . . he always had a good word for the down and out musician, and also a handout, if they asked for it, and lots of times when they didn't ask for it. He was truly a charitable person. And I give Joe Frank the credit for putting the Grand Ole Opry in the big time class and prestige and also the big time money."[30] Not only had he brought the Golden West Cowboys to the Opry in 1937, but also East Tennessee recording artist Roy Acuff in 1938, who would become the show's first network radio host in the fall of 1939. Frank, by then based in Nashville, helped plan the big Camel Caravan shows in 1942, and went along on those extensive tours to U.S. military installations with the acts he'd booked: Minnie Pearl and the Golden West Cowboys (with young vocalist Eddy

Arnold). A Camel Caravan tour, passing through Fort Worth in 1942, gave the diminutive and personable accordionist Frankie "Pee Wee" King, Mr. Frank's son-in-law, his first opportunity to meet Ernest Tubb—on a hotel elevator, of all places.[31] Without knowing it at the time, the two would soon be fast friends and frequent road companions, working for the same manager.

From Mr. Frank's point of view, as he placed his calls to Gadsden and Birmingham to book Ernest Tubb that weekend at the tail end of 1942, Tubb's reputation as a handsome young jukebox star was enhanced by a glowing report of Tubb's Birmingham performances he got from Constance Keith on the scene. Constance, "Connie" to her friends, was, like Floy Case, a columnist for Dixie Music's *Mountain Broadcast and Prairie Recorder* magazine, was generally knowledgeable about the country music scene, and headed Roy Acuff's fan club at the time. She had a good rapport with Acuff's mentor, Mr. Frank, and called him in Nashville about Birmingham's sensational response to Ernest Tubb. A week or so later, when Elaine Tubb met Constance Keith for the first time, she could truthfully write to Floy Case about her, "She has really been nice to Ernest."[32]

On the Gadsden show Friday, New Year's Day 1943, Tubb received his highest pay yet ($150). Besides working with Chester Studdard, Toby Reese, Johnny Toma, Ray "Kemo" Head, and the other Gadsden Melody Boys, he shared the stage for the first time with Pee Wee King, Eddy Arnold, and the other Golden West Cowboys. In fact, they provided his accompaniment, as they would for most of the next six months. Tubb's self-made Atlanta booking was staged the next day, Saturday, January 2, at WSB's Saturday night Barn Dance in the city's Erlanger Theater with Hank Penny and other acts. But Mr. Frank wanted more from and for his newfound Texas Troubadour. He asked Ernest, just as he had Roy Acuff five years earlier, "Would you like to appear on Nashville's Grand Ole Opry?" To which Ernest replied, "Would I?!" and readily agreed. He played a Friday night show in Jackson, Tennessee, on January 15, with Roy Acuff, Billie Walker, Minnie Pearl, the Golden West Cowboys, Gene Steele, Ford Rush, and Jamup & Honey. Then he and the several Opry acts in that group drove the 120 miles eastward to Nashville for Ernest Tubb's Grand Ole Opry debut the next night.

GRAND OLE OPRY

Ernest Tubb made his initial Grand Ole Opry guest appearance on the show's prime half-hour, the 9:30 to 10:00 P.M. NBC Network portion sponsored by R. J. Reynolds's Prince Albert Smoking Tobacco. The date was January 16, 1943, and the place was the Opry's home since 1939, the downtown War Memorial Auditorium. Joe Frank was in the wings to bolster Tubb's courage; contemplating such a huge radio audience, Tubb suffered from understandable stage fright. Word had been passed along by the Opry's stage manager Vito Pellettieri for Zeke Clements and others not to sing any Ernest Tubb hits that night: Tubb himself would be on the show. Roy Acuff, Frank's 1938 protégé, brought out the latest model when he introduced Tubb to warm applause. Seven-year-old son Justin, who would first grace the Opry stage himself within the next two years, was listening down in Fort Worth at Jimmie and Cherry Short's house, holding the antenna in his hand for better reception. "To me, that was [when he became] a star: to be that far away, and pick him up on the radio."[33] Apparently his dad's old employer, KGKO, the NBC affiliate for Dallas–Fort Worth, did not yet carry the Opry's network feed.

Tubb always said afterward that he didn't remember anything about his Grand Ole Opry debut: he was too frightened. He was told that he took encores, which would indeed be exceptional for the tightly scripted and closely timed network broadcast. Whatever the War Memorial Auditorium's audience response was, Mr. Frank had little trouble convincing Opry founder Judge George D. Hay, station manager Harry Stone, and network producer Jack Stapp that this Tubb fellow deserved a closer look. Ernest was asked to come back to the Opry as much as he could over the next month. He was booked into Chattanooga for Saturday and Sunday of the next weekend (January 23 and 24), where Elaine met him after spending a week back in Texas with the children. With only one Opry appearance under his belt, he must have had some sort of verbal agreement with the management, because in a letter written to Floy Case on Monday, January 25, 1943, just before they boarded a train from Chattanooga to Nashville, Elaine Tubb says this: "We are planning on moving to Nashville. We are going to look for an apartment or house this next week . . . Ernest will be on the Grand Ole Opry every Saturday night from now on until he goes back to Hollywood. He is thinking about working with Mr. Joe Franks [sic]."[34]

Not only was he "thinking about" it, he was booked to do just that, with an Evansville, Indiana, concert for Friday, January 29, a return engagement in Gadsden for Sunday, January 31, and a big Cincinnati package show with Pee Wee King, Bill Boyd, and others for February 7. After he played the Opry January 30 and February 6, the management made Tubb's joining the cast official at the February 13 show. According to Justin Tubb, "They've got it listed somewhere that his official joining date is February 13 . . . I think he tried to get it close to his birthday, you know. To make it official, around that week."[35] The Opry's records on this matter square with Tubb's own recollections of a four-week tryout, so this must be right, even though Elaine knew it was coming as early as January 25. A brand-new, forty-year chapter in Ernest Tubb's career had opened.

10

The First Year in Nashville

MOVING ON UP

Ernest Tubb's first movie, *Fighting Buckaroo,* appeared for one day only at the New Liberty Theater in Fort Worth, February 5, 1943. Elaine Tubb watched it and took snapshots of the marquee for her good friend Floy Case, who had moved with husband J. C. Case to Arlington, Virginia, where he had war work at the Naval Observatory. Ernest was already in Nashville, living at the Clarkston Hotel, playing the Opry and touring with the Golden West Cowboys, until Elaine and the children could come up with the furniture. He found a house to rent in mid-February with a few acres around it on Route 1, Campbell Road, a mile and a half from Madison, Tennessee (just north of Nashville), and Elaine, her stepfather, and the children left Fort Worth on March 2, 1943. After blizzards, rain, and a blowout on their trailer, they finally came into Nashville in a freight truck fifteen minutes before midnight, Friday night, March 5. Jimmie and Cherry Short accepted Ernest's invitation to come to Nashville and for Jimmie to work for Ernest; after a few weeks in the Memorial Apartment Hotel, they too found a house, out on Dickerson Road.

In a letter written late in March 1943, Elaine Tubb gives Floy Case the earliest Tubb Opry schedule, including two studio shows prior to the 8:00 Opry opening: "Ernest and the Golden West Cowboys are on every Saturday at 6:30 P.M. and then again at 7:45 P.M. Then they come on again between 9:30 to 10:00 P.M. (that is the network part); sometimes they come on right after 9 P.M. And they come on again around 10:30 to 11:00 P.M. When they are leaving out on the train for their Sunday Show they generally come on for their last part on the show at 10:30 P.M."[1] About Jimmie Short, in the same letter she says, "I think that Jimmie sang on one of the early programs last Saturday night. Now I'm not for sure. But so far he hasn't sang on the Op'ry. He plays for Ernest on the Op'ry. And too he may sing on some of the personal appearances."[2]

By midyear, Jimmie was gone, visiting kinfolks in Texas, and Leon, in the service since late 1942, had been transferred from Oklahoma to a camp near Augusta, Georgia. On furlough, Leon saw Ernest July 4 at an Atlanta personal appearance, in part at least to talk about returning to Ernest's employ as soon as Uncle Sam permitted. On August 3, 1943, after months of furnace and other problems in their rented house, the Tubbs bought a ranch home on two lots (in 1945 they bought five more adjacent lots) in the Crestview Estates on Cedar Crest Road off Anderson Lane, just off Gallatin Road north of Madison and not far from their rented place. Justin, barely turned eight years old, was placed in Castle Heights Military Academy in Lebanon, Tennessee, that fall, thirty miles east of Nashville, and only came home some weekends. Tubb, meanwhile, with J. L. Frank's help, had finally built his own band, the first group of Texas Troubadours.

THE EARLIEST TEXAS TROUBADOURS

When Ernest Tubb accepted Mr. Frank's offer to come to Nashville, with the incentive of a 50,000-watt radio station as home base from which to tour, a whole new tour territory opened for this red-hot jukebox sensation. The Golden West Cowboys, managed by Joe Frank, became the first touring band that Ernest Tubb used. Some remember that he may have used them for as long as six months, and sure enough, radio schedules don't list separate Ernest Tubb shows on the Opry or in other WSM time slots before June 1943. Billy Byrd, Nashville pop and jazz guitarist who had worked some on the Opry since the late thirties, remembers the early close Tubb-King alliance and puts a different slant on it. Normally the story goes that Tubb was the new kid on the block, being given a boost by the colorful, well-established Opry band, the Golden West Cowboys; and of course there's some truth to that. But Byrd says that Mr. Frank used Ernest Tubb, the new jukebox and film star, as a way to boost his son-in-law's fortunes. As Billy explained it, "If you booked Ernest, you had to take Pee Wee."[3] Newspaper ads for shows on their early tours bear out Tubb's star status and top billing. If anyone on those shows got higher billing, it was network Opry comic Minnie Pearl, not the Golden West Cowboys. Their 9:00 P.M. Grand Ole Opry sponsor, Royal Crown Cola, put Tubb and King on an equal footing from the start; a telling photo from 1943 has Tubb and King flanking Opry founder George D. Hay, with all three men holding bottles of the sponsor's product.

A humorous anecdote from one of their joint tours the next year (November 1944) comes from a time when there was no doubt who was the bigger star. Tubb, the Golden West Cowboys, and a package that included Minnie Pearl, the Duke of Paducah (Whitey Ford), Curly Fox and Texas Ruby, Jamup & Honey, and the DeZurick Sisters played a lucrative booking for promoter Oscar Davis in the old National Armory in Louisville before a huge crowd. The show grossed $5,000 to $6,000, but the next night they were booked into Pee Wee King's hometown of Milwaukee, "his first local appearance in nine years," *Billboard* reported after the fact. In Milwaukee, though, the gate sank dismally; even *Billboard*'s normally sanguine reports only mentioned a "fair crowd" for the two days there, never more than 2,500 fans.[4] When the Milwaukee gig was over, the troupe had lost all they had made in Louisville, prompting Tubb to remark good-naturedly to Pee Wee, "The next time you want to go home, just let me know, and I'll pay your way up there and back."[5]

Whether because of resistance from Nashville's musicians union, a bad problem with ulcers (as Harold Bradley remembers), or a disagreement with Tubb (of which there would be several over the next four years), Jimmie Short was no longer Tubb's lead guitarist when the first Texas Troubadours band was formed. Bradley, a Nashville teenager, had the task of playing the indispensable electric lead guitar for the duration of his 1943 summer break from high school. When Bradley left that fall, there was still no Jimmie Short: Herbert McBride "Butterball" Paige got the job. He's called out by Tubb as "Tommy" (yet another of his nicknames) and "Little Man" (later these would include "Nature Boy" and "Cute Little Rascal") on a September 4, 1943, Opry recording, the earliest extant Tubb Opry performance. No lead guitarist is mentioned in Floy Case's January 1944 *Mountain Broadcast and Prairie Recorder* report, written some weeks or months before: "Ernest Tubb, Texas' Own Smiling Troubadour, [has] with him a group of musicians known as the Texas Troubadours. There's Jimmy [*sic*: Johnny] Sapp pulling the fiddle bow, Ray Kemo Head, who plays a steel guitar, Toby Rees [*sic*], the comedian, and Chester Studdard, who hails from Gadsden, Alabama, playing the bass fiddle. Ernest and the boys are also making personal appearances throughout the country, so be sure and see them when they come your way. In the meantime, if you haven't seen *Fighting Buckaroo,* make it a point to do so. His latest picture, *Riding West,* should be released soon."[6]

The nucleus of Tubb's first Texas Troubadours came not from Texas but from Gadsden, Alabama, of all places. There a group called the Melody Boys had held forth for several years on local radio and in area schools and was a favorite Sunday afternoon group on the Southeastern package shows for which Joe Frank furnished acts. In fact, the main man for the Melody Boys, emcee Chester Studdard, had been the one sent by Frank to Birmingham to ask Tubb to play the Gadsden show a week after the December 1942 Birmingham show. At that time, the Melody Boys, who always backed Rex Griffin when he came home to Gadsden, had just finished a seven-month tour in Canada and were looking for regular work. Frank asked three of them (Studdard, Reese, and Head) to come to Nashville and work for Tubb, and sometime in the late spring of 1943 they did.[7]

Studdard occasionally played guitar and joined the singing, but for the most part he served as emcee, a role he shared with folks like the Duke of Paducah on Frank's package shows. He was also a straight man for the comedy of his close friend Vernon "Toby" Reese, guitarist-singer-comic for the group, who formed an integral part of the first Texas Troubadours. Reese, raised in Gadsden by his machinist father, had worked as a millwright before beginning a musical career with Studdard about 1937. They stayed together for the next thirteen years, including their few months with Tubb. Adept at singing comic songs and always dressed in the classic rube garb of the "Toby" character, his comedy often relied on Chester as the straight man. An extant script from those years, saved on Ernest Tubb's professional stationery, consists of their version of the then-popular Abbott and Costello "Who's on first?" routine.

Not very many months elapsed before Chester and Toby both were gone. Joe Frank explained to Tubb that he didn't really need an emcee, Chester's only strength, but when Chester was let go his good friend Toby left with him. Judge Hay found them a little more WSM work, with a tour of military bases in a troupe that included several other performers. Before the war ended, both men were back in Gadsden, where in 1947 they started a successful radio barn dance.

A third member of the original Texas Troubadours to come from the Melody Boys of Gadsden would stay with Tubb somewhat longer than the other two—steel guitarist Ray "Kemo" Head. Though "Kemo" was a nickname, based on the Hawaiian guitarist Kemo Kiloi,[8] his full name was often listed as "Ray Kemo." Kemo spent about a dozen years employed at the Goodyear plant in Gadsden before he moved into professional musicianship in the Melody Boys. Occasionally he'd play an Hawaiian instrumental, but an unobtrusive slide was all he could do for fills, so Kemo gratefully left the real work to the electric guitarist, which suited Tubb just fine. The mutual loyalty between Ernest Tubb and Kemo Head lasted many years. Staying with Tubb for three years the first time, Kemo went into the grocery business in Louisiana and returned to Nashville at Tubb's behest to fill in on steel in the mid-1950s.

The first full-cast photo of the Texas Troubadours shows that Norman Zinkan, brother to the Golden West Cowboys' bass player Joe, was the band's first stand-up bass player. Like Chester Studdard, Toby Reese, and Harold Bradley, Norman Zinkan stayed in the band only a very short time. Rounding out the first group was a fine radio fiddler from Louisville, a brown-eyed, black-haired, dark-complected man, Johnny J. Sapp, usually called "Johnny Boy." Sapp was a topnotch fiddler, possibly the best musician of the bunch, often a featured instrumentalist on shows and audible with fine fiddle fills on many of Tubb's mid-forties recordings. Except for a stint of World War II military service, during which time Hal Smith took his place, Sapp was a Texas Troubadour for three years.

By the beginning of 1944, at the time that Studdard and Reese left, both Short brothers had rejoined Tubb. When the group went to Hollywood in January 1944 for a recording session and to make the movie *Jamboree,* Leon and Jimmie were on hand, and Butterball Paige had moved over to string bass and comedy. Jimmie, as before, took over the lead guitar work, while Leon provided rhythm guitar (in Toby's place) and sang with Jimmie on duet numbers. Though Jimmie was gone again through much of 1944 and the early part of 1945, Leon stayed and played the lead part about as well as his big brother.

NASHVILLE RADIO: A.M. WEEKDAY SHOWS

Before he had a Grand Ole Opry time slot in his own name, Ernest Tubb appears in the Nashville newspaper radio logs as hosting the first of his fifteen-minute weekday programs on WSM. His first one ran the longest in the same slot, airing at 6:45 A.M. Monday through Saturday, live with occasional transcribed exceptions. It began June 21, 1943, and is last listed a year later (June 17, 1944).

For about five years, morning radio was a regular part of Ernest Tubb's workload, though of course the time slots changed and several months might elapse between series. These quarter-hour shows, lasting for an average of three months per series, five or six days a week, were sponsored by the various *Ernest Tubb Radio Song Books,* which sold by mail for 50 cents apiece (see the next section). Tubb and his boys featured three to four songs in each show, sandwiched around the song book commercials. WSM's strong signal that early in the morning reached a good many listeners in the outlying farm areas, north into Kentucky and south into Alabama. Tubb and his boys rose with the farm folk, working almost all of these shows live (precious few exist today) to sell a very popular product: the 50-cent mail-order song book.

ERNEST TUBB PUBLICATIONS

Working the Memphis fairgrounds with Roy Acuff in August 1942, Ernest Tubb saw Roy's boys haul out washtubs full of money from the sale of Roy's song books. Tubb knew he wanted a piece of that action, but arrangements had to be made with his new publisher on the West Coast, Sylvester Cross.

Cross, owner of American Music (BMI) and Cross Music (ASCAP), had taken a chance on Ernest Tubb when no one else would, though he was at first dubious of a man named "Tubb" dressed in a tuxedo for his publicity shot.[9] Tubb's earliest song copyrights and the first American Music song book date from 1941, the year of "Walking the Floor over You." A second *Ernest Tubb Song Folio of Sensational Successes* appeared in 1942, with twenty more new songs; like the first, it sold for 50 cents. Inspired by Acuff's example, Tubb wanted a line of products closer to home, printed in bulk. So after Tubb's move to Nashville and the management agreement with Joe Frank, Cross granted his permission for Tubb to market a new line of song books over Nashville radio, a strategy Frank was eager to exploit. In the first of what proved to be five *Ernest Tubb Radio Song Books,* Tubb wrote this: "To my dear friend, Sylvester L. Cross, president of American Music, Inc., 9153 Sunset Boulevard, Hollywood, California (exclusive publisher of all my songs), I want to express my deep appreciation for permitting me to publish this Radio Songbook for my radio friends."[10]

Frank knew that the mass market approach was what made the money. The first two American Music *Song Folios of Sensational Successes* were aimed at the fellow artist as much as the fan: "And to you, Artists," Tubb wrote in his foreword, "who have been so kind to feature my songs on radio and records in the past, may I offer my humble thanks. I sincerely hope that you find these songs in my Number Two Folio worthy of your hearty approval."[11]

The experienced Mr. Frank blanketed all of Tubb's radio audiences with song book pitches. The weekday morning shows sold each book in turn to the morning listeners, and for three years the 11:15 to 11:30 Opry time slot, sponsored by Ernest Tubb Song Books, peddled the books to the larger Opry audience. Early bandsman Chester Studdard recalls the volume of song book orders: "He was getting so many song book orders, and they were just 50 cents then. We'd sort out the fan mail from the song book orders, and two or three of us would have to go to the post office and get it, because one person couldn't do it by himself, to get it back to the house at that time . . . He had two or three girls who worked all the time on that, looking after the mail . . . Course he sold his books on his show dates."[12]

The song books themselves gradually got bigger, but only because there were a few more reruns each time. The first (1943) had eighteen songs; the second (1944) had twenty, as did the third (1945). The fourth radio song book ballooned to thirty songs, "10 favorites, and 20 new songs." Various promotional bonuses were used to heighten the appeal of each book: pull-out photos, extra song lyrics, and one (the fourth book, 1946) offered a book for the kiddies, from which they could cut out doll figures of and clothes for "Ernest and Justin Tubb, The Texas Troubadours, Stars Of The Grand Ole Opry." In January 1975 Ralph Emery found a file copy of this cutout book and said he thereby got the idea to interview father and son for a week's worth of his radio shows. Ernest's reaction:

"I hope the show does better than the paper doll book did, Ralph. The folks who were nice enough to put these out, they printed 100,000 of them, and the last time I saw the man with that company, he asked if I wanted to buy 80,000 of them real cheap."[13]

The same *Ernest Tubb's No. 4 Song Book* came with an "official certificate" for those who chose to enter the Ernest Tubb Radio Song Poem Contest. First of sixteen prizes for the "most original and adaptable song poem" was a Shetland pony, with saddle and blanket, a "250.00 value, delivered to the winner, regardless of address." All the rest of the prizes were various denomination Victory bonds, in values from $200 down to $25.

Prince Albert Opry host Roy Acuff, thanks to the work of his wife, Mildred, and his publishing partner, songwriter Fred Rose, watched his firm Acuff-Rose flourish during those years with a stable of writers and a growing catalogue of hit songs. By the time Acuff quit the Opry over a salary dispute in April 1946, Tubb was arguably the bigger star, but somehow the time, temperament, partners, or connections to make him a big-time song publisher were lacking. As those requests wrapped around quarters rolled in, Tubb was content to market books containing only his own songs. But the books got harder and harder to produce: the supply of new songs was tapering off, and the publication quality of the books was getting a little worse each time, as paper quality and song arrangements deteriorated. Also, the sheer workload involved in preparing new books and selling them through the mail was becoming more than Tubb's now home-based operation could handle. Not surprisingly, Tubb was open to a lucrative offer to do business another way. When his contract with Sylvester Cross expired (well before publishing his final radio song book), he took the advance money of the Aberbach brothers, Julian and Jean, and joined the growing list of major artists copublishing through Hill & Range.

SATURDAY NIGHT BROADCASTS

The Carter's Champion Chicks Show

On the Opry stage no single artist—not even the big ones like Ernest Tubb—worked more than two appearances per Saturday night. That meant that Tubb could perform at most six songs, fewer if he chose to feature his bandsmen; the radio listeners and auditorium crowds expected these to include the three or four songs they knew best. Naturally, then, Tubb and his Texas Troubadours jumped at the chance to star in their own half-hour, pre-Opry studio show Saturday nights at 7:00, starting on October 2, 1943, for Carter's Champion Chicks. Tubb co-hosted the show the previous month with the Golden West Cowboys, his R.C. Cola co-hosts, but then he took over with his own band. Except for occasional leaves of absence (such as for his Hollywood trip to make the film *Jamboree* in January 1944, when Eddy Arnold and his Tennessee Plowboys filled in), Tubb would star on this show from WSM's Studio B until into the 1950s.

The sponsor, Mr. Otis Carter, ran a farm in Illinois from which he shipped baby chicks; he first saw Ernest Tubb on a concert date in his home area. Justin Tubb tells the story: "Dad went up and played a show on a tour, and the man fell in love with him, and got him and hired him, sponsored his show on WSM . . . I was just a kid, and I used to sing on that show. That was where I got my start, really, at WSM . . . The mics wouldn't let down, so I had to stand in a chair, which made me furious."[14]

WSM listener Jerry Langley remembers the Carter's show as Ernest Tubb at his best. Unless the loquacious Mr. Carter happened to be on the broadcast, thereby taking precious airtime away from the music, Tubb could always feature his bandsmen and an occasional guest like the great Rex Griffin.[15] Best of all, Tubb himself got to sing a wide variety of songs, old and new, that he did not have time to perform on the Opry. Memories from fans like Langley and the invaluable logs kept by Nebraska listener Dick Hill reveal the range of song material Tubb performed on the Carter's show. Many of the songs he never recorded commercially.

In short, the half-hour Carter's Champion Chicks show was for four years the sort of Ernest Tubb forum that the *Midnite Jamboree* then became. Perhaps not coincidentally, Tubb's broadcast for Carter's Champion Chicks dropped to a quarter hour in July 1947, a few months after he purchased his first Saturday midnight time. Six years later, in 1953, Tubb's Carter time remained the 7:00 to 7:15 quarter-hour, though he soon relinquished the show to other artists.[16]

On the Opry

After the Carter's Chicks show came the Grand Ole Opry itself, staged 8 P.M. to midnight (first at the War Memorial Auditorium and then, after June 1943, in the Ryman Auditorium). Tubb at first shared the various time slots with the Golden West Cowboys as listed in the Elaine Tubb letter. Later that year, the Nashville newspapers jointly listed Tubb and the Golden West Cowboys only in the 9:00 P.M. R.C. Cola half-hour. Tubb eventually inherited the R.C. Cola show as his own, hosting it from December 1944 to August 1946. But his first full-fledged sponsor was himself. Making its debut October 16, 1943, the Ernest Tubb Song Book segment ran from 11:15 to 11:30 P.M. and held that time slot for almost three years.

Bringing in Jimmie Short and later that first year using Harold Bradley and

Butterball Paige, Tubb featured an electric guitar from the start of his Opry career, whatever other instruments might chime in. If an electric instrument bothered the tradition-minded "Solemn Ole Judge," George D. Hay, he never let on. Chester Studdard recalls that it was a drum that Hay couldn't stand; he knew the electric guitar was crucial to Tubb's style, and if he hadn't wanted it on the Opry, he wouldn't have agreed to hire Tubb. When Hay sat down to write about his "tall Texas Troubadour" for his first *Story of the Grand Ole Opry* (1945), he used only glowing words. "His Texas drawl topped off by a twinkle in his eye and a kindly sense of humor plus his ability to interpret the songs of the soil have endeared him to millions of Americans . . . It has been our pleasure to work with Ernest on the Grand Ole Opry and in personal appearances throughout the country. He is a very courteous and generous young man, a straight shooter and a mighty fine friend to have. From where we sit it looks like Ernest is really going places."[17]

Hay knew from the start what all but Opry idolaters have to admit today: that Ernest Tubb did more for the Opry in his early years there than the Opry did for him. He was a star when he came, with three or four records burning up the nation's jukeboxes and movies to his credit. Of the entire Opry cast, only Roy Acuff had comparable credentials. Ernest Tubb brought the Opry a new sound, a new type of song, and its first genuine example of a Western image (discounting those Alabama and Wisconsin cowboys, Zeke Clements and Pee Wee King).

On the other side of the ledger, the Opry gave Ernest Tubb a much-needed home base, cut adrift as he had been just before he came. If Hollywood couldn't use him full time, then Nashville, with its 50,000-watt station and central location for touring the eastern half of the United States, would be a fine substitute. Occasional radio network exposure boosted his record sales, he told an interviewer a quarter of a century later: "I became a member in 1943 and the first six months I was there, my record sales doubled. And they were selling pretty good when I went to the Opry."[18] The many regionally popular entertainers based there (Acuff, Minnie Pearl, Jamup & Honey, the Duke of Paducah, Bill Monroe, besides the Golden West Cowboys) afforded a good choice of "touring partners" for road work, and the WSM Artist Service Bureau, even with its 15 percent fee, did provide assistance with arranging bookings.

The best thing for Tubb about the Opry in the beginning, though, was the man who had brought him there, J. L. Frank. While Mrs. Marie Frank was helping Elaine Tubb furnish their rented house, Joe Frank was keeping Ernest Tubb busy at the Opry, with morning radio, and on the road. He was doing for Ernest Tubb what he'd already done for Gene Autry and Roy Acuff, and what Carrie Rodgers could never quite do back in Texas: provide experienced, full-time, hands-on career direction.[19] No wonder Tubb put this paragraph on the inside front cover of his first songbook:

> To My Friend, Mr. J. L. Frank,
>
> I extend my sincere gratitude for the many ways in which he has helped me. J. L. Frank is a friend to many world-famous entertainers and has been a great factor in their rise to success, and he deserves more credit than any of us could possibly give him, a true lover and believer of American folk songs and entertainment and a great showman to boot. My hat is off to J. L. Frank.
>
> *Ernest Tubb*

11

Records, Radio, and Fan Clubs

THE WARTIME TRICKLE OF RECORDINGS

Just as Ernest Tubb began to really make his mark as a recording star—when jukeboxes in every part of the nation were reporting heavy plays on his Decca records, especially "Walking the Floor over You," "I'll Always Be Glad to Take You Back," and "When the World Has Turned You Down"—a double blow fell upon that key part of the Tubb career. Two catastrophic circumstances quite beyond his control conspired to keep Ernest Tubb out of the recording studios for spans of eighteen and then sixteen months, punctuated by a single intensive session, and also to limit his number of releases and sales for months beyond that. These blows were, first (and foremost), a recording strike by the American Federation of Musicians and second, the severe shortage of shellac for record manufacture, brought about by the Pacific war and consequent government rationing.

Tubb had been a card-carrying, dues-paying member of the American Federation of Musicians (AFM) for barely two years at the time of the recording strike. Few hillbilly musicians, in fact, were union members during the 1930s, while Tubb worked his way up through the Texas beer joints and low-wattage radio stations. The venues and stations didn't want to pay them anything like a union scale in the first place; beyond that, many local chapters didn't want to lower their standards by allowing hillbilly or other "strictly by ear" musicians to join. When he and the Short brothers finally joined the union in Waco in April 1940, en route to that first Decca session in Houston, it was only because the word had come out from Dave Kapp of Decca that he could no longer record nonunion musicians. Just two years later, at the end of July 1942, the very union that Tubb had joined in order to make records told him and all other union musicians that they could no longer make them. That is, not until union boss James C. Petrillo was satisfied that, one by one, the record companies had met the union's compensation demands. The strike, which came to be known as the Petrillo ban, dragged on so long that within months there were calls for Congressional investigation and action. Petrillo's own shady past did not make the union's public relations job any easier.

Whatever Ernest Tubb felt about the strike, its causes and aims, it could not have come at a worse time for him. His name dominated *Billboard*'s weekly jukebox reports for much of 1942, in the midst of which (on August 1), the strike came. Ernest Tubb would not record again until January 1944, some eighteen months after his previous session, and accordingly the number of his new releases radically dropped off. During the war, Tubb's Decca output of singles was as follows: in 1940, four releases; in 1941, six; in 1942, hot as he was, only five (well, seven, counting the two new Bluebirds of 1936 material); in 1943, two; in 1944, one; and in 1945, three.

Compounding the problem, and in Tubb's case a factor well beyond the duration of the strike, was of course the war and the serious shortage of shellac. Deemed essential for bomb production, shellac was unfortunately irreplaceable then for record production. Washington bureaucrats in charge of such things blew hot and cold for the war's duration as to domestic shellac supply, so the record companies were correspondingly inconsistent with the number of new releases and the number of copies of each that they could press. "Record supply outlook" became a common feature of media reports. The shortage was at its worst in the early part of 1943, with the weeks' reports varying between "none at all," "frozen for the duration," to as much as "15 percent." For most of the war, Decca only pressed 10 percent of the orders received.

Finally some good news came.

November 4, 1944—No Lack of Shellac Now. The government has turned the task of importing shellac back to private interests as of October.[1]

Not right away but gradually things got better. Still, a lot of damage had been done. Hal Smith says of Tubb that "the one problem that kept him from being the biggest act ever was World War II. Decca allocated a 100,000-unit ceiling on those wartime releases, and the jukeboxes bought up most of those. Besides which, Ernest gave about half of his allocation away to younger artists on the label."[2]

THE WORLD BROADCASTING SYSTEM AND
THE END OF THE PETRILLO BAN

Two bright spots lightened this very dark wartime recording picture, for Decca Records artists at least: Decca's comparatively early settlement with Petrillo and the union, and their purchase of a transcription company, the World Broadcasting System, Inc. Decca came to terms with the union by October 1943: *Billboard* on the 23rd of that month reported that "Bing Crosby and the Andrews Sisters have just made a recording (Decca) of 'Pistol Packin' Mama,' one of the first recordings since the new pact was signed with the AFM."[3] Even in their case, the strike had lingered for more than fourteen months; that it would last longer for the other majors, Columbia and Victor, was to Decca some consolation. With the new-release field to themselves for much of 1944, Decca's profits for the first nine months of that year were $743,382. For the same period a year later (when the shellac situation improved), profits had fallen dramatically to $40,289, with competition on new releases from the other majors the only conceivable factor in such a drop-off.[4]

When the AFM gave Decca the all clear for new recordings, there was a great deal of catching up to do, and the main work outlet they found for their artists was building the catalogue of their new transcription company. World had been a major player in the programming service business since its founding in 1929 by Percy L. Deutsch and other entrepreneurs and electrical engineers.[5] World recorded all types of music and other radio entertainment for subscribing radio stations nationwide; in effect, stations "rented" a library from World. The big sixteen-inch, vertical-cut, 33⅓ rpm discs were never sold to the general public but were "licensed for use by, and rented to radio stations for broadcast purposes only,"[6] at a time when commercial records often weren't—and with a better quality of sound reproduction.

Decca Records bought the World Broadcasting System in early 1943 for some $750,000, a bargain price in the midst of the strike. Decca then became the first company to settle with the AFM that fall. Under the terms of their settlement, new recording could commence as long as the masters were first used by World.[7] The earliest World recordings after it became a Decca subsidiary date from October 1943; Decca artists worked for World through mid-1946.

Jukebox operators and the home market still suffered from the shellac rationing and the lingering strike, but radio, especially those stations supplied by World, had a two-year bonanza. Ernest Tubb's own World recordings—115 over two intensive series of sessions, sixteen months apart—besides being the only ones Tubb made between July 1942 and August 1945, illustrate a creative interplay between Decca's purposes and his own.

A MOVIE AND THE FIRST WORLD SESSIONS: JANUARY 1944

Tubb's first World recordings, and his first of any kind in eighteen months, came in conjunction with his third Hollywood movie trip. *Billboard* reported on December 4, 1943, that "J. L. Frank arrived in Hollywood early last week to confer with producers at Columbia and Republic Studios on picture contracts for Ernest Tubb and his Texas Troubadours and Pee Wee King and his Golden West Cowboys."[8]

Tubb got time off from his broadcast and touring schedule for much of January and headed for Hollywood with four Troubadours: fiddler Johnny Sapp, guitarists Jimmie and Leon Short, and bass player–rube comic Butterball Paige. They gave first priority to filmmaking, shooting a picture for Republic entitled *Jamboree*. The film was a madcap musical identity mixup with Freddie Fisher and the Schnicklefritz Band, in which Tubb and his boys, surrounded by a great deal of different musical talent (besides Freddie Fisher, there is another Fisher, Shug; the Music Maids; and Rufe Davis), perform only two songs: "You Nearly Lose Your Mind" and "Walking the Floor over You." *Jamboree* was actually released before his second Columbia Western, *Riding West* (*Jamboree* on March 15, 1944, and *Riding West* May 18, 1944).

Finishing *Jamboree*, Tubb and his four Texas Troubadours, with no help this time from California musicians, then proceeded to make up for many months of lost time with eight separate recording sessions held at Decca's Melrose Avenue studios over five working days. Tubb cut forty songs, all for World, nine of which were eventually released on Decca. Many and great were the songs recorded that week, but the best known today remains Redd Stewart's "Soldier's Last Letter." Tubb's only 1944 Decca release, it stayed on the charts for twenty-nine weeks and at number one for four weeks.[9] The song came from Sergeant Stewart, then in the Army, to Joe Frank, who took it to Tubb. Given the wartime reality of husbands, brothers, fathers, and friends in the service and mothers in his crowds who had received the same type of unfinished final letter that the song describes, "Soldier's Last Letter" was a huge and immediate success. Tubb knew it was a smash from audience reaction: "I know this song was a true story to a lot of mothers, for I met quite a number of them and autographed their 'last letters' for them, 1944–1945."[10] Charlie Walker describes its impact on a New Orleans crowd in what he believes was its first public performance.

> I never forgot that, because that's the night on that show that he intro-
> duced on the stage for the first time "Soldier's Last Letter." Right in the
> middle of the war, I had just turned seventeen. I thought that was the
> prettiest song I ever heard, and that's one of the greatest ovations I'd
> ever seen for anybody, and I've seen them all. Everybody in that au-
> dience had either a son in the service, or a cousin or a nephew, and at
> the end of that song, if you remember the lyrics, "And dear God, keep
> America free." When he closed that, and that light man worked different
> colors, as each verse progressed and he got down to that last part

where she knew that her darling had died, he had like a pale orange color or something. When he finished, they were just like sitting there in shock, and all of a sudden they just broke out applauding and it was unbelievable, the reception he got. So I got this song and took it back, I was the first guy to sing it on the radio, because I learned it and got it and took it to Dallas and started singing it on the radio the next day, soon as we got back.[11]

TOURING AND BROADCASTING

Ernest Tubb turned thirty on February 9, 1944; he was in concert that night at the Thomaston (Georgia) Tabernacle, back out on the road after the movie and transcription trip to Hollywood, though he had stopped off in Texas for a family gathering to say farewell to his big brother. On Ernest's birthday C. R. Tubb Jr., though thirty-seven years old and the father of seven (including twin girls less than a year old) was inducted into the Navy. He was gone for over a year, serving in and around some of the same Pacific campaigns with his oldest son, Talmadge. By August 1945 C. R. was stateside again, touring that month down through Florida with the Ernest Tubb road show.

Weekends almost always found Tubb and the boys in Nashville, with the regular Saturday broadcasts to do, even if they had to leave immediately for the next tour. Two-day engagements, often covering a Monday and Tuesday, were common in 1944, in cities like Raleigh, Altoona, and Jacksonville, in the company of his regular tour mates that year: Minnie Pearl, the Golden West Cowboys, Curly Fox and Texas Ruby, Jamup & Honey, and sometimes the Duke of Paducah. Cindy Walker, whom he'd met in Hollywood in 1942 and who at this time also recorded for Decca, played several shows with Tubb and these other acts that summer, including a Norfolk engagement June 4–5, 1944, the two days prior to D day. Tubb made his first of what became annual swings to the Northeastern open-air parks in August and joined a big part of the WSM cast in the WSM Grand Ole Opry Tent Show #4 that took them to Alabama and Georgia between late August and October.

With a war going on, there were changes that year in the Texas Troubadours personnel. Fiddler Johnny Sapp spent much of 1944 after making *Jamboree* and the first World transcriptions in the Army. He returned in early November but had been replaced first by a mysterious figure named Fred Turnage[12] and then by Hal Smith, over from the Golden West Cowboys. When Jimmie Short left the band to take his own program on Nashville's WLAC at 6:15 A.M. weekdays on July 3, 1944, his brother Leon stayed with Ernest to play the lead guitar. Steel guitarist throughout the year was Ray "Kemo" Head, but the main new additions to the

Texas Troubadours late in the year—October 28, 1944, was their first regular appearance on Tubb's Carter's Chicks show[13]—were the Drake brothers, Jack and Bill. They had worked with Cousin Emmy and other artists as a featured duet attraction in and around Atlanta, Chattanooga, Louisville, and St. Louis before this, but came to Tubb from the Golden West Cowboys. Rhythm guitarist Bill Drake didn't stay long with Tubb's entourage (as he would not the next time around either, in 1947–1948); published listings for the Tubb act in Minnie Pearl's monthly *Grinder's Switch Gazette* drop "Drake Brothers" for "Jack Drake" in March 1945. This left a basic lineup of Sapp, Leon Short, Kemo, and Jack Drake, augmented by Jimmie Short's return in the summer of 1945.

By 1945 Tubb was a big enough star for J. L. Frank to split him off from the Opry's other big names and build around him a package of Opry newcomers. For most of that year, the "new faces" on Tubb's road shows were a sister duet, the Poe Sisters, and a comic named Rod Brasfield.

Ruth and Nelle, the Poe Sisters, were Mississippians who had done most of their earlier radio (and even some TV) work in the Northeast before coming to the Grand Ole Opry on June 17, 1944. Frank hired them to tour with Tubb the following January. Nelle played guitar and Ruth mandolin, and they sang sentimental and heart songs, mostly, throwbacks to an earlier style that made for a pleasing contrast with Tubb, who tried unsuccessfully to interest Dave Kapp at Decca in recording them.[14] Nelle Poe's handwritten account of their days with Ernest Tubb sheds light on the early career of a future show business legend, a former Tampa, Florida, dogcatcher who might easily have become Tubb's manager.

> We had another road manager, Thomas A. Parker, hired by Mr. Frank, to go ahead of us to promote our show. He got radio time, ads in newspapers & booked us in auditoriums and theatres and had our Hotel rooms reserved and waiting when we arrived. We often ate with "Uncle Tom," as we called him . . . We liked him, and he'd often go to our shows and come down into the audience as E.T. was on stage. He'd put on an old black hat and have a dusting broom, brushing off the shoulders of people in the audience and causing quite an audience response; as he got closer to the stage, the people laughed and applauded. He looked like the character "Frog" that was Gene Autry's side kick in the movies . . . Then he'd go on stage and talk some with Ernest Tubb. The audience liked that a lot.[15]

Smithville, Mississippi, native Rodney Leon Brasfield, "the Teller of Tall Tales," was a veteran comic with repertory and tent show experience who left his brother Boob's show to make it on his own, in the vein of the Opry's comic star Whitey Ford (the Duke of Paducah). A handwritten note in Nelle Poe's scrap-book says that Brasfield made his Opry debut the very same night they did, June 17, 1944. Clearly by November 11, 1944 (the first date that young Dick Hill stayed up late enough to log the contents of Tubb's 11:15 Song Book program), Tubb had Brasfield as his regular guest. Soon he was touring with Tubb and doing a weekday broadcast with Eddy Arnold, *The Checkerboard Fun Fest,* in addition to Eddy's main Opry show, for Purina at 8:00 P.M. Rod went on to great things at the Grand Ole Opry, replacing Ford as the Prince Albert Opry comic (even co-hosting the show with Red Foley for a time in the late 1940s), a role he enjoyed until his death in September 1958.

Tubb's own broadcasting career grew considerably in 1945 with the debut of a national program, *Opry House Matinee,* sponsored by Purina's heated cereal product, Shredded Ralston. This was Ernest's first work for Brown Radio Produc-tions, a spinoff of the ad agency run by brothers Charles and Bill Brown. They handled the Purina account and pitched Opry talent for national radio work to the company's home office in St. Louis. Tubb and Eddy Arnold were the main Nashville beneficiaries, as both stars got Purina shows. Arnold's was *The Check-erboard Fun Fest,* sponsored by Purina's livestock feeds: a quarter-hour show transcribed for Mutual from the WSM studios before a small live audience and broadcast three days a week.[16]

Tubb, at that time a much better known star,[17] also transcribed his program, a half-hour show done at the Ryman Auditorium on Saturday nights, just before the 8:00 P.M. Grand Ole Opry began. Other Opry acts were regular features of the show, and Jack Baker, formerly of NBC's *Breakfast Club,* was the announcer. Most Mutual stations carried Tubb's program, *Opry House Matinee,* around midday on Saturday. About Tubb's show, Floy Case wrote this in June 1945: "A new show here in the Southwest is the Sat. morning 11:30 A.M. program of OPERA HOUSE MATINEE [*sic*], a transcribed show on WFAA, KPRC, WOAI, WKY, and KVOO featuring ERNEST TUBB and THE TEXAS TROUBADOURS and other WSM enter-tainers, with JACK BAKER formerly of the NBC BREAKFAST CLUB as M.C. on the air for a breakfast food concern. It's 30 minutes of fun and music."[18]

A NEW FAN CLUB

A casualty of Ernest Tubb's first two years in Nashville was his original Texas-based fan club. Floy Case first mentioned the original club in her November 1942 *Mountain Broadcast and Prairie Recorder* column: "Faye Flanagan, Route 1, West-brook, Texas, has organized a fan club in his honor—contact her for details."[19] The name of Faye Flanagan crops up occasionally thereafter in Elaine Tubb's correspondence with Mrs. Case. "The fan club is coming along swell," she said in

November 1942; but problems are hinted at in the next mention (February 19, 1943). "Had a card from Faye the other day. I must write her. I am so glad that Lucile [Ritz] is going to help Faye with the paper. She needed someone to help her along; as you say, she is just a kid. And I'm sure she didn't realize what a job she took upon herself. Not ever having any experience on such. I'm sure that everything will come along fine. I think she is a sweet girl, she'll come out on top I'm sure."[20]

Real trouble is at hand when Elaine wrote this on November 4, 1944, only weeks before the formation of a second and different club: "About the fan club. Honest, more people have written asking about the club. Saying they hadn't received their paper in months. Some say they've wrote her two or three times and they haven't received any answer."

A new club in new hands was the news that Elaine could gratefully report in a letter of April 14, 1945: "Yes, Floy, I was so pleased with the first issue of the club paper that Norma put out. I truly believe the right person has a hold of it now. She seems to be the right one. I will say I am glad that Norma has it now instead of the Flanagans . . . I am sorry that it all had to happen like it did. But then, things like that can't be avoided sometimes."

Norma Winton, a young lady in Moffett, Oklahoma, admitted later that she had really started the club in the fall of 1944 for her own circle of friends and pen pals. But the demand for a full-fledged Tubb fan club was so great that she widened its scope, planned a regular publication, and, so as not to step on her predecessor's toes, at first called it the Ernie Tubb Fan Club No. 2. "Ernie" soon gave way to "Ernest," and the "No. 2" vanished also. The first published "Our Roll Call" lists thirty members, all but three of whom are women. Though promised as a bimonthly, the first issue was dated quarterly, January-February-March (1945), a change later explained by Norma as due to wartime problems with her publisher.

In her column, "At the Ranch House," Norma states her dreams and purposes for the club. She solicits suggestions for a club motto (the winner later was "Boost Our Star in All Ways, Always"); floats the idea of club stationery; asks for snapshots; and dreams of club secretaries in each state, an annual club get-together, and membership benefits including a newsletter and Tubb photos and snapshots.[21]

The second issue brought a column from Ernest himself, with this advice: "I want to say a great big WELCOME to each of our members. Your interest and support is deeply appreciated. I want you to know that this is your club and you can make it a GREAT fan club, or just another club . . . I just know that we are going to have the best club in the country, and I hope it will be the largest."

Later in the column came this statement of Tubb's views as to what the club's guiding principles should be:

> Big of Soul, Big of Heart, Big of Mind. NEVER belittle a fellow artist; instead, always stand ready to lend a helping hand to those who need it. A word of praise for those who deserve it. And if we can't say something good about our fellow man, let's just leave the space blank in the paper. This can't hurt anyone. Let's NEVER let jealousy or selfishness creep into our paper, for these things are akin to smallness of heart and soul, of which we want no part. Let's always be humbly grateful to all who help us carry out our plans for this club, based on these principles.[22]

THE CHICAGO WORLD SESSIONS

Almost as much time elapsed between Ernest Tubb's two intensive World sessions—sixteen months—as had elapsed between the start of Petrillo's strike and the first World session (eighteen months). But in May and June of 1945, with a somewhat different group of Texas Troubadours, Tubb made seventy-five new recordings for World at Chicago. Jimmie and Leon Short, who made twenty-five World recordings of their own in these weeks, are still prominent in Tubb's band, but Leon this time around does the lead guitar work in place of big brother Jimmie.

Tubb's work for World in Los Angeles in January 1944 and Chicago in May–June 1945 totaled a whopping 115 songs, only a handful of which ever appeared on the Decca label. Thus, tracking down copies of the big discs became a labor of love for Tubb's more serious collectors. Young Bill French wondered why, even after there was an Ernest Tubb Record Shop, he couldn't order so many of the Ernest Tubb songs he heard on the radio. He later found out they were World transcriptions. Ultimately he rounded up copies from radio stations and from other collectors doing the same, and, being mechanically minded, he devised a turntable and needle to play at home the oversized, "inside-out," vertically cut discs. French's main complaint after years of patient searching was: "They never put Ernest's material on both sides of a World disc, which meant you had to find that many more of the records."[23]

THE V-J DAY SESSIONS

Tubb returned to Chicago with the same group of Texas Troubadours for two days of recording August 14–15, 1945. Decca's logs list the sessions as September 11, but a Tubb letter of September 4, 1945, looking back on the sessions, proves that date is in error. He says, "We were in Chicago the week Japan gave up. In fact, we recorded the day it happened and finished the next day."[24] The Case family was most pleased to learn from the letter that Ernest, among the eight cuts, had included Floy Case's "I'm Beginning to Forget You," which he had done for World the previous May. Tubb himself wrote five of the eight songs from the August session. One of them, an all-time Tubb classic, came from the challenge of roadmate Nelle Poe to write a song about a phrase he commonly used, "There's a little bit of everything in Texas." Justin Tubb tells the story: "Every time they'd go into Texas, he'd say, 'Well, you know there's a little bit of everything in Texas.' And he would talk about the coast, about the mountains, and the plains, and East Texas . . . and down around Austin . . . And he would never quit talking about it, and every time they'd go back into Texas he would bring it up again, and she'd say, 'You gotta write that song.' So he did, I think he wrote it in '45, and it came out in '46, and that was when they were working with him, and they were members of the Opry then."[25]

Nelle Poe's scrapbook contains a postcard from the Stephen F. Austin Hotel on the very tour on which the song was finished, a Ralston-sponsored Texas tour. Her note beside the card says that he finished it after their Austin show date of July 10, 1945. To his fan club just a few months later, he left it up to them if "There's a Little Bit of Everything in Texas" would supplant "Walking the Floor over You" as his theme song. It was a huge hit, selling over 200,000 copies by July 1946.[26] But neither this nor any other song would ever knock "Walking the Floor over You" out of its top spot.

The other classic Tubb composition first recorded at this time was "It's Been So Long, Darling." Tubb often told how he was inspired to write it.

> We all get ideas for songs. He was an aviator in WWII, and I rode back with him on a train from California. We gave up our seats to ladies and spent the night in the train's washroom, and he told me this story. He'd been gone a long time, and was engaged to be married. The closer he got to home the more he wondered, "Will she still love me? Will we be married? Will I love her? Will we even know one another? The closer I get to home, it just scares me to death." So I got the line, "It scares me through and through." . . . When I got home, by that time I had it in my head and wrote it down.[27]

A NEW *OPRY HOUSE MATINEE*

Ralston Purina of St. Louis sponsored a series of Tubb's Texas personal appearances that summer, to plug his transcribed *Opry House Matinee*. On November 17, 1945—the Saturday that "It's Been So Long, Darling" entered the record charts—Eddy Arnold and Tubb began doing their Mutual shows live, back-to-back, from Nashville's downtown Princess Theater. The entire hour took on the name of Tubb's old show, *Opry House Matinee*. After a special "sneak preview" the night before, this first staging took place at noon in the Princess, though it was transcribed for later broadcast on some stations. Arnold hosted the first half-hour for Checkerboard, and Tubb hosted the second half-hour for Ralston,[28] though the full hour was not broadcast in all markets, including Nashville.

On the first few Princess Theater shows, Tubb hosted WSM talent like Becky Barfield (she of the Golden West Cowboys), Opry fiddler-mandolinist Mack McGarr, and of course the Texas Troubadours. Tubb's regular Mutual cast changed the next year to include a couple touring with him, Radio Dot and Smoky; comic relief from blackface stars Jamup & Honey; gospel stylings from Wally Fowler; and to give things a Western flavor, music from the Oklahoma Wranglers (the Willis Brothers). As a national broadcast, *Opry House Matinee* from the start brought in big-name guest stars. Curley Bradley, who at that time was for Mutual "the Tom Mix of Radio," headlined the very first show and posed for publicity shots backstage with the two hosts and producer Charlie Brown. Later guests included Smiley Burnette, Tex Ritter, and Jack Guthrie. But always there was ample time for Tubb to sing three or four of his own songs and to announce upcoming tour dates in areas covered by network affiliates. At one point in the series, he even sang the top song of the week; Tubb's renditions of the Merle Travis hits, "Divorce Me C.O.D." and "So Round, So Firm, So Fully Packed," seem to have sparked enough fan interest that Tubb featured them for years. He ultimately recorded the latter.

In the summer of 1946, *Opry House Matinee* took to the road with Ernest Tubb, as we shall see, just as Ralston had sponsored his summer 1945 tour. But that fall, with Tubb back in Nashville, the title reverted to *Checkerboard Jamboree* as a single half-hour show (a lone program, that of November 23, 1946, survives on a Radiola LP).

12

The Great Popularity

In 1946, "after the war was over," Americans readjusted to a peacetime way of life, and their favorite country singer, gauged by several key indicators, was Ernest Tubb. His songs spoke to the hopes, the dreams, the fears of post-war Americans, with a combination of directness, simplicity, explicitness, and warmth that made his "message" that much more appealing. The success he enjoyed proves that he was touching some nerves and sounding some new themes, as we shall see.

The fact of his popularity is indisputable. If he wasn't quite what one of his newspaper ads that year claimed for him, "America's No. 1 Singing Cowboy and Western Movie Star," he probably was America's favorite hillbilly or country recording artist. A California magazine, from the very heart of Merle Travis, Gene Autry, and Jack Guthrie country, named Tubb America's Tophand Ballad Singer, their top award, in June 1946. Whether one looks at record sales, jukebox chart performance, song book sales, listenership of his several regular national broadcasts, or to the number of artists singing and recording his songs, Tubb comes out on top or mighty darn close. Ernest Tubb was, if only for a while, at the top of his profession after more than a decade's struggle to get there.

A BUSY MAN: RADIO AND ROAD

Tubb's busiest radio year of all—with morning shows, Saturday night shows, and yes, the Saturday midday Mutual *Checkerboard Jamboree* broadcasts—was probably 1946. Early and late in the year, Tubb and his cast did those shows from Nashville's Princess Theater. But at midyear he took his act on the road and did the broadcast from auditoriums, fairs, or wherever he happened to be on Saturday, with local Mutual affiliates piping the show nationwide. The Opry allowed

Tubb his first of several leaves of absence to take his show on the road that summer. They lost Roy Acuff that spring to a salary dispute and his desire to do less-restricted touring; not wanting to lose their other major star, they showed Tubb a surprising leniency. The first out-of-town *Checkerboard Jamboree* came from Tubb's former hometown, Fort Worth, at a big show on June 15. Rex Griffin, Jim Boyd (Bill's brother), and Okeh Records star Ted Daffan were on the North Side Coliseum show, which followed the national broadcast. One of the last of that summer's shows found him back in the Dallas–Fort Worth area, at the Arlington Downs Rodeo on August 31.

Tubb's road crew had grown to the point that even the long funeral home touring car they used no longer sufficed. Replacing the Poe Sisters was a West Virginia couple who came up to Nashville from work at KWKH Shreveport, Radio Dot and Smoky, Lewis and Dottie Swan in real life. They did comedy in addition to the Lulu Belle and Scotty style of heart songs. The Short Brothers were often billed as an added attraction, since they fronted the shows and were trying to get their own recording career going for Decca. Rod Brasfield, "the Plum Tree Patch Philosopher," also known then as "Uncle Poody's Favorite Nephew," remained in the touring cast, and Opry legend Uncle Dave Macon even made a few trips with Tubb that year. To move this entourage from city to city, Tubb bought a used school bus and painted on its side in big black letters "Ernest Tubb and his Texas Troubadours. WSM Grand Ole Opry." The star usually traveled in his own car, driven by his brother C. R., who was now out of the Navy and working as the official road manager for ticket and song book sales, pocket money for the band, and so forth. Years later Ernest Tubb told a story about his school bus, one of the first used by a country artist.

> At one show I played in Florida with Uncle Dave Macon, I had just acquired a bus for traveling. At that time most country performers traveled in cars. It was an old school bus with poles down the middle. Uncle Dave would brag and brag on my bus, and in Florida he said, "How about me riding in that bus to Boston with you?" So he went to Massachusetts on the bus with us, and coming back through Washington D.C. or Virginia, the weather was bad. I was riding in my car following the bus. On a rise, the bus hit an icy spot and the wheels spun. The bus slid backwards down the hill a ways and ended up in a ditch, leaning way over. No one got hurt, but on the bus Uncle Dave had grabbed a pole and had nearly bent it double. When the bus stopped, he headed for the door and got off. When we started back up, Uncle Dave said, "No, thank you," and he never got on my bus again.[1]

Late in the year, Minnie Pearl, Tubb, and Tubb's manager Oscar Davis (he took over Tubb's career when Joe Frank dropped him to concentrate on Pee Wee

King and Roy Acuff) formed a road partnership to split the proceeds, and with Davis's promotional skills were doing quite well. But the marriage bug broke up this fine partnership.

> We formed a business together and traveled around doing shows. We never had a loser and made some good money each night. I got so aggravated at that woman, though. She was going with Henry Cannon then. In fact, she met Henry when she was working with me. Henry had the first charter airplane service out of Nashville. He wanted Minnie to stay home and let him fly her to the bigger dates. Every night I'd go through the same talk with Minnie going back to Nashville. She would ask me if she should go off the road, but I couldn't imagine Minnie Pearl staying at home and cooking for Henry and not going on stage. Oscar Davis, my manager, said to me, "You better talk to Minnie, or she's going to mess a good thing up." Every week I'd talk her out of staying home, but it came to the point where she'd start talking about it even before we left the auditorium. Finally, I said to her, "I think you ought to stay home with Henry. Oscar won't like it, but go ahead." She left soon afterwards. I told her, "Minnie, I know what's gonna happen. You'll be happy for a little while, but I'll give you two months and you'll be back on the road." As it turned out, it took about that long before she went back on the road.[2]

The Texas Troubadours' lineup underwent a few changes over the course of the year. Zeb Turner played most of the summer *Checkerboard Jamboree* tours with the band, sometimes on steel but usually on guitar. Tubb was without a steel guitarist just then: Ray "Kemo" Head left sometime between the February and September recording sessions. By the time the latter rolled around, Tubb had hired Wayne Fleming away from the Milton Estes band: Fleming played steel on the September session and toured for a few months after that, until Tubb hired arguably the nation's best on that instrument, Jerry Byrd.

On fiddle, Johnny Sapp left in the spring of 1946 after a heated dispute with Tubb. Norma Winton described to Floy Case what she knew of Sapp's departure: "Haven't heard what the trouble was, and won't ask, for it's none of my truck, of course. But it wasn't a bit nice of him to hit Ernest. Why, Johnny could beat him to a pulp before he knew it, because he is so much bigger."[3] Tubb's new fiddler was a real showman, a King Records artist and a veteran of the Larry Sunbrock tours with Cowboy Copas and Rusty Gabbard: "Fiddlin'" Red Herron. When Norma Winton saw their show in Fort Smith on May 30, she said of new men Zeb and Red, "Both are real musicians, I assure you. We especially liked 'Zeb's Mountain Boogie' and Red's 'Listen to the Mockingbird.'"[4]

Large crowds turned out for the road shows, particularly on Sundays in the big cities. Floy Case wrote, "Ernest Tubb has been playing to full houses on his appearances in southeast Texas, Houston, Beaumont, etc. One writer at Beaumont spoke of Ernest's singing being the type that 'long haired musicians' listened to and liked, but turned the dial quickly if they heard a step on the porch!"[5]

At midyear Norma Winton reported that Ernest Tubb Fan Club membership had risen to fifteen hundred, mostly women, in only eighteen months of existence,[6] which certainly squares with Charlie Walker's memory: "But he was popular, I'm gonna tell you. Anybody that didn't get a chance to see him in the mid-forties, really missed something. 'Cause I mean, I've seen Elvis, and all the guys from every generation, the young girls trying to get to them after the show. Ernest, he had those thirty-year-old good-looking women trying to knock the door down to get to him, he had them—he had the young ones too, but I mean, Ernest was really popular. He was tall, and thin, and had those sharp-looking Western outfits."[7] Fiddler Hal Smith remembers: "You had to see him to know this. I remember women keeling over in Louisville when he sang there—they had to take them away on stretchers. He was as big as Sinatra, only with a different, country audience."[8]

Ernest Tubb was clearly Decca's biggest asset in the hillbilly field, and almost their biggest asset, period. "From 1940 to 1950—I'm not bragging, I'm telling you what Decca told me—I didn't have a record to sell less than 300,000."[9] If that's right, with twenty-two Decca releases to his credit by this point, over six million sales resulted, even with all the problems of wartime pressing restrictions. He would match or exceed that total just in the two big years, 1946 and 1947, rivaling Bing Crosby as the company's top seller. Jack Gordon wrote in the Fort Worth paper at the time of his August 31, 1946, appearance in Arlington, "Ernest Tubb, the former $25-a-week KGKO singer, whose earnings reached $150,000 last year, will need a washtub to carry home his pay this year." When he came back to the Dallas–Fort Worth area the next summer, touring with his new film *Hollywood Barn Dance,* and with a good many more records on the market, Frank X. Tolbert wrote in the July 26, 1947, *Dallas Morning News,* "This year Tubb expects to sell four million records," echoing Harry Clark's comment in a competing paper at that same time: "Tubb and his frolicking crew record discs for Decca and it is reported that Tubb 'platters' bow only to Bing Crosby in point of sale for that company. Over 3,000,000 of his records are said to have been purchased so far this year."[10]

NEW RECORD RELEASES

The pace of Tubb's new releases picked up markedly in 1946, with a nearly normal supply of shellac available for pressing. For the year four new releases appeared (plus the luxury of two reissues), and from these eight new songs, three became tremendous hits, though released almost simultaneously in the fall: "Rainbow at Midnight," "Filipino Baby," and "Drivin' Nails in My Coffin."

The last mentioned, Jerry Irby and Floyd Tillman's great song, had been released by Irby on Globe Records and by Floyd Tillman on Columbia (for which Irby gave him half the song) in early 1946. For Tubb it fit in well with earlier songs like "I Ain't Going Honky Tonkin' Anymore" and was a harbinger of many to come, like "Warm Red Wine" and "Two Glasses, Joe." The other two were also "cover" versions of earlier records, a new practice for Tubb at the time but something he would soon be doing a lot more often. At his September 1946 session, he actually recorded both sides of a current Cowboy Copas record: "Filipino Baby" (the mid-1930s Billy Cox favorite, based on a Spanish-American War original) and "I Don't Blame You," which Alton Delmore wrote under his alias "Jim Scott." Copas plugged "Filipino Baby" with all his might, but Tubb's version sold the most records.

"Rainbow at Midnight" was Tubb's cover of another current song, in this case recorded for King by the Carlisle Brothers. The song was the creation of Knoxville legend Arthur Q. Smith, who sold his rights in it to a Knoxville radio performer named Lost John Miller. In spite of Lost John, Arthur Q., and the Carlisles' record, "Rainbow at Midnight" today is almost exclusively identified with Ernest Tubb, not only because he sold the most records at the time (probably a half million), but also because he featured the song in stage performances for the rest of his long career. East Tennessean Jack Greene, a future Texas Troubadour, only knew "Rainbow at Midnight" as the Carlisles' record, but he admits "Ernest had the national hit."[11] Tubb even wrote an "Answer to Rainbow at Midnight" which he recorded the next year.

Because Tubb had the national hit on "Rainbow at Midnight," sociologist George Lipsitz consistently called the song "Ernest Tubb's" when he used it for the title of his study, *Rainbow at Midnight: Labor and Culture in the 1940s.* Lipsitz makes of the song a veritable anthem for the postwar aspirations of millions of Americans. Some of his comments bear quoting here.

A former road construction worker from Texas captured some of that national ambivalence between fear and hope in a song that he recorded in 1946. Ernest Tubb's country-and-western hit, "A Rainbow at Midnight" [*sic*] recounts the feelings of a soldier returning home from overseas on a troop ship. His vision of a rainbow in the night sky reminds him of the woman he left behind when he went to war, and it makes him think of her love, to which he is returning . . . A distinctly male fantasy, "Rainbow at Midnight" offers the possibility of restored patriarchal authority as the penultimate reward for wartime sacrifice. World-weary and somber despite its optimism, Tubb's song conveyed a promise that the dark and trying present might merely be a prelude to an idyllic, romantic future.[12]

Clearly "Rainbow at Midnight," like Tubb's earlier "It's Been So Long, Darling," captured the mood—the "fear" and "hope," as Lipsitz put it—of the postwar American. Though it may be "a distinctly male fantasy," many of Tubb's legion of women fans dreamed of that little "home in the country" and "baby or two" as often as the men did; after all, they'd endured deprivations of their own during the war.

"Rainbow at Midnight" and "Filipino Baby" were the A sides of consecutive Decca releases in their new 46000 hillbilly series. Tubb, normally consulted about the sequence, contents, and timing of his releases (since the success of "Walking the Floor over You") was upset, fearing that simultaneous releases like this would in effect cancel each other out by cutting into the expected sales and response to both songs. He called Dave Kapp, who explained his action: "Ernest, I didn't ask you because I knew you'd disagree, but they both should be out. We didn't want to put them together [on the same disc] 'cause we knew we could sell two records. But if they don't sell as many as your last release did, in the long run—maybe they won't sell as fast—I'll apologize to you." Tubb admitted later, "Sure enough, eventually, they both sold the same amount that I'd been selling."[13]

REASONS FOR THE GREAT POPULARITY

Why, then, was Ernest Tubb so popular at this time? Of course he had been a star in the country music firmament since at least 1941, with big jukebox records, then three movies, national broadcasts as early as 1943, and an ever-widening circle of tour itineraries. Profit from his popularity was largely postponed by wartime problems, as we have seen, but by 1945–1946, Tubb was clearly at or near the top of his field (gracing *Billboard*'s cover, a rare feat for a hillbilly artist, once in each of those years).[14]

The times were right for Tubb. If indeed he had been hurt by the war's onset at a time when he was just getting hot, he was at least well positioned to take advantage of the lack of competition just as the war ended. Before long the Tubb imitators made their appearance on radio and records (as we shall see), but in 1945, who else was making his type of music? The other popular country stars had more of a Western or western swing flavor, with larger and more polished bands featuring multiple fiddles, jazzy steel guitars, whole rhythm sections, and sometimes even horns; witness recordings by Elton Britt, Jimmie Davis, Red

Foley, Bob Wills, Spade Cooley, Al Dexter, and even many of the singing cowboys. Tubb had none of these things: just a straightforward, no frills, drawling and believable baritone, framed only by the insistent, piercing melody line of an electric guitar.

Sociologist Lipsitz is on the right track, ascribing some of Tubb's popularity to the message and mood of his songs, so closely attuned to what large parts of the nation were either experiencing or hoping for. But more important than the message was the messenger. No single song, no group of songs, made Ernest Tubb a star, though many were important. Eddy Arnold once voiced a memorable retort to those who said the Grand Ole Opry made him: "If the Grand Ole Opry made me, why didn't it do the same for the Fruit Jar Drinkers?" If "Walking the Floor over You" *made* Ernest Tubb, why didn't it do the same for Bob Atcher (who had a cover version)? Why didn't "Rainbow at Midnight" sell half a million copies for the group that cut it first, the Carlisle Brothers? It sounds trite, but the top factor in Ernest Tubb's popularity was Ernest Tubb: those qualities of personality or voice that made him unique and instantly recognizable.

A quick list of those characteristics, exemplified by what his fans were actually saying about him, is not hard to formulate. His voice had its technical flaws; particularly pronounced in those years was its tendency to drag the tempo and to slide down from a sustained pitch after a few beats, even though this too added to its distinctiveness. But there was a warmth, a believability to it. From his broadcasts or from his records, one got the assurance that the man enjoyed singing, and he knew how to make the listener enjoy his singing. A fan, Terri Lenzen of Duluth, Minnesota, had these comments published in the second issue (April-May-June 1945) of *Melody Trails,* echoing Hal Smith's evaluation of Tubb's hold on women fans: "Ernest Tubb is my Frank Sinatra. I cry when he sings 'Soldier's Last Letter,' and swoon when he sings 'You Nearly Lose Your Mind.' That deep drop he takes on the word 'trifle' just sends me out of this world."[15] Another fan, Peggy Hobbs of Pardee, Virginia, said virtually the same thing in the next issue, adding the importance of Tubb's rapport with a live audience. "You really don't know how to appreciate Ernest's singing until you see him when he sings 'You Nearly Lose Your Mind.' That low note he does on 'trifle' just simply sends me."[16] Mrs. Mae Loosier won the fan club's What I Like Best about Ernest Tubb contest at the end of 1945 with this entry:

> What I like best about Ernest Tubb is his friendly voice. I have never heard as pleasant a voice, and I could listen to him for hours. Not just singing, but also speaking. His voice never grates on the nerves like some voices but has a restful quality that really makes him stand out among singers. Really, I think this is where most of his popularity lies, because a voice really only shows how a person's mind and heart feels.

And it seems as though Ernest really likes the folks who have helped put him where he is today . . . I envy his personal friends because they get to hear his speaking voice more than the rest of us.[17]

Tubb's voice, then as later, conveyed a warmth of personality that was only enhanced by personal contact, and this endeared him to the fans. The distinctive drawl, something that observers from Judge Hay to Floy Case pointed out, made him instantly recognizable: despite the presence of a good many imitators back then, listeners knew an Ernest Tubb performance the minute they heard it.

But his fans not only identified Tubb when they heard him: they identified *with* him, and this in at least a couple of ways. His concerns were their concerns, voiced without frill, without metaphor, without simile, in a sparse, rough-hewn, down-to-earth style so different from the day's pop stars Sinatra, Crosby, and Como. Tubb, on hit after hit, laid all his cards on the table; listeners knew what he was singing about and identified with his viewpoint. Whether it was love gone wrong, the problems of rebuilding relationships after long wartime separations, dreams of an idyllic life in a newly peaceful world, the woes or the joys of drink, Tubb had a hit song about it.

With voice and instrumentation, he'd found a style that was all his own. A young fan growing up in Marshall, Arkansas, Fred Daniel, recalls how distinctive that spare Ernest Tubb sound was, with just that unique voice and an electric guitar ringing out the melody. "Nobody else was doing that. The minute you heard it, you knew it was Ernest Tubb. I sure wanted to sound like that in my own little band, and just about everybody I knew felt the same way."[18]

In seeking to explain Ernest Tubb's popularity during his heyday, Tubb himself joyfully conceded one factor that can't be omitted: that some jukebox customers played Ernest Tubb records as an ego boost, for self-gratification, thinking "He's a big star, and I can sing as well as he can." The customers who believed this were not necessarily Ernest Tubb fans, and he never would have become a star on the strength of their patronage. But once he was a star, this factor kicked in with something like a snowball effect. Tubb always enjoyed recounting episodes of meeting the "fans" who felt this way, brushing off their hostility and ill will with a laugh at his own expense, and taking their nickels to the bank just like anybody else's.

IMITATORS

Ernest Tubb, then and throughout his long career, clearly had a warm, pleasant, and distinctive voice that begged to be imitated. Between 1945 and 1947 especially, a lot of people were trying to do just that.

Bobby Osborne, who grew to fame as a bluegrass musician with his younger brother Sonny, started out with a radically different sound: he was one of the many Ernest Tubb imitators, fronting a little group in Dayton, Ohio. "When I was 11 or 12 years old, I saw Ernest Tubb in person, and that's when I really got interested in playing music. I played electric guitar with a thumb pick and tried to sing like Tubb . . . I played electric guitar, Dickie Potter played electric mandolin, and Junior Collett played rhythm guitar."[19] Oddly, when young Bobby Osborne's voice later changed, it got higher. "When I was about sixteen (1947) my voice changed and I had to take to something else."[20] As bluegrass stars, Decca label-mates, and Tubb's fellow Opry cast members, the Osborne Brothers remained close to Ernest Tubb through the years, sometimes touring with him and always including a goodly number of Tubb songs on their recordings. On their latest recording project (1995), eleven years after Tubb's death, the Osborne Brothers pay tribute to the Ernest Tubb influence with an all-Tubb package.

Artists across the board, country and even a few pop singers, recorded Tubb's songs. Covering at least one or two Tubb hits in these years were artists as diverse as Jimmy Lawson, T. Texas Tyler, Ford Lewis, Red Murrell, Hank the Yodelling Ranger (Snow), Scotty Harrell, Texas Jim Robertson, Johnny Bond, and Tex Johnson, among others. In one energetic period around August or September 1946, a young West Virginian destined for great things, Hawkshaw Hawkins, recorded sixteen of Ernest Tubb's songs for King Records at his producer Syd Nathan's insistence.

Bennie Hess, a Houston-area singer adept at mimicry[21] who knew the appeal of Tubb's style, cut a regionally popular hit called "Tonight and Every Night." His own composition, it was done in a style indistinguishable from Tubb's, even aping such mannerisms as saying "Pick it out, son" on the steel player's instrumental break. First recorded for Houston's Opera label (#106), "Tonight and Every Night" proved popular enough to be recut by Hess and his band, the Nation's Playboys, on Chicago's new Mercury label (#6121). Mercury, in fact, became almost a "second home" for Ernest Tubb imitators, since they also signed Tubb clone Allen Flatt in 1954, after his earlier discs for Jamboree, Tennessee, and Republic. Hal Smith recalls that Flatt had live radio programs on WKDA, a Nashville station.[22] Imagine that: Ernest Tubb so popular that he was mimicked in his own city!

On radio, with so much live performance by countless obscure artists in those years, Tubb imitators were legion—far more numerous than on recordings. A young Tubb fan, Jerry Langley, who lived then in southern Kentucky and could get Tubb's WSM broadcasts easily, recently opined: "Just about every small radio station right after the war had somebody who tried to sing like Ernest Tubb."[23] This was a development that Tubb himself welcomed: broadcast performances of his songs meant payments directly to him, besides stirring up more sales for Tubb's own recordings. In the September 1945 *Mountain Broadcast and Prairie Recorder,* Floy Case was among the first to notice this phenomenon: "And I'll venture to say that Ernest Tubb is the most 'imitated' singer in radio today . . . He is to the field of hillbilly or folk music, what Sinatra is to the realm of popular music. His fans love him! The gals 'swoon' over him."[24]

Tubb's early fan club publications often note artists who feature his songs. Of Lloyd Cornell in Indianapolis, Viola Myers wrote, "Lloyd Cornell gives 'Soldier's Last Letter' full justice. Lloyd does 'Wond'ring How' [*sic*] nicely, as well as other Ernest Tubb compositions."[25] In the same article, speaking of Chuck Harding (co-writer of Tubb's "When Love Turns to Hate"), Viola says, "When Chuck sings 'Soldier's Last Letter,' he sounds so much like Ernest himself." She goes on to include one of Ernest's heroes and role models, Rex Griffin (at that time in Chicago), as in some sense a mid-forties Tubb clone. "Rex's rendition of 'They'll Do It Every Time' [*sic*] sounds so much like Ernie's that you'd have a difficult time distinguishing it from Ernie's. Don't know whether Rex and Chuck patterned off of Ernie, or from Jimmie Rodgers, but anyway, they remind me a lot of Ernie."[26] In her next article for *Melody Trails* (October-November-December 1945), Viola Myers added young Rex Allen to Tubb's list of Chicago-area radio admirers: "Rex Allen is the latest pro to join our outfit [i.e., fan club]. He's really making a name for himself with his yodeling, singing, and friendliness. Rex does 'Blue-Eyed Elaine' beautifully."[27]

Texas Bill Strength, destined for a notable country music career himself, was an early friend and admirer of the Texas Troubadour who borrowed heavily from Tubb's style and repertory as he launched his radio career. From a letter to the Ernest Tubb Fan Club printed early in 1946: "Those of you who have heard my 34 broadcasts weekly, over station KFEQ, St. Joseph, Missouri, already know just how much I boost Ernest's songs over the air . . . His encouragement and heart-warming assistance has meant so much to me that I could never express it into words. So I'll just say, 'Thanks, Ernest, from the bottom of my heart.' "[28] Later that year, Strength would actually front a band that Norma Winton sang with in the western Arkansas and eastern Oklahoma area, the Melody Trail Riders. Not surprisingly, *Billboard* reported of Norma that "She specializes in the Ernest Tubb songs as well as the Jimmie Rodgers yodels."[29] Lee Thomas, Ernie Lee, Carl Story (Fort Worth's "Palomino Kid"), and countless other radio singers of lesser note acknowledged their debt to Tubb for his inspiration and his help.

TUBB JOINS THE HILL & RANGE EMPIRE

By mid-1946, operation of Ernest Tubb Publications was becoming more than Ernest's household staff could manage. True, they'd done four successful radio song books, sponsoring radio programs on the Opry almost since the time Tubb came there, and different series of morning programs as well, with their contests, giveaways, and cutout books. But there were always headaches involved in securing copyright permissions, finding good quality arrangements on the newer songs, and agreeing on which (and how many) photos to use. Tubb by this time had less and less interest in publishing his own song books (though he would publish a fifth and final *Radio Song Book* in early 1947), and began to cast an eye toward the retail record business. Accordingly, he was open when the offer came that year from the Aberbach brothers to buy up his new copyrights, give Tubb his own publishing company, and manage it for him. This was the same deal that began to prove irresistible to a great many prominent country artists about this time.

Julian J. and Joachim Jean Aberbach were Austrian Jews who emigrated to the United States after working in music publishing in Europe. Jean Aberbach, the elder, learned the business from the bottom up; he started work in the mailroom of Chappell Music in Paris, then transferred to the New York office in 1936. Julian came to the United States in 1940, and a few years later the brothers bought a half-interest in Biltmore Music from the Chicago transcription firm of King and Blink. When they later acquired full ownership, they renamed the company Hill & Range Songs, Inc., to characterize the direction they planned to take their firm: toward the relatively wide-open country music world. Julian headed the day-to-day operations in California, with advice and input from Jean, who stayed on at Chappell in New York until 1948.

Early they settled on a modus operandi that would prove astoundingly effective: approach the country stars with generous sums of advance money[30] to handle their publishing. "Don't worry about it: we'll handle everything. Just keep writing or finding good songs." Of course they signed writers to exclusive contracts with less generous advances, but with the stars they usually set up personalized companies, affiliated with and co-owned by the parent company, Hill & Range. Artists not only liked the advance money in and of itself, but some reasoned that the Aberbachs would have to work that much harder to promote the stars they signed once they had money invested in them.[31]

Soon the latest Hill & Range signings became regular news in *Billboard*'s "American Folk Talent" column. Bob Wills Music was incorporated in July 1946. Red Foley took a reported $10,000 advance from Jean Aberbach to start up what became Home Folks Music for Foley's publishing in July 1947; and about that same time Eddy Arnold agreed to an advance plus a regular draw from Hill & Range, not to start a new subsidiary, but to bring Hill & Range the songs that came his way.[32]

Between February and September 1946 (based on the first appearance in Tubb's discography of "Ernest Tubb Music" material), Ernest Tubb struck his deal with the Aberbachs close to the later Foley model. There was no fancy, evocative company name in Tubb's case; his co-owned subsidiary company was simply named Ernest Tubb Music, and though in print the company name always appeared followed by an "Inc.," diligent lawyers on the Ernest Tubb probate case forty years later could find no proof of incorporation, neither in New York, California, nor Tennessee. This, plus the absence of trade paper fanfare in his case, makes it impossible to pinpoint the date or exact terms of the deal.

With Bob Wills, Red Foley, Ernest Tubb, and Eddy Arnold all under contract before the end of 1947, the Aberbachs had arguably the four top stars of the country field on their roster, and this impressive list made it that much easier for performers of slightly lesser note to take the advance money and sign. Without a doubt, the brothers Aberbach were generous in some ways, preferring expensive gestures public or private that were calculated to impress. They seldom forgot to send birthday gifts to their major stars (Tubb among them), or even to their artists' children in many cases. In the early 1950s, when the company was still based in Hollywood, a typical gesture was to throw a lavish dinner at the Riverside Rancho for their artists touring in southern California, such as Hank Snow or Lefty Frizzell.[33]

Nagging questions of low or nonexistent royalties (a practice by no means confined in those days to any one company) and the Aberbachs' fondness for litigation lowered their stock in the industry's eyes as years passed. They sued Acuff-Rose for the lucrative Pee Wee King–Redd Stewart classic "Tennessee Waltz" in 1951, claiming that Stewart had been under exclusive contract with Ernest Tubb Music when he wrote it. They lost that case and had similar bad luck when they were sued by cowboy songwriter Tim Spencer in 1953. A judge's subpoena with an order of *duces tecum* ("bring your papers," rendered colloquially as "deuces take 'em") was more than they cared to face. Literally by dark of night, they took the files in question and moved their offices to New York City to avoid compliance.[34]

Ernest Tubb, like his close friend Hank Snow, remained loyal to the Aberbachs and to his own Ernest Tubb Music almost to the end—at least until Hill & Range was sold to Jean Aberbach's old employer, Chappell Music, in 1975. He appreciated the advance money and the birthday gifts, the song books they printed (four over an eight-year period: 1948, 1950, 1953, and 1956), and it was nice to be free of the hassles of running his own publication company.

ENJOYING "THE GREAT POPULARITY"

The year 1946 marked the midpoint of a three-year period of great popularity. As 1947 began, Tubb had not one but two smash hits on the market, "Filipino Baby" and "Rainbow at Midnight." He was touring the country on lucrative personal appearances with Minnie Pearl as part of their Oscar Davis partnership, using one of country music's earliest tour buses. The only thing that dwarfed 1946 was 1947, a new year that would find Ernest Tubb making a final motion picture (this one in a starring role), releasing more Decca records (fourteen) than in any other single year of his career, selling between three and four million of his own records, and going into business as a record retailer. Nor is this all. In 1947 Tubb would bring country recording to Nashville, and bring country music to Carnegie Hall. It never got any better than this for Ernest Tubb.

13

A Year of Milestones

Perhaps the only single calendar year that really merits its own chapter in the Ernest Tubb story is the one we come to now, 1947. It was truly a year of milestones.

A FINAL FILM: *HOLLYWOOD BARN DANCE*

Ernest Tubb, though clearly one of country music's three or four biggest stars in 1945 and 1946, made no additional films in those years. His surprising three-year drought was finally broken with the March 1947 filming of *Hollywood Barn Dance.* Tubb signed the contract with independent producer Jack Schwarz and writer-director Bernard B. Ray to make this one film, his only starring role.[1] Tubb's manager Oscar Davis bought the script and name rights to *Hollywood Barn Dance* from Cottonseed Clark, host of a radio show by that name. Texas Troubadours' steel guitarist Jerry Byrd recalls that moviemaking wasn't all that they did: there were some personal appearances in California. They played the Riverside Rancho and at least two others: a Bakersfield show and one in Oakland on the Sunday before filming began on a Monday. "We had to fly in two small planes back to L.A. so as to be there on Monday A.M."[2]

Plotted around "Ernie Tubb's" fictitious rise to stardom over paternal objections, with the Texas Troubadours playing themselves, Tubb and his troupe sparkle on thirteen songs (nine by him and two each by the Short Brothers and Radio Dot and Smoky)—a far cry from the four songs in each of the Starrett Westerns. Tubb's good friend and "Oklahoma Hills" star Jack Guthrie makes his only film appearance, singing "Oakie Boogie" as a special guest toward the end. Guthrie died less than a year after filming.

Hollywood Barn Dance, copyrighted July 1, 1947, was hyped on the Interstate

Theater Circuit with in-theater personals by the star himself (again on leave of absence from the Opry), beginning with its premier at Dallas's Rialto Theater July 23. Dallas's biggest air personality, "Pappy" Hal Horton of the *Hillbilly Hit Parade,* emceed these festivities,[3] which featured "eight acts, two bands, and all that makes for a flash opening," said *Billboard* of August 2. Tubb stayed a week in Dallas and got plenty of press as "the Small Boys' Sinatra,"[4] then moved on to other theaters on the circuit, promoting the film for the next six weeks. Toward the end of the year, yet another Tubb tour promoted the film.[5]

Together the two tours were wearing out Tubb and his band. Red Herron quit that summer, replaced by Hal Smith, a Golden West Cowboys veteran. "Red got tired of the heavy touring schedule with that movie," Hal remembers. "Oscar Davis was working them to death . . . I remember that by December 1947 . . . I had already played nine hundred shows on that theater circuit with Ernest and his movie . . . but it was a nightmare. Sometimes no people would show up for those afternoon matinees; sometimes the little theaters were crackerbox sized."[6]

Young Justin, though, who turned twelve in August, loved going along on the summer tour, watching *Hollywood Barn Dance* and a generous sampling of his dad's stage shows. "I traveled with him in the summertime when those [also including *Jamboree*] were released, and he was working with the film, and I'd sit and watch it four or five times a day. And he'd do shows in between."[7] Another future country music star, Bill Anderson, recalls the joy of *Hollywood Barn Dance,* though without the Tubb stage show: "I remember going to the Decatur Theater in Decatur, Georgia, on a Saturday morning at 10 o'clock, 11 o'clock, whenever they opened, and seeing *Hollywood Barn Dance* six times. There were several songs in there . . . that I just had to see him do. Finally my parents had to come and drag me out at the end of the day. God, I loved that."[8]

THE ERNEST TUBB RECORD SHOP

In the spring of 1947, Ernest and Elaine Tubb made a decision whose impact and ramifications would be long-lasting and far-reaching. Clearly it was the best business decision they ever made, but beyond that, this move has had more impact on country music's growth than any comparably sized venture. Since his death, it has kept Ernest Tubb's name before a large public, perhaps even to a greater extent than his surviving recordings. I refer, of course, to the opening of the Ernest Tubb Record Shop in Nashville.

Several factors weighed into their decision to open the Record Shop. Elaine needed and wanted something to do after losing interest in a florist shop venture that she and secretary Billie Miller had tried. Tubb's tax man Charles E. Mosley was supportive of the idea; he agreed to invest in the business and to keep its books. Though he continued his work as a freelance tax accountant, the former IRS agent set up shop at the home of the new business, 720 Commerce Street, and moved with it in August 1951 to its longtime 417 Broadway location.

The key factor in starting the venture, though, was Tubb's own sense of the difficulty that fans across the nation were having in buying country records. Here he was on to something, something record buyers of today have a hard time even imagining. He'd heard the complaints from fans on the road and from those who wrote to him: "Where can I find Bill Monroe records? Roy Acuff records? Your records?" As son Justin Tubb put it years later, "My father started the Record Shop, not to make money, but as a convenience to the fans."[9]

In Nashville itself, home of the Grand Ole Opry, buying a country record was no easy task in the mid-1940s. Current records by just a handful of the top country stars are mentioned in record shop ads of the day,[10] but such a tiny sampling is hardly representative of the number of artists then making country records. A young fan from those years, Jerry Langley in Greenville, Kentucky, while admitting that he was just a naive kid at the time, says, "I didn't think of the Opry acts I heard on the radio as recording artists. [Of course a great many *weren't!*] Records, to me, meant Vernon Dalhart and Jimmie Rodgers."[11] When he got old enough to drive down to Nashville with a friend, he says that the only place they could find any country records was from a jukebox operator who sold used copies. This is pretty close to what Ernest Tubb himself recalled of the Nashville situation: "There was only one place in Nashville, Tennessee, for instance, where you could buy country music records and this was a juke box operator with the Hermitage Music Company."[12]

Wartime shortages and distribution problems were expected; but by 1947 the war was two years past, and country music careers were being hurt by this lingering shortage of available country records. Tubb's records were selling, to the tune of at least 300,000 per release; but hearing the things he heard from his own fans, he knew how scarce must be copies of the minor artists' releases. Tubb must also have wondered how many more copies of his own discs would be sold if country product was marketed more aggressively. He decided to do something about it and become a record retailer himself.

Undoubtedly there were those who advised him against opening his own record store. The up-front capital and ongoing costs would be great; a record shop might serve as a permanent distraction from the more important business connected with his own career. Going into such a business could possibly alienate fellow artists and would certainly anger a lot of the existing record outlets, what with newfound competition from a big-name star. There was truth in all these cautions, as experience proved. The expense was the major drawback; when Tubb chose to replace records broken in mailorder shipment, he opened the floodgates to early losses that averaged about $10,000 per year for the first five years.[13] Son Justin thinks that about 50 to 60 percent of the records shipped out came back broken: "He almost lost the farm when he started, because of breakage. I don't know what kind of insurance you could have had in those days for those. Maybe the post office wouldn't insure them. That would run the cost up too high, [and] he didn't want to charge them for that. But he just, he paid for it out of his pocket. If they got there in one piece, great, if they didn't, he would replace them . . . It took several years before the record shop got into the black, was up in the fifties."[14]

Hal Smith remembers it the same way, adding that the popularity of the new, unbreakable 45s was the saving factor. "I remember seeing great piles, stacks of broken records in a corner of that shop. They might not have made it but for one thing: the 45. I well remember Charlie Mosley standing on the corner of 7th and Union with what looked like a little piece of a record, saying 'This is our answer.' He was holding one of the first 45 rpm records."[15]

And yes, Tubb made record retailers mad: "I made everybody in the music business mad at me, because I put in a Record Shop! . . . Decca . . . received complaints [from dealers] saying they would never sell another Ernest Tubb record. Even in Nashville, the juke box operator . . . was offended because I put in a Record Shop, and all he was doing was running his juke boxes and selling some used records . . . They were upset because I was a recording artist and they thought I was going into competition with them."[16] But from the start, Tubb made it clear that he was only trying to give fans "a place where they could order their favorite records." "Order" is the key word; at its beginning, the Ernest Tubb Record Shop was solely a mailorder operation, with no real plans for an over-the-counter operation, much less a live show inside the shop: "A lot of people thought I was wrong, but actually I spent a lot of money advertising records and I think that within six months they all saw that I was creating a bigger demand for records by advertising over the Grand Ole Opry. So it helped everybody in the long run."[17]

The young fan Jerry Langley bears out the truth of Tubb's assessment of his shop's impact: "I had never heard of Tex Ritter or Johnny Bond until Ernest Tubb plugged their records on his show. Then I figured if Ernest Tubb liked their music, they must be pretty good."[18]

If dealers got mad at Tubb for opening a record shop, then he soon had plenty of company. All-country record shops launched by country artists soon became the rage. Between 1948 and 1950, some half-dozen country artists opened their own record shops: Eddy Arnold in Murfreesboro, Tennessee; Jimmie Skinner in Cincinnati; Clyde Moody in Washington, D.C.; deejay Fred Edwards in Dallas; Cliffie Stone in Hollywood; Wilma Lee and Stoney Cooper in Wheeling,

West Virginia; Carl Story (the bluegrass performer: not the Fort Worth radio singer who wrote "I'm with a Crowd but So Alone") in Knoxville; Rosalie Allen in New York City; and Pee Wee King and his brother opened King's Record Shop in Louisville. Only the Jimmie Skinner Music Center in Cincinnati and King's Record Shop in Louisville even came close to enjoying the success and longevity of the Ernest Tubb Record Shop.

Tubb's manager Oscar Davis saw to it that the official opening of the Ernest Tubb Record Shop, its beginnings as an over-the-counter operation and as the second most important place for country music fans to visit, was indeed a "grand opening." This self-styled "Folk Music Headquarters" on 720 Commerce Street (Hewgley's Music Store today, in the building joined to Chambers Garage) welcomed an array of Nashville celebrities to the WSM microphone on Saturday, May 3, 1947. "I know on opening day we had a broadcast in the afternoon over WSM, say like from 3 to 4 o'clock or from 4 to 5 o'clock—the initial opening, grand opening of the Record Shop."[19]

Photographers on hand captured the array of stars present that day to wish Ernest Tubb well in his new venture, although Nashville newspapers said not one word about it. Eddy Arnold, then neck-and-neck with Tubb in national popularity, came with his manager Tom Parker. One picture captures the two stars amicably swapping autographed copies of their latest records: Eddy hands Ernest "It's a Sin," while Ernest hands Eddy "I'll Step Aside." WSM manager Harry Stone had a few words for the broadcast, wishing Ernest well and welcoming a business that would soon become one of WSM's longest-running buyers of airtime. David Cobb, who had worked Tubb's morning shows and also his 11:00–11:15 Ernest Tubb Song Book portion of the Grand Ole Opry, announced the event.

Clyde Moody came, who, like Eddy Arnold, soon followed Tubb's example and opened his own record store. The Opry's Curly Fox and Texas Ruby graced the proceedings, as did Lew Childre, "That Boy from Alabam." Milton Estes, a Pee Wee King veteran who then led the Musical Millers, also appears in the all-star group shots taken on the occasion. The biggest surprise guest seems to have been West Coast film, radio, and Columbia Records star Johnny Bond, writer of Tubb's "Tomorrow Never Comes," "Love Gone Cold," "I Spent Four Days in a Dallas Jail," and the current Ernest Tubb hit, "I'll Step Aside."

The two main Texas Troubadours, Jimmie and Leon Short, Tubb cohorts off and on since San Angelo days, were prominent in the photos. Decca artists themselves by this time, within months they would leave Tubb to try to make it on their own.

Nashville newspapers may have said nothing about it, but the event filled the cover of the June 14, 1947, *Billboard,* with a caption that began "The Ernest

Tubb record shop in Nashville is only the latest of top folksinger Tubb's many successful show biz activities."[20]

Ernest Tubb kept as close an eye on Record Shop matters as his career permitted. Though entrusting much of the preparatory work to wife Elaine, the erstwhile shop manager, and the day-to-day operation to investment partner Charles Mosley, Tubb recalled "driving to Memphis myself to pick up some records in June," the month after the grand opening,[21] which was surely not the only such trip he made.

But for the most part he had to rely on the staff that he and partner Charles Mosley chose. From Tubb's own household came wife Elaine and her live-in personal secretary, Billie Miller. Mosley brought in the shop's main clerk, one of his tax customers and a young woman who was also no stranger to Tubb, Dollie Dearman. She was a Nashville dancer, girlfriend to WSM's Harry Stone, and the future wife of WSM's Jim Denny. At that time she handled song book sales at the Grand Ole Opry in a little room backstage. Tubb knew her from that Opry song book connection, having autographed a photo for her in 1946; he clearly agreed with Mosley's choice of the pretty and personable Dollie for the store job. She knew the stars, but was far from starstruck: growing up in Nashville, she had studied serious dancing and as a schoolgirl actually considered Grand Ole Opry "the pits," to quote her own more modern expression.[22]

As Dollie tells the story, Elaine and Billie, though ostensibly the top-level management, didn't do much of the day-to-day record selling, though they would borrow from the cash register for shopping or lunch money.[23] Mosley ordered the record stock, and Dollie and her helpers sold the records. Their biggest over-the-counter sales were on Saturdays, when the Grand Ole Opry crowd was in town, though all accounts agree that mailorder sales, the shop's first operation, remained its most important source of revenue. An April 1948 report has mail-order accounting for 70 percent of sales.[24]

A BIG YEAR FOR RECORDS

Ernest Tubb could stock his new record shop with a lot of his own titles because 1947 was his busiest recording year yet, excluding of course the 1944–1945 World transcriptions. In 1946, Tubb had made thirteen recordings in two sessions; for 1947, he recorded twenty-seven. It was Tubb's all-time busiest year for releases, too: fourteen singles, including four boxed together for his first album. Tubb's new material that year came from a variety of sources.

Tubb himself was still writing good songs. Noting things from the life of a family man and a touring musician that might make for a good song, he would sit on his sofa for hours on end, go through a pack of cigarettes and a pot of coffee with guitar in hand, turning a phrase just right or polishing up the melody. That was his home method. On the road, a hurried note scrawled or dictated (depending on whether he was driving) had to suffice, and would be polished up at home. Of his many new copyrights that year, "Don't Look Now (But Your Broken Heart Is Showing)," inspired by a poorly concealed bottle in the pocket of one of his bandsmen ("It could have been any of them," Justin told me), was one of his all-time best.

After the great success of "Soldier's Last Letter" and "Tomorrow Never Comes," Tubb certainly listened to material by other writers and slackened his own furious songwriting pace somewhat. Redd Stewart and Johnny Bond, writers of these two songs, were favorite sources. Bond's titles we have already listed, and Stewart, having tasted success with one tune for the Texas Troubadour, agreed to collaborate on a few more songs with Tubb. In 1947, shortly after co-writing "Tennessee Waltz" with Pee Wee King (as later litigation established), Stewart signed an exclusive writer's contract with the new Ernest Tubb Music, Inc.[25] The two songs this arrangement produced (both in 1947) were "Two Wrongs Don't Make a Right" and "It's a Lonely World." The former was prominently featured in Tubb's 1947 movie, *Hollywood Barn Dance,* and the latter became an Ernest Tubb favorite, but only after several years had passed and a later (1955) issued recording was made.

With anywhere from 300,000 to 400,000 sales for each single release in these years, small wonder that Bond, Stewart, and other writers wanted Ernest Tubb to record their songs. The list of those who successfully pitched him songs during these years is long and impressive. In most instances, Tubb simply covered songs he liked already out on records, many of which he found from his own Record Shop stock.

Young Hank Thompson, a former fan in Waco of Tubb's KGKO broadcasts, and a protégé of Dallas deejay "Pappy" Hal Horton, sent four of his songs on Bluebonnet Records via Pappy Hal to Tubb in Nashville in mid-1947: "A Lonely Heart Knows," "Whoa Sailor," "Swing Wide Your Gate of Love," and "Starry-Eyed Texas Gal." The deal that Horton presented to Tubb was that Tubb could buy the songs for his own new company, Ernest Tubb Music, if he would promise to get them recorded on a major label. Tubb bought three of them, all except "Starry-Eyed Texas Gal," and kept his end of the deal. He recorded "A Lonely Heart Knows" in August 1947 and at the same series of Decca sessions at Nashville's Tulane Hotel he got Milton Estes to record "Whoa Sailor" and "Swing Wide Your Gate of Love." Thompson remembers today that Tubb's version of "A Lonely Heart Knows" probably sold about 300,000 copies, "the equivalent of a million today," but that Estes's records sold considerably less.[26]

Other up-and-coming young country artists provided Tubb with some of his bigger songs of the era. "Let's Say Goodbye Like We Said Hello (in a Friendly Kind of Way)" and "Yesterday's Winner Is a Loser Today" came from a Cincinnati-based Kentuckian who had just begun recording for Radio Artists Records, Jimmie Skinner. Like Tubb an admirer of the great Jimmie Rodgers, he had befriended Mrs. Rodgers through the mail and says this about "Let's Say Goodbye Like We Said Hello": "I had sent this song to Mrs. Jimmie Rodgers, and after listening to it, she sent it on to Ernest in Nashville, Tennessee."[27] The two men became close friends for many years, and Skinner, whose singing in his early years showed some affinity with Tubb's, also emulated the Texas Troubadour by opening a very successful country music record shop, the Jimmie Skinner Music Center in Cincinnati. Jimmie's early favorite, "Will You Be Satisfied That Way?" was also popular for Tubb in the mid-1950s.

Ernie Lee, a Renfro Valley and Cincinnati (WLW) favorite for whom Tubb secured an RCA Victor contract about this time, wrote and recorded "Takin' It Easy Here," a song to which Tubb took an immediate liking. Tubb cut a demo version of it with Nebraska songstress Texas Mary, and at year's end made a master recording for Decca. Though that version was not issued, Tubb sang it on broadcasts for years and finally put it in a 1967 album.

A radio singer and Tubb disciple in Fort Worth named Carl Story (who recorded for the same Bluebonnet label that Hank Thompson did) got a song to Ernest through wife Elaine titled "I'm with a Crowd but So Alone." Elaine, in company with Tubb's niece, Anna Ruth Collier, heard Story sing it on his Fort Worth radio show, and she offered to bring it to Ernest's attention. Tubb liked the song and made only a few minor changes in it. He recorded it December 14, 1947, and published it with Elaine as Story's listed co-writer, since she'd brought it to him and liked the song so well. The rest of the song's history is best told by Carl Story, who talked to Kevin Coffey about it: "Ernest recorded this song in '47, and he recorded it just before the musicians strike of 1947. And he told me later, 'I'm not gonna release it; they don't want me to release that song right now because I made over 50 songs to get ready for the musicians strike. And I just sounded tired, and it showed up in the record.' I think really he was just telling me this because in the meantime he and Elaine had gotten a divorce. And I think he had remarried, or was fixing to get remarried to Olene."[28] Any possible objections by Tubb's future wife Olene didn't prevent his recutting it in June 1951 (the hit version), nor again for a much later *On Tour* album. So the song itself has long since entered the Tubb canon. Like Stewart, Bond, and Skinner, Story subsequently placed other songs with Ernest Tubb, in his case after the passage of many years: "Go to Sleep Conscience (Don't Hurt Me This Time)" (1961) and "Miles in Memories" (1973).

During these big years, Tubb would still occasionally attribute a good song to Mrs. Carrie Rodgers, his mentor and one-time manager to whom he owed so much. He had done this from the beginning of his Decca career, with "I Cared for You More Than I Knew" in 1940, and "I'm Missing You" (lucrative flip side of "Walking the Floor") in 1941, though he rerecorded neither of them for World. The year 1947 brought the best, and surely the most interesting, of the lot. "A W-O-M-A-N Has Wrecked Many a Good Man" was set to the tune of the one Jimmie Rodgers lost recording, "Prohibition Has Done Me Wrong," a pressing of which, on loan from Mrs. Rodgers, Tubb himself broke during his early years of their association. At least as late as 1956, Tubb admitted his accident to friends who were record collectors, but downplayed its importance, still believing then that RCA had Rodgers's master recording somewhere in their vaults. Tubb had "Prohibition Has Done Me Wrong" long enough to learn it quite well; he could still sing most of it in the mid-1950s, and he told close friends that Rodgers's record may not have been released because of lyrical references to morphine and co-caine.[29] Doing what he could to atone for the breakage, Tubb attributed the tune's authorship to Rodgers's widow, taking justifiable half-credit himself for completely new lyrics. Tubb's song bears a close melodic similarity to the only surviving recording of the older Rodgers song, band leader/fiddler Clayton McMichen's unissued (but rescued) 1931 Columbia master.

Using songs written by Texas Troubadours made sense when they were good, and Tubb had done this as early as 1941 with "Time after Time" by the Short Brothers. Sticking to this tradition of getting songs from his lead guitarist, Tubb wrote a pair of songs with the great singer-guitarist who often filled in for Jimmie Short in the mid-1940s, Zeb Turner. One was "Texas in My Soul." Young Justin Tubb, barely eleven years old at the time, remembers helping his father and Zeb Turner put that one together by jogging their memories of Texas place names.[30] It was for Ernest Tubb a natural follow-up to his big hit, "There's a Little Bit of Everything in Texas," but Tubb himself (though he put the song in his first Aberbach song book, *Ernest Tubb Folio of Recorded Hits No. 1*) never recorded it. Tex Williams for Capitol and Hank Penny for King put it out on disc. Tubb did record the other tune he wrote with Zeb Turner, one of two songs he premiered in the film *Hollywood Barn Dance:* "You Hit the Nail Right on the Head."

From his former bass player, the man who replaced Jimmie Short on lead guitar, Tommy "Butterball" Paige, Tubb got "Heart, Please Be Still." Paige was in between stints with Tubb, leading a band called Butter Ball and the Red River Boys on KLCN in Blytheville, Arkansas, when he co-wrote "Heart, Please Be Still" with Baby Stewart of that station's Stewart Family (Four Star recording artists later).[31] "Heart, Please Be Still" also made it into the *Ernest Tubb Folio of Recorded Hits No. 1,* though it was not a hit for Tubb, whose 1947 cut was not issued. In

1949, Paige himself made the first released version of the song, for Bullet. Babia "Baby" Stewart would write other songs in later years for Tubb.

Two other writers of note, actually of more importance for songs they would write later, had their first songs placed with Ernest Tubb just prior to the end of 1947 and the second Petrillo recording ban. Cindy Walker was an established songwriter when Tubb cut his first of her songs: he had known her since 1942 and toured a good bit with her in 1944. But his first commercial recording of a Cindy Walker song came in late 1947, "How Can I Forget You." Unfortunately, it follows the familiar pattern of other songs I've just mentioned: included in *Ernest Tubb Folio of Recorded Hits No. 1* and recorded, the recording was not released. It is only important as the precursor of so many more to come: "Warm Red Wine," "Two Glasses, Joe," and "Hey Mr. Bluebird" among them.

More successful for Tubb at the time was the maiden songwriting effort of his eldest nephew, Quanah Talmadge "Billy" Tubb, naval veteran of World War II and in 1947 still sailing the waves for the U.S. Merchant Marine. Inspired to write songs by his famous uncle's career, and undoubtedly having time to kill on the ocean, Talmadge (as he is best known) wrote "Seaman's Blues" and sent it to his kinsman for consideration. Ernest reworked it just enough to take half-credit and recorded it December 14, 1947. The Tubb family now tells the story that Talmadge was ashore in some far-flung seaport when from a blaring jukebox he heard the strains of his own "Seaman's Blues" and knew not only that it was recorded, but that it must be a hit.[32] It was. "Seaman's Blues" reached the best-seller and jukebox charts the summer of 1948 and remained a staple in the Tubb repertory for the rest of his career. And it was only a foretaste of what was to come from Talmadge's pen: "Jealous Loving Heart," "(I'm Gonna Make My Home) A Million Miles from Here" (both written about this time), besides the immortal "Waltz across Texas."

THE RECORD INDUSTRY COMES TO NASHVILLE

By 1947, Tubb had been in Nashville four years but had never once recorded there—only in Hollywood, Chicago, or (once) New York. But in the summer of 1947—August 11 and 13, to be exact—Tubb took a break from his tours with *Hollywood Barn Dance* to hold his first two Nashville recording sessions, at the Castle Studios in the city's downtown Tulane Hotel. *Billboard* reported on August 30, 1947, that "Milton Estes and Red Foley cut their first Decca platters in Nashville two weeks ago. Previously all cutting was done in Chicago, but many waxeries are now using WSM's new studios. Majestic also cut a series of sides there."[33] It's odd that Ernest Tubb, a far bigger record seller than Estes or (at this point) Foley is not mentioned in this article, because the same held true for him.

What are called here "WSM's new studios" were actually begun and operated by three engineers on their own time and for their own profit: George Reynolds, Aaron Shelton, and Carl Jenkins. This entrepreneurial venture made much of Nashville's later growth possible, but their move was dictated by the growing body of talent, vocal and instrumental, already beginning to call Nashville home.

Decca's new itinerant producer of country records, Paul Cohen (formerly of their Chicago and Cincinnati offices), relied heavily for this, his first of many Nashville trips, on the advice and musical talents of WSM staff bandsmen Owen Bradley and Beasley Smith.[34] They lined up many of the session musicians and suggested some of the arrangements, while Cohen worried mostly about A&R (artist and repertoire) concerns, matching artists with songs and nixing songs he felt to be unsuitable. In Bradley's eyes, Ernest Tubb was the big factor in Decca's making the move to Nashville recording: "If Ernest had said no, we wouldn't have done it. He was that big."[35] And big he certainly was in Decca's estimation: a September 1947 *Billboard* account says, "Tubb is reported to have collected over $50,000 in Decca royalties the first six months of this year."[36]

Of course there was really no reason Tubb would have said no. Beyond doubt, he pushed the idea. He was Nashville's biggest Decca star—second biggest on the whole label, after Crosby—and his many long trips to earlier Decca sessions had been rife with problems over equipment and expenses. Beginning with these two August 1947 Nashville sessions, Tubb for the rest of his career (thirty-five more years) would do *all* of his recording in Nashville, except for the one Andrews Sisters session in early 1949. Decca thus became the pioneer among the major companies for Nashville recording, and Tubb was their biggest country star.

Despite the disappointingly high number of unused titles from the August and December Nashville sessions, the issued cuts made the next year, 1948, Tubb's biggest yet on the jukebox record charts. On the personal side of things, though, the story was very different.

14

The Fight for Respectability

Few professional entertainers are satisfied with commercial success in and of itself. Some are satisfied with peer acceptance. But many want more—they want the respect, if not the love, of the public at large and respect from entertainers in other fields. Ernest Tubb, atop the country music field in 1947, had all the commercial success he ever could have wanted, but he craved for his field the respect it had never been accorded.

MALONE'S THESIS

Country musicians from the beginning faced this challenge, in a particularly acute fashion. Bill C. Malone has written a short, wonderfully suggestive book about this problem and the two main images that early country singers used to get around it: *Singing Cowboys and Musical Mountaineers* (University of Georgia Press, 1993). As he points out, the musicians were generally Southerners, born with the Civil War's stigma of defeat, which runs counter to the American philosophy of win, win, win. Many of the early performers came from very poor backgrounds and had very little formal education (Ernest Tubb is a case in point). Making matters worse, country musicians in many ways come close enough to the American mainstream—WASP male performers historically, who often affirm basic American values in their songs—to make any lack of respect they encounter that much more galling. Rhythm and blues performers, and later rock and roll stars, never expected mainstream acceptance and hence never really felt the lack of it. But the perception by the broader public of an inherent inferiority in country music has most acutely pained its performers over the years. Historically they and their music simply have not been taken seriously by the media and by the larger public.

Because of his background and character, it seems inevitable that Ernest Tubb would be a leader in this fight. From boyhood he had a fondness for the underdog or the stepchild.[1] How natural, then, that he would fight for his chosen profession, seeing that it was the stepchild of America's entertainment business. As he launched his career, Tubb knew derision firsthand, as we have also seen— from family members, highway passersby, and San Angelo club owners, among others.

One of Malone's two respectability routes worked fairly well for Ernest Tubb, when he finally started making some money by singing: the cowboy image, played to the hilt on Texas radio and in the two Starrett Westerns. But when Tubb made his third film (his first non-Western) in January 1944—*Jamboree* for Republic—he shed the cowboy's mantle of respectability and found himself scripted face-to-face in a battle for his music's dignity against a novelty band that in real life recorded for the same Decca label that he did: Freddy Fisher and the Schnicklefritz Band. Fisher's disdain for the Texas Troubadours drips from this acrid line in their first face-to-face encounter: "You call that music? If I couldn't play any better than that, I'd quit." After a comic mix-up (the core of the plot) in which each band tries to ape the other's style to impress talent scout Don Wilson with the sound they think he wants, both bands finally learn their lesson, one that Tubb applied to his whole life and career: "Don't try to be something that you're not."

What Malone discusses as the other route to respectability, that of musical mountaineer, Tubb saw as the very opposite of a positive image. He would not have understood Malone's points about hillbillies as self-sufficient, independent, defiant, quasi-romantic Anglo-Saxon stock. To call the music as a whole "hillbilly" was to Tubb an outrage: too many people used that word as an insult, a putdown. A "hillbilly" by definition was dirty, ignorant, and isolated, was he not? To call the music by that name was to belittle it, to denigrate it. That was not a solution to the respectability problem: that was a major part of it.

"SMILE WHEN YOU CALL ME A HILLBILLY"

What could be done about the "name" aspect of the problem? Would there ever be a generic name for this kind of music that all could agree upon? If using the term "hillbilly" to lump together the cowboys, the mountaineers, the swing bands, and the jukebox singers was not acceptable, and was, in fact, worsening the respectability problem, what were the alternatives? Tubb discussed this question with the one man he knew in a position to do something about it: Decca's Dave Kapp. Tubb had already used his commercial clout to claim the privilege of sequencing and timing his record releases. Now he consulted with Kapp over the possibility of changing the catalogue name for the music.

To this point Decca had gone along with the general industry practice. Under the label "Hill Billy Records," a 1940 Decca catalogue supplement (the year Tubb joined the label) used subheadings for these different styles: "Old Time Singing," "String Bands," "Sacred," "Fiddlin'," and "Old Time Dance." Right on through the January 1946 *Dealers' Quick Reference List,* "Hillbilly" (now one word) vied with "Blue Label Popular," "Sepia," "Race," and "Hispana Series" as Decca's popular categories. But by the summer of 1948, things had changed. Decca offered dealers that summer "A Complete Listing of COUNTRY and Sepia Records," offering as subgenres a mixed bag of "Ballads, Blues, Folk Songs, Spirituals, Country Tunes, Gospel Songs." Ernest Tubb leads the way among the pictured "Country Artists," with forty-four listed titles. Red Foley comes next with twenty-eight titles, followed by Jimmie Davis with twenty-four.[2]

What had happened between 1946 and 1948? Ernest Tubb had one or more conversations with Dave Kapp about the use of that word "hillbilly" in Decca's catalogues, and by 1948 it is nowhere to be seen. Here is Tubb's account of the substance of their conversations.

> I talked to Dave Kapp . . . Course Red [Foley] never did like the 'hillbilly' either . . . but they asked me, 'What would you call it?' I said, 'Well, I don't know, but most of us are from the country originally—call it country music.' Dave said . . . but see back then they had the Sons of the Pioneers, cowboys, what we call cowboy music, you know. Western, or cowboy. He said, 'Well, the Pioneers, we couldn't call them country music.' I said, 'Well, what about 'Western'? 'Country and Western'? He said, 'Now that may be all right' . . . They started doing it when they put their releases, you know, the sheets. And so the other companies, they just . . . the other companies quit using it [hillbilly] too, and started calling it 'Country & Western.'[3]

Tubb's "Country & Western" compromise with Kapp is reflected in a March 1951 Decca supplement and was still in use in a July 1954 supplement. And, as Tubb said, other companies (and the trade papers, he might have added) followed suit. But the days of "Country & Western" were numbered, as cowboy movies and music faded in popularity, giving way to "serious" TV Westerns.

With Judge Hay at the Grand Ole Opry, Tubb's argument was the same.

> I got Judge Hay, I asked him, I said, 'Let's quit saying hillbilly,' explained to him why. Cause we all used to say 'hillbilly,' you know. What's happening there: a lot of people don't understand what hillbilly means; they think of somebody sitting out somewhere making moonshine liquor, something out there in the hills, barefooted, with a long beard and making moonshine—they call them hillbilly. It looks like they think of

our music as an inferior type of music, and I said, 'I think we can elevate it a lot if we quit using the word . . .'[4]

RESPECT FROM THE TRADE PAPERS

Paralleling these conferences with Decca executives and Grand Ole Opry emcees—and actually preceding them—were Tubb's efforts to get his type of music adequately recognized in the trade papers. It boggles the mind now, but when Ernest Tubb first broke into stardom, the kind of music he made was largely ignored even by the record industry weeklies. Tubb was among the first to do something about that: "There weren't any awards when I started; there weren't even any country music charts in the trade magazines. I remember Bob Austin way back when he was trying to start a country music chart in *Cash Box* magazine. I'm one of the people who helped him. He wrote me and asked me what I thought about it, and if I'd give him some information on how the records were doing. This was back in 1944: there weren't even any charts then."[5]

According to Frank Hoffmann, *Cash Box* charted some records as early as 1942, but those early charts were built around songs rather than the individual recordings—yet another of the great chasms that separates the music business and its press in the 1940s from today's.

The situation was a little better at *Billboard*. Well ahead of *Cash Box, Billboard* had started a separate chart for country records, the small but important "Most Played Juke Box Folk Records" list, which first appeared in January 1944. Tubb's records were among the hottest for the first several years of that chart, and he also got plenty of mentions in the "American Folk Tunes" columns. "Folk," which of course has for scholars an entirely different meaning, *Billboard* dropped in 1949 from their charts in favor of "Country & Western," which survived at least in the abbreviated "C&W" form until 1962. Tubb's original suggestion, "country," has reigned ever since in the "Hot Country Singles" chart.

CARNEGIE HALL—"THIS PLACE SURE COULD HOLD A LOT OF HAY"

"Folk artists get their first Gotham concert break September 18–19 when a troupe headed by Ernest Tubb plus Minnie Pearl, the Short Brothers and Rosalie Allen work Carnegie Hall. Tickets go for from $1.20 to $3.60. Tubb is reported to have collected over $50,000 in Decca royalties the first six months of this year."[6] So reported *Billboard* magazine in their September 20, 1947, folk music column of a special event that has grown in significance with the passing years, a key battle won in the ongoing fight for country music's respectability.

For accuracy's sake, if this was a "first" at all, it was the first all-country concert in New York's venerable bastion of culture. Denver Darling, based in New York at the time, performed country songs as part of a 1945 Carnegie Hall concert. But looking back on it, this concert has grown in importance as perhaps country music's "coming of age." The Opry's founder, "Solemn Ole Judge" George D. Hay, puts it in perspective at the beginning of his wonderful 1953 report on the Carnegie Hall concert: "When the Opry started, our boys and girls made personal appearances in country school houses, town halls, courthouses and small auditoriums. Then came appearances in small theaters in many states. From that time on the sky has been the limit."[7]

New York promoters Sol Gold and Abe Lackman arranged with Tubb manager Oscar Davis to bring an Opry troupe those two nights into Carnegie Hall. Besides the headline acts listed in the *Billboard* account, the Texas Troubadours, by then a trio separate from the Short Brothers (Jack Drake on bass, Hal Smith on fiddle, and Tommy Paige on lead guitar when Jimmie Short wasn't there and steel when he was), were given two songs; Radio Dot and Smoky sang one. Judge Hay, introduced by Oscar Davis, spoke some welcoming remarks. In his account, Hay refers to an unnamed New York country disc jockey, left off the printed program, whose "nice talking job . . . fit into the picture beautifully."[8] He must mean Dave Miller, left off the program but mentioned in the *Cash Box* review (see below).

Hay writes of a dinner given by Davis the afternoon of the first concert and the nerves that plagued the veteran cast: "Brother Davis was host at a small dinner given just before the first night's show. Cousin Minnie Pearl and the Judge were somewhat concerned about how the show would be received by a New York audience . . . here we were in New York City, America's largest town, getting ready to serve plain corn to an audience about which we knew nothing. Somehow or other we got to Carnegie Hall in a cab."[9]

Despite his nerves, Hay felt warmly welcomed when the big moment came to blow his steamboat whistle and give the opening remarks for the 8:30 P.M. show. The program's list of "musical numbers" tells us that the Short Brothers led off with "Stay a Little Longer," "Old Indians Never Die," and "As Long as I Live." Hal Smith then fiddled "Sally Goodwin," Jack Drake sang (yes, sang: he had been the vocalist the year before on the Texas Troubadours' lone Bullet record) "It's a Shame," then Radio Dot and Smoky did their number, "Gold Mine in the Sky."[10] Local favorite Rosalie Allen sang "The Old Ferris Wheel" and "Guitar Polka," and then the star, Ernest Tubb, came out and offered this classic ice-breaker: "Boy, this place sure could hold a lot of hay." Tubb, who had been to New York City at least once before for his September 1946 recording session, was clearly not awed by the big crowd and the venue's fabled past.[11] In later interviews, he never explained his motive for the famous remark, but he did recount the audience reaction.

Oscar Davis was my manager then, booking agent . . . He liked to watch the people . . . He'd stand in the lobby . . . He'd walk through the audience just to hear people talking, see what they were saying . . . And he was walking through the aisle when I mentioned this—he was out in the audience. And he said a lady had one of those binoculars, one of those eyeglasses on a string. Very dignified, you know. And he said when I said, "Boy, this place sure could hold a lot of hay," he said she dropped her eye-glass, and she punched a lady next to her and said, "My God! Talking about putting hay in Carnegie Hall!" We had about, let's say, 2 percent curiosity seekers; we had 98 percent country music fans.[12]

Tubb's set began with "You Nearly Lose Your Mind" (his usual opener before the days of "Thanks a Lot") and featured "There's Gonna Be Some Changes Made Around Here," "You Were Only Teasing Me," "Filipino Baby," then "Rainbow at Midnight." Minnie Pearl came on for comedy and her version of "Maple on the Hill," and Tubb was back to close the show with (what else?) "Walking the Floor over You." Even before then, he had them in the palm of his hand: "It was the greatest responsive audience that I ever had 'til I went to Korea. When I'd say, 'I'm gonna sing "Rainbow . . . ," ' I couldn't get the title out, they would start applauding before I'd even get to the 'Rainbow at Midnight.' It was the greatest audience I'd ever worked to, until Korea."[13]

Hay says, "The show went over beautifully both nights, with a handful of empty seats out of several hundred on the first night and standing room only on the second. I thanked God, from whom all blessings come!"[14] *Cash Box* echoed the Judge's sentiments:

They came, they saw, they conquered . . . a troupe of stars from Grand Ole Opry, WSM, Nashville, played Carnegie Hall in New York before jam-packed, capacity audiences . . . The crowd whistled, applauded and cheered Ernest Tubb, Rosalie Allen, Minnie Pearl, Dave Miller and a host of other stars. Tubb, Allen, and Pearl repeatedly came back for curtain calls. The show played before throngs of highly critical and blasé New Yorkers for two days, and was regarded as one of the most successful engagements to ever appear in the nation's largest metropolis.[15]

The New York media reaction was somewhat mixed; the *Times* carried paragraph-size mentions each night for those who might want to go, but no review.[16] Years later Tubb recalled that media interest picked up once they saw the size and enthusiasm of the crowd. "I thought the people who booked us were going to lose money on the deal. All they bought was two small ads in a New York newspaper. We played two nights, and turned away huge crowds each night . . . That was one of my greatest thrills. The radio and newspaper people ignored us the first night we were there, but we'd turned away 6,000 people, so the next night every radio and newspaper reporter was there."[17]

This would not be the last big country concert at Carnegie. T. Texas Tyler, Tubb's friend and the writer of "You Were Only Teasing Me," which Tubb included on his historic concerts, staged his own Carnegie Hall show the next year (April 25, 1948), as he rode the crest of "Deck of Cards." The Sons of the Pioneers played Carnegie in June 1951, and three famous concerts were staged there in the 1960s: the Opry troupe of November 1961 that included Bill Monroe, Faron Young, Grandpa Jones, Jim Reeves, and Patsy Cline; the Flatt & Scruggs concert of December 1962; and Buck Owens's celebrated 1966 concert.

Barely a month after Tubb led the first Opry package into Carnegie Hall, Eddy Arnold headlined two shows in a single night at Washington, D.C.'s Constitution Hall, a huge Connie B. Gay promotion. There the larger 4,500-seat hall (Carnegie held about 2,700) sold out twice to see Arnold, Minnie Pearl, Rod Brasfield, the Oklahoma Wranglers, and musical funny men Lonzo and Oscar.[18] Though the days of the schoolhouses, the tent shows, and the county fairs were by no means over (Tubb spent most of the summer of 1948 with Jamup & Honey on a tent show), Grand Ole Opry packages headed by such proven stars as Tubb and Arnold could now go uptown anytime they chose.

Trade paper coverage, the beginnings of a new name, and packed houses in Carnegie Hall and Constitution Hall: country music, beginning to boom as never before, was accorded a grudging, newfound respectability, in no small part due to the efforts of its hottest star, Ernest Tubb.

15

On the Personal Side: The Late 1940s Watershed

The very longevity of Ernest Tubb's career, matched by his fans' unwavering loyalty and devotion, tends to obscure the fact that for him as for most of the long-term achievers, there were several valleys, or doldrums, which he converted into successful turning points. In fact, Tubb was not very far into his peak years when he first felt the downward pressure. For several reasons, many of them personal, 1948 proved to be a pretty tough year.

THE SILVER LINING: RECORDS IN 1948

Tubb made no recordings in 1948. James C. Petrillo's American Federation of Musicians went on strike again, banning all recordings with instrumental accompaniment as of January 1, 1948—the second such strike in a six-year period. Of course the record companies had warning and, remembering the length and severity of the first strike (over two years for most companies), did what they could to stockpile new recordings by their major artists toward the end of 1947. As things turned out, the second strike ended within the year, and companies hardly felt the pinch this time around.

The biggest hit of Tubb's 1948 crop (three chart hits) was his recycled 1933 pop song, "Have You Ever Been Lonely (Have You Ever Been Blue)," which first made the charts December 11, 1948, and climbed as high as number 2 on the jukebox chart. But except for this limited record success, 1948 brought for Tubb no landmark events comparable to the many of 1947—at least, no positive landmarks.

PROBLEMS ON THE ROAD

Even though he was one of country music's three or four top stars, Ernest Tubb had a hard time keeping together a touring band in 1948. When Jerry Byrd left him to work for Red Foley and stay off the road, Tubb filled the slot by bringing back Ray "Kemo" Head. But before the year was out, he'd hired young Don Davis, a former Golden West Cowboy who'd just returned to Nashville from a West Coast junket. "I got a call from Hal Smith at Satsuma, Alabama, and he said, 'Ernest wants you to come up.' I was still only about seventeen years old. Somehow his band, he wasn't happy with them, because Leon and Jimmie Short had left, and gone to Baltimore, I think it was. And Ray "Kemo" Head was playing steel with him, and I don't think he was the greatest in the world."[1] The band when Davis came in to play steel had Hal Smith on fiddle, Jack Drake on bass, Bill Drake on rhythm guitar, and Butterball Paige on lead electric guitar. Bill Drake left, and in October Tubb had replaced him with Hal Smith's wife, Velma Williams Smith, a talented guitarist and singer with the Opry's Williams Sisters and more recently with Roy Acuff's Smoky Mountain Boys and Girls. Velma says now, self-deprecatingly, "Ernest only hired me so Hal and I could work together."[2]

One problem keeping people steadily in his employ was Tubb's erratic behavior. Davis, a big boy from Mobile, Alabama, whom Tubb always called "Kid," soon found out one of the reasons he was hired: with his two-hundred-pound frame, he could help keep Ernest in line. Though largely unknown to his public, the fact is that Ernest Tubb until he was fifty had a problem with alcohol, and under its influence, he was rowdy and hard to handle—a totally different person, as new band members soon learned. Davis tells his story.

> C. R. [Jr.] was on the road with Ernest . . . ticket taker, he kept everybody in line. He would assign me to do stuff with Ernest. I was like an eighteen-year old, two hundred pounds, like a linebacker, and Ernest would get rambunctious when he was drinking. C. R. would have Butterball with him, and put me in the limo [back seat] with Ernest. I couldn't figure out why, but I found out! Ernest had a thing about kicking the windows out. He had a big diamond ring with "E.T." on it, and when he was gonna start some shit he'd start tapping the window. I made $55 a week—$5 extra for this duty—plus what I made on song books . . . Well, those were '48 limos, seven-passenger limos, and those windows were thick! But when he'd start tapping, you knew he was gonna kick the windows out. That was my signal—grab him! I'd wrestle his ass to the floor.[3]

Don Davis soon learned that a little reverse psychology might save him considerable energy. "I finally learned how to deal with that. I told him, 'Look, Ernest, I'm gonna kick them windows out. I don't like them windows. They shouldn't be here, we need to be free spirits, to breathe.' And I had cowboy boots, just like he did, and I'd rear back to kick them, and I'd let him restrain me! He held me from Murfreesboro, Tennessee, to Miami. Kid, you're not gonna kick my goddam windows out. This is *my* car.' "[4]

They all tell the same basic story. Danny Dill: "Ernest had a problem with alcohol, there's no doubt about that . . . And Ernest had a fetish for glass, he couldn't stand glass . . . It didn't matter what kind of glass. I take it, if it was a mirror he sure got it, because he didn't want to see himself, I guess—I don't know. I'm psychoanalyzing him now, but any kind of glass he would break it if he got his hands on it . . . He couldn't stand glass around him when he drank . . . There's many stories about him breaking out doors and windows and stuff . . . if he got drunk enough. I don't think it was like he had a few drinks, but if he'd been at it for two or three days."[5]

Jerry Rivers, best known as Hank Williams' fiddler later, heard most of the "war stories" from the Short brothers, who hired him a year or so after they'd left Ernest. "It was obvious they left Ernest Tubb on less than good terms . . . They didn't have kind things to say about Ernest Tubb . . . it became obvious that there was no friendship left there . . . Ernest would get pretty rowdy. He was the well-liked, loved Ernest Tubb when he wasn't [drinking]. But more than one have told me this: it was a fetish with E.T. to kick out the windows of the tour car when he got upset and drunk. They [the Shorts] told me that was one of their jobs—to put glass back in the tour car."[6]

Ernest Tubb's problem with the bottle was long-standing, an occupational hazard, one might almost say, for a man who sang for tips around Texas beer joints and who once owned one himself. Edward Linn, with a frankness uncharacteristic of most of the early literature about Ernest Tubb, said in his fine 1957 article for *Saga,* "Young performers go to Ernest with their troubles, not only because he has a notoriously big heart, but because they know that he has been through the mill . . . Ernest has had his skirmishes with the bottle and didn't always win."[7] Drink cost Ernest an appearance on one of the early, key Oscar Davis package shows, Linn alone reported: "Ernest was supposed to appear next at a Davis promotion in Little Rock, but he got drunk and missed the show. Luckily, Davis didn't hold it against him, since drinking is practically an occupational disease among country singers."[8]

Tubb's drinking was at its worse in the years 1947–1948 and undoubtedly contributed to the instability in his band about that time. Early in 1949, Tubb disbanded altogether, keeping only Butterball as his lead guitarist and using local musicians for his road gigs. Hal Smith remembers that manager Oscar Davis advised this move: "We went out on a tent show tour, but the business just wasn't as good as it had been. Then Oscar Davis told Ernest, 'I can get just as much money for you and Butterball alone—why don't you let the rest of these guys go?' And that's what he did."[9] Opry newcomer George Morgan hired them all: Jack Drake, Don Davis, Hal and Velma. It may have been prearranged, both to help Morgan and let the musicians land on their feet. But by that time, Tubb's drinking had wreaked its havoc on the home front. It proved to be both a cause and an effect of his deteriorating marriage, which dissolved in 1948 after fourteen years.

PROBLEMS AT HOME

Drink was one of the problems in a marriage failure for which there was plenty of blame to go around. Merwyn Buffington said, "I never thought Ernest and Elaine would divorce; they seemed made for each other," but he also admitted that Ernest had a fondness for certain of his female fans—and this from the early days of his marriage, when he was singing for tips in Texas beer joints.[10] Elaine had a proclivity from the start to "bail out" when things got difficult; from wherever they were living in their Texas days—Midland, Corpus Christi, San Angelo, Fort Worth—she could catch a ride back to San Antonio with her truck-driving stepfather, Mr. Webber, or with some of his friends and co-workers.[11] Some sources swear that Elaine was leaving Ernest when she and a nurse had the accident near Fredericksburg that killed seven-week-old Rodger Dale Tubb in September 1938. Elaine heading back to San Antonio from Fort Worth partly caused the fret that inspired Ernest to write his biggest song, "Walking the Floor over You." And who knows how many of his sadder love songs of that period came from personal experiences? "Try Me One More Time"? "That's When It's Coming Home to You"? "You're Going to Be Sorry"? "This Time We're Really Through"? "I Don't Want You after All"? "You May Have Your Picture"? "Mean Mama Blues"? (He even used the phrase "Mean Mama" in a picture he signed for her, which she still has.)

After the move to Nashville, more marital tension came from the perils of prosperity. Ernest Tubb's great-niece, Debbie "Snooky" Tubb, opines, "When they got money, they probably did spend it. They had been poor. They were just like anybody else; the first time you get big money, you always make mistakes. Money's part of it."[12] Like other husbands, Ernest was ambivalent about having his wife work: sometimes he wanted her to, sometimes he didn't (as she alleges in the divorce complaint). She helped in the song book business—for over a year she kept office hours for Ernest Tubb Publications in #224, Bennie Dillon Building—and was a prime mover behind the Record Shop. But co-worker Dollie Dearman remembers that Elaine and her personal secretary Billie Miller had a fondness for borrowing cash register money for lunch or shopping trips on which their favorite items were bras, slips, slippers, and housecoats. The shopping habit may have been one reason that Ernest asked her to quit the Record Shop, which she did, only a year after it opened.[13] Of course in that first year, the shop had lost money hand over fist, so maybe some staff cutbacks were in order anyway. Capitol artist Wesley Tuttle alludes to another possible reason for the

dismissal: Elaine's over-fondness for the Tennessee-area Capitol Records distributor. Tuttle says that this is what broke them up; Ernest moved out of the
house when he learned of it.[14]

Examine some of the songs Tubb wrote in Nashville, and see if they don't say
it all pretty plainly: "I'm Free at Last," "A House of Sorrow," and what about the
warnings in "There's Gonna Be Some Changes Made around Here"?[15]

Besides slips, slippers, and bras, shoes of all sorts appealed to Elaine; her
large collection became the target of Ernest's drunken rage on one memorable
occasion. Kin and bandsmen tell the story a little differently, but they agree on
the basics of what happened. Ernest was home from a tour and wanted to take
her to a movie. Maybe he'd already been drinking, but when she declined, saying
she didn't have the right shoes to wear, Tubb went on a rampage. He hauled
every pair of shoes she owned to the middle of the living room floor and proceeded to rip them to shreds with what is variously described as a pocketknife or
an icepick. Another variant of the story has Ernest tossing each one out the back
door as he ripped them up, only to have the faithful family dog fetch them back.
Snooky Tubb heard years later that her grandfather, Ernest's brother C. R., had to
be called over from his McGavock Pike home to help calm him down and stop the
destruction of property.[16]

As this episode demonstrates, whatever Elaine's faults, Ernest Tubb was
very difficult to live with. Home for a week, then out for two; fan mail to answer;
deals to cut; records and song books to sell; other artists to help—and every
problem magnified by his love of drink. Like many other stars, he couldn't find
time for a home life, to be a good husband and father. Justin and young Elaine
were shipped off to schools for much of the year, so that for a time the Tubb
household consisted more of employees and extended family than of Tubb children. There was Leon Short, a Tubb live-in from the time he got out of the service
in 1943 until his parents moved to Nashville. There was secretary Billie Miller
("Aunt Billie" to the Tubb children), the old San Angelo friend who moved up to
help Elaine; she stayed with the Tubbs until she remarried in 1948. Niece Anna
Ruth Collier moved up from East Texas for her 1947–1948 George Peabody College year, worked in the new Record Shop, and lived with Uncle Ernest and Aunt
Elaine until their separation.

On August 13, 1948, Lois Elaine Tubb sued Ernest Dale Tubb for divorce,
alleging in her complaint that "Defendant has become absolutely estranged from
complainant and is living separate and apart from her, and it is apparent from his
actions that he has no affection or love for complainant, and has so announced
to her, falsely accusing her of being the cause of his actions." She goes on: "She
has heretofore tried to work, and did work at employment agreeable to the

defendant, and upon his objection quit such employment and remained at home with her children, and now has no income, or means of support, except from the defendant . . ."[17]

First Circuit Court Judge Richard P. Dews heard the case on October 16, 1948. Tubb was represented by attorney Dudley Porter Jr., though none too energetically, it would seem. Tubb's side conceded his desertion and did not really contest the divorce. If there had been adulterous behavior by either party, it is not in the court record. Judge Dews's account says at one point, "the defendant having been represented by counsel but having put on no proof"; Elaine's side called witnesses, whose names and testimony have not been preserved; counsel for the defense called none, though he did apparently question Elaine's witnesses.

Not surprisingly, Judge Dews found for Elaine, granting the divorce and ordering alimony in the form of the defendant's entire interest in the Cedar Crest Road homeplace, its household furnishings and furniture. Elaine got the custody of the two children, which she'd sought, and child support payments of $200 per month, although Ernest got generous visitation rights, as specified in their separate property settlement agreement: "at reasonable times and places during such school years, and with the understanding that said children can be with him during the vacation period between such school years . . ."[18]

Oddly, the Ernest Tubb Record Shop is not mentioned in the property settlement; maybe it had lost so much money in that first year that Elaine wanted no part of it. The homeplace went on the market; Elaine had already moved the kids to San Antonio, where she would live, and Ernest moved in with his brother on McGavock Pike, which was not exactly a haven of privacy either. C. R. and Margie had four sons at home, five-year-old twin girls, and a daughter on the way, besides the occasional presence of other extended family members. Small wonder that Ernest loved the road.

A marriage that had endured so many hard times broke apart on the rocks of prosperity. Elaine, for her part, continued to love Ernest, though she remarried. Today a large photo portrait of Ernest Tubb in his prime hangs over her bed, and in the living room of her home hangs a fan's tapestry of the couple together, although it oddly juxtaposes an older Ernest (circa 1975) with a youthful Elaine (circa 1945). Always they had the common interest of the two children. For about ten years, Tubb stopped singing "Blue-Eyed Elaine" but niece Anna Ruth Collier Husky saw him perform at a West Texas club about 1959 and announce, when fans kept requesting the song, "Well, it's been ten years. I guess that's long enough."[19] In 1978–1979, Tubb overdubbed a tender "Sing it for your mother" to Justin's verse on their "The Legend and the Legacy" duet version of the song.

OTHER PROBLEMS

Not only did his marriage collapse in 1948; so too, for much of that year, did his fan club, the second time within five years that Ernest experienced serious fan club trouble. In those years Ernest Tubb probably had too many fans for any one club or club president to successfully handle. Faye Flanagan and Lucille Ritz had found this out before; Norma Winton found it out in 1947–1948, after such a promising beginning. The early issues of her fan club newsletter, *Melody Trails,* those printed between 1945 and early 1947, were truly top-notch: fun, fact-filled, thick bulletins, which (in accord with their star's wishes) were never exclusively about Ernest Tubb. But after a January 1947 twenty-three-page *Melody Trails* (volume 3, number 1), comes a gap of some twenty months before *The New Melody Trails* appeared, dated "fall edition" (1948) (curiously, also numbered volume 3, number 1), with Gene Autry on the cover. A postwar paper shortage, mentioned in some of Norma's explanatory columns, was part of the problem. The distractions of Norma's move to Nashville during that time (spring 1947) to help the Tubbs set up the Record Shop business was another factor. So too was her personal life; she moved back to Fort Smith, Arkansas, tried a singing career of her own, and married Henry Barthel on March 13, 1948.

But in fairness to Norma, another big part of the problem with keeping the fan club running with anything like a normal printing schedule, be it monthly or quarterly (she tried both in those early years), was Tubb himself: his attitude toward fan clubs in general and his own in particular. Since Tubb promoted other artists' careers so energetically, he expected his fan club publications to do the same, even though that meant a lot of extra work for the beleaguered club president. And he knew he was not in a position to lend it much aid. His attitude was, "If this is what the fans want to do, great." He was flattered that someone wanted to start such a club and that several thousand people wanted to join, but he took a wait-and-see posture. Tubb was a long time coming to a proper appreciation of the value of his fan club.

Perhaps that sounds uncharacteristically selfish on his part; it certainly differs from the way artists view fan clubs today, when most are operated from the star's own office. But it gets back to Tubb's root modesty more than to any aloofness or selfishness, a wonderment that he ever became a star in the first place. He no more expected to involve himself in the fan club's operations than he would have lobbied for an award (yet another difference between Ernest Tubb and some stars of today). We might draw an analogy with the tentative way he hired new bandsmen: his line was always, "Well, son, we'll try you for awhile and see how you work out." It appears he felt the same way about the fan club; he never gave Norma's efforts over the years his unqualified support, though he expected it from the club. Wasn't that what fan clubs were for?

Fan clubs, still quite new in those days (Bill "Cowboy Rambler" Boyd, Gene Autry, and Roy Rogers had just about the only extant clubs in the country field before Tubb), were fraught with potential drawbacks. Tubb seemed in the beginning more aware of these than of the free promotional possibilities of fan clubs; his gaze seemed to be fixed on the negative side of the coin. If clubs weren't handled just right, they could alienate more fans than they would attract. There were a lot of ways this could happen: untimely or discontinued publications; unanswered mail; even (in later years) changes in the star's itinerary made after a publication went to press, and the subsequent confusion and hurt feelings. In the final issue of the first *Melody Trails* run (January 1947), Tubb dwelt on these problems, while praising Norma's efforts at a tough job.

> If you should know of any person or persons who have joined our club and have voiced regret of doing same . . . I would like to return to them the dues they have paid to date . . . The past two months have brought a few very sarcastic letters that were reeking with criticism for the way Norma has been running the club. These people also expressed their regrets for ever joining the club. NONE of these letters were signed, so I have no way of knowing from whom they came. If I knew, I could write them personally and return their dues . . . I feel in my heart that Norma has done the very best that she could to keep this club the way she feels I want it to be. She has had a tough job of it with paper shortage and a number of other handicaps that I won't take time to mention . . .

Then he waxes philosophical about the purposes of fan clubs:

> the success of the club, which can only mean the success of the STAR, is the only reward there is. But after all that is, or should be, the sole purpose of any fan club. People should only join a fan club when they have faith in the Star, and feel that they can in some way be of help to pushing him, or her, to greater success, and by all means, WANT to be of some help. If they feel any other way than this, they should never become a member of such a club.[20]

Ernest is preaching here to the faithful few, the chosen—the only ones he wanted in his fan club. It mattered more to him that his club members be loyal and dedicated—"Ask not what your star can do for you; ask what you can do for your star"—than that they double their membership, from three thousand to six thousand, as one club contest about this time sought to do.

In her follow-up editor's note to this letter, Norma pleaded with the fans to help keep Ernest out of club problems in these words: "Let's work this out among ourselves and not have Ernest in on any part of this unsatisfied part. He isn't responsible, and he won't have to pay . . . now will he? . . . And let's not cause Ernest to have to write this way ever again."[21] She may or may not have known "the way [Tubb] wanted [the club] to be," but she knew by this point at least the way he *didn't* want it to be. Tubb's fears and doubts became a sort of self-fulfilling prophecy, as *Melody Trails* dropped so long out of publication. In the early 1950s, its publication schedule became even more erratic.

BIRTH OF AN INSTITUTION: THE *MIDNITE JAMBOREE*

If 1948 brought its share of setbacks and reverses for Ernest Tubb's life and career, it also brought at least one very big highlight: the first appearance at the Ernest Tubb Record Shop of a new program that evolved into a country music institution: the *Midnite Jamboree.*

Exact dates for the basic chronology have proven elusive. Different persons give different accounts; Tubb himself gave contradictory accounts from his memory of the show's development. Even the information trail from trade papers and fan magazines—what few there were then—is confusing.

Some evidence indicates that Ernest Tubb owned a slice of that precious Saturday midnight, post-Opry airtime, dubbed by him the *Midnite Jamboree,* as early as January 1947, even before he'd opened the Record Shop.[22] Tubb believed in buying WSM airtime for his own purposes, proved by the earlier Ernest Tubb Song Book segment of the Grand Ole Opry. It is quite possible that to build interest in advance for mailorder sales from his shop Tubb bought separate airtime for that purpose; mailorder operation of the Ernest Tubb Record Shop was probably going on weeks or months before any over-the-counter sales.[23]

Nashville newspaper radio logs, though, during the early months of 1947 list a "Dave Minor" as using the WSM time slot immediately after the Opry. It is May 31, 1947, before the midnight time slot says *Grand Ole Opry,* even then not mentioning Ernest Tubb or his Record Shop by name (they finally would in 1953).[24]

Accounts in *Billboard* further muddy the issue of the *Midnite Jamboree*'s origin. Therein are several mentions of the Record Shop from the spring of 1947 onward, but no mention of any radio program before the April 10, 1948, issue, which says "Ernest Tubb, the Decca star, reports that he is now doing a disk jockey seg every Saturday night from his Nashville record shop, with the program going on right after the Grand Ole Opry. Ernest reports that his record shop, now a year old, is going great guns, with 70 percent of the business mail order."[25]

Anna Ruth Collier, a 1947–1948 Record Shop employee while attending George Peabody College, remembers that on those nights when Tubb himself was out of town for personal appearances, Elaine Tubb and Billie Miller brought copies of the week's featured records to the Ryman Auditorium as the Opry show wound down and took positions in the glassed-in control room as virtual dee-jays. David Cobb then announced the program from the Ryman stage. Her recollection of a disc jockey show that early (predating the *Billboard* mention) is backed up by Johnnie Wright of the Opry's Johnnie & Jack, who left Nashville for Shreveport at the beginning of 1948 with partner Jack Anglin (only to return four years later). He remembers plugging their Apollo releases (1947) by chatting with host Tubb on a midnight show from the Commerce Street record shop. Hal Smith, the fiddler who joined Tubb in mid-1947 and worked with him right through 1948, says, "I remember that we first did the midnight show from WSM's Studio A on the fifth floor of the National Life building. [That] went on a few weeks, a few months at the most, after I joined the band, before he made his operation over-the-counter at 720 Commerce Street."[26]

If we put these accounts together, it appears that Tubb launched a records show in early 1947, which did some shows from the Ryman stage immediately after the Opry and others (when Tubb was in town) from WSM's Studio A. In the early part of 1948, that broadcast, still not yet an hour in length, moved into the Commerce Street store; despite the crowded conditions, live performances by Tubb and by his guests began to be featured. The Record Shop was close to the Opry (one block north and two blocks west), so it was easy for fans to drop by and shop, especially with the incentive of the new live show. This was just about the only other thing the country music fan could then do on a whirlwind Nashville visit in those years, besides or in addition to attending the Grand Ole Opry.

When Ernest was in town, he would perform some of his own songs on the midnight show, but he still had the Opry and the Carter's Chicks shows on which to do that. At midnight the emphasis was other artists' records. Rather than spin them all, Tubb and his boys actually performed several of them on each show. Odd as that may sound today, for years a regular part of Tubb's broadcast from the shop was his renditions of songs of the day. Sometimes they were hits, but more often they were songs that he liked by second-tier artists, songs that he could sing, from current records that needed this sort of boost or plug to energize the sales. Tapes by collectors survive of Ernest Tubb singing a good many such songs from his *Midnite Jamboree*—even more interesting because they are songs that he never recorded commercially.[27]

Evolving from a deejay-and-guest format, the *Midnite Jamboree* always featured guests, as time allowed. Often, it was an Opry star just dropping by. By 1949, when the broadcast had lengthened to forty-five minutes, that night's Opry big-name guest would usually come by, especially if that artist (as frequently happened in the late 1940s) was a non-Opry act in town for Red Foley's network portion. Acts like Floyd Tillman, Elton Britt, Jimmy Wakely and Margaret Whiting, Tex Ritter, Ernie Lee, Wesley Tuttle, Johnny Bond, Tex Williams, Tommy Duncan, or Tennessee Ernie Ford appeared on those early Midnite shows. Tuttle says that when he came to Nashville for the weekend, he was booked onto three programs: the Prince Albert NBC *Grand Ole Opry,* Ernest Tubb's *Midnite Jamboree,* and the next day's *Sunday Down South,* a network show from the WSM studios.

Tubb as host sang fewer and fewer current songs by other artists as time passed and as his voice deepened. More and more of these records were played by the engineer, then plugged by the announcer. And while records are still played on the *Midnite Jamboree* today (approaching a half-century, only the Opry itself has been on radio longer), over time this practice gradually and naturally evolved into bringing on the artists themselves as guest stars to sing and plug their own songs. In this way, the *Midnite Jamboree* slowly became what it is widely thought to be today: if not exactly a talent show (clearly not an amateur show), then at least a place where the newcomer, the young artist with one or two records out, can get a break.

The demographics (to use a rather barbarous modern phrase never thought of back then) of the midnight radio audience were perfect to make it that sort of show. Saturday midnight was a time at which barhoppers and nightlifers all across the South were beginning to head home. With most local stations off the air by then, a great many of these folk tuned their car radios to clear-channel 650 kilocycles, WSM radio in Nashville, to hear the goings-on at the Ernest Tubb Record Shop. There they were: a ready-made audience before whom the newcomer, the young hopeful, could strut his stuff.

The announcers on this famous program became legends in their own right, a powerful fraternity that included (in order, going through Tubb's lifetime), David Cobb, Jud Collins, Grant Turner, Hairl Hensley, and Keith Bilbrey. All were living and present at a fortieth-anniversary celebration for the Ernest Tubb Record Shop, held at Nashville's Convention Center in May 1987. But as anyone who listened to the program knows, when Ernest Tubb was in town, he did most of the talking, with song dedications, his own itineraries, and recognition of fans in the shop's audience and of many listening by radio.

In spite of consistent success in trade paper record charts with his new releases, 1948 was a down year for Ernest Tubb, personally and professionally. At home he endured a divorce. Professionally, because of a strike, no new records were made; his fan club died a brief death; and his band was restructured. At the same time, however, the Ernest Tubb Record Shop, though losing some $10,000 annually at its outset, nevertheless became the home of a radio institution, as Tubb branched out from record retailer to talent booster with the *Midnite Jamboree*. It was a harbinger of the many good things that would make 1949 a terrific comeback year. And it was only one of several ways that Ernest Tubb boosted deserving talent, even that far back. The next chapter explores his earliest efforts to do just that.

16

A Helping Hand

If you look at the long course of Ernest Tubb's career, several consistent threads interweave the whole tapestry, from beginning to end. Never did his love of performing flag: in good health or poor, the joy with which he did his work was a constant. Always he went out of his way to please his fans, signing all the autographs, posing for all the pictures. He knew the fans "paid the freight," that they were the ones who got him out and kept him out of the cottonfields (or the drugstores, or the beer trucks, for that matter). There was, as we have seen, a dedication to his profession in terms of its acceptance and respectability, a desire that it always be worthy of at least a grudging respect from other parts of the entertainment industry. Not only did he work for that respect in the early days when it was in such short supply, but it remained an ongoing concern of his, evident in published statements in the very last days of his career.

Just as consistent as any of these, and maybe the single best remembered aspect of Ernest Tubb aside from his music, is the helping hand he always extended to the deserving newcomer. Country music never had another such tireless altruist. Mrs. Rodgers had helped him through his long and difficult musical apprenticeship; so, looking down from the pinnacle once he made it, he asked her how he could possibly repay her. Of course he did kind things for her, as we have seen. But her answer to the question, "What can I do to repay you?" was a simple "Just do the same for others." And he always did. Whatever ups or downs Tubb's own career was going through, this remained constant. Not that he wouldn't have been generous with his time and experience anyway—we have seen that compassion for the underdog was an early and strong character trait. And helping others was yet another way that he strengthened the industry of which he was such a big part. But when he was asked about his famous generosity, he always gave Mrs. Rodgers credit for the inspiration and motivation.

We have seen already his efforts to help songwriters who supplied material, bandsmen who wanted to make it on their own, and acts in his touring troupe. Acts like the Short Brothers, the Poe Sisters, Rod Brasfield, Radio Dot and Smoky, Ernie Lee and Pete Pyle[1] owed Tubb thanks for various favors. Tubb also played the role of record producer for an unlikely old-time duet, Rebe and Rabe. Alabamians much in the style of the Blue Sky Boys, Revin "Rebe" Gosdin and J. C. "Rabe" Perkins were protégés of former Texas Troubadour Chester Studdard on his Saturday night Gadsden show, the *Dixieland Jamboree,* and also worked Birmingham radio and schoolhouse dates at the time Tubb met them. As a favor to them and to Chester, Tubb arranged a recording contract for the boys with MGM, then set up and supervised their session of January 28, 1949, at the Castle Studios in Nashville's Tulane Hotel, where so many of his own 1947–1953 sessions were held.[2]

Best known of the early artists he helped, though, were three Hanks who became legendary stars in their own right: Thompson, Williams, and Snow. Tubb tried to make them all Opry stars and succeeded in the case of the last two. Though all three men had the talent and determination to become great country stars on their own, which Tubb and others saw clearly, still his boost to each man came at propitious moments.

HANK THOMPSON

Henry William "Hank" Thompson, eleven years Tubb's junior, was WACO radio's "Hank the Hired Hand" about the same time that Tubb was KGKO's "Gold Chain Troubadour." Thompson remembers listening to Tubb's 7:15 A.M. show before going to school in Waco, and as we've seen, he lists Tubb right up there with Jimmie Rodgers, Gene Autry, and Roy Acuff as his early inspirations.

They met for the first time when Thompson was in the Navy on the West Coast during World War II. Tubb was playing the famous Venice Pier when Jimmie Short introduced them. Tubb did not recall that meeting in later years, but hero-worshiping Thompson certainly did. After the war, Hank went back to Waco radio work and made his first recordings for Globe and Bluebonnet. Dallas disc jockey "Pappy" Hal Horton took over Thompson's career about this time, publishing his earliest recorded songs through his Metro Music. Among the things Horton did for Thompson—besides ranking his records high on the Hillbilly Hit Parade—was pitch his songs to major artists, among them Ernest Tubb.

The recording ban put a stop to the song deals for a while, but Tubb during that time (1948) worked more closely with Thompson than he ever would afterward. The Brown brothers, still looking for top country talent to sponsor on radio through Purina, at Hal Horton's suggestion turned to newcomer Hank

Thompson, who agreed to the deal and came to Nashville to star in their show, *Smoky Mountain Hayride*. It first aired September 11, 1948, over the Mutual network, with a rather eclectic cast of Thompson, Annie Lou and Danny Dill (who would later tour extensively with Tubb), black gospel stars the Fairfield Four, and a dixieland band. Thompson guested on the Opry and the *Midnite Jamboree* a good bit at the time.[3] He also hosted a six-day-a-week morning show on Nashville's WLAC with Donna Jean, a pop singer down from WLW in Cincinnati.[4]

Within the next few weeks, Hank Thompson made some far-reaching career decisions. Manager and mentor Hal Horton died on November 28, and *Billboard* reported Thompson's indecision about continuing *Smoky Mountain Hayride*.[5] Tubb tried to get Hank to stay in Nashville. They went to Grand Ole Opry manager Jim Denny, who agreed to give Thompson an Opry slot if he'd leave the *Smoky Mountain Hayride* and WLAC, which he did. How different country music history might have been: but Hank Thompson stayed on the Opry only until he saw the size of his first check. "After withholding, it came to less than $10.00—I think it was $9.40." Thompson quit the Opry, but before heading back to Waco to begin doing personal appearances, he ran into another Hank, MGM's Hank Williams, who couldn't believe Thompson's decision. "Man, Ernest Tubb got you on the Grand Ole Opry, and you're *leaving?* Some of us would kill for that!" To answer the other artists who would surely tell him the same thing, Thompson planned to frame his whopping $9.40 check, but says, "I needed the money too bad." He adds, "Back then, I just didn't feel at home on the Nashville music scene, though Ernest argued with me to stay. I didn't feel that I could have developed my music there: Nashville then didn't have the musicians to handle western swing the way I wanted to do it."[6] To which one of his biggest fans and backers, Tubb's niece Anna Ruth Collier Husky, replies, "He could have brought musicians! Ernest Tubb did! . . . I was crushed. I loved the Opry, and I was crushed that he wouldn't stay . . . Uncle Ernest didn't tell me that it [Hank's leaving the Opry] hurt him, but I'm sure it did."[7] But in a very real way, Hank Thompson has always expressed his gratitude for the help that his idol Ernest Tubb tried to give by recording several Tubb songs in his long association with Capitol Records.

HANK WILLIAMS

Second of our trinity of Hanks is the immortal Drifting Cowboy, Hiram "Hank" Williams, in all likelihood country music's most meteoric and charismatic star. While no one could maintain that Ernest Tubb was a huge factor in Williams's ascent, their paths crossed at several early points, and Tubb was the key Opry artist lobbying for Hank to be hired.

Charlie Walker says that Hank's first encounter with Tubb was in Fort Worth.

Williams had come over from Alabama with a group of teenagers selling magazines. They got as far west as Fort Worth when one of their party absconded with the money, leaving the rest to get back to Montgomery as best they could. Walking around one of the city parks with a friend, trying to figure out how they could get back, Williams saw a sign announcing a concert that day in that park by Ernest Tubb, the Gold Chain Troubadour. So he stayed and watched Ernest Tubb for the first time.

Not too many years later, when Hank had become a big enough star to tour with Tubb, he admitted to the great impact Tubb's music came to have after that first meeting: "I listened to that Grand Ole Opry, and I heard Roy Acuff, and I thought, man, that's the greatest thing I ever heard in my life. I learned to sing just like him . . . Then all of a sudden, here you come on there with that electric guitar, and I thought, my God, *that's* the greatest thing I've ever heard, right there. So then I started to sing just like *you.*" At that point, as Tubb recounted it in later years, Williams leaned over with a grin on his face and said, "You know what I finally done? I just got me a style right in between you two so-and-so's, and I kinda like it."[8]

Williams first got Ernest Tubb's attention at a concert where Tubb was the featured attraction. "He stole my show from me in 1943 in Montgomery. He was on the station down there, and he opened my show. You remember Uncle Joe Frank who brought me here? We'd use local radio talent to plug the show, I think Joe gave him $50 to plug the show on his radio show all that week, and be on our show. When he opened the stage show, he got about three encores . . . I told Joe, 'You'd better help this kid.' "[9] Frank responded, "I agree with you. He's got a lot of talent. But we can't get him to straighten out. He's got a little problem—drinking problem."[10] This was the hurdle Williams would have to clear with Opry management, even after he had one of 1949's biggest hits with "Lovesick Blues."

On his trips to Nashville up from Shreveport to make records or to do business with his publishers Acuff-Rose, Williams came by the Ernest Tubb Record Shop to enlist Tubb's help in getting on the Opry. It was on one of those visits that he chastised Hank Thompson for walking away from the chance he was dying to get. Shop clerk Dollie Dearman remembered her first encounter with an almost recognizable Hank Williams about this time. "It was a Saturday on Commerce Street. This fellow came in with a felt hat, a shirt with a collar open, and dark trousers. He was sorta stoop-shouldered. He said, 'Is Ernest Tubb here? I'm Hank Williams.' I thought, 'Hank Williams—sure!' I said, 'Well, let me go see.' I knew Ernest was there; we had an office in the back. And I said, 'Ernest, there's somebody up there who says he's Hank Williams.' And he said, 'Let me take a peep.' And sure enough, it was."[11]

By the spring of 1949, Williams, who was tearing up the crowds every week at Shreveport's *Louisiana Hayride,* could no longer be ignored by the Opry if it wanted to remain the nation's foremost country music program. He had several powerful lobbyists on his behalf: his publisher Fred Rose and artists besides Tubb who also brought back to Nashville accounts of Williams's new-found sobriety. Tubb, Red Foley, Cowboy Copas, Minnie Pearl, and Rod Brasfield had (in various combinations) played some Oklahoma and Texas show dates with Williams in April and May 1949, just as "Lovesick Blues" was so hot for the Shreveport star, and they'd seen a change in Hank.

"It took me a year to get the power people to bring him in to the Grand Ole Opry," Tubb remembered.[12] What finally got Hank in the Opry's door? A sobriety promise: they didn't need anyone else with Tubb's problem. "Give me three months. Promise me you won't drink for three months." Tubb got the promise, and, as he told the story in later years, Williams was even better than his word. "And he did for eleven. Everybody grew to love him. I figured if he could stay there three months he could show them what he could do, and the people—he'd have so many fans they'd be a little more tolerant of him. They wouldn't kick him off if he took a drink. But I told him, 'Don't tell me you'll quit forever, just say you'll do it for three months.' "[13] Tubb was the one who first introduced Williams to an Opry audience, on the June 11, 1949, Warren Paint Opry segment,[14] and events soon followed Tubb's script, as Hank rose to Opry stardom.

On the road or at the Opry, Hank often offered Ernest his latest song creations. Tubb recalled: "Every song he wrote after I met him, he didn't want to record it. He wanted me to record it. You know what? The one regret I have—he wanted so bad for me to sing one of his songs, record one, and I never did, as long as he lived. Cause every time he'd write one, it'd be too good for him. I'd say, 'No, Hank. It's good, but you gotta record it. That's your song.' "[15] "Every song he wrote" reflects exaggeration in Tubb's account; surely part of Hank's motivation (he used the same ploy on other artists) was to find out if a particular song was any good. Even so, the anecdote highlights Hank's high regard for Tubb.

In Williams's short career, he recorded three Ernest Tubb songs for radio transcription that were released posthumously: "First Year Blues," "It Just Don't Matter Now," and "I'm Free at Last." Beyond these, he clearly "borrowed" the melody of "Time after Time," the Short Brothers' song cut by Tubb in 1941, for his own "Never Again Will I Knock on Your Door." And in the last few weeks of his life, Williams admitted to two Tubb relatives that for one of his final great creations, "Your Cheating Heart," he had borrowed Ernest Tubb's great image of walking the floor. The Tubb cousins, Justin and Douglas Glenn, were his guests for what may have been his final show, at the Skyline Club in Austin, and "Your Cheating Heart" wasn't even on the market yet when he sang them this song (and

"Kaw-Liga") and made the admission. "I stole a line from your daddy, Justin. 'You'll walk the floor, the way I do. Your cheatin' heart will tell on you.' "[16]

Hank helped himself to Tubb's melodies and images, but he felt free to ask Tubb for advice, which was given unstintingly. Hank asked Ernest about the retail business. When he and wife Audrey thought about opening a Western clothing store in Nashville, they asked Ernest how much money he was losing in the Record Shop. " 'In the first two years, I lost $10,000 a year.' 'Well, that won't be too bad, if I only lose $20,000.' "[17] So on June 16, 1951, they opened their Hank & Audrey's Corral, close to Tubb's Record Shop. Jerry Rivers remembers, "Hank and Audrey put their Western clothing store right down by it, and they would plug each other . . . That's why Hank and Audrey put their shop there, to draw upon all those folks walking around between the Opry and the Record Shop. If Hank and Audrey hadn't had their problems, that might have been as big as the Record Shop, because there were no other clothiers then. There'd have been no Alamo, or Loretta Lynn [The Alamo and Loretta Lynn's Western Wear, later Nashville Clothiers]."[18]

Tubb was also free with personal advice. Hank's biographer Colin Escott says that Tubb was one of the few people that Hank opened up to about his drinking problem. Williams's fiddler Jerry Rivers is sure of it: "I always thought Ernest was like a big brother to Hank. I didn't hear these conversations, but I got the feeling that Ernest's point to Hank when he'd get drunk was, 'Hey, I tried that, and I didn't get anywhere . . . You're not gonna get anywhere doing that. Take it from one who knows . . . Boy, you're gonna be big, but you can kill it.' "[19] Hank, who wanted to stay sober so badly, even asked Ernest if he should take a dangerous medical cure.

> He hated drinking, and he wanted to take this cure. You'd take this medicine, and you had to carry a letter in your pocket. If you're taking this medicine and you take a drink, if you don't get to a hospital quick enough it'll kill you. He asked me if he should do it, take this cure. I told him, "This you have to decide, 'cause if I advise you to do it and you get off some place late at night and you fall off the wagon, and start drinking, you could wind up dead and I'd feel responsible." He knew he was an alcoholic. Then it dawned on him.[20]

Well, Hank didn't take the cure, and by and large he couldn't stay sober. Rivers said, "Yes, Ernest was probably disappointed with the way Hank's career went. But there wasn't anything he could do. Hank wouldn't go out drinking with them, or with anybody else. He'd go off by himself: out on the road somewhere, or up at the Tulane Hotel . . . He was a loner."[21] When Jim Denny finally fired Hank

Williams from the Opry cast in August 1952, Tubb was in Denny's office when he placed the call to Hank at his Natchez Trace residence. "When I was in the parking lot, I ran into Mr. Craig (National Life chairman Edwin Craig, the insurance company that owned WSM and the Opry). He knew, and he said, 'What do you think, Ernest?' I said, 'Well, I hate it, but I saw tears in Jim's eyes . . . He told me he was going to try to get Hank to straighten up.' Mr. Craig said, 'I'm sure Jim means well, but it may work the other way. It may kill him.' I was feeling the same way."[22] Less than five months later, Hank Williams was dead of heart failure related to his alcoholism.

HANK SNOW

Third and last chronologically of the three Hanks to whom Ernest Tubb reached out a helping hand—and the one for whom that hand did the most lasting good— was a Canadian star and fellow Jimmie Rodgers disciple, Clarence Eugene "Hank" Snow. After years of hard knocks climbing the professional ladder in his native Nova Scotia, Snow finally won a Canadian reputation as "Hank, the Yodelling Ranger," but he found it nearly impossible to win a following in the United States. He got nowhere with ventures to Wheeling in 1944 and California in 1947, each time having to recoup his fortunes by going home to Canada. Finally, the American offices of his record company, RCA Victor, relented and issued some of his records in the U.S. market, and Snow's foray to Dallas in late 1948 and early 1949 found a fairly receptive audience.

On February 2, 1949, as a $25 extra act on a show at Fort Worth's North Side Coliseum, Snow finally met one of his favorite American stars and his long-time correspondent, Ernest Tubb. Snow loved the music of Ernest Tubb from the day he heard "Try Me One More Time" and "You Nearly Lose Your Mind." "I could hear the Opry in eastern Canada pretty well . . . So I wrote to him care of the Grand Ole Opry and got a nice letter back, and from that we corresponded. Not frequently, but probably a couple of times a year."[23] Snow says in his recent autobiography that he "mailed Ernest a couple of my Canadian records."[24] One of Snow's wartime recordings was of Tubb's great "Soldier's Last Letter."

Awed by finally meeting Tubb, Snow was immediately put at his ease in conversation. "Very, very polite and very, very friendly . . . It just seemed like I had known him all my life." After letting Snow play his famous Jimmie Rodgers guitar, Tubb talked about the situation in Nashville. Tubb told him he was on a leave of absence from the Grand Ole Opry, heading for the West Coast with his guitarist Butterball Paige (to record with the Andrews Sisters, among other things); would he, Snow, like to fill in for him at the Opry in his absence? The offer took Snow's breath away, but Opry manager Jim Denny and Harry Stone (WSM station manager) wouldn't go for it.[25] Tubb phoned them long distance, argued, cajoled; he even had his Record Shop send them copies of Snow's records. "Well, what do you think?" Tubb asked Harry Stone a couple of days later. Stone's only comment was, "He sounds too much like you." "Ah, don't give me that stuff. I'm talking long distance and I'm spending my money. I'll argue with you when I get home. He sings like he's a Jimmie Rodgers fan—same type of thing I do. But with that Canadian brogue he can't sound like me."[26]

Their debate continued. Snow remained largely unknown in the United States, though the Dallas area had warmed to his "Brand on My Heart." In June of 1949, Tubb recorded a Hank Snow song in the vein of his earlier hit, "Filipino Baby," called "My Filipino Rose." Snow says of this in his autobiography, "I went around telling everybody, 'The great Ernest Tubb has recorded my song.' That really gave me a completely new outlook on life. I wasn't thinking about the royalties I'd get as writer, I was thinking about how Ernest was a true friend to me. He didn't have to record my song. There were hundreds of good songs being written, and because of his popularity he was being pitched songs by the best writers and publishing companies in the country. Besides, Ernest was a real good writer himself, and he could make more money by recording his own songs. It was a great feeling to know that such an unselfish person was working on my behalf, and I was confident that, if it was in the stars for me to get on the Grand Ole Opry, Ernest would be the one to make it happen."[27]

By year's end, Snow's recording of Jenny Lou Carson's "Marriage Vow" made a one-week appearance on *Billboard*'s best-seller chart (December 31, 1949). Just about that time, Snow's phone rang in Dallas; it was Ernest Tubb in Nashville. "I believe I've got you placed on the Grand Ole Opry. Can you come up here right away?" "Just as fast as my car will bring me there." He met Ernest at the Record Shop, and they went to WSM for two interviews: one with Jim Denny, and one with the Opry's network producer Jack Stapp. Denny agreed to give Snow a chance and to throw in a publicity campaign—a press kit for radio stations, promoters, and talent buyers, and ads in all of the key trade papers.[28]

Snow's first Opry appearance came exactly one week after his chart debut: January 7, 1950. The payment of $75 per week (far better than Hank Thompson's union scale) seemed to Snow a bonanza, but the lukewarm Opry audience response to his first few shows discouraged Hank almost to the point of quitting. Snow's wife Min talked him out of it: "You can't quit now. You can't let Ernest down. Give it a try at least. Ernest has done a lot here for you and it would be a big disappointment for him."[29]

Hank didn't quit, and Ernest Tubb did all he could, giving Snow appearances on his *Midnite Jamboree* and plugging his records over the airwaves. But the Opry bosses were not impressed with Snow's early efforts: Tubb, on a Northwestern tour, had to ride the long distance phone again. "Hell, it took me a year to get you to hire him. You can't fire him yet. Wait until I get back."[30] For all of Tubb's efforts, Snow would have been fired anyway had not his record of "I'm Moving On" hit when it did (chart debut July 1, 1950). "It hit right then, it was perfect timing. I've been there ever since, thanks to one song, and with a big boost from Ernest Tubb."[31]

A terrific country music career was finally off and running, and the two men forged a lasting friendship, almost a partnership. Later chapters will show just how much the two men had in common, particularly in the 1950s: a famous joint trek to Korea; cofounding the Jimmie Rodgers festivities in Meridian; shared management for a time by Dub Albritten; a joint investment in a pair of radio stations with WSM's Bill McDaniel; and Snow's partial emulation of Ernest Tubb the businessman, with his 1958 opening of the Hank Snow Music Center.

17

Out of the Doldrums: The Comeback of 1949

Early in 1949 Tubb "cleaned house" in terms of his Texas Troubadours. Sometime shortly after his January 23–24, 1949, Nashville recording session (if those dates are right: they could be postdated strike sessions), steel guitarist Don Davis, fiddler Hal Smith, his wife, Velma Williams (rhythm guitar), and even Jack Drake were let go, on the advice of manager Oscar Davis. More properly, they were given away: shipped en masse to Grand Ole Opry newcomer George Morgan to become his first band. None of the musicians had hard feelings: Drake, in fact, was confident that he'd get another chance. Hal Smith remembers him saying, "Well, I'll just wait by the phone."[1]

With all of Tubb's financial reverses of the previous year, the absent salaries and reduced travel expenses for a time were propitious. Driving with Butterball Paige in a single car to most of their dates, Tubb hired local musicians to handle steel, bass, and rhythm. Musicians all over the country were playing Ernest Tubb songs anyway, so he wasn't taking much of a chance that they wouldn't know his repertory.

Tubb and Butterball drove westward toward California for tour dates at the end of January and all through February; for the new year, Tubb was taking his summer leave of absence in the late winter. In Texas on the way, they played Fort Worth's North Side Coliseum and met Hank Snow for the first time. In California, besides tour dates, they were booked for a mid-February recording session with the Andrews Sisters. Decca Records was famous for pairing up the company's roster in creative ways to sell more records, which of course made economic sense; if done so as not to offend either artist's fans, you could sell the record to both sets. The plans had been to record Tubb with Decca's Mr. Big, Bing Crosby. But when Tubb and Paige got to California, Crosby was away on a hunting expedition. Dave Kapp suggested the Andrews Sisters as an alternative, and Tubb was ready: he'd brought a song with him from a country group, the Range Riders in Cleveland, Ohio, called "I'm Bitin' My Fingernails and Thinking of You." Their leader and one of the song's co-writers, Ernie Benedict, had just recorded it for Victor; it probably helped that they were Hill & Range affiliated.

Countriest of the two arrangements was their cover version of Eddy Arnold's big hit, "Don't Rob Another Man's Castle." The second verse of "I'm Biting My Fingernails and Thinking of You," sung by the Andrews, emphasized their sound and style. The record was issued in the pop series, used the Andrews' regular producer Victor Schoen, and gave them top billing: "The Andrews Sisters & Ernest Tubb." But looking back on it in later years, Tubb was adamant that "I wasn't gonna sing and try to make a pop record with their music—they had to sing and make a country record with me." It was a matter of necessity, as Tubb explains: "I had the sheet music, and really I learned the thing by ear—I learned it from a record—and I wasn't singing from the copy. And they were singing note for note off the sheet music, and finally they said, 'We got two different tunes here.' I said, 'You better change y'all's, then, cause I can't read that thing.' So Patty just threw the music away and said, 'Let's learn it from Ernest.' So they learned the way I was doing it and they did it."[2]

Tubb was back on the Opry by the late spring, and before June he'd made the call and rehired his old bass player, Jack Drake. Publicity photos made early that year show only Tubb and Butterball; by midyear, Jack joined up to make it a trio. By the date of his next recording session (June 12, 1949), Tubb had added two other musicians: a fine young steel player named Dickie Harris, and (of all things) a mandolinist, Clarence "Mack" McGarr. Harris was a Nashvillian, barely nineteen at the time of the session, but already a veteran of the Paul Howard and Robert Lunn bands on the Opry and of morning radio shows with Tubb's former guitarist, Zeb Turner. Except for a six-month hiatus in Miami later that year, Harris would be Tubb's steel player for almost seven years. Kentucky-born Mack McGarr was a great musician (once a featured fiddler on the Prince Albert Opry and part of Owen Bradley's staff band on Tubb's *Opry House Matinee*), but he was in poor health. Tubb hired him both for musical and humanitarian reasons.

> This was one of the things you do because you like someone and the man wasn't in too good health, and I wanted to give him work. I didn't want the fiddle . . . so I said, "Mack, can you play something else? Play mandolin." So I let him play on "Warm Red Wine," and this was one of the highlights of his life. He said, ". . . I've been playing all my life, and this is the first time anybody ever called my name on a record." And he was just thrilled to death. He didn't live too long after that . . . He had

asthma so bad he couldn't hardly breathe. He went west and it was too late. He started having hemorrhages and finally came back home and died.[3]

BROWN-EYED OLENE[4]

By the time of the June 12 session, Tubb had something to sing about: a brand new bride. On June 3, he married Olene (sometimes "Olean") Adams Carter, like himself divorced, but only twenty-three years old (to Tubb's thirty-five). They tied the knot in Rossville, Georgia, just across the Tennessee state line, where a lot of Tennesseans made "quickie" marriages.

In a 1965 interview Olene gave this account of their first meeting: "I wrote to the Record Shop for a song book, and I ended up with Ernest. It was a hot day, I had been out cutting grass, and I was in the middle of washing my hair when the telephone rang and it was Ernest. We talked, and he wanted to meet me right there and then, but there I was with my hair all streaming down wet, and had to tell him no." Reporter Dixie Deen narrates the rest of the story: "Ernest, by some sixth sense however, seemed to know this was the girl for him, and wouldn't take no for an answer. He drove right on over, met Olene (complete with streaming wet hair), fell in love with her, and five months later down in Georgia, they tied the knot."[5] Five months must be a slight underestimate: she wouldn't have been cutting grass in January.

Some members of his family he told of his impending nuptials, and some he didn't. Tubb niece Anna Ruth Collier had gone back to Texas after the Ernest-Elaine split, and with help from Uncle Ernest and his friend Hal Horton found work in the fall of 1948 in a Dallas store, The Record Shop, on Main and Ackerd Streets. When her uncle, with Cowboy Copas, Red Foley, and Hank Williams (over from the *Louisiana Hayride*) came to Dallas for a big Sportatorium show on May 4, 1949, they found time for an autograph session at her shop. This was only weeks before Tubb's remarriage, but to Anna Ruth, Tubb said not one word about Olene or their upcoming marriage. And yet she remembers that Olene flew out to California to meet him for a premarital rendezvous about this time, and also to San Antonio to meet Ernest's mother, Mrs. Ashton, for her approval.

What were Ernest's children told in advance of Olene? "Nothing," says Justin Tubb bitterly. "We knew nothing about her. She just, all of a sudden, there she was. I think we came back one Christmas, and the next summer we came up, they were married. Maybe [at Christmas] she stayed out of the way or something, because I only stayed for ten days or so . . . But anyway, she was a complete culture shock to us."[6]

The fan club published no report of the marriage for some six months.

Norma Barthel's report in the winter 1950 *Melody Trails* says: "We are happy to let you know that Ernest Tubb married lovely Olene Carter, of Old Hickory, Tennessee, a few months ago . . . We hear that Olene is mighty sweet and we're sure she is or Ernie wouldn't have picked her. Right?"[7]

For his own part, Tubb was proud to the point of gloating about his "new mama," and poured it into song. "My Tennessee Baby" became the immediate hit song of the June 12, 1949, session. Written some time before the actual marriage, the song contains a Jimmie Rodgers reference: "T for Texas, T for Tennessee / my Tennessee baby's put her brand on me. / We're gonna get married, and it won't be long, / if I can convince her where we should make our home." Tubb's home demo of a song he never commercially recorded, "Brand New Mama," is even more gloating.[8]

But things weren't immediately rosy for the new couple. Billy Byrd recalls, "There were about seven or eight months that I didn't think they were going to make it. And after about seven or eight months she got him curled under that little finger and she told him when to breathe. And no matter what Red Foley, or Cowboy Copas, or any of his close friends would tell him or say, or Vito, no matter who told it, her word come first."[9]

On April 11, 1949, almost two months before the marriage and undoubtedly looking ahead to it, Ernest Tubb paid $12,000 cash for a home and lot at 331 Lawndale Drive, Glencliff Estates in suburban Nashville. Over the next eighteen months, the new couple spent $4,850 on short-term notes to buy four adjacent lots.[10] For seventeen years, as they brought five children into the world, this was their home. Song tapes, awards, fan's gifts, and other assorted memorabilia forced them to seek more space in 1966,[11] although the Lawndale property remains in the family at this writing.

A NEW LEAD GUITARIST

Ernest Tubb's secretive and abrupt remarriage was handled the way it was, niece Ruth Husky theorizes, to avoid negative publicity. Neither party was underaged, the usual reason for Tennessee couples to marry out of state, but of course each had been divorced. With Nashville media's legendary neglect in those days of country musicians, one wonders why they bothered to be secretive; but if the purpose was to avoid possible scandal at the time, they certainly succeeded. The same cannot be said of Herbert McBride "Butterball" Paige's woman troubles, which finally got him fired by Tubb.

Paige was single, living then at Delia "Mom" Upchurch's Boscobel Street rooming house, which became famous as the first Nashville home of so many struggling hillbilly musicians. But his short, round frame and winsome personality won him a good many female admirers. Tubb teased him about it with stage comments during his instrumental breaks: "Aw, come in there, Butterball . . . We call him 'Nature Boy.' . . . He's a cute little rascal, ain't he?" Paige, who'd been out of the Texas Troubadours once before (between 1944 and 1947), clearly kept an eye out to once again lead his own band; even in Tubb's presence, he'd ask venue owners to hire him.

All this Tubb would have continued to tolerate, though: Paige played the key instrument, and played it well. But only days after the very successful June 12, 1949, session, Butterball was gone, victimized unfairly, some feel, because of the unsought attentions of a married woman: Connie, wife of Grand Ole Opry newcomer Jimmy Dickens. "Ernest told him to stay away from her, and I think Ball was actually right; he said, 'Now, I'm not having anything to do with her, but she comes on to me all the time.' "[12]

Fired in June, Butterball promptly landed on his feet with a contract to record for Bullet Records. His new band, the Red River Boys, consisted of steel guitarist Dickie Harris, plus Ken Custer on bass, Randy Hughes on guitar (future Patsy Cline manager and pilot), and Roy Justice on fiddle. Manager Murray Rose found regular work for the band in Miami[13]—on TV station WTVJ, at the Biscayne Palace club, and on a Sunday afternoon sightseeing boat. Unfortunately, these plush gigs lasted only a few months. Harris left the band at year's end to go back to his native Nashville and rejoin Tubb. Butterball bounced from radio work in Baltimore (1950) to Raleigh (1951), then back to Baltimore for a job on WMAR-TV. There he joined two of Tubb's other ex-lead guitarists, Jimmie Short and Zeb Turner. Paige remained in the Baltimore area for the rest of his life.

Nashville-born jazz guitarist William Lewis "Billy" Byrd, who had played the Opry for years on either side of World War II naval duty with a number of artists (Herald Goodman, Sarie and Sally, Paul Howard, Bradley Kincaid, Jimmy Dickens, George Morgan), was just back in town from Shreveport work for Curley Kinsey and Curly Williams when he asked Ernest Tubb for a job in the summer of 1949. Though bereft of Butterball, Ernest was reluctant to hire him, Billy remembers, because he had his eye instead on a Detroit guitarist. Ernest asked his right-hand man, bassist Jack Drake, if Billy could do the job. "Well, the boy can play real fine guitar, play jazz and all of that, real fine guitar. But he couldn't cut your part. He couldn't do your, there's no way in the world he could play like that." Fortunately for Billy (and ultimately for Ernest), he decided, "Well, the boy seemed real sincere. I think I'll give him a shot at it." Just before leaving town on a West Coast tour with Red Foley and his men Grady Martin and Billy Robinson, Tubb told Byrd to go down to the record shop, take all of his records home, "and see if you can learn a few of them."[14] Ten years later, Billy Byrd was still Ernest Tubb's guitarist.

Billy's first Ernest Tubb session came late that August, when he and Jack Drake, a rehired Don Davis (Dickie was gone with Butterball, remember) a rhythm guitarist (probably Jack Shook), and a vocal group called the Beasley Sisters (Alcyone Bate Beasley, Evelyn Wilson, and one other) helped Tubb record what became a seasonal classic, "Blue Christmas." The song had been around a couple of years without making a big splash for any of the artists who cut it, Doye O'Dell and Riley Shepard among them (the ban prevented any 1948 versions). Flip side of the record and the only other song on the Tubb session was Irving Berlin's "White Christmas," which Tubb had tried to record back in 1947. It was then much better known than "Blue Christmas," and accordingly was treated by Decca as the record's A side.

The smooth female harmony sound was a throwback to the Andrews Sisters duets from earlier that year, and also presaged much of that sort of thing in coming years: a favorite Owen Bradley touch. It sure worked this time: Tubb's "Blue Christmas" was a runaway hit, reaching number 1 on the jukebox charts, in competition with two Gene Autry records ("Here Comes Santa Claus" and a new thing called "Rudolph, the Red-Nosed Reindeer"). The country Christmas tradition had been born. For Tubb, "Blue Christmas" would hit again each of the next two yuletides.

The newlywed worked himself to the point of exhaustion that fall, touring the West Coast with one of the first Opry troupes to go out there in September (Tubb himself had of course worked the Coast several times as a soloist, on movie or recording trips). *Billboard* mentions that he was coming off several weeks of "complete rest" in mid-October. Maybe "complete" is an exaggeration, because while he rested up for recording work scheduled in early November, Ernest Tubb took his first and last major fling at being a celebrity disc jockey.

Beginning October 25, 1949, and running until late April of the following year, *Ernest Tubb's Record Roundup* with Tubb and Jerry "Tex" Thomas aired weekday afternoons from 3:00 to 4:00 P.M. on Nashville's WMAK (and at other hours on several outlying stations in syndication). As a record shop proprietor and *Midnite Jamboree* host, besides his credentials as a singing star, Tubb was uniquely qualified to offer opinions on the top country hits and artists of the day, and on this show that's exactly what he did, in a freewheeling, fun format. Justin Tubb, up from San Antonio for a Christmas holiday visit at the end of 1949, remembers that a week's worth of shows was transcribed at one session, minus the actual playing of records, which was always dubbed in later. For Justin particularly, the show was fortuitous, since Jerry Thomas later became his first radio boss, hiring him for disc jockey work in 1953 at WHIN in Gallatin.

The main thing this break in Ernest Tubb's touring schedule afforded was preparation for a big recording session. Paul Cohen came to Nashville for another series of Decca recording sessions early in November 1949, just before his other main Decca act in Nashville, Red Foley, led an Opry gang to Europe over Thanksgiving. In keeping with the experimental bent that had seen Tubb record with the Andrews Sisters and then do Christmas songs, there were more surprises on tap for these Tulane Hotel sessions. Even *Billboard* knew something was afoot, but their guess or source of information was wrong: they reported in the October 15 issue that "Tubb will do a kiddie album for Decca."[15] It would have been interesting; a home recording exists of Tubb singing "Go 'Long Mule" for his baby daughter, Scooter Bill. The burgeoning crop of baby boomers might have made for nice sales. But Paul Cohen had other plans for Tubb, just as far from the norm and equally intriguing.

Tubb's ensemble, slightly different for each session this busy year, consisted in November of Billy Byrd on lead guitar, Don Helms on steel, Mack McGarr back on mandolin, Jack Drake on bass, and Dale Potter on fiddle. At least this was the lineup for Tubb's three solo recordings: "Letters Have No Arms," "Throw Your Love My Way," and "I'll Take a Back Seat for You," a new Tubb composition.

RELIGIOUS RECORDINGS: DECCA'S FAITH SERIES

One of the two major studio experiments by Tubb that week was the making of six religious recordings on the last day of the sessions (November 10). Word apparently came down from Decca's New York office to include the label's two main country stars, Ernest Tubb and Red Foley, in what they would call the Faith Series. *Billboard* reported on the project in its March 4, 1950, issue.[16] Decca in this instance pioneered the incursion of the straight country singer into sacred material in a big way. For decades after this, most of them would record at least one "sacred" album, and Tubb and Red Foley were the trailblazers in that regard.

From his control room seat at the November sessions, Tubb was touched by his favorite of the Foley recordings, the Negro spiritual and recitation, "Steal Away," whose recitation Hank Williams later as Luke the Drifter called "The Funeral." Foley, singing with his eyes closed and unaware of the presence of anyone else, had Tubb, Cohen, and his own wife Eva in tears.[17]

Tubb, by contrast, did not seem as comfortable with the six sacred songs that he sang. Maybe it was too much of a departure for him. Gospel or hymn material never shows up on his earlier Grand Ole Opry performance logs, or on the earliest *Midnite Jamboree* shows that were recorded. Ernest Tubb was a Southwestern jukebox singer who just wasn't turned that way. Consequently, Tubb's sacred releases weren't big sellers: they didn't click with Tubb's normal jukebox market. Interestingly, Tubb's measure of Foley's greatness as a sacred singer was the fact that Red's records *did* make it, "onto every jukebox in the country."[18]

Maybe religious recordings by Ernest Tubb was not such a great idea. But Paul Cohen had one more trick up his sleeve for the November 1949 sessions, which worked quite well: a pair of duets, the first of some seventeen over a four-year period, by Ernest Tubb and Red Foley.

THE TUBB-FOLEY DUETS

The two men had a lot in common: the Grand Ole Opry, a fondness for booze, Decca contracts, and links to Hill & Range, the Aberbach brothers' publishing empire. But they were also very different: Foley's trained voice always tempted him to go pop, a problem Ernest never had. This alone made pairing them on duets a chancy venture. Perhaps for that reason only two songs were cut on their first session: "Tennessee Border No. 2," Homer and Jethro's reworking of Foley's big hit of that year, and Cindy Walker's "Don't Be Ashamed of Your Age," which Bob Wills had recorded for MGM in 1947.

Both songs are pure fun, lacking the tone of mock acrimony that came to characterize later Tubb-Foley recordings. This first record was issued November 14, 1949—a scant six days after the probable session date, which indicates how high Decca's hopes were pinned on their all-star country pairing. *Billboard* hailed the Tubb-Foley duets with a cover photo of the two men at a Decca microphone placed on the Ryman Auditorium stage for the December 10, 1949, issue.

While by hindsight we can say that both men's November 1949 solo material outshone the duets, this initial pairing was popular enough to justify their recording of fifteen more songs (fourteen of them released) between 1950 and 1953. And as these first examples already made clear, putting Ernest Tubb and Red Foley together on records seems such a natural move—their chemistry was so good—that one wonders why Decca with its duet history didn't try it sooner. The two were obviously great friends who enjoyed singing together, and the contrast in voices and styles, though great, somehow pleased. Tubb's deep, drawling baritone is unable to contain the chuckles over Foley's best lines; Red, on the other hand, showcases that smooth, trained voice that slipped easily into boogie or pop styles. Foley covered the harmony parts every time. In fact, Tubb never sang a harmony part on any duet, whether with the Andrews Sisters, Foley, or on later ones with the Wilburn Brothers and Loretta Lynn. Though he knew his basic guitar chords and could master a melody by ear, Tubb could neither read music—something he always admitted with pride—nor find harmony.

In the great show business tradition of Burns and Benny, Hope and Crosby, country's only comparable "friendly rivalry" was born. As the years passed this carried over into Grand Ole Opry performances, Red Foley's drop-in appearances on Tubb's *Midnite Jamboree,* and even into the days of Red's *Ozark Jubilee* TV work, well past the four years of their joint recordings. Foley would have greater commercial success later with Kitty Wells, as Tubb did much later with Loretta Lynn. But their joint recordings helped to cement a lifelong friendship and gave fans of each man a glimpse of just how versatile they could be.

When it was over Ernest Tubb could look back on 1949 as a real turnaround or comeback year. He had a new home, a new wife, a new band lineup, and the best year of his career in terms of chart records (eleven different songs).[19]

Small wonder that fan club president Norma Barthel could write in her fall 1949 *Melody Trails,* under a new Tubb photo, "I thought you might like this new pose of Ernest Tubb, 'cause I sure do! It's so nice to see him looking so happy these days and he reports that he feels wonderful, too. Maybe that accounts for those extra nice records he has been turning out lately—reckon?"[20] Yes, Ernest Tubb and his fans had a lot to be smiling about as the 1950s began, large with promise.

18

Good Songs and Good Times

For all the accomplishments of the forties, all the great songs and the hard-won national prominence, Ernest Tubb still had things to prove and obstacles to overcome. But with a new wife, a new purposefulness, and a new streamlined show band, the 1950s began for the Texas Troubadour full of promise, hope, and determination.

By and large, Ernest Tubb did not disappoint his growing body of fans. The early 1950s were good years for Ernest Tubb and good years for country music as a whole, with a wave of new young talent and a commercial prosperity heretofore untasted. Because of this, looking only at Tubb's record chart listings gives a distorted picture of his true performance. Yes, Tubb's records in the 1940s generally rose higher in the charts and stayed there longer. But by the early 1950s there was a raft of younger competition, while the various trade paper country charts still limited their coverage to fifteen or twenty songs. Weaker chart performance by itself does not prove a career slump.

Tubb's mounting competition for record success is illustrated by a comment *Billboard* reported in November 1952: "Carl Shook, WKYW Louisville veteran, did a little private research. Between May 8 and October 8, 1952, Shook received 440 new country and western records, 880 sides, which averages to six new sides per day. Shook feels that this over-releasing is not giving the DJ a chance to air all the good tunes sufficiently to really give them a public test."[1] Besides burying the newcomers on independent labels—a fate Tubb fought with his *Midnite Jamboree*—the glut to which Shook refers hurt even the big stars. Tubb was one of its victims in terms of chart popularity, though his records sold almost as well as ever. Niece Ruth Husky remembers Tubb telling her that his sales were so consistent, Decca didn't even bother to itemize individual records on the royalty statements they sent him—one sold as many as another,[2] and the figure was consistently high.

RECORDINGS 1950–1952

Though overshadowed by his own earliest hits even more than by the work of younger "competitors" like Hank Williams, Hank Snow, Lefty Frizzell, and Carl Smith, Ernest Tubb's Decca recordings from the early 1950s nevertheless included some of his very best work.

Tubb wrote very little in those years, but the last few songs from his pen were good ones, "I'll Take a Back Seat for You" and "Give Me a Little Old Fashioned Love" especially. Of the songs he accepted from other writers, one recurring theme was a fondness for "baby" songs. His own first baby, son Justin, by this point a teenager with an obvious musical flair himself, suggested to his dad during summer vacation visits to Nashville certain songs he thought appropriate for his father's style. Ernest took Justin's advice on a couple of baby songs, and listening to them now one has to say that Justin was right, although their chart success was limited at the time.

The first was a cover version of a pop song by Bob Merrill and Terry Shand that Moon Mullican had previously recorded in the country field, "You Don't Have to Be a Baby to Cry." Red Foley attended the 1950 session at which Tubb recorded it, chatting in the control room with producer Paul Cohen. Speaking of the recurring low note in the song, Cohen ribbed Foley, "Don't you wish you could do that?" Foley, one of country music's few trained singers at the time and Tubb's great friend and duet partner, rejoined "Don't he wish *he* could do that?" Years later, Tubb told that story on himself with great good humor.[3] In all honesty, Tubb's reach for that low note comes up a little bit short, but Ernest Tubb fans were and are very forgiving on that score. Another baby song that Justin successfully lobbied his famous father to record was Lee Roberts's "Precious Little Baby," a great song and done by Tubb in fine fashion.

As with "You Don't Have to Be a Baby to Cry," a good many of Tubb's best songs in the early 1950s (really, ever since about 1946) were cover versions of songs other artists had out on records first. All the major stars did this in those days of a song-driven record industry: hit songs of the day, pop or country, were usually recorded by half a dozen artists, each label determined to get a piece of a good song's action. A song Tubb cut that originated in the country market but that certainly got pop covers was Stuart Hamblen's big hit, "(Remember Me) I'm the One Who Loves You." Its appeal for Tubb and his producer Paul Cohen—besides being simply a great love song, one of the best ever written—was in all probability the low note on the word "one," reminiscent of the drop in Tubb's own "You Nearly Lose Your Mind" and his more recent cover of "You Don't Have to Be a Baby to Cry."

Tubb had more of a conscience about the practice of covering hits than some other artists showed. He consistently tried to give a record time to sell all that it was going to sell for the original artist, especially if that artist was a struggling newcomer. As proprietor of the nation's main country record store, Tubb was in a position to know when a record's sales had peaked. An early 1950s example was Arthur Q. Smith's "Missing in Action." Smith, the pen name of Knoxvillian James Arthur Pritchett, was one of country music's best songwriters (surreptitious writer of Tubb's huge hit, "Rainbow at Midnight"), but owing to his penchant for selling his best songs for ready cash, his name almost never shows up on a country record label. When Tubb chose to cover Jim Eanes's Blue Ridge record of Smith's Korean War ballad, "Missing in Action," Smith's name actually appeared on the release. It had *not* been listed on Eanes's Blue Ridge record, which was actually a big regional hit.[4]

Young Texan Ray Price had a song out on Columbia that same year (1951) which he co-wrote, entitled "Hey La La," a sad lament for a deceased lover. Tubb chose to record the song for Decca with help from one of the first vocal choruses he ever used on records; Price had done it the same way, so this was not an innovation on Tubb's part. No doubt young Price welcomed the royalties that Tubb's cut brought him, but this was only the beginning of Tubb's helping Price, about which more in due course.

Not only was Ernest Tubb fond of songs about babies in the early 1950s, be they kids or sweethearts, he even had a favorite songwriter who went by the nickname "Baby." She was Babia "Baby" Stewart Howard, part of the singing Stewart Family based on station KLCN in Blytheville, Arkansas, and who, for a time, recorded with Four Star. She co-wrote "Heart, Please Be Still" with Butterball in the late 1940s, and her two fine contributions to the Tubb career were the 1950 "I Need Attention Bad" and Tubb's 1952 release, "I Will Miss You When You Go."

Another Ernest Tubb friend and contact in the northeastern Arkansas community of Blytheville during these years was a singer-writer-disc jockey also on KLCN, Don Whitney, whose song "Don't Stay Too Long" Tubb recorded in 1951. Whitney, who, like the Stewarts, recorded then for Bill McCall's Four Star Records, booked Tubb into Blytheville for performances, including one during Blytheville's National Cotton Picking Contest in October 1951. Danny Dill of Annie Lou and Danny, who were fronting Tubb's entourage for that trip, remembers this show because a man walked out of the arena right past the security guards with Tubb's guitar. The guitar later turned up, but the thief never did.[5]

Writers who had or would have considerably more name recognition than Whitney or the Stewarts placed songs with Ernest Tubb in the early 1950s, among them a young man who had just moved to Nashville to plug songs for Tannen Music. Boudleaux Bryant was his name, and he had already penned country hits, for Jimmy Dickens mostly ("Country Boy"), when Tubb waxed his

"Somebody's Stolen My Honey." As well as any other cut of these years, "Somebody's Stolen My Honey" exemplifies the point about fine Tubb recordings making comparatively less chart impact than earlier recordings had. Tubb was in particularly good voice for this one, and he delivered the lyric with captivating sincerity. The harmony twin guitar break by Billy Byrd and Grady Martin is as fine an instrumental break as graces any Tubb recording. It would be the only Boudleaux Bryant song Tubb ever cut.

If Bryant was the promising newcomer among country songwriters in 1952, Lou Wayne was one of the established veterans, friend from San Antonio days, and writer of Tubb's "Careless Darling" and hits for several other country artists. Wayne was back in San Antonio in the early 1950s, and he teamed up with KMAC's popular disc jockey Charlie Walker to write a few songs, since Walker was trying to get a recording career with Imperial Records off the ground.

One of the songs they co-wrote Walker saved for Ernest Tubb's consideration: "Fortunes in Memories." This wasn't the first song he sent to Ernest, but it was the first one Ernest liked. "Is the publishing open on that one? I like it and might record it." "Well, no," Charlie had to admit, "I assigned it to Acuff-Rose." "Well you're a strange one," Ernest replied. "You send me all these songs, I finally find one I like, and you've put it with Acuff-Rose. But I don't care; I plan to cut it anyway."[6] He did, and "Fortunes in Memories" became one of his best songs of that or any other period, hitting number 5 on *Billboard*'s jukebox chart in the fall of 1952.

Another Tubb release from this time (flip side of "Somebody's Stolen My Honey") was also a favorite for disc jockey Charlie Walker, because its writer was a San Antonio resident and one of his listeners: Justin Wayne Tubb, number one son of Ernest. "My Mother Must Have Been a Girl Like You" was Justin's first of many recorded songs. He'd almost had a country novelty cut by the master of that genre, Jimmy Dickens, titled "I'm Gonna Whip the Living Daylights out of You." Dickens held it for consideration before passing on it. But at the ripe age of fifteen, and with just a little touching up from his dad, Justin wrote "My Mother Must Have Been a Girl Like You" after that line jumped out at him from a movie in which an orphaned boxer spoke it in praise of his girlfriend. Justin, young and not motherless himself, admits that he was probably in love with some girl at the time he wrote it. He recalls that he and sister Elaine were riding out to Arizona on a summer vacation with their dad and stepmother (August 1951) when father and son (but mostly son) were whipping it into finished form.[7]

Decca Records embraced two new speeds for their recordings in 1950: they pressed their first 45s that summer, and were soon manufacturing ten-inch albums at 33⅓ speed. This new LP technology made feasible Tubb's first real album collections. Released almost simultaneously in early 1951 were eight-song collections (in boxes of 78s and 45s, besides the single ten-inch record) of religious songs (all six of the 1949 recordings, plus two new ones) and, for the first time, Jimmie Rodgers songs. *Billboard* reported that Ernest Tubb "is fulfilling a lifetime wish with his forthcoming album of the late Jimmie Rodgers songs. The foreword of the album will be written by Mrs. Carrie Rodgers, his widow, now residing in San Antonio."[8]

ON THE HOME FRONT

In Nashville, Tubb had plenty to keep him busy, between the demands of business, broadcasts, and home. Down at the Record Shop, there was always business to talk over with co-owner and tax man Charlie Mosley. At the Record Shop fellow artists hit him up constantly for favors, advice, money, song suggestions, and drinks, but in and around that, he had records, song books, and pictures to sell, tours to map out, *Midnite Jamboree* shows for which to line up guests, weekday broadcasts to do, and recording sessions at the Tulane Hotel for which to prepare. The shop itself moved in August 1951 from 720 Commerce Street to a larger location at 417 Broadway, primarily to accommodate the crowds that wanted to see the *Midnite Jamboree* shows.

Nashville radio—and after August 1950 WSM-TV—gave Tubb all the work that his tour schedule allowed. Until April 1950 he had his one-hour weekday program on WMAK, *Ernest Tubb Record Roundup* with Jerry Thomas. The early-morning shows were (thankfully, I'm sure) long past, but now there was occasional midday work, live or transcribed. Tubb and his band were frequent guests of John McDonald on his *Noon Time Neighbors* farm show; various quarter-hour "Ernest Tubb" slots show up from time to time in the newspaper listings.[9] The *Friday Night Frolic* made its debut in these years;[10] this was done live, just like the Opry itself, though from the WSM studios and with a smaller, nonpaying audience. On Saturday nights, Tubb still had the Carter's Chicks program at 7:00, while his Grand Ole Opry sponsors and time slots varied over the years. His semiregular TV spots in those years of a single Nashville TV station included appearances on *Western Corral, Tennessee Jamboree,* and *Uncle Amby's General Store.*[11]

In their new brick home at 331 Lawndale, Ernest and Olene Tubb started their family with daughters born a year apart. Erlene Dale Tubb arrived Easter Sunday, March 25, 1951; Papa Ernest was playing the Sports Arena in Toledo, Ohio, that day, and didn't see his baby daughter until he made it back to Nashville the next weekend. Mrs. Rodgers came, though, establishing a tradition that would hold for all the children of Tubb's second family. "No, my stay in Nashville was not in the capacity as 'nurse,'" Mrs. Rodgers wrote to Jim Evans the following May 18. "They had a very capable nurse and housekeeper. I was simply invited to share with them their expectations and joy at that time. I had a wonderful visit."[12]

Mother Olene's recollections fourteen years later actually mixed up the two daughters, but, with needed corrections by me, the story of Erlene's birth reads this way: "When Erlene Dale came into the world, Ernest was driving to Toledo, Ohio. Olene had driven him to the Record Shop, where he had to leave to go on the road, then she took the car home and called the hospital. Erlene Dale was born at 1:00 o'clock the next afternoon. Ernest hadn't been able to sleep as usual in the car, and as they pulled into Toledo he glanced at his watch . . . it was one o'clock. When he walked into the Sports Arena, Mrs. Jimmie Rodgers was on the line to tell him his 'little boy' was a girl."[13]

Olene Gayle, the next daughter, came on March 4, 1952, a Tuesday night, when Ernest was at home in Nashville. "Olene was fixing Ernest a T-Bone steak at six o'clock. She said she couldn't have him go to the hospital without supper, because once there she knew he wouldn't eat. Having put supper on the table, she went to lie down while Ernest ate. Then she called the ambulance and Olene Gayle was born at 8:30 [P.M.]. At 10:30 Olene told Ernest he could go home."[14]

On the quiet days—few and far between for a man who logged about one hundred thousand miles annually with his Texas Troubadours—Tubb could retire to his upstairs ranchstyle den to work on new songs, listen to the hundreds submitted for his consideration, or tackle some correspondence. A rare published account of the Tubb home at the time says of the den, "It is full of guitars, recording equipment, and Western furniture. Thousands of records, many of them by Jimmie Rodgers, line the walls. The pictures of Rodgers, Mrs. Rodgers and their daughter, Anita, have a place of honor in the home. The long horns of a Texas steer soar over the fireplace."[15] Photos by Don Cravens and Walden Fabry, which appear in the newspapers and in Tubb's later Hill & Range song books, nearly always show Tubb, with or without his band, at home in the upstairs den. Billy Byrd remembers many practice sessions in that den, during which Tubb familiarized the band (sometimes just Billy) with new songs. But always, "At home and abroad, the Texas troubadour wears nothing but Western clothing—boots, colorful shirts, tight pants, ten-gallon hat. He has 12 pairs of embellished boots, made for him in Wichita Falls at $75 a pair. 'I never owned but one pair of slippers in my life,' Tubb says. 'I bought them to attend a funeral.'"[16]

To a degree that amazes in today's world of reclusive celebrities, Tubb's home was open to his oldest, most trusted fans. Norma Winton Barthel describes for the fan club in detail visits she made to the Tubb abode, twice in fact—a November 1945 visit in the Madison days of "Blue-Eyed Elaine" and a November 1953 visit to 331 Lawndale. And she prints in her book *Ernest Tubb: The*

Original E.T. Carl Dieckman's account of the March 1956 visit that he and Jack Spiegel, fans from the Midwest, made.[17]

A star of his magnitude was instantly recognizable wherever he went, of course, unless he went to some lengths to disguise himself. When his doctor ordered him to take it easier, to slow down his pace, he did for the first time take extended vacations. In August 1951, Ernest, Olene, baby Erlene, and Justin and Elaine (during school vacation) headed to Texas, New Mexico, and Arizona for three weeks (the trip that produced the finished product of Justin's "My Mother Must Have Been a Girl Like You"). It was during this trip that the Ernest Tubb Record Shop was moved from Commerce to Broadway, all in one night and mostly by brother C. R. and his boys.

More health woes plagued Ernest in March 1952, soon after the birth of his and Olene's second girl. He was hospitalized in San Jose, California, with a severe bronchial infection and flu, then flown back to Nashville for rest.[18] So in October of 1952, Tubb and wife Olene took a ten-day vacation, back to the same South-western states that he loved. Seeking anonymity, he let his beard grow for three days and drove the back roads. At an isolated little beer joint somewhere in New Mexico, Tubb stopped for a drink and chatted with the members of a house band setting up for the evening's performance. "How you gonna get a crowd way out here? There's nobody else in sight," Tubb asked them. "Oh, you just wait, mister. When eight o'clock rolls around, they'll be here for dancing." "Well, I wish I could stay to see it. But good luck to you. By the way, I'm Ernest Tubb from the Grand Ole Opry." Tubb shook hands with all the men, and as he went out the door, he heard one of them say, "Ernest Tubb, my foot!" Laughing about it with Olene, she had the last word: "Well, you said you didn't want to be recognized, and you weren't."[19]

Back home the following month, Tubb followed with great interest the presidential election, and was saddened when his beloved Democratic Party lost both chambers of the U.S. Congress and the White House for the first time in twenty years. Against the odds, Tubb put his money where his political sympathies lay. It wasn't his first presidential bet: Roy Acuff had bet him that Dewey would win the 1944 election. "I'll never forget how in 1944 he bet me $100 on Thomas E. Dewey against Roosevelt, who was running for his last term," Tubb recalled. "On election night, he invited Pee Wee King and several of us out to a club he or one of his boys had out on the Louisville highway. I went to pick up my mail before the polls closed, and Roy had already put my $100 in my mailbox. We've been friends ever since that election, because I remember kidding him about it. I told him he knew he'd lost when he bet me. I also accused him of betting on Dewey and voting for Roosevelt."[20]

Watching Acuff and Eddy Arnold head a *Celebrities for Eisenhower* telecast from the Ryman Auditorium on election eve (the first live telecast from the Ryman), Tubb, emboldened by the bottle, called Arnold late at night to lay a wager for Adlai Stevenson. "He started calling me," Arnold remembers.

> Ernest was a boozer, and I wasn't. He started calling me at 2 o'clock in the morning. He called me two nights to have fun with me. But I don't wake up too well; so when he called me the third time, I didn't even say "Hello," I said, "Yes, Ernest. Listen, if you need me, I'll be there, but you bastard, you don't call me at two o'clock in the morning." He was drunk, but he never called me again; he wasn't too drunk to know what I was talking about. That was the wager, and he lost, and he sent me a check. I never cashed it; I still have it somewhere. It was his idea; he was also betting with somebody else, seems like it was with Henry [Cannon], Minnie [Pearl]'s husband. He found out that we were for Eisenhower . . . But Ernest was honest enough to send the check. I never cashed the check, didn't need the check; had no intention of cashing it.

And he does still have the faded check, tucked away in a desk drawer—for $200, dated November 10, 1952.[21]

ON THE ROAD

The year 1950 brought a new lineup of Texas Troubadours, a trio with lead guitar, steel guitar, and bass, augmented in the studio by various talented session regulars and on the road by different opening acts or front men. This three-man Texas Troubadours band, sparse though it seems, had Jack Drake on bass, Billy Byrd on lead guitar, and Dickie Harris on steel. It was an ensemble small enough for Tubb to keep the single road car that he and Butterball had used without going back to anything like the old stretch cars or school bus he had used in his early salad days. Three bandsmen and their instruments, plus Tubb himself if the trips were under three hundred miles,[22] filled up the one car for tours. The opening act—Annie Lou and Danny, for example—traveled in a separate car. When Tubb flew to faraway dates, he'd often take Billy Byrd with him on the plane, whether commercial or chartered. Touring or not, his three bandsmen got their basic $75 a week; if they weren't touring, broadcasting or recording for him, they were free to do so with other artists.

THE FRONT MEN

Now the industry calls them "opening acts," and it's considered a career-maker if you can land that spot for Garth Brooks or Alan Jackson, let us say. In the early

1950s, they were called "front men"; in Tubb's case, these were the singers that he'd take on the road to round out his show. Because they were hired on a per tour basis, it would be impossible without a complete Tubb itinerary to say when a given act began to fill this role and when it ceased to do so. But here are the main acts that traveled with the early 1950s Texas Troubadours to open or "front" the shows.

Arthur "Rusty" Gabbard was a Kentuckian who teamed for years with Cowboy Copas and a fiddler (sometimes Natchee the Indian and sometimes Red Herron, before he worked for Tubb) in a hillbilly trio barnstorming the nation for promoter Larry Sunbrock. Adopting the popular Western persona, Gabbard became "Arizona Rusty" for a time, but he was "Art Gabbard" on the first records he made (for Dixie). He had met Tubb at least as early as January or February 1949, when Ernest and Butterball came to Wichita Falls, Texas, en route to the West Coast.[23] Gabbard made his first MGM recordings in 1950 and seems to have worked a short time then as front man for Tubb. He rejoined Copas later that year and after that found radio station work in Houston and Beaumont before filling the front man role for Ray Price (1953–1954). While with Price, Gabbard wrote his best-known song, "I'll Be There," which became a big hit for Price. Gabbard joined Ferlin Husky's Hush Puppies when Ferlin came to the Grand Ole Opry in late 1954, but was back with the Texas Troubadours by mid-1955.[24]

Tubb's 1950s counterpart of Radio Dot and Smoky was a West Tennessee husband and wife duo, Annie Lou and Danny. They came to the Grand Ole Opry at the beginning of 1946, very much in the Lulu Belle and Scotty mold, after Danny had toured for a time with the Opry's Duke of Paducah. Their earliest confirmed tours with Tubb were in 1950, and they worked a great many of his shows over the next two years. When Annie Lou temporarily dropped out of the act to give birth to their daughter Ava Tyanne (born November 3, 1952), Danny continued working for Tubb as a single, traveling with the band. He made the Korea trip in March 1953 and worked the first two Jimmie Rodgers Festivals in Meridian.

As Danny explains it now, "Ernest had a pretty good deal with us." For a total of $75 a day, plus hotels and gasoline costs, they traveled in their own car with the band in another. Besides providing a top-quality opening act, Danny emceed the show from start to finish and stayed on stage during Tubb's set playing rhythm guitar, something Eddy Arnold on earlier tours wouldn't let him do. Tubb, though, thought enough of Danny's rhythm playing to use him on a couple of Castle Studios sessions in the very early 1950s, though Danny now can't recall which ones. Dill made his major mark in country music as a songwriter, in the wake of a 1954 song he wrote for Carl Smith, "If You Saw Her through My Eyes (You'd See Her Differently)."

ROAD STORIES

Travel by car or plane had its hazards, of course: the Opry folk, Tubb included, were remarkably free from accident throughout the 1950s, although their luck worsened with the famous fatalities of the next decade. Tubb and Eddy Arnold flew to a Sunday show date in Detroit booked by Oscar Davis in the late 1940s and were delayed in Cincinnati on the way by inclement weather. They forgot to notify anyone in Detroit, and Davis told a hushed crowd that no one knew if Tubb and Arnold were safe, and called for prayer. About that time, the two stars showed up, and the whole thing made for a good story in *Billboard*. Later stars traveling by plane would not be as fortunate.

The Tubb entourage, with "Uncle C. R." at the wheel, lost the touring car briefly to repairs in 1950 on a Montana junket when an approaching car crossed the center line and sideswiped their back bumper.[25] This was the Northwestern tour, it seems, on which Billy Byrd remembers Ernest riding the telephones to keep the Opry management from firing Hank Snow, just before "I'm Moving On" took care of that problem.

With his basic three-piece band, Tubb played very few clubs in those years. The lion's share of his personal appearances were in auditoriums, armories, coliseums, ballparks, and open-air recreational parks in the Northeast. Tubb's far-flung and frequent tour dates clearly reflect his great popularity; he was still a big box-office draw in the early 1950s, with or without the hot newer stars on the same package. Typical are these *Billboard* notices:

> Ernest Tubb played a show for Biff Collie in Houston April 20 [1950] to 2,200 patrons, with about 600 turned away.
>
> Alex Campbell, WASA, Havre de Grace, Md., reports Rainbow Park, near Conowingo, Md., did 7,000 at 75 cents each July 23 [1950] with Ernest Tubb.
>
> Connie B. Gay of WARL, Arlington, VA., will play one of the biggest hillbilly shows yet when he takes over the 38,000 seat Griffith Stadium, Washington, to do a two-day (September 22–23, 1951) show which will feature Lefty Frizzell, Ernest Tubb, Lester Flatt and Earl Scruggs, Moon Mullican, Carl Smith, and the Duke of Paducah.
>
> Connie B. Gay's Griffith Stadium promotion drew 14,000, probably a record for that area.
>
> The Georgia Crackers, WHKC, Columbus, Ohio, report that their G-Bar-C Ranch outside Columbus did good business in its second year [1951]. Biggest grosser was Ernest Tubb, who worked there twice.
>
> Ken Ritter, nephew of Tex, KFDM, promoted big show in Beaumont—capacity crowds for four shows on April 30 [1952], starring Er-

nest Tubb, Hank Williams, Duke of Paducah, plus other Opry acts. The police department sponsored it: 10,000 came, 2,500 turned away.

Valley View Park near Wheeling had a record crowd on July 6 [1952] with Ernest Tubb, Wilma Lee and Stoney Cooper.

The Tower Theatre, whose capacity is 1600, did capacity business for three shows November 2 [1952] with Ernest Tubb.

Mack Sanders, KFBI, Wichita, Kansas, reports he emceed an Ernest Tubb package October 24 [1952] that did 10,000 payees.[26]

Chart performance may have been down, but if these quotations are a reliable indication, Tubb experienced in the early 1950s no real decrease in popularity. Working the road, he drew packed houses and stayed just as busy as he wanted to be—or as busy as his doctor would let him be. By 1953, he had sold some fifteen million Decca records, a third of that total since 1950. He had grossed more than $1 million, and could look back on ten years of Grand Ole Opry stardom.[27] More big things were just ahead—a trip to Korea and the first of the Jimmie Rodgers Festivals—that made 1953 another landmark year in the career of the Texas Troubadour.

19

A Tough but Memorable Year

When the year began with the death of a good friend, a younger man he'd inspired and helped to stardom, Ernest Tubb might have suspected that 1953 was going to be tough. That's how Tubb's year began, with the country music world rocked on New Year's Day by news of Hank Williams's death from heart failure at the age of 29. At the huge Montgomery funeral on January 4, Ernest Tubb sang the appropriate "Beyond the Sunset," one of Hank's immortal Luke the Drifter numbers. Tubb was not in good voice; one suspects the problem was due to Tubb's own grief and the probability that he'd "had a few," as son Justin puts it.[1] In later years he described it as the toughest thing he ever had to do; he vowed then and there never to sing at another funeral.

Son Justin, though only seventeen, was a journalism major at the University of Texas in Austin at the time of Hank Williams's death. In fact, he was attending the Cotton Bowl game in Dallas (Texas vs. Tennessee) on New Year's Day as the news was spreading. Only weeks before, he'd seen Hank for the last time at the Skyline Club in Austin as Hank's guest—along with his cousins, who made up a Dessau Hall family band, The Tubb Boys and the Hootenanny Scratchos.[2] Justin, already neglecting his studies because of the entertainment bug, was a huge Hank Williams fan and, devastated by the news, set out to write a personal tribute in song, which finally took shape as "Hank, It Will Never Be the Same without You." Justin says that after the Cotton Bowl game, "I went on back to Austin, and immediately started writing the song. And I . . . I just quit going to classes."[3] With "My Mother Must Have Been a Girl Like You" already to his credit, Justin sent the song to his father, who "rewrote it; he changed it. I wrote it from my viewpoint, and he rewrote it from his viewpoint, since he was gonna record it . . . He didn't want anybody to think he was trying to capitalize on Hank's death to have a hit record, [so] we donated all the royalties to Hank Jr., set up a trust fund for him, because he was, like, three years old, and we were afraid Audrey was gonna steal all the money, and Hank Jr. wasn't going to get nothing."[4] Ernest recorded it at the end of February, with "Beyond the Sunset" cut for the flip.

The new year continued to be tough on Grand Ole Opry performers. Two days before that February 24 recording session, Ernest Tubb had played a Louisville benefit for a Grand Ole Opry star nearly killed in a January auto crash, Bill Monroe. Two Sunday shows at Louisville's Armory, starring a host of Opry talent in addition to Tubb (Red Foley, Carl Smith, Hank Snow, Moon Mullican, Roy Acuff, the Carter Sisters), drew seventeen thousand people and netted over $8,600 for Monroe. In a famous photograph, Tubb holds the money in his hat as one of a group of stars gathered around Monroe, who is flat on his back in a body cast with nineteen fractures and a broken back.

In early April another Opry star needed a benefit show to help with medical expenses: James Clell Summey, "Cousin Jody," formerly with Roy Acuff and Pee Wee King, by this time a comic star on his own. Jody had lost some fingers in an accident around his trailer home, and it was not known if he'd ever play his "biscuit board" dobro again. Barely three months along, 1953 already must have seemed like "the year of benefit shows." The Opry was alerted to its need for a trust fund, and toward the end of the year a gang of Opry talent went back to Louisville, led this time by the fully recovered Monroe, to raise money for a Grand Ole Opry benefit fund. Jody's benefit show was held in Chattanooga on April 5, with Tubb, Hank Snow, and Lew Childre on hand, though they had returned only three days before from a month-long benefit of a different sort: a tour of the Korean War zone.

OFF TO KOREA

American involvement in defense of South Korea began under UN auspices when North Korean forces crossed the 38th parallel in June of 1950; the three-year war became the first conflict to bring hillbilly entertainers to actual fighting fronts. Several country artists had toured Korea before Ernest Tubb and Hank Snow led a Grand Ole Opry troupe there in March 1953, near the end of the fighting (the armistice came four months later, in July). Connie B. Gay, who handled the details of the Tubb tour, had earlier arranged a March 1951 tour by Grandpa and Ramona Jones with Mary Klick. Elton Britt went to Korea in May 1951, and Carolina Cotton played there over the 1952 Christmas season.

Billboard's first notice of a possible Korean tour by Opry talent appears in its December 20, 1952 issue: "Hubert Long, manager of Hank Snow, reports that the Victor warbler may play Korea and Japan along with Grandpa Jones and Lew Childre in March. Connie Gay, the Washington DJ, is lining up the tour."[5] Jones had already been to Korea; sometime between this report and the actual tour in March, his place was taken by Ernest Tubb. Snow remembers now that he personally went to Tubb with the idea.

> Now it was me that started that thing off, so I had nobody but myself to thank for the mess we got in. But I decided through a bunch of military people that I knew, who said, "Why don't you go over there and entertain them people? They would love a taste of home." So that put that in my mind and then I got an attorney here in town by the name of R. B. Parker, he went with me and then I went to Ernest and said, "I'm going to go to Korea, would you like to come along?" He had asked me to come along on the [Jimmie Rodgers] monument, so I wanted to get back at him. He said, "Hank, I can't give you an answer on that right now, cause we're real busy on the road . . . but I'll let you know."[6]

Tubb finally said yes and freed up his entire month of March for the trip, asking his three musicians (Billy Byrd, Jack Drake, Dickie Harris) and Danny Dill (without Annie Lou, who'd given birth to daughter Ava Tyanne in November 1952) to come along. Snow took his Rainbow Ranch Boys, Childre worked solo, and the only other Nashville traveler was WSM's Bill McDaniel, the trip's energetic publicist. Tubb and Hank Snow each took home movie cameras along and took hours of film over the course of the thirty-day trip.

The flight out of San Francisco stopped at Hawaii and then at Wake Island before landing in Tokyo. In the Wake Island airport restaurant in the early morning hours, having flown thousands of miles already, Tubb was accosted by a young man plugging a song. Cameras were on hand to record his audition; Snow listened in to part of it. Danny Dill fondly recalls the story: "This guy was serving us, and there were four of us in there. He approached Ernest about a song, and said, 'Hey, I've got a song. I wish you would listen to it.' And as he was going to get his ukelele or whatever it was, Ernest said, 'My God! I'm in a little island in the middle of the Pacific Ocean and I can't get away from these guys.' But he was nice enough to listen to the boy's song."[7]

In Tokyo, coming and going, the entourage was lodged at the Dai-Ichi Hotel, where they heard a local group perform "Walking the Floor over You." Danny Dill remembers, "They was playing in the coffee shop, or playing as entertainment in this room where people ate . . . He sung 'Walking the Floor over You' in perfect English, it was all right. Somebody said, 'We'd like to go up there and congratulate these boys, how good they did.' 'You can go, but they won't know what you're talking about, because they don't speak English.' And they didn't, but they loved the song. That really happened."[8] Publicist Bill McDaniel says the group was made up of women in Sears-Roebuck cowgirl outfits, and he adds the variation that Tubb heard "Walking the Floor over You" sung perfectly in northern Japan by a seven-year-old boy, whose mother told Tubb that the boy spoke no English.[9]

Once in Korea, each day's itinerary was crowded. Usually they played several shows per day, many in open-air, fenced-off, makeshift hillside "theaters" packed with appreciative GIs. Small planes or helicopters took the entertainers to most of their show sites, though sometimes the equipment came separately in jeeps. Once a North Korean patrol forced rerouting of the equipment caravan, making it an hour and a half late. As they got closer and closer to the front lines, UN jets zooming past and mortars or other small-arms fire sounding off became more common. On at least one occasion, Snow tells of a show abruptly halted by the imminence of enemy raiders; if several hundred marauding North Koreans had gotten past a security fence, there could have been a slaughter, of performers and GIs alike. Another place, known as the Rice Bowl, was blown to bits the day after the Opry entertainers had played there. At Panmunjom, in a so-called peace zone, artillery fire overhead competed with the show's amplification.

All told, the troupe played to some seventy-five thousand soldiers on their twenty-thousand-mile round trip. Thousands came in person, and many thousands more heard the entertainers on a series of broadcasts over two armed forces networks, the Far East Network and the Korean Network.

Tubb himself stayed completely sober during the trip, quite a feat for him at the time and remarkable in light of the tough circumstances and the generous offers of libation from their accompanying Special Services offer, seldom refused by Snow, Byrd, and Dill.[10] An interesting sidelight of the Korean trip was the revelation that Ernest Tubb's music was used by the North Koreans for propaganda purposes. One of the GIs gave Bill McDaniel a copy of what was purported to be a handwritten, unsigned letter back to Mom from an American soldier that had actually been duplicated and dropped behind UN lines by communist pilots. "Instead of making up a letter of their own, the Reds used the words of Ernest Tubb's song, 'Soldier's Last Letter,' and changed the wording a little to fit their own purpose. So many Allied troops were familiar with Tubb's song the propaganda was recognized as a hoax immediately."[11]

The trip was great for morale, military officials told McDaniel, and hopes were expressed for regular Korean visits by Grand Ole Opry acts. Roy Acuff took his show there the following October, some four months after the armistice. Part of the morale boost from the first trip was the personal attention that the two main stars lavished on the troops. Hank Snow, whose most requested song on the tour was "My Mother," offered to contact the mothers of servicemen for whom he could get addresses. Expecting a few hundred such requests, he got over seven thousand, and faithfully sent a form letter to each mother after he got back.

Tubb's favor was, if anything, even more costly, thankless, and heartbreaking. He volunteered to contact the wives or sweethearts of those men who asked him to do so, conveying a message that their soldier was safe and well. Justin Tubb remembers that his dad came back with a briefcase full of such requests—easily several hundred—and that he did indeed, on his own time and at his own expense, call or write the women. Many were no doubt happy to hear such news, and from so famous a messenger, but what always stuck in Tubb's recollection were the many indifferent or thankless women, and the multiple instances of children answering his calls who either didn't remember Daddy at all or didn't know where Mommy was.

As Justin Tubb put it, the Korea trip had a tremendous impact on his father: "He talked about it for years." Ernest himself always ranked it as one of his career highlights, just as Hank Snow still gets emotional writing about the trip forty years afterward. Tubb told the Nashville *Banner* in December 1956, "I would not trade what it meant to me for a million dollars—those GI's, those hungry Korean children in that desolate land, and the gratitude they showed to us for bringing them something to be happy about. We've never had an audience anywhere to compare with those grateful GI's standing in the snow—within a mile and a half of the front line." As late as 1977, Tubb described the Carnegie Hall crowd as his most receptive "until Korea."[12] For him, nothing before or since compared to that experience.

After playing their final shows on the return trip through Japan at Tokyo's Ernie Pyle Theater ("best sound and lighting systems in the world," Hank Snow says),[13] they finally flew home, arriving in Nashville the morning of April 2, with press photographers and fellow Grand Ole Opry stars on hand to greet them.[14] The exhaustion and heartbreak of all the follow-up work that Tubb had volunteered for, in addition to the resumption of a regular touring schedule, sent Ernest Tubb into a real tailspin. Dry on the trip itself, he made up for it afterward, with an extended drinking binge that made it impossible for him to attend what otherwise was a dream come true for him: the first Jimmie Rodgers remembrance in Meridian , Mississippi.

REMEMBERING JIMMIE RODGERS

No one worked harder to enhance the memory and reputation of Jimmie Rodgers than Ernest Tubb. Since Rodgers was his inspiration, and Mrs. Rodgers his guiding light during some very tough years, Tubb felt that he owed that much to

Jimmie's name and fame. But he never approached his efforts on behalf of Jimmie Rodgers as paying off a debt: it was truly a labor of love. Much as any great fan would, Ernest Tubb wanted to share with all who would listen the music of the man he had virtually worshiped. After 1941 or so, Ernest Tubb, unlike most Rodgers fans, was in a position to do just that, on a large scale.

Using the $1,500 Martin 0045 guitar, with Jimmie's name down the neck in mother-of-pearl and "Blue Yodeler" by the tuning keys, was one obvious way that Ernest Tubb intentionally reminded fans of his debt to Jimmie Rodgers. Tubb insisted on using it in his films and in the publicity shots for those films, over the objection of some. Johnny Bond's note on *Riding West* in his autobiography says, "Director didn't want Tubb to use Jimmie Rodgers' guitar. Tubb wouldn't yield."[15] In a group photo promoting his final film, *Hollywood Barn Dance,* Tubb holds the Martin, but he'd either been convinced to apply tape to Rodgers's name, or the photo was doctored prior to release. Tubb tried (unsuccessfully) to interest filmmakers in the life of Jimmie Rodgers well into the 1950s, proposing himself for the title role as long as that was feasible.

More successful were his lobbying efforts with RCA Victor to put Rodgers's records back into production after World War II. By war's end, with all of its attendant record production problems, not a single Jimmie Rodgers record was in the company catalogue, for all his great success between 1927 and 1933. Rodgers fans, not content with the scratchy old records they still had, organized to do something about it, with Ernest Tubb's support and encouragement. In September 1947, a printer in Lubbock, Texas, Jim Evans, started the Jimmie Rodgers Society to serve a network of Rodgers fans worldwide with whom he was already in touch. Their correspondence convinced him of the need for such a society; he asked Ernest Tubb to inaugurate one, but Tubb, then at the very peak of his stardom, suggested that Evans, with more time available, could capably do it himself. Jointly lobbying for Rodgers reissues from RCA was a goal they agreed upon: Evans had the fan network that he could mobilize, and Tubb soon had the forum of his midnight broadcasts from a mailorder record store that could push Rodgers sales very hard. Tubb told Jim Evans in a letter of July 2, 1948, "I'm still after Victor to get the Album out. I can hardly wait myself . . . I only have about thirty of them [Rodgers's records] left, and they are worn pretty badly."[16]

Mrs. Carrie Rodgers wrote to Evans on April 5, 1949, "This is authentic—Victor is issuing a Jimmie Rodgers Memorial Album the latter part of this month. It contains 'Blue Yodel,' 'Daddy and Home,' 'Never No Mo' Blues,' 'Brakeman's Blues,' 'Away out on the Mountain,' 'Frankie and Johnny.' Here's hoping it will lead to more releases."[17] Mrs. Rodgers received the first copy of this *Jimmie Rodgers Memorial Album* on Harry O'Connor's *Hillbilly House Party* radio show of

May 2, 1949, given by record distributor H. L. Alexander.[18] True to his intention, Tubb immediately plugged the album with all his might on the *Midnite Jamboree,* beginning a tradition of including Jimmie Rodgers records on that program that endures to this day. Hank Snow remembers, "Both of us told Steve Sholes, who was then head man at RCA, that we were very pleased and that we would certainly do the Jimmie Rodgers songs and boost the albums any chance we got."[19]

Tubb kept that part of his promise also, despite his conviction that without the yodel, he couldn't really do justice to Rodgers's songs himself. He cut "Frankie and Johnny" for World transcriptions in 1945, "Waiting for a Train" late in 1947, and in 1950 began work on his album of Rodgers's songs.

Ernest Tubb was solely responsible for bringing back into print Mrs. Rodgers's affectionate biography, *My Husband Jimmie Rodgers.* In 1950, fifteen years after the original vanity press run, he brought out his Ernest Tubb Publications edition and sold it through the Record Shop. He said this about the book in a letter to Jim Evans of the Jimmie Rodgers Society: "I will be happy to sell you the J. R. books at wholesale price, which is the cost of printing plus a small royalty for Mrs. Rodgers. I am bearing the cost of the first edition printing my self, as well as the airtime I'm devoting to this book. But it is something that I've always wanted to do for Jimmie's fans. The book will cost you .75 per copy plus postage. But it cannot be sold for over $1.50; this I do request of you."[20] Mrs. Rodgers had told Evans a few months earlier that the book "will be the same as the 1935 edition except for some added pictures and a paper binding. It is Ernest's idea."[21] As an initial promotion, Tubb offered free copies of the book to the media.[22]

Boosting Mrs. Rodgers's income through book royalties and added record royalties from reissued or rerecorded Jimmie Rodgers songs did not exhaust Tubb's generosity toward her. "Harry (Mushmouth) O'Connor, WBOK, New Orleans, reports that Mrs. Jimmie Rodgers . . . visited him recently. She arrived in a new cadillac presented to her by Ernest Tubb."[23]

THE FIRST JIMMIE RODGERS DAY

The seed for a Jimmie Rodgers Day on May 26, 1953, the twentieth anniversary of Rodgers's death, was planted in 1951, when Ernest Tubb first approached his friend and fellow Rodgers disciple Hank Snow about a monument to the Blue Yodeler's memory. Snow says, "Ernest came to me and he said, 'I'm going to have a life-sized monument made of Jimmie. We're gonna have it made in Italy. Would you like to become a part of it?' " When Snow said yes, Tubb added, "Well, we don't want to get too many people in on this, so we'll just—do you want to go half with me?" "Sure, how much is it gonna cost?" "Well, the monument is gonna cost $5,000." Snow adds, "So that meant I was supposed to shell out $2,500, which really I couldn't afford at the time, but I desperately wanted to do it, so I didn't let him know how bad off we were financially."[24] In Snow's words, Tubb had argued, "We need to do this for Mrs. Rodgers, as well as to the memory of the late Jimmie Rodgers; he was the daddy of country music." Of all people, Snow needed no convincing of Jimmie Rodgers's importance. But as things turned out, besides paying for half of the monument, Snow actually did a lot more of the actual legwork as the big day for the unveiling ceremony approached, and a different sort of event grew up around that.

Early in 1952, Snow made the first of several trips to Meridian, Mississippi, city of Rodgers's birth, to meet with officials about the possibility of placing the monument there. The two stars had hoped to have it placed on Meridian's court-house lawn, but as Snow relates in his autobiography, city officials balked at that: two statues were there already. Mr. Nate Williamson, local attorney and brother to Mrs. Rodgers, was a powerful ally in their quest to overcome local obstacles. As these meetings continued on a periodic basis, Tubb and Snow continued to talk up the Rodgers legacy as best they could. On May 26, 1952, Tubb, Hank Snow, Mrs. Rodgers, and Ralph Peer were interview guests of disc jockey friend Don Owens of WEAM, Arlington, Virginia, on an hour-long Rodgers memorial broad-cast.[25] In another year's time, Jimmie would be dead twenty years. Would every-thing with the statue and with Meridian officials fall into place by then?

Looking back on it in 1977, Tubb recalled, "We wanted a monument, really, we didn't know what we were starting. We wanted to keep it a secret, even from Mrs. Rodgers . . . but the news got out and people started writing us, 'When are you going to have the Jimmie Rodgers Day?' So we called to Mrs. Rodgers, and she'd been hearing from people, and didn't know what they were talking about."[26] Meetings with Meridian officials continued; when Ernest finally could attend one of those gatherings along with Snow, he was more favorably im-pressed by the city's recommended site for the monument (near an industrial district) than Snow had been. "Well, this place isn't all that bad. It would be an ideal spot to make a nice rest area or roadside park for the people passing Meridian, going east or west. It's a pleasant setting, with all these beautiful pine trees around, and when tourists stop they'll see the statue. So if the city can't do any better and we can't pressure them, I believe we should settle for this."[27] They did. Meantime, their ideas of what events should surround the unveiling were growing. Plans began to form of a big country music show, with invited music industry and political celebrities and large enough crowds and sufficient media attention to make the festivities an annual event.

Soon the Meridian citizenry knew that plans were afoot. On November 5, 1952, a newspaper account of city council doings mentions, "A national move-ment to present the city with a statue of the late Jimmie Rodgers, world renowned recording artist, was revealed at the meeting [that day] by attorney Nate Williamson. Hank Snow . . . was introduced as one of the sponsors of the project . . . The sponsors are seeking only a suitable location for the statue. Mayor Paine appointed a committee to work with Williamson and Snow on the event. The unveiling ceremony will bring to Meridian many stars of the entertainment world, including Snow, Ernest Tubb, Louisiana's ex-Governor Jimmie Davis, plus Gov. Hugh White."[28] Fan club president Jim Evans learned about the plans from Mrs. Rodgers. In a letter written later that month, which enclosed the above clipping, she begins, "At the time I told you all about the monument, I felt that I may be a little premature in mentioning it—but I was so pleased with the news I just couldn't keep it. But it was okay, as when Ernest called me last Friday night he mentioned that I should tell you—and in your way, you could tell the fans that you are in contact with and invite those that can and want to to be present at the unveiling ceremony. It will be the night of May 26, 1953."[29]

Word of all this leaked out slowly but surely through the Jimmie Rodgers Fan Club and the media. Before the big day came, Tubb and Snow were actively seeking media publicity to ensure a larger crowd at the unveiling. Tubb told Evans in a letter of February 3, 1953, that Roy Acuff, Cowboy Copas, Red Foley, Jimmie Davis, Jimmie Skinner, Webb Pierce, George Morgan, and Tommy Duncan were on the planned program, and "I still plan to invite Lefty Frizzell if I can ever catch him in one spot long enough to get a letter to him."[30] Contributions from fans toward the cost of the monument and the day's events were allowed, though not necessarily encouraged. Mrs. Rodgers conveyed to Jim Evans Ernest Tubb's wishes to have it worded this way in the fan club publication: "It is not necessary, but any others who care to contribute toward this cause, even a small amount, have a part in (or something to that effect), can send to: Jimmie Rodgers Memorial Fund, c/o Jim Evans, President, Jimmie Rodgers Fan Club (address)." She adds, "But he [Ernest] says the main thing to stress is the invitation to be present. You might add ways of learning details from time to time or last minute changes etc., through you and Ernest's midnight show. There is to be a page or two in *Billboard* about it as the time draws nearer. Some will learn that way."[31]

Billboard, at the behest of Ernest Tubb and Hank Snow, ran the news in their May 16, 1953 issue. There was a full two pages plus, with articles by Ralph Peer, Mrs. Rodgers, Hank Snow, and Ernest Tubb on "Rodgers' Influence on Country Music"; a short biography (plugging Mrs. Rodgers's book, available from Ernest Tubb Publications, P.O. Box 817, Nashville, for $1.50); blurbs on the fan club and on Rodgers's first royalty check; a list of songs composed by Rodgers; his twenty-four available recordings (by this time four three-record albums had been released); plus a write-up on the six extant guitars that Jimmie Rodgers used.

Country Song Roundup ran a feature on the upcoming event, and the normally staid and silent Nashville *Tennessean* even ran a series of three articles in May issues of their Sunday magazine: the first on Rodgers, the second on Ernest Tubb, and the third on Hank Snow. Their profile of Tubb was (to the best of my knowledge) the very first feature-length article on the Texas Troubadour that a Nashville paper ran on him, after ten years' residence in the city. Snow was comparatively fortunate, having been there only three years at the time.

Ernest Tubb was sick, tired, and often inebriated in the aftermath of Korea; Mrs. Rodgers wrote to Jim Evans on April 22, 1953, "Ernest hasn't been at all well since his return from Korea—cold plus dental trouble."[32] Consequently, Tubb attended very few of the final preliminary meetings in Meridian with city officials. Snow had done his drinking *in* Korea, Tubb only afterward; as he says in his book, Snow often made two or three seven-hundred-mile round trips from Nashville to Meridian by car in a week's time that spring, to wrap things up with the help of "Mr. Nate" Williamson. What he doesn't say in his book, but freely admitted in an interview, is that Tubb's sickbed phone calls from Nashville to Snow's Meridian hotel room often got tedious. "I was in Meridian, Mississippi . . . and it was *cold* in my room . . . and the phone wouldn't be by my bed, it's across the room. So I had to get up and go over there . . . I'll tell you the God's truth. I was on that phone with Ernest Tubb for three solid hours, I swear to God, and freezing, and I was doodling on this paper—I've still got that somewhere here as a souvenir of that—and he's still talking." (About anything in particular?) "Nothing in particular, and talking and repeating the same thing over and over. 'Now, lookee,' that was his favorite word. 'Now, lookee.' " (Was he just passing the time, wanting somebody to talk to?) "He was just *drunk.*" (And there was no diplomatic way for you to get out of this—"Look, Ernest, I want to go back to sleep"?) "No, if I'd a tried that, I think he would have kept me on there longer."[33]

Unfortunately, Ernest Tubb was in the same condition when the big day finally came, and had been for days before. He told interviewers in later years that he had "pneumonia in my right lung,"[34] and son Justin says that he probably did: that and other complications brought on by a drinking binge.

> He was a binge drinker, at the Jimmie Rodgers, because I went down and took his place, and unveiled the statue. It was because he was drinking. He would go like months and wouldn't touch a drop, and then all this stuff would build up that he'd want to get straightened out and get settled, and then he'd start drinking and for a couple of weeks maybe he'd sit there in that house and call everybody he was mad at, and tell them what was wrong, and what they oughta do to change it . . . He was drinking, and he just did not want to go down there, and he couldn't get

straightened up in time to make it, because it took him two or three days to get back to normal . . . And he asked me to go, because I think Jimmie Snow [son of Hank] and I had gone to New York, to meet the boy from England [Ian Lee], who they had brought over, for the first Jimmie Rodgers day. Jimmie Snow and I went to New York, we were on *The Eddie Fisher Show* . . . went to see the Chicago Cubs play the Brooklyn Dodgers at Ebbetts Field, this was a big deal for me, man! But anyway, we had just gotten back, and he was still going through this little period, and decided he wasn't gonna go, so he called Hank Snow and said, "Do you mind if Justin goes and takes my place?" . . . It [drinking] has an effect on your kidneys, and on your liver, and of course it affects everything. And he was the kind that when he drank like that he didn't eat.[35]

It was a tragedy that Ernest Tubb had to miss the day he had worked so hard to bring about. As the big day unfolded, Hank Snow and master of ceremonies Eddie Hill phoned regular reports of the festivities to the Tubb home. "Eddie Hill at the time was the all-night DJ on WSM. He gave us a lot of publicity in advance," Snow says.[36] Some twenty-five thousand people descended on Meridian, taking up all available lodging within a seventy-five-mile radius, for what was dubbed nationally Jimmie Rodgers Day and National Hillbilly Music Day,[37] but locally Jimmie Rodgers and Railroadmen Memorial Day.

A selling point with the Meridian city officials had been to honor all of Meridian's deceased railroad workers with this big event. A special rail line was laid from the city out to the monument site to bring in the dignitaries on a steam locomotive (making its last run that day) to the 1:30 P.M. ceremonies, emceed by Tom Dunn. Mrs. Casey Jones, ninety-four years young, and Casey's aged fireman, Sim Webb, appeared on the program along with the main local sponsors, the Junior Chamber of Commerce and the Meridian *Star* newspaper, plus the politicians. Mississippi's governor and lieutenant governor, Governor Frank G. Clement of Tennessee, and Louisiana's ex-governor and Decca recording star Jimmie Davis were on hand. Mrs. Rodgers made a short speech for network radio microphones, as did Jimmie's old publisher and producer, Ralph Peer. RCA Victor was represented by Mr. J. B. Elliott, who helped Ralph Peer dedicate a flagpole and markers around the fenced-in monument and retired steam locomotive. Newsreel cameras recorded the ceremony, and many radio microphones were set up; but the remote feeds back to WSM radio in Nashville emphasized the evening's concert at 7:00 from the Junior College Stadium. Tubb's February list to Jim Evans had lengthened to include Minnie Pearl, Little Jimmy Dickens, Carl Smith, Lew Childre, Bill Monroe, Marty Robbins, and Moon Mullican, plus such additional non-Opry acts as Englishman Ian Lee, Rodgers mimic Bill Bruner (who that night gave his Jimmie Rodgers guitar to Hank Snow's singing son, Jimmie Rodgers Snow), disc jockey Nelson King, the original Carter Family, new sensation Jim Reeves (fresh off a May 23 Grand Ole Opry guest shot singing his big hit, "Mexican Joe"), Slim Willet (of "Don't Let the Stars Get in Your Eyes" fame), Justin Tubb singing in his father's place (he had only just moved back to Nashville from Austin, working at WHIN in Gallatin), and friend of Mrs. Rodgers, San Antonio disc jockey, Imperial Records artist, and co-writer of "Fortunes in Memories," Charlie Walker. Small wonder that the show went on for four hours! WSM's Bill McDaniel, publicist of the Korea trip, was on hand taking photos. Incidentally, it was the *Tennessean*'s H. B. Teeter who composed the wording carved onto the Rodgers monument.[38]

May 26, 1953, was a Tuesday. Snow's published account says that the big night went over so well that a lot of the musicians stayed around for most of the rest of the week in a festive, jam-session mood, beginning what became (as they had hoped) an annual event. Governor Clement and Roy Acuff had expressed the hope that 1954's National Hillbilly Music Day might be held in Nashville, but for the next six years the Meridian event highlighted each year's country music calendar, alongside the late fall disc jockey convention in Nashville. For various reasons—outside exploitation, Mrs. Rodgers's declining health, rock and roll, and some Meridian opposition—the Jimmie Rodgers festivities vanished between 1960 and 1969, but have come back strong since. Throughout its 1950s heyday, Tubb and Snow were actively involved. Later in 1953, with Nate Williamson's help, the state of Mississippi chartered the Jimmie Rodgers Memorial & Health Foundation, a tax-exempt fund to receive monies contributed through Jim Evans. As Tubb explained in a letter to Evans dated August 22, 1953, "All the money we can raise will be used to keep the name of our Jimmie alive, and take care of the Statue, and perhaps add to this Memorial in the future, and also, this money will be used to help suffering people. Especially those with T.B. . . . We plan to charge for the show next year, and all profits will go to the fund."[39]

As for his personal health, Tubb wrote to his own fan club's *Melody Trails* that summer.

> I am happy to report that I feel much better, though still a little weak . . . However, I have been back on my midnight show and plan on returning to the Opry in the near future. My doctor told me I had to take it easy for awhile and I have been trying to do just that. He has also got me playing golf and it is doing wonders for me. I just love it. Everyone has been so very kind and thoughtful to me while I have been laid up. I didn't know I had so many friends . . . It broke my heart to miss the Jimmie Rodgers Day . . . but that was Dr.'s orders. My heart was there, at least . . . Mrs.

Rodgers said the artists seemed to have worked twice as hard to sort of make up for me not being there. She was so proud of our tribute to her Jimmie. By the way, tell the members to check with their local theatres concerning the newsreel coverage of the Memorial event. It was covered by Universal-International, and has already shown in Meridian . . . I can hardly wait to see it myself.[40]

A MUSICAL FAMILY

Though Ernest Tubb was on the sick list for much of 1953—from April well into the summer, as we've seen—his very illness gave him the time and opportunity to further the nascent musical career of his eldest son, Justin Tubb, and to help start one for his first daughter, Violet Elaine "Scooter Bill" Tubb. The same year saw two of his nephews, Douglas and Billy, make strides toward musical careers, much as their songwriting half brother Talmadge already had.

At Brackenridge High School in San Antonio, Justin had worked on the school paper; at the University of Texas, ostensibly he was studying journalism. He hoped to get into sports journalism, either from the print or broadcast end of things, having soured on his musical career between ages three and eleven as "the Little Texas Troubadour." But in Austin he was joined by two cousins (C. R.'s boys), Douglas Glenn and Billy. Glenn, though several weeks older than Justin, was still in high school when he moved down to Austin: both were only seventeen, and Billy was fifteen. Glenn thinks he was sent down there to look after Justin; Justin thinks that part of his responsibility was to look after Glenn, and both tried hard to keep young Billy out of trouble. Nevertheless, if by "trouble" one means neglecting school work, forming a family band and playing the Austin club scene, then all three young men got into trouble.

The three Tubbs plus three other musicians made up the house band at Dessau Hall in nearby Pflugerville, Texas. When Austin's biggest country deejay, KVET's C. V. "Red" Jones heard them, he offered them his managerial direction and even suggested the band name, the Tubb Boys and the Hootenanny Scratchos. They never made records as a group, but in addition to working Dessau Hall they worked area clubs and shows in their hometown of San Antonio, drove up to Shreveport and the *Louisiana Hayride* with Goldie Hill and her brothers, and worked Slim Willet's Mid-State Jamboree in Abilene. They were the guests of Hank Williams and his mother at Austin's Skyline Club in December 1952, purportedly Hank's last concert, which Goldie Hill also remembers attending.

Justin and Glenn both remember when Shreveport disc jockey Jim Reeves, the new Abbott recording artist, was booked into Dessau Hall and they were to be his backup band. The Tubb Boys and their Hootenanny Scratchos worked hard to learn the handful of records that Reeves had made, only to have him come in and fill up his first set with Ernest Tubb songs. "Jim, aren't you gonna sing any of your songs?" they asked him. He didn't think they'd know them, but was confident that they'd know Tubb tunes. In the second set, he sang his own songs. On another occasion, they split the evening with Jimmy Dickens and the Carlisles.[41]

When Hank Williams died, a despondent Justin Tubb went into a funk, but the family band stayed together a while longer. In the January 3 *Billboard,* Red Jones reported that "Ernest Tubb's son, Wayne Justin [*sic*], who is attending school at the University of Texas, is a mighty fine guitar picker himself." By month's end, Jones reported to the same publication that he was "promoting dances at Dessau Hall." On February 24, Ernest Tubb recorded Justin's "Hank, It Will Never Be the Same without You," a fact duly reported to *Billboard* by Jones,[42] then left for Korea for the whole month of March. During that month, Justin's two cousins bailed out and returned to Nashville. Sometime during April, back from Korea, Ernest Tubb placed a 2 A.M. long distance call to his son in Austin. Justin remembers it well: "And I was sitting there: I hadn't been to class in probably two months. And he called and said, 'Well, how ya doin'?' I said, 'Well, not too well. Why did you call?' He said, 'I had a feeling something was wrong.' . . . When he called me I was down in the dumps. He called and said, 'Well, what do you want to do?' 'I'll come up there.' So I moved to Nashville. That's when I went to work for WHIN in Gallatin."[43]

Justin had done enough singing at sorority parties and night clubs to know that he wanted to be a singer, but once back in Nashville and living with his father and stepmother, his dad told him all the bad things about being a country singer: not to discourage him, Justin points out, but only to open his eyes. "Remember, you won't make it unless you have the ability, regardless of who tries to help you."[44] Ernest Tubb gave this slant on their conversations years later: "He said to me, 'Daddy, all I'll ever ask you is advice. Keep up my allowance for six months, and if I can't make it in music, I'll go back to college.' "[45] Justin hosted a good many *Midnite Jamboree* shows during his father's troubles those first few months back from Korea, and in well under six months Justin had gainful employment as disc jockey at WHIN in Gallatin, Tennessee (about twenty miles out of Nashville), hired at Ernest's recommendation by his old co-host on *The Ernest Tubb Record Roundup,* Jerry Thomas, then the program director at WHIN.

One of Father Tubb's first bits of advice to Justin was to get some on-mic experience, to learn how to talk to fans, just as he himself had done through the Carter's Chicks show, the *Midnite Jamboree,* and the *Ernest Tubb Record Roundup.* Justin began his WHIN program on May 4, 1953, coincidentally just as Ernest

Tubb began a week of personal appearances in Texas booked by Red Jones, Justin's former Austin manager.[46] That summer, writing his column for the fan club, Ernest Tubb gave Justin's WHIN schedule, plus a bit of good news: "Justin has a disc jockey show over WHIN, Gallatin, Tenn., Mon. through Fri., 4:05 to 5:00 p.m. Then on Sat., he has a live program from 3:05 to 3:30 p.m. His cousin, Billy Tubb, plays electric lead guitar for him. (Real good, too.) Justin is drawing more mail than anyone who has ever been on that station. I am real proud of him. He is to record for Decca this fall—as is little Elaine. Decca asked for them—I'm not pushing them."[47]

Both siblings were living with their ailing dad, Olene, and their two little sisters, but Ernest indeed was not pushing them with Paul Cohen and Decca. In Justin's case, the connection was Justin's songwriting and demo recordings. Ernest brought them to Cohen, trying to get the songs placed with other Decca artists, but Cohen said, "Hell, he sings good enough; let's record him."[48] Some within the Decca Records hierarchy may have balked at the idea of a star's son signed to the same label; Gary Crosby, Bing's boy, had already made a few less-than-successful Decca discs. But through Paul Cohen, Decca got not one but two Tubb children. Both made their first recordings on August 5, 1953, at Tulane Hotel sessions. For Elaine, then a weekly regular on the *Midnite Jamboree,* her first two recordings would also be her last: the pop-flavored "Mean Age, In-Between Age Blues," well-suited to a thirteen-year-old's adolescent woes, and a country cover of the Jean Shepard/Ferlin Husky hit, "A Dear John Letter," with her dad doing Ferlin's recitative part. Justin's four songs recorded that same day were only the beginning of a six-year association with Decca and a great career as a singer-songwriter.

Billy Tubb, as noted by his Uncle Ernest, went more into the instrumental line as Justin's lead guitarist. As "Ronny Wade" (King Records, 1957–1958) and later as "X. Lincoln" (Time Records, 1962; this is now his legal name), he sang with a smooth vocal style, but he has spent most of his career as a guitarist. Between Billy Byrd and Leon Rhodes, as we will see later, he worked as his uncle's lead guitarist,[49] though he never recorded with Ernest Tubb.

Douglas Glenn Tubb, meantime, had also followed his hillbilly muse back to Nashville from Austin, where his father still lived (in early 1953) on a farm off Donelson Pike. He soon teamed up with an area nightclub singer, Roy Duke, and Duke's brother Frank. Roy was the writer of "My Wasted Past," which Tucker Robertson at the Ernest Tubb Record Shop (along with Mrs. Rodgers) brought to Ernest Tubb's attention; Tubb recorded it at the pre-Korea, February 24, 1953 session. This trio, plus fiddler Mack Smith of Russellville, Alabama, hit the road later that year with Bill Bailey's Minstrel Show as the hillbilly act to hold the crowds between animal acts and clowns in Cy Ruben's Circus. They were sold on this idea by "a wild Cherokee Indian" named Ted Edlin, later the booker and manager for Hawkshaw Hawkins, Jean Shepard, and Cousin Jody. To promote the tour and to have something to sell from the stage, Douglas Glenn Tubb as "Doug Tubb" made his first records in Birmingham for Ted Edlin's Mart label: "Deaf, Dumb, and Blind" and "The World Is a Monster."

After the tour, a mutual friend and successful songwriter and plugger, Vic McAlpin, arranged for Doug and Roy to make a better-distributed Dot Record ("Standing at the End of My World" was the duet side), which proved to be a stepping-stone to Decca contracts for both men. Douglass Glenn Tubb then dropped the "Tubb" name altogether and became "Glenn Douglas." Professionally, he wanted no part of the Tubb name, any more than his brother Billy did or as his half brother Talmadge had when he recorded for Decca as "Billy Talmadge." Doug puts it well for all his brothers when he says of his famous uncle, "Those were pretty big boots to be sloshing around in." His pseudonym inverts the order of his first two names, in part because "Douglas Glenn" was too close to the then-popular "Darrell Glenn" (of "Crying in the Chapel") and in part because "Douglas" was a more common and better-sounding last name.[50] The Decca recordings of Glenn Douglas have something of a cult following now, though none were hits at the time. He later recorded for other labels, but as a songwriter he has since made a huge impact on country music.[51] He furnished a lot of Justin Tubb's early Decca material, and his Uncle Ernest subsequently recorded several of his songs, from "I'll Be Walking the Floor This Christmas" (1954, co-written with Justin) to "Tommy's Doll" (1969), with others in between.

20

Changing Times

In November 1953, Decca Records announced in a press release: "Ernest Tubb . . . has been signed to a new four-year contract with Decca Records. The singer has been with Decca for 13 years."[1] That same month, *Billboard* magazine named Ernest Tubb to its first Honor Roll of C&W Artists, a list of eight past and present greats. He received the honor on the stage of the Grand Ole Opry November 21, 1953, during the second deejay festival, while his mentor Mrs. Rodgers accepted the same award for Jimmie; Mrs. W. W. Stone, mother of Hank Williams, brought four-year-old Hank Williams Jr. to the Opry stage to accept for his late father. The other inductees, like Tubb, were living and active: Eddy Arnold, Roy Acuff, Red Foley, Carl Smith, and Hank Snow.[2] This capped a busy year which, if not the best for his health,[3] was certainly memorable for the trip to Korea and the first Jimmie Rodgers Day in Meridian. Ernest Tubb was at the very top of his professional form, a proven draw on the road if no longer dominant on the record charts. Neither he nor anyone else could have foreseen how changes just ahead in the music industry would so seriously impact that career within the four years of this new Decca contract.

Tubb's career was certainly busy enough to need a manager. In the tradition of Mrs. Rodgers, Joe L. Frank (who had died in May 1952), and Oscar Davis, Dub Albritten assumed Tubb's managerial reins at the end of 1953. From offices in the Ernest Tubb Record Shop, Albritten agreed to direct both Tubb and Hank Snow, as the *Pickin' & Singin' News* announced.[4] But the arrangement proved to be more than Albritten could handle, as the Tubb fan club announced in the fall of the next year, 1954: "Dub Albritten is no longer mentor of Hank Snow and Ernest Tubb, and has gone to Springfield, Mo., to manage the business affairs of their very good friend Red Foley, who is now starring on ABC out of Springfield. They found that managing two very popular artists was a little too much for one person and both Hank and Ernest agreed it would be better for him not to try it."[5]

The vacuum left by Albritten's departure would soon be filled, in Tubb's case by Gabe Tucker and in Snow's by Tom Parker, Eddy Arnold's ex-manager.

COUNTRY TUNE PARADE

Early in 1954, Tubb had a new weekly national broadcast of his own, though it lasted only some thirteen weeks. Here is the report from *Pickin' & Singin' News:* "The NBC Radio Network replaced the Eddy Arnold Show January 23[6] with a new country music program featuring 'The Texas Troubadour,' Ernest Tubb, with Miss Goldie Hill. The presentation is aired with a live audience as part of the Friday Night Frolic over WSM . . . and is transcribed for release to the NBC Network at 9 P.M. CST following the Prince Albert Grand Ole Opry show Saturday. In addition to Tubb and Miss Hill, 20, . . . special guests will be featured on each program. The sponsor is an insecticide manufacturer."[7]

Though only twenty, Goldie Hill was already a country music veteran: busy in a family band around San Antonio (where she'd known Justin, Doug, and Billy Tubb), a one-time *Louisiana Hayride* regular, and signed to Decca Records (through Webb Pierce) since July 1952, she would join Justin Tubb for some very successful Decca duets later that year. Her memories now of *Country Tune Parade* are not altogether fond ones: "I don't remember who got the show going: probably Ernest, Jim Denny, and Norm Riley [her manager] together. I didn't know Ernest well, and we never talked much about a show before we'd do it, although we'd have to rehearse songs with his band. Ernest would sing a song, then [stop for] a commercial; then he might sing another, then [stop for] a commercial. Then I'd do mine."[8] Goldie Hill's job was primarily to cover the "female" hits of the day, usually country but sometimes pop, as this story shows: "When I heard Loretta Lynn the other night sing 'Secret Love,' it reminded me that I'd sung it on that radio show. And as I recall, the minor chords really were a problem for Ernest's band . . ."[9]

Off to a good start, in terms of the stations that carried it, *Country Tune Parade* faded rather quickly. "Our show replaced 'The Eddy Arnold Show,' which had been on 75 stations, about March 6, 1954, with a network of 117 stations. But it only lasted about thirteen weeks, if I remember correctly."[10]

Norma Barthel at the Ernest Tubb Fan Club was naturally enthusiastic, praising *Country Tune Parade* for a characteristic it actually shared with the *Midnite Jamboree* at that time: Ernest Tubb singing other artists' hits.[11]

IN THE RECORDING STUDIO

Ernest Tubb naturally hoped to record more new hits of his own that winter, as he reached his fortieth birthday. Despite its heavy load of recording work (twenty-two masters), 1953 witnessed a pretty steep decline in chart activity. Even including the Red Foley duets in these totals, Tubb had slipped steadily each year so far in the 1950s: from his career high of twelve new charted songs in 1949 and 1950, he dropped to four in 1951 (Hank Williams that year had twice as many), moved up to five in 1952 (only one fewer than Williams, Snow, and Arnold), then back down to two in 1953 (when Carl Smith, with seven, was the big winner).[12] At this point his most recent chart toppers had been "Blue Christmas" in 1949 and the Foley duet "Goodnight, Irene" in 1950.

Even with a new four-year contract in hand, Tubb's recorded masters in 1954 dropped to ten, fewer than half of the previous year's twenty-two, and two of those ten were Christmas songs. Best remembered of the other eight is "Jealous Loving Heart," a love song from the pen of nephew Talmadge Tubb. After some five years of *Midnite Jamboree* performances, Ernest had finally worked "Jealous Loving Heart" into an arrangement he liked. The song, warmly accepted by Tubb fans, did not make the record charts at the time but became a wonderful up-tempo opener for stage shows and broadcasts.

His first big hit from Cindy Walker's pen, "Two Glasses, Joe," was the other record highlight of 1954. Tubb sang it the rest of his life; when flattering mimics set out to "do" Ernest Tubb, "Two Glasses, Joe" was often the song they chose. *Billboard*'s anonymous reviewer says, "Tubb has one of his strongest releases in some time here. Juke box reports are particularly favorable, although there is no lack of excellent retail action as well."[13] And from the same issue, "Tubb has come through again with a record which is headed for the charts . . . If there were more such consistent artists making money, the record business would be a cinch."[14] "Two Glasses, Joe" did make the charts, topping at number 11 on the best-seller list.

TELEVISION

Ernest Tubb and his Texas Troubadours were frequent guests on WSM-TV programming, for three years (1950–1953) Nashville's only TV station, owned by his bosses at WSM radio and the Grand Ole Opry. But Eddie Jones, the radio and TV critic of the Nashville *Banner* at that time, expressed a widely held view that WSM-TV did not properly use the pool of local talent available to it for live programming, relying more and more on network feeds as time passed. All along, it seems, there was the belief in the boardrooms of WSM radio that too much TV exposure would kill the appeal of their venerable Grand Ole Opry. This didn't sit well with the artists themselves, who could see the coming boom in television and wanted to be a part of it.

This comment was printed at the time that Tubb and Snow hired Dub Albritten: "[He] is reported to be concentrating on obtaining more transcribed shows and television appearances for the luminaries."[15] On that front 1954 was a year of unrest: before it had passed, Albritten had moved to Springfield, Missouri, to guide Red Foley successfully into the television medium via the *Ozark Jubilee,* and Tubb, hoping to see more action on that front in Nashville, said this to his fan club: "We are all anxious to do more television shows and I believe this will come to pass in the near future. I think we will be doing some TV film shows and also some network shows by the first of the year."[16]

Flamingo Films: *The Country Show*

"Well, at last we are making a few TV films. The Texas Troubadours and I will be featured about every six weeks in this series to be called 'Stars of the Grand Ole Opry.' The first one should be released January 15th."[17] This was the news that Ernest Tubb had for his fan club that winter. He doesn't say that he had debated with, pleaded with, and cajoled recalcitrant WSM executives to accept the deal offered by Flamingo Films, a Hollywood company represented in the negotiations by producer Albert Gannaway. "We negotiated for months before finally signing a five-year contract on August 18, 1954," Gannaway remembers. "Ernest Tubb and Roy Acuff were very much in favor of the project, wanting the TV exposure. Generally speaking, the higher up the chain you went with National Life, the less enthusiastic they were—fearing that TV exposure would kill the radio show."[18] The restive Tubb, speaking for several of the other artists, must have thought by this time that *any* TV deal was better than continued inactivity. All of the parties to the negotiations knew by then that the *Ozark Jubilee* in Springfield was about to switch from radio to TV, with Red Foley at the helm. Arguing that a contract now would not preclude similar live network TV for the Opry at a later date, Tubb and others convinced WSM officials to strike the deal. Filming began in November 1954 and continued until December 1956.

The first films were shot in black and white at the Ryman Auditorium, but sound problems there proved insurmountable. Then the switch was made to a much more compact theater on the campus of Vanderbilt University, complete with hay bales and other barnyard paraphernalia. *Billboard* reported that the first TV markets began showing *The Country Show: With Stars of the Grand Ole Opry* the week of January 20, 1955, which was the very same week that *Ozark Jubilee* began on ABC-TV.[19]

Ernest Tubb appeared on the show much more frequently than "every six weeks," as he had originally announced. Tubb, always so ready with a smile and a laugh, had the warm, genial ways that made him the show's favored host, appearing in that role twenty-four times out of the series' total of ninety-two half-hour shows. He guested on another eighteen episodes. Producer Gannaway recalls also that Tubb's promptitude, his ability to keep a show going and then to wrap it up on time, helped establish him as favorite host. "He had his boys ready, and there was no fooling around—Tubb set the record for fastest filming of a single episode: 37 minutes to film a 22-minute show. That was why Ernest hosted *by far* the most shows in the series."[20] Union regulations demanded payment rates of $100 per session for the leader (star), $50 per three-hour session for each sideman, and a hefty 25 percent extra per quarter-hour of overtime. When Tubb hosted, Gannaway had to pay very little overtime. Gannaway filmed his shows in widely scattered busy weeks,[21] during which a star would earn $3,000 if he worked a heavy five sessions per day over a six-day week.

The special demands of television could be difficult for radio-minded Opry stars to adjust to. Because of problems with light glistening off his shiny mandolin, Ira Louvin of the Louvin Brothers was asked to have it sprayed. Fearing the effect of that spray on his instrument's sound, the temperamental Louvin stormed off the set after a single half-hour's performance. They never again worked for Gannaway.[22] Tubb's lead guitarist Billy Byrd recalls that Gannaway's time consciousness meant that he sometimes asked the musicians for shorter instrumental breaks. To Byrd, who always cut his breaks as short as possible anyway ("Folks pay to hear Ernest Tubb sing, not to hear me play"), this was particularly off-putting; he even kidded Gannaway once with a wonderful reason not to make his break shorter: "It tells a story."[23]

Pillsbury Flour sponsored the broadcast over most of its stations and in the spring of 1956 also sponsored a four-week Southern tour with Ernest Tubb, the Wilburn Brothers, and Marty Robbins to promote the TV films. Soon Opry radio sponsor Martha White Flour began squawking about Opry talent promoting a competitive brand, so the tours (and ultimately the show) came to a halt by year's end.

Gannaway recalls that he had overextended his credit lines by that time, else he'd have loved to fulfill the contract and film shows for the remaining three years of his five-year deal. As things turned out, WSM could not syndicate their talent on TV for those three years since Albert Gannaway and Flamingo Films still had the exclusive rights. Small wonder that the relations between Gannaway and WSM became strained, to put it mildly. During the late 1950s, Gannaway put his energies into low-budget movies, using Opry (or ex-Opry) talent such as Marty Robbins, Webb Pierce, Faron Young, and Carl Smith in B Westerns. In later years WSM sued (and lost) over Gannaway's continued syndication of the shows in periodic reruns without further payment. Apparently his original contract with the Nashville musicians' local was airtight: the local accepted a lump sum contribution to its pension fund up front and forfeited any claims to rerun rights, figuring in those days of primarily live TV that there never would be any. In fact, they came back quite successfully as *Country Music Caravan* in 1967 and *Classic Country* in the 1980s. Many of the shows, edited and remixed, are now available on home video, truly classic performances from an era long gone. For their historic value, the shows are treasured by many of the living artists and sidemen, the ones not overly embittered by no rerun money. A maverick artist who prospered leaving the Opry soon after the Gannaway days, Faron Young, takes perverse delight in Gannaway's huge personal fortune: "Gannaway is the only man who ever really put one over on WSM."

Ten months after the *Ozark Jubilee* debut, the Grand Ole Opry, bringing up the rear, broke into network television with a monthly hour on Saturday nights sponsored by Ralston-Purina, done live from the Ryman Auditorium with special sets. The first show aired October 15, 1955, and Tubb was one of the headliners. Ernest was almost as frequently called on for this show as for Gannaway's films; of twelve monthly shows, airing through the summer of 1956, Tubb hosted four.[24] Network TV, then as now, believed that big-name pop guest stars on country music shows would attract more viewers and better ratings, and typical were those first episodes Tubb hosted. Les Paul and Mary Ford were the big shots on the debut show; on January 7, 1956, he welcomed Tony Bennett to the program saluting Hank Williams. Jimmy Dickens, Slim Whitman, Bill Carlisle, and an unknown female singer in town for her second recording session, Patsy Cline, also appeared on that show.

RECORDINGS: A LITTLE DIFFERENT SOUND

On October 2, 1954—during Ernest Tubb's August-to-November sick leave, when he was hosting the *Jamboree* but not playing the Opry—his midnight show welcomed a young singer named Elvis Presley and his two musicians, Scotty Moore and Bill Black. Over from Memphis, they were plugging their only record release on Memphis's Sun label, "Blue Moon of Kentucky"/"That's All Right, Mama." They had played the Grand Ole Opry during the 10:15 segment, to no great response; Opry boss Jim Denny, according to Presley biographer Peter Guralnick, admitted the boy's talent but told Sun owner Sam Phillips that night that Presley didn't fit the Opry mold. Phillips had previously arranged their *Midnite Jamboree* appearance, and when Elvis met Ernest Tubb, he was effusive in his admiration for the Texas Troubadour. Recreated from several sources (and based largely on Tubb's own account), they had this basic conversation:

(Elvis) "They tell me if I want to make any money, I've got to sing this way."

(Tubb) "Have you always been poor?"

(Elvis) "Always."

(Tubb) "Well, son, you go ahead and do what they tell you. Make your money, and then you can sing the way you want to. But tonight on my show, sing 'Blue Moon of Kentucky.' "

Whatever Elvis's reception on the *Midnite Jamboree,* he was grateful for the chance to sing there and to meet Ernest Tubb, especially after his Opry disappointment. And for the rest of his life, Ernest Tubb was impressed with Presley's gratitude: "Of all the people who've been on my show, he is the only one who wrote me a thank-you note." Texas Troubadour Lynn Owsley (steel, first joined 1974) remembered that even in his last days, Elvis "was a fan of the old man's. Ernest's birthday was February 9. Every birthday until the year Elvis died, Elvis would send him a big heart-shaped box of chocolate candy, because he knew the old man liked chocolate."[25]

In 1954, Presley certainly was doing something new and different, something that rapidly won favor with younger record buyers, many of whom had been fans of country music before this time. "That's All Right, Mama" was a song straight out of rhythm and blues, a roots-based black style that on its own merits was winning numbers of young white fans. In short order, Tubb's young Grand Ole Opry mate, Marty Robbins, recorded a Columbia cover version of "That's All Right, Mama," and Tubb's old western swing idol Tommy Duncan was singing "Hound Dog" on Intro Records; the deluge had begun.

Ernest Tubb's own recorded repertory even showed some slight effects of the trend. His 1955 releases dropped to five singles (from six in 1954); one was a gospel single with titles cut in 1953, but three of the others featured songs of black origin: "Kansas City Blues," "The Yellow Rose of Texas" (stretching it, I know, since this 1830s tune so popular in Tubb's home state was *about* a mulatto), and a new Chuck Berry hit, "Thirty Days (To Come Back Home)." The similarity of Norma Barthel's review of "Thirty Days" and that of an earlier release, "Have You Seen (My Boogie Woogie Baby)," illustrate Tubb's flirtation with the new sound.

> Ernest's new record is "It's a Lonely World" . . . a lovely, sad number he has been doing for quite a while. Back side of the record is "Have You Seen My Boogie Woogie Baby?" a bouncy little boogie number that the Troubadours especially like! (July 1955)[26]

> Ernest has a new record out for Decca . . . First is a fast-stepping little number called "Thirty Days," which the Texas Troubadours really like

(They're always wanting Ernest to record something fast!). The flip side is a very pretty new one by Miss Cindy Walker called "Answer the Phone." (November 1955)[27]

Tubb had one foot in the old style and his other in the new. He'd sung "It's a Lonely World" ever since Redd Stewart wrote it for him in 1947; "Answer the Phone" was his third regular made-to-order Cindy Walker song. But it was "Thirty Days," its flip, that got the country chart action[28]—a sign of the times. While Ernest Tubb was not going as far as Robbins or others (Marty had cut Berry's "Maybelline" and Little Richard's "Long Tall Sally" by this time), even going this far toward R&B was a big surprise to son Justin.

> Well, that was Paul [Cohen]'s idea. That was back I guess at the begin-
> ning of, not artists or records crossing over, but songs. Artists in the
> country field cutting pop hits or rhythm and blues hits, and people in
> the pop field cutting country hits. And I didn't particularly go along with
> this one. I was a big Chuck Berry fan. Because I thought he was as close
> to a country songwriter as they had in rock and roll or rhythm and
> blues, 'cause his songs had stories. They had meaning to them, they
> had lyrics, clever lyrics, and I loved the song "Thirty Days." . . . He
> [Ernest] sold some records on it, and it was a good jukebox record for
> him, because there were a lot of jukeboxes that catered to the country
> field that liked the song, but they wouldn't put Chuck Berry's record on
> there. But Paul talked him into doing it. There were a couple that he did:
> "My Boogie Woogie Baby," and there was another one that I came to like
> better, "What Am I Living For." Now I didn't like the idea of him doing
> that at first, but once he got the record out and I listened to it a few
> times, it seemed to fit him more than "Thirty Days" did.[29]

Ernest Tubb's recordings the next year, 1956, show the same mixture of old and new, as he kept a foot in each of the stylistic camps. A heavy drumbeat marks most of the new songs, at least one side of each single release for the jukeboxes and disc jockeys. Examples of these are Johnny Cash's "So Doggone Lonesome," A side of his first 1956 single. Even heavier on the drumbeat was one side of Tubb's next single, a Jimmie Rodgers remake, of all things: "Jimmie Rodgers's Last Blue Yodel (The Women Make a Fool out of Me)." This is particularly curious, since, as young singer Stonewall Jackson (about whom more in due course) remembers, Ernest was angry with how Webb Pierce had "jazzed up" Jimmie's "In the Jailhouse Now" to make it 1955's monster hit. "He didn't speak to Webb for a year, I know."[30]

The flips on these records stayed closer to the established Tubb style. "Will

You Be Satisfied That Way" from 1955 was Jimmie Skinner's great song, set to the tune of "Just a Closer Walk with Thee," while Vic McAlpin's[31] "If I Never Have Anything Else" is highlighted by Tommy Jackson's smooth fiddle work.

Most of Tubb's studio work that year, though, was very much on the traditional side: twelve songs for his first twelve-inch album, *The Daddy of 'Em All,* which was finally released in 1957. Ernest was persuaded to pose on a makeshift throne with scepter in hand for the album's cover photo. The songs were for the most part country music standards that he had sung on radio and stage for much of his career. He did, though, mix in a couple of cover versions of fairly recent songs: Jack Toombs's "You're the Only Good Thing" (popular later for George Morgan) and a song Wade Ray had out on RCA Victor, "There's No Fool Like a Young Fool."

Tubb was proud of the album, and eager for its release, as he wrote to his fan club.[32] The songs finally appeared on three extended-play 45s in late March 1957, and *The Daddy of 'Em All* LP was finally issued July 1.

GABE TUCKER

Dub Albritten had been in Springfield several months when Ernest Tubb brought in a new manager, Texas radio personality and former Grand Ole Opry sideman Gabe Tucker. Tucker was working for Cliff Gross in Louisville when he first met Ernest Tubb during the war, and the two men came to know each other well after Tucker joined Eddy Arnold's first Opry band in 1943. Tucker was a born showman: trumpet player, bass player, standup comic, and much besides. "I remember Gabe done a tour with us, maybe several tours," Hank Snow recalls. "But if anybody ever talked really Southern, with a Southern drawl, it was Gabe . . . He'd go on the stage dressed in tails, and them people's expecting some high-faluting deal from New York, and start 'How y'all doin?' out there in tails. But he was a good showman, really good showman."[33] In Texas during the early 1950s, Gabe had emceed barn dances in the Houston area and worked as a flamboyant deejay on several radio stations. With a flair for publicity, Tucker saw that it was duly reported in *Billboard* (June 6, 1953) that he had played a very special request, "Ramona," for a listener while she died. Tucker was at KRCT in Baytown when he made the decision to move to Nashville and, from offices in the Ernest Tubb Record Shop, manage the careers of Ernest and Justin Tubb.

Tucker applied a pretty firm hand to the Tubb careers from the outset. Leaving the Houston area May 1, 1955, and setting up in Nashville three days later, he secured Justin a spot on the Grand Ole Opry's roster September 10 of that year, after booking Justin's very busy summer of personal appearances. Ernest's summer was highlighted by a very successful show in—of all places—

Nashville, drawing a crowd of nearly twenty thousand to a free outdoor show held at Centennial Park. Though he wasn't the only attraction (he brought along a newcomer down from D.C. named Patsy Cline) and admission was free, this was Tubb's largest crowd to date, surpassing a turnout of eighteen thousand at a favorite outdoor venue, Harry Smythe's Buck Lake Ranch in Angola, Indiana.[34]

Tucker tried to apply more discipline in the area of Tubb's cash-flow control. Tubb was amazed when Tucker offered him a 6 percent note for a $1,000 balance on the purchase of Tubb's Fleetwood Cadillac, a car with only about seventeen thousand miles on it when Tubb planned a trade-in. Tucker remembers, "He looked at me and said, 'I don't need that.' I said, 'Well, yeah, you do, too.' He said, 'You know, that's the first one I ever had.' I said, 'Well, frame that mother until I can get it back . . . Ernest, I could die tomorrow, and you've got a thousand dollars coming.'" Then there was the matter of the short walk over to lunch from the Record Shop to George & Gus's (what later became Linebaugh's). "So, me and Ernest'd be going down the street, and you know back in those days $5 was $5. He couldn't go from his store down there, and it wasn't half a block, without it cost him $5. Winos would hit him up, and goddamn, it'd cost him $5. And I said, 'Ernest, I could go down there, get us something to eat and come back, and we could both eat cheaper than what you give away.'"[35]

Looking at the big picture, Tucker was concerned that with possible hard times ahead, Ernest needed to build up a nest egg.

> When I went there, he didn't have no cash. And I looked the situation over, and I thought, God damn. And back then, it wasn't too damn easy to book a country artist. Right in there, 'cause Elvis had really started going good . . . Course with an old—I called Ernest the old rock of Gibraltar, because he's the most consistent man on draws there, at that time . . . So I got busy and I just worked my butt off and I got him about eighty-something thousand dollars in the bank, all of his bills paid up. And I don't mean that I done it all, hell, he went and worked, but I booked enough dates. Man, I was really proud of myself. What I was trying to do was to get Ernest a pile of money set up to where that I didn't have to take just anything that come. I figured that Ernest had paid his dues, and he was due the best dates in the business, but I couldn't do it if he didn't cooperate with me and save his money to where he could be independent. But I never could get that over to him.[36]

As Tucker put it, "Ernest was his own worst enemy. I believe, if he had that bus full of money, he'd have to hire somebody to go wreck it, get rid of it." That's exactly what he did this time.

When the next year came around, Tucker's publicity acumen put this face on the news that Ernest Tubb would indeed be very selective with his 1956 bookings. The fan club announced, "According to Gabe Tucker, Ernest will limit his personal appearances during 1956. He is going to make three tours in the spring and three tours in the fall, and that's all . . . so that he will have more time to devote to his business ventures in Nashville and elsewhere."[37] Limiting Tubb's tour schedule was of course in part making a virtue of necessity, as Tucker eloquently explained. Tubb had even told some of his boys, "I may not be doing this next year," implying layoffs that naturally didn't sit too well with them.[38] Tucker's rather imperious ways didn't sit too well with them, either. Billy Byrd recalls, "I liked him all right, till he got to be manager, and got to running the boys. You know, you can be manager and do it in a nice way, but you can't tell Ernest's boys or anybody else's boys when to leave and how to leave, and get on the road right away, and all this stuff: that don't work."[39]

But Tucker and others did eye certain choice places to park Ernest's growing nest egg. The Record Shop and Ernest Tubb Music were long since going concerns; it was the business ventures outside of Nashville that captured 1956's headlines. Most of Tubb's nest egg went into an investment in radio stations, made jointly with Hank Snow at the urging of publicist Bill McDaniel, who quit his WSM job to oversee the two co-owned stations. It did not have Tucker's blessing.

> A fellow by the name of McDaniel, worked up at WSM radio station, found two little old radio stations up in the hills of Kentucky [sic], come down there and made a big presentation like he's selling NBC, you know . . . Ernest said, "Gabe, would you come down tonight and sit in on this? You've been around radio for a long time; I'd appreciate your advice." . . . Went by, and he said, "What do you think?" I said, "Ernest, don't touch it. I wouldn't have the damn radio stations if you give 'em to me. It's a headache from the word go." And you know what? He and Hank went ahead and bought 'em, and they lost their butts. I said, "Now Ernest, if you do buy 'em, as soon as they get in trouble don't look to me to go up there and straighten 'em out, 'cause I ain't got time to fool with them." But I'll tell you, he's got guts; he never asked me to go up there. But he run poor old Charlie Mosley up there![40]

One of the stations was in the hills of Kentucky, at Whitesburg—WTCW, a 1,000-watt station on the air since February 1953. Tubb, Hank Snow, and McDaniel bought it from Kenneth Crosthwaite, newspaper man and soft-drink bottler in Whitesburg, for $95,000 in mid-April 1956. The seller's brother, Don Crosthwaite, was to remain as station manager.[41] The other station, WHBT, was in the hills of East Tennessee at Harriman, about forty miles west of Knoxville. Snow candidly agrees that Tucker's advice to Tubb was correct. "That was a very, very bad investment for us both. One was in a little 250-watt station in Harriman, Tennessee . . . And run by two brothers—both—one at each station. But that really turned out to be a big flop. And Ernest and I went up there and we went around and visited with all the merchants throughout the place, throughout both places, but we both sold our investments and got out of it smiling."[42] The closing assessment doesn't quite square with his opening sentence, the one much closer to Tucker's "they lost their butts."

If Gabe Tucker had any preferred investments for the Tubb nest egg, the only one that ever surfaced was in a Rio Grande Valley grapefruit ranch, and for this Tubb actually invested no money and made none, in spite of Tucker publicity to the contrary. He only "invested" his name, really, with a friend of Tucker's who owned and operated a grapefruit ranch in the valley. The key to marketing the fruit was the phrase "shipped directly from the Ernest Tubb Ranch," as though Tubb himself owned the ranch.[43] Actually, Tubb had nothing to do with the day-to-day operations, never even saw the ranch, but plugged the fruit on his *Midnite Jamboree*. Things were going pretty well until a drunken deejay at that fall's convention in Nashville blurted out to Tubb something close to the truth: that Tubb's name was being used for somebody else's free advertising. Tubb didn't like the look of the deal after this and wanted out of "the Ernest Tubb Ranch." The collapse of this arrangement was the beginning of the end for the Tubb-Tucker relationship, though already there were rifts. The previous spring, Tubb had forced Tucker to take on the management of the Wilburn Brothers. "I didn't want 'em. But he forced 'em on me, which I wasn't happy about."[44]

So after a year and a half, as of December 31, 1956 ("to keep my taxes straight"), Gabe Tucker left the scene and headed back to Texas. "By mutual consent," *The Country Music Reporter* had it, "his management contracts with Ernest Tubb, Ernest Tubb Music, Inc., Justin Tubb, and the Wilburn Brothers were being terminated."[45] Maybe it was a good time to go, with the coming of rock and roll, a shakeup at WSM (Artists' Service was in disarray, with the firing of Jim Denny the previous September), differences between the two principals, and unrest in the band. Tucker went back to the Houston area for radio and nightclub work, kept a hand in talent management (signing RCA's Hank Locklin in April and red-hot Bobby Helms of "Fraulein" fame in June), and eventually linked up with Houston music impresario H. W. "Pappy" Daily.

As for his former clients, Ernest Tubb included, Tucker gave his old buddy Hal Smith (then managing Ray Price and Jim Reeves) advance notice of his plans to leave Nashville. "I told Hal, 'I'm a nervous wreck, and I'm not gonna have a heart attack. So I'm gonna turn every damn artist I got loose except Bobby Helms, and I'm gonna send them a wire the last week in December, and they'll be available as of January 1, 1957 . . . Well, hell, Hal, I won't tell anybody I'm aleaving, but you. I don't want you to go hit 'em up to manage 'em until January 1, but January 1, if you want 'em, I feel like you can get 'em.'" Hal got them: "Every damn one of 'em."[46] Ernest's old fiddler became his booking agent in the new year 1957. Smith's booking agency, Curtis Artist Productions, and its successors would book Ernest Tubb on more shows than all his earlier agents combined, in the full quarter-century that remained of his career. That quarter-century didn't exactly get off to a great start, though: because of rock and roll and personal problems, 1957 would be Ernest Tubb's toughest year since 1948.

21

The Good That Men Do

FAMILY MAN

Already we've seen that Ernest Tubb was country music's most altruistic, unselfish, and least jealous individual. If Tubb believed in a newcomer's talent, and saw that he needed a break, Tubb would go out of his way to see that he got it. Helping others was almost his main industry activity, but as we've also seen, Ernest Tubb was just as giving on the home front.

"He didn't tell me this," Hank Snow said, "[but] it comes from pretty straight people that he supported about seven families in Texas. They were kin in some way, probably a cousin or niece or nephew."[1] Likeliest candidates for this ongoing support were two sisters (Jewell and Opal), his mother, his father, and then those in Tennessee: Olene and his own growing new family. Ernest and Olene were blessed with their long-awaited first son on December 12, 1956. So sure was Ernest that they were going to have yet another girl that the arrival of Ernest Dale Tubb Jr. cost Ernest, a natural gambler, handsomely: $20 steaks to all his band and a hand-tooled guitar case to songwriter Eddie Noack.[2]

Noack's good friend and Ernest Tubb fan Dr. Byron Baker witnessed this transaction as the three men talked about the blessed event in the lobby of Houston's Rice Hotel, where Ernest had made his first Decca records over sixteen years before and was staying while performing in the Houston area. Dr. Baker adds that the loss of the guitar case was something "which Olene later objected to."[3] Noack, Houston's young but famous writer of "These Hands" (the huge Hank Snow hit), was doubtless pitching Ernest songs that night; the next month, Tubb cut Noack's "God's Eyes."

Ernest Jr. soon got the nickname "Tinker" from a babyish trait: "Well, he was always tinkering with things, from the time he embarked in his walker, he was into the cabinets and the pots and pans."[4] But the name was still just Ernest Jr.

when Tubb proudly said to his fan club, "I just wish you could see the 'Boss' of us all, E.T. Jr. We're all so proud of him! . . . And remember, BE BETTER TO YOUR NEIGHBORS AND YOU'LL HAVE BETTER NEIGHBORS. Sincerely yours, ERNEST TUBB SR. (How about that title?)"[5]

STARS OF THE FUTURE

For Ernest Tubb, then, charity began at home; but that was *only* the beginning. As the industry's greatest altruist, Ernest Tubb stood ready at all times with a helping hand for the deserving newcomer. Whatever it took, whatever the need was—professional advice, a spot on the *Midnite Jamboree,* a sandwich, a loan, a gift. "He was one of the most unselfish people that I've ever known," Hank Snow recalls. "And helped more artists than you can shake a stick at—I mean from Pee Wee King right on down the line to some of them that's on the Opry right now . . . And would neglect his own work to do so."[6] Neglect his own work, yes, and spend from the fund of goodwill that he had built up in an industry that owed him so much. Seldom, in other words, did Ernest call in favors on his own behalf, but very often he did so for others.

In keeping with the tradition he'd established with such artists as Hank Thompson, Hank Williams, and Hank Snow, he continued to hold a hand out to the talented younger performer, maybe even more regularly as the mid-fifties brought trying times to the straight country singers. The *Midnite Jamboree,* week in and week out, showcased four or five acts—some of them Opry stars, to be sure, but most were newcomers with that first or second small-label record on the market, having very little luck attracting the attention of disc jockeys or major label producers. Many or most would never be heard from again, but a few made it. And for some of these few, Ernest Tubb went the extra mile, opening doors and insisting that well-placed people give a special listen.

PATSY CLINE

That Ernest Tubb was an early booster of Patsy Cline is indisputable. What has been the subject of some dispute since the publication of Margaret Jones's recent Cline biography is the extent of the boost he gave. There, Gabe Tucker questions Tubb's role in Cline's ascent. "Ernest gets credit for all this bullshit for what he done for Patsy. It's very unlikely he helped her pick any songs or did anything for her because if he had a good song, unless it was strictly a girl's song, he ain't going to give it to nobody. He'd do it himself."[7] To this writer, Tubb claimed only to have been present at that June 1, 1955, Coral session, not to have provided any song material.[8] And when Tucker goes on in Jones's book to talk about the grandiose plans he had (after a first meeting, mind you) for Patsy as part of a package tour with Ernest, the Wilburns, and even Bobby Helms, he's plainly blowing smoke. In 1955, the Tucker-Tubb partnership did not include the Wilburn Brothers: Tubb forced them into the deal nearly a year later (spring 1956), and against Tucker's wishes, if he told me the truth in 1977. And Bobby Helms? After some *Midnite Jamboree* appearances late the following year, Helms was signed to a Gabe Tucker managerial contract in the spring of 1957, months after Tucker had severed his ties with the Tubbs and returned to Texas.

Tucker's account of Patsy's coming to Nashville for the first time is basically right. In town for her initial recording session, she was brought to his attention by an advance call from her Washington, D.C. mentor Connie B. Gay, one of Tucker's former employers and a frequent booker of Ernest Tubb. Gay asked Tucker to find a spot for her on the *Midnite Jamboree,* which he did—Tucker trusted Gay's judgment of talent. But he couldn't do it without some juggling and only after making the poor girl sing her song four different times in rehearsals—a first time by herself, twice for Gabe, and a fourth time for Ernest, who agreed with Gabe's assessment: "Damn, you are right. She *is* a female Red Foley."[9] With her first *Midnite Jamboree* performance behind her, she was assured she could return to the show whenever she was in town. Only weeks later she was back, singing on the Sunday morning June 26 program and then guesting on the big Centennial Park free show headlined that Sunday afternoon by Tubb. *Billboard*'s July 15 account of that concert, following the lead of the Nashville newspaper that sponsored the event, misspelled her name "Kline," but as most agreed even then, Nashville would be hearing a lot more from this young woman. The next Saturday, July 1, she sang on the Grand Ole Opry for the first time, performing the feature song from her June 1 session, the still-unreleased Eddie Miller song, "A Church, a Courtroom, and Then Goodbye." Then at Ernest Tubb's invitation, Patsy performed on a big July 4 package show at Memphis's Russwood Ball-park,[10] with Texas Bill Strength, Faron Young, the Wilburn Brothers, Goldie Hill, and a host of other artists.

Starring on Connie B. Gay's *Town & Country Time Jamboree* back in Washington, Patsy Cline came to Nashville on a fairly regular basis in the months that followed. She played the November 1955 Fourth Annual Disc Jockey Convention there, and just after New Year's came back for another recording session. She probably played the *Midnite Jamboree* again, but this time Tubb (no doubt with help from manager Tucker) did her even better: they got her an appearance on ABC-TV's monthly *Grand Ole Opry* show, Saturday night, January 7, 1956. Press accounts of the program don't mention her, and until recently no footage from this show had been found; but as photographs in the Opry's archive and newly found footage prove, co-host Ernest Tubb practically held Patsy's hand through this, her first national TV appearance. The other co-host, Jimmy Dickens, strolls over to where Ernest and Patsy are sitting and asks Ernest if this is the new girl singer "he's been talking about so much." Ernest owns up to it and goes on to brag about Patsy, who then sings "A Church, a Courtroom and Then Goodbye" to the two stars. She stays around while Ernest, with Billy Byrd's help, serenades her with his new hit, "Answer the Phone." And in the show's finale, when the whole cast has gathered in tribute to Hank Williams, Patsy stands to Tubb's immediate left and begins to sing the second verse of "I Saw the Light" when time runs out and the producer hustles the Cedar Hill Square Dancers onto the stage, who nearly knock Tubb over in their haste.

In the seven years that remained of her life, Patsy Cline rose from obscurity to stardom on the strength of her own great talent, Owen Bradley's production abilities, and wonderful songs in the early 1960s from Hal Smith's Pamper Music. As Tucker says, Ernest Tubb did not find her songs—for years she was tied up contractually with Bill McCall's Four Star Music—and apparently they never toured together. But Patsy Cline returned Tubb's favors by recommending a steel guitarist whom Tubb ultimately hired, Virginian Elmer "Buddy" Charleton.

JOHNNY CASH

Ernest Tubb was "introduced" to Johnny Cash by a record left inside his front door. It was "So Doggone Lonesome," Cash's second Sun release, placed there by Tucker Robertson, a former Record Shop employee who thought the song would be great for Tubb. Ernest must have agreed: he recorded the song shortly there-after (January 24, 1956).[11]

Their first joint tours came shortly after that, during which Cash got some valuable lessons in stage delivery: " 'Make those people know that you believe in what you're singing. When you're singing "Folsom Prison Blues," don't smile. Make them feel the misery of the lyrics; but when you're singing "I Walk the Line," give them a twinkle in the eye once in a while and let them know it's light-hearted.' I still think of those things Ernest told me when I'm onstage from time to time, and remember the lesson he gave me."[12]

Edward Linn, for his *Saga* feature article on Ernest Tubb in 1957, got this same story from Cash, whom Linn called "the hottest country singer at the moment." "Ernest coached me all through the tour . . . My big trouble was that I really didn't know the point I was trying to get across in the songs I was singing. I didn't know what I was supposed to be accenting."[13]

With Tubb's help—"I had to convince 'em that Johnny belonged"[14]—Cash joined the Grand Ole Opry for what proved to be a two-year stint in July 1956, a move clearly aimed to draw a younger crowd to the show. Linn's article, written so soon after the event, gives this account, using the word "country" where I think he means "rock": "When he got back to Nashville, Ernest began pushing Cash to the Opry. It took a hit record to get Cash up there, though ['I Walk the Line']. His main problem was that as soon as it became evident that he was the kind the girls scream over, everybody advised him to become a little more 'country,' to mold himself after Presley. Tubb told him to stick to his own style and be himself. 'You've got the whole family,' he said. 'What do you want to lose anybody for?' "[15]

Cash's deep voice ensured a high degree of compatibility between his song material and Tubb's. Tubb was clearly a Cash influence, as biographer Colin Escott points out: "Cash was obviously influenced by other singers who worked the low vocal range with minimal instrumental support, artists like Ernest Tubb and Jimmie Skinner."[16] But starting with "So Doggone Lonesome," Tubb recorded Cash's material far more often than Cash recorded Tubb's. Douglas Glenn Tubb, who toured a great deal with Cash early and co-wrote songs with him, such as the fine "Home of the Blues," plugged several Cash tunes to his uncle. A year after "So Doggone Lonesome," Tubb cut Cash's "My Treasure" for a single and "Home of the Blues" for an EP.[17] Douglas Glenn was still plugging Johnny Cash songs to Ernest Tubb as late as the early 1970s, when he successfully pitched him Cash's "Say Something Nice to Sarah."[18] Meantime Tubb had made album cuts of four other Cash songs. Two First Generation tribute duets cut with Tubb in 1979, "Jealous Loving Heart" and "Soldier's Last Letter," are Cash's only recordings of Ernest Tubb songs.

THE WILBURN BROTHERS

Teddy and Doyle, the Wilburn Brothers, were already Decca artists with three charted records when Ernest Tubb took them under his wing in 1956. As children in the Wilburn Family, they had played the Grand Ole Opry in 1940 and recorded for Four Star in the early 1950s. Signed with Decca in 1954 through the assistance of their boss at the time, Webb Pierce, the boys were touring as a duo in Faron Young's entourage by the time of Webb's big 1955 hit "In the Jailhouse Now" (which featured their uncredited vocals). *Billboard* on March 10, 1956, reported, the "Wilburn Brothers confirm that they're on their own after touring for 15 months with Faron Young. They played their last date with him February 26, 1956. They parted on friendly terms . . ."[19]

The Grand Ole Opry didn't see fit to add them to their list of artists at that time, either, so Tubb went to work on that, first taking them on the aforementioned Pillsbury Flour tour in April and May 1956. As Edward Linn described the sequence of events, writing in 1957, "Despite their reputation, the Wilburns were ready to quit only a short time ago and go back home. They weren't getting airtime over the Opry . . . Ernest, who felt they were being squeezed, immediately put them on his midnight show and took them on tour. Then he fixed it so they got back on the Opry."[20]

Not only would the Wilburns tour with Ernest almost constantly for the next couple of years, but he recorded four songs with them in 1957, including the chart hits "Mister Love" and "Hey, Mr. Bluebird."

STONEWALL JACKSON

Last of these mid-fifties future stars boosted by Ernest Tubb was the Moultrie, Georgia, farmboy who came to Nashville with a satchel full of songs in his pickup truck: Stonewall Jackson. In his autobiography *From the Bottom Up,* Jackson recalls coming to town on a Wednesday and pitching songs to Acuff-Rose, trying out with Judge Hay and Dee Kilpatrick (Jim Denny's successor) for the Grand Ole Opry on Thursday, and playing his first *Friday Night Frolic* the next night backed by the Texas Troubadours. Writer Walt Trott placed that Friday Opry debut on November 2, 1956, and as Jackson now says about this sequence of events, "The Good Lord or somebody was looking out for me. I didn't waste no time."[21]

Jackson proudly admits that Ernest Tubb right away became the main "somebody" looking out for him. Olene Tubb, listening at home to that Friday broadcast as her husband introduced this complete unknown who immediately won over the studio audience, took Stonewall for someone that her husband should help. "I'd like for you to kinda take him under your wing, and see that he gets a chance." "I'll be glad to; I think he's got something too."[22]

"The first thing he done, he bought me some clothes. That happened, like, the next Monday . . . After we got on the road he bought me quite a bit more stuff . . . and got me outfitted real good." And that was only the beginning. "I'd be on the [Opry] portion with Ernest all the time. I done the Record Shop . . . and I went out and opened up Ernest's shows for about a year and a half." The road shows paid Stonewall "$20, $25 a night," generous considering "I wasn't of any value to him—if you can't sell a ticket, you're no value! And if they don't know who you are, you don't sell no tickets." To help cover living expenses at home, Tubb put Jackson on a retainer with Ernest Tubb Music in return for a few of his songs. "Like, $25 a week, so I could help pay my rent and have eating money and stuff like that . . . Then later on, like my fourth hit, was 'Why I'm Walking.' But it had been in his company all this time . . . He didn't know it would make him any money or anything, but when people do good things it comes around."[23]

As with most of the other young singers he helped, Tubb had for Jackson good advice about stage delivery. In Stonewall's case, the first thing he had to do was to quit trying to sing like Hank Williams. "I was always heavy into Hank Williams, so I just trained myself to sing like him, even that little break he did. So Ernest told me, 'I want you to do one thing for me. I want you just to turn loose and sing like yourself. Just sing like you would if you're not thinking about anybody.' That did away with the little break, because you have to kinda work to do that . . . He said, 'Because I tell you what. You sing so much like Williams, they'll just love you to death for just a little while, then they'll drop you like a hot potato, because there's already a Hank Williams.' "[24]

On the early tours, Tubb kept a close eye on Jackson's singing and delivery. "He checked me out, buddy. And he would tell me stuff, like, 'If you get an audience and they're not very responsive, you can always pick out one or two people out there that's really enjoying what you're doing. Concentrate on them. Concentrate on somebody that's got a positive look in their face, and just concentrate on that person. And that'll get you through it. Ninety-nine times out of a hundred, you'll win the rest of them over."[25]

Tubb even helped the unknown Opry newcomer land a record contract with rival Columbia Records. Ernest and Dee Kilpatrick of the Opry lined up a series of auditions with several labels; Decca, although interested in Jackson, was not on the list. " 'I didn't call Decca in on it,' " Jackson remembers Tubb saying, " 'because I'm afraid that'll look too much like you're just being pushed by me . . . Decca would sign you, they've already heard about you, they would sign you just from hearing about you, and hearing you on the Opry. But I wouldn't want to push you where you're that close to me.' So they set up auditions with Columbia, RCA, and different ones. Three or four different ones, and I wound up on Columbia."[26]

Charlie Walker remembers that though Don Law of Columbia appreciated Stonewall's talent and would come to do so even more later, he would have signed Jackson just on the strength of Tubb's recommendation. He had passed up a chance years before to sign Tubb himself, and wasn't about to pass up a Tubb protégé.[27]

Jackson says today, "I loved Ernest like a Daddy, like a second Daddy . . . He was as near to a second father that I would ever have, Ernest Tubb was." And, like a father, Ernest even concerned himself with Stonewall's personal life. "I had a girl that I met when I first came here . . . He'd see me downtown, see me at a restaurant with her, and say, 'I don't think you oughta do that. I seen you with that same girl.' . . . He wanted me to kinda stay away from that until I could get established, you know . . . Of course that relationship worked out [it was his future wife, Juanita] . . . My wife never liked him for a while, till after she got more acquainted with him . . . He just thought it might be some girl I'd found down there around Linebaugh's or Tootsie's: fresh off a barstool at Tootsie's, for all he knew."[28]

Also like a good father, Ernest Tubb was concerned with Stonewall's personal appearance. Besides buying the Western clothes, Tubb bought Jackson a $100 Stetson hat on one of his first outfitting sessions. "And I had it on," Jackson remembers, "riding down the road with it, and he kept looking at me. And he said, 'Let me see that.' You know, the window on them old buses just pushes back. He just sailed that out the window! And he'd just give a hundred dollars for it. He said, 'You're like Hank Williams. You ain't got sense enough to wear a hat.' And I guess I about had it down on my ears a little bit there. Evidently he thought I looked better without a hat, so I never wore a hat a lot."[29]

Jackson hit the road with Tubb right away, for a tour of the Northwest in November 1956, although his role as a regular on Tubb's long tours would not come until 1958. By that time, his 1957 and 1958 Columbia recordings were starting to sell, "Not real big, but thirty thousand, forty thousand records at a time, till I hit. And each one would do a little better." The "hit" came in the fall of 1958 with a song he and George Jones had written around a tag line given them by a Tennessee prison inmate, "Life to Go."

When the autograph lines for Jackson at package shows got as long (or longer) than Tubb's, Tubb had another fatherly talk with the young singer. "I seen how you did out there with all those pictures and that big line you got out there. I think it's probably time that you put you a little outfit together and go out on your own."[30] That's exactly what he did, and the next year brought Jackson the huge crossover hit "Waterloo." Another career was in high gear, thanks in no small part to help from the Texas Troubadour.

22

More Tough Times: Rock and Roll

As early as 1955, the year of Bill Haley's "Rock around the Clock" and the first full year of the Elvis Presley phenomenon, country music disc jockeys were debating about a new influx of "rhythm and blues" and pop songs into the music they loved and played. The purists who wanted to stay with traditional country sounds were sometimes dubbed "hardliners" whose attitude was described by *Billboard* at one point as "antiprogress . . . some C&W deejays . . . refuse to play anything even faintly tinged with a pop or rhythm and blues flavor, even when recorded by a C&W artist."[1] Some real hardliners might not have played Tubb's rendition of a pop song ("Till We Two Are One," 1954) or an R&B tune ("Thirty Days," 1955), especially since these featured heavier beats and jazzier guitar licks.

But this mid-fifties crossover of songs soon became a crossover of singers too. Marty Robbins cut R&B songs in an R&B style, such as "Long Tall Sally" and "Maybelline," and Eddy Arnold became a straight pop singer with a new version of "Cattle Call" that used Hugo Winterhalter's orchestra. And in 1956, when two more Sun artists, Carl Perkins and Johnny Cash, came up with smash hits in this new style so beloved of affluent baby boomers, some heretofore country artists, often with a push from their A&R men, took a fling with rock or at least with that more country hybrid that was later dubbed "rockabilly." George Jones of "Why Baby Why" fame recorded a couple of wild ones, "How Come It" and "Rock It," using the name Thumper Jones. Fiddling Jimmie Loden of Alabama's Loden Family (they played Ernest Tubb's big Memphis show in August 1942), now billed as Sonny James, cut a smash teen hit that had nothing country about it: "Young Love." That year the country charts were dominated by the new sounds: Presley racked up roughly half of 1956's number 1 country records with five of them, while Perkins and Cash each had one, and Marty Robbins's pop-tinged "Singing the Blues" also made the list. Many country deejays objected to the dominance on *Billboard*'s chart of the new sounds, but there wasn't much they could do about it, given the buying and listening habits of the new generation. If they tried a boycott (as some did) and refused to play "objectionable" recordings, competitor stations gladly took up their slack to meet the demand.

While the purists could point with pride to the occasional success of a Ray Price or Louvin Brothers record, times got tough in a hurry for hard-core country artists. Ernest Tubb's manager in 1955 and 1956, Gabe Tucker, said, "Rock and roll was eatin' our damn lunch. They damn near put us out of business."[2] These were the days, remembers Wesley Rose of Hickory Records and Acuff-Rose Publishing, that his staff had so little business to transact they whiled away much of the good weather months playing softball or golf. Ernest Tubb, Stonewall Jackson says, was hurt by the decline of traditional country music's appeal and his own pulling power on the road. "I've seen it at the Ryman where you'd only have a few rows of people up front. This really hurt Ernest, it hurt him deep. And he was like a man grieving, like he'd had a couple of kids die. It was really a grief-type situation."[3]

On records, Tubb for a time tried to have it both ways, as we've seen, with singles that often featured an up-beat, newer-styled song paired with a more traditional love song. But as far as chart performance was concerned, there was no need to bother. His large and loyal following kept the sales of his three 1956 singles respectable, but nothing like what the new artists were doing and nothing like his own peak sales figures of a decade earlier. Tubb, unlike many of the older traditional country artists, continued to make records throughout this tough period, but 1956 became the first year since *Billboard* started country charts in 1944 during which not a single Ernest Tubb record appeared.

Times were tough for Tubb on the road too. It wasn't simply "to look after business interests," the stated reason, that Tubb cut back on his touring that year, to "three tours in the spring and three tours in the fall." The demand simply wasn't there. Hank Snow disbanded for awhile, and Tubb thought about doing it; Dickie Harris recalled Tubb's warnings, "Boys, I may not be doing any touring next year."[4] Hal Smith, booking Tubb from the beginning of 1957, remembers that a time came when Tubb seriously considered getting out of the business: "Well, things were on the decline: not to where we were starving, but certainly not doing as well as we had. TV was red hot all of a sudden. Well, Ernest and I had just about reached the end. He came out here to the 119 Two Mile Pike office [and] we talked everything over. We came this close to concluding that the best thing to do was to get out of the business! . . . Well, his brother was in the insurance business in Texas by then, so Ernest said, 'I could go into business with Bud, but this is all I've ever done.' It was so sad."[5] Stonewall Jackson, touring with Tubb, saw it firsthand and made this assessment.

> The gravy got a little bit thin there . . . I can tell you that was the lowest ebb that I've ever seen country music at. When Presley hit, and it got all the attention on Presley, and the other singers that was doing that same kind of stuff—it just preempted country to the lowest amount that I've ever seen it preempted . . . You could take a big package, not just a few of us, out, and you could still not have very much of a crowd. And Ernest would get, he would just be so hurt . . . It hit its knees, though, and I suppose more than hurting Ernest, it scared him too. He was really concerned, because we'd go out there in Oklahoma, and Texas, and places where he was supposed to be strong. And we just wouldn't have them . . . It was only like a year in there, but it was a tough year. And you don't know the future. When you go off a cliff like that, you think, "Boy, this could be it."[6]

Ernest Tubb confined his one printed statement about rock and roll to what follows, mild in view of the music's effect on his career. The two-part question, submitted through his fan club, was "Do you like rock and roll music? Do you think it should be played on country music record shows?" His answers hinge on a distinction between "liking" and "appreciating" music, and a philosophy of the local and representational role of the disc jockey.

> This is a hard one! Let's say I like, to some extent at least, music in any form. Some I can appreciate, some I cannot, including R&R. As to whether R&R should be played on country music shows let me say that Jimmie Rodgers had a strip pasted on his guitar which read, "Variety is the spice of life." I refuse to disagree with that. So, I feel that if the majority of a Country Music DJ's listeners wanted some Rock and Roll, then they should play some. If the majority didn't want it, then I don't think the DJ should play it. They should have their own opinion, but not force their opinions on others. Frankly, for everyday listening, give me good old Country Music.[7]

PACKAGE TOURS AND A NEW BUS

The package tour, as implied in Stonewall Jackson's last-quoted comment, was the main response of Ernest Tubb and other country artists to the slackening demand for personal appearances. Extra names on the marquee, it was hoped, would draw enough extra ticket buyers to offset splitting the take so many more ways. With all or at least most of the acts traveling together in a caravan, travel costs were cut and safety enhanced. Talent on the RCA Victor roster had used a single-bus, caravan approach as early as 1954. Johnnie & Jack, Kitty Wells, and Roy Acuff headlined a touring package show for most of 1955 and 1956—a totally logical team, seeing as how Kitty was Johnnie's wife, and Roy and Kitty were just then recording duets for Decca. These early country package tours could hardly be called responses to rock and roll, though, since the Wells-Acuff group even played three dates with Presley, who was rudely treated by the erstwhile King of Country Music, Mr. Acuff.[8] Just as Tubb was starting his own traveling package show, the Philip Morris tobacco company blazed the trail with their Philip Morris Show, with country singers (Carl Smith, Goldie Hill, Red Sovine), an announcer (Biff Collie), a comedian (Bun Wilson), even a rock singer (Ronnie Self). Unlike any country tour before or since, this show, with full corporate sponsorship, charged no admission price beyond proof of purchase of a pack of Philip Morris cigarettes. Small wonder that this angered the more traditional bookers and promoters; going up against a "free" show is always tough, and this came at a time when rock and roll had everybody crying anyway. Philip Morris, to be sure, would never have done it but to attempt to salvage their image in the South after published reports that they had given money to the NAACP.

While Tubb had played package shows well before the mid-fifties—going all the way back to those 1941–1942 Oscar Davis shows, in fact—he never traveled as part of one before the beginning of 1957, when his group, including the Wilburn Brothers, joined up with the Kitty Wells and Johnnie & Jack troupe (Acuff, maybe at the right time, had tired of road work for the time being) for a one-year series of tours booked by Tubb's new agent Hal Smith and the Johnnie & Jack manager, Frankie More.

Tubb was quoted three months into his own package show saying that this idea was proving a godsend for the WSM artists and would be the wave of the future. The piece may be largely hype in the face of the rock crisis, and the title might be a case of whistling past the graveyard: "Tubb Predicts Opry Artists Entering Best Tour Season." But here are some of Tubb's printed thoughts: "A complete Grand Ole Opry unit means more of our Opry artists are getting opportunities to work regularly . . . It's far better than the former system of having one or two Opry stars, and a number of non-Opry performers to make up a show, that would carry the Grand Ole Opry label because the Opry star was headlined. I look for the package plan to grow and grow as it proves its success."[9]

Tubb took his group in a newly purchased flex bus, his first of any kind since the ill-famed school bus of ten years earlier, and something that his boys had wanted him to get for some time. He announced it to the fans: "Well, the Troubadours and I will be traveling in the big bus that I bought from my good friend, Pee Wee King, during this new year. It is in the shop, as I write this, being remodeled inside. When completed, it will have twelve seats, folding couches that will sleep three people, clothes closets for our costumes, an ice box for cold drinks, a place to make our coffee, and a rest room. We are all so happy over the comfort this bus will give us on the many long tours we plan to make this year."[10] Eyeing such comfort, the boys had pressed the boss for some years to buy a bus and outfit it in just such a manner. In their efforts they were not above enlisting Tubb's good friends to join the lobbying, one of whom was Michigan booker and bandleader Casey Clark, who already had a bus. Clark agreed, and Tubb was finally convinced that he too could afford such comfort.[1]

The bus he bought was Pee Wee King's gasoline-powered, six-cylinder flex bus. King remembers, "I traded him the bus. I bought it in Iowa and the boys didn't like the bus, so we went back to the limousines. So consequently, Ernest had a Cadillac and said, 'I'll give you this as a down payment and give you $500 a month for six months,' and he did. So that's how we made the deal: he got the bus and I got the Cadillac."[12]

After the proper renovations, the bus was ready to roll on the package tour at the beginning of February 1957, after publicity pictures were taken in front of the Ernest Tubb Record Shop. Tubb put his boys (Rusty Gabbard, Ray "Kemo" Head, Jack Drake, and Billy Byrd) and the Wilburn Brothers on the bus, while Johnnie and Kitty followed in a brand-new Lincoln that they owned and Jack Anglin and their band (Shot Jackson, Joe Zinkan, Ray Crisp) in a second car. It's a good thing the cars were along: the bus sometimes literally needed a boost uphill, Johnnie Wright remembers.[13]

The bus motor finally gave out in San Diego, according to Wright. His steel guitarist, Shot Jackson, probably the best mechanic on the tour, pulled the whole engine out and loaded it into the bed of a pickup truck to get it overhauled or swapped for a new one. Unable to resist the lure of nearby Tijuana, Mexico, Jackson and some of the boys left the loaded pickup on the U.S. side of the border, only to return and find the pickup in place but the engine stolen. "Shot never did live that down . . . Ernest kept after him, 'Shot Jackson, you took my motor off in that truck and sold it.' "[14] The engine's former owner, Pee Wee King, remembers that Tubb rented a car to get back to Nashville, leaving one of his boys with the engineless bus in a California garage, and on a WSM broadcast made the following plea: "Whoever's got my motor bring it back, because my boy and the bus, they want to come back home."[15]

Wright recalls that most of the dates were quite successful. "Usually we'd do good. I don't think we ever made a flop . . . I'd say if we made $500 apiece clear a week, that was about average; $500, after everybody; that'd be me, Kitty, and

Jack, maybe wind up with anywhere from $250 to $500 each a week, after paying the hotel bills and the gasoline. It was a lot of money back then; the admission price was so low: $1.00 in advance, $1.50 at the door."[16]

Gate receipts, then, held up pretty well, although Tubb's bus repair and telephone bllls cut into his take considerably. "Ernest was on the telephone one night, how many hours? About fifteen hours one night, talking to Olene, solid!" Of course, he was drunk to begin with to do such a thing, because of which he almost missed the next night's show (and probably should have, given his condition and performance). "Billy Byrd kicked off something, and Ernest, he started singing something else. And he turned around, 'Billy Byrd, you kicked off the wrong song.' He never did get straight that night. That's the only time I ever did see him like that."[17]

Another drain, increasingly after buses even made it possible during travel, was his gaming losses. Tubb had gambled from an early age. One source recalled Ernest's gambling binges with his father and brother, holed up in a Dallas hotel room. From the days of the big cars, Dickie Harris recalls driving down the road with the overhead light on, so that Tubb and various band members could play cards in the back seat. And not just the usual poker games, although there were plenty of those, but bets of chance. Kemo told Johnnie Wright of a particular game they devised with empty beer cans in their hotel room.

> He said he and Ernest and a bunch of them was in the room one night after a show, and they was all drinking beer, and they got to betting they could throw a beer can off the wall, and it'd fall into the trash can . . . If it didn't, you lost a quarter or whatever. It made so much racket, Kemo said, that the desk clerk called up and said, "You're gonna have to cut that racket out, it's waking all the people up next door." Ernest said, "All right, we'll stop that." So they took the mattress off the bed and set it up against the wall. Then they'd throw the can up and hit that mattress, and it'd drop down there.[18]

PERSONAL WOES

Fatherhood

If rock and roll's heyday was tough on Ernest Tubb professionally, the period was also a trying time on his personal life. His first two children reached marriageable age, always cause for concern to a loving parent. Teddy Wilburn remembers that a few of Ernest Tubb's marathon phone calls back to Nashville from hotel rooms on the 1957 tours were to his daughter, Violet Elaine. In his October 1956 fan club journal, Ernest Tubb said of Elaine, "She has no recent recordings but plans to make some new ones in the near future."[19] Two months later, *Melody Trails* reported that "Ernest's oldest daughter is doing fine after her serious accident several weeks ago. She has returned to Nashville after a visit back to Texas to recuperate . . . Elaine sings nearly every week on the Midnight [*sic*] Jamboree and is making preparations for a recording contract deal soon, I understand."[20] A contract never materialized: that one 1953 single was all she would ever make.

Justin's career on Decca Records, tours, and on the Opry was going along just fine: at least until rock and roll hit. Living in a "bachelor house he had built last year, here in Nashville, when not on tour,"[21] in 1956 he cut an up-tempo version of "You Nearly Lose Your Mind," the first (and one of the few) Ernest Tubb songs he recorded. It would not be the last rock- or pop-styled Justin Tubb recording. In mid-1957, he cut an album of traditional country songs, "Country Boy in Love," in the new style, which included his Dad's "Try Me One More Time." The project was a compromise he worked out with Paul Cohen: newer accompaniment to older songs of Justin's own choosing. His father urged Justin to go through with the project despite misgivings, thinking he should not make waves with the company.

Playing the Jimmie Rodgers Festival each year was about the only contact on the road between father and son, though of course Justin was an Opry and *Midnite Jamboree* regular. At the 1957 Jimmie Rodgers Festival—moved up to May 21 and 22 owing to scheduling problems with too many artists for the 26th, a Sunday that year—Justin sprang a surprise on his father and his fans: he was no longer a bachelor. Though not yet twenty-two, he married a Nashvillian, Mary Beatrice "Bea" Swift, at Tulumbia, Mississippi, en route to that year's Rodgers festival. "Porter Wagoner was my best man," he recently recalled to Otto Kitsinger.[22]

The Jim Denny Episode

The May 21–22, 1957, Fifth Annual Jimmie Rodgers Memorial Day Celebration gave Ernest Tubb a daughter-in-law; but it's also memorable for sparking the most dramatic confrontation of Ernest Tubb's life and career, one that was potentially devastating.

Tubb and Hank Snow lined up their usual array of top talent for the two-day event: Johnnie & Jack, Kitty Wells, Jim Reeves, Roy Acuff, Ray Price, the Wilburn Brothers, Charlie Walker, Justin Tubb, and many others. For the first time, awards were given: Marty Robbins won the Jimmie Rodgers Achievement Award as the outstanding male entertainer in country music (tradespeople and fans voted for this), while Kitty Wells took the same award for female entertainer.

Industry voters selected winners of the Jimmie Rodgers Hall of Fame Award, for persons contributing the most to country music over the last five years (i.e, the lifetime of the festival). Festival cosponsors Tubb and Snow shared the award, the first of its kind. The festival's short history after this, coupled with the birth the next year of the Country Music Association, tends to obscure the fact that Tubb and Snow were hall of famers even before there was a Country Music Hall of Fame.

These were the highlights. But problems arose when Jim Denny, the fired Opry Artist Service Bureau chief, now the head of Cedarwood Music and the Jim Denny Artist Agency, brought to Meridian the very same week the Philip Morris Country Music Show, "free" admission and all. Tubb and Snow had fought its coming, objecting to Denny's underhanded tactic of drawing from the crowd that they had worked for five years to build up. Denny did it anyway, staging a spectacular at the Junior College football stadium May 22, second night of the festival, complete with a radio hookup and a speech from Tennessee Governor Frank Clement. "We weren't the only ones on the free show," Johnnie Wright remembers. "They had probably half of the Grand Ole Opry people on there that night . . . Ernest and Jim Denny fell out completely. They didn't speak to each other for a long, long time. Really, I think Ernest was right on it, myself. I'll have to give him credit for doing the right thing. Because they were there first; I think to put a free show in against something that's charging for to get in was really bad."[23]

Hank Snow is still upset about it, almost forty years afterward, without naming names or years; but he says this was one reason he and Ernest lost interest in staging the Rodgers festivities. "It was no fault of little Johnny [Call for Philip Morris], but the Philip Morris company was one of the culprits who used the celebration to do their advertising. They took a free ride on what we had worked so hard to build. To me that was very cheap. Did they do anything to help Ernest and me in getting the event established? No. Not one thing."[24] No event was held in 1958; there was a festival in June of 1959, but by then Mrs. Rodgers's health had seriously declined. Tubb and Snow never again hosted the Meridian festivities, which only resumed years later.

The more immediate consequence of this Philip Morris flap was a tragicomic, pseudo-confrontation between Ernest Tubb and Jim Denny. Billy Byrd remembers that even before Tubb left Meridian at the week's end, he had resorted to drink. "Ernest got drunk, and the more he thought about it, the madder he got. So he gets back to Nashville, and he's still drunk."[25] On Sunday night/ Monday morning, May 26–27, back in Nashville, still mad and still drunk, Tubb called Jim Denny at home, woke him up, and cussed him up one side and down the other. Johnnie Wright thinks that Denny offered the suggestion, "Well, why don't we just meet up here on Union Street at WSM, and we'll settle this once and for all?" At that point, Denny "just took the phone off the hook, and laid it over there so Ernest couldn't wake him up anymore."[26] With no intention of going down to the National Life Building, Denny went back to sleep and put the matter out of his mind. But it was far otherwise with Ernest.

Tubb reached for something he'd only recently taken from Grady Martin in payment of a debt: a .357 magnum, complete with belt and bullets. "So Ernest straps that on him, in his house shoes, gets in his '56 private Fleetwood Cadillac, beautiful powder blue bottom and a light cream top, his own car. He drives it up, and the radio station back in those days was on the fifth floor of the National Life Building [7th and Union, downtown]. Ernest gets out in his house shoes and socks, and you never see Ernest without some kind of a boot on . . . And he walks in those house shoes into the lobby of the National Life Building, and you go to the elevator, and you go up to the fifth floor. Well, when he got into the lobby, there's a great big tall fellow, he must have been close to seven foot tall, called Mr. Lawrence."[27] "Ernest, you can't have that gun in here," Mr. Lawrence told him. "The hell I can't." "Well, you sure can't fire it." "Like hell I won't."[28] "Ernest looked at the elevator, and he fired a shot up over the elevator. Mr. Lawrence went running this way; wasn't but two or three in there, but they was running every which way, getting out of the way."[29] The newspaper accounts take the story from here: "Police Sgt. J. W. Irvin who directed the investigation of the incident, said police responded to a call at 5:30 a.m. that a man with a gun was at National Life. 'We found Ernest in the middle of the floor with a pistol,' he said. 'It had been fired once. There was a bullet hole in a window frame. Mr. Tubb was drunk. Mr. Tubb said he came there because he had a phone call from somebody threatening to kill him.' "[30]

WSM news director Bill Williams was in the lobby and said in later years that he was Tubb's mistaken target. "Today," Opry historian Jack Hurst wrote in 1975, shortly before Williams's death, "Williams recalls that he had just walked into the lobby of the National Life Building to go to work when a shot from a .357 Magnum pistol was fired over his head. Badly frightened, he turned and saw Tubb and shouted, 'Ernest, what are you doing?' All he can remember Tubb answering is, 'My God, I've shot the wrong man.' "[31] Newspaper accounts at the time vary as to just what Williams was doing: the Nashville *Banner* account has him on the elevator with WSM announcer David Cobb and night watchman A. H. Roberts;[32] the Nashville *Tennessean* says that "Williams was broadcasting when he heard the shot and went to the lobby immediately."[33] Hurst's account adds that "an engineer already on duty upstairs in the WSM studios called the police as soon as he heard the shot . . . and they arrived almost immediately." In any event, Williams went to the phone and called station manager Jack DeWitt to tell him what had happened. "Well, you've got to get Ernest home." "Oh, it's too late for that—the police are already here."

Williams, target of the shot according to his later recollection, indisputably became Tubb's shepherd at that point, at the behest of his boss, Mr. DeWitt. Arrested on two counts—carrying a pistol and drunk and disorderly conduct—Tubb was taken to the city jail (Johnnie Wright believes he was taken to jail in Lebanon, Tennessee, 30 miles away, in the company of his manager, Hal Smith, to avoid undue publicity), and WSM sent Williams with him. "While Williams waited for him to complete the mandatory three hours incarceration for public drunkenness, Tubb bought cigarettes for the other inmates and sang to and with them, Williams recalls."[34] Tubb was released on bond at 9:00 A.M., the *Banner* reported in that afternoon's edition, and an hour later forfeited the $60 bond by failing to appear for trial in city court ("$10 for drunk and disorderly conduct and $50 for carrying a weapon").[35]

Bill Williams is the man that the local press went to for answers, but there wasn't a lot he would divulge. "It was accidental," he told the *Tennessean* for the next morning's edition. "There was nobody in the lobby with Ernest at the time. He apparently had come inside the lobby to see if the person who called him was there. The bullet went high into the wall over a door."[36] The *Tennessean* added, "Station authorities declined to identify the caller. They said it was a person with whom Tubb had had differences." Their protective spin at the front of the story is obvious: " 'It had nothing to do with the station,' Harri Anne Moore, public relations director said. 'Mr. Tubb was not here in connection with a performance at the time. It was more or less a private matter with Ernest.' "[37] The *Banner*'s account on the afternoon of the shooting is more revealing of the caller's identity, still without naming names: "Tubb was quoted as saying he had come there to meet a man no longer connected with Station WSM."[38] That was as close as Tubb himself ever came to revealing his caller's identity, though it was well known to anyone close to the business. Bill Williams told Jack Hurst in 1975 that it was Denny. "Jim said he finally had told Ernest to meet him in front of the National Life Building at 4:30 or so, thinking that Ernest would show up and then get tired of waiting and go home. He had forgotten that some of us would be coming to work early in the morning."[39] Hurst was the first to publish Jack DeWitt's belief, whether well founded or not, that Denny had engineered the whole incident to embarrass DeWitt, WSM, and the Opry, for his being fired the previous fall.[40]

Tubb never talked about the incident in later years, at least not to the press. Friends say that as Jim Denny was dying of cancer in 1963, Tubb made a successful effort at reconciliation. Others hint that third parties got them together with the lure of a profitable card game, each man thinking, "Well, that's all right. Maybe I can win some money off of the son of a bitch."

Jack Hurst in his 1975 Opry history is content to say this about Tubb's role: "Needless to say, the incident in the National Life lobby was out of character for Ernest Tubb."[41] I'm not so sure of that, and not just for the reason that in the course of researching this book I have unearthed a great many tales of Ernest Tubb's drunken escapades. His police record for minor offenses stretched back to at least April 26, 1954, when his car "snapped a telephone pole on North First Street near Berry."[42] On New Year's Eve 1957, several months after the Denny episode, he crashed "his 1957 Cadillac into a tree on Lynwood Terrace at Lynwood Boulevard," being "plenty drunk" at the time—an incident that also landed him once again in county jail and that time cost him $250 in bonds.[43]

Such episodes are not why I think the Denny encounter may not have been out of character. Though he could be mean when he drank, Tubb was certainly lucid in the sense of telling everybody what he thought. As Justin said, "He would go like months and wouldn't touch a drop, then all this stuff would build up that he'd want to get straightened out and get settled, and then he'd start drinking and for a couple of weeks maybe he'd sit there in that house and call everybody he was mad at, and tell them what was wrong, and what they oughta do to change it."[44] There is a clear element of seeking to right wrongs in the Denny episode. While Johnnie Wright doesn't necessarily endorse Tubb's shooting, he does feel that Ernest was right to be mad about Denny's sending in the free show on top of a festival he'd worked five years to promote.

Folklorist and critic Joe Wilson goes even further than Wright in defending Tubb's action, in this passage from his *Journal of Country Music* review of Randall Riese's *Nashville Babylon:* "That Ernest Tubb shot up the WSM lobby is told, but not why. The poor reader is left to surmise that ET may have been a bit erratic when he'd had a few drinks. Nothing could be further from the truth. ET took his sixshooter down there because it was the right thing to do, an epic attempt at public service, a cowboy hunting a businessman, offering a you-go-first-shoot-it-out to an adversary he thought a sleazeball."[45]

23

Years of Transition

Weathering the flood tide of rock and roll, life and career went on for Ernest Tubb. He still had a routine of broadcasts, tours, recordings, other business, and hobbies ("taking pictures with my movie camera, collecting records, and collecting pictures taken with my fans";[1] in this instance he failed to mention golf), all punctuated by the constant demands from other people for bits of his time—whether for advice or loans. He described this routine in answer to a fan's question for the summer 1957 *Melody Trails:* "We spend very little time rehearsing, except for recording sessions (however, we should). Business takes up some of my time, but Mr. Charles Mosley (manager of the record shop) has been my 'right hand' for 12 years. Hal Smith and others relieve me of most of these responsibilities. Olene is a great help to me too. As for personal appearances, we are making them at a rate of 18 to 20 a month. I answer 90% of my mail. So, you see, I don't have much time left with my family and that is a part of this business I don't like. But I try to make the most of every moment I do have with them."[2] He was using some of those moments to make more family members; a second son, his fourth child by Olene, Larry Dean Tubb, was born May 28, 1958. "Ernest was home and playing golf, so Olene finished her wash, fixed his supper and then called the ambulance . . . There was quite a race to beat Larry Dean to the hospital, and Olene says she 'rode Broadway on two wheels.' . . . Larry Dean was born as the elevator reached the 2nd Floor of Vanderbilt Hospital."[3]

There were a few out-of-the-ordinary jobs to break Tubb's routine. He must have been pleased to help Hank Snow formally open the Hank Snow Music Center on January 24, 1958. One photograph of the big event shows Tubb and the Wilburn Brothers behind the WSM microphone as Snow looks on approvingly. Snow had purchased the old Kendle Music Company at 810 Church Street in Nashville late in 1957, and on December 20 began a weekly 11:00–11:30 P.M.

broadcast from the store. Therewith ended the similarities to the Ernest Tubb Record Shop; avoiding any possible competition, Snow's store primarily sold instruments and gave lessons, but sold no records.

As always, even with the fall-off occasioned by rock and roll, and as that fan club answer indicates, Tubb spent most of his time on the road. Tubb and the Texas Troubadours still had his flex bus at the beginning of 1958, though that particular bus did not last the year. They posed with the bus in front of the Record Shop with the new cast for the February 1958 tour: George Jones (booked, *Billboard* said, for "12 appearances a month with the new Ernest Tubb package"),[4] the Louvin Brothers, Stonewall Jackson, singer Rita Robbins, and, billed as a separate attraction, his front man Rusty Gabbard. By March, though, when the tour hit Texas and New Mexico, travel was by car. This was the end of the line for the first flex bus; Tubb sold it to his niece's husband, G. A. Husky of Lubbock, who planned to use it as a rolling office in his construction business. Soon, the Huskys gave up on it too, bought a private plane, and sold the bus to Lubbock entertainer Jimmy Mackey. By a twist of fate, Mackey's drummer/driver on his new bus was one James "Hoot" Borden, a 1970s mainstay of Ernest Tubb's road show.

By March 1958, Rita Robbins had given place on the Tubb package to a different female singer, Skeeter Davis, formerly of the Davis Sisters and now hoping to make it as a solo star with RCA and the Tubb troupe. Skeeter and Stonewall flew with Tubb on an enviable tour of Army installations and private promotion dates in Hawaii at the beginning of April. Jones and the Louvins were scheduled to go too, "but due to a foulup in plane transportation, they . . . turned back from Farmington, New Mexico."[5] Stonewall Jackson today recalls that Jones stayed behind because of illness and adds that his fellow Opry newcomer even in those days had "a touch of the grape" and that Ernest would "kinda be on George about that. He didn't like him drinking them beers, or people seeing you do it . . . George was kinda, back that far, like he'd just come out of the brush." As to the Louvins, Tubb had "as good a relationship as you could have with Ira." Almost apologetically, Stonewall adds, "But he [Ira] sure could write songs! You always have to add that, don't you?"[6]

CHANGES IN THE BAND

Between the February and March tours, Tubb permanently lost another of the featured acts—his front man, rhythm guitarist, and sometime bus driver, the well-liked Rusty Gabbard. Gabbard left over a trivial episode brought on no doubt by Tubb's bottle and frayed road tempers. Gabbard quit when Ernest gathered the band in his hotel room and demanded that each bandsman sit on the floor. "Son, sit down in here on that floor." "I'm not gonna sit on the floor." "I said, sit on that floor, son." "Now Ernest, I love you, but I'm not sitting on the floor for nobody." "If you don't sit down on that floor, you're fired." "Well, goodbye." Johnnie Wright, telling the story, adds that manager Hal Smith, traveling with the group, was a witness to this exchange, and that Rusty never again worked for Ernest Tubb.[7]

By the time of Tubb's May 1958 recording sessions, he had hired Howard G. "Johnny" Johnson to front his shows and play rhythm guitar. By July, Johnson had Gabbard's old featured-act billing on the tour dates. A veteran country show-man by then, Johnson led a group in the 1940s called the Carolina Sunshine Girls, which featured his first wife, Jerry Leary (sister of Wilma Lee Leary Cooper). He had played with Wilma Lee and Stoney Cooper's Clinch Mountain Clan, and then in Jimmy Dickens's fine Country Boys group of 1955–1956; when Dickens dis-banded to join the Philip Morris Country Show, Johnson joined Smiley and Kitty Wilson and guitarist Paul Yandell in the Louvin Brothers' band. Tubb hired and kept him for four years: Johnson and old hand Jack Drake were the constants over the next four years as the band completely changed around them.

The major change at just about the time Johnny came was Kemo's retire-ment and the hiring of steel guitarist Buddy Gene Emmons. Barely twenty-one when hired (born January 27, 1937), Emmons was already a steel guitar legend. Far from being jealous at Emmons's arrival, lead guitarist Billy Byrd says that in 1956, when Dickie Harris quit and Ernest rehired Kemo, "I almost got down on my knees and begged Ernest to hire Buddy Emmons . . . I just told him, 'Well, he'd make you sound better, he's so good himself.'"[8] Emmons played state-of-the-art instrument models (Fender, National, even custom-made Grigsbys) and had al-ready gone into partnership with Shot Jackson to build the famous Sho-Bud Guitars by this time. Like Johnson, he was a veteran of Jimmy Dickens's great Country Boys band: Dickens brought Emmons to Nashville in July 1955, after an apprenticeship in his native Indiana and some work with Casey Clark in Detroit (where Emmons met Dickens coming through on tour). While with the Country Boys, Emmons played on their four instrumental recordings for Columbia, in-cluding the popular "Buddy's Boogie," and made four other records under his own name for that label.[9]

Why was Byrd's 1956 plea in vain? "He didn't want to hire Buddy Emmons, because he was kinda wild . . ."[10] Overcoming his hesitation, Tubb took the plunge in the spring of 1958, and the Texas Troubadours now featured the best steel guitarist around, who became a crowd pleaser and a special target of Tubb's teasing. Tubb wrote to the fan club at the end of that year, "Well, the

Texas Troubadours are all doing fine. I do think they sound better than ever these days . . . Buddy Emmons, the youngest member of the Troubadours, is a big hit everywhere we go, especially with the teenagers. He is considered about the best on the steel guitar, by most country musicians . . . I'm very proud of all the boys but I kid Buddy so much on our shows that I just thought I should say something nice about him for a change!"[11]

Having Buddy Emmons made quite a difference in the Texas Troubadours sound. No longer would the electric guitar be the sole dominant lead instrument. When "Half a Mind," which featured Emmons's steel throughout, became Tubb's first legitimate hit in roughly four years, this change became permanent: the pedal steel had come to stay in the Ernest Tubb sound. "Half a Mind" was big enough, in fact, to require sharing more of its history.

"HALF A MIND"

In 1958 Roger Dean Miller was an up-and-coming twenty-two-year-old songwriter who'd been in Nashville just a few years from Fort Worth, where he did most of his growing up. He had replaced Van Howard as Ray Price's tenor singer about this time, which was quite a job in view of the many big Price hits that featured that sound. Miller's Nashville running buddies included Ernest Tubb's nephew and son, Douglas Glenn and Justin. Miller's boss Ray Price was managed by Tubb's booker Hal Smith; Price and Smith about this time jointly invested in Pamper Music. By mid-June 1958, Price, not surprisingly, was booked onto some of the same shows as Ernest Tubb, since Smith was doing both stars' bookings. Miller, therefore, had several tie-ins with Ernest Tubb, both on the road and through the Tubb family. Legend has it, though, that when Miller had come up with a piece of a song called "Half a Mind," he called Ernest up and sang the part he had over the telephone in the wee hours of the morning.

How Miller came up with his part of "Half a Mind" has been disputed. A friend of his, musician Harold Morrison, remembered working with Miller to "write something with 'half a mind' in it. After awhile I told Roger, 'I can't think of anything,' so he went on later and wrote 'Half a Mind' on his own and it was a hit for Ernest Tubb."[12] Not quite on his own, says Douglas Glenn Tubb. "Well, this is not something the public knows about. Roger and I had been friends for a long time. We had run around, and I'd pitched a lot of his songs . . ." One was "Invitation to the Blues," to Rex Allen.[13]

But back to "Half a Mind":

I went in Mom's Cafe [which later became Tootsie's Orchid Lounge] . . .
and Roger was sitting there drinking a beer, and a boy named Hutch

Hutchinson was sitting there, and I got a beer and sat down. We got to talking, and he [Miller] said, "I've got an idea for a song. Let's write it." And I said, "OK, what is it?" He said, "I've got half a mind to leave you, but I've only got half the heart to go." "Well, that shouldn't be hard, let's do it." He said, "Oh, it's too noisy in here. Let's go somewhere else." Hutch said, "You guys come on and just get in the back seat, or one of you get in the back seat with the guitar, and I'll just drive you around, and you can write it in the car, and I'll shut up." So he did, and we drove around for two or three hours, drinking our beer, and wrote the song.[14]

Bill Anderson and Billy Byrd agree that when Roger took the song to Ernest Tubb, it wasn't in its final form. Anderson, yet another of Miller's good buddies in those days, says:

I remember very vividly about that, because the song is a three-verse song: it's not a verse-chorus-type song. The way Ernest recorded it, he sang a verse, then the second verse, then there's that great steel break by Buddy Emmons, and on that third verse: did you know that Ernest wrote that verse? . . . Roger for all his talent was somewhat undisciplined, both as a person and as a writer, and Roger would write the "inspiration" part, but the "perspiration" part he didn't want to have a whole lot to do with . . . Jim Reeves I think had to finish "Billy Bayou," or sit down with Roger and make him finish it. So he had these great two verses to "Half a Mind," and Ernest I know wrote the third.[15]

Tubb went into the studio with his finished version of "Half a Mind" on June 11, 1958. His nephew ("Doug honey"), Douglas Glenn Tubb, was on hand for the session that began at 8:50 P.M., in part because his Uncle Ernest was scheduled to record Doug's "Next Time." Surprised to hear "Half a Mind" being cut also, he thanked his uncle. "'For what?' I said, 'For doing our song.' He said, 'Doug honey, your name's not on here.' I said, 'Me and Roger wrote it the other night.' He said, 'Well, what do you want me to do? You want me throw it out?' I said, 'No, don't throw it out. It sounds like a hit song to me. If Roger can live with it, I can live without it.' Course I could have lived with it a lot better at that time, but . . . Regardless of what I told E.T., I got pretty upset about it. And I left the session at that point . . ."[16]

The song was a hit, climbing to number 8 on *Billboard*'s newly consolidated Hot C&W Singles chart. And Ernest Tubb made Roger Miller some money. His later release of Douglas Glenn's "Next Time" actually spent more weeks on the chart (fourteen to "Half a Mind's" eleven), but peaked outside the top ten at number 14.

SONG PLUGGING

About this same time, Ernest Tubb played song plugger to his friend, fellow Texan and touring partner, Roger Miller's boss Ray Price, in a celebrated episode that had a great impact on the two friends I just mentioned, Miller and Bill Anderson. Sometime in May 1958, Tubb and Ray Price were driving out to the links for a golf game when WENO radio in Madison played Dave Rich's new RCA record of a song Bill Anderson had written and recorded for TNT, "City Lights." Anderson tells the story:

> After it had played, Ernest told him, "Son, that's a song you need to record." And at the time, Ray had a record scheduled to come out, "Invitation to the Blues," Roger Miller's song. Roger had even told me; he was working with Ray Price at the time, and we were very good friends, and he said "I've got Ray Price's next record." And I thought, "God, that must be wonderful." And then the way I heard the story, all the way around that golf course, Ernest just wouldn't let Ray alone. "Son, you better cut that song." So about the seventh or eighth hole, Ray told him, "I'll cut the song. Just hush . . . get off my back about it."[17]

Ray had cut "Invitation to the Blues" in a scheduled four-song session on May 6, 1958; on May 29 came the special session to cut the one song, "City Lights," and the two were paired on Columbia 41191, released June 9. "They put Roger's song on the flip, on the B side, and I don't think Roger ever forgave me for that either," Anderson recalls.[18] "City Lights" became the bigger hit, staying at number 1 for thirteen weeks, while "Invitation to the Blues" climbed to number 3 in the last days of *Billboard*'s separate disc jockey list, on what must have been the strongest double-sided hit in years. "But Ernest had a quality about him: he sensed what the public liked in so many ways," Anderson gratefully recalls. "And I don't mean just music, or just himself—look at all the talent he boosted. He had his finger on the pulsebeat of the public, maybe more than anyone else at that particular time, and he recognized that song as a hit, and he matched it with Ray Price. Thank goodness! If it had rained out their golf game that day I might still be in Commerce!"[19]

Anderson referred to the talent Tubb boosted. About this time he did one of his biggest favors, the latest of several for his San Antonio deejay friend, Charlie Walker. Tubb got him a Decca contract at the beginning of 1954, but the coming of rock and roll and the swollen size of Decca's country roster led to Walker's termination in 1956. After a brief try with Mercury, Walker joined Columbia, with a good word from Ray Price.

In Nashville for his first Columbia session, he and Price were going over song material when Ernest Tubb phoned. "Have y'all found anything for Charlie to record?" Ray said, "Yeah, we've found two or three things that he likes." Ernest said he had some songs and asked them to come out to his house, which they did. One of the songs they brought was "Pick Me Up on Your Way Down," a tune submitted to Ray's and Hal Smith's new publishing company, Pamper Music, by a Californian named Harlan Howard.

> But the song was written for Kitty Wells; said, "Pick me up on your way down, for I love my country boy" . . . He wrote it for Kitty, but he had turned it over to Ray Price . . . So Ernest put it on, and said, "Naw, that's a girl's song, you can't do that." I said, "Play it again; we're gonna have to change a few lines in it," so I played it again. "Naw, that's a girl's song." He was looking for a song that you could just change from "her" to "him" or something like that . . . Finally, about the third time, he gets to hit his hand on his head, and said, "Hey, wait a minute. Yeah." . . . He and I and Ray Price fed each other [ideas], and kinda made a change or two in there, and after we finished, he said, "My God, that's gonna be a good song. When I first heard it, I never thought it would work."[20]

Walker recorded it on June 5, 1958, and as he remembers, "After I cut it, Ernest was over there grinning with Price and some of them. I walked over and said, 'What do you think?' He said, 'Well, I'll tell you what I think. I think you just cut a hit. I'll tell you how much I think it. I'm gonna give you three months: if you ain't sold in three months, I'm cutting it myself." That's about what he needed, Walker recalls, "And then it really took off."[21] The rock and roll tide was about to be turned, in part by such a stone-cold country hit. "And nobody could figure why it was such a big hit. 'Cause it had two fiddles, steel guitar, had that old, kind of an updated Bob Wills sound . . . Shortly—a few months—after that, Ray Price hit with 'Heartaches by the Number,'[22] and then we had like a ten-year period: every record you heard was a shuffle beat! And then it faded out, and you didn't hear it again for ten, fifteen years, and now it's back again. All these kids are doing the line dance and the two-step, and the shuffle."[23]

SKEETER

Tubb's "new" singer, Skeeter Davis (Mary Frances Penick), he had known for several years. In the days of the Davis Sisters and their great success in 1953 with "I Forgot More Than You'll Ever Know," Skeeter and B. J. (Betty Jack) had guested on Tubb's *Midnite Jamboree*. But Betty Jack Davis was killed in the August 2, 1953, car wreck near Cincinnati that seriously injured Skeeter, just about the time their big record was taking off. And though a new Davis Sisters tried a comeback with

Betty Jack's real-life sister Georgia joining Skeeter (they were not related to Skeeter), the chemistry and the music were not the same. Emotionally unsettled, Skeeter retired from music for awhile and sought solace in the life of a homemaker. This didn't work either, but RCA Records was patient enough to retain her under a solo contract throughout it all.

One of her first solo records barely cracked *Billboard*'s disc jockey chart on February 24, 1958: "Lost to a Geisha Girl," the answer to Hank Locklin's hit on Lawton Williams's "Geisha Girl." Skeeter then joined the Tubb tour when Ernest was tipped off by son Justin that a certain female singer in Covington, Kentucky, was looking for work. Ernest Tubb phoned and asked her to come along on a forty-two-day tour to Hawaii and the West Coast. To Skeeter's surprise, husband Kenneth Depew readily agreed to the idea, and a close two-year association with Ernest was begun.

Tubb offered Skeeter much the same helpful advice he had given to Stonewall Jackson, who was still on Tubb's tour when Skeeter joined it: "From the start of the tour, he could sense that I was nervous. So one night he advised me to spot one or two faces in the crowd and sing directly to them, rather than trying to sing to everybody or nobody. What I had been doing was staring out above the crowd and avoiding any eye contact whatsoever. I tried his suggestion during the very next performance, and it worked like a charm."[24]

Ernest was protective of his touring girl singer. He let her stay on the bus when she preferred not to sing in nightclubs; and when one night a drunk tried to join her on the bus and Skeeter got away screaming into the nightclub, Tubb stopped his show, announced a short break, and had Johnny Johnson take her to a hotel room. "We ain't never leaving her on the bus again. We were fools to do it in the first place."[25] Tubb urged her to spend more of her money on herself and stop sending all of it back to her husband. She did so, buying a set of golf clubs to keep up with Ernest and the boys.

The indifference that her first husband showed to their touring, and to Skeeter's career in general (as long as she sent the money back), inspired Tubb to play for her a record from the jukebox at a truckstop cafe, Carl Belew's "Am I That Easy to Forget?" released in the spring of 1959, which Skeeter immediately made a part of her repertory. She had a hit with it a year later.

For her part, Skeeter furnished Tubb song material in an indirect way. She writes in her autobiography of suggesting R&B material for Tubb to cover, two songs in particular that he did release on singles.

I overheard him tell Hawkshaw [Hawkins] one day, "If you want to know what the kids and colored folks are listening to, just ask Skeeter. She's a walking, talking *Billboard* magazine." I wasn't about to change my taste to please Ernest. "Yeah, that's right. Why, I heard a song just last night you oughta record," I told E.T. "If you don't, I'm going to." At the next stop, I found it for him on the jukebox. The song was "What Am I Living For?" Ernest liked it and covered it country. I had repaid the favor for "Am I That Easy to Forget?"[26] I even found his follow-up song, Laverne Baker's "I Cried a Tear." Those songs were a long way from "Walking the Floor over You" and the other Ernest Tubb tunes up until that point. Both of E.T.'s next country hits came directly off of rhythm-and-blues radio.[27]

Though Billy Byrd recalls that Ernest could be a trifle overly friendly with Skeeter if he was "in his cups,"[28] she became a close friend to Olene and the young Tubb children: "I guess I may as well go ahead and confess. I slept in Justin Tubb's bed. Justin wasn't in it, of course. By the time I moved to Nashville, Justin was already grown, out on his own, and probably raising himself, too. When we came in off the road, Olene Tubb would invite me to stay with her, Ernest, and the kids rather than go back to my empty trailer . . . The Hula Hoop was the rage of 1959. I'd get out in the front yard and Hula-Hoop with the younger Tubb children while E.T. made movies of us. I was still a kid myself."[29] Hula hoops went along on some of the road trips about this time, too. Fan Beulah Marie Harris published this account of a Tubb road show in *Melody Trails,* spring 1959: "I got to see Ernest when he was in Kansas City on October 30 [1958]. Also on the show were Ray Price, Skeeter Davis, Roger Miller, the Cherokee Cowboys, and the Texas Troubadours . . . I guess the hula-hoop craze had hit the Troubadours, as Buddy Emmons had one backstage which he and Roger Miller seemed to be having a time with."[30]

Ernest made Skeeter a regular on a Saturday morning network radio show that premiered in January 1959, *Ernest Tubb Jamboree,* which also starred Ray Price and featured guests. "The new Ernest Tubb Jamboree originates from the Ernest Tubb Record Shop every Saturday morning from 10:30 to 11:00. You are invited to take in the show anytime you're in Nashville and go back again that night to visit the Midnight [*sic*] Jamboree . . . it is broadcast over a multi-system of radio stations." Bill Anderson, a 1958 *Midnite Jamboree* guest with cohort Chuck Goddard, remembers "a show Ernest hosted out of the Record Shop on Saturday mornings, over a network, and he put me on that show real early in my career."[31] The show was renewed for a second run of thirteen weeks, then seems to have vanished.[32]

Skeeter stayed on Ernest's road shows through the end of 1959, sharing the bill the latter part of that year with Charlie Walker. By then, her pay from Tubb had risen from $25 to $100 per show, on the strength of her mid-1959 hit, "Set Him

Free." Tubb knew by year's end it was time to set Skeeter free, as he had Stonewall Jackson in mid-1958 after "Life to Go," and as he would later do with Jack Greene after "There Goes My Everything." Davis, who found country-pop stardom in the 1960s, has never forgotten her debt to Ernest Tubb, coming up to him late in his career and asking, in the words of Scotty Wiseman's song, "Have I told you lately that I love you?" and praising him almost as a father figure in her recent autobiography.[33]

RECORDINGS

LP technology and the growing demand for twelve-inch stereo recordings were the forces driving much of Ernest Tubb's recordings from the late 1950s forward. Tubb signed a new Decca contract at the end of 1957 as his previous four-year contract expired. Length and terms (as usual) were not made public,[34] but apparently the contractual volume of recording was raised so that Tubb could meet the demand for LPs. Thirty-six masters were made over eleven different sessions in 1958 alone, all of them under the full direction of Owen Bradley, who was named in April of that year to replace Paul Cohen as Decca's first Nashville-based C&W A&R director.[35]

In sessions stretching from May to October, Tubb and his Texas Troubadours, augmented by studio drummers, the guitar of Grady Martin, and Floyd Cramer's piano (Bradley played very little after becoming Tubb's full-fledged producer), laid down twelve songs for his next album. "I hope to have a new album out in about three months," Tubb wrote to the fan club quite prematurely in early 1958, before any of the recordings had been made. *The Daddy of 'Em All,* its predecessor, had been heavy on the old songs; this next one would be a more even mix, though all would be "new" for Tubb. "I don't know yet just what the numbers will be. The plans are for six old favorites and six new songs."[36] A full year after writing this (January 1959), the album was released. Tubb liked everything about it except its title and its cover photo: "I hope all of you like the new LP album that was released in January. I don't know who dreamed up the title [*The Importance of Being Ernest*] but I hope that it will meet with your approval. Also I don't like the cover picture and haven't the slightest idea where they got it. I don't believe that you will like it either, but trust that you WILL like what's inside the cover well enough to make up for this picture and the title. Be sure to write and let me know . . ."[37]

A hatless Ernest grins off-camera to his left in the suspect cover photo, alongside the title whose clever literary allusion is lost on Tubb. Had he known the Oscar Wilde play (and someone must have mentioned it after this published statement), he still might not have approved of the wordplay, since in the drama two male suitors vie for the heroine's love by adopting her favorite male name, "Ernest"—a name that we know from that first *Mountain Broadcast* letter (November 1940) Tubb never cared for. Really, *most* of his 1950s LP titles didn't fare well with him. "Ernie" in *Red and Ernie* (1956) he liked even less than "Ernest," and *The Daddy of 'Em All* (1957), with its pretentious title and cover photo, leaves us all bewildered. One wonders in view of these why Decca's New York office, culprit in these actual examples, named his next big album project *The Ernest Tubb Story,* and not *Tale of a Tubb.* When the folks in the New York offices wandered any distance at all from such totally safe terrain as *Ernest Tubb Favorites* (1956) and *The Ernest Tubb Story* (1959), they generally wandered too far.

At least the vinyl contents of *The Importance of Being Ernest,* as Tubb had hoped, did generally please his legion of fans: Tubb blends the promised mix of old and new tunes into his own timeless style. We know that he worked mighty hard to get them to his own liking, whatever the fan response. "Your Cheatin' Heart" took eleven takes, "San Antonio Rose" took eight, and Tubb's own new composition, "All Those Yesterdays," required no fewer than twelve takes.[38]

Sessions for *The Importance of Being Ernest* overlapped with work on *The Ernest Tubb Story,* an ambitious project that Tubb first described to the fans in these terms: "Also, we have started re-recording some of the old songs for a big Album which is supposed to amount to about 36 songs. This big Album probably won't be released until 1959 and all of the songs will be numbers that I have recorded in the past. I won't re-record all of the 36 songs, but I'd say at least half of them, especially the real old ones like 'Walking the Floor over You,' 'I'll Get Along Somehow,' etc."[39]

Somewhere between the first project sessions (May 1958) and the last almost a year later (March 1959), the plans changed. Thirty-six titles, or a three-record set, were cut down to twenty-four for a two-record set, and all of them were remakes: no originals were included. Decca Records explained their thinking in the liner notes.

> The 24 songs making up this package are new recordings. It would have been much easier to have collected the old masters, extending back over the years, in order to package this collection of hits. Decca, however, decided to give this edition of Tubb's performances the advantage of modern, stereophonic recording techniques . . . Hence, this becomes a definitive edition, cut by the artist during the peak of his career, using the best studio facilities. While adding the advantage of modern engineering, the new performances retain stylistic authenticity, with typical instrumental accompaniment.[40]

So far, so good. And the next line anticipates the existence of stringent truth-in-advertising laws when it warns, "In line with modern trends, it will be noted that some arrangements include a choral group." We'd now replace the word "modern" with "passing," but at the risk of heresy, *some* of the remakes—usually the ones without choral groups—are indeed better than the originals. After all, in 1958–1959 Tubb still had Billy Byrd, and he never had a finer steel guitarist than Buddy Emmons. Tempo problems, voice problems, and such factors as Dick Ketner's lack of an amplifier had weakened several of the originals remade here—remakes of such cuts as "It's Been So Long, Darlin'," "Last Night I Dreamed," and "I Love You Because" are distinct improvements. Tubb could not possibly have improved his earlier cuts on most of the others, though—"I'll Get Along Somehow," "Letters Have No Arms," "Rainbow at Midnight," and "I Will Miss You When You Go" among them. One wonders why he tried.

Times and industry conditions demanded it, one supposes; but remakes of this type became the bane of the latter-day record collector, who usually has no warning.[41] And Decca Records was the chief offender, overlooking none of their top stars in the quest for remakes: Ernest Tubb, Jimmie Davis, Red Foley, Webb Pierce, Kitty Wells. After *Ernest Tubb Favorites* in 1956, Tubb could never convince Decca to compile an all-originals oldies package again, though he certainly tried. The tracks on *Ernest Tubb's Golden Favorites* (1961) came straight out of *The Ernest Tubb Story,* and *Ernest Tubb's Greatest Hits* and *Greatest Hits Vol. 2* were mixed bags of originals and remakes. Decca's numbered series of *All-Time Hit Performances* usually included originals, as the title implies, but these were various-artist packages; to get the Tubb cuts one had to buy the entire series.

ON THE ROAD: BUILDING A DANCE BAND

With enough recording done by March 2 to last for the rest of 1959, Ernest Tubb and the Texas Troubadours spent the rest of that year outside the recording studio, working personal appearances and weekend broadcasts. A lengthy winter junket marked the first time that Roy Acuff and Ernest Tubb toured together, although Ray Price and Skeeter Davis remained regular attractions on that trip. On two different "Hap" Peebles Midwestern tours that year (August/September and again at Thanksgiving), Tubb and the boys were joined by a young singer named Jed Starkey. Chuck Stripling also worked that first tour, then veteran western swing bandleader Johnnie Lee Wills, a Peebles favorite, joined them in November. Charlie Walker, though still based at KMAC in San Antonio as the Southwest's favorite country disc jockey, joined Tubb and Skeeter Davis for a tour of Michigan in October on the strength of his "Pick Me Up on Your Way Down."[42] Hawkshaw Hawkins and Jean Shepard, separate single acts and not yet man and wife, joined Tubb and Skeeter Davis at the very end of 1959 and the beginning of 1960.

Tubb, though, was nearing the end of a three-year stint as headline package-tour attraction. Times were getting better for touring country acts, so there was accordingly less economic need for the all-in-one-unit Opry package show. It was becoming economically feasible once again for acts to tour separately, which also gave promoters flexibility to book whatever name acts they might want for big-ticket shows. In Ernest's case, although there would be a few package tours per year for quite some time yet, returning to solo touring with a new and improved Texas Troubadours unit this time around opened up a whole new world of venues: the dance clubs. And this was the solution suggested by booker Hal Smith at the "crisis conference" held with Ernest to which I have previously alluded. I quote Mr. Smith's recollection of what he told Ernest: "Ernest, I know of one thing we could try. I know you've never wanted to do this. We could go into the ballrooms. I know you don't want to; you don't want to do those three- and four-hour sets you've seen Bob Wills and Spade Cooley do. I think we can get you shorter sets than that. But you'll have to carry a bigger band."[43]

Hiring Buddy Emmons had been a move in that direction; there would be several more such moves from 1959 to 1962, a period of great flux for the Texas Troubadours. So much so in that first year, in fact, that it's probably a good (or at least necessary) thing that Tubb did no recording after March 2.

On January 31, 1959, Tubb and his band (Byrd, Emmons, Drake, Johnson) appeared as guests on one of southern California's top country music TV shows, Nat Nigberg's *Country America* (KABC-TV). There it was announced that Billy Byrd had signed a contract with the new Hollywood firm, Warner Brothers Records, to make instrumentals under his own name.[44] This was the beginning of the end for Byrd's ten-year term as Ernest Tubb's lead guitarist. Sensing his worth in light of the contract, Byrd asked Tubb to raise his $75 weekly pay—the same salary he was hired for in 1949—and was refused, so he quit on two weeks' notice. This was in the summer of 1959, after Tubb's Decca sessions for that year. Byrd worked a short time for Ferlin Husky, then accepted Gordon Terry's offer to move to California and join his band at Bonnie's Foothill Club in Long Beach. "Course he offered me a lot more than playing for Ernest, you know." Not content to hire one ex-Texas Troubadour, Terry went after another one, steel guitarist Buddy Emmons. Byrd recalls, "Gordon flew into Nashville and said, 'I'm gonna bring Emmons back with me.' I forgot how much he offered him: he was making about the same thing . . ."[45]

But the California job in Terry's band didn't last long for either man. "I worked for Gordon, and Gordon got real important, 'staritis,' as we called it." Terry lost his lucrative Long Beach gig on New Year's 1960, so only a few months after moving West, both Byrd and Emmons were out of work. Billy moved back to Nashville, and though he continued to record a while for Warner Brothers, his main work in the 1960s consisted of driving a taxi for Yellow Cab and playing guitar at Shakey's Pizza Parlor.

Emmons too came back to Nashville, not waiting for Terry's demise. "After six or eight months I started getting homesick for Nashville. One night I heard Jimmy Day playing on a Skeeter Davis record; it kinda tore me up, and made me decide that I really wanted to get back into what was happening there. Then I heard about Ray Price being at Bonnie's Foothill Club in Long Beach with Jimmy Day. They had a lot of room in their bus, so I loaded all of my things on Ray's bus and finished out the tour with the Cherokee Cowboys. For some reason, Ray didn't have a bass man with him and was picking up one in each town, so I played bass on my steel, by tuning my strings down."[46]

Did the Texas Troubadours survive the double loss of Byrd and Emmons for most of 1959? Barely. For steel guitar, Tubb (or Jack Drake, who usually made such decisions) brought in two veterans of Jim Reeves's band: Jimmy Day and then Bobby Garrett. Replacement lead guitarist was Tubb's nephew, Billy Lee Tubb, a graduate of the Tubb Boys and the Hootenanny Scratchos and Justin's earliest Gallatin guitarist. Ernest had complimented his playing for Justin back in 1953, but as things turned out, his tenure as a Texas Troubadour was brief. As "Ronny Wade," he was already a recording artist in his own right, having recorded for King in 1957–1958. By the time of Tubb's Michigan tour in the fall of 1959 (with Charlie Walker, Skeeter Davis, and Ray Price), Ronny Wade had joined the Texas Troubadours and was helping Johnny Johnson front the shows.

At the other end of his brief tenure, Wade appears as lead guitarist to Jimmy Day's steel in April 1960, when Ernest Tubb filmed episodes of a quarter-hour TV show called *Community Jamboree* for the National Guard. But his brother Douglas Glenn recalls, "Billy had a problem with showing up on time. He didn't think all that was that important."[47] His uncle Ernest naturally thought differently, and had to make a change. By 1962, Billy had again changed names, this time to "X. Lincoln," made some more records, and found his longest stint as front man for the Leroy Van Dyke road show. He has more recently worked in that capacity for John Anderson.

When Ronny Wade left the Texas Troubadours, Buddy Emmons was talked into coming back. Emmons, having ridden Ray Price's bus back into Nashville, would later work regularly for Price, but only after this second stint with Ernest Tubb. Emmons got a call from Jack Drake, who told him their guitar player (Wade) was leaving. "Bobby Garrett was then playing steel. Since I knew enough of Ernest's old tunes, he said I could play lead guitar. I did that for four or five months, until Garrett left, and I went back on steel."[48] Tubb's many recordings between March and June 1960 feature Garrett's steel work.[49] Grand Ole Opry recordings from those few months prove that Tubb often featured Garrett and Emmons on twin steel guitars: showy, though quite a departure from the traditional Tubb sound. On sessions, Grady Martin often played the twin electric lead guitar with Emmons, as he had done for some years with Billy Byrd.

When Garrett left the band in the summer of 1960, his place was taken by another Dallas native, lightning-fingered Leon Rhodes, hired away from Dewey Groom's club as lead guitarist. Emmons was then freed up to return to steel, and Tubb could boast of his best band yet. Completing the move in the direction of a dance band, Tubb hired his first road drummer, Billy "Bun" Wilson, at about the same time as Rhodes; for both men, their first Tubb recording session was September 21, 1960. Farris Coursey or Murray "Buddy" Harman had played drums on Tubb sessions since at least 1950 (a light snare can be heard on the best reproductions of "I Need Attention Bad"), but "Bun," veteran of the Philip Morris Country Music Show and later the comic on TV's *The Ernest Tubb Show,* was the first drummer to travel as a Troubadour.

Charlie Walker, among others, was impressed by Tubb's moving toward a "hot band," something that Billy Byrd and Dickie Harris had each urged him in vain to do years before. Walker makes the same point as Hal Smith: that Tubb could play a wider range of venues with a dance band. "They knew they could work those dance clubs more with a good dance band than they could with a show band . . . They had the best dance band in the business . . . That's why he was able to work all those clubs out there: cause he had such a good band that they'd just book him and the band, and the band would play sometimes the whole dance, or half of it. He had a knocked-out band there at one time."[50]

The Texas Troubadours had come through three or more years of flux and transition into a new era, sporting a new style (with as many intros and breaks by pedal steel as by electric guitar, especially on the albums) and playing before new audiences in the dance halls. Before long, the Texas Troubadours would have almost as many fans as Ernest Tubb did.

From 1960 forward, Ernest Tubb's road itinerary is dominated by an ever-increasing round of club dates, from Texas, Oklahoma, and Louisiana out through Colorado and California and most states along the way. Fairs, auditorium shows, and the outdoor park dates were still there, even an occasional road package, especially for Mr. Peebles in the Midwest. But Ernest Tubb's road show found itself booked more and more into the NCO clubs around the nation and such nightspots as the Cabaret Club in Bandera, the Esquire Ballroom in Houston, and the Club Rendezvous in Lubbock (to take three recurring Texas examples). Ernest Tubb had brought his music back to the setting in which it was born.

The new clubs were generally larger and nicer than those in which he began; he and the band were not in fear of life and limb, and the sizable guaranteed fees were nearly always delivered.[51] Tubb refers to the new venues in an early 1962 letter to the fan club: "we have been playing a lot of Night Clubs the past two years and have received some very good compliments on the Troubadours for playing such good dance music."[52]

At the same time that he "went home" to the club circuit, Tubb also returned on records to his root sound. After 1960, there were no more pop covers and very few studio experiments. His only remaining duet partner, Loretta Lynn, was as country as he was: some called her a female Ernest Tubb. With a voice that was a bit more subdued (probably a combination of his age and the changeover to stereo), and at tempos that, to put it mildly, are not rushed, Tubb settled back into a stone-country groove with his best band yet, and a career renaissance was the result. Hard country music was back in the 1960s, and Ernest Tubb's resurgence was a big part of that.

Somewhere on the road, Ernest Tubb and his nemesis, the bottle (Country Music Foundation)

Blue-eyed Elaine as cowgirl. (Photo by Walden S. Fabry, Country Music Foundation)

Elaine in real life. (Country Music Foundation)

C. R. Tubb Jr. and nephew Justin in 1947 behind one of country music's first buses, the "Texas Troubadour Special." (Courtesy Mr. David McCormick)

"Hollywood Barn Dance" lobby card, 1947

Tubb and Eddy Arnold swap their latest records on grand opening night: Tubb hands Eddy "I'll Step Aside," Eddy hands him "It's A Sin." (Courtesy Mrs. Loretta Jordan)

Carnegie Hall marquee the first night of the big show. (Photo by William Gottlieb, Courtesy Mr. Marcus McFaul)

Manager Oscar Davis and his wife flank the Tubbs at the May 3, 1947 record shop opening. (Courtesy Mrs. Loretta Jordan)

Grand opening on May 3, 1947 of the Ernest Tubb Record Shop, 720 Commerce Street, Nashville. Standing, from left: Texas Ruby (foreground), Clyde Dilleha (background), Johnny Bond, Milton Estes, Eddy Arnold (background), Ernest Tubb (at WSM mic), David Cobb, Mrs. Elaine Tubb, Curly Fox, Clyde Moody, Jimmie Short, Leon Short. (Courtesy Mr. Richard Weize)

Behind a theater in Waco, Texas in 1947, Tubb poses with Waco newcomer Hank Thompson. They are leaning against Thompson's truck. (Courtesy Mr. David McCormick)

Early broadcast of the *Midnite Jamboree* from Commerce Street, circa 1948: (from left) Bill Drake, "Butterball" Paige, Jack Drake, Tubb, and the back of fiddler Hal Smith. (Country Music Foundation)

C. R. Tubb Jr., Mrs. Carrie Rodgers, Ernest Tubb, and partner Charles Mosley celebrate in 1949 the release of the first Jimmie Rodgers reissue album at the Ernest Tubb Record Shop. (Courtesy Mrs. Dollie Denny)

Tubb flanked by his only two regular musicians, Butterball Paige (left) and bassist Jack Drake, in early to mid 1949. (Courtesy Mrs. Ruth Husky)

The Record Store, Main and Ackerd Streets in Dallas, May, 1949: (from left) Hank Williams, Cowboy Copas, Red Foley, store manager Bob Jones, Ernest Tubb, and Tubb's niece Anna Ruth Collier—an employee there. (Courtesy Mrs. Anna Ruth Collier Husky)

Tubb's future road act, Annie Lou and Danny Dill, around the time they came to the Opry in 1946. (Courtesy Mrs. Dollie Denny)

Mother and sons on the couch at Ernest's Nashville home, late 1949.

A night on the town: Hank Williams (background), Mrs. Rodgers and Ernest Tubb (right foreground), all others unknown. (Courtesy Mr. David McCormick)

Tubb's pose for a life-size standup cuout, so that fans at the Record Shop could always have their picture made with Ernest. (Photo by Walden S. Fabry, courtesy Mrs. Dollie Denny)

Professional band shot in the early 1950s in Tubb's Lawndale Drive attic studio: Tubb, Dickie Harris seated at steel, Jack Drake behind him, and Billy Byrd on right. (Photo by Walden S. Fabry)

Ernest the ballplayer, in full stage attire.

Typical *Midnite Jamboree* look from the new location at 417 Broadway. Packed crowd hems Tubb and his boys (Byrd, Drake, Dickie Harris) onto the corner platform.

Ernest Tubb Record Shop at 417 Broadway, shown from the street in the 1950's. (Country Music Foundation)

The Tubb Boys and the Hootenanny Scratchos at Dessau Hall, Pflugerville, Texas, early 1953: (from left) Justin Tubb, Billy Lee Tubb, Todd—, Billy—, Doug Tubb, Buddy—. (Courtesy Mr. Douglas Glenn Tubb)

Employee of Pan American Airlines pitches a song to Hank Snow and Ernest Tubb during a stopover in their flight to Korea, March 1953.

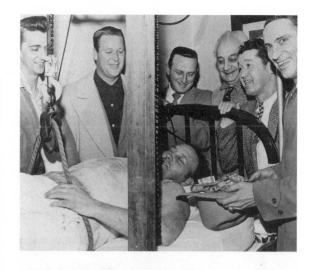

Brown-eyed Olene Tubb, snapped by her husband on vacation, circa 1951. (Country Music Foundation)

Tubb's own hat bears an offering for the injured Bill Monroe. Circling Monroe's hospital bed in early 1953 are (from left) Carl Smith, Eddie Hill, Jim Denny, Vito Pelletieri, Roy Acuff, and Tubb. (Courtesy Mrs. Dollie Denny)

Korean concert with friendly warplane overhead (as explained by WSM publicist Bill McDaniel's handwritten note). (WSM photo by Bill McDaniel, courtesy of Mr. Jerry Strobel, Grand Ole Opry Archives)

Here is one of the times Tubb left his Troubadours on the road and played the Grand Ole Opry with a pick-up band (but a pretty good one): Grady Martin (far left), Tommy Jackson (fiddle), and Don Helms (steel). (Courtesy Mr. Jerry Strobel, the Grand Ole Opry Archives)

This oddity graced the 1954 postcards of the Jimmie Rodgers Memorial Society, from that year's Rodgers Festival: (from left) Tubb, Mrs. Rodgers, Jim Evans, and Hank Snow, with a ghostly Jimmie superimposed. (Country Music Foundation)

Tubb and his manager, Gabe Tucker, confer in Tucker's office at the Ernest Tubb Record Shop in the mid 1950s. (Courtesy Mr. Richard Weize)

Finale of the January 7, 1956 "Grand Ole Opry" ABC TV show: (from left) June Carter, Tony Bennett, Ernest Tubb, TV magazine official, Patsy Cline, Ray Price, Bill Carlisle, and Slim Whitman. (Photo by Jeanne Gordon Studios, courtesy Mr. Jerry Strobel, the Grand Ole Opry Archives)

Lined up by the new bus for a tour, January 1957: (from left) Billy Byrd, Ray "Kemo" Head, Ernest Tubb, Jack Drake, Rusty Gabbard, Kitty Wells, Johnnie Wright, Jack Anglin, Shot Jackson, Ray Crisp, Joe Zinkan, Teddy Wilburn, Doyle Wilburn. Stonewall Jackson looks longingly out of the Record Shop window—his turn would come the next year. (Courtesy Mr. Richard Weize)

Inside the Record Shop to promote the 1958 tours: (from left) Ira Louvin, Charlie Louvin, Rita Robbins, and Ernest Tubb. (Courtesy Mr. Richard Weize)

Tubb with his 1958 band: (from left) Buddy Emmons, Jack Drake, Billy Byrd, Johnny Johnson. (Courtesy Mrs. Ruth Husky)

One of the first great Texas Troubadours show bands, 1961: (from left) Buddy Emmons, Jan Kurtis, Johnny Johnson, Jack Drake, Leon Rhodes, and the boss man. (Photo by Sid O'Berry, courtesy Mr. Jan Kurtis)

Tubb unveils the first Country Music Hall of Fame plaques on the Opry stage, November, 1961. (WSM photo by Les Leverett, courtesy Mr. Jerry Strobel, Grand Ole Opry Archives)

The passionate golfer, early 1960s. (Photo by and courtesy of Jan Kurtis)

The passionate smoker not long before he quit, shown backstage at Borger, Texas on January 27, 1965. (Photo by Dub Waldrep, courtesy Mrs. Ruth Husky)

Loretta Lynn and Ernest Tubb cut one of their classic duets, January 1965. (Photo by Les Leverett, courtesy Mr. Jerry Strobel, Grand Ole Opry Archives)

"The Great Band" and their boss in an upbeat moment: (from left) Jack Drake, Cal Smith, Ernest Tubb, Jack Greene, Leon Rhodes, Buddy Charleton. (Country Music Foundation)

Smith, Charleton, Drake, Tubb, Rhodes, and Greene shown with their "Singing Bus Driver," Johnny Wiggins, and his bus on June 21, 1965. (Photo by Les Leverett, courtesy Mr. Jerry Strobel, the Grand Ole Opry Archives)

A smiling Tubb makes his way to the stage of Nashville's Municipal Auditorium for his Country Music Hall of Fame induction on October 22, 1965. (Country Music Foundation)

Hal Smith, Ernest Tubb, and Haze Jones celebrate in 1967 Tubb's first ten years with Smith's booking agency. Two years later, Smith sold out to Haze Jones who formed Atlas Artists. (Courtesy Mr. Randy Piland, Nashville *Tennessean/ Banner* library)

Family reunion in Texas, 1968: the Tubb "children" stand in order of age (from left) behind their Dad: C. R. Jr., Jewell, Lucille, Opal, Ernest. (Photo by G. A. Husky, courtesy Mrs. Ruth Husky)

Eschewing his own hat but armed with eyeglasses and guitar, Tubb records in the 1970s. (Photo by Les Leverett)

Billy Parker got his way: the briefly hatless Texas Troubadours play a Lubbock club date on July 4, 1969. (Photo by G. A. Husky, courtesy Mrs. Ruth Husky)

The 1974 band of seasoned veterans: (from left) driver Hoot Borden, Tubb, Billy Byrd, Junior Pruneda, Wayne Hammond, Don Mills, Don Helms. (Courtesy Mrs. Ruth Husky)

Long-time partners Charles Mosley and Ernest Tubb cut the ribbon for a second Ernest Tubb Record Shop on Demonbreun Street in Nashville on June 2, 1976. (Courtesy Mr. Randy Piland, Nashville *Tennessean/Banner* library)

Producer Pete Drake and Ernest Tubb flank their piano pounder, Owen "Half Moon" Bradley, at the time of Tubb's move to First Generation Records, 1977.

"Hurry up and wait": Tubb and his boys patiently await instructions during the April 1979 Ryman Auditorium filming of the Academy Award winning *Coal Miner's Daughter*. (Courtesy Mr. Randy Piland, Nashville *Tennessean/Banner* library)

Willie Nelson and Ernest Tubb share a laugh at the Austin press conference before Willie's 1979 Fourth of July picnic. (Photo by Rick Henson)

A rare sight, seen only in the later days, Justin Tubb and his Dad perform together at the Grand Ole Opry. (Photo by Judy Mock)

The author and Ernest Tubb at the Ernest Tubb Fan Club Picnic at Two Rivers Mansion in Nashville on June 10, 1980. (Photo by Robert K. Oermann)

Socializing at the Tennessee Governor's mansion on September 20, 1981 before the Roy Acuff Roast, with Acuff (left) and Gene Autry (who is standing in front of Tubb's escort, his daughter Karen). (Photo by Les Leverett)

Mourners surround the flower-bedecked coffin of Ernest Tubb minutes after the funeral service at Nashville's Two Rivers Baptist Church on September 10, 1984: Bill Monroe, Porter Wagoner, and Teddy Wilburn (left); Karen Tubb and Mrs. Olene Tubb (near center); Carl Butler, Hank Williams Jr., and Carl Smith (right). (Courtesy Mr. Randy Piland, Nashville *Tennessean/Banner* library)

Ten years after his burial, a cross to "Daddy"
and a single flower mark the spot where Tubb
lies, Hermitage Memorial Gardens, Hermitage,
Tennessee.

24

The Great Band:
The Troubadour Chapter

It took a few more years, but by the end of 1962, Ernest Tubb had in place the five men who formed unquestionably his greatest band of Texas Troubadours. For sheer musical ability they were unsurpassed; electric guitarist and steel guitarist formed a tight team on the instrumentals, as well arranged and well rehearsed as any in the business. The drummer and rhythm guitarist, capable on their instruments, were talented singers, each of whom would go on to stardom with their vocal abilities. Jack Drake, Tubb's bass player for all but a few months since the fall of 1944, though average at best as a musician, was the man who put the band together, the man who hired each of the talented newcomers. Leon Rhodes came in 1960 and the other three—steel player Buddy Charleton, drummer Jack Greene, and front man Cal Smith—in 1962. For nearly five years these men were the Texas Troubadours, and before they went their separate ways, they were recording artists with a fandom of their own, besides making possible Ernest Tubb's notable 1960s career resurgence. Here's how it all came about, man by man.

LEON RHODES

First hired of the new men was electric lead guitarist Leon Rhodes, a Dallas native. Leon was twenty-eight when he joined the band in 1960 (born March 10, 1932), but he already had twelve years of professional experience in his home area. A natural musician, Rhodes joined the staff of the Big D Jamboree in 1948 (at sixteen) after an audition of boogie-woogie guitar stylings. He played on recordings by Lefty Frizzell, Ray Price, and others in the 1950s, and found all the regular work he wanted as drummer, guitarist, and vocalist on the club scene, besides touring occasionally on short hops with Bobby Williamson, Buddy Griffin, Sonny James, and others. For all his natural ability, music then was more of a lucrative sideline—the work he preferred was professional fast-pitch softball. At $25 a game, he was good at that too, pitching and playing infield for a team that finished second twice in world tournaments.

In 1960, Leon was the regular drummer and sometimes guitarist with a trio that played afternoons and with a larger group that played Sunday evenings in Dewey Groom's 3,500-seat Longhorn Ranch; one Sunday night Ernest Tubb and the Texas Troubadours came to Dallas to headline a show there. Playing his weekly gig, Rhodes was called to the side of the bandstand by a man he didn't know, who asked if the band could do an Ernest Tubb song with Leon playing the lead part. When the man insisted, Leon finally asked the vocalist if he knew any Tubb songs. "A chorus of one; I'll sing it twice, and you do the turnaround in between," came back the reply. The stranger vanished right after the song ("Well, thank you very much," Leon thought), but came back later with somebody else, asking Leon to join them at their table. He did, and the men turned out to be Jack Drake and Buddy Emmons, who implored Leon to join the Texas Troubadours. "We want to offer you a job. How'd you like to move to Nashville, Tennessee, and go to work playing guitar?" "Playing guitar? I'm not the guitar player here, I'm the drummer." To which Emmons's reply was, "Naw, man, you're a guitar player." At the time Rhodes refused: "I can't leave Texas, no way." Tubb and the Troubadours did their show and left, but Jack Drake didn't give up, phoning Rhodes four different times. The fourth time, Rhodes remembers, Drake said, "Leon, we want you to come up here. We're going on a thirteen-day tour, we'll send you the money. We've already talked to Ernest and told him how great we thought you were. We'll pay your way up here. I'll pick you up at the airport, we'll go out on a thirteen-day tour, and just see how you like it." Rhodes agreed, envisioning this tour as a needed vacation; he never moved back to Texas and spent almost seven years as lead guitarist for Ernest Tubb.[1]

ELMER "BUDDY" CHARLETON

Very early in 1962, the second tenure of Buddy Emmons as Texas Troubadour steel guitarist was drawing to a close. No one denied Emmons's genius on the instrument, or the pivotal role he played in bringing steel guitar to the fore in Ernest Tubb's sound. But his free-spirited personality had caused more than one clash with his fellow musicians and, more importantly, with the boss. As his successor Buddy Charleton remembers, "Buddy had a reputation for being the type who'd get to jamming around and wouldn't come back for a job. So they were getting a little aggravated with him." And for his part, Emmons told Charleton at a Tubb date in Virginia that he was chafing under Tubb's stylistic restrictions: "I'm getting a little burned out with the way I have to play." So the discontent was mutual.[2]

That same night, to Charleton's surprise, Jack Drake asked him if he'd be interested in playing steel guitar for the Texas Troubadours. Charleton was "the Buddy Emmons" of Hunters Lodge near Fairfax, with several years' experience in Virginia club work. A self-admitted disciple of two earlier Buds on the steel guitar—Isaacs and Emmons—young Elmer "Buddy" Charleton was a bricklayer by day. The Grand Ole Opry's female sensation at the time, Patsy Cline, had once been backed up by a Winchester band, the Country Crackers, which included Charleton, and as the Emmons situation deteriorated for Tubb, she recommended Charleton to him. Two months after Drake's initial offer to Charleton at Hunters Lodge, Emmons was fired after an angry confrontation with Tubb and his brother C. R. That very night, Drake made the long distance call to Virginia and the contact number that Charleton had given him. Charleton had no phone at the time; his contact was Hunters Lodge impresario and well-known area disc jockey Eddie Matherly. For Tubb, Matherly was willing to part with Charleton immediately; the next day, despite a snowstorm, he was on a plane to Oregon for a Tubb show date.[3] Of the great sixties band members, steel guitarist Buddy Charleton had the longest tenure, staying more than eleven years, from the spring of 1962 to the fall of 1973.[4]

JACK GREENE

Jack Henry Greene, born January 7, 1930, in Maryville, Tennessee (about fifteen miles south of Knoxville), began singing professionally while still in high school over station WGAP ("World's Greatest Aluminum Plant," Alcoa's plant near Maryville). Always determined to make it as a singer, Greene bided his time in a variety of groups, taking his turn at the mic and playing whatever instrument most needed playing: guitar, then string bass and, for several years, drums. After two years of Army duty during the Korean War, Greene joined an Atlanta group called the Peach Tree Cowboys as drummer and vocalist, and when rock and roll knocked most live country music off Atlanta television, he turned entrepreneur as co-owner of a nightclub, The Covered Wagon.

While working a day job for an Atlanta glass company, he decided to base his musicianship at East Point's Dixie Jubilee, where a great many of the big-name Nashville acts played when they came to the Atlanta area. Through long-time friend and Atlanta native Pete Drake, Greene came to know Pete's older brother Jack, and when Ernest Tubb and the Texas Troubadours played East Point on December 30, 1961, Jack Drake asked Greene if he'd like to be the band's drummer. Current drummer Jan Kurtis (real name Jan Kurtis Skugstad), a fine musician and the immediate successor of Bun Wilson, had given a six months' notice, so Drake was on the prowl.

Modestly, Greene adds that his main qualifications were not musical at all: from his Army days, he'd learned a lot about diesel motors and could drive and repair Tubb's bus! But the band needed another singer, as Johnny Johnson was the only one they had and he was feeling the heat from his wife to quit the road after more than four years with the band. Six months later (June 1962), Greene got the phone call to come on up; before moving his family to Nashville, he drove up and auditioned immediately after listening to an Ernest Tubb session at Bradley's Studio. "Leon wanted to know if I could play the fast ones . . . then Ernest got out his guitar and we did some of his things."[5] After that he took a "trial tour," much as Leon Rhodes had done and with the same result: Jack Greene, "the big-eared singing drummer," was now a Texas Troubadour.

CAL SMITH

Johnny Johnson finally did quit the Texas Troubadours (only when his wife threatened to leave him, which she later did anyway); he worked his last Ernest Tubb recording session on August 30, 1962. It was almost four months later that his permanent replacement was hired, a California club singer and former disc jockey, Cal Smith (real name Grant Calvin Shofner). An Oklahoma native, Smith was eleven when his family moved from Gans, Oklahoma, to California during World War II, where his mother found work in the shipyards.

Unlike Rhodes and Greene, Smith was a long-time Ernest Tubb fan. He even gave up a singing job at Mitchell's Club in San Jose to see Ernest Tubb perform at San Jose's Tracy Gardens in 1948.[6] But Smith kept singing; he was a vocalist with Uncle Phil Philley and his Big Western Jamboree Band when it played San Quentin Prison on the same big show that is most famous for featuring Johnny Cash and the Tennessee Two (January 1958).[7] He was also one of the popular country disc jockeys on KEEN in San Jose.[8] But his long-delayed first actual meeting with Ernest Tubb came in 1961, some thirteen years after the Tracy Gardens show, through ex-Texas Troubadour Bill Drake, brother of Jack and then living in California.[9]

Quite a bit of time elapsed between this first chance for Smith to sing with the Tubb group (1961) and Jack Drake's call to San Jose hiring Smith to replace Johnson. Smith cites December 26, 1962, as the big day. For almost six years, Cal Smith fronted Ernest Tubb's road show and slowly rose to prominence for his singing on Kapp Records and television's *The Ernest Tubb Show.* Working for his hero was more than a little traumatic for the nervous Smith, who has graphically described in interviews how active his bowels were during his days with Tubb.[10] Though working for Ernest unsettled Smith's intestines, Tubb did have a calming, fatherly influence on the general direction of Smith's life. His years of club work had left him something of a fight-prone hell-raiser; slowly, Tubb calmed him down and, in the great Tubb tradition, coached him on vocal delivery. Tubb told him, "You're too mechanical. You're just standing out there singing. Put a little feeling in your singing."[11]

Smith's account of the advice is more detailed: "Scared me to death, you know, because I figured, 'Man, I'm fixing to get fired!' He said, 'You're too automatic with your singing, you know. Find one word and make that word mean something. Start putting some feeling into a song; you sang in those old nightclubs in California so long that you don't know the meaning of feeling.' So I immediately started taking his advice, and I'd try to find that word that meant something."[12]

Those who remember Smith's singing when he joined the band recall that it was nearly identical to Hank Thompson's. No doubt, as he had talked Stonewall Jackson out of sounding like Hank Williams, Tubb had to remind Smith that there was already a Hank Thompson and that Cal Smith needed to sing like Cal Smith. Cal found his own style by copying not one but two originals (Thompson and Tubb), much as Hank Williams "merged" Roy Acuff with Ernest Tubb to become distinctive.[13]

THE TROUBADOURS ON RECORD

On Tour

Just as this great band was beginning to take shape, Ernest Tubb and the Decca executives agreed that it was time to spotlight the road show with a "live" album from a large road venue. "Owen Bradley at Decca said, 'Ernest, it's about time to get the Texas Troubadours' name out there. Let's experiment, see how it goes. What we better do is let the Troubadours do half of it and you do half of it, which will help the sales and keep Decca happy,' "[14] remembers Buddy Charleton (brand-new to the band then and billed as "Bud," so people wouldn't think he was Buddy Emmons).

The site chosen was Tulsa's Cain's Ballroom, legendary dance hall and home between 1934 and 1942 to Bob Wills and the Texas Playboys and afterwards to Bob's brother, Johnnie Lee Wills and his fine western swing band. Tubb and the boys played Cain's December 16, 1961, and Decca made a genuine attempt to record their show for a live album. Band members recall that too much crowd noise ruined those recordings, so it was back into the Nashville studios in March and April to recut the songs: "We cut it live, but the crowd was so noisy and rowdy we couldn't use it. Decca was there and everything, but they were just wild—they always were at Cain's when Ernest was there. They took it back to the studio, but they couldn't clean it up enough. So we had to go into the studio and cut it again."[15] The six Texas Troubadour performances for the planned album—instrumentals or vocals by various members of the band—were cut between March 1 and 4, 1962, two months after the club date and only about a week before the return trip to Cain's for picture taking.

Liner notes say, "In this album, recorded live at the famous Cain's Ballroom in Tulsa, Oklahoma, you'll hear a typically exciting performance . . . featuring the one and only Ernest Tubb, his Texas Troubadours, and the over 2,000 happy fans who flocked to the ballroom for this appearance." Well, the two thousand happy fans were live, at least. A few years later Tubb came short of calling these "live" albums (*Midnite Jamboree* from 1960; this one; and 1965's *Hittin' the Road*), using the term "informal" instead: "one of those informal albums, featuring actual audience participation, introduction of songs onstage, etc. that you seem to like so well."[16]

Buddy Charleton, brand-new to the band at the time of the recording sessions, was floored by one particular song Ernest wanted them to arrange for the album, "Steel Guitar Rag"; but the arrangement Leon found for it proved to be one of the best,[17] an old one from his early Dallas days.[18] Charleton and Rhodes remember that the song's creator (or at least first popularizer), Leon McAuliffe, was knocked out by their recording.[19] Rhodes says "Ralph Emery'd play it every 15 minutes; he [McAuliffe] said, 'I have never heard nothing this great before.' "[20]

ERNEST TUBB PRESENTS THE TEXAS TROUBADOURS

The new band of Texas Troubadours had made their first real mark as recording artists in their own right, and they were plenty good enough to get another shot at it the next year, in the first full album of their own. By that time, the new lineup was in place, with Jack Greene, Cal Smith, and even their "Singing Bus Driver," Johnny Wiggins, all to join Leon Rhodes on the vocal work. Rhodes and Charleton worked out their instrumental numbers in hotel rooms during the many and long road trips; in fact, the whole album, *Ernest Tubb Presents the Texas Troubadours,* was recorded in two days (July 23–24, 1963), squeezed between typical long Tubb road trips.

In his affectionate liner notes, Tubb concluded with this appraisal: "I think you will feel like the many fans that write to me every week to say that they think I have the best band that I've ever had. And you know what? I AGREE WITH THEM."

Wiggins, Rhodes, and Cal Smith did some great singing on *Ernest Tubb Presents the Texas Troubadours,* but the hit vocal was undoubtedly Jack Greene's version of the old Rex Griffin classic, "The Last Letter"; it was pulled off the album and issued as a single, something practically unheard of at the time. As before, Rhodes and Charleton sparkled on the instrumental numbers, which they arranged with some help from Leon's Dallas buddies, Clay Allen and George McCoy.

Decca took a wait-and-see attitude toward the Texas Troubadours as a recording act: after all, this had been a one-time deal. When the results were in, sales and airplay (exemplified by the Greene single) justified further projects. Between 1964 and 1969, two more Texas Troubadour albums (plus *Hittin' the Road,* which they shared with their boss) appeared on Decca. By the time of the last one, though, only Buddy Charleton remained from the lineup of what I've called "the great band."

For four full years—from the time Cal Smith came in December 1962 until Leon Rhodes left late in 1966—Ernest Tubb had his finest band. Tubb knew it (as we've seen), his fans knew it (as their letters to him proved), and, in all modesty, the band members knew it too. Fellow artist Bill Anderson remembers the special electricity of a night at the Opry with Ernest Tubb and these great Texas Troubadours on the bill, adding that their success was a big part of the reason other bands got to record, including his own Po' Boys Band on the same Decca label.[21]

Several times the Texas Troubadours had to play an entire club date themselves, if Tubb was drunk or sick; fans, club owners, or promoters seldom complained. "And that man would have us back; if he had a crowd, the crowd didn't leave. And I'll tell you something else," Leon Rhodes continues. "We had as many fans coming to see the Texas Troubadours—I shouldn't say that—but I think we had as many as Ernest had." Bluegrass fiddler and Opry announcer Eddie Stubbs, interviewing Rhodes when he made that comment, adds one from his old disc jockey friend Red Shipley, a great line with which to end this chapter: "The Texas Troubadours were what every other hillbilly band wanted to be, but wasn't."[22]

25

The Last Good Years

Ernest Tubb's own early 1960s odyssey, while building his great band, is a story of personal lows and professional highs. Ironically, the tables completely turned later in the decade: he cleaned up his personal life to a degree that few of his friends, peers, or bandsmen thought possible, just as a long, slow career decline began.

GOODBYE TO MRS. RODGERS

On the personal side, Ernest Tubb was a grandfather twice over when the 1960s began. Justin and Bea Tubb presented him his first, Leah-Lisa, on April 30, 1958; the next year, on October 1, 1959, daughter Elaine and her husband, songwriter Wayne Walker, welcomed Capri Walker into the world. Ernest and Olene finished their family with the birth on May 1, 1960, of Karen Delene Tubb, whose coming was afterward a bittersweet recollection. Ernest was not there—being away on a Canadian tour—but once again Mrs. Rodgers was, and "Karen" was as close as Mrs. Rodgers would let them come to naming the child for her. "She had never liked her own name Carrie, so we named our youngest daughter Karen for her."[1]

By then Mrs. Rodgers's health was in serious decline; in 1959, she found she had colon cancer and underwent an operation in Meridian. Charlie Walker recalls, "I was the one that got her to go to the doctor . . . She kept looking thin and yellow, pale looking, pallor look . . . So they operated on her. She wanted to be operated on in Meridian, said, 'If anything happens to me, I want to be there, that's where I want to be buried.' . . . And she was operated on down there, and came back to San Antonio, and she lived a couple more years, two or three pretty good years after that."[2]

As Walker said, she lived some two years after the surgery. Her poor health was the major reason for the 1960s demise of the Jimmie Rodgers Day festivities in Meridian; Snow and Tubb didn't have the heart to carry it on without her. Soon her friends, unbidden of course, stepped in to help with her medical expenses. Charlie Walker arranged a benefit held September 17, 1961. Walker recalls, "I asked her permission to do it, though. I said, 'I'm gonna get these guys together. We won't advertise it that we're doing it as a benefit to you, we'll just do the show. And give you the money.' . . . We had Ernest Tubb, Hank Snow, Hawkshaw Hawkins, Wilburn Brothers. I just got everybody . . . Johnny Cash was on it, Jimmy Newman, Bill Anderson." The San Antonio performance raised some $6,000, Walker remembers, minus what the state of Texas collected as a venue tax.[3]

Though Mrs. Rodgers looks almost well in the pictures taken at that event (she stands between Ernest Tubb and promoter Billy Deaton in the one most widely circulated), she lived barely two more months, just long enough to know that her husband had been one of the first three members elected to the new Country Music Hall of Fame. Ernest Tubb helped unveil the plaque bearing his idol's likeness on the night of November 3, 1961, at the Country Music Association's Third Anniversary Banquet. Mrs. Rodgers received a certificate bearing the wording of her late husband's plaque. Before the month was out, she was gone. Ernest Tubb sent this wire to his fan club president: "Dear Norma, Mrs. Jimmie Rodgers passed away quietly at 10:18 A.M. November 28th in San Antonio, Texas. Funeral services will be in Meridian, Mississippi, Friday, December 1st at 3 P.M., Webb Funeral Home. Your Friend, Ernest Tubb."

A longtime Tubb fan in Louisiana who used the pen name "Alice from Dallas" attended Mrs. Rodgers's Meridian funeral and described it in detail for the fan club journal, emphasizing that "Ernest was so tired and looked so bad but, bless his heart, he held up better than we expected."[4] Tubb's appraisal of her passing, from the next page of the same *Melody Trails* issue, shows the depth of his loss.

> I am still half way in a daze over the loss of Mrs. Rodgers. Even though we all knew the end was near doesn't make the fact of her passing any easier to bear. I can still hardly make myself admit that she is lost to us forever. But her great spirit seems to still be with me. I am so grateful that I can feel her there behind me in spirit, to give me the courage that I will need to carry on in my work. As she would say, the show MUST go on. So that is what I will try to do. Olene was my tower of strength during this heartbreaking experience. She took care of so many of the details for me and was such a great help by just being there by my side. I know she was deeply saddened but she was able to hide her true feelings throughout most of the ordeal and remembered to remind me that I should be

grateful for having Mrs. Rodgers as long as I did. Which, of course, is the right way to look at it. My life has been truly so much richer for having known this great lady. For this I will be forever grateful.[5]

DRINKING AND GAMING

Emotional burdens like this one were not his only or even his major problem. As he neared age fifty, fatigue from the many and lengthy tours took its toll on Tubb's physique, making his fondness for alcohol and tobacco that much more damaging. A young, sober man would have been hard-pressed to maintain vigorous health with a road schedule like the one the Texas Troubadour had. Jack Greene, from the great 1962–1967 band, remembers the longest trip (time-wise) was three-and-a-half months, working four hours (or more) per night for all but three or four of the nights away.[6] Though drink was by no means Tubb's only diversion (more about cards, dice, and darts shortly), it was a major one up until 1964.

"He was the kind of man who might start drinking on a Friday, and he'd have to keep going until he got to slobbering; until he got to that point, he couldn't quit," Buddy Charleton recalls. "He might go two weeks and not touch a drop; but if he took one drop, he had to go through that cycle until he'd quit." Normally he kept his bus well-stocked, Charleton remembers: not just for himself, but for bandsmen if they wanted moderate, after-show amounts. Tubb himself drank "beer, whiskey—good whiskey; Jim Beam, bourbon." But if the supply ran low, Tubb would stop the bus en route to buy, or sometimes even to borrow, a drink, as Charleton relates.

> I remember sometimes we'd be going down the road, and he'd say, "Boys, I got to have a drink. Stop the bus, go up to that house, and ask that man for a drink." This is when Johnny Johnson was with us. And Johnny said, "Ernest, I can't go up there and ask that man for liquor." Ernest would say, "I can tell by looking at his house that that man's got some liquor." Course he'd already been drinking, but he had run out. "Tell that man Ernest Tubb wants a drink." And I'll be doggone if he didn't go up there and come back with a pint or a half-pint![7]

Going as far as he usually did when once he started drinking, Tubb virtually became a different person under its influence. Jack Greene points out the dramatic contrast between Ernest Tubb sober and drunk: "Yeah, Ernest had those times, and when he got on one, it seemed like he never run down. He'd be going for days and nights. But he always, he was the exact opposite; he was a Jekyll-and-Hyde. One of the kindest, most grateful men I've known in my life, to be one of the most obnoxious, mean bastards you ever met in your life when he was drunk. And he would find every fault in you that you could think of. He was a Jekyll-and-Hyde; he was two exact opposites."[8] Greene says that some of Tubb's worst bouts were almost predictable because of a certain geographic regularity about them. "Ernest had these places: he had San Antonio and he had San Francisco and he had Seattle and Washington, D.C., and I believe that's all, the four places there was always a three-day drunk. Always! No matter what time of the year, those particular places, there was somebody or something that was in his bag, I don't know, never knew. But you knew it was gonna happen."[9]

Rarely in the 1960s, with the big bus and ultimately the professional drivers, was Tubb in a position to jeopardize lives behind the wheel of an auto, as he sometimes had been in the 1950s. Occasionally, though, the bus broke down and the entourage traveled in cars. From one of those times Leon Rhodes recalls pausing for a nap in the back of the instrument car, only to awaken with a drunken Tubb at the wheel, heading uphill on the wrong side of a two-lane highway. Shaken for hours afterward, Rhodes somehow managed to convince Tubb to pull over for a bathroom break and relinquish the wheel.[10]

More commonly, the damage from Tubb's drinking was confined to scenes on the bus or in the hotel rooms. Rhodes recalls, "A lot of times we'd leave the hotels in the morning and go down and get on the bus, and ET wouldn't be on it. And I'd sit on the bus, and we'd sit sometimes for an hour. Jack Drake would be sitting there by me, 'Go up and get him.' I'd say, 'Naw, you go get him.' . . . They said, 'If you don't go on and get him, we're gonna be late for the show. We've got 350 miles to drive,' or whatever. And finally I'd say, 'Ok, I'm gonna go get him this time, but I ain't gonna do this no more.'"

The bedrooms would often be in frightful shape, as Rhodes continues.

I'd go up and knock on the door, and he'd come and open the door. And he would be up all night, sipping; he'd have the lamps broke up, and he'd have the beds all turned upside down . . . I'd just walk in the room and say, "Now, ET, this is enough. I mean, it's enough. Now you get yourself out of this room and you go down and get on the bus; we've got a job to play." And he'd look at me with them wild eyes, and he'd say, "OK, son." . . . And when I'd get out in the hallway with him, I'd say "Give me $100." He'd run his hand in his billfold and give me $100. Put his billfold back up, and I'd get him on the elevator, and get him downstairs, and when I got to the desk going out, I'd hand the lady or the man there $100, I'd say, "You got a broke lamp, and a bed turned upside down upstairs. This will take care of it. If there's any more, if we owe you any more, just call the office or write the office. You've got the phone number."[11]

Charleton for one never believed that Ernest Tubb would be able to quit drinking. But quit he did, as Tubb said in 1974: "And since 1964, I haven't had a drink. Like my daddy said, 'When anything gets bigger than you are, you better quit.' So I did."[12] He didn't say, of course, that this decision came in the aftermath of one of his worst episodes, one that almost cost him the employ of his band's two best singers, Cal Smith and Jack Greene.

Greene recalls that Tubb was too drunk on his bus to play a date with the band at a fire hall in Maryland, somewhere north of Washington, D.C.

> So we just played the whole date . . . Jack Drake was always the one that called the shots: he said, "We're going home, boys." Cause when Ernest got on one, it was over.
>
> So I come by the bus . . . and I heard Cal say, "I love you, you old son of a bitch, but you ain't gonna slap me." And I said, "Oops. Tilt! There's something going on here." And Cal come off the bus with his stuff, and he got in somebody's car and went on to Washington, D.C. [to catch a commercial bus].

Well, the Tubb bus was a few hours down the road, into the mountains of northern Virginia, when Greene, trying to keep to himself and avoid the ruckus, was approached by Ernest: " 'Move over. I want to talk to you.' He sits down and starts to tell me all my problems . . . what I had to do to straighten out my problems, and I said the wrong thing. I said, 'Ernest, I can live with my problems, but you better take care of yours too.' And he said, 'Well, when you get to Nashville, you no longer work for Ernest Tubb.' I said, 'I don't have to get to Nashville. I can get off right here.' He said, 'Stop the bus!' "

Greene got off, dressed only in his brown, rhinestone-studded gabardine stage costume—he'd never had a chance to change or get a jacket—while Johnny Wiggins crept the bus alongside him for five or ten minutes, imploring him to get back on. To make matters worse, some of the ones left on the bus were betting as to whether he'd get back on, Tubb included. Ernest bet $50 that he wouldn't get back on, and he was on the winning side. Wiggins finally gave up, and Greene walked for a solid hour to an all-night diner in Warrenton, Virginia, which he learned to his relief was also the bus stop.

"So it was still dark when the bus came by, and I went up, I said, 'How much is a ticket to Nashville?' He said, '$25.' " All Greene had was a $20 bill. " 'How much to Knoxville? Mama lives there.' About that time somebody slapped me in the back of the head and said, 'I'll loan you $5, big ears.' It was Cal! He'd caught a Greyhound back at the bus station in D.C."[13]

The two men talked all the way back to Nashville of their career plans, now that their days in the Texas Troubadours were over. By then, they each had records out and, figuring they could make it, were determined not to rejoin Ernest under any circumstances. But they did, as Tubb phoned them with a bit more remorse than was typical after such episodes.

> Ernest called and I said no, I'm through. He said, "Well, would you come down and talk about it?" I said, "No, I wouldn't care to talk about it. I appreciate everything you've done for me; I think I can make it on my own." "Well, I always hurt the ones I love most; I promise you I'll never drink another drop in my life. Just come down and talk about it; meet me at the Opry tonight." And he looked so bad; he'd been on one of them three-day drunks, and he looked so bad. Cal and I both came down . . . What's funny is, we never talked. We never said a word about it; we just went back to work. We saw how bad he looked, and how bad he felt, and he just had that guilty look, we felt so sorry for him. Because he was sick . . . But he told me on the phone, "I promise you I'll never drink another drop." And he didn't.[14]

Here, as before, his looks did his apologizing for him; it was almost as if, to this point, his drinking bouts were just something he expected band members to take as part of the job. Of course it might have been too painful to talk about them in retrospect, or he might not have remembered all of the sad details. But he was not one to discuss his own problems (just everybody else's, when he was drunk), or to offer thank yous or apologies. When Leon Rhodes would finally get Tubb out of the hotel rooms and onto the buses after a bad night, "most of the time [he'd] go back there and go to sleep. And by the time that night came, he'd be all right. And he'd never, he'd *never* mention it."[15]

Tubb was equally reticent regarding Leon's honesty about always returning the huge sums he won from Ernest betting on dartboard tosses. "I could hit that bullseye just about every time. And I won as much as $3,000 off of Ernest . . . And the next morning, I'd put it all in an envelope . . . I'd lay it over in his lap and I'd say, 'This is yours.' Then I'd sit down over there. Wouldn't open his mouth! But I'd watch him: he'd get it, take it, put it in his coat, or put it wherever . . . And not one time did he ever say thank you. He never admitted that he'd done anything wrong, never said, 'Well, hey, I shouldn't have been drinking last night, I shouldn't have done this, that or the other.' "[16]

Other bandsmen and visiting artists felt differently about the sums (usually less than $3,000, of course) they could win from Ernest. He loved to while away the weary miles at hands of cards or throws of dice. With the dice in crap games, Ernest by all accounts could more than hold his own.[17] But he'd usually have to be that good with the dice to make up for his losses at cards. "[He was] not good at cards. Ernest was one that couldn't turn over. He'd bet on a come, knowing he was beat," Jack Greene remembers. "In other words, if he had two aces showing, and that's all he had, and the guy sitting over here's got three showing, he'd still bet on the come. If he hit three, he couldn't beat him! But he was that kind of a guy; he loved to gamble, and he loved to shoot craps, and loved to play golf."[18]

Porter Wagoner beat Ernest at the crucial moment in a traveling card game neither man ever forgot. "Pro, this time I got you boy," Wagoner recalls of the Tubb boast. "I said, 'Well, you probably have, I ain't got much of a hand . . .' He said, 'I've got a good hand; I've got aces full, got three aces and two eights.' And I said, 'Well, I've just got two pair.' And he reached to get the money, and I said, 'Wait a minute. Both pair have got nines.' And I laid out them four nines." Ernest was a good loser, especially then, as Wagoner remembers. "He got as big a kick out of that, out of me getting it on him, as honest to God, if it had happened to me . . . He would walk by me on the Opry, for months after this had happened, and say, 'Two pair, huh?' "[19]

Much later Tubb "lost" his whole bus to steel guitarist Lynn Owsley for a few days during a New England tour. "We got to gambling, and he run out of money . . . 'Ernest, I can't carry this credit like this, I've gotta have something to show for it.' He said, 'I've got a bus here, don't I?' 'Well, I'll take a note on that bus.' He wrote it out for me, and I loaned it [money] against the bus. A substantial amount, though I'm not really in the moneylending business, as I explained to Ernest. So after I got the note on the bus, I told him, 'Ernest, there's gonna be some changes made around here. I hope you sleep good on a bunk, 'cause I'm taking your room. We're gonna be stopping at some different places.' " Needless to say, Tubb won his bus back, and Owsley didn't reveal the price he had to pay in retribution.[20]

Tubb's fondness for gaming became pretty widely known shortly after his death through Hallway Productions' *Thanks, Troubadour, Thanks* TV documentary and also via the recollections of Texas Troubadours on various other TV and radio Tubb tributes. Far less has been said about his drinking problem, out of respect, no doubt, for his stature in the business, the help he gave to so many, or the fact that he eventually put it all behind him. Some who now talk about it (like Johnnie Wright), are not even comfortable calling it a drinking "problem." Wright reserves that term to those like Hank Williams or George Jones whose careers were more seriously impacted by drinking.

To the direct question Why was Tubb's problem with alcohol so little known, at least to the fans? Jack Greene's answer was, "Well, it didn't affect his singing, for one thing. He could get pretty drunk and still sing good. It didn't affect his singing like some people, you know; as soon as they have a couple of drinks their tongue gets so thick they can't make it work . . . And he probably timed it better, too, [drinking] after the show." (The fans?) "No, they didn't see it. Course most of it went on in the hotels, after the shows, and on the bus."[21]

TOBACCO

More devastating to Tubb's career than drink and gambling were the long-term effects of his cigarette smoking. Ernest Tubb, as we have seen, was rolling smokes in his teens, at the time he stood in line for manual labor in San Antonio. With few exceptions, fan snapshots from the 1940s to the mid-1960s, catching Ernest Tubb at the Record Shop or right around concert time, show him holding a cigarette. On a recorded 1951 *Midnite Jamboree* (and this must be typical, though few recordings of the show survive), Tubb admits to being "caught" at the end of a record break still holding a cigarette, which he has to quickly pass off to a bandsman to continue the show. Son Justin Tubb remembers that his father, during his prolific songwriting days, wrote at home, on the couch or in bed, with the aid of a pot of coffee and multiple packs of cigarettes.

Of course this fairly common habit never bothered his bandsmen (most of whom also smoked) or adversely affected his behavior. But as the years passed smoking certainly took its toll on Tubb's singing voice. Typically, smoking lowers the speaking or singing voice, and it seems to have done so for Tubb. To state the obvious, this former yodeler sang in a much higher register in 1942 than he did in 1962 (or most of the years between). But the big problem was the hacking cough from a fluid buildup in the throat that required frequent clearings. Jack Greene, a smoker then himself, recalls calling Ernest's problem "smoker's cough" or "smoker's wheeze": "Back then I don't think we even knew what emphysema was."[22] By the time Greene joined the band, Tubb was down to a couple of packs a day, which Greene did not consider really heavy smoking. But Tubb's cough certainly wasn't getting any better, and in January 1966 the matter came to a crisis.

"I smoked for years and years and when I first started getting sick, I was laying on the bed one night and I started to cough. Well, after a minute, I couldn't breathe, and I got scared. I truly thought that I would die. I quit the next day, and I haven't even wanted one since," adding, "Why, I'm just like a preacher when it comes to quitting smoking."[23] Ten years after quitting, he could remember the minute that he gave it up: "[I] quit January 6, at 2:06 a.m., 1966. I'm six foot and I weighed 129 pounds at the time and coughed all night, every night. I gained to 178 in three months and now I'm steady at 165. Don't miss it a bit."[24]

His long-time physician, Dr. George Duncan, admired Tubb's determination and felt that his firm decision prolonged his life. "Once he made up his mind to do something, he did it . . . and I feel sure that his life was prolonged at least five or six years because of his firm decision to quit."[25]

Jack Greene remembers that it was one of the hardest decisions Ernest Tubb ever had to make, and that sticking to it was not easy with so many bandsmen (like Greene) and visiting poker players smoking around him constantly. "When he had to give up cigarettes he'd chew chewing gum, and he'd chew up a big pack of chewing gum a day. He'd put it all in his mouth. He couldn't even talk for that chewing gum. And I was smoking at that time; I'd smoke a cigarette in front of him where he could see it, and he grabbed me around the throat one time, and said, 'Greene, you can smoke a cigarette better than anybody I ever saw.' "[26] Candy was another alternative to cigarettes, Cal Smith recalls: "Ernest decided to quit smoking, and in fact I have his cigarette lighter. Six months after he quit, I asked him what he done with his cigarette lighter, and he said, 'I have it right here [in my pocket].' But he quit smoking, and he'd go into a store and buy gum and candy, and he wouldn't buy just a few bars, he'd get a sack that high."[27]

Even though he'd quit smoking, the candy never caused a weight problem. Obesity was certainly one physical ill that Ernest Tubb avoided throughout his seventy years. A denture wearer by this point, he didn't have to worry about gum and candy rotting his teeth, either.[28]

FROM PERSONAL LOWS TO PROFESSIONAL HIGHS

So much for the personal woes and Tubb's eventual conquest of these besetting sins just past age fifty. In the meantime, his career surged to levels he hadn't seen since the early 1950s, a full decade before.

Part of Ernest Tubb's 1960s resurgence was due to changing conditions, a swing of the pendulum that brought hard country music back into favor. Nashville's *Music Reporter* magazine used almost those very words in a front-page editorial dated August 14, 1961.

> Listeners Tired of Raucous?
> Country in Wide Comeback
> The pendulum has swung again and country music which was sniffed at
> by many teenagers and young adults four or five years ago has bounced
> back hard to become today's most loved and most merchandisable
> product. Every major label and most indies too recognize the fact, and
> are expanding their country output.[29]

And it wasn't just country music as a whole that was coming back, but a harder-edged style of singer, more along Tubb's line. Topping *Music Reporter*'s own twenty-five-song All Country chart for that same week was George Jones's "Tender Years," with records by Claude Gray, Frankie Miller, Bill Anderson, and Carl Smith rounding out the top five. On *Billboard*'s January–November tabulations of the top fifty records of 1961, Jones, Buck Owens, Webb Pierce, Faron

Young, even Kitty Wells, figure prominently. And though Tubb was not on the list for that year, his star was rising as his style was coming back. With the great band under construction that year and the next, he only needed the right songs, and several good ones were soon forthcoming.

One of Nashville's fastest-rising publishers in those years was Pamper Music, co-owned and operated by Tubb's booking agent, Hal Smith of Curtis Artists Productions. Pamper was clicking with songs from three of the town's most talented newcomers: Harlan Howard, Hank Cochran, and Willie Nelson. And though most of their big songs were going to other artists (Jim Reeves, Patsy Cline, Ray Price), Tubb got first crack at a few by Harlan and Hank. "Through That Door," written by Cochran, made the top twenty late in 1961, a fine follow-up to Tubb's record of son-in-law Wayne Walker's "Thoughts of a Fool."

Harlan Howard once told Justin Tubb, "When I first started writing songs, I wrote every song for Ernest Tubb,"[30] the man who, as we have seen, helped make Harlan's "Pick Me Up on Your Way Down" such a huge hit for Charlie Walker. And Tubb had the first singles on several good Harlan Howard songs in the 1960s and 1970s, though none made *Billboard*'s Hot C&W Sides: "A Guy Named Joe," "Little Ole Band of Gold," "Christmas Is Just Another Day for Me," "I Never Could Say No."

It took an oldie from 1949 to get Ernest Tubb back into the top twenty, in the fall of 1962: Art Gibson's "I'm Looking High and Low for My Baby." The song became a staple of Tubb's stage repertory, highlighted by the lead guitar break on which Tubb names his guitarist (Leon Rhodes at that time) by saying, "Now you look awhile, Leon."

After some success with Ralph and Eddie Davis's "Mr. Juke Box" came Tubb's biggest hit in over a decade. "Thanks a Lot" was Tubb's first record to go as high as number 3 on *Billboard*'s chart since "Missing in Action" in 1952, and his first since "Soldier's Last Letter" in 1944 to spend as many as twenty-three weeks on those same charts. Everything about "Thanks a Lot" was remarkable— the way Tubb found the song, coincidentally from a future Texas Troubadour; the dominant six-string "tick tack" bass licks on Tubb's version; and the fact that it soon displaced "You Nearly Lose Your Mind" as Tubb's favorite concert opener.

Tubb and the boys were driving through Oklahoma on one of their many swings through that state when he heard a record he liked on the bus radio: Billy Parker's recording of a song written by Eddie Miller (of "Release Me" fame) and Don Sessions entitled "Thanks a Lot." His Cimarron single broke fast country and pop, but with limited distribution it had not been a big seller. Tubb liked what he heard, tracked Parker down,[31] and got a copy of the record from him. Parker says that Tubb assured him he wouldn't cut it if in Parker's judgment it would hurt the sales of his own record, but Parker readily gave his go-ahead. "Thanks a Lot" began its chart ascent and long chart stay for Tubb on September 28, 1963.

Tubb was in no rush to dilute such a hit with a subsequent single; seven months passed before the follow-up came. But when "Be Better to Your Baby" appeared, it soon won a favored place in the Tubb canon as well. It was a natural for Ernest Tubb, written especially for him by number one son Justin, then one of the hottest songwriters in country music. In fact, Ernest had just released an album, *Thanks a Lot,* largely composed of Justin Tubb songs: "Lonesome 7-7203," "Big Fool of the Year," "Stop Me If You've Heard This One Before."

Justin built "Be Better to Your Baby" around his father's favorite spoken expressions, all of which he'd heard time and time again on the *Midnite Jamboree:* "By crackee," "Doggone ya," "Lest I should forget"; the title idea came from his famous "Be better to your neighbors, and you're gonna have better neighbors, doggone ya." Harlan Howard urged him to write it, Justin says. "I sung it for Harlan, because he kept after me, he said, 'Boy, you need to write your Daddy one just for him.' And that was it, I was working on it at the time, and I sung it for him, and Harlan said, 'Boy that's great.' He was as big a student of what he [Ernest] said and did as I was."[32]

Tubb had a succession of good records after this. Beginning with "Mr. Juke Box" and for the remaining time he had his great band, each of Tubb's A sides reached *Billboard*'s Hot Country Singles chart for at least a short while. "Pass the Booze" stayed on for seventeen weeks and eventually made his *Greatest Hits Vol. 2* album. His cover of Ned Miller's "Do What You Do Do Well" (with trio harmony from Cal Smith and Jack Greene) was fairly successful, though not as big as Miller's more pop-styled smash for Fabor. It was certainly well-suited for Tubb's low range. With "It's for God, Country, and You, Mom (That's Why I'm Fighting in Viet Nam)," a ballad from veteran San Antonio cowboy singer and tunesmith "Red River Dave" McEnery, Ernest Tubb sang about the third war fought during his extended career. From "Soldier's Last Letter" and "Are You Waiting Just for Me?" in World War II, through "Missing in Action" and "A Heartsick Soldier on Heartbreak Ridge" from Korea, to this, his only song about Vietnam, he sang about them all. New Deal Democrat Tubb was naturally a fan of fellow Texan and Great Society architect Lyndon B. Johnson and hence a supporter of America's Vietnam effort at its outset—or at least as long as it was directed by a Democratic administration. With Richard Nixon at the helm of a waning war effort in the early 1970s, I well remember Tubb's warm endorsement of antiwar songs that his former protégés the Wilburn Brothers were then featuring on the Grand Ole Opry: "Little Johnny from down the Street" and "The War Keeps Dragging On."

Singer/songwriter Arleigh Duff, of "Y'All Come" fame, was an Austin, Texas, disc jockey at the time Ernest Tubb had a top-twenty hit with his beautiful song, "Another Story." Duff says of the song, "I wrote this one at Honeycomb House in Austin. Ernest Tubb made it a hit. Thanks Ern. I think I'll dedicate this one to an old girl friend, real or imaginary . . . I'm thankful to Ernest Tubb for recording this song, because he is one of my favorite people."[33] "Another Story" rode the charts to its peak of number 16 just as 1966 was ending, by which time Leon Rhodes had become the first of the great band members to leave. As a solo artist, Ernest Tubb would never again have a top-twenty hit. Tubb's Decca album with "Another Story" as its title cut was one of his better late-1960s sellers, racking up sales of 37,021 units.[34]

"WALTZ ACROSS TEXAS"

A final single from the years of the great band deserves special mention, more for its enduring popularity than for its chart success at the time, which was minimal. Ernest Tubb's record of "Waltz across Texas" spent only seven weeks on the *Billboard* chart in the fall of 1965, never climbing higher than the thirty-fourth position. But as Tubb himself could truthfully say ten years after its release, "It's become a classic. Outside of 'Walking the Floor over You,' it's my most requested song."[35] By the end of his career, according to a statement Ernest Tubb made to son Justin, "Waltz across Texas" had passed "Walking the Floor over You" and had become his most requested song.[36] It was special to Tubb, of course, "because it's about my home state of Texas, and was written by my nephew Talmadge Tubb."[37] To Ernest Tubb fans everywhere, but especially to the many in Texas, the song became very special indeed. Many second- or third-generation Tubb fans are to this day surprised to learn that "Waltz across Texas" was neither a 1940s classic, one that Ernest Tubb had practically "always done," nor a big hit at the time of release.

Ernest Tubb said of the song, "He [Talmadge] didn't have it quite finished, and it laid around my den for about eight or ten years, and I dug it out and started fooling with it and liked it, so I rewrote the chorus and added a verse, and I decided to do it for my own pleasure, because it's about my home state of Texas."[38] As this quotation implies, the song itself has an interesting history. There is no copyright on the song prior to Ernest and Talmadge Tubb's joint copyright of 1965, shortly after its release. Some testimony points to a Corvair Records release (Talmadge's company, managed for its brief existence by Roger Miller) of the song by Bill Mundy in about 1960, but no hard evidence supports that claim. *Billboard* reviewed only one Bill Mundy record, Corvair #100, in its March 7, 1960, issue: "Whirlwind"/"I Won't Blame You." Copies of that review and of the actual recording are on file at the Country Music Foundation, and neither song was written by Talmadge Tubb or bears the slightest resemblance to "Waltz across Texas" (ruling out a *Billboard* misprint). No one interviewed for this book who recalls that Mundy released "Waltz across Texas" on Corvair Records—Talmadge Tubb (who remembered "Whirlwind" as its flip), Douglas Glenn Tubb, Anna Ruth Collier Husky—owns a copy. Ernest Tubb's recollection of its unfinished state and the absence of any prior copyright further corroborate the tentative conclusion that it was not released before Ernest Tubb cut it.

A little different sound on Tubb's recording helped set it apart: Leon Rhodes took the second half of the instrumental break (after Buddy Charleton's steel part), playing an acoustic guitar. "I said, 'Ernest, I sure would like to do it on the flattop guitar and not the electric.' He said, 'Aw, I don't know son; that ain't never been done before.' And I said, 'Well, would you let me just play the turnaround, and then we'll listen to the playback, and then if you don't like it, or if it's not working, then I'll pick the lead back up and play it on the lead?' He said, 'Well, go ahead and try it.' And so I did . . . and it came out so beautiful that Owen Bradley came out of that studio and he started walking towards me and Ernest—I'd already walked towards Ernest and was listening—he said, 'E.T., that guitar sounds great, man, great. You oughta leave it like that.' . . . E.T. liked it. But I think when Owen Bradley came out and made that statement before anything was ever said, that just cinched it right there."[39] Something akin to a Texas anthem had been born. Not for nothing has "Waltz across Texas" remained for the last seven years (as of this writing) on the KIKK (Houston) list of its top ten most requested songs.[40]

ALBUMS

Ernest Tubb took good care of his bandsmen, they all admit, by finding them plenty of lucrative studio employment in the 1960s, and most of it (as the discography in the back of this book proves) was done to fill a steady succession of long-play albums. Tubb's albums from this period, what I've called his last good years, are the best that he ever made. Generally speaking, the choice of material is good: each album's concept or theme is fresh, and the songs are well-suited to his voice, which is far better than it would be just a few years later. Producer Owen Bradley stuck almost exclusively to that great band, using very few tricks or frills in these comeback years for hard country; piano (which he had used for years) and electric bass were just about it.

One can arbitrarily classify (for discussion purposes) Tubb's early 1960s albums into three basic groups: informal, OPH (for "other people's hits"), and specialty. Remakes, a fourth category for which Decca was especially infamous, covers only three Tubb albums, outside the scope of this era: 1959's *Ernest Tubb*

Story, 1961's *Ernest Tubb's Golden Favorites,* and, for the most part, *Let's Turn Back the Years* (1968).

Informal LPs (I've introduced the use of this term already from Tubb's own pen) were those pseudo-live productions that featured guest artists, various Texas Troubadours, audience applause, and spoken introductions of singers and/or songs. In this category were *Midnite Jamboree* (1960), *On Tour* (1962), and *Hittin' the Road* (1965). When Tubb himself coined the term "informal" in a letter to his fan club, he alluded to their popularity with his fans, but Decca/MCA company sales figures for the most part fail to back him up. No figures are available on the first one, but *On Tour* sold only 8,755 and *Hittin' the Road* only 8,512—well below his average sales for the period.[41] Maybe the fans who wrote him expressing their approval of such LPs were not backing up this expression with purchases, preferring albums that were either all Tubb or all Texas Troubadours.

The OPH albums are numerically by far the largest grouping. This was a favorite, and largely inevitable, approach to album recording by the Decca label with all their artists, though it was a practice by no means confined to Decca. Paraphrasing a statement Tubb's fellow Decca star Bill Anderson made, "An Ernest Tubb fan doesn't think a song's been sung until Ernest Tubb sings it." Of course there were always a great many country hits that, because of style or vocal range, Ernest Tubb couldn't sing; but this fan loyalty was what Decca was banking on as they ground out album after album of this type. This table of album sales seems to show that Decca was justified in their faith:

ALBUM	YEAR	SALES
Ernest Tubb Record Shop	1960	14,204
All-Time Hits	1961	38,074
Thanks a Lot	1964	14,010
My Pick of the Hits	1965	26,469
By Request	1966	21,116
E.T. Sings Country Hits Old and New	1966	25,494
Country Hit Time	1968	25,061

Not listed here is the aforementioned *Another Story,* since one of Tubb's own hits was its title song. But it too largely consisted of OPHs, as did such later albums titled for Tubb singles as *Saturday Satan Sunday Saint* (1969), *One Sweet Hello* (1971), and *Say Something Nice to Sarah* (1972).

Specialty albums in Tubb's case include three basic subcategories (though barely more albums than that), all of which he had used in the 1950s for his earliest albums: tribute, religious, and Christmas.

In 1950–1951, Tubb paid tribute to his idol and inspiration, Jimmie Rodgers, with *Ernest Tubb Sings the Songs of Jimmie Rodgers.* Early in 1963, he released

Ernest Tubb Sings Just Call Me Lonesome, a twelve-song tribute to Rex Griffin, which Tubb described in advance to his fan club the year before.[42] Tubb fans seem not to have been as familiar with Griffin or his material as Tubb might have liked: sales totaled a disappointing 10,383 units.

At the very end of 1967, Decca released *Ernest Tubb Sings Hank Williams,* the third and last tribute album of Tubb's long career. Williams's legend and songs have a perennial appeal and have been recorded countless times by countless artists. But Williams, dead fourteen years when this album was made, was younger than Jimmie Rodgers and Rex Griffin and younger by nine years than Ernest Tubb. Here we have a rare instance of an idol paying tribute to a worshiper: the master, if you will, singing the songs of a protégé. This belated tribute to a special friend and touring partner must have been especially meaningful for Tubb, who turned down first crack at more than one Hank Williams song when the ink on Hank's paper wasn't dry. Fans of Ernest Tubb and fans of Hank Williams each bought this one: sales far outstripped those for his Griffin tribute, hitting 41,821 units.

Tubb first recorded religious songs in 1949, when Decca Records launched its 14000 Faith Series, and in 1951 he released an album of sacred material. He returned to that theme for the second and final time in 1963, issuing *Family Bible* some three months after his Rex Griffin tribute appeared. Low sales seem to have precluded any further forays for Tubb into this field, as *Family Bible* sold only 10,028.

Tubb had helped pioneer Christmas singles in the country field after his huge success with "Blue Christmas" in 1949. Between then and 1954, they were an annual event for Tubb, revived again with releases in 1962 and 1963. So it was not surprising when in 1964 Decca finally issued a twelve-inch Ernest Tubb Christmas LP, titled (predictably enough) *Blue Christmas.* Made up entirely of past singles, the album became a big catalogue item for the company, eventually selling 32,275.

Blue Christmas, confined as it was to holiday favorites, was the first instance since 1956's *Ernest Tubb Favorites* of the Decca label's consenting to an all-reissue package of Tubb material. Yes, on their budget-line Vocalion label they had packaged some older Tubb hits in *Ernest Tubb and the Texas Troubadours* (1964), and Vocalion would issue a few more (*Stand by Me,* the early gospel material, and *Great Country,* a repackage of *The Daddy of 'Em All*). But the main Decca label had an aversion to reissuing a collection of all originals once Tubb had remade most of his old hits.

In 1963, Tubb thought he had them talked into it: "I have finally talked Decca into releasing an album sometime this year or next of the old numbers of the early forties, including 'Yesterday's Tears,' 'I'll Never Cry over You,' 'I Ain't Going

Honky Tonkin' Anymore,' and other favorites of that era. This one will probably be titled 'For Collectors Only' and will contain the ORIGINAL recordings, just as the fans have told me they want."[43] It never happened, although Tubb, whose word had formerly been gospel with the Decca brass, fought for years to get it.

A final set of albums in the specialty category I reserve for separate consideration in the next chapter, wherein I describe his duets with Loretta Lynn as one of several mid-1960s Ernest Tubb milestones.

26

Loretta, a Gold Record, the Hall of Fame, and a TV Show

In a busy eight-year period, between 1949 and 1957, Ernest Tubb recorded with several other Decca acts, as we have seen: the Andrews Sisters, Red Foley, daughter Elaine, and the Wilburn Brothers. Tubb and Foley were the country pioneers in Decca's strong tradition of pairing up acts in different combinations to keep up the interest of record buyers. Duet hits showed their first signs of returning to favor in country music with Carl and Pearl Butler's huge hit late in 1962, "Don't Let Me Cross Over," even though Pearl's part consisted only of harmony on the title words in the chorus. Their subsequent releases were labeled "Carl Butler and Pearl," and the duet trend was infused with new life.

George Jones and Melba Montgomery hit in 1963 with "We Must Have Been out of Our Minds," and by the early weeks of 1964, Johnny and Jonie Mosby were having success.

Tubb fan club president Norma Barthel says that the initial idea for Ernest Tubb to record with a female was Decca's: "When the boy-girl duet craze broke out a few months back, Decca began looking for a girl to team with E.T." She describes Tubb's choice as experimental: "He suggested Loretta because he knows her as a sincere little country girl with a lot of talent."[1] Loretta Lynn's account from her autobiography makes Tubb's choice considerably more emphatic. "Ernest Tubb, who recorded on Decca, was looking for a duet album, and he had his choice of women singers. Just on Decca alone he could have sung with Kitty Wells or Brenda Lee. But he chose me, after I'd had just a couple of hits. I remember Ernest chose me because, he said, I was an 'honest country performer who sang with her heart and soul.'"[2] Barthel is surely right when she goes on to describe the doubts or misgivings of pairing these two. "At first it seemed doubtful that the high, clear notes of Loretta Lynn could possibly blend with the deep, mellow voice of the Texas Troubadour. But they tried it, and the result was a hit."[3]

Loretta Lynn was a Kentucky girl, twenty-one years Tubb's junior, though not so young as Tubb implied in his liner notes to their first album: "I never inquire about a lady's age, so I can't say for sure that Loretta Lynn hadn't been born as yet when I signed my first contract with Decca on April 4, 1940."[4] In fact she turned five that month. A few more years passed and Ernest Tubb became one of her very favorite Grand Ole Opry stars: Loretta tuned in to the Saturday night broadcasts from her home in the hills of Eastern Kentucky. She began her own singing career in the clubs of Washington State, and her first record, *Honky Tonk Girl* on the Zero label, actually hit the *Billboard* chart and brought her on a promotional tour to Nashville. Though Ernest Tubb was clearly among the first to recognize Loretta Lynn's talent, he was out of town, working an NCO club date near San Antonio for Billy Deaton, when Loretta first played the Grand Ole Opry and Tubb's own *Midnite Jamboree* on September 17, 1960. It was Tubb's own protégés, Teddy and Doyle Wilburn, who took Loretta into their special care, negotiating her Decca contract through Owen Bradley and making her a regular cast member of their syndicated TV show, which premiered in 1963. Before her Tubb duets, she'd racked up hits with "Success" (1962), "The Other Woman," "Before I'm Over You" (1963), and "Wine, Women, and Song" (1964).

Their first "experimental" session was held March 10, 1964. Loretta Lynn was pregnant, five months away from giving birth to twin girls: "And here I am trying to keep it hid, see, I didn't want Ernest to know I was pregnant. I was afraid he wouldn't record with me. I wore this great big old sweater, and I thought, 'He ain't gonna know I'm pregnant.' He'd a had to been blind . . ."[5] For Loretta Lynn it was such a thrill to work with her idol that she didn't want to jeopardize it. And for his part, Ernest certainly wanted a hit or two for his own sake, but also for hers. Buddy Charleton says, "I don't know whose idea it was to do those duets, but I know that from his point of view, he was trying to help get her career off the ground, 'cause she hadn't been in town very long."[6]

From the outset an album was envisioned, but an initial 45 was the trial balloon on the Tubb-Lynn pairing: Decca 31643, "Mr. & Mrs. Used to Be" and "Love Was Right Here All the Time." Issued June 11, 1964, the record stayed on *Billboard*'s Hot Country Singles for twenty-three weeks, almost the entire second half of the year. Loretta gave birth to her twin girls, Peggy and Patsy, on August 6, 1964, so she was in no condition to tour or in any other way promote the record that summer until late August, as the Ernest Tubb Fan Club reported.[7]

There is little evidence that Ernest Tubb and Loretta Lynn ever did many joint tours during the days of their recording. Buddy Charleton remembers, "They'd sing duets on the Opry some, and occasionally they happened to be on the same road show, but they never really toured together, or promoted those records—not like Loretta and Conway did later."[8] Charleton's recollections of frequent Opry duets is certainly borne out by an Opry performance log meticulously kept by fan Johnny Shealy. If both artists were booked for a given Opry, Lynn would nearly always appear on Tubb's portions, and a duet was a must. Introducing one (transcribed) performance, Tubb says that he promised fans at his last personal appearance that "if Loretta was on the Opry tonight, we'd sing." They may have toured together more after the days of their duets. In her 1976 autobiography, Lynn says, "Nowadays I sing my duets with Conway Twitty, but I usually arrange for Ernest to make one tour with me each year."[9]

About the duets themselves, Loretta says in the same book, "Ernest never tried to hog the songs. He'd just share the melody with me, without getting fancy, and I still think they're some of the best songs I ever did."[10] Shared melodies, yes; but of course if there was any harmony singing to be done, Loretta did it, just as the Andrews Sisters, Red Foley, and the Wilburn Brothers had before this. And the songs were even better on their second series of sessions. About "Our Hearts Are Holding Hands" writer Bill Anderson remembers that "Connie Smith and I cut the demo on that together, which is rare, because she and I never recorded together, but that was about the time I found her, and I had just written the song."[11] "Our Hearts Are Holding Hands" hit number 24 on *Billboard*'s chart, but on the Opry, the two sang "We're Not Kids Anymore," Loretta Lynn's composition on the single's other side, more frequently.

Sales on the album reflect just how popular the twosome were and assured that there would be more joint recordings. Decca DL 4639, *Ernest Tubb and Loretta Lynn* (prominently subtitled *Mr. & Mrs. Used to Be*), came on the market March 5, 1965, and ultimately sold 86,569 copies—a huge total compared to most other Tubb LP sales of the era (see the list in the previous chapter). There were two more albums, *Ernest Tubb and Loretta Lynn Singin' Again* (1967) and *If We Put Our Heads Together* (1969), which sold 81,660 and 48,428, respectively. Reflecting a final fading of their joint popularity was not only the 30,000-unit slump in the sales of their last album, but the fact that their final single, "If We Put Our Heads Together"/"I Chased You til You Caught Me" (1969), was the only one they made that did not reach the charts.

Throughout the years of their association, on the strength of such hits as "Blue Kentucky Girl," "Fist City," "You Ain't Woman Enough," "Don't Come Home a'Drinkin' (With Lovin' on Your Mind)," Loretta Lynn rose to become country music's dominant female artist (alongside a 1966–1967 newcomer, Tammy Wynette). Ernest Tubb, for all his past stardom, was clearly no longer in her league as a hitmaker during the years they recorded together, and when the slump in sales hit with the 1969 product, all parties concerned—Decca Records, Loretta

Lynn, and Ernest Tubb—must have known that the experiment had had its day and that if Loretta were to make any more duets with a Decca roster artist, it wouldn't be with Ernest Tubb. Whatever Decca Records executives said to Tubb about it, Loretta says she went to him and sought his permission to record with Conway. Of course he was glad to give it: by all accounts, Tubb "bowed out" gracefully, and welcomed the great 1970s success of the Conway Twitty/Loretta Lynn team. An overdubbed performance with Lynn on the 1979 *The Legend and the Legacy* project was the last time they recorded "together."

ACCOLADES

A Gold Record

Overdue recognition was accorded in 1965 for Tubb's top-selling record, "Walking the Floor over You," when he received from Decca Records a mounted gold record for the song's one million sales. The surprise came at a celebration given by Decca for Tubb's twenty-fifth anniversary with the company—a luncheon at New York City's Friar's Club on April 29, 1965. Decca president Milton Rackmill, Owen Bradley, and other company officials presented Ernest with two special tokens: a gold record for "Walking the Floor over You," mounted on red velvet inside a case (they mounted the most recent 45 version), and a thirty-nine-jewel Tiffany watch with an inscription recognizing his quarter-century with the company.[12]

The Recording Industry Association of America never officially certified "Walking the Floor over You" as a gold record, simply because it took nearly a quarter-century for the song in several different versions to sell a million copies. Decca generously counted all versions and kept in mind the special circumstances that limited sales of the first release.

The Country Music Hall of Fame

Nashville's Country Music Association (CMA), founded in 1958, first voted members into their Country Music Hall of Fame in 1961 with the induction of Jimmie Rodgers, Hank Williams, and Fred Rose. Only weeks before Mrs. Jimmie Rodgers died, Ernest Tubb was there to unveil those first three plaques. In 1962, Roy Acuff became the first living member inducted, but no one, living or dead, garnered enough votes the next year for election.

During the disc jockey convention in November 1964 at Nashville's downtown Tennessee Theater, anticipation built as the winner was to be announced. The two primary candidates, it seemed, were Tubb and CMA President Tex Ritter. As Tubb recalls, "They told me to get him [Ritter] there, but they had told him to get me there."[13] In his biography of Tex Ritter, Johnny Bond says that slips of paper left on the floor after a CMA meeting, all with "Ernest Tubb" written on them, had convinced Tex that Tubb was the winner.[14] Bond makes no mention of Ritter's being entrusted to get Tubb to the event, only that Tex saw Ernest in the fifth row and thought only of Ernest as the winner's plaque was being read.

> "One of America's most illustrious and versatile stars of radio, television, records, motion pictures, and the Broadway stage." (Tex thought, "That fits Ernest Tubb all right. They may have made a mistake about the Broadway bit, but surely they meant Carnegie Hall.") "Untiring pioneer and Champion of Country and Western industry. His devotion to his God, his family, and his country is a continuing inspiration to countless friends all over the world." ("That's Tubb in a nutshell!") "Ladies and Gentlemen, I am honored to present to you the newest member in the Country Music Hall of Fame . . ." (Tex, beaming with joy, began to walk toward the spot where Ernest Tubb was sitting, with hand outstretched.) "TEX RITTER." Half-way to Ernest Tubb, amid the thunderous applause, Tex stopped and looked back to see if he had misunderstood. It was no mistake. He had been had again. It was their way of keeping the news from him.[15]

If Ernest had any hint it would be Ritter, he was right, and the big surprise was on Tex. But as a result of these CMA shenanigans, Tubb must have known that he was the favorite for 1965.

When the big night came the next year—Friday night, October 22, 1965, at Nashville's Municipal Auditorium, Ernest Tubb became the sixth member of the Country Music Hall of Fame, only the third living member, elected at the peak of his renewed popularity.

CMA Executive Director Jo Walker unveiled Tubb's plaque, as CMA Board Chair Frances Preston read a laudatory speech, which rightly called Tubb "one of the most popular choices of all time."[16] What Tubb said on this momentous occasion was short but apt: "Thank you very much. I don't think I deserve this, but I'm glad somebody thinks that I do."[17]

THE ERNEST TUBB SHOW

Several of the Grand Ole Opry's most popular acts were demonstrating the appeal and profitability of doing syndicated TV shows when Ernest Tubb did likewise at the behest of his booking agent, J. Hal Smith. *The Porter Wagoner Show* (1961) and *The Wilburn Brothers Show* (1963) had begun their long runs in nationwide TV markets, and soon Martha White Flour launched the popular *Flatt and Scruggs* program. It was a former Martha White salesman, A. O. Stinson, who branched out into gospel music TV syndication in Atlanta and then came back to Nashville to work for WSIX-TV whom Hal Smith approached in 1965 to head up his own TV venture.[18]

Smith now says, "I did that show to help Ernest, to promote Ernest . . . I think Ernest got a second wind out of that show . . . It gave him something new to do, new exposure."[19] Taped at WSIX-TV studios—producer Stinson's former employer—the first episodes of *The Ernest Tubb Show* were made in the summer of 1965 and premiered to press and industry invitees that August. A production schedule of four programs taped together at sessions roughly four weeks apart, for a full fifty-two shows per year, was launched. This meant a lot more work for Tubb and his boys, given their road and recording commitments, but in the beginning at least, Tubb loved it.

The artists in the cast were at that time booked by Smith: Tubb, Jack Greene (still the Texas Troubadours' drummer, but already a Decca artist), Pamper writer and new (1964) Grand Ole Opry star Willie Nelson, comedian and first Tubb drummer Bun Wilson, Decca artist Linda Flanagan (in the first few shows, though she soon moved over to a different Smith production, *Country Music Carousel*, and was replaced by Epic and later MGM artist Lois Johnson), Cal Smith, and the old "pug-nosed fiddler," Wade Ray (then working for co-star Willie Nelson). The show gave great exposure to Smith's acts, but Smith says, "I did the show for Ernest, and only secondly to help the acts we booked."

Some people might consider the exposure to young Willie Nelson the most important thing about the show. "We had billed Willie as Ernest's co-star; that's the way Ernest wanted it, to help Willie," Hal Smith recalls. But it wasn't helping: "Nothing we ever did for Willie seemed to help him! His records then weren't going anywhere . . ."[20] Billed as the show's co-host, the taciturn Nelson was seriously miscast. "You know Willie Nelson was my co-star on that show, and the producer kept after me to get Willie to say something. I said, 'You get him to say something. I can't.' Willie's a great singer, but he didn't have just a whole lot of exuberance on TV."[21] Seeing that it wasn't working, Willie went to Smith later and asked to leave the show; his exit, Smith now believes, probably hurt Ernest—at least, it bothered him that he hadn't really been able to help.[22]

Tubb's young children, Tinker and Karen at least, got onto the program from time to time. Tinker, nine years old when the show debuted, had already been singing on the *Midnite Jamboree* for some time and would later travel with the band on summer vacations, as Justin had done in the middle 1940s. And what I have called the great band of Texas Troubadours undoubtedly widened their following with exposure on the TV show. Grand Ole Opry and *Midnite Jamboree* listeners who hadn't bought the albums or seen a road show (if any such existed) could now put faces to the names Leon, Buddy, the two Jacks, and Cal.[23]

Jeannie Seely, wife of Pamper songwriter Hank Cochran and a new Grand Ole Opry star (future Jack Greene duet partner), joined the cast before the show went out of production, replacing Lois Johnson. Otherwise, cast and format were pretty much the same from start to finish of the show's three-year run. The initial *Music City News* report praised its "smooth pacing . . . low-key lighting . . . excellent camera work . . . and overall production."[24] Tubb kept things moving and always seemed to enjoy the other performers, leading the sparse applause (studio audiences ranged from small to nonexistent). After Willie Nelson left, Jack Greene was the closest thing to a co-host, singing a song and then usually bringing Tubb back on.

Tubb loved to be the butt of Bun Wilson's routine, always held on the front porch of "Bun's Cafe." His laughter was so hearty that it usually ended in a fit of coughs; these were the last days of his chain-smoking and the first days after he quit.

In slightly under three years 139 shows were made. A pure syndication product, the show had no sponsor (as Porter Wagoner did with the Chattanooga Medicine Company) and thus had to charge a higher rate than those who did. Network baseball TV overruns hurt the show in about half of its markets (forty to fifty total stations at its peak); "It wasn't so bad if you were preempted one week," Smith recalls, "but if it happened two, three weeks in a row, people start to forget you—to figure you'll never be on again."[25] Some stations dropped the show on rumors that it was going out of production; with those losses, Smith recalls, they were forced to stop production in the early part of 1968. Smith was getting out of his many other music ventures, in view of the inroads made in Nashville by outside money; at about the same time, he sold Pamper Music, Gibson Music, Hal Smith Artists (formerly Curtis Artists Productions), and Boone Records.[26]

For several years, viewers in different parts of the country saw the show in reruns. The Nashville Network paid $200,000 in the middle 1980s to run twenty-six of the shows, introduced afresh by son Justin—the only network exposure the show ever received.

Looking back on the show ten years after its production, Ernest Tubb summed up his feelings: "It was a lot of extra work, to come in off the road and do a week's worth of shows. I liked TV work all right . . . but I guess the agency that was handling the promotion and marketing was understaffed. We just never got enough markets to make it real profitable."[27]

Of the shows 113 are still in existence—thirteen were lost when master tapes got reused, and thirteen more to shipping damages. They remain in Hal Smith's office vaults at Goodlettsville, Tennessee, waiting for the right deal to air again.

27

Decline Sets In

Ernest Tubb could look back on 1965 as "my best year" for many reasons; it had been a year of accomplishments and accolades, as we have seen. But one reason 1965 stood out in Tubb's memory was that he never again had another year like it. After this mid-1960s resurgence, a steady decline set in. Maybe it was inevitable that a singer in his fifties who had been a major star in the country music world for a quarter-century would slip from the limelight as a new generation of performers came to the fore.

Part of the problem was Tubb's aging voice. With emphysema complicating the normal ravages of age and overuse, Tubb's voice lost its strength and took on a raspier, breathier sound with less power to sustain tones. Confined to the same low range he'd used since at least the mid-1950s, he was also limited in his song selection by this as well as the fact that he hadn't written his own songs for years. He had "edited" songs submitted for his consideration and, as we've seen, sometimes given away the products of this editorial flair, as in the case of "Pick Me Up on Your Way Down" or "Half a Mind." He told the fan club in 1957 in answer to the question, "Do you write songs anymore?" "Yes, once in awhile. But I seldom like what I write, so I don't record them."[1]

LATER SONGS

Without new songs of his own, Tubb depended on songs he could find. Sometimes he resorted to older songs: Jimmie Rodgers's "In the Jailhouse Now"; the Jimmie Skinner/Jesse Rodgers song that Tubb had first tried (unissued) in 1947, "Yesterday's Winner Is a Loser Today"; a ten-year-old Skeets McDonald single when he released "One More Memory" in 1969; a remake of "Dear Judge" in 1970; and "Shenandoah Waltz," the 1940s Clyde Moody favorite.

Tubb kept his Ernest Tubb Music, Inc. alive on BMI's books with a trickle of new songs that he chose for recording, songs submitted to him without prior publishing commitments, and these were sometimes retouched by his editorial pen. Among these were songs from newer writers like Hap Howell (pseud. for Hal Bynum) ("Nothing Is Better Than You") and Jack Ripley ("Too Much of Not Enough"), while some were new songs from older writers, men who had supplied Tubb with tunes for years: Billy Hughes ("Just Pack up and Go," "Mama, Who Was That Man?," "Somebody Better Than Me") and Carl Story ("Miles in Memories").

Loretta Lynn and her mentors, the Wilburn Brothers, found many of the Tubb-Lynn duet tunes (1964–1969). Lynn herself wrote one of Tubb's last charted songs, "I'm Gonna Make Like a Snake," in 1968. Son-in-law Wayne Walker contributed a few more memorable songs to the Tubb corpus in these years, such as "Saturday Satan Sunday Saint" and "I Chased You Till You Caught Me" (both 1969).

Other highly reputed writers got new songs to Tubb, too, though from 1970 through 1972 *none* of his singles hit *Billboard*'s chart. Besides Harlan Howard's "Don't Back a Man up in a Corner" (1970) and "Baby, It's So Hard to Be Good" (1972), Merle Haggard furnished "One Sweet Hello," and Eddie Miller (of "Thanks a Lot" and "Lots of Luck" fame) wrote "When Ole Goin' Gets a-Goin'." Tubb's protégé Johnny Cash was at the height of his fame when he wrote "Say Something Nice to Sarah," which was pitched to Tubb by his nephew Douglas Glenn for a 1972 single recording.[2] Marty Robbins, whose lengthy performances on the Grand Ole Opry's final segment regularly delayed the start of Tubb's *Midnite Jamboree* over WSM, wrote "In This Corner." Another Opry star, Porter Wagoner, who turned to songwriting with a vengeance beginning about the middle-1960s, penned a cute novelty for his old poker buddy, written as though it were autobiographical by Tubb: "The Texas Troubadour" (1973). Tubb's first charted record in almost four years (and it barely made it, at number 95) was the first of two Shel Silverstein songs that Tubb would feature on MCA singles after Decca was absorbed: "I've Got All the Heartaches I Can Handle" (1973), which became the title selection of his first MCA album. Don Wayne was hot as the hit writer of Cal Smith's "Country Bumpkin" when Tubb cut Wayne's "Don't Water down the Bad News" (1974).

BREAKING UP THE GREAT BAND

Tubb's aging voice, the availability and selection of songs, and the competition from younger artists were of course not the only reasons for his relative decline as the 1960s waned and the 1970s came on. Part of his descent, whether cause or effect, can be ascribed to the turnover in his Texas Troubadours band. Between the latter part of 1966 and the middle of 1968, every member of Tubb's great band left him, except for steel guitarist Buddy Charleton. This doesn't mean that capable musicians weren't hired in their places; in most cases, the new men were quite talented. But the team spirit, the camaraderie, and the overall quality of the musicianship were lowered. From this point onward, there was more turnover in the band in a given year than there had been for long stretches of years before this. Drums and bass, in particular, became trouble spots with a continuously high turnover after the two Jacks (Greene and Drake) left. Road weariness and related home-front problems caused most of the attrition.

Leon Rhodes was the first member of Tubb's great band to go, toward the end of 1966. Jack Drake picked Leon as the guinea pig to ask Tubb for a $5 raise (from $30 a day to $35), knowing that if Leon got it they'd all get it. Two weeks or so after being refused, Leon decided to quit the road and work recording sessions in Nashville full time. Tubb was supportive of his decision and appreciated the fact that Leon was willing to teach his replacement the intros and turnarounds. Rhodes even lengthened his notice to a full month, to give Tubb time to find a replacement. "And I left, and they got Steve Chapman, and he never asked me to show him anything, or nothing. So I didn't say anything else about it."[3]

Rhodes found session work, and regular work with Spider Wilson as part of the growing Grand Ole Opry staff band, but Tubb and Rhodes had a subsequent falling out over *Midnite Jamboree* work. According to Leon, Mrs. Tubb was telling Opry musicians like George Morgan and Skeeter Davis not to use Leon on their *Midnite Jamboree* performances. An attorney Leon consulted urged him to sue Tubb over this: "If you'll just say the word, we can get everything Ernest Tubb's got." Not wanting to go that far, Leon took the matter before the local chapter of the American Federation of Musicians and won his case. With or without Record Shop work, Leon Rhodes made more money away from the Texas Troubadours than he ever had with the band: "The first three months that I was off the road, I made more money than I made the whole twelve months I was with him. The last year I worked for him I made $7,130; and I made more than that the first three months I was off the road."[4]

Next to go, under considerably happier circumstances, was the singing drummer, Jack Greene. Tubb himself eased Greene out of the band while Greene's own singing career was taking off. Shortly after the release of his "The Last Letter" (1964) from the album *Ernest Tubb Presents the Texas Troubadours,* Greene was signed to a Decca contract, and with the forum of Tubb's far-flung personal appearances and regular slots on his Grand Ole Opry and *Midnite Jamboree* shows, Greene's first releases, "Don't You Ever Get Tired of Hurting Me" and "Ever Since My Baby Went Away," achieved some popularity. But of course it was his late-1966 record of Dallas Frazier's "There Goes My Everything," a runaway number 1 smash (at the top of the chart for seven weeks and the CMA's first Single of the Year at their fall 1967 awards), that established Jack Greene as a star in his own right. Even before he left the band, Greene was allowed to work some dates on his own. "They'd come in and play the Opry, and he'd let me go out and work dates on my own, because the same booking agent was handling both of us . . . it was great that Ernest helped me plan all this . . ."

Greene took advantage of this dual role, but the time finally came in May 1967 when Tubb had to kick him out of the nest. "We played the biggest club in Texas, which later became Gilley's. At that time, it was called Shelly's Club. And we played Shelly's Club the weekend that the 'There Goes My Everything' album came out." In keeping with the Troubadours' habit of selling their LPs (almost never Ernest's) on the road, Greene had picked up four boxes in Dallas the day before from a Decca distributor there. "I sold four boxes of albums that night from the stage, and Ernest told me on the way to the South Louisiana Hayride—we were going to play there the next night [Shelly's on May 19; the South Louisiana Hayride in Ponchatoula on May 20]—he said, 'I think it's time to go, son. You got a good base built under you now, you can go out there and pay for your kids' education and make yourself a good living. And if you can't make it, you can always come back and be a Troubadour.' "[5] Greene didn't have to come back.

A year later, Tubb's other featured vocalist, Cal Smith, who like Greene had stayed on after the embarrassment of the drunken double firings, left the band. Cal's recordings on Kapp Records were steadily increasing in popularity, though he had nothing to match "There Goes My Everything" by the time he left the band July 7, 1968. His fourth Kapp single to make the *Billboard* chart (the first of them to crack the top forty), "Drinking Champagne," prompted Cal to leave, although the record had not yet hit the charts when he did. "I left as a result of 'Drinking Champagne' . . . in July of 1968 . . . Ernest and I had talked about it, and it kinda came unexpected to Ernest because one night we were in Texas and I just figured, 'Well, it's time for me if I'm gonna do it, I may as well do it, you know.' So I told Ernest—we had two weeks to go on the tour—and I said, 'Ernest, I want to give you my notice. I'm gonna try it on my own . . . The next day he called [booking agent] Haze Jones and told Haze, 'Get to work on Cal right quick because he's leaving the band. He's got two weeks to go with the band.' And Haze like to have fainted! 'Couldn't he give us three or four months to get some bookings for him?' "[6]

Even before Smith's superstardom, which came between 1972 and 1975 with hits like "The Lord Knows I'm Drinking," "Country Bumpkin," "It's Time to Pay the Fiddler," and "Jason's Farm," Tubb predicted his rise to interviewer Jackie Pyke. "He is a good, solid singer. He will not be an overnight success. He will not put out à big hit next week. But I think he will keep climbing slowly but surely and become a well-established country music star. As of now, each record that Cal has put out has outsold the last one. I think everything is working out as I predicted it would for him. I still say that Cal Smith will be one of our best country music stars over a period of time and he will last a long time, in my opinion."[7]

For health reasons, Jack Drake finally left the band early in 1968. Although he continued to record with Tubb through April 1968, the March 1968 fan club newsletter, *Keeping up with Ernest Tubb & the Texas Troubadours,* reporting on his replacement, Buck Evans, adds "We miss Jack Drake something awful but if he had to be replaced for awhile, Buck is the one to do it. He will be a guest in the Texas Troubadours next Decca album, along with Bun Wilson and former Troubadour Jack Greene."[8] A heavy smoker, Drake lived on four more years before dying of emphysema, though some recall it was a stomach ailment that made him quit the road and devote his time to business ventures with brother Pete Drake. The Tubb fan club reported in its March 1969 issue that Jack was working "with a music publishing company [Window Music], Stop Records, recording sessions, and some personal appearances."[9]

Except for a brief departure in 1949 when Tubb kept only Butterball Paige as his whole band, Drake had been with Ernest Tubb since the fall of 1944—twenty-four years. Still in his forties, the veteran Drake had permanently established his reputation as Tubb's top band talent scout, since he had been responsible for picking and hiring *all* the members of what became Tubb's best band: Rhodes, Charleton, Greene, and Smith. And though these younger musicians generally had no high regard for Drake as a musician, they loved him as a man and could certainly appreciate the way he looked out for the group. Leon Rhodes said, "Well, you know, Jack wasn't the best. He was kinda one of these guys that, he played his instrument, but he didn't, he couldn't advance on it. He just had certain things that he could do, and it was good enough to work. He wasn't the greatest, but he wasn't the worst either. He had his own little style of playing . . . You could sit down and try to show him something new, and three or four different changes in a little song that you could add to and make the song a little bit better. And for some reason he couldn't grasp it real quick; it'd take a thirty-day tour for him to get on to where you're going there."[10]

But they loved him nonetheless. "Jack Drake could sit right here and cuss you out, and you'd like it. He could say the dirtiest and the nastiest words, the ugliest words to you that you'd ever heard, and they just come out of his mouth sounding sweet. It wouldn't make you mad, with him cussing you out. Somebody said one time, I believe talking about Jack, said Jack owed him $50, and he said he really got mad one night and shoved him up against the wall, and told him he was gonna beat him up if he didn't give him that $50 he owed him. But he said, 'Before I got away from him, he borrowed fifty more from me.' "[11]

Jack Drake died April 30, 1972. The *Nashville Banner,* in its obituary of May 2, gave his age as only forty-three, although that's probably as much as six years understated. The Reverend Dave Rich, minister of the Christ Gospel Church (first to cover Bill Anderson's "City Lights" for a major label), officiated.

RHYTHM SECTION AND FRONT MEN

After this point, turnover was marked in the Texas Troubadours' rhythm section. Bass, electrified after Drake's departure, had a measure of stability with two tenures from Texas native Junior Pruneda (1969–1974, then 1976–1977). Between Drake and Pruneda's first tenure came Buck Evans and Noel Eugene Stanley. Between the two Pruneda terms came Benny Whitten and Buck Evans again. When Junior left for the last time after his 1976–1977 stay, the floodgates were opened: Randy "Panda" Woolery, Larry Emmons (son of Buddy), Ronnie Dale, and Jack Leonard all played electric bass between 1977 and Tubb's retirement late in 1982.

On drums, Don Mills played for five years (1972–1977), but before and after his stay, drummers came and went. Between Jack Greene and Mills there were Wayne White, Bill Pfender, Wayne Jernigan, Hoot Borden, Chuck Sprenger, and Sonny Lonas; after he left, Bobby Rector, Chuck Browning, Jimmy Heap Jr., and Jerry Don Borden (son of Hoot) had the job between 1977 and 1982.

Even Tubb's front-man slot, after Cal Smith's departure in mid-1968, was problematical for the rest of Tubb's career. The first to take it was Billy Parker. Tubb had stayed in touch with Parker ever since tracking down "Thanks a Lot" from him in 1963. Tubb even secured for Parker a Decca recording contract in 1967. So in the summer of 1968, Parker got the call, direct from the man he was asked to replace—Cal Smith. "I always wanted to go to Nashville, to make it as a star, to be on the Grand Ole Opry—but I hadn't thought I'd do those things as Ernest Tubb's front man," Parker remembers. But he adds ruefully, "I discovered what I probably already knew: that I didn't like road work."[12]

There was something else Parker didn't like about being a Texas Troubadour: wearing the Western hat. "I'm about five-feet-ten, and I'd never before worn a hat in my life. That hat made me look like Jimmy Dickens [i.e., even shorter]."[13] As spokesman for the boys, he approached the boss man with a simple question about the hats, and got a now-famous answer.

> I had talked to the guys, I'd become brave, I'd been with him long enough that I was a little braver and could talk to him a little freer . . . I said, "E.T., one thing I've really been wanting to talk serious with you about." And he said, "Son, what is it?" And I thought, "Boy, this is good, he's in a good mood." I said, "Is there any way that us boys could kind of

quit wearing the hat?" And really even in the old bus with the engine running . . . you could have heard a pin drop . . . And I think everybody was listening down in the front seat. And E.T. said, "Yeah, son, there is a way." Then my hopes were really built up, I thought, "This is it." "There's a way to quit wearing the hats of the Texas Troubadour. And that's leave the band."[14]

It's a great story, and wonderfully told by Parker. Soon, though, Tubb relented, and for a time the Texas Troubadours went hatless, as photos in the fan club journals prove.

The road, rather than hats or their absence, wore out Billy Parker. "I actually stayed six months longer than I intended to, waiting for Ernest to find my replacement." Parker stayed on in Nashville for awhile even after Tubb hired his replacement in the late spring or summer of 1970, another Oklahoman, fiddling Leon Boulanger: "I stayed and helped Haze Jones book Ernest Tubb at Atlas Artists Bureau. It was at that point strictly a two-man operation." Jones, brought on board in the early 1960s by Hal Smith, in 1969 bought out Smith's booking arm, Atlas Artists. But Parker didn't stay with Jones for long. "Those few months were a stopover on my way back to Oklahoma." In September 1970 he went back into country radio at KTOW in Tulsa and soon became KVOO's all-night deejay, a job he held for the next eight and a half years.[15]

Boulanger, a multi-instrumentalist best remembered for his fiddle playing,[16] was a country music veteran when Tubb hired him to fill the role of front man. A 1964 *Billboard* column mentions "Leon Boulanger and his western swing band" working a syndicated radio show out of Minneapolis. Boulanger was popular with the crowds, even for a time fiddling in his stage act while bus driver James Price did a jig dance.[17] Other bandsmen (Junior Pruneda in particular) believed that Boulanger came to feel that his own show was as important as Tubb's, and finally he was let go.

After Boulanger, the Texas Troubadours' featured singer for five years was Wayne Hammond. He was succeeded by Ronnie Blackwell (formerly with Porter Wagoner), Rusty Adams, Ernest Tubb Jr., Ronnie Dale, and finally Jack Leonard. Most of these were veterans on the way down rather than young men on their way up, indicative of Tubb's own distance from the limelight. Blackwell and Adams were not in good health when they had the job; Blackwell, in fact, died soon after leaving Tubb in 1978, and Adams really only took the job as a favor to Ernest. Tinker, who had gone on his father's summer tours since about the time he could first walk, was a better guitarist than singer; Ronnie Dale (real name Ronnie Dale Rotroff) was an old cohort of Johnny Paycheck's who had made records for two decades when he joined Tubb; and Jack Leonard, Tubb's last front man, like Dale had a professional singing career stretching back to the late 1950s. He joined the band in Tubb's last active year (March to December 1982), but even so, working for Tubb fulfilled one of Leonard's long-time dreams.[18]

LEAD GUITAR AND STEEL

Heart of the Texas Troubadours band, of course, was the lead guitar and the steel, and for his final fifteen years, Ernest Tubb managed to fill these slots with a capable combination of young and veteran musicians.

Steve Chapman, a blonde, blue-eyed Virginian, came over from Charlie Louvin's band as lead guitarist when Leon Rhodes left. A talented musician, he still could have used some of Leon's offered help to learn particular songs.

> The first job I ever worked with E.T., we were in Oklahoma somewhere. I was just in awe of the man. I'd always heard of him, but I didn't know a lot of his material. [I] walked in and he got off onto something called "There's a Little Bit of Everything in Texas." And I got off into trying to play that thing, the turnaround, and I got into a wrong key, I was so scared, and my mouth was dry, and I was stumbling and falling, and completely missed it. E.T. just walked over there while I was struggling, and he said, "You'd sell this damn job pretty cheap right now, wouldn't you?"[19]

Chapman stayed from late 1966 into 1969. When he left, Tubb (with difficulty) coaxed a return engagement out of the legendary Billy Byrd. Tubb wanted to know if Billy had quit drinking, but he hired him back even without that assurance,[20] a full ten years after he'd quit. Maybe Billy's playing had lost some of its edge, or maybe it was just jealousy from bandsmen who resented Byrd's legendary status—for whatever reason, Byrd and Buddy Charleton did not hit it off. Charleton criticized what he saw as Byrd's overeagerness to kick off a song, and they couldn't stay together on duets. Byrd found fault with some of Charleton's playing too, pointing out that on one break of "Walking the Floor over You" Charleton was in the habit of playing a third part rather than the basic harmony.[21]

Sometime in 1970, after barely a year back, Billy Byrd was gone again. If Charleton had tried to get him out, he managed to succeed. As Buddy admits today, toward the end of his Tubb tenure he was having run-ins with many of the musicians he was trying to lead; the responsibility of bandleader, filling Jack Drake's shoes, was a heavy one. His own burnout, plus the frustration of seeing good musicians so quickly tire of the road and quit, was taking its toll.[22] An even worse confrontation occurred when Charleton left a stage in disgust at drummer

Hoot Borden's drumming; Tubb asked him to apologize, but Charleton never did.[23] Junior Pruneda acknowledges that by that time sentiment in the whole band was running pretty much against Charleton: he was never happy with the best that they could do. Soon, Charleton realized it was time for him to go.

> One day we were getting ready to play a show at Opryland, at the Park; I was putting on my uniform, and Ernest came up to me and said, "Son, are you getting tired of the road?" That's when it hit me, and I said, "Yeah, I guess I am." He said, "I've been watching you, and you been getting all of the boys in the band uptight. They want to please you, give you what you want, but you're not letting it go at that; you're still riding them. I just thought I'd ask and see if you were a little tired of the road." "Well, I guess I am. Give me some time to think about it." He didn't say quit or stay, he just wanted me to give it consideration. So after that we played the Opry, and then the Record Shop, and I went to him and said, "I think I've had enough." . . . Since Eddie Matherly didn't want a two-weeks' notice when I went with Ernest, maybe that was part of the favor he did.[24]

That was it. On a fall night in 1973, after almost twelve years in the band, Buddy Charleton went home to Virginia to be closer to his ailing dad. The last member of the great band was gone.

Lead guitar had been capably handled meantime by a Detroit-area picker, Jack Mollette, and then by a fast-fingered Oklahoman named Bobby Davis. Davis was a top-flight guitarist who, by his own admission, had trouble adapting to the simple Tubb style. "He was a great guitar player," Billy Byrd remembers. "He would make Leon [Rhodes] stand up and notice, he played so great. But Bobby could not play Ernest Tubb style. And he went to Ernest and told him, 'The hardest thing I ever done in my life was try to play for you, your style.' He couldn't do it."[25]

About the same time Buddy Charleton left the band, Bobby Davis went back to Oklahoma—temporarily, he hoped—to console his wife, whose mother had just been killed by a burglar. So who did Ernest Tubb call as a fill-in on lead guitar? For the third and final time, Billy Byrd.

> Of course I didn't have any intentions of going back the last time. Ernest asked me again, so I feel pretty honored that he called me twice to come back. Really, I wish I hadn't gone back that last time, but I worked about a year. I got tricked into it . . . [Bobby Davis] had told Ernest he was coming back, but he never did. And I'd ask Ernest every three or four weeks [When is Bobby coming back?] . . . I was only doing it as a favor. I

was only supposed to go for thirty days to begin with. I lasted about a year, and he finally hired Pete Mitchell. I helped him every way in the world, and Pete was a good little guitar player, especially for Ernest. I spent a lot of time, a few days there, working with Pete, trying to help him, and then I did leave.[26]

Billy's 1973–1974 colleague on steel guitar was another veteran that Tubb had begged to help him out, a man Byrd found much more compatible than Buddy Charleton. In fact, he was a man whose work on records with Ernest Tubb dated back to Billy's first year with Ernest (1949): Don Helms. Helms remembers how and why he was asked to take the job.

Well, Buddy Charleton had left kind of suddenly and I had been traveling with Cal Smith. I wasn't playing, but I had been going with Cal and collecting his money and making the hotel reservations—just company, more or less; he was traveling alone. Well, Buddy Charleton left Ernest Tubb at the same time that Loretta Lynn and Conway Twitty formed United Talent and started touring together. They asked Cal Smith to come and tour on the package. And Cal Smith told Ernest, "I've got just the man. Your old friend Don Helms will take Buddy Charleton's place." So it all kinda happened within a few days. Ernest called me, and I said, "Yes sir, I'll do it. I'm not doing anything."[27]

Helms may or may not have taken on the job as a temporary, like his cohort Billy Byrd. But for a man his age, the road was a tough pill to swallow. "I told my wife that if he hadn't been on the road so doggone much I would have stayed with him. Somebody said, 'I thought you were on the road with E.T.?' I said, 'Well, I was, almost a year, then he finally come through town and I got out.' Ernest saw me later and told me, 'You son of a bitch, you couldn't take it, could you?' " In the same lighthearted vein, Helms jokes now about how he and Byrd raised the band's average age. "You talk about old folks week! You get Ernest Tubb, Billy Byrd, and Don Helms together, it was like the rest home!"[28]

Younger blood was on the way to Tubb's two key instruments, though. Pete Mitchell (real name Peter Michaud) was a French Canadian picker from Blind River, Ontario, who had worked in country music (with Ray Price) and in pop-rock (with the Big Beats, Bobby Dean and the Gems) before settling into a "sit-down" job at Fort Worth's Stage Coach Inn. There he played behind Cal Smith, who got booked into the club as a single act around the time of his hit with "The Lord Knows I'm Drinking." Cal hinted that he might find work in Nashville for Pete, and Pete naturally assumed that meant working for Cal. After "Country Bumpkin" hit, a call came to Fort Worth from Nashville, and Mitchell assumed it was Cal. To his surprise, it was Ernest Tubb. Pete replaced Billy Byrd in September 1974 and stayed with Tubb the rest of his career.[29]

Lynn Owsley, an Alabamian in his mid-twenties but already with considerable professional experience, replaced Don Helms on steel at about the same time that Mitchell took Byrd's place. For a brief period in the late 1970s, because of stomach problems and the need for a lighter road schedule and better diet, he and Johnny "Dumplin' " Cox switched jobs between Tubb's and Cal Smith's band; except for that, Owsley with Pete Mitchell formed the Texas Troubadours' main instrumental tandem the rest of the way. So closely were the two linked that the final *Midnite Jamboree* announcer, Keith Bilbrey, jokes that "Lynn was actually Mitchell's last name. His first name was 'Peton' . . . Pete 'n' Lynn.' "[30]

AN INDUSTRY HEADING IN NEW DIRECTIONS

Compounding Ernest Tubb's problems in the early 1970s with the voice, song selection, and band turnover were factors even less amenable to his control: trends in the country music industry, not at all favorable to the style of music that he performed. As the pendulum swung to bring hard-edged, honky-tonk music back into favor in the early and mid-sixties, the decade to follow (roughly 1965 to 1975) brought to ascendancy styles and sounds with which Ernest Tubb had little sympathy or compatibility: the smooth, cosmopolitan "Nashville sound" and its most popular reaction, the so-called outlaw movement.

When Ernest Tubb's old friend and roadmate Ray Price recorded a straight pop version of "Danny Boy" and tried to pawn it off as country in 1967, he endured a firestorm of protest from country's traditional fans. Some of it, then and later, came from Ernest Tubb. "Let 'em do what they want to do, but don't call it country. Ray Price, one of my good friends in country music, he wound up with a thirty-piece orchestra and he apologized to me. I said, 'Don't apologize to me. Apologize to your fans. They're the ones who are disappointed. I don't give a damn whatcha do. I don't care, Ray, but your fans come to me and say, "What's happened to Ray Price?" I said you're trying to go pop.' "[31]

Ernest Tubb had been among the first country artists to use a string section (on "Kentucky Waltz" with Red Foley in 1951) and backup singers (even before that). "I did it because it was a novelty, but I didn't do it on all my songs, just certain ones. Then everybody else started doing it too."[32] And he raised no objections to Jim Reeves, Patsy Cline, or others when they pioneered the Nashville sound in the late 1950s and early 1960s. Unlike some purists, Ernest Tubb believed that the right artist could in fact make a country record with strings and horns, as long as there was a country core somewhere. Performance style was the key. "You can have a lot of musicians back there, as long as they play it simple and don't put too big arrangements on it . . . You can have 20 fiddles, if they play it country, that's great."[33] In another place, Tubb said, "I don't mind six fiddles in a band, but I sure don't want six violins."[34] Key to his thinking was the fans: *they* knew what was country and what wasn't, and they were the ones deserted by the would-be pop artists. "I try not to be a fanatic, though, and say it all has to be one type of country. I like anything that's good. But what I don't like is the way people like Ray Price and Eddy Arnold have deserted country fans to try to appeal to the pop fans."[35]

What about the coming of the mid-seventies outlaw movement, the Austin sound, and the rise of "Waylon, Willie and the boys," so clearly a reaction to Nashville's country-pop? Did Ernest Tubb race to embrace it, especially since another of his younger protégés, Willie Nelson, was its central figure? Hardly. His sympathies with this set of "cosmic cowboys," judging from published comments, were clearly limited. Musically, he probably preferred it to the Nashville sound, but the image of the country musician that these "outlaws" were projecting was antithetical to what Tubb had always stood for. "They call themselves 'outlaws,' but that's just gimmickry. They say I was something of a rebel myself because I was the first person at the Grand Ole Opry to use an electric guitar. Willie and Waylon have some good ideas, and I like 99 percent of what they do. Maybe they brought some of the hippie-types to the music, but they are still country. I'd record with them if we could do it without the gimmicks." And he did, on *The Legend and the Legacy* and "Leave Them Boys Alone," which preached a special "outlaw" tolerance that Tubb himself had not always shown.

Some parts of the outlaw image really turned him off, particularly the stage behavior of Kris Kristofferson and David Allan Coe: "Now, Kris Kristofferson— I've got a bone to pick with that boy. As a songwriter, I can't take anything away from him, but as a person—well, that's something else. I just don't like the way he conducts himself. I heard some pretty bad things about him at the Dripping Springs Festival down here last year [1972]. Standing up on stage—supposed to be representing country music, you know—with a beard, and using four-letter words in front of children . . . it's just a shame. I didn't know a Rhodes Scholar could be so dumb!"[36] With Coe, the problem (as Tubb saw it) was much the same. "Those people like Coe who use those four-letter words on stage with women and children in the audience are hurting this business. As soon as they get out, the better off country music will be. I can't see the purpose of foul language. If they have talent, they don't have to go through with all this to get attention."[37]

This same sort of image problem was the reason Ernest Tubb supported the Grand Ole Opry's relocation to the new Opryland amusement park. It took the show away from its close proximity to his long-time 417 Broadway Ernest Tubb Record Shop location, home of the *Midnite Jamboree*. But it also took the show (and more importantly, the fans) away from Nashville's then-notorious "lower Broad," haven for pawn shops, peep shows, and so-called adult movie houses. "Even if the Opry wasn't movin'," he told a reporter in 1972, "I'd be concerned about what's happenin' to the block. They've ruined this whole section with the peep shows and all. It used to be only Tootsie's, Linebaugh's, the record shop and some souvenir places."[38] But Tubb also told the press he had no plans for his Record Shop to leave lower Broad: "The new Opry House is wonderful, but just because the show has moved, we're not closing. In fact, we're gonna continue to have the Midnite Jamboree there after each Saturday Opry. I do plan on opening a new place when the motel [i.e., Opryland Hotel] is completed . . . Then we'll have the Jamboree there and concentrate on mail order business at the Broadway shop."[39] And that's exactly what he did.

On the night of the big move, Tubb, by then a thirty-one-year Opry veteran, worked out his busy schedule to be on the show when it opened in its new home on March 16, 1974. This was the famous night in which Watergate-beleaguered President Richard Nixon was on hand for the festivities, playing the piano and yo-yoing with Roy Acuff. Indicative of Tubb's political sympathies was his reaction to the question Bill Anderson put to him that night. "Ernest, you've been here all these years. Did you ever think you would live to see a president of the United States come to the Grand Ole Opry?" "Naw, I never did. But just between me and you, I wish it had been another president."[40] Two years earlier, Tubb wrote to friend Bill French, "I like you—even if you have let tricky Dick trick you—you'll wise up some day."[41]

By 1975, Ernest Tubb found himself something of an elder statesman, fighting a rearguard battle for country music's image, sound, and dignity, and also a slightly embittered, battle-weary veteran, busier than ever in his early sixties while watching an industry he had helped to create pass him by. Two of the hardest blows fell in 1975, as two long-term relationships came crashing down around him. At home his twenty-six-year marriage to Olene dissolved in legal separation; that same year he made his last records for MCA, the conglomerate entertainment corporation that was heir to Decca Records, thus ending a thirty-five-year relationship.

28

The End of Long-Term Relationships

Ernest Tubb had good reasons to bid a less-than-fond adieu to the year 1975 when he wrote this on November 3 for his fan club's yearbook: "So, let's just kick Old 1975 in the pants and pray for a much better year in 1976."[1] Why so glum? In this letter, he listed a few of his reasons: the deaths that year of George Morgan, Lefty Frizzell, Sam McGee ("among others," Tubb adds; he could have mentioned Bob Wills, whose funeral he attended that May in Tulsa, and his former manager Oscar Davis); Hank Williams Jr.'s near-fatal fall off a mountain in Montana, and his mother Audrey Williams's death (reported to Tubb by son Justin on the phone as he was composing the letter).

Closer to home, Ernest Tubb had even better reasons to rank 1975 as one of his worst years—things he does not tell the fan club. National news that summer was his legal separation from wife Olene, something Tubb barely hints at in this passage: "Then, my children's grandmother, 'Mom' Adams, or 'Big Mama,' as they affectionately called her, passed away this summer. She was such a sweet person. We all loved her and will miss her very much." No mention of Olene and no description of Mom Adams as his mother-in-law.[2]

LEGAL SEPARATION

Band members and persons close to the family were always aware of a certain amount of stress and strain in the second Tubb marriage, most of it centered around two factors: Ernest's drinking and Olene's spending. If anything, the long periods of separation for his touring probably prolonged the marriage. Friends tell how Olene seldom bought just one of anything, from food to kitchen appliances, with money her husband brought in from the tours. And though both partners were fond of using the telephone, family members swear that after a certain point Olene kept his personal telephone under lock and key. The faults surely ran both ways; as great-niece Debbie "Snooky" Tubb says, "You can't blame Olene for everything." Living with Ernest Tubb (*any* Tubb man, says Snooky) could be difficult.

With the coming of five children, with Olene's ongoing role of booking *Midnite Jamboree* talent, and with the purchase in the mid-1960s of a huge new home (two-in-one, in fact) for the growing family on Wakefield Drive near suburban Brentwood, there was little public hint of a rift until the actual split came in 1975, after twenty-six years of marriage. Olene had taken over the family bookkeeping about 1972 in an attempt to save money, and she saved it, all right: for whatever reasons, unbeknownst to Ernest, income taxes were not paid for 1972, 1973, and 1974. Interest and penalties caused the tax bill to mount: ten years later it still stood at $236,033.37.

Two days after Olene filed for legal separation, the *Nashville Banner* (May 8, 1975) account alludes to money woes as the heart of the problem. "The wife of country music entertainer Ernest Tubb has filed for legal separation from her husband, claiming she is a pauper, but the singer says his wife 'can't live on a budget.' Mrs. Olene Tubb, 49, of 5402 Wakefield Drive, is citing her husband of 26 years with destruction of their property and cruel and inhuman treatment." Charges were filed in the Davidson County Circuit Court the afternoon of May 6, 1975. Part of Tubb's quoted response from the same article follows.

> I've done everything under the sun. I've still got three children in school and I hesitate to make this too public. But my wife has been ill for several months and she may need medical help. I've offered to send her to any clinic she wants to go, but I don't get any answers from her. But the real breaking point came when our accountant placed us both on a budget. She had been keeping the books and for the last couple of years things had been fouled up. After our accountant put us on a budget, she was never happy. That's when I had to leave home.[3]

Court records date this separation on or about the previous March 25. In the interim, Tubb had lived in Room 109 of the Murfreesboro Road Holiday Inn, trying to clean up and occupy their empty home on Lawndale Drive. "I was cutting the grass and my wife refused to give me a key inside. That is why she is saying I destroyed property. The first thing I knew of her attitude was last month when she filed a peace warrant against me. I was in Texas at the time. I don't know why she did it. I didn't do anything. I haven't had a drink in 11 years and she has all my hunting guns in the house."[4]

The warrant, Tubb told reporter Hance, was never served, but Olene won her restraining order the next day (May 7), alleging that since the Lawndale property was now in their children's names (and it was, though Ernest later claimed he had not been privy to that action), he had no right to continue "changing its present purpose or purposes for any other use than is now in being."

In this May 6 petition for "separate maintenance and support," Olene sought a decree of separate maintenance that would include child support, alimony, and attorney's fees, since she claimed pauperism. On June 10, Tubb filed his own "petition for injunctive relief," which sought to restrain Olene by court order "from in any way or manner disposing of, destroying, encumbering or mortgaging any of the property of the parties, either real or personal." The restraining order was granted the same day.

On July 9, Olene filed a copy of the family's most recent (1974) tax return. As housewife and Record Shop employee, her contributions to the family income were nonexistent, while his gross income for that year totaled $257,439.72—almost all of it ($248,846.00) from personal appearances. After all deductions, interest, expenses, and depreciation, his total tax bill on an income of $65,301.45 was $24,710.73, only $8,332.79 of which was paid at filing.

Also on July 9 Olene filed with the court a list of her estimated monthly expenses sought in the separate maintenance petition. The list, on public file as part of the separation case, seems to prove Ernest Tubb's contention to the press that Olene could not live within a budget. Besides the expected catalogue of utilities, groceries, insurance, taxes, a house payment of $600, a car payment of $255, and children's expenses ($3,000 for that), she lists doctor bills ($330 per month), beauty shop costs ($120 per month), "personal female necessities" of $200 per month, "yard help" of $350 per month, "household help" of $600 ("doctor has told me I am going to have to have help at home"), then "Miscellaneous" ("for clothing, etc.") of $1,000. The grand total, though not tallied on the typed affidavit, comes to $9,782.35 per month. In view of this, the judge's final award of $2,500 per month does not seem quite so exorbitant.

At a final hearing held July 31 before Judge J. William Rutherford of the First Circuit Court for Davidson County, Tennessee, Ernest Tubb's attorney agreed that Olene was entitled to separate maintenance; that was not contested. The only question was the amount. The final decree came the next day. It set the monthly sum at $2,500, gave Olene Tubb permission to reside at the Edmondson Pike home (sometimes listed more correctly as Wakefield Drive), gave Ernest Tubb permission to reside at the Lawndale Drive home, stipulated that Olene may have the out-of-print recordings once jointly owned, while Ernest could keep (to sell on the road) some 916 LPs (and 120 eight-track tapes) of in-print, current recordings. The judge refused to rule on the contested question of whether Olene Tubb could attend the *Midnite Jamboree* (Ernest wanted her ousted), but he decreed that neither party could dispose of "any properties pending further orders of the Court." This last provision caused Ernest Tubb untold misery over the last nine years of his life: staring at a huge tax debt, he couldn't sell his bus, the house that the decree granted him, or property he had purchased in Texas for various relatives. The house he lived in over his last decade he bought in daughter Gayle's name (over Olene's stern objections).

Tubb was expected to reduce the tax bill with help from MCA royalties; but in a five-page petition drawn up December 26, 1975, by Tubb's attorney Robert H. Schwartz, Tubb complained that he had been unable to negotiate any monies from MCA toward the retirement of his tax debt. Olene planned to retire the tax bill with a Commerce Union Bank loan secured against earnings from the Ernest Tubb Record Shop, which Tubb refused. As part of her response to her husband's petition, Olene sought more support, claiming that he grossed over $400,000 in 1975 (a substantial increase over 1974) and used none of it to retire the tax debt, adding that he "has squandered funds over the last six (6) months by buying automobiles, refusing to move into the Lawndale property as the Court directed he should, and in fact did purchase a new home, and further he paid all the costs for one of his grandchildren to be placed in a school where it costs some Two Thousand ($2,000.00) Dollars per month to maintain the child in the school." The upshot of her complaints was that she wanted her maintenance and support payments raised from $2,500 per month to $4,000 per month.

There is no record of subsequent legal action by either party. Ernest Tubb never moved back into the Lawndale house, which was never sold to retire the tax bill and remains to this day Olene's property. The house Tubb bought was the one in Antioch put in daughter Gayle's name. "Legally separated," which in many ways seems the worst of all possible worlds (all the costs of marriage without any of the benefits), continued to be Ernest Tubb's marital status until the day he died, although Justin and others begged him to seek a divorce. He wouldn't do it; from his point of view, Olene was seriously ill and in need of financial support, though hardly the pauper that she claimed to be.

THE BREAK WITH MCA

As his estrangement from Olene was dragging through the court that summer of 1975, Ernest Tubb made what proved to be his last recordings for MCA, corporate successors to Decca. Music Corporation of America purchased effective control of Decca's stock back in 1962, but for several years Tubb's albums, like all Decca LP product, simply noted at the bottom "Decca Records, Inc., A Subsidiary of MCA, Inc." The label changeover from Decca to MCA took place in the spring of 1973.

The new label never had much time or promotion money for its many veteran country music stars: Webb Pierce, Kitty Wells, Jimmie Davis, nor for the man with the longest continuous affiliation, Ernest Tubb. At midyear Tubb made his first single in over a year and his first album in two years. The single was "If You Don't Quit Checking on Me," and the album was simply titled *Ernest Tubb*. But as with several releases past, there was little promotion and, for the album at least, sales of only 9,835 units, well down from the 20,208 units sold by his only previous MCA album, *I've Got All the Heartaches I Can Handle*.

Tubb signed a new five-year contract with MCA at the time of these May and June sessions. At the time he signed his previous contract (for ten years, in 1965), he had a prophetic conversation with Norma Barthel, looking ahead to its expiration: "Whoever heard of a 60-year-old man making records and traveling all over the country, putting on one-night shows three weeks out of every month?"[5] Well, when 1975 came, Ernest Tubb was doing just that, but his recording future by then, as he had guessed, was considerably more problematical. Besides his age and unfavorable industry trends, there was Tubb's request for large chunks of back royalties (or at least advances against future royalties) to help retire his huge tax bill.

The regular fan club publications for months held out hope of new recordings that never came, then hinted at a rift between Tubb and MCA, which was gradually confirmed by press accounts; 1976 became the first year since 1948 (date of the second Petrillo ban) to come and go without any new Ernest Tubb recordings made, and by that year's end, Tubb confirmed everything that the fan club had reported as rumor. He'd bought his way out of the new five-year contract, severed his ties with MCA, and was a free agent, so to speak, in search of a new record deal.

> First off, they became so big. They merged with MCA and got involved with motion pictures and mostly television. I can't understand how they think. We had no mutual relationship. I'm not knocking Decca. I had some very good years with them. But they got to the point they couldn't care less what I wanted released. After 36 years, you're not going to have a hit record every three months. They became more concerned with people like this Newton-John . . . uh . . . Elton John. They're more concerned with that. Decca hasn't spent an ad dollar on me in the last 20 years. Every artist has a month, a month in which he is promoted in the trade magazine . . . but never me.[6]

Tubb's side of the contract negotiations is as follows. "I'd been there 35 years, and they wanted me to sign a ten-year contract . . . I said, 'Let's make it five.' So we signed that; then the next year we began to have little disagreements . . ."[7] Tubb was never too specific about those disagreements, but he did say, "They came up with a lot of new ideas that I didn't like. I have thought for a long time that our product couldn't be any better than it is now, and so I just asked them to let me out of the contract."[8] "It took me another year, but in 1977 they let me out of my contract. The people I knew have all gone, they've moved upstairs or gone."[9]

The old guard at Decca was indeed gone: only weeks apart in the early months of 1976, Owen Bradley left Decca/MCA after a thirty-year association, and Dave Kapp, long out of the Decca picture, died in a New York City hospital.[10] Milt Gabler, Milton Rackmill, Marty Salkin, and other New York-based Decca executives had stepped aside in favor of West Coast MCA executives,[11] the movie and TV people to whom Tubb referred. Their objectionable "new ideas" for Ernest Tubb records included more pop touches (strings, backup voices), less use of the Texas Troubadours on recordings, and maybe even a different type of song.

After the split, other record companies came forth with offers, but they all wanted these same types of new touches to any Tubb records they might produce. "Columbia wanted to talk to me, Victor wanted to talk to me, Capitol wanted to record me; they all wanted to record me, but they all wanted to change me, maybe bring me up to date in a modern manner. I said, 'Well, Pete [Drake], tell them to forget about it.' . . . Now if they don't like what we're recording, then they're out of luck, because this is all I can do, all I'm gonna do. I wouldn't change or do a gimmick or all that stuff, if I knew it would sell five million albums tomorrow."[12]

The same thing was happening to other veteran country artists[13]—Kitty Wells, Webb Pierce, Jimmie Davis, and the Osborne Brothers all were dropped by MCA, and with other labels the story was much the same. If you weren't "Nashville sound" or an "outlaw," they didn't want you. Pete Drake, as we shall see, had a pretty large pool of veteran talent—not just Tubb—from which to build his new label venture, the aptly named First Generation Records.

RETIREMENT?

Whether or not he would ever record again, Ernest Tubb had no thoughts of retiring from roadwork and disbanding the Texas Troubadours, even though he was in his sixties and the press continually asked him about it. To the question he offered several cogent reasons why retirement was not for him, though he never mentioned the obvious one of financial need. Implied in much of what he said on the subject is a touch of resentment that the question was asked at all. When he says "The fans will tell me when to quit," one hears an implied defiance:

You, the ladies and gentlemen of the press, will not tell me. "I'm gonna let the people decide. I told an old boy in Tulsa who asked me that, 'I'll sing as long as you pay to come through that door.' "[14] Often the reasons he gave were more pragmatic, even health related. "I'd get too nervous being in an office. Besides I'm too lazy to work. I like being out and meeting the people."[15] Or, "You know, the doctors claim when you're busy at any profession, any job, for 35 or 40 years and then you quit, you'll live six years no matter what your health is. I want to live longer than six years."[16]

Friends of his had tried to retire and failed. "It's like anything else—you're either in or you're out. I've seen people try to slow down before, and after awhile they're out. I like what I do. If you keep a band, they have to make a living. You have to work to live and you have expenses to meet, like my bus—it costs me $100 a day to move by bus. And by working, you get new fans and keep old ones."[17] "I got my answer to that from Sally Rand, the fan dancer. She worked a club in New Orleans last year on her 69th birthday, and somebody asked her why she didn't retire. She said, 'People only retire from jobs they don't like.' "[18]

If Sally Rand was his example of how best to handle retirement, Tubb often evoked the negative example of his old Opry friend, Roy Acuff. "You know, Roy Acuff has retired five times, and next month he's going to Vietnam. As long as my health holds up and people want to see me, I'll keep at it. I'm doing what I love to do."[19]

NEW BUSINESS VENTURES

After his separation from Olene, there were even more offices for Ernest Tubb to "keep out of" by staying on the road with his Texas Troubadours. One was a new music publishing venture with son Justin (1975); the next year there was expansion and incorporation for the Ernest Tubb Record Shop.

Cary & Mr. Wilson Music was the new publishing venture, a name drawn from Justin's youngest son (Cary Justin Tubb) and Arthur Wilson, the mentor of a business acquaintance. The new company, with Justin doing most of the day-to-day work, opened its Music Row office in July 1975 at 700-B 18th Avenue South.[20] Besides publishing new songs that Ernest and Justin might write or record, Cary & Mr. Wilson Music eventually bought up the catalogue of Hill & Range's old Ernest Tubb Music Company, as Justin Tubb explained. "In the 1940s, Hill & Range bought all the older American Music songs, and formed Noma Music for them. Ernest Tubb Music, formed and put under Hill & Range, took care of his songs thereafter. When Hill & Range sold out to Chappell [about the time the two Tubbs formed their company], Cary & Mr. Wilson Music acquired the Ernest Tubb Music songs, but Chappell got the older songs, the ones that had gone to Noma Music, and they still have them. We've thought about acquiring these too, but it depends on how much Chappell thinks they're worth."[21]

An even more significant business venture at that time for the Tubbs involved the Ernest Tubb Record Shop. In 1976, a second store was opened on Demonbreun Street near the Country Music Hall of Fame. The idea was to get the *Midnite Jamboree* crowd away from the seedy and lonely lower Broad area and to tap into the (then) sizable tourist crowds (between 350,000 and 500,000 per year) drawn to Music Row by the Hall of Fame. Partners Ernest Tubb and Charles Mosley cut the ribbon to the new store on Wednesday, June 2, 1976, and the venerable *Midnite Jamboree* had a new home as of Saturday, June 12.[22]

The Demonbreun location was never envisioned as more than a temporary home for the show; ultimately it would move back in close proximity to the Opry, near Opryland USA park and Opryland Hotel. Indicative of these plans (to which Tubb had referred as early as a previously quoted March 1974 piece) is the fact that when the Music Valley Shop opened less than three years after the Demonbreun store in May 1979,[23] it immediately became the number 2 shop; the Demonbreun store, which stayed open, then became number 3.

By that time, Ernest Tubb Record Shops added an "Inc." to their name by incorporating. In October 1976 the long-time two-man private firm filed a stock plan with the state of Tennessee, dividing ownership among four persons: the two original owners (Ernest Tubb and Charles Mosley) plus Justin Tubb and Gary David McCormick, Record Shop manager since 1973. Their stockholders agreement, dated October 13, 1976, locked the corporation basically into those four hands, with Mr. Mosley agreeing that upon his death, his shares would go to Ernest Tubb, and that at Tubb's death, his total shares would go to his heirs. The ownership division is not spelled out, but it wasn't equal quarters: there is a three-year waiting period from the date of the agreement for McCormick to increase his ownership share to 20 percent, or one-fifth.[24]

Even before he became a corporation stockholder, Justin Tubb had become the active manager of the *Midnite Jamboree* show, though of course his father hosted the show whenever he was in town.

> But when he and Olene separated, he more or less turned it over to me. And he came to me first, and asked me to do it, take it over, book the guests and listen to all the tapes, and schedule them . . . He said, "I want you to do it." I said, "I don't want to do it. I don't want to get caught in the middle of a situation like, with her [Olene]." So he kept asking, and turned it over to David. "Well, I'll just get David to take care of it." But he kept after me.[25]

BETTER TIMES A-COMIN'

The mid-1970s were, arguably, a tough time for America—recall the disenchantment, the cynicism, and the malaise that followed Watergate and the fall of Vietnam, all of which made Jimmy Carter possible. Clearly it was a controversial and divisive time for country music as well. In 1974, the Country Music Association gave its top awards to John Denver and Olivia Newton-John, which sparked a firestorm of protest and gave birth to a short-lived rival Nashville organization, ACE (Association of Country Entertainers), with which Tubb had some sympathy. He said in 1978, "Roy Acuff, Hank Snow and I have been fighting for years to get the networks to do country shows that are authentic,"[26] implying of course that the CMA, the Academy of Country Music, and their predecessors had long since dropped that ball with network TV.

Whatever the status of the nation or of country music, it is beyond argument that the 1975–1977 period was not a good one, personally or professionally, for Ernest Tubb. One silver lining to his many dark clouds was that he drew closer to his eldest son Justin because of Cary & Mr. Wilson Music and the incorporation of the Ernest Tubb Record Shops. Though father and son still didn't tour or perform together, they were now near neighbors in suburban Antioch, Tennessee.

Still, these years were so dark—his darkest since the heyday of rock and roll in 1957–1958 twenty years before, or perhaps even since his first divorce in 1948—that Tubb was surely glad to see the cycle turn again. By sticking to his guns, and continuing to "keep on keeping on," Tubb, staying busier than ever on tour, saw the press attention and the adulation of a grateful public and industry come around once more. Beginning about 1979 and lasting the few more years of his active career (through 1982), Ernest Tubb became widely recognized and touted for what he truly was: a legend with a legacy.

29

A Legend with a Legacy

BACK ON RECORDS

Ernest Tubb had been out of the recording studios for nearly two years and was only just free of his MCA contract when an old friend, Merle Haggard, got him back into the studio for a spur-of-the-moment duet. None of the sides with Tubb were ever released, though Haggard's project when released did feature several Tubb songs (see discography).

Barely a month later, in late March and early April 1977, another of Tubb's old friends, steel guitarist and Music Row entrepreneur Pete Drake, scheduled sessions for Tubb and his Texas Troubadours at his Pete's Place studio. For Tubb these were the first of their kind—almost like trial or demo sessions. After forty years of making records, here was Ernest Tubb, laying down tapes with which Drake planned to "shop him around" to the major labels.

In five separate sessions between March 23 and April 5, Tubb, his Texas Troubadours (at that time Wayne Hammond, Lynn Owsley, Junior Pruneda, Pete Mitchell, and Bobby Rector), and a handful of studio musicians taped and re-taped eleven songs: five new ones and six Tubb oldies. After initial inquiries to all the major labels, Drake had decided to record Tubb himself, hoping to have more success with a finished product.[1] There were still no takers, so in spite of Drake's earlier failure in the business with Stop Records in 1972, Drake was once again a label owner. This time he dubbed the company First Generation Records, because of signing Tubb and such other veteran artists as Ferlin Husky, Billy Walker, Jan Howard, Ray Pillow, Charlie Louvin, Vic Willis, Jean Shepard, and Tubb protégés Stonewall Jackson and the Wilburn Brothers.

The first Tubb release was a single, FGS 001, "Sometimes I Do"/"Half My Heart's in Texas," issued on September 19.[2] "Are you excited about it?" WSM disc jockey Hairl Hensley asked Tubb. "Pete's excited! But after all these years, I don't get very excited about anything. If it sells anything, then I'll get excited."[3] On December 17, 1977, it actually cracked *Billboard*'s Hot Country Singles as a double-sided entry and stayed there seven weeks, peaking at number 79. It was his first charted single in over four years. The album, *Ernest Tubb: Living Legend,* came out just before Christmas, with an album of remakes planned for mailorder sale via radio and TV.[4]

Almost a year later (August 14, 1978), Tubb and his latest Texas Troubadours were still remaking classic Tubb favorites at Pete's Place. Tubb was told only about the TV direct-sale album plans; but Pete Drake had some surprises up his sleeve, as Tubb found out and explained to the press a few weeks later.

> Pete said he wanted an album of old songs, ten or fifteen or twenty . . . They called me in the office—I thought presumably to listen to the playback of what we'd done that night. This was last week, wasn't it? (Yeah) So they started playing something I'd done last year—"Waltz across Texas." I thought maybe they'd made a mistake till I heard Willie Nelson come in singing on it! I thought, "Oh me." And they kept playing tape and song after song: they had about seven different—Willie Nelson, and Waylon Jennings, Johnny Paycheck, Loretta Lynn—they had come in and recorded with me on those tapes . . . I was really surprised, a very, very nice surprise, to think these people wanted to come in and do that. That Pete, Pete Drake is a little bit tricky, you know, you gotta watch him. He fooled around with them Beatles too long, I think. Ha Ha![5]

Beginning on or about July 11, Nelson, Jennings, and Paycheck led the parade to Pete's Place. George Jones and Marty Robbins worked sessions into their busy schedules, and ultimately Conway Twitty, the Wilburn Brothers, Charlie Rich, Ferlin Husky, and son Justin (an overdub, yes, but the first and only time they recorded together) joined the project.

With all these big names, Drake clearly hoped to interest a major label in the finished product. "Drake says he is negotiating with major labels, including several that turned him down a year ago, for release of the album. He says he hasn't yet decided whether to lease it to a major label or release it on 1st Generation."[6] Drake's optimistic hopes were to have the album out by that fall. "If we can get all the rest of the releases from the labels, I would like for it to come out in October. I'd like to get it out about DJ Convention, if there was any way. We've got most of the releases."[7]

Besides the guest singers on the duos and trios (many artists sang on two songs), Drake hired a bevy of all-star musicians, background singers, and guest engineers as well (see discography). Chet Flippo of *Rolling Stone* magazine wrote the epigrammatic liner notes, the same job he'd had for country music's first platinum album three years earlier: *Wanted: The Outlaws.*

Delays in the album's release, as Drake unsuccessfully shopped the big project to other labels, actually proved fortuitous, since the ultimate release (on First Generation) coincided with Tubb's sixty-fifth birthday. The setting was a gala birthday party for Tubb at Nashville's Exit Inn on a snowy February 9, 1979. Jim Sasser, first-term Tennessee U.S. Senator from Tubb's beloved Democratic Party, was probably the biggest dignitary on hand, though cards and congratulatory telegrams from several were read, including one from President Jimmy Carter. Musician friends from the Opry were prominent among the few hundred invited guests: Jack Greene, Jeannie Seely, Loretta Lynn, George Jones, and Charlie Louvin. Peter Fonda was on hand, posing for photos with the birthday boy and commiserating with Justin Tubb about what it was like to be the son of a legend and working in the same profession. Oddest and best publicized of the many gifts presented that night was a Texas-shaped guitar designed by Shot Jackson of Sho-Bud and handed to Tubb by his faithful booking agent of ten years, Haze Jones.[8]

The critics were mostly favorable to the all-star compilation once it finally did hit the stores and the radio stations. "Tubb has been around for so long, and still plays so frequently, that it's easy to forget why countless musicians and fans consider this lean, tall man something of a yardstick, a standard."[9] Praising some of the duet blends—Haggard's, Cash's, and Lynn's—this critic added, "The key on a Jimmie Rodgers tune is much too low for Conway Twitty, as he himself admits to Ernest in a recorded aside at the end. Charlie Rich's smooth and light voice goes along with Tubb's style about as well as barbecue and whipped cream." Part of the difficulty of singing with Ernest Tubb was captured by this wonderful metaphor: "Tubb has sung these songs for so long they are like that old armchair that your grandad always sits in. The chair fits him perfectly, but it gives you a backache if you're in it longer than five minutes."[10]

Canada's Cachet Records, a firm that specialized in TV direct-mail sales, later released a shortened version of the album, *The Legend and the Legacy Volume 1,* which went gold by selling over $500,000 worth of product (half the U.S. certification level). By year's end, Cachet had pulled two singles from the album: Tubb duos and trios on "Waltz across Texas" (with Willie Nelson), and "Walkin' the Floor over You" (with Haggard, Atkins, and Charlie Daniels). The former got only to number 56 in the summer; the latter did better, making it to number 31 in the fall.

After *The Legend and the Legacy,* Ernest Tubb never again placed a record (single or LP) on trade magazine charts, though he continued to record for Pete Drake and First Generation. Almost all of his remaining Pete Drake recordings were remakes of his older hits, though there were a few new songs by other writers ("I Ain't Been Right Since You Went Wrong," "Sad Songs & Waltzes") and even a final Ernest Tubb composition, "One More Day."[11]

None of these later First Generation recordings were released in Tubb's lifetime. Pete Drake was also dead (having died in 1988) when in 1992 his widow Rose licensed the entire corpus of this material—several with new duet partners and 1990s-style sound mixes—to California's LaserLight label as the five-volume *The Legendary Ernest Tubb & Friends*. Already out of print by 1995, it did not receive the loving treatment, by most accounts, that even this later material deserved. The sound mix is inconsistent, to say nothing of the quality of Tubb's voice on several of the heretofore unreleased songs. The latest word is that Mrs. Drake plans more repackagings of this material, one at least without any guest vocal overdubs.

Besides the Pete Drake-produced recordings, Tubb began to appear as a guest on other people's records. In 1979, Tubb joined a dozen artists, "biggest" of which were Justin, Charlie Louvin, and Charlie Walker, on three tracks by a Haze Jones entourage called the Atlas Artists Cowboy Rhythm Band. (For a complete list of the artists, see the note to this session in discography.) Legendary broadcast personality Biff Collie produced the records for the Award label. This small-scale replication of the *Legend and Legacy* project, assembled strictly to promote the booking agency, soon faded out of sight when nothing approaching a hit emerged.

After this there were four occasions in the very early 1980s when Tubb agreed to sing with friends one-on-one. In 1981, he sang with Sammi Smith on her LSI recording of Guy Clark's "I'll Be Your San Antone Rose." Later that year he joined his great contemporary and fellow Texas legend Floyd Tillman on a Gilley's label recording of a new Tillman song, "One Way Love." Ernest's part was recorded at Pete's Place in Nashville, although the western swing musicians (Herb Remington, Johnny and Dick Gimble, Clyde Brewer, and Leo Dolan) and Tillman cut their parts at Gilley's famous nightclub in Pasadena, Texas—then at the peak of its *Urban Cowboy* fame.

During his last active year, 1982, Tubb recorded with more close friends, only a few weeks apart and shortly before he had to give up regular touring. With ex-Texas Troubadour Billy Parker on the Soundwaves label, Tubb sang "Tomorrow Never Comes" for Parker's album, *Something Old, Something New*. And last of all—final recording of a forty-six-year career—was the popular cut with outlaws Waylon Jennings and Hank Williams Jr., "Leave Them Boys Alone." Released as a single in 1983 on Williams's Warner Brothers label, the song (co-written by Dean Dillon, Hank Jr., Gary Stewart, and Tanya Tucker) climbed to number 6 on *Billboard*'s Hot Country Singles chart. Tubb, though in poor voice because of the ravages of emphysema, was the perfect father figure for this recording, bestowing his paternal blessings upon the nonconformists of this later age. It was an appropriate role, really, with which to bow out of the recording world, a fitting musical last will and testament.

CULT HERO AND ELDER STATESMAN

Even before the release of *The Legend and the Legacy,* Ernest Tubb was entering a phase of his life and career that might be dubbed the "cult hero" period, where, as one of country music's true elder statesmen, he was showered with awards and accolades and accorded what was for him an unprecedented media notoriety.

Tubb returned to the silver screen in what became the Best Motion Picture of 1980, his part filmed in April 1979. Tubb played himself in the familiar role of introducing Loretta Lynn, portrayed by Sissy Spacek in the film adaption of Loretta's autobiography, *Coal Miner's Daughter.* It was the easiest of his movie roles; he had aged, but his attire and style were much the same as they had been twenty years before. Performing on the Ryman stage or in the lower Broad Ernest Tubb Record Shop was old hat to him. His bandsmen, though—Mitchell, Owsley, Heap, and the rest—had to shed their long hair to get an authentic early-1960s Texas Troubadour look. "I haven't seen the boys' ears for years," he quipped to reporter Laura Eipper.[12]

An embarrassing incident several weeks before with the lead actress might well have jeopardized Tubb's involvement. Sissy Spacek, an Opry guest the night of January 27, 1979, later joined her hostess Loretta Lynn on the *Midnite Jamboree,* then held on Demonbreun Street near the Hall of Fame. As part of the on-air banter, Tubb poked fun at his fellow Texan's ethnicity. "What kind of a name is Spacek, hon?" No answer from the smiling actress. "I know what it is: it's a Polack name, isn't it?"[13]

Tubb got a further publicity boost of sorts from Hollywood in 1980 when Steven Spielberg released one of the all-time box office winners, *E.T. (The Extra Terrestrial).* To veteran country music fans, "E.T." would always and only stand for "Ernest Tubb." Country complaints about the cute little usurper of those famous initials were predictable and took the form of at least one song—David Houston's "E.T. Still Means Ernest Tubb to Me"—and a book often quoted in my early chapters, Norma Barthel's privately published, affectionate biography of Tubb's early life, *Ernest Tubb: The Original E.T.*

More frequently than ever Tubb appeared on national telecasts as his career wound down. In 1976, seven years into the show's long run, he made his first guest appearance on *Hee Haw,* and in June of 1981 taped a second and final appearance. There were half-hour concerts for *Austin City Limits,* broadcast in 1978 and 1982. Canada's long-running country music showcase, *The Tommy Hunter Show,* taped Tubb and his boys November 19, 1981.

Also, fellow Opry stars were eager to have Tubb on their syndicated shows. He was featured guest on the *Marty Robbins Spotlight,* and was interviewed twice by Bill Anderson on his syndicated *Backstage at the Grand Ole Opry* (in the fall of 1980 and again in May 1982).[14] In March 1982 he spent two days in St. Paul, Minnesota, with Garrison Keillor on his NPR show, *Prairie Home Companion.*

Increasingly, the lifetime or career awards came his way. Besides election to the Country Music Hall of Fame as the sixth member in 1965 and the Nashville Songwriters Hall of Fame in 1970 in their first batch of twenty-one members, Tubb took home International Fan Club Organization's Second Annual Tex Ritter Award in 1975. He won the *Music City News* Founder Award in 1978, which happened to be the first year of its national telecast. And in 1981 the Academy of Country Music in Hollywood gave him their Pioneer Award, ACM's equivalent to the Country Music Hall of Fame.

Summing up his career for all the nation to see was a two-hour syndicated TV tribute taped March 10, 1982, and aired on different dates in different markets that fall. The Dick Clark Production *Ernest Tubb: An American Original* used some old film and TV clips, and spoken reminiscences and tribute songs from current friends and peers.

The program's opening and closing stood out. For the beginning, the camera followed a show-goer to Nashville's TPAC Theater in Billy Byrd's Yellow Cab, as Billy gave a brief running commentary on the Tubb career before finally revealing just who he was and how he knew so much about Ernest Tubb. The finale brought the Texas Troubadour on stage to a standing ovation. In labored breath he uttered his thanks to all concerned, then sang a poignant version of "Waltz across Texas" (by then his most requested song, remember), backed by his current band (something Tubb *always* insisted upon for TV appearances), plus son Justin and former Troubadours Jack Greene and Cal Smith.

PRESTIGIOUS VENUES

On the road, where Tubb and his boys spent the lion's share of their time toward the end, gigs included several of the more prestigious, high-profile venues on their Atlas Artists Bureau itinerary, along with the many fire halls, dance clubs, and auditoriums in all fifty states. On Sunday night, June 4, 1978, they played the Smithsonian Institution, one of a handful of artists to do so in the Smithsonian's American Country Music series. The concert handlers wanted rehearsals and sound checks; they wanted Tubb to come out at 8:00 sharp, without a band warm-up; and they asked that he talk about each song performed by way of a career overview. Reluctantly, Lynn Owsley recalls, Tubb granted the last two but refused rehearsals and sound checks. Future Opry announcer Eddie Stubbs, fifteen years old at the time, was among the select few hundred in attendance and recalls being powerfully moved by the whole night, but particularly by Tubb's story and performance of "Our Baby's Book." Eddie had just lost a younger brother to cancer.

Less prestigious perhaps than the Smithsonian Institution but considerably more visible and better attended were concerts at the Lone Star Cafe in New York City and Willie Nelson's annual Fourth of July picnics near Austin. Tubb played each several times.[15] Once he was recorded for radio transcription by *Live at the Lone Star Cafe,* and another time in New York City (at the Mudd Club) he and his band had the "privilege" of meeting the group Molly Hatchet. Lynn Owsley, when told that Molly Hatchet was backstage, said, "Well, bring her on out."[16] Front man and bass player Ronnie Dale recalls, "We were just in awe. It was a hard rock, hard metal band that opened for us. And we walked in with our outfits and our cowboy hats and we play 'Waltz across Texas' and 'Thanks a Lot' and these kids go completely crazy. I thought we were in the wrong place! These guys walked in with the spikes and all different colored hair, but they loved him, they simply loved him."[17]

Willie Nelson acknowledged his debt to Tubb by booking him for the big picnics; for the huge throngs Tubb came as nothing less than a conquering hero. Bus driver Hoot Borden's firsthand account of their first (1979) performance for Nelson is classic.

> Well, friends, we played our first Willie Nelson 4th of July Picnic this year, and it was something! 90% of you wouldn't believe it if I wrote it and the other 10% was there. 30,000 goat ropers and hippies all together! 200 bathrooms, 4 semi-trailers loaded with beer, 50 medical teams, 5 helicopters, 300 armed guards, 5 field kitchens set up, 150 stage personnel, and the P.A. set alone was bigger than a basketball court. The reception and news conference, on July 3rd, outdid everything I've ever seen . . . E.T. was easily the Star of the show. All 30,000 stood the entire time he was on . . . The crowd had waited 12 hours to see Willie and E.T. and they let them know it, too.[18]

No wonder Cachet Records chose to pull the Tubb-Nelson duet of "Waltz across Texas" as a single from their album that year, or that Tubb was invited back to Austin in 1980.

Tubb had played the famous Gilley's Club in Pasadena, Texas, for years, even before it became Gilley's in 1971. It was still Shelly's Club when Jack Greene worked his final night as a Texas Troubadour there in May 1967. When Gilley's became the center of the *Urban Cowboy* craze, Tubb's appearances there became events: no one was better received. Three days after the 1979 Nelson picnic, on July 7, 1979, Tubb and the Texas Troubadours set an attendance record at Gilley's with six thousand paying fans. They would come back three to four times each of the next three years, and always to great response.

TALES OF A ROAD WARRIOR

With so much time spent on tour, Tubb and his bandsmen had a road lifestyle which, wearisome though it could be, included certain pleasures and diversions beyond that of entertaining. Many and colorful are the tales of the road, fondly recollected by former Texas Troubadours.

Tubb was foremost a man of business, strictly seeing to his accounts and making sure that everyone was properly paid. No Troubadour, early or late, ever questioned Tubb's honesty as a boss. "See, Ernest never mailed money home . . . he kept it all [with him]," Jack Greene recalled. "When he had to do business, he'd be back just behind me . . . He had a briefcase over there, and he had all of his paperwork, and he would keep track of everything, every day that everybody played, how much he owed everybody, how much money he took in, how much the agency got . . . And on these long tours he'd put this money in an envelope: he'd put Haze Jones's money, my money, Cal's money, in envelopes, and put it in his briefcase. There ain't no telling how much money he had in that briefcase . . . checks wasn't popular at that time. Everybody used cash."[19]

Besides the money in the briefcase, in envelopes or not, were the ledger books to keep track of sums: money in, money out, and money on loan. "Advances" or loans to band members, paid back through salary deductions, were common—sometimes for their personal needs like homes and cars, but more commonly to keep the card games going. Lynn Owsley remembers both, and says that Tubb was like a father in knowing when to lend, for what, and to whom. For gambling, loans were always easy to come by: Tubb himself wanted the games to continue at all costs.[20]

As much as he loved the gambling, Tubb seldom (if ever) made any money at his boys' expense; if he knew he'd cleaned them out, he would lend money to keep the games going until they had won back their losses.[21] But except for the fans, those cards came first. Ronnie Dale remembers how games were suspended, the cards carefully guarded on the table, while everyone worked a show.[22]

Tubb loved all games of chance—cards, darts, dice—but he also loved to eat. Though he never gained much weight, favorite foods he ate with passion: good Mexican food in the Southwest, steak and red beans whenever he could get them, and can after can of Wolf Brand Chili, warmed on his bus stove. Owsley remembers that his boss iced cans of fruit cocktail and packages of cookies in a certain spot in the big ice chest.[23] These, in addition to the candy bars and gum, bespeak Tubb's considerable sweet tooth, post-alcohol and post-tobacco.

There were other diversions to lighten the load of the long road trips. The favorite outdoor recreation continued to be golf; indoors, besides the games, Ernest Tubb loved movies. Toward the end, he could view videotapes on the bus's television set. In a letter to fan, friend, and collector Bill French, Tubb ordered videotapes of eight films, indicative (one supposes) of his motion picture tastes: *Albuquerque, Key Largo, To Have and Have Not, The Maltese Falcon, Butch Cassidy, The Sting, Every Which Way but Loose,* and *Electric Horseman.*[24]

Before the days of video, though, he and the band were lucky to see favorite films on the road. Owsley remembers that one kindly theater owner in Nebraska opened his business for an unscheduled afternoon showing of John Wayne's *The Cowboys,* only too happy to accommodate Ernest Tubb and the Texas Troubadours. One film Tubb didn't like was the original *M*A*S*H.* "He walked out about halfway through that one; he thought they were making fun of our servicemen. And he never would say anything good about that [TV] show! He thought it was a Commie,"[25] Buddy Charleton remembers.

For TV viewing, limited for the most part to daylight traveling hours, soap operas were Ernest Tubb's must-see programs—particularly *General Hospital* and *One Life to Live* (parodied by bandsman Junior Pruneda as *General Horseplay* and *One Wife to Give*). If motel check-out times came during one of these shows, Tubb on occasion rented rooms for an extra day to use just long enough to watch. If they were already en route, the bus TV usually sufficed, though with it there were the distractions of card games and/or poor reception. "I've seen him tell the driver to back up or turn around if the reception was getting bad," Owsley remembers. "Those Friday afternoon 'cliffhangers' were especially important. He'd go out of his way to see those. And sometimes if he just had to miss them, we'd get him a *TV Guide* or something like that to catch up on the plots."[26]

In addition to viewing Walter Cronkite on the TV evening news, Tubb kept abreast of current events with local newspapers. If the band had traveled all night and Tubb had slept on his bunk, somebody had to wake him up in the morning with coffee, juice, and a morning newspaper: no easy task, since Tubb was a heavy sleeper.[27]

But Tubb was interested in more than current events. Late nights in his bunk, when the games were over, he read books voraciously. "Ernest would go back there and he'd read all night long," Buddy Charleton remembers. "Just novels, mostly. You couldn't really pinpoint one."[28] As far back as he can recall, son Justin remembers his dad's avid reading. "He read all kinds . . . he liked

Westerns. . . ."[29] Tubb said of his reading once, "I'm still doing it. We have all these long trips, and it makes the time pass better. I might recommend the one I'm reading now, *I'm Not Much, but Baby I'm All I've Got . . .* I haven't finished it yet, but it's good."[30] His most complete statement on his reading came in a 1977 interview: "I've half-way tried to educate myself. I had no formal education, I didn't have a chance, I had to pick cotton and work on the farm . . . So I read the best of the best-sellers, anything that's a little off the beaten path . . . I guess half that bus is full of books, in my little room back there. And I've even got some of the Troubadours reading now; they'll borrow some of mine. If we've got a long trip, like to the West Coast, I take a couple of good books. I read till I get sleepy."[31]

Thus did Ernest Tubb spend the bulk of his last days, cruising the interstates in "the Green Hornet" [nickname for a series of several bright green tour buses], eating, sleeping, reading, gaming, TV-watching—when he wasn't standing on some far-flung stage (prestigious or otherwise) or giving his views to journalists. With fans and writers, he was always the picture of civility, whether giving autographs, interviews, or photo ops. And he expected his bandsmen, around the fans, to behave likewise, enforcing strict rules that carried penalties for violation. Ronnie Dale recalls, "You didn't kiss nobody. I kissed my sister . . . by the bus, by the door, and that was forbidden. I heard him lean over and say, 'That's one,' meaning $100. It didn't dawn on me what he was doing . . . and I gave her a kiss and got up in the wheel-well of the bus . . . and he said, 'That's two. Good thing you didn't get to three because you'd have been gone.' . . . You just didn't do anything like that around the bus, cause these other people didn't know that she was my sister. You kept up the respect and the face of the Texas Troubadours."[32]

Courtesy, respect to the fans, and promptitude—all were enforced by fines. Buddy Charleton remembers the promptness rule. "If you didn't show up at a certain time he'd give you to show up, you had to pay a dollar for every minute you was later getting back to the bus. And then after the period of a month would go by . . . the ones who had the less credit, points, would get the money."[33] To which Jack Greene adds, "You know who paid the biggest fine of anybody? Ernest Tubb! Ernest was an hour late. You remember when the time changed [Daylight Savings Time] we was in a hotel in Fort Worth, and he come out on the bus, and everybody had this grin on their face, and he wondered, 'Oh oh; what happened now?' . . . He was about an hour and two minutes late. Dollar a minute, Ernest!"[34]

On their own time, bandsmen could do anything they liked, provided it didn't interfere with promptness and work performance. Tubb too would let his hair down as we have seen, even after his drinking days, indulging not only in the card games and practical jokes, but in coarse language that poured forth without malice, almost as second nature. Fans never saw or heard that side of their beloved E.T., but occasionally a worshipful young guest musician would be treated to it, set up for the fall usually by the Texas Troubadours for their amusement. "We set up 'Little Lulu,' Allen LeLeu, a Cajun-born guitarist, by putting him in E.T.'s bus seat, telling him it was all right, to make himself at home. Allen idolized E.T.—he'd never seen this side of him. Sure enough, the bus pulled out, away from those fans, Ernest came up there, no hat on, wearing glasses, and he leaned over and said, 'Now get out of my seat, you little wormy bastard.' "[35]

The tough side of this life was its never-endingness: the tours seemed to stretch on forever. When one ended, another began. Ernest Tubb's schedule wore out many a younger musician; family men could seldom endure it for long. But this grinding life that Tubb lived for so long became a part of his appeal. He was a rock, a given, a permanent part, it seemed, of the country music landscape. Whatever or whoever else came and went, Ernest Tubb would go right on, playing and singing to his old fans and making new ones. "I've worn out a lot of them, and I'll wear out these guys too," Tubb said of one of his later, long-haired aggregations of Texas Troubadours. New artist Junior Brown spoke of this assumption, shared by Tubb and his fans, when we talked about Ernest Tubb: "I wish he'd lived forever. I kinda thought he would, you know, he just died on me . . . I thought the old man would live forever, I really did. When he was gone, there was just a big chunk that went right out of country music."[36]

The end of the long road was just ahead.

30

The Curtain Falls

During 1982 it became apparent, through the notices in a normally adoring press and even more clearly to those attending his shows, that Ernest Tubb's singing was labored and raspy. A concert review that fall says, "He was just released from the hospital last week where he was treated for everything from pneumonia to exhaustion . . . No interviews this trip. He was saving his voice for his first performance since he left the hospital."[1]

Normal breathing was tough enough, evidenced by his weak speaking voice, but singing gradually became almost impossible for Tubb, as his volume and sustainability all but vanished. "In Sunday afternoon's show, pleading a summer cold, he sounded worse than ever. He made frogs sound like Elvis Presley. It was awful . . . Folks still enjoyed hearing classics like 'Walking the Floor over You' and the Jimmie Rodgers song 'In the Jailhouse Now,' but you could tell they were barely tolerating that voice."[2] Even short shows tired him out and sent him back to the bus and the oxygen tank. The emphysema Tubb had battled since the mid-1960s finally had the upper hand, and his days were numbered.

The end came that fall, with a whimper and not a bang. Cancellations, rare even in his heavy drinking days, became the rule rather than the exception after the summer. He made his last Grand Ole Opry and *Midnite Jamboree* appearances on August 14. On August 29 he played a big Ernest Tubb Day show in Memphis, Texas (in West Texas, between Fort Worth and Lubbock). Many members of his family were there: brother C. R. Tubb Jr. and his son Talmadge Tubb came, all the way from Arizona; faithful niece Anna Ruth Collier Husky came from Lubbock. It was the last time they ever saw him perform. And he was well below par: an affectionate Amarillo newspaper account said, "The performances were not necessarily easy for the singer and a number of his fans. Tubb had suffered several days from laryngitis and was forced to limit his appearance. He remained inside his air-conditioned bus as long as possible as a means of preserving his voice."[3]

Rather than cancel many of the fall shows already booked, Haze Jones prevailed upon Justin Tubb, Cal Smith, and Jack Greene to substitute when they could, which kept the Texas Troubadours working and kept the 15 percent commissions rolling in. And too, Tubb himself hoped for several months—hardly stopped hoping—that he'd feel well enough to hit the road again. After a hospital stay and several weeks at home, Tubb decided he'd try a weekend tour around Veterans Day—November 11–13, 1982—which took him into three different Midwestern states: Holt, Missouri, on the 11th; Carlyle, Illinois, on the 12th; and Berlin, Ohio, on the 13th. Son Justin Tubb worked the first two shows with him but had a previous engagement on the last night. The show in Berlin's Highland High School proved the last of the more than four thousand personal appearances that Ernest Tubb made.

"When he got sick, and he asked me to use the Troubadours, I did that for one reason," Justin says today. "It gave him something to hope for. Long as that band was hanging in there together, and I was working the Opry (and I used them on the Opry from '82 on until he died in '84 . . .) he could more or less tell himself, 'Well, I'm gonna get better here, and I'm gonna get back up and get on the road.' "[4]

The Ernest Tubb Fan Club kept up an optimistic tone for many months thereafter, hoping against hope that the Texas Troubadour would sing again. From the winter 1983 *Ernest Tubb Fan Club*: "After the first of the year, Ernest hopes to resume touring on a limited basis but it is very doubtful he will be able to make those long tours as in the past. We have been begging him to slow down for years and hope that he will do so, now."[5] Fan club president Norma Barthel checked out published reports that he had returned to a light touring schedule early the next year and found them to be false: "I talked with Ernest again on March 6th and he hadn't been able to start back to work yet and said it would be May or June before he can, due to him having been on the oxygen machine for so long, etc."[6] Even with 1983's summer weather, Tubb felt no better: "I talked with Ernest again recently, and he said he is still about the same . . . no better actually, but no worse."[7]

Ernest Tubb's final months, in a retirement forced upon him by illness, were not altogether unhappy ones. Justin says, "He didn't suffer so much with pain. They had medications to take care of that. He suffered from being cooped up, tied down, not able to get up and go and do the things he loved to do, but he had a ton of exercises to keep his lungs flexible, anything to make him breathe."[8]

For a time he still saw visitors—former bandsmen and fellow artists—and off the road he drew closer than ever to family. Justin's family lived only about three blocks away from his dad's little home in Antioch, and Olene's children were also frequent visitors. Justin told *Country Music* magazine of his father's continued interest in musical goings-on, lasting almost to the end.

> He kept up with things at first and then the last six or eight months, he quit listening to the Opry. I think the last thing he quit listening to was the Midnite Jamboree. He told me that he started goin' to bed a little earlier. But he actually got to the point that if he couldn't be a part of it, he didn't want to hear it. He did watch his old television show, which I introduce, on the Nashville Network . . . He was very strongly unhappy with the way things were goin' in Nashville. But he loved Ricky Skaggs and George Strait, Gene Watson, Moe Bandy . . . Merle Haggard was his favorite. I think he felt better about things after Ricky hit.[9]

Loretta Lynn encouraged him to the last, and was unsparing in her help. "I told him when he got well that we was gonna go do some more shows together, get on my bus, and I said, 'I'll give you my room. You can stay in my room.' He said, 'No, I ain't gonna take your room.' But he was really ready, right up until Ernest passed away, he was ready."[10]

Tubb gradually lost the taste for visitors as his condition worsened. Talking came to take too much out of him, and his pride was such that he didn't want old friends to see him in such bad shape. "There were false rumors that a lot of the artists he had helped never came around to see him," Justin added. "I'd tell Daddy that so-and-so wanted to come out and see him, and he said, 'Thank 'em for me,' but, he said, 'I really would rather not have any company.' "[11] Junior Pruneda felt honored that on one of his trips to Nashville, he got word that "the old man" wanted to see him. But as months passed and Tubb's health worsened, even visits from old Opry friends like Roy Acuff and Hank Snow were discouraged. "I wish I hadn't a went," Snow says of a visit he made with Roy Acuff, Haze Jones, and one other singer whose name he couldn't recall. "Ernest looked awfully, awfully bad. And he was sitting there with this thing to breathe strapped on his back . . . And [he] talked a few words, and then breathed. I wish I hadn't gone out there. And he was there all by himself."[12]

It was certainly not the case that Ernest Tubb was forgotten by the country music world in his retirement. On national TV, Willie Nelson in a moment of triumph remembered Ernest: accepting the 1983 CMA Entertainer of the Year Award, Nelson added a simple "Get well, Ernest." Tributes in print and on records flowed in from all quarters. Long-time fan club president Norma Barthel published her loving and useful look at his early career, *Ernest Tubb: The Original E.T.,* first as a fan club project and then (at Tubb's behest) she offered it to a wider public. Several interesting records appeared: David Houston took Barthel's angle with his "E.T. Still Means Ernest Tubb to Me"; Tommy Collins cut "Ernest Tubb 78s," a song whose lyrics made clear that these were the narrator's most prized possessions; Donnie Rohrs sang "E.T.: A Tribute to Ernest Tubb" on Leap Frog Records; and Jerry Hanlon, one of so many younger artists that Tubb had done his best to help, cut "E.T. We're Missing You."

"COUNTRY MUSIC PIONEER UPDATE" EMBARRASSMENT

Justin Tubb's reference to "false rumors" about artists not going to visit his ailing father stems almost certainly from a major embarrassment that darkened Ernest Tubb's dying days, a final difference between him and his estranged wife Olene.

The publication responsible was a short-lived venture using Clyde Moody's name and prestige to (among other things) build interest for a planned alternative to the Country Music Hall of Fame and its library: a Country Music Pioneer Association. Laudable as the attempt may have been—and as genuine as its concerns over country music's direction were—it didn't have the chance of the proverbial snowball in hell, given its well-established predecessor and the slashing, cutting style of its own printed invective. Here's a sample from the premier issue (April 1984) of the *Country Music Pioneer Update:* "Nashville is a great town for rumors. Rumors are dangerous but sometimes true." In the *Update*'s short life it would print plenty of them, with about as much regard for truth and objectivity as this premier editorial showed for reader reaction: "Each month the Editor will voice his views on the Condition of Country Music. Some readers will like it— some will not. But frankly we don't give a damn one way or the other!"[13]

In a signed "Letter from the President" on pages 1 and 2 of the third *Country Music Pioneer Update,* Clyde Moody opined that the industry was "recklessly ignoring a pillar from its very foundation," meaning the ailing Ernest Tubb. "He is now confined to his home, supported by oxygen 24 hours a day and in need of around-the-clock care. He is without funds or income. He is in debt beyond recovery. The IRS has a lien on his heavily mortgaged house, which is in a state of deterioration and sitting in the middle of an overgrown, weed-ridden yard. He can not help himself."

In the key passage, Moody said that the time for help was now, while Tubb lived. "The debtors will be identified after E.T. is gone. They will come forward in ranks, claiming friendship, telling stories of who worked with who and when; the road stories will abound. They will have great plans for benefits, memorials, Halls of Fame and honors galore. E.T. will go down in Country Music History as the greatest of all. We'll even have an E.T. day. Everyone at the Opry will bow their heads in a moment of silence." Rather than name Tubb's debtors (which he was sorely tempted to do), Moody placed the blame on the entire industry, "a selfish, self-centered bunch of hypocrites that apparently don't care about anything, but filling their beds, egos and pocketbooks," and he prescribed a cure. "First of all, the entire Country Music industry must clear this man's slate; allow him to maintain his image and dignity; make it possible for him to go out with his head as high as he always held it. If we fail to do this, we will create a blight on Country Music that can never be erased . . . If we forsake Ernest Tubb, we might as well close up shop."

Mr. Moody's source of information for Tubb's woes (made explicit in the next issue) may be gleaned from certain telling phrases in this passage.

> We are no longer talking about a man who has deteriorated to 100 pounds, who is broke and can hardly buy food or medicine; who is overwhelmed with debt; who is lonely and abandoned; who has finally been sapped of the last ounce by the vultures; who has no more to give, therefore has lost his appeal; who without the love and care of his wife, Olene, who attends him day and night, makes the excuses and fends off the "pickers," would have no way of existing; who is probably lying there in total confusion, wondering what happened and why it all went wrong. We are talking about Ernest Tubb. The single most influential name in Country Music.[14]

The dying Tubb was outraged and deeply hurt by this publicity. In another "Letter from the President" in the next issue (July-August 1984), Moody names his sources, and chronicled the reaction.

> The article and the facts were given to CMPA by Mrs. Ernest Tubb and confirmed by Ernest's daughter and several other people seemingly close to the matter . . . The response, very frankly, was minimal, which caused great concern by CMPA. However, we did get a strong reaction from Mr. Haze Jones, Ernest Tubb's booker, from Justin Tubb (E.T.'s son and a CMPA member), and from Hank Snow. These three gentlemen requested a meeting with the staff of Update. All three contradicted Mrs. Tubb and others. They stated that Ernest is sick but not life threatening [or so they said]. That he is not destitute nor without money to buy food and medicine. That E.T. does have outstanding bills but also owns property and can handle his own affairs. They also stated that the articles injured E.T.'s pride and did irreparable damage to his spirit . . . Upon contacting Mrs. Tubb again, she says she stands by her original statements . . . Update did receive a phone call from Ernest Tubb. He did not deny or confirm the Update stories, but he did say that Haze Jones could speak for him.[15]

Faced by these contradictions, Moody concludes that "there is more to the situation than Update or the public should be involved in. It is obviously a family and personal matter." Requesting that "anyone who decided to help E.T. please not do anything at this time," Moody closed his letter with the odd justification that he might be right next time: "Update will be more diligent in the future for the facts, but it will not hesitate to come forward. Next time it may be accurate and if we hesitate somebody may die of neglect."[16]

The very next issue reported Tubb's death, in a "Letter from the President" addressed to Ernest Tubb at the "Golden Jamboree in the Sky," and smugly informed the departed star of the many who waited until he was gone to discover what a great star he was.[17] While faulting those who were "touching the hem" and using Tubb's death to advance their own purposes, the *Update* on its third page, in an article entitled "Now Is the Time To Rally," clearly did that very thing: "When all of the Ernest Tubb's are gone, and they are passing rapidly, then the music we love so dearly will be gone . . . If we do not support CMPA and organizations like it, there will be no voice . . . We need a rallying point, a symbol to guide us . . . What better symbol than Ernest Tubb? His passing does not have to be a tragedy . . . Let us take this opportunity to join together to support CMPA . . . IF YOU LOVE COUNTRY MUSIC, YOU SHOULD BE A MEMBER OF THE COUNTRY MUSIC PIONEER ASSOCIATION."[18]

Despite using Ernest Tubb's death for fundraising purposes, the CMPA died an early death, folding after publication of its November-December 1985 issue.

THE FINAL CURTAIN

Dr. George Duncan admitted Ernest Tubb to Nashville's Baptist Hospital for three long stays in 1984—January 3–11; July 23–August 2, and then for the last time on August 10. "When he went in for the last time, we didn't know it, but I think we all felt it," Justin recalled.[19] Olene, watching for the vultures, was in his room much of the time, and, as his condition permitted, she allowed some celebrity visitors. Porter Wagoner tried to cheer Tubb with talk of a return to the golf course; Tubb's reply, as Wagoner remembers it, was "Pro, I don't believe I'm gonna make it this time. I really don't think so. I'm just so weak."[20] Cal Smith remembers from his last visit, "Ernest reached over and got me by the hand, and squeezed my hand, and said, 'Don't worry. I'll be all right.' "[21] Smith's friend and Texas Troubadour contemporary, Jack Greene, felt an urge to go see Tubb just before the end.

> After he got in the hospital, it was so hard for him to talk. He couldn't even talk on the phone, it was such a strain for him to get anything out. But I woke up one morning, and the Spirit said, "Go see Ernest." So I

called Olene and she was there, and she said, "Yeah, come on up." So I went up there in the afternoon. He was just laying there, he had just dried up to nothing, skin and bones, I really didn't recognize him. He looked another person, he really did—his hair was all messed up . . . I didn't talk much, just more or less let him know that I was thinking about him . . . He got up and used the bathroom while I was there, and came back. And I mean just walking ten steps to the bathroom and back was just like he'd been running fifty miles. Just wore him out. His skin looked so bad, and he wasn't getting any oxygen at all, you know; they had him on the tube and everything else. So the next morning he got up to go to the bathroom and sat back down on the bed, and just bent over [dead]—the next morning after I went to see him. Something just told me to go see him.[22]

Something told several other people to be there the next day, September 6, 1984, when Ernest Tubb died at about 11:00 A.M. that Thursday morning. The *Nashville Banner* account that afternoon quoted eyewitness Porter Wagoner: "He was unconscious. He just quit breathing. He took a breath and that was all." Jack Greene and Jeannie Seely were "outside the door," the *Banner* said, with wife Olene, "their sons and a granddaughter" in the room.[23] With more time to prepare, the *Tennessean*'s account from the next morning, written by Bob Oermann, quoted hospital spokesman Gil Cawood as saying, "He had been conscious up until almost the very end. There were several members of his family with him when he died." From manager/agent Haze Jones, present "at the bedside," Oermann listed son Justin, daughter Elaine, brother C. R., "several grandchildren, and nephew Glen Douglas [*sic*]." Among the stars at the hospital at the time of death were Mel Tillis, Cal Smith, Porter Wagoner, Jack Greene, and Jeannie Seely.[24] Douglas Glenn Tubb remembers Dr. Duncan's final pronouncement: "The world's just lost a great man."[25]

For three days Tubb's body lay in state at the Madison Funeral Home—across the street from the Kitty Wells and Johnny Wright Museum—where hundreds of mourners filed by. The Opry that weekend noted their fallen star. "We are sure there will be no other like him," Opry manager Hal Durham noted. "Tonight we're going to do as E.T. would have wanted us to do—go ahead with the Opry."[26]

At 2 P.M. on Monday, September 10, about fifteen hundred mourners gathered for the funeral at Two Rivers Baptist Church, just across Briley Parkway from the Opry House. As expected, it was a star-studded farewell. The pallbearers alone included Bill Monroe (who sang a haunting, a capella "Swing Low, Sweet Chariot" in the service), Cal Smith, Carl Smith, Hank Williams Jr., Teddy

Wilburn, Carl Butler, Jack Greene, Billy Parker, Junior Pruneda, Porter Wagoner, and brother C. R. Tubb Jr. In attendance besides were Roy Acuff, B. J. Thomas (who gave a spoken tribute and sang "Tomorrow Never Comes"), Little Jimmy Dickens, Kitty Wells, Billy Walker, Hank Snow, George Hamilton IV, Jim Ed Brown, Connie Smith, Lorrie Morgan, Charlie Walker, Jeannie Seely, and others. Tubb lay in an open casket, with one of his white cowboy hats resting at one end, thus displaying the unusual sight of his hatless head, his hair grayer than anyone could remember. Floral arrangements surrounded the fallen singer, and the church's sound system reverberated with a medley of appropriate Tubb recordings chosen for the occasion: "If We Never Meet Again," "Beyond the Sunset," "I Love You Because," "I Will Miss You When You Go," "Stand by Me."

A RESTING PLACE

When it was all over and the Reverend Billy Moore had said his piece, Tubb was laid to rest in Hermitage Memorial Gardens, and a new controversy was born that brews to this day. No one expected a gravesite marker to be erected right away, but the fact that to this writing nothing marks the spot of Ernest Tubb's final resting place remains a festering sore to his millions of fans. If you want to see the gravesite, ask the staff at the Hermitage Memorial Gardens; they might show you, or they might not, but they know where it is. George Newsom was kind enough to show me (see my photo in this volume). Faithful friends, fans, and the Grand Ole Opry Trust Fund have done all they can to try to place a marker there, but the widow has blocked it every time.

Justin wrote to the Ernest Tubb Fan Club on July 1, 1986, "Well, no one is more embarrassed and ashamed about this than I am. But the truth is this. Although they [Ernest and Olene] had been legally separated, and not living together, for over nine years, according to the laws of the state of Tennessee, his wife was his legal heir. And apparently she and only she can put a marker down, and so far she has not done so. I even went so far as to work out a plan to acquire a marker, and the offer was turned down by her, I am told. So please don't blame me. I've done everything I can."[28] To a later fan club question, "Why don't Mrs. E.T. put a marker on his grave?" Justin's reply was, "I wish I had an answer. Maybe she does. Write her at 5402 Wakefield Drive, Nashville, TN., 37220."[29]

A TANGLED ESTATE

Ernest Tubb's estate is still not closed as of this writing, having dragged through probate court for more than a decade. The primary fight has concerned which, if any, existing will has validity. Olene, named by the court as estate executrix on

November 13, 1984, brought forward a will dated July 22, 1983, witnessed only by her brother, Robert G. N. Adams (by then conveniently dead), which praised Olene in glowing terms. What newspaper accounts described as "three crudely typed pages on blue 'Texas Troubadour' stationery" contained the following: "I have let her down many times, but she has never let me down. She has always been there when I needed her." The document left Olene 70 percent ownership of the three Ernest Tubb Record Shops and 61 percent of two music publishing companies. Probate Judge Jim Everett threw it out in short order: state law required that a will be witnessed by at least two persons.

Not only was this will disallowed, but Olene was removed as executrix after only two weeks in that post when Justin came forward with his copy of a September 26, 1979, will, "the original having been lost, destroyed, or suppressed by persons unknown."[30] In this will, which named Haze Jones, Commerce Union Bank of Nashville, and Calvin Grant Shofner (Cal Smith) as trustees, Olene was to have received all household effects and a third of the estate in one trust, while Tubb's seven living children were to have divided the remaining two-thirds in equal shares. Separate from the estate, according to this will, was stock in music companies (100 shares to Anita Rodgers Court, 510 shares to Justin, and 390 shares divided equally among the other six children) and ownership of the Ernest Tubb Record Shops.

The will dispute was far from settled when other wranglings came to the fore. Mrs. Olene Tubb and two of her children, Karen Delene and Larry Dean, in February 1985 sued her daughter Olene Gayle Tubb Key Guidry and her husband Patrick Guidry to prevent their sale of the last house Ernest Tubb had lived in— the little house at 105 Cedarcroft Court in Antioch, purchased in Gayle's name. Tubb bought the house in 1975 and put it in her name "in an obvious effort to hide the fact that he was the purchaser," the suit alleged, claiming he put $21,441 into the purchase and lived there until he could no longer care for himself. The suit requested that title to the house be transferred from the Guidrys to the Ernest Tubb estate.

Meanwhile the claims against the Tubb estate had mounted. The IRS alone had a claim of $236,033.37. There were doctor bills, hospital bills, some $16,250 for funeral expenses (including $5,250 Olene used to purchase gravesites, her control of which has caused so much controversy), and $30,000 for Olene's annual support. Persons to whom Tubb had loaned money vanished, but the ones who'd loaned it to him came out with a vengeance after he died, claiming it against the estate. Among others, there was over $60,000 in unrepaid loans and open accounts which the Record Shops or the Texas Troubadour Western Store had advanced either to Ernest or to family members.[31] Together, these claims swelled the total claims against the estate to $334,188.00.

At first no one knew the asset size of the estate against which these claims were made. Olene Tubb had estimated a ludicrously low $50,000 figure while she was the executrix, which was soon laughed out of court. But just how big was it? Exactly which properties or monies belonged to the estate and which did not— the Record Shops? the music companies and their song royalties? the Antioch house? Each became the subject of separate court fights.

Disposal of the Ernest Tubb Record Shops was of course a major concern for all parties involved. A yearend 1984 balance sheet submitted to the probate court listed assets, fixed and current, for the three Nashville shops at $126,306.77, and Justin Tubb estimated a 1982 gross sales figure in excess of a million dollars. By July 31, 1987, total assets had grown to $211,716.43. Was it a part of the estate, or was it not? Gary David McCormick and Justin Tubb jointly alleged that it was not, citing the 1976 incorporation and partnership agreement. Since Charles Mosley predeceased Ernest Tubb, Tubb owned 70 percent of the corporation at the time of his death. McCormick owned 20 percent and Justin Tubb owned 10 percent; no one questioned their shares being outside the Ernest Tubb estate. But what of the 70 percent? McCormick and Justin Tubb filed suit, claiming the agreement gave them right of first refusal to purchase that stock from the estate upon Ernest Tubb's death. Book value of the stock was contested along with everything else.

By this time, the tangled estate was in the hands of a new administrator, Commerce Union Bank giving place in January 1986 to attorney Frank S. King Jr. of Nashville's King & Ballow law firm. On the estate's behalf, King sued to have the 1987 Record Shop ruling (which was in favor of McCormick and Justin Tubb) overturned. He lost, so that by the end of 1989, that question was settled: Ernest Tubb Record Shops, Inc., was totally outside the wranglings of the Ernest Tubb Estate. The former Tubb stock was all eventually purchased by McCormick. In the fall of 1993, Justin's ownership share was back down to 10 percent, and in the wake of Justin's declaration of bankruptcy, McCormick soon bought the rest. Gary David McCormick, in sum, is the only clear winner in the tangled Tubb estate fight; he came out with the prize that eluded every Tubb family member, though he bears as a consequence the enmity of those he bested in the court wranglings. Douglas Glenn Tubb in 1995 launched a rival mailorder operation, emphasizing the family name he had once eschewed as a country singer: Tubb Country Records, P.O. Box 291331, Nashville, TN., 37229-1331.

Despite everything, the Ernest Tubb Record Shops have flourished, with annual sales routinely topping the million-dollar mark. A fourth store opened in Pigeon Forge, Tennessee, in the Great Smoky Mountains, in 1988, a fifth in Branson, Missouri, in 1991, and a sixth in the Fort Worth stockyards in October 1993. A separate mailorder and corporate offices opened at 1024 17th Avenue South (on Music Row) in January 1991, and in June 1995 the expanded Music Valley Drive Ernest Tubb Record Shop #2, home of the *Midnite Jamboree,* moved into larger store quarters alongside the new Troubadour Theater.

Matters have not been so tidily settled on the other disputed points. A 1986 newspaper account titled "Tubb Estate Picked Clean by IRS, Debts" said it all: at that time it truly had been.[32] Cash on hand was less than the $334,188.00 claimed against it. But the debts were slowly paid off by the regular income that rolled in year-in and year-out. In 1985 alone, royalty income from MCA Records, BMI, and the Harry Fox Agency totaled over $48,000. Between December 20, 1989, and April 12, 1994 (the longest and latest period for which I found figures), the estate's receipts totaled $513,507.52.

FAMILY WRAP-UP

Ernest Tubb's grave in Hermitage, Tennessee, still has no marker, but in 1986 the Ernest Tubb Fan Club, which limped along a few years after Tubb's death,[33] placed an imposing $436 plaque at the Crisp (Texas) Community Center. The Community Center no longer stands (to say nothing of the actual Tubb birthplace), but the plaque is now placed in a rather isolated but visible spot by the side of the road, not far from the "Crisp" sign.

All of Ernest Tubb's siblings are dead. Jewell died in Kaufman in 1970 while he was still living; Lucille Tubb West died in March 1988, and Opal "Blondie" Collier died in April 1989. The eldest, his beloved "Bud," brother C. R. Jr., was the last to die, inheriting the largest share of their parents' longevity.[34] He died July 4, 1994, only weeks short of his eighty-eighth birthday and less than a year after his long-time wife Margie died. His large family, amply endowed with Tubb musical talent as we have seen, has also had its legal bouts and fallings-out over the hefty estate C. R. Jr. accumulated in the insurance business.

Justin Tubb still tours occasionally and marked forty years on the Grand Ole Opry in September 1995, though he plays the Opry rarely and the *Midnite Jamboree* never, in view of his differences with David McCormick. He had good response to a wonderful 1986 MCA-Dot album, which, though titled simply *Justin Tubb,* was entirely a tribute to his father. Between 1985 and the early 1990s he hosted an annual *E.T. Radiothon* with Opry guest stars in the wee hours of Sunday morning after the Opry to raise funds "F.O.R.E.T.": "For Ongoing Research & Emphysema Treatment." Divorced three times (twice from second wife Carolyn), he lives with his mother, "Blue-Eyed" Elaine, in Madison, Tennessee. He hopes to someday write a book of his experiences, but meanwhile to write song hits for his son Cary Justin Tubb, an aspiring singer.

Violet Elaine Tubb Walker Burgett Wingerter works at the 417 Broadway

Ernest Tubb Record Shop. Her son Darryn Chance Walker, after sowing considerable wild oats as a lad, had some success as a songwriter (Mel Tillis's "Lying Time Again," 1980) but never made it as a singer. Her daughter Capri Walker married into the music business, to drummer Ed Chambliss. She works in Porter Wagoner's office, as she has for years.

Of Ernest Tubb's younger children, born to Olene, the two oldest girls (Erlene and Gayle) never showed any musical ambitions. Ernest Tubb Jr., "Tinker," gave up his interest in singing when a school coaching job beckoned, even while his father was still touring. Larry Dean, a talented photographer who took loads of pictures of his dad late in life, now works as Charlie Daniels's personal bus driver. The youngest, Karen Delene, Olene's look-alike, was the only family member present when David McCormick and the Ernest Tubb Record Shop recently dedicated the revamped Green Hornet bus for exhibit at store #2 out on Music Valley Drive near the Opry House.

31

---

*A Summing Up: Legacies—Lasting
and Otherwise*

This book has covered a life history and five decades of career facts; it's time
now to step back and take a closing look at their significance. Readers may, of
course, form other and better conclusions from the story I've told. I hope they
will. These, for now, are mine.

REASONS FOR ERNEST TUBB'S POPULARITY

I approach this evaluation with trepidation. If becoming a country music star and
then remaining one for forty years were all that "easy" to figure out or to understand, I suspect there would be more people doing it and fewer books written on
the subject of how to make it in the music business. And in Ernest Tubb's case
there are particular difficulties. His fans find themselves all too often on the
defensive against critics who ask, "Why? Why do you listen to him? What do you
hear in that voice to make you like him?" Or, from a longer historical view, the
question might be, "How did Ernest Tubb hold the country audience as long as
he did?" Tubb's fans are asked to justify their admiration in a way few country
fans are.

Ernest Tubb was an individualist, a stylist, a singer whose voice was instantly recognizable. Even when he tried to sing like Jimmie Rodgers, he sounded
only like himself. Tubb and all the great country stars had that individuality.
When you heard an Ernest Tubb record on the radio or jukebox, you knew immediately that it was Ernest Tubb. Such individuality is at a premium in country
music today, far rarer than it once was. A cookie-cutter mentality in today's music business seems intent upon turning out a succession of clones, sound-alikes,
or even (in this age of video) look-alikes, trimmed down to just a few set patterns.

Most of Ernest Tubb's unique sound was his "improbable" voice, as historian and musician Doug Green called it, "frank, worldly-wise, avuncular, singing with unflinching directness—and sometimes with a wink and a grin." Green was not the first, but one of the most articulate, to notice "the peculiar trailing off of that authoritative, resonant voice at the end of each phrase."[1]

But Tubb was also linked inseparably to a distinctive instrumental sound. Best known, says Green, for "the ritualistic, mantric four-note guitar lick" of his lead guitarist, this sound made Ernest Tubb's music instantly recognizable and totally distinctive. It did for Tubb what Don Helms's high-register, three-identical-note tag on the steel guitar did for Hank Williams.

George Hamilton IV called Ernest Tubb "Mr. Sincerity" in the title of a Tubb tribute album he recorded for RCA Victor in 1965,[2] and no one could argue that Ernest Tubb's utterances, musical or otherwise, were sincere, sometimes to a fault. He said what he thought, and as songwriter and singer he dealt with things that either had happened to him or could have. This gave him a believability on stage, an artist-audience rapport, which again is characteristic of the greatest country artists.[3] Ernest Tubb had no "moves," no gyrations—in fact a certain "woodenness" was sometimes critically mentioned—and certainly no other gimmicks, unless you count the widely used Western attire. But with the aforementioned sincerity, believability, and audience rapport, his no-frills, stand-and-deliver stage style became his greatest strength as a country music performer. Justin Tubb offers an articulate explanation of Tubb's performance strengths.

> He definitely was a jukebox singer, more than a radio singer. But even more than a jukebox singer, he was a live performer. He came across better on stage than he ever did on records. He had a charisma that went right to those people sitting there in that audience. And he could communicate when nobody else could get to them, or knew how to get to them, or what to do to get to them. All he had to do was walk out there and start talking and singing, and he had them in the palm of his hand. And you can't explain it, you can't describe it, it was just there.[4]

Technically, he was not a "good" singer. Everybody knew this, Tubb best of all. "He would be the first to tell you that he wasn't," Justin remembers. "He sung flat, he sung sharp, he sung out of meter . . . He was working a show . . . and used the house band's guitar player. So he got up there and did this show . . . The guy came off stage, and said, 'Mr. Tubb, I don't know if you realized this, but on that one song . . . you got out of meter just a little bit there.' And he said, 'Oh well, I didn't realize that, son. But I'll tell you what. If I do it again, you just get right out of meter with me.' "[5]

Long-time front man, emcee, and opening act Danny Dill of Annie Lou and

Danny says much the same thing about Tubb's basic ability to communicate. "As much as I loved Ernest, he was never a singer, ever. He just wasn't a singer, mechanically. But communicate! Nobody else I ever saw, except [Hank] Williams, on stage could communicate what he was feeling as well as Ernest. And that's all it took . . . He was a better in-person singer than on records—by any stretch of the imagination . . . And they loved him, and they heard him. It didn't matter what came out of his mouth, you heard it, and you heard what he meant. And I'm afraid I can't say that about me, and I can't say that about a lot of other people."[6]

Tubb's longevity is itself a mighty achievement. How many recording artists in any field of music can boast of first and last recordings forty-six years apart? You can count them on two hands. This was made possible in part by good fortune, of course, but in large part by the fact that Ernest Tubb cultivated loyalty from his fans and received it in return. Because he was so loyal to them, going out of his way for them, they remained loyal to him. Danny Dill says, "Ernest was more aware of his people than anybody I ever knew. I mean he was more aware of his dependence on his fans. He had to have them, his fans. They understood him, and he understood them. And they were loyal. I never saw anybody as loyal as an Ernest Tubb fan."[7] The amazing fact that for forty-plus years he had the same fan club president is only one instance of that loyalty.

Cal Smith tells one of the classic stories of how far Ernest Tubb would go to accommodate a fan.

> We was in Florida one time, getting ready to play a show, and I mean it was raining cats and dogs. And there was a lady came and knocked on the bus, out in this pouring down rain, and she said she didn't have enough money to buy a ticket to the show but she said she'd like to have her picture taken with Ernest Tubb. And Ernest put on that white hat and jumped out there in the pouring down rain, and had his picture taken with this lady. And when he got back in the bus, I said, "Ain't many people woulda done that." And he said, "If she thinks enough of me to drive out here in this rain to get a picture, well the least I can do is get out and take it with her."[8]

LEGACIES: LASTING AND OTHERWISE

Such, in my view, were the qualities that made Ernest Tubb a success. But what lives on in the musical legacy of Ernest Tubb? His records we'll always have and always treasure, to be sure. But the man is dead; the on-stage communicator (by all accounts his greatest talent) is no more. How, if at all, can we say that country music to this day is different, or perchance better, because of Ernest Tubb?

Many previous journalistic evaluations of the Tubb legacy—chief among them my own, I must admit—have "majored in the minors," I now believe, when assessing Ernest Tubb's lasting impact. How important is it, for example, to say that Ernest Tubb was the first regular Grand Ole Opry star to feature the electric guitar? Even some Opry members had experimented with it before he came, and Tubb used it because of his previous success with that sound on records. If you were going to have Ernest Tubb at all, you were going to have an electric guitar. That's why his bringing it raised no sterner objections from Judge Hay and the Opry string band traditionalists. The amplified guitar was a purely technical innovation whose day was bound to come to the Opry, as it did everywhere else. Billy Byrd, Harold Bradley, Grady Martin, Hank Garland, Jabbo Arrington, and others were backstage at the Ryman jamming on the electric guitar shortly after Ernest Tubb came, and it wasn't Jimmie or Leon Short that they were listening to and learning from, wonderful as they were for the Ernest Tubb style: they listened to the greats of jazz and swing, the men who'd been the first to plug in.

Tubb's use of Western or cowboy clothes on the Opry did get a good deal of mileage from WSM's publicity machine: "Now here's that tall, good-looking Texan who learned to sing while roping and branding cattle as a boy." But Zeke Clements had used the cowboy image at WSM years before Tubb came, as had J. L. Frank's Golden West Cowboys. In the 1950s, ex-movie cowboy Tubb toned down his Western outfits considerably, keeping the hat and boots always but wearing only a checkered shirt and string tie in the warm weather months and rather conservative solid-color suits with Western trim the rest of the time. Tubb never went for the gaudy, spangled Nudie suits popularized by Hank Snow or Porter Wagoner, which became the rage in the 1960s, but are so largely out of fashion now.

And what about the 1947 performance at Carnegie Hall? Recent research brought to light the fact that Decca country artist Denver Darling was part of a show there in 1945. Even if we say that Tubb headlined the first all-country show, or the first Grand Ole Opry package to play there, the question again becomes "What of it?" Only a few country artists followed Tubb into that bastion of high culture—T. Texas Tyler, the Sons of the Pioneers, Flatt & Scruggs—and Tubb's appearance made no permanent New York City inroads for himself or for country music. Carnegie Hall is chiefly significant, it now seems to me, as a gauge of the high-water mark of Ernest Tubb's intense postwar popularity. He'd not have played there had he not been on top of the country music world then.

What, then, were the lasting legacies from Ernest Tubb? Where is his name writ large, or where are his footprints most clearly seen, in the country music world of the 1990s?

Honky-Tonk Innovator

Tubb spent his long career making a style of country music known by a single, somewhat elusive term in the general histories: "honky-tonk." Yes, a honky-tonk is a place, which often enough figures literally in the action (and even in the titles) of Ernest Tubb songs: "I Ain't Going Honky Tonkin' Anymore," "Honky Tonk Heart," "Warm Red Wine," "Drivin' Nails in My Coffin," "Two Glasses, Joe," "Don't Brush Them on Me." But a honky-tonk song is more than simply a beer-drinking song. There is clearly a shift of themes here from an older type of country song that grew out of the folk song or the Victorian parlor ballad. Stripped of all sentimental veneer and all symbolism, a honky-tonk song conveys in direct, hard-hitting, explicit language the day-to-day lives of working-class people. Tubb's hits presaged the times when country music (like today) would be more clearly known as a music of class (the working class) than a music of region (the South).

For the first time, as part and parcel of the social upheaval consequent upon World War II and its aftermath, country songs, honky-tonk songs, with Ernest Tubb one of their chief purveyors, began to deal forthrightly with divorce, with infidelity, with despair, with alcoholism, with the challenges of modern life in general. Pop songs were a long time yet in making this leap, but in country, the honky-tonk song drove all before it, and it remains to this day country's predominant type.

But honky-tonk is music as well as song, a sound at least as much as a theme or story or narrative stance. And here Ernest Tubb can best be assessed in relation to the other honky-tonk pioneers: Al Dexter, Floyd Tillman, and Ted Daffan. These three men came of age in the same basic Texas musical culture at the same time as Ernest Tubb (or slightly before), and they all wrote and performed great honky-tonk songs. Dexter was the first to use the word in a song title ("Honky Tonk Blues," 1936), and certainly his "Pistol Packin' Mama" (1942) has to qualify as one of the biggest honky-tonk hits. But for all his greatness, something in Dexter's ultra-nasal voice and his accompaniment suggested a novelty act. Entertaining as his records were, they lacked the believability of an Ernest Tubb original. They come off as humorous tales.

Tillman and Daffan, by contrast, were masters of despair in what they wrote. How much more despairing can one get than Tillman's "It Makes No Difference Now" or Daffan's "Born to Lose"? Tillman's "Slipping Around" became the great country anthem on infidelity. As a singer, Floyd Tillman was every bit as distinctive and idiosyncratic as Ernest Tubb—some have even noted similarities—but he approached his singing with more of the wild, improvisational feel of a western swing jazz musician, a quality that actually became more pronounced as he aged. He didn't want to stay on the beat, whereas poor Al Dexter probably wanted to but couldn't; he simply had no sense of meter and was always a session musician's nightmare for that reason. And Daffan? He didn't sing at all; he played the steel guitar and hired smooth, pop-influenced vocalists, Chuck Keeshan chief among them, for his great Okeh Records.

Along comes Ernest Tubb, whose "Walking the Floor over You" was a smash jukebox hit at about the same time as Daffan's "Worried Mind." I speak under correction, and I certainly do not mean to detract from his great forerunners and contemporaries. But I have to believe that Ernest Tubb's direct, on-the-beat, clear, believably rendered lyric with that spare single electric guitar accompaniment hit the nickelodeon crowd from Detroit to Los Angeles to Richmond like a revelation: "Here's the real thing at last, the genuine article. Daffan and Dexter and Tillman were saying the right things; Tubb says them the right *way.*" In short, Ernest Tubb brought the honky-tonk song part way out of the western swing tradition, gave it a new, sparer sound and in the process an even greater believability. This winning formula would reap great benefits for Tubb, of course; but it has since done the same for countless country artists, in fact for nearly all of the great ones since Tubb's heyday: Hank Thompson, Hank Williams, Webb Pierce, Ray Price, Buck Owens, Merle Haggard, Gene Watson, George Strait, Randy Travis, and so many others.

TALENT SCOUT

I save for last a final glance at the most common, recurring thread from these many pages. At any stage of his career—from the time he first "made it" right through the last touring he did—Ernest Tubb tried to help others. Buddy Charleton put it well: "He'd help you if you asked him; sometimes even if you didn't ask him."[9] He often helped promoters who didn't make enough money on a Tubb date. He didn't want anybody to lose money on Ernest Tubb, and it wasn't simply a question of pride: he believed that the way for country music to grow was for everybody to make money at it.

The best-known instances of his helping others, and which surely had the most lasting impact on the country music world, were his offers of help to fellow artists and to the many talented and determined young men and women who aspired to be his fellow artists. That was the main reason for the *Midnite Jamboree:* to get records played and songs sung by newer artists who needed the exposure. Most of the guests he had on that show never got very far, to be sure: but the many who did changed the face of country music.

Call the roll of the ones he helped in this and other ways. We've met them in chapter after chapter, and my list, as long as it is, could not possibly be complete:

Rod Brasfield, the Short Brothers, Rex Griffin, Pete Pyle, Hank Thompson, Rebe & Rabe, Jimmie Skinner, Ernie Lee, Hank Snow, Hank Williams, Carl Smith, Justin Tubb, Rusty Gabbard, Elvis Presley, Patsy Cline, the Wilburn Brothers, Bobby Helms, Stonewall Jackson, Skeeter Davis, Charlie Walker, George Hamilton IV, Loretta Lynn, Cal Smith, Jack Greene, Bobby Lewis, Billy Parker. Most of these artists would probably have made it anyway; but imagine country music without these folks, and then you'll realize a big part of the difference that Ernest Tubb made. "He helped a lot of people," Eddy Arnold admits, "and I admired him for that."[10]

Asked to assess his father as talent scout, Justin Tubb said, "One of the best. He knew good talent. He mainly had a feeling for what the people would like, whether it be a song, or a band, or a singer, or what. He had a feeling for what the country music fan would like, and what they would buy. He didn't miss too many times, either."[11]

So, besides the great music he left us—ironically, more of it, available now than at any time during his life[12]—Ernest Tubb helped shape the very course of country music behind the scenes, and not just as talent scout. The city of Nashville owes its adopted star a huge debt of thanks. The sound and the look of the Grand Ole Opry were different after Ernest Tubb came there. Nashville first became country music's recording capital in the late 1940s, in large part because Ernest Tubb lived there. Country music gradually ceased being the music industry's stepchild, because Ernest Tubb boosted its sales, more widely distributed its records, and helped at least one trade paper to chart those records. He even helped find a more palatable and less pejorative name for the music he loved.

A NEW INTEREST IN ERNEST TUBB

Small wonder that now, more than a decade after his death, tributes are still being paid to the Texas Troubadour. If anything, there is more interest in his career at this writing than at any time since the weeks after his death. TNN frequently airs tributes to Tubb's memory: there were salutes on *Nashville Now* and more recently on *Music City Tonight; Thanks, Troubadour, Thanks* and a more recent documentary first shown there in February, 1996, *The Life & Times of Ernest Tubb* that was produced by Vello Nickolauo for Greystone Productions. WSM, the Grand Ole Opry's home station, has saluted Ernest Tubb and his now reactivated Texas Troubadours on at least three programs of the weekly *Nashville Nights with Carol Lee* in 1994–1995, and in June 1995, the Ernest Tubb Record Shop #2 first offered for public view the revamped Green Hornet bus inside its newer, larger quarters.

The *Midnite Jamboree* has a large new home, the first one built specifically for it: the new Troubadour Theater. And yes, the Texas Troubadours (at least one group of them) are back on tour part time after a decade of being scattered to separate pursuits. The first of what it is hoped will be annual reunions of the Texas Troubadours took place in June 1995, in conjunction with the bus remodeling and store expansion. A gentleman named Austin Church hopes to create a one-man Ernest Tubb stage show—a biographical foray akin to what Hal Holbrook did for Mark Twain and James Whitmore did for Will Rogers.

Lynn Owsley, coordinator of the 1995 Texas Troubadours reunion and one of the reconstituted Troubadours, remembered Ernest Tubb once saying "A person's not really dead, as long as he's remembered."[13] Even if our concept of immortality goes no further than this, it's safe to say that Ernest Tubb will never die.

NOTES

PREFACE

1 Albert Jay Nock, "The Purpose of Biography," *The State of the Union: Essays in Social Criticism* (Indianapolis: Liberty Press, 1991), 6.

2 Ibid.

3 C. S. Lewis, "On Criticism," *Of Other Worlds* (New York: Harcourt, Brace Jovanovich, 1966), 50.

1 FAMILY AND EARLY LIFE

1 Quanah Talmadge Tubb, comments, August 1994.

2 Ruth Husky, interview by the author, April 21, 1994.

3 Debbie Tubb, interview by the author, April 22, 1994.

4 Douglas Glenn Tubb, interview by the author, May 4, 1994.

5 Quanah Talmadge Tubb, comments, August 1994.

6 Ernest would sign photos to any of his siblings "Your Bud" or "Your Little Bud."

7 Quanah Talmadge Tubb, comments, August 1994.

8 *Ernest Tubb Folio of Recorded Hits No. 1* (Hollywood: Ernest Tubb Music, Inc., 1948), 23.

9 Norma Barthel, *Ernest Tubb: The Original E.T.* (Privately published, 1984), 2.

10 Townsend Miller, "Ernest Tubb," *Stars of Country Music* (Urbana: University of Illinois Press, 1975), 228.

11 Dalene Husky, interview by the author, February 25, 1995.

12 "The Star of the Week—September 16, 1961—Ernest Tubb—Favorite Foods," *The Troubadour* (fall 1962): 9.

13 Ibid.

14 Ruth Husky, interview by the author, February 24, 1995.

15 Ibid.

16 Barthel, *Ernest Tubb: The Original E.T.*, 3.

17 Miller, "Ernest Tubb," 224–225.

18 Ibid., 228.

19 Dr. Gentry's files, which he used to compile *A History and Encyclopedia of Country, Western, and Gospel Music* (1961), came to the Country Music Foundation Library, Nashville, in December 1994.

20 Miller, "Ernest Tubb," 228.

21 Barthel, *Ernest Tubb: The Original E.T.*, 4–5.

22 Ruth Husky, interview, April 21, 1994.

23 Barthel, *Ernest Tubb: The Original E.T.*, 7.

2 JIMMIE RODGERS

1 Peter Guralnick, "Ernest Tubb: Still the Texas Troubadour," *Country Music* (May 1977): 66.

 2 Ibid.

 3 Ibid.

 4 Floyd Tillman, telephone interview by the author, January 2, 1994.

 5 Ernest Tubb, interview by Hairl Hensley, *Inside Music City,* October 29, 1977.

 6 Norma Barthel, *Ernest Tubb: The Original E.T.* (Privately published, 1984), 8. She erroneously gives "Blue Yodel No. 2" as the subtitle for "The Brakeman's Blues." They were in fact opposite sides of the same record, Victor 21291.

 7 Ibid., 9.

 8 Frederick Burger, "Texas Troubador Still Walkin' Floor," *Miami Herald,* September 13, 1981, n.p.

 9 Barthel, *Ernest Tubb: The Original E.T.*, 9.

10 Ruth Husky, telephone interview by the author, November 4, 1993.

11 Debbie "Snooky" Tubb, interview by the author, April 22, 1994.

12 Barthel, *Ernest Tubb: The Original E.T.*, 10–11.

13 Ibid., 11–12.

14 Ibid., 12–13, 77.

15 Nolan Porterfield, *Jimmie Rodgers: The Life and Times of America's Blue Yodeler* (Urbana: University of Illinois Press, 1979), 306, 310.

16 "T. Tommy Interviews Ernest Tubb," *Melody Trails* (January 1956): 13.

17 Ernest Tubb, interview by the author, October 4, 1977.

18 Ernest Tubb, interview by Hairl Hensley, *Inside Music City,* October 29, 1977.

19 Porterfield, *Jimmie Rodgers: The Life and Times of America's Blue Yodeler,* 437.

20 Ernest Tubb, interview.

21 Ernest Tubb, interview by Hairl Hensley, *Inside Music City,* October 29, 1977.

22 Transcribed from a tape of Tubb's home recording in the possession of the Bill French family.

23 Merwyn J. Buffington, interview by the author, November 29, 1977.

24 Barthel, *Ernest Tubb: The Original E.T.*, 15.

25 Ibid., 16.

26 Ernest Tubb, interview.

27 Barthel, *Ernest Tubb: The Original E.T.,* 16.

28 *Ernest Tubb Song Folio of Sensational Successes No. 1* (Portland, Oreg.: American Music, 1941), 16.

29 *Ernest Tubb Song Folio of Sensational Successes No. 3* (Hollywood: American Music, 1943), 34.

30 Merwyn Buffington, interview.

31 Stan Crawford, "Borger Is Brightened by Troubadour Visit," *The Troubadour* (spring 1965): 4, quoting the Borger, Texas newspaper, on the occasion of his first-ever concert there, January 27, 1965.

32 Barthel, *Ernest Tubb: The Original E.T.,* 35.

33 Ernest Tubb, interview.

34 Elsie McWilliams, "The Passing of Jimmie Rodgers," copyright Southern Music, 1936. Recorded by Ernest Tubb October 27, 1936, and released on Bluebird 6693.

3 SAN ANTONIO DAYS: "BLUE-EYED ELAINE" AND "JIMMIE'S WIFE"

1 Merwyn Buffington, interview by the author, November 29, 1977.

2 Ibid.

3 Norma Barthel, *Ernest Tubb: The Original E.T.* (Privately published, 1984), 17–18, 77–81.

4 Douglas Glenn Tubb, interview by the author, May 4, 1994.

5 See photo in the photo section of Tubb in Benjamin holding this guitar.

6 Ernest Tubb, interview by the author, October 4, 1977.

7 Barthel, *Ernest Tubb: The Original E.T.,* 19.

8 Ibid., 20.

9 Elaine (Tubb) Lemieux, interview by the author, April 18, 1994.

10 Barthel, *Ernest Tubb: The Original E.T.,* 21–22.

11 Ibid., 22–23.

12 Ibid., 21, 23.

13 Merwyn J. Buffington, interview.

14 "Professional Career of George W. Ing," reminiscences sent to the author by Tracy Pitcox of Brady, Texas.

15 Elaine (Tubb) Lemieux, interview.

16 Charlie Walker, interview by the author, November 1, 1994. The "wife" Charlie Walker refers to is Tubb's second wife, Olene.

17 Ibid.

18 Nat Green, "American Folk Tunes," *Billboard* (May 5, 1945): 67.

19 Charlie Walker, interview.

20 Floyd Tillman, telephone interview by the author, January 2, 1994.

21 Mildred Pollard, interview by the author, January 14, 1995.

22 Barthel, *Ernest Tubb: The Original E.T.,* 27.

23 Ibid., 29.

4 BLUEBIRD RECORDS AND A TOUR

1 Copy enclosed with letter to author from Bill French, April 23, 1985.

2 Norma Barthel, *Ernest Tubb: The Original E.T.* (Privately published, 1984), 36.

3 Russell Sanjek, *American Popular Music and Its Business: The First Four Hundred Years.* Vol. 3, *From 1900 to 1984* (New York: Oxford University Press, 1988), 133.

4 Ernest Tubb, interview by the author, October 4, 1977.

5 Mildred Pollard, interview by the author, January 14, 1995.

6 Ernest Tubb, interview.

7 *Ernest Tubb Song Folio of Sensational Successes No. 1* (Portland, Oreg.: American Music, 1941), cover. Carrie's publicity shot is found inside the front cover.

8 Norma Barthel, *The Ernest Tubb Discography: 1936–1969* (Privately published, 1970), 30.

9 Ernest Tubb, interview.

10 Barthel, *Ernest Tubb: The Original E.T.,* 34.

11 Ibid.

12 Mildred Pollard, interview.

13 Ibid.

14 Barthel, *Ernest Tubb: The Original E.T.,* 31.

15 "The Star of The Week—September 16, 1961—Ernest Tubb—Most Embarrassing or Unusual Experience," *The Troubadour* (fall 1962): 9.

16 Carrie Rodgers, notes to *Ernest Tubb Sings the Songs of Jimmie Rodgers,* Decca DL-5336, 1951.

17 "A Personal Foreword by Mrs. Jimmie Rodgers," *Ernest Tubb Song Folio of Sensational Successes No. 1,* inside front cover.

18 Quanah Talmadge Tubb, taped comments, received by the author August 31, 1994.

19 Douglas Glenn Tubb, interview by the author, May 4, 1994. See also a letter written by Tubb to Floy Case re a Chicago meeting with Peer rep Bob Gilmore in August 1945. Tubb clearly felt Peer was not paying Mrs. Rodgers adequate royalties and used a lawyer to secure them for her.

20 Johnny Sippel, "Folk Talent and Tunes," *Billboard* (April 12, 1952): 34.

21 Ernest Tubb, "Jimmie's Wife," *Mountain Broadcast and Prairie Recorder* 2.5 (June 1941): 10.

5 DETOURS

1 Merwyn Buffington, interview by the author, November 29, 1977.

2 Ernest Tubb, interview by the author, October 4, 1977.

3 Ibid.

4 Ibid.

5 Merwyn Buffington, interview.

6 Norma Barthel, *Ernest Tubb: The Original E.T.* (Privately published, 1984), 37.

7 Merwyn Buffington interview.

8   Ernest Tubb, interview.

9   Merwyn Buffington, interview.

10 Edward Linn, "Country Singer: The Ernest Tubb Story," *Saga* (May 1957): 71.

11 Merwyn Buffington, interview.

12 Linn, "Country Singer: The Ernest Tubb Story," n.p.

13 Mrs. Merwyn Buffington, interview by the author, April 23, 1994.

14 Merwyn Buffington, interview.

15 Elaine (Tubb) Lemieux, interview by the author, April 18, 1994.

16 Merwyn Buffington, interview.

17 Ernest Tubb, interview.

18 *Standard-Times* (San Angelo), various issues, January through September 1938.

19 Ernest Tubb, interview.

20 Ernest Tubb, interview by Hairl Hensley, *Inside Music City,* October 29, 1977.

21 Ernest Tubb, qtd. on *The Ralph Emery Show,* January 7, 1975.

22 "San Angelo Babe Car Wreck Victim," *Standard-Times* (San Angelo), September 11, 1938, p. 1.

23 Mrs. Merwyn Buffington, interview.

24 Ibid.

25 Ernest Tubb, interview.

26 Ibid.

27 Elaine (Tubb) Lemieux, interview.

6   "SWELL SAN ANGELO"

1   Grant Turner, qtd. on *Thanks, Troubadour, Thanks,* Hallway Productions, 1987.

2   Charlie Walker, interview by the author, November 1, 1994.

3   Cliff Kendrick, interview by Kevin Coffey; shared by Coffey with the author from tape of May 11, 1992.

4   Ernest Tubb, qtd. in Leon Fleming, "Singer Recalls Old Days When He Lived in San Angelo," *Standard-Times* (San Angelo), October 11, 1959, p. 1.

5   Renay San Miguel, "Tubb's Voice Echoes in Angelo," *Standard-Times* (San Angelo), September 9, 1984, p. 1A.

6   "Singer Recalls Old Days," p. 1.

7   Elaine (Tubb) Lemieux, interview by the author, April 18, 1994.

8   Ibid.

9   Ernest Tubb, interview by the author, October 4, 1977.

10 Ibid.

11 In all his Decca career, which began that next spring (1940), Tubb yodels only once, as a tag at the end of his "Mean Mama Blues" (1941), and never on any of the many Jimmie Rodgers tunes he would later record.

12 Ernest Tubb, interview by the author, October 4, 1977.

13 Elaine (Tubb) Lemieux, interview.

14 Lyrics transcribed from tape of Tubb's home demo recording.

15 Ernest Tubb, interview. Tubb revealed that Eddie Hill was the friend who told him this in a broadcast interview with Hairl Hensley later that month for *Inside Music City,* October 29, 1977.

16 Floy Case, "Jimmy and Leon Short," *Mountain Broadcast and Prairie Recorder* 9 (September 1946): 16.

17 Ernest Tubb, interview.

18 Elaine (Tubb) Lemieux, interview.

19 Case, "Jimmy and Leon Short," 16.

20 "Singer Recalls Old Days," p. 1.

21 "Tubb's Voice Echoes in Angelo," p. 4A.

22 Ernest Tubb, interview by Hairl Hensley, *Inside Music City,* October 29, 1977.

23 *The Ralph Emery Show,* January 9, 1975.

24 Ernest Tubb, qtd. on *The Ralph Emery Show,* January 7, 1975.

25 Ernest Tubb, qtd. on *The Ralph Emery Show,* January 9, 1975.

26 Ernest Tubb, qtd. on *The History of Country Music,* 1970.

27 "Singer Recalls Old Days," p. 1.

28 "Swell San Angelo," *Ernest Tubb Song Folio of Sensational Successes No. 1* (Portland, Oreg.: American Music, 1941), 31.

7 DECCA RECORDS: THE FIRST TWO SESSIONS

1 Bob Kendrick, interview by Kevin Coffey, June 6, 1992.

2 Charlie Walker, interview by the author, November 1, 1994: Walker's version of the way Ernest Tubb told it to him.

3 Russell Sanjek, *American Popular Music and Its Business: The First Four Hundred Years.* Vol. 3, *From 1900 to 1984.* (New York: Oxford University Press, 1988), 132.

4 Ronnie Pugh, "Decca Records and Country Music," notes to the CD-set *Decca Country Classics from the Vaults: 1934–1973,* MCAD3-11069, 1994, p. 2.

5 Ernest Tubb, interview by the author, October 4, 1977.

6 Norma Barthel, *Ernest Tubb: The Original E.T.* (Privately published, 1984), 41.

7 Charlie Walker, interview.

8 Ernest Tubb, interview.

9 Charlie Walker, interview.

10 Ernest Tubb, interview.

11 Charlie Walker, interview.

12 Ernest Tubb, interview.

13 Ibid.

14 Ibid.

15 Cut by Autry August 27, 1941, for Okeh 06549 (and Conqueror 9807); after World War II it was issued twice on red-label Columbia, 37425 and 20152.

16 Ernest Tubb, letter, *Mountain Broadcast and Prairie Recorder* 2.3 (November 1940): 7.

17 Norma Barthel, "Correction from Last Issue," *The Troubadour* 21.3 (summer 1965): 5.

18 Ernest Tubb, interview.

19 Douglas Glenn Tubb, interview by the author, May 4, 1994; and Talmadge Tubb, taped comments, c. August 31, 1994.

20 Barthel, *Ernest Tubb: The Original E.T.,* 43–44.

8 FORT WORTH DAYS

1   Quanah Talmadge Tubb, taped comments, August 1994.

2   Douglas Glenn Tubb, interview by the author, May 4, 1994.

3   Floy Case, "My Friend—Ernest Tubb," in *Ernest Tubb: The Original E.T.* by Norma Barthel (Privately published, 1984), 70.

4   Talmadge Tubb, taped comments.

5   *WFAA-KGKO-WBAP Combined Family Album: Dallas–Fort Worth, 1941* (Dallas, 1941): 29. This volume, the only one I have seen, makes no mention of Ernest Tubb: it must have "gone to press" before he was hired.

6   Ernest Tubb to Floy Case, February 11, 1941. Copy on file at the Country Music Foundation Library, Nashville.

7   Ernest Tubb to Floy Case, February 18, 1941. Copy on file at the Country Music Foundation Library, Nashville.

8   Vernon Young, telephone interview by the author, June 23, 1994.

9   Letter and document from the Floy Case collection. Copies on file at the Country Music Foundation Library in Nashville.

10 Norma Barthel, *Ernest Tubb: The Original E.T.* (Privately published, 1984), 70–71.

11 Floy Case, "Down Blue Bonnet Way," *Mountain Broadcast and Prairie Recorder* 2.4 (April 1941): 11.

12 Ernest Tubb to Floy Case, February 11, 1941. Copy on file at Country Music Foundation Library, Nashville.

13 Merwyn J. Buffington, interview by the author, November 29, 1977.

14 Ernest Tubb, interview by the author, October 4, 1977.

15 Ibid.

16 Ibid.

17 Smith had only been in the Red Hawks a short time; he's not their guitarist in the 1941 *WFAA-KGKO-WBAP Family Album* picture.

18 Ernest Tubb, interview.

19 Ibid.

20 Ibid.

21 Ibid.

22 Floy Case, "Down Blue Bonnet Way," *Mountain Broadcast and Prairie Recorder* 2.5 (June 1941): 3.

23 Floy Case, "Down Blue Bonnet Way," *Mountain Broadcast and Prairie Recorder* 2.6 (September 1941): 6.

24 Vernon Young, telephone interview.

25 Hank Thompson, telephone interview by the author, January 24, 1994.

26 Talmadge Tubb, taped comments, August 1994.

27   Charlie Walker, interview by the author, November 1, 1994.

28   Marie White, *Melody Trails* 2.2–3 (April-May 1946): 10. A decade later, a Tubb performance of that same mixed-up version of "I Saw Your Face in the Moon" was recorded from a *Midnite Jamboree* broadcast.

29   Ernest Tubb, interview.

30   Coffee Grinders member who prefers to remain anonymous.

31   Joe Frank Ferguson, conversation with the author, November 23, 1994.

32   "Popular Radio, Recording Artist Entertains Here," *Daily Gilmer Mirror* (Gilmer, Texas), October 22, 1941, n.p.

33   Ernest Tubb, interview.

34   Ernest Tubb, qtd. on *The Ralph Emery Show,* January 6, 1975.

9 MOVIES AND PACKAGE SHOWS

1   Ernest Tubb, interview by the author, October 4, 1977.

2   Floy Case, "Down Blue Bonnet Way," *Mountain Broadcast and Prairie Recorder* 2.7 (December 1941): 11.

3   Tubb's handwritten manuscript was still in Mrs. Case's possession when she died in 1988; a copy is on file at the Country Music Foundation Library in Nashville.

4   Mildred Pollard, telephone interview by the author, January 14, 1995.

5   Floy Case, "Down Blue Bonnet Way," *Mountain Broadcast and Prairie Recorder* 3.1 (March 1942): 6.

6   "American Folk Records," *Billboard* (March 7, 1942): 61.

7   "American Folk Records," *Billboard* (April 18, 1942): 63.

8   "American Folk Records," *Billboard* (June 27, 1942): 77.

9   "American Folk Records," *Billboard* (July 25, 1942): 99.

10   Cindy Walker recalls meeting Ernest Tubb on that trip at a luncheon her parents gave for Tubb and his publisher, Sylvester Cross of American Music, embarrassing herself by spilling a glass of tea in her lap. Cross published some of her songs and all of Tubb's then; and though Ernest took none of her songs then, she would ultimately become the most-recorded songwriter (after himself) in his repertory.

11   Wesley Tuttle, telephone interview by the author, January 20, 1994.

12   Ernest Tubb to Mrs. and Mrs. J. C. Case, July 9, 1942. Copy on file at the Country Music Foundation in Nashville.

13   Floy Case, "Down Blue Bonnet Way," *Mountain Broadcast and Prairie Recorder* 3.3 (November 1942): 3.

14   Nat Green, "Hillbillies Heat with Helium," *The Billboard 1943 Music Year Book* (New York: Billboard Publications, 1944): 102.

15   Case, "Down Blue Bonnet Way" (November 1942): 4–5.

16   *Commercial Appeal* (Memphis), August 21, 1942, p. 4-A; August 23, 1942, IV, p. 7.

17   Ernest Tubb, interview.

18   Ernest Tubb to the Case family (now in Arlington, Virginia), December 6, 1942.

19   Ernest Tubb, interview by T. Tommy Cutrer, *Music City U.S.A.,* March 30, 1971.

20 Wesley Tuttle, telephone interview.

21 Ernest Tubb, qtd. on *The Ralph Emery Show,* January 8, 1975.

22 Ernest Tubb to the Case family, December 6, 1942.

23 Ernest Tubb, interview.

24 Ernest Tubb to the Case family, December 6, 1942.

25 Chester Studdard, interview by the author, August 20, 1993.

26 Ernest Tubb, interview. Interestingly, Hal Smith, Tubb's future fiddler, booking agent, and TV producer, was in the group that booked Tubb into Montgomery. He was playing on Birmingham station WSGN at the time; the December 27 show there marked their first meeting (Hal Smith, interview by the author, July 25, 1995).

27 Letters from Elaine Tubb to Floy Case.

28 Alton Delmore, *Truth Is Stranger Than Publicity: Alton Delmore's Autobiography* (Nashville: Country Music Foundation Press, 1977), 110.

29 Ibid.

30 Ibid., 110–111.

31 Ernest Tubb, interview; and Pee Wee King, interview by the author, November 18, 1993.

32 Elaine Tubb to Floy Case, January 10, 1943.

33 Justin Tubb, interview by the author, August 8, 1994.

34 Elaine Tubb to Floy Case, January 25, 1943.

35 Justin Tubb, interview.

10   THE FIRST YEAR IN NASHVILLE

1 Elaine Tubb to Floy Case, undated, circa late March 1943.

2 Ibid.

3 Billy Byrd, interview by the author, May 3, 1994.

4 Nat Green, "American Folk Tunes," *Billboard* (December 9, 1944): 63.

5 Billy Byrd, interview.

6 Floy Case, "Down Blue Bonnet Way," *Mountain Broadcast and Prairie Recorder,* no. 18 (January 1944), p. 6.

7 Since Harold Bradley is in the first photographs with Chester, Kemo, Johnny, Toby, and bassist Norman Zinkan, the Melody Boys were in place by summertime anyway.

8 Ray Head, interview by the author, August 17, 1977.

9 Ernest Tubb, interview by the author, October 4, 1977.

10 *Ernest Tubb No. 1 Radio Song Book* (Nashville: Ernest Tubb Publications, 1943), inside front cover.

11 *Ernest Tubb Song Folio of Sensational Successes No. 2* (Portland, Oreg.: American Music, 1942), inside front cover.

12 Chester Studdard, interview by the author, August 20, 1993.

13 Ernest Tubb, qtd. on *The Ralph Emery Show,* January 10, 1975.

14 Justin Tubb, interview by the author, August 8, 1994.

15 Jerry Langley, interview by the author, December 21, 1993.

16 Pictured in a 1956 *Life* photo essay on the Grand Ole Opry is the Lonzo & Oscar bus on a Montana tour, proudly listing their Carter's Champion Chicks radio sponsor.

17 George D. Hay, *A Story of the Grand Ole Opry* (Nashville, privately published, 1945), 56–57.

18 Jackie Pyle, "I Talked with Ernest Tubb," *Ernest Tubb Discography: 1936–1969* by Norma Barthel (Privately published, 1970), 17.

19 In fairness to Mrs. Rodgers, one must say that at least now Tubb had a career to direct.

11 RECORDS, RADIO, AND FAN CLUBS

1 "No Lack of Shellac Now," *Billboard* (November 4, 1944): 66.

2 Hal Smith, interview by the author, July 25, 1995.

3 "American Folk Tunes and Tunesters," *Billboard* (October 23, 1943): 66.

4 "Decca Records Report Lower Net Earnings than in 1944," *Billboard* (November 17, 1945): 79.

5 Russell Sanjek, *American Pop Music and Its Business: The First Four Hundred Years.* Vol. 3, *From 1900 to 1984* (New York: Oxford University Press, 1988), 131.

6 David Kressley, "Catalog of World Transcriptions," *Record Research* 89 (March 1968): 1. Much of what follows regarding World transcriptions history draws upon Kressley's article.

7 Sanjek, 219.

8 "American Folk Tunes and Tunesters," *Billboard* (December 4, 1943): 63.

9 *Joel Whitburn's Top Country Singles: 1944–1988* (Menomonee Falls, Wisc.: Record Research, Inc., 1989), 329.

10 Dorothy Horstman, *Sing Your Heart Out Country Boy* (New York: E.P. Dutton, 1975), 281.

11 Charlie Walker, interview by the author, November 1, 1994.

12 Named in Minnie Pearl's earliest *Grinder's Switch Gazette* Opry programs as a Tubb bandsman. An unknown man who shows up in a couple of group shots from 1944 is probably Turnage, though a handwritten identification on the back of a print at the Country Music Foundation calls this man "Eddie."

13 Dick Hill, "The Grand Ole Opry, 1944–45. A Radio Log Kept by Dick Hill of Tecumseh, Nebraska," *Journal of Country Music* 5.3 (fall 1974): 95–97.

14 Dave Kapp to Ernest Tubb, August 27, 1945; saved in Nelle Poe's scrapbook, now at the Country Music Foundation Library, Nashville.

15 Nelle Poe, handwritten account of the Poe Sisters' career, prepared February 20, 1991, donated to the Country Music Foundation Library.

16 "Floy Case Reports" of September 1945 in *Mountain Broadcast and Prairie Recorder* (new series 5, p. 23) mentions that in Fort Worth it aired over WBAP at 6:45 A.M. Monday, Wednesday, and Friday.

17 Arnold had his first recording session in December 1944, delayed over a year by the Petrillo ban.

18 Floy Case, "Floy Case Reports," *Mountain Broadcast and Prairie Recorder,* new series 4 (June 1945): 9.

19 Floy Case, "Down Blue Bonnet Way," *Mountain Broadcast and Prairie Recorder* 3.3 (November 1942): 3.

20 Elaine Tubb, correspondence with Floy Case, dates cited in text.

21 Norma Winton, "At the Ranch House," *Melody Trails* 1 (January-February-March 1945): 2.

22 Ernest Tubb, column, *Melody Trails* 2 (April-May-June 1945): 3.

23 Bill French, homemade video narration made in the late 1980s, supplied to the author in November 1993 by Mr. French's daughter, Mrs. Donna DiVito.

24 Ernest Tubb to the Case family, September 4, 1945. The dates were confirmed by information recently unearthed from Decca by Bear Family's Richard Weize.

25 Justin Tubb, interview by the author, August 8, 1994.

26 "American Folk Tunes," *Billboard* (July 13, 1946): 114.

27 Ernest Tubb, qtd. on *The Ralph Emery Show,* January 7, 1975.

28 "Opry House Matinee," *Melody Trails* 1.5 (January-February-March 1946): 19.

12   THE GREAT POPULARITY

1 Don "Ramblin'" Rhodes, "Long Music Career Full of Memories for Ernest Tubb" (Augusta) *Chronicle,* May 11, 1975, p. 1C.

2 Ibid.

3 Norma Winton to Floy Case, May 4, 1946.

4 Norma Winton, "Memorial Day: Of a Most Memorable Occasion," *Melody Trails* 2.4 (June 1946): 6.

5 Floy Case, "Floy Case Reports," *Mountain Broadcast and Prairie Recorder,* no. 7 (March 1946): 12.

6 Norma Winton, "Ernest-ly Yours," *Melody Trails* 2.4 (June 1946): 2.

7 Charlie Walker, interview by the author, November 1, 1994.

8 Hal Smith, interview by the author, July 25, 1995.

9 Ernest Tubb, interview by T. Tommy Cutrer, *Music City U.S.A.,* April 2, 1971.

10 Newspaper clippings from 1946 to 1947 in the possession of Mrs. Ruth Husky of Lubbock, Texas.

11 Jack Greene, interview by Hairl Hensley, *Midnite Jamboree* special tribute to Ernest Tubb, September 9, 1984.

12 George Lipsitz, *Rainbow at Midnight: Labor and Culture in the 1940s* (Urbana: University of Illinois Press, 1994), 45–46.

13 Ernest Tubb, interview by the author, October 4, 1977.

14 "American Folk Tunes," *Billboard,* April 14, 1945, and August 3, 1946.

15 Terri Lenzen, letter, *Melody Trails* 2 (April-May-June 1945): 5.

16 Peggy Hobbs, letter, *Melody Trails* 3 (July-August-September 1945): 8.

17 Mae Loosier, "What I Like Best about Ernest Tubb," *Melody Trails* 1.4 (October-November-December 1945): 7.

18 Fred Daniel, interview by the author, December 9, 1994.

19 "The Osborne Brothers: Getting Started. An Interview with Bill Emerson," *Muleskinner News* 2.4 (July-August 1971): 2–3.

20 Neil Rosenberg, "The Osborne Brothers," *Bluegrass Unlimited* 6.3 (September 1971): 5.

21 Yes, the same Bennie Hess who years later convinced Jimmie Rodgers's biographer Nolan Porterfield that he had a mysterious Rodgers recording—which was, in fact, Hess himself aping the Rodgers style.

22 Hal Smith, interview.

23 Jerry Langley, interview by the author, December 21, 1993.

24 "Floy Case Reports," *Mountain Broadcast and Prairie Recorder* new series 5 (September 1945): 12.

25 Viola Myers, "From Illinois," *Melody Trails* 1.3 (July-August-September 1945): 3.

26 Ibid.

27 Viola Myers, "From Illinois," *Melody Trails* 1.4 (October-November-December 1945): 7.

28 Texas Bill Strength, letter, *Melody Trails* 1.5 (January-February-March 1946): 2.

29 "American Folk Tunes," *Billboard* (November 16, 1946): 94.

30 Bar Biszick, who has done the most research on the Aberbach Brothers and Hill & Range, tells me that the advance money came from their earliest hit songs, "Shame on You" and "Detour," as well as from BMI.

31 Interviews with songwriters Ben Weisman and Zeke Clements, and former Hill & Range staffer Grelun Landon were most useful in sketching out this overview of the Aberbach approach.

32 Eddy Arnold, interview by the author, November 23, 1993.

33 "Folk Talent and Tunes," *Billboard,* various issues, 1951.

34 Grelun Landon, interview by the author, June 21, 1994.

13 A YEAR OF MILESTONES

1 Signing is pictured on page 23 of *Ernest Tubb Folio of Recorded Hits No. 1* (Hollywood: Ernest Tubb Music Inc., 1947).

2 Jerry Byrd to author, December 20, 1994.

3 See *Ernest Tubb Folio of Recorded Hits No. 1,* p. 46.

4 Frank X. Tolbert, "The Small Boys' Sinatra," *Dallas Morning News,* July 26, 1947, p. D-1.

5 "American Folk Tunes," *Billboard* (December 27, 1947): 84.

6 Hal Smith, interview by the author, July 25, 1995.

7 Justin Tubb, interview by the author, August 8, 1994.

8 Bill Anderson, interview by the author, June 2, 1994.

9 Mary Hance, "Tubb Began Record Shop for the Fans," *Nashville Banner,* May 2, 1987, p. A-4.

10 The Record Mart (Ernie's), 179 3rd Avenue North; Hermitage Music Company (the jukebox operator), 423 Broad Street (in the same block where Tubb's shop would move in 1951!); Buckley Amusement Company (another jukebox company), 141 8th Avenue North. A few of the top hillbilly artists (Acuff, Autry, Arnold, Ritter, Tubb) had

between three and five listed titles, selling for 63 cents or 79 cents, at Sears, Church Street at 8th Avenue North.

11 Jerry Langley, interview by the author, December 21, 1993.

12 Jackie Pyke, "I Talked with Ernest Tubb," in *Ernest Tubb Discography (1936–1969)* by Norma Barthel (Privately published, 1970), 18. Langley, interestingly, says that Ernie's on Third Avenue was the place to buy the used jukebox records.

13 Ibid., for the $50,000 five-year total. The $10,000 per year figure is mentioned by Tubb on *The Ralph Emery Show,* January 10, 1975.

14 Justin Tubb, interview.

15 Hal Smith, interview.

16 Pyke, "I Talked with Ernest Tubb," 18.

17 Ibid.

18 Jerry Langley, interview.

19 Ernest Tubb, interview by the author, October 4, 1977.

20 *Billboard* (June 14, 1947): cover.

21 Ernest Tubb, interview.

22 Dollie Dearman Denny, interview by the author, February 25, 1994.

23 Ibid.

24 "American Folk Tunes," *Billboard* (April 10, 1948): 114. Mailorder sales would constitute as much as 75 percent of the business as late as 1965, though with the rise of Nashville's country music tourism, that figure had dropped to 30 percent of a $1.8 million business in 1989.

25 Pee Wee King recalls that Tubb loaned Stewart the down payment for a house and structured the song deal so that royalties would constitute repayment (Pee Wee King, interview by the author, November 18, 1993).

26 Hank Thompson, telephone interview by the author, January 24, 1994.

27 Jimmie Skinner, "A Few Words about Ernest Tubb," *Melody Trails* (summer 1953): 8.

28 Carl Story, interview by Kevin Coffey, March 1, 1995. Assuming Story had this conversation about 1949, the sequence of events would be exactly right—and by then, Story would have surely been wondering why it hadn't been released.

29 Carl Dieckman of Alton, Kansas, to Jim Evans of Lubbock, Texas, April 24, 1956. Evans papers at Country Music Foundation Library.

30 Justin Tubb, interview.

31 See note to the discography entry on this recording. Stewart figures in this narrative later as writer of "I Need Attention Bad" and "I Will Miss You When You Go."

32 Ruth Husky, interview by the author, November 4, 1993.

33 "American Folk Tunes," *Billboard* (August 30, 1947): 109.

34 Bradley plays on Tubb records at least as early as 1949 and knew Tubb from his earliest Nashville days and then of course from leading the *Opry House Matinee* house band. But Hal Smith in a recent (July 25, 1995) interview said that he thought pianist/arranger/songwriter Beasley Smith arranged all the earliest Nashville sessions.

35 Owen Bradley, interview by the author, March 20, 1981.

36 "American Folk Tunes," *Billboard* (September 20, 1947), reporting on the Carnegie Hall concert.

14 THE FIGHT FOR RESPECTABILITY

1 Norma Barthel, *Ernest Tubb: The Original E.T.* (Privately published, 1984), 4–5.
2 Decca Records catalogues and catalogue supplements on file at the Country Music Foundation Library, Nashville.
3 Ernest Tubb, interview by the author, October 4, 1977.
4 Ibid.
5 Ernest Tubb, qtd. on *The Ralph Emery Show,* January 9, 1975.
6 "American Folk Tunes," *Billboard* (September 20, 1947): 121.
7 George D. Hay, *A Story of the Grand Ole Opry* (Nashville: privately published, 1953): 44.
8 Ibid.
9 Ibid.
10 Oscar Davis got free concert publicity from a New York newspaper personality who wrote "Gold Mine in the Sky," in exchange for including it on the program!
11 Oscar Davis said in later years that to Tubb, Carnegie Hall originally meant nothing: it might just as well have been any honky-tonk in America.
12 Ernest Tubb, interview.
13 Ibid.
14 Hay, *A Story of the Grand Ole Opry,* 44.
15 *Cash Box* (October 27, 1947): 25.
16 *New York Times,* September 19, 1947, p. 2: "Music Notes. Events tonight: 'Grand Ole Opry,' program of folk music, Ernest Tubb, George Dewey Hay, Minnie Pearl, and others, Carnegie Hall, 8:30 o'clock." And that's the expanded version, with more detail than the previous day's notice. By an odd coincidence, on the same page with the first night's concert mention by the *Times* is a whiskey ad with an endorsement by Hal Horton of Dallas, one of Tubb's great boosters on the KRLD *Hillbilly Hit Parade* and *Cornbread Matinee.*
17 *Dayton Journal Herald,* April 21, 1979.
18 Hay, *A Story of the Grand Ole Opry,* 44.

15 ON THE PERSONAL SIDE: THE LATE 1940S WATERSHED

1 Don Davis, interview by the author, January 21, 1994.
2 Hal Smith, interview by the author, July 25, 1995.
3 Don Davis, interview.
4 Ibid.
5 Danny Dill, interview by the author, January 26, 1994.
6 Jerry Rivers, interview by the author, August 19, 1994.
7 Edward Linn, "Country Singer: The Ernest Tubb Story," *Saga* (May 1957): 70.
8 Ibid., 73.

9   Hal Smith interview, July 25, 1995.

10 Interviews by the author with Merwyn J. Buffington (1977) and Mrs. Buffington (1994).

11 Elaine (Tubb) Lemieux, interview by the author, April 18, 1994.

12 Debbie Tubb, interview by the author, April 22, 1994.

13 "Not working at the Record Shop anymore" is all that Elaine Tubb said about it in a letter to Floy Case of June 7, 1948.

14 Wesley Tuttle, interview by the author, January 20, 1994.

15 The lyrics to a fine song Tubb wrote but never recorded, "I'm Gettin' Tired," tell the story even better.

16 Billy Byrd, Debbie "Snooky" Tubb, and Justin Tubb were my sources for this account.

17 Divorce papers, "Elaine Tubb vs. Ernest Tubb," Davidson County (Tennessee) Court.

18 Ibid.

19 Ruth Husky, interview by the author, February 21, 1995.

20 Ernest Tubb, letter, *Melody Trails* 3.2 (January 1947): 3.

21 Norma Winton, editor's note, *Melody Trails* 3.2 (January 1947): 3.

22 Bill Graham's column on Nashville news in King Records' *Record Roundup* (volume 1, number 3, March 1947) specifically names the *Midnight Jamboree* and says that in January 1947 Tubb turned over part of his time to help with a March of Dimes drive.

23 Hal Smith, interview.

24 Microfilmed copies of the *Nashville Banner,* Vanderbilt University's Jean and Alexander Heard Library; spot-checked for the years 1947–1953.

25 "American Folk Tunes," *Billboard* (April 10, 1948): 114.

26 Hal Smith, interview.

27 Three examples, with original recording artist appended, make the point: "Tearstains on Your Letter" (Hank Penny), "I Wasted a Nickel Last Night" (Shorty Long), "Give Me a Hundred Reasons" (Ann Jones).

16   A HELPING HAND

1   Pete Pyle, Bluebird Records artist and Opry member when Tubb came, was a writer on Tubb's "When Love Turns To Hate."

2   Session sheet faxed from Polygram Studios by Hank Williams biographer Colin Escott, July 7, 1992. See also Ivan Tribe's notes to the Rounder LP *New Sounds Ramblin' from Coast to Coast. The Early Days of Bluegrass. Volume 3.* I have also relied on my interview with Chester Studdard, August 20, 1993.

3   Hank Thompson, telephone interview by the author, January 24, 1994.

4   Johnny Sippel, "Folk Talent and Tunes," *Billboard* (October 30, 1948): 31.

5   Johnny Sippel, "Folk Talent and Tunes," *Billboard* (December 18, 1948): 32.

6   Hank Thompson, telephone interview.

7   Ruth Husky, interview by the author, April 21, 1994.

8   Recounted by Charlie Walker in my interview of November 1, 1994.

9   Ernest Tubb, qtd. on *The Ralph Emery Show,* January 10, 1975.

10 Ernest Tubb, interview by the author, October 4, 1977.

11 Dollie Dearman Denny, interview by the author, February 25, 1994.

12 Ernest Tubb, interview.

13 Ibid.

14 Colin Escott, *Hank Williams: The Biography* (Boston: Little, Brown & Co., 1994), 106.

15 Ernest Tubb, interview.

16 Douglas Glenn Tubb, interview by the author, May 4, 1994.

17 Ernest Tubb, qtd. on *The Ralph Emery Show.*

18 Jerry Rivers, interview by the author, August 19, 1994.

19 Ibid.

20 Escott, *Hank Williams: The Biography,* 178–179.

21 Jerry Rivers, interview.

22 Escott, *Hank Williams: The Biography,* 209.

23 Hank Snow, interview by the author, February 1, 1994.

24 Hank Snow, with Jack Ownbey and Bob Burris, *The Hank Snow Story* (Urbana: University of Illinois Press, 1994), 290.

25 Ibid.

26 Ernest Tubb, interview.

27 Snow, *The Hank Snow Story,* 301.

28 Ibid., 318.

29 Hank Snow, interview.

30 Billy Byrd, interview by the author, March 10, 1994.

31 Hank Snow, interview.

17 OUT OF THE DOLDRUMS: THE COMEBACK OF 1949

1 Hal Smith, interview by the author, July 25, 1995.

2 Ernest Tubb, interview by the author, October 4, 1977.

3 Ibid. McGarr played on Tubb's June, November, and December 1949 sessions, then must have left for the West. He died in Nashville on May 20, 1951.

4 Never a song title, this was what Dollie Dearman called Olene, after so many years of referring to Elaine as "Blue-Eyed Elaine."

5 Dixie Deen, "The Woman behind the Man," *Music City News* 3.3 (September 1965): 9.

6 Justin Tubb, interview by the author, August 8, 1994.

7 Norma Barthel, letter, *Melody Trails* 6.1 (winter 1950): 2.

8 "I've got a brand new mama, about twenty-three; / a gal that thinks the whole world of me. / So why should I worry since you have gone? / I don't need you baby, I can always get along. / As long as I've got money, and diamond rings, / I just don't need another doggone thing."

9 Billy Byrd, interview by the author, March 10, 1994.

10 Public records of the Registrar of Deeds, Davidson County, Tennessee.

11 The Tubb family moved into 5402 Wakefield Drive on or about June 6, 1966, leaving dirty dishes in the sink and children's bicycles in the yard on Lawndale exactly as they were.

12 Billy Byrd, interview.

13 Outfitted by girlfriend Connie, as Oscar Davis remembered.

14 Billy Byrd, interview.

15 Johnny Sippel, "Folk Talent and Tunes," *Billboard* (October 15, 1949): 119.

16 "Decca puts Andrews Sisters, Bing on Religious Wax Series," *Billboard* (March 4, 1950): 18.

17 Ernest Tubb, interview.

18 Ibid.

19 *Joel Whitburn's Top Country Singles: 1944–1988* (Menomonee Falls, Wisc.: Record Research, Inc., 1989), 329.

20 Norma Barthel, letter, *The New Melody Trails* (fall 1949): 14.

18 GOOD SONGS AND GOOD TIMES

1 Johnny Sippel, "Folk Talent and Tunes," *Billboard* (November 15, 1952): 59.

2 Ruth Husky, interview by the author, February 25, 1995.

3 Quoted here from Tubb's account to Ralph Emery on *The Ralph Emery Show,* broadcast January 7, 1975.

4 It was big enough to justify major label executives offering big money for the master and the whole Blue Ridge company thrown in. One offered label owner Noah Adams of North Wilkesboro, North Carolina, $50,000. He refused, figuring if it was worth that much to the big boys, it must be worth more to him. Bill Clifton, who told this story to radio personality Eddie Stubbs, added that he was one of three persons who eventually bought the company in the mid-fifties from Adams for a figure considerably below $50,000.

5 Danny Dill, interview by the author, January 26, 1994. See also Whitney's account, reported in *Billboard*'s "Folk Talent and Tunes," November 3, 1951.

6 Charlie Walker, interview by the author, November 1, 1994.

7 Justin Tubb, interview by the author, August 8, 1994.

8 Johnny Sippel, "Folk Talent and Tunes," *Billboard* (December 9, 1950): 26.

9 WSM, 12:15–12:30, airing in early June 1952; definitely transcribed, as I compare those dates with his tour schedule.

10 Earliest for which I have found newspaper listings is June 6, 1952, at which time Ernest Tubb's half-hour came at 8:30, following Hank Williams's at 7:30 and Roy Acuff's at 8:00. Pretty good Friday night lineup, eh?

11 Recollections of resident fan Jerry Langley.

12 Mrs. Jimmie Rodgers to Jim Evans, May 18, 1951.

13 Dixie Deen, "The Woman behind the Man," *Music City News* 33 (September 1965): 9.

14 Ibid.

15 H. B. Teeter, "Nashville's Texas Troubadour," *Nashville Tennessean Magazine* (May 3, 1953): 9.

16 Ibid.

17 Carl Dieckman, "Two Fans Visit Ernest Tubb," *Ernest Tubb: The Original E.T.* by Norma Barthel (Privately published, 1984), 74.

18 It was during this incapacitation that Tubb's bandsmen Jack Drake and Billy Byrd were able to accompany Hank Williams to New York City and work *The Kate Smith Evening Hour.* Notice of Tubb's ailment is found in *Billboard* (April 12, 1952).

19 Ernest Tubb, qtd. on *The Ralph Emery Show,* January 9, 1975.

20 Jack Hurst, "Acuff and Tubb: 'Rediscovered' by crossover fans?" *Chicago Tribune,* October 11, 1979, n.p.

21 Eddy Arnold, interview by the author, November 23, 1993. The check was actually shown more recently—May 1995—to Don Cusic, who relayed the exact date and amount to me.

22 Ernest Tubb, interview by the author, October 4, 1977.

23 See photo on page 235 of Paul Kingsbury, ed., *Country: The Music and the Musicians* (Nashville: CMF/Abbeville Press, 1988).

24 Gabbard chronology pieced together from the "Folk Talent and Tunes" column in *Billboard,* 1950–1954. Nashville *Tennessean* newspaper account of Tubb's June 1955 Centennial Park concert has Gabbard with the band by that date.

25 Dickie Harris, interview by the author, June 4, 1994.

26 Johnny Sippel, "Folk Talent and Tunes," *Billboard* (May 13, 1950): 124; (September 2, 1950): 33 and 101; (September 29, 1951): 40; (October 20, 1951): 79; (November 10, 1951): 92; (May 24, 1952): 89; (August 2, 1952): 100; (November 29, 1952): 47; ibid., 131.

27 Teeter, "Nashville's Texas Troubadour," 9.

19 A TOUGH BUT MEMORABLE YEAR

1 Justin Tubb, interview by the author, August 8, 1994.

2 Douglas Glenn Tubb, interview by the author, May 4, 1994.

3 Justin Tubb, interview.

4 Ibid.

5 Johnny Sippel, "Folk Talent and Tunes," *Billboard* (December 20, 1952): 40.

6 Hank Snow, interview by the author, February 1, 1994.

7 Danny Dill, interview by the author, January 26, 1994.

8 Ibid.

9 "Plea for More Country Music Brings Op'ry Stars Half-Way 'Round World to Korea; 75,000 United Nations Men Entertained by Tubb, Childre, Snow," *Pickin' & Singin' News* 1.1, 8.

10 Hank Snow, with Jack Ownbey and Bob Burris, *The Hank Snow Story* (Urbana: University of Illinois Press, 1994), 345. Confirmed in my interview with Danny Dill, January 26, 1994.

11 Eddie Jones, "Reds Snitch Song, but Plan Fizzles," Nashville *Banner,* May 15, 1953, n.p.

12 Ernest Tubb, interview by the author, October 4, 1977.

13 Snow, *The Hank Snow Story,* 348.

14 Photo in Nashville *Banner* of April 2, 1953; a WSM photo of the homecoming has Tubb amused by the welcoming messages on hand-held signs by Marty Robbins, Tommy Sosebee, and others.

15 Johnny Bond, *Reflections: The Autobiography of Johnny Bond* (Los Angeles: JEMF Special Series no. 8, 1976), 27.

16 Ernest Tubb to Jim Evans, July 2, 1948. Evans's correspondence is now part of the Country Music Foundation collection.

17 Carrie Rodgers to Jim Evans, April 5, 1949.

18 "S.A. Singer's Discs Reissued," San Antonio *Light,* May 3, 1949, p. B-10.

19 Hank Snow, interview.

20 Ernest Tubb to Jim Evans, May 6, 1950.

21 Carrie Rodgers to Jim Evans, February 17, 1950.

22 Johnny Sippel, "Folk Talent and Tunes," *Billboard* (June 3, 1950): 33.

23 Johnny Sippel, "Folk Talent and Tunes," *Billboard* (April 12, 1952): 34.

24 Hank Snow, interview.

25 Johnny Sippel, "Folk Talent and Tunes," *Billboard* (July 12, 1952): 43.

26 Ernest Tubb, interview by Hairl Hensley, *Inside Music City,* October 29, 1977.

27 Snow, *The Hank Snow Story,* 353.

28 Meridian *Star,* November 5, 1952, p. 2.

29 Carrie Rodgers to Jim Evans, November 14, 1952.

30 Ernest Tubb to Jim Evans, February 3, 1953. All of these acts did perform, plus more that I will list later.

31 Carrie Rodgers to Jim Evans, undated (early 1953).

32 Carrie Rodgers to Jim Evans, April 22, 1953.

33 Hank Snow, interview.

34 Ernest Tubb, interview by Hairl Hensley.

35 Justin Tubb, interview.

36 Hank Snow, interview.

37 Mississippi Congressman W. A. Winstead had steered a resolution to that effect through the U.S. House of Representatives. Tubb surely was not happy that the word "hillbilly" got into the event's designation.

38 "25,000 Fans Attend Rodgers Dedication," *Pickin' & Singin' News* 1.2 (June 13, 1953): 1 and 6. Teeter's monument inscription—monument and engine now stand in Meridian's Highland Park, much closer into town, adjacent to the Jimmie Rodgers Museum—reads, "His is the music of America. He sang the songs of the people he loved, of a young nation growing strong. His was an America of glistening rails, thundering boxcars and rain-swept nights; of lonesome prairies, great mountains, and a high blue sky. He sang of the bayous and cotton fields, the wheated plains, of the little towns, the cities, and of the winding rivers of America. We listened. We understood."

39 Ernest Tubb to Jim Evans, August 22, 1953.

40 Ernest Tubb, letter, *Melody Trails* 8.3 (summer 1953): 3.

41 Otto Kitsinger, notes to *Justin Tubb: Rock It on Down to My House,* Bear Family records box, 1994.

42 Johnny Sippel, "Folk Talent and Tunes," *Billboard* (January 3, 1953): 59; (January 31, 1953): 40; (March 14, 1953): 48.

43 Justin Tubb, interview by Otto Kitsinger, April 13, 1994.

44 Ben A. Green, "Ernest Tubb Walks in Steps of Jimmie Rodgers to Win Fame; Justin Follows Dad," Nashville *Banner,* December 15, 1956, p. 3.

45 Ernest Tubb, qtd. on *The Ralph Emery Show,* January 8, 1975.

46 "Folk Talent and Tunes," *Billboard* (May 9, 1953): 39.

47 Ernest Tubb, "We Hear from Ernest Tubb," *Melody Trails* 8.3 (summer 1953): 3 and 8.

48 Quoted by Kitsinger, *Justin Tubb; Rock It on Down to My House.*

49 Tubb says "Aw, Ronny, now" as the camera cuts to him on a TV appearance, *Community Jamboree* for the National Guard, filmed in the spring of 1960.

50 Douglas Glenn Tubb, interview.

51 He is best known for "Skip a Rope" and "Two-Story House."

20 CHANGING TIMES

1 *Pickin' & Singin' News* (November 28, 1953): 3.

2 "Country Deejays Pick 8 All-Time Greats," *Billboard* (December 5, 1953): 48. Across the page from this story (on page 49), Ernest Tubb rates a full-page ad, plugging his last three Decca singles and listing Dub Albritten at the Record Shop address, along with James Denny at WSM, as contact for his bookings. The Albritten managerial announcement was delayed until the New Year, however.

3 Tubb was confined to bed with a "serious virus infection" the very next Saturday, November 28, according to the December 14 *Pickin' & Singin' News.*

4 "Tubb, Snow Said to Have Same Manager," *Pickin' & Singin' News* (December 24, 1953): 1–2.

5 Norma Barthel, "Country Music News and Notes," *Melody Trails* (fall 1954): 15.

6 Two other sources (see below)—a clip in the possession of Goldie Hill Smith and Norma Barthel's *Melody Trails*—indicate that the first broadcast of *Country Tune Parade* did not come until March 6.

7 "Tubb, Hill Take Eddy Arnold Spot on NBC Program," *Pickin' & Singin' News* (January 30, 1954): 1.

8 Goldie Hill Smith, interview by the author, January 27, 1995.

9 Ibid.

10 Ibid.

11 Norma Barthel, " 'Country Tune Parade' on NBC," *Melody Trails* 10.2 (spring 1954): 8.

12 Compiled from *Joel Whitburn's Top Country Singles, 1944–1993* (Menomonee Falls, Wisc.: Record Research, Inc., 1994): 384–385.

13 "This Week's Best Buys," *Billboard* (September 25, 1954): 57.

14 Ibid.

15 "Tubb, Snow Said to Have Same Manager," *Pickin' and Singin' News* (December 24, 1953): 1.

16 Ernest Tubb, "Our Star Writes," *Melody Trails* 10.3 (summer 1954): 3.

17 Ernest Tubb, "We Hear from E.T.," *Melody Trails* 11.1 (winter 1955): 3.

18 Albert Gannaway, interview by the author, February 15, 1994.

19 Bill Sachs, "Folk Talent and Tunes," *Billboard* (January 22, 1955): 16.

20 Albert Gannaway, interview by the author, February 15, 1994.

21 Typical is this mention from the February 12, 1955, "Folk Talent and Tunes" column in *Billboard:* "Flamingo Films shot its second group of TV films in Nashville last week. Featured were . . . Ernest Tubb . . ."

22 Howard Miller, *The Louvin Brothers: From Beginning to End* (Nashville: privately published, 1986), 51.

23 Billy Byrd, interview by the author, March 10, 1994.

24 October 15, January 7, March 31, and June 23.

25 Lynn Owsley, qtd. on *Nashville Nights with Carol Lee,* April 29, 1994.

26 Norma Barthel, "News about E.T.," *Melody Trails* 11.3 (July 1955): 11. Remember, Billy Byrd was a jazzman and Dickie Harris, in Tubb's own words, was a "hepcat."

27 Norma Barthel, "News about Our Star—E.T.," *Melody Trails* 11.7 (November 1955): 10.

28 Peaked at number 7 on the jukebox chart and number 10 on the disc jockey chart, according to *Joel Whitburn's Top Country Singles,* p. 385.

29 Justin Tubb, interview by the author, August 8, 1994.

30 Stonewall Jackson, interview by the author, March 28, 1995.

31 The song is credited to Vic's wife Lily so that Ernest Tubb Music could have the publishing.

32 Ernest Tubb, letter, "We Hear from E.T.," *Melody Trails* 12.6 (June 1956): 3.

33 Hank Snow, interview by the author, February 1, 1994.

34 Nashville *Tennessean,* issues of June 22, 26, and 27, 1955.

35 Gabe Tucker, telephone interview by the author, November 22, 1977.

36 Ibid.

37 Norma Barthel, "News about Our Star—E.T.," *Melody Trails* 11.6 (October 1955): 15.

38 Dickie Harris, interview by the author, June 4, 1994.

39 Billy Byrd, interview by the author, May 3, 1994.

40 Gabe Tucker, telephone interview.

41 "Hillbilly Stars Buy Station," Nashville *Tennessean,* April 20, 1956, n.p.

42 Hank Snow, interview.

43 *The Country Music Reporter* (November 10, 1956): 15.

44 Gabe Tucker, interview.

45 "Tubb, Wilburns and Gabe Tucker Tear Up Contract," *The Country Music Reporter* 1.9 (January 5, 1957): 2.

46 Gabe Tucker, interview.

21 THE GOOD THAT MEN DO

1 Hank Snow, interview by the author, February 1, 1994.

2 Dixie Deen, "The Woman behind the Man," *Music City News* 3.3 (September 1965): 9.

3 Byron Baker, telephone conversation by the author, May 9, 1994.

4 Deen "The Woman behind the Man," 9.

5 Ernest Tubb, letter, "To All E.T.F.C. Members Everywhere," *Melody Trails* 13.1 (winter 1957): 3.

6 Hank Snow, interview.

7 Margaret Jones, *Patsy: The Life and Times of Patsy Cline* (New York: Harper Collins, 1994), 90–91.

8 Ernest Tubb, interview by the author, October 4, 1977.

9 Jones, *Patsy: The Life and Times of Patsy Cline,* 90.

10 Ibid., 93.

11 Ernest Tubb, qtd. on *The Ralph Emery Show,* January 8, 1975.

12 Johnny Cash, "Special Tribute to Ernest Tubb," *Country Music* (January/February 1985): 43.

13 Edward Linn, "Country Singer: The Ernest Tubb Story," *Saga* May, 1957: 70.

14 Ernest Tubb, interview.

15 Linn, "Country Singer: The Ernest Tubb Story," 70.

16 Colin Escott with Martin Hawkins, *Good Rockin' Tonight: Sun Records and the Birth of Rock 'n' Roll* (New York: St. Martin's Press, 1991), 109.

17 One of many mistakes in my previously published Tubb discography articles was to call his "Home of the Blues" unreleased.

18 Douglas Glenn Tubb, interview by the author, May 4, 1994.

19 Bill Sachs, "Folk Talent and Tunes," *Billboard* (March 10, 1956): 58.

20 Linn, "Country Singer: The Ernest Tubb Story," 70.

21 Stonewall Jackson, interview by the author, March 28, 1995. Jackson's recreation of their conversation, as told to him later.

22 Stonewall Jackson, interview.

23 Ibid.

24 Ibid.

25 Ibid.

26 Ibid.

27 Charlie Walker, interview by the author, November 1, 1994.

28 Stonewall Jackson, interview.

29 Ibid.

30 Ibid.

22 MORE TOUGH TIMES: ROCK AND ROLL

1 Quoted by Margaret Jones in *Patsy: The Life and Times of Patsy Cline* (New York: Harper Collins, 1994), 102.

2 Ibid.

3 Stonewall Jackson, interview by the author, March 28, 1995.

4 Dickie Harris, interview by the author, June 4, 1994.

5 Hal Smith, interview by the author, July 25, 1995.

6 Stonewall Jackson, interview.

7 Ernest Tubb, letter, "E.T. Answers Our Questions," *Melody Trails* 14.1 (winter 1958): 12.

8 Johnnie Wright and Kitty Wells, interview by the author, April 6, 1995. Presley, late for a matinee show date in St. Louis, rushed back across the street to the hotel where he'd

left his billfold, Johnnie Wright remembers. Acuff insisted that the show start without him and finish without him, although he got back in plenty of time to come on. At Acuff's insistence, Presley was docked his $75 fee by promoter Oscar Davis. Kitty Wells remembers that Elvis was hurt: "I've never been treated that way in my life." To salvage his ego, Acuff would have been best served if Presley had been kept off the other shows as well. As opening act, he proved impossible to follow; after the third date, Acuff had him dropped from the tour altogether, vowing never to work with him again.

9   Ben A. Green, "Tubb Predicts Opry Artists Entering Best Tour Season," *Nashville Banner,* April 20, 1957, pp. 1–2.

10 Ernest Tubb, letter, "To All E.T.F.C. Members Everywhere," *Melody Trails* 13.1 (winter 1957): 3.

11 Casey Clark, interview by the author, August 16, 1994.

12 Pee Wee King, interview by the author, November 18, 1993.

13 Johnnie Wright and Kitty Wells, interview.

14 Ibid.

15 Pee Wee King, interview.

16 Johnnie Wright and Kitty Wells, interview.

17 Ibid.

18 Ibid.

19 Ernest Tubb, letter, "Ernest Answers Our Questions," *Melody Trails* 12.10 (October 1956): 10.

20 Norma Barthel, "Latest News of Our Star," *Melody Trails* 12.12 (December 1956): 3.

21 Norma Barthel, "Ernest Answers Our Questions," *Melody Trails* 12.11 (November 1956): 5.

22 Justin Tubb, interview by Otto Kitsinger, April 13, 1994, tape furnished to the author by Mr. Kitsinger.

23 Johnnie Wright and Kitty Wells, interview.

24 Hank Snow, with Jack Ownbey and Bob Burris, *The Hank Snow Story* (Urbana: University of Illinois Press, 1994), 358.

25 Billy Byrd, interview by the author, May 3, 1994.

26 Johnnie Wright and Kitty Wells, interview.

27 Billy Byrd, interview.

28 Douglas Glenn Tubb, interview by the author, May 4, 1994.

29 Billy Byrd, interview.

30 "Shooting by Tubb 'Private Matter,'" Nashville *Tennessean,* May 28, 1957, n.p.

31 Jack Hurst, *Grand Ole Opry* (New York: Harry N. Abrams, 1975), 282.

32 "Texas Troubador Arrested on Pistol Shooting Charge," Nashville *Banner,* May 27, 1957, n.p.

33 "Shooting by Tubb 'Private Matter,'" n.p.

34 Hurst, *Grand Ole Opry,* 282.

35 "Texas Troubadour Arrested on Pistol Shooting Charge," n.p.

36 "Shooting by Tubb 'Private Matter,'" n.p.

37   Ibid.

38   "Texas Troubadour Arrested on Pistol Shooting Charge," n.p.

39   Hurst, *Grand Ole Opry,* 286.

40   Ibid.

41   Ibid., 285.

42   "Ernest Tubb Suffers Cut Lip in Car Crash," Nashville *Banner,* April 27, 1954, n.p.

43   "Ernest Tubb Charged as Drunk," Nashville *Tennessean,* January 1, 1958, n.p.

44   Justin Tubb, interview by the author, August 8, 1994.

45   Joe Wilson, review of *Nashville Babylon: The Uncensored Truth and Private Lives of Country Music's Stars,* by Randall Riese, in *Journal of Country Music* 12.3 (1989): 51.

23   YEARS OF TRANSITION

1   "E.T. Answers Our Questions," *Melody Trails* 13.2 (April-June 1957): 11.

2   "E.T. Answers Our Questions," *Melody Trails* 13.3 (summer 1957): 3.

3   Dixie Deen, "The Woman behind the Man," *Music City News* (September 1965): 9. Dean Tubb, as he's now known, was his father's main photographer for the last years that the Texas Troubadour was on the road.

4   Bill Sachs, "Folk Talent and Tunes," *Billboard* (January 27, 1958): 93.

5   Bill Sachs, "Folk Talent and Tunes," *Billboard* (April 21, 1958): 55.

6   Stonewall Jackson, interview by the author, March 28, 1995.

7   Johnnie Wright and Kitty Wells, interview by the author, April 6, 1995.

8   Billy Byrd, interview by the author, May 3, 1994.

9   "Buddy Emmons: Pedal Steel King," *Guitar Player* (May 1976): 16.

10   Billy Byrd, interview.

11   Ernest Tubb, letter, *Melody Trails* 15.1 (winter 1959): 4.

12   Eddie Stubbs and Walt Trott, notes to the "Johnnie & Jack and the Tennessee Mountain Boys," Bear Family box, p. 62. BCD-15553. "Biographies of the Key Musicians: Harold Morrison."

13   Douglas Glenn Tubb, interview by the author, May 4, 1994.

14   Ibid.

15   Bill Anderson, interview by the author, June 2, 1994.

16   Douglas Glenn Tubb, interview.

17   Bill Anderson, interview.

18   Ibid.

19   Ibid. An interesting *Billboard* reference to Anderson from this time is found in the May 5, 1958, "Folk Talent and Tunes" column: "A new rockabilly trio comprising Bill Anderson of WJJC, Commerce, Georgia, Chuck Goddard of Trepur Records, and Dickie Henderson, young drummer, has been working personals through Georgia in recent weeks . . . Anderson's newest release on the TNT label couples 'No Song to Sing' and 'City Lights.' Deejays may obtain a copy by writing to TNT Records, 1422 W. Poplar Street, San Antonio."

20   Charlie Walker, interview by the author, November 1, 1994.

21 Ibid.

22 Another Harlan Howard tune! First charted May 11, 1959.

23 Charlie Walker, interview.

24 Skeeter Davis, *Bus Fare to Kentucky: The Autobiography of Skeeter Davis* (New York: Birch Lane Press, 1993), 179–180.

25 Ibid., 180.

26 Skeeter's chronology is off here. Tubb's "What Am I Living For," Decca 30759, predates Belew's "Am I That Easy to Forget," Decca 30842, by several weeks.

27 Ibid., 195.

28 Billy Byrd, interview by the author, March 10, 1994.

29 Davis, *Bus Fare to Kentucky: The Autobiography of Skeeter Davis,* 194.

30 Beulah Marie Harris, "I Saw Ernest Again," *Melody Trails* 15.2 (spring 1959): 5.

31 Bill Anderson, interview. Anderson knew Pete Drake in Atlanta; through Pete's brother Jack they got the *Midnite* gig, with the possible extra assistance of the show's announcer, Grant Turner. Turner played host at WSM each week to a visiting deejay, "Mr. DJ USA," and this was the week Goddard won that distinction. Typically, each winner played Tubb's *Midnite Jamboree.*

32 "Country Clippings," *Music Reporter* 3.43 (May 25, 1959): 52.

33 Davis, *Bus Fare to Kentucky: The Autobiography of Skeeter Davis,* 179.

34 Charlie Lamb, "Charlie's Column," *Music Reporter* 2.19 (December 23, 1957) 2, says, "Ernest Tubb has re-inked with Decca Records for another long term. Started there in 1940 and in this business, that's a long tenure."

35 "Owen Bradley Named C&W A&R Director For Decca Records," *Music Reporter* 2.35 (April 14, 1958): 1 and 10.

36 Ernest Tubb, letter, "Our Star Writes," *Melody Trails* 14.1 (winter 1958): 3.

37 Ernest Tubb, letter, *Melody Trails* 15.1 (winter 1959): 9.

38 Information combed from the Decca tape vaults for the Bear Family reissue set, *The Yellow Rose of Texas,* BCD-15688 (1993).

39 Ernest Tubb, letter, "We Hear From E.T.," *Melody Trails* 14.3 (fall 1958): 3.

40 Notes to *The Ernest Tubb Story,* Decca DXB-159 (1959).

41 The "warning" quoted above about these being "new recordings" was placed on the *inside* of the fold-out double album; therefore you could easily buy it before you knew *The Ernest Tubb Story* was all remakes.

42 From this October 1959 Michigan tour comes Walker's recollection of Tubb breaking his upper dental plate by biting into an apple on the golf course.

43 Hal Smith, interview by the author, July 25, 1995.

44 "Warner Bros. Signs Billy Byrd," *Music Reporter* 2.28 (February 9, 1959): 17.

45 Billy Byrd, interview.

46 "Buddy Emmons: Pedal Steel King," 38.

47 Douglas Glenn Tubb, interview.

48 "Buddy Emmons: Pedal Steel King," 38 and 40.

49 Tubb's only "Aw, Bobby, now" comes on "The Kind of Love She Gave to Me."

50 Charlie Walker, interview.

51 Many are the stories told of Ernest Tubb's returning his fee to a luckless promoter after a bad night. But he did this of his own choice; the band got paid just the same, out of Tubb's pocket.

52 Ernest Tubb, letter, "Ernest Tubb Writes," *Melody Trails* (January-February 1962): 3.

24 THE GREAT BAND:
THE TROUBADOUR CHAPTER

1 Leon Rhodes, interview by Eddie Stubbs, March 27, 1995.

2 Buddy Charleton, interview by Eddie Stubbs, January 2, 1994.

3 Ibid.

4 Ibid.

5 Jack Greene, interview by the author, April 24, 1995.

6 Cal Smith, qtd. on *Music City Tonight,* June 17, 1994.

7 "Folk Talent and Tunes," *Billboard* (January 27, 1958): 93.

8 Bob Pinson, interview by the author, April 26, 1995. Then a listener and neighbor of Smith in San Jose, he is now a senior colleague of mine at the CMF.

9 Cal Smith, qtd. on *The Ralph Emery Show,* March 26, 1973.

10 Cal Smith, qtd. on *Music City Tonight.*

11 Ernest Tubb, qtd. on *The Ralph Emery Show,* January 10, 1975.

12 Cal Smith, qtd. on *Nashville Nights with Carol Lee,* March 11, 1994.

13 Cal Smith, qtd. on *The Ralph Emery Show.*

14 Buddy Charleton, interview by Eddie Stubbs.

15 Ibid.

16 Ernest Tubb, letter, *The Troubadour* (summer 1965): 7.

17 Ibid.

18 Leon Rhodes, interview by Eddie Stubbs.

19 Buddy Charleton, interview by Eddie Stubbs.

20 Leon Rhodes, interview by Eddie Stubbs.

21 Bill Anderson, interview by the author, June 3, 1994.

22 Leon Rhodes, interview by Eddie Stubbs.

25 THE LAST GOOD YEARS

1 Dixie Deen, "The Woman behind the Man," *Music City News* 3.3 (September 1965): 11.

2 Charlie Walker, interview by the author, November 1, 1994.

3 Ibid.

4 [Alice from Dallas], letter, *Melody Trails* (January-February 1962): 2.

5 Ernest Tubb, letter, *Melody Trails* (January-February 1962): 3.

6 Jack Greene, interview by the author, April 24, 1995.

7 Buddy Charleton, interview by Eddie Stubbs, January 2, 1994.

8 Jack Greene, interview.

9 Ibid.

10 Leon Rhodes, interview by Eddie Stubbs, March 27, 1995.

11 Ibid.

12 Marshall Falwell, "E.T. Remembers," *Country Music* 2.8 (April 1974): 76.

13 Jack Greene interview. Cal Smith, in his version of the story on *Thanks, Troubadour, Thanks,* said that the date was in Fairfax, Virginia, that he had been drinking as well as Tubb, and was told to leave the bus after their heated exchange. He had to borrow $20 from Johnny Wiggins to help buy his bus ticket (and ultimately, part of Jack's), and the Justice boys were the two men who drove him to the D.C. bus station.

14 Ibid.

15 Leon Rhodes, interview by Eddie Stubbs.

16 Ibid.

17 Cal Smith, qtd. on *Thanks, Troubadour, Thanks,* TV documentary, Hallway Productions, 1987.

18 Jack Greene, interview.

19 Porter Wagoner, qtd. on *Thanks, Troubadour, Thanks.*

20 Lynn Owsley, qtd. on *Nashville Nights with Carol Lee,* March 11, 1994.

21 Jack Greene, interview.

22 Ibid.

23 Falwell, "E.T. Remembers," 76.

24 Jack Rice, "Ernest Tubb Walks On and On," *St. Louis Post Dispatch,* April 11, 1976, n.p.

25 Dr. George Duncan, qtd. on *Thanks, Troubadour, Thanks.*

26 Jack Greene, qtd. on *Thanks, Troubadour, Thanks.*

27 Cal Smith, qtd. on *Music City Tonight,* June 17, 1994.

28 Charlie Walker recalls seeing Ernest break his plate biting into a golf-course apple in 1959 (interview by the author, November 1, 1994). Cf. note 42, chap. 23.

29 *Music Reporter* 6.3 (August 14, 1961): 1.

30 Justin Tubb, interview by the author, August 8, 1994.

31 Parker today thinks he was still in Tulsa at the time, but contemporary sources usually call him "an Oklahoma city boy," and Thurston Moore's *Country Music Who's Who* gives his deejay affiliation then as KLPR, Oklahoma City.

32 Justin Tubb, interview.

33 Arleigh Duff, *Y'All Come—Country Music: Jack's Branch to Nashville* (Austin, Texas: Eakin Press, 1983), 186.

34 Sales figures supplied by Ping Hu of MCA Records, September 14, 1994.

35 Ernest Tubb, qtd. on *The Ralph Emery Show,* January 8, 1975.

36 Broadcast statement made by Justin Tubb on the *Midnite Jamboree,* January 1, 1995.

37 Ernest Tubb, qtd. on *The Ralph Emery Show,* January 8, 1975.

38 Ibid.

39 Leon Rhodes, interview by Eddie Stubbs.

40 Broadcast statement by Justin Tubb on the *Midnite Jamboree,* January 1, 1995.

41 All quoted sales figures come from MCA files, released by Ping Hu via John Carmichael, both of MCA, Inc., in a fax transmitted September 14, 1994. Unfortunately, they furnished only album sales figures.

42 Ernest Tubb, "A Message From E.T.," *The Troubadour* (fall 1962): 3.

43 Ernest Tubb, "E.T. Writes," *The Troubadour* 19.2 (summer 1963): 3. From a letter written to the fan club on his forty-ninth birthday, February 9, 1963.

26 LORETTA, A GOLD RECORD, THE HALL OF FAME, AND A TV SHOW

1 "Loretta Lynn," special pamphlet, *The Ernest Tubb Fan Club, 1964*, p. 2.

2 Loretta Lynn with George Vecsey, *Coal Miner's Daughter* (Chicago: Henry Regnery Company, 1976), 120.

3 Barthel, *The Ernest Tubb Fan Club 1964*, 2.

4 Ernest Tubb, notes to *Ernest Tubb and Loretta Lynn*, Decca DL 74639 (1965).

5 Loretta Lynn, qtd. on *Thanks, Troubadour, Thanks*, TV documentary, Hallway Productions, 1987.

6 Buddy Charleton, interview by Eddie Stubbs, January 2, 1994.

7 Barthel, *The Ernest Tubb Fan Club 1964*, 2.

8 Buddy Charleton, interview by Eddie Stubbs.

9 Lynn, *Coal Miner's Daughter*, 120.

10 Ibid.

11 Bill Anderson, interview by the author, June 2, 1994.

12 "E.T.'s Gold Record," *The Troubadour* 21.3 (summer 1965): 4.

13 Ernest Tubb, qtd. on *The Ralph Emery Show*, January 6, 1975.

14 Johnny Bond, *The Tex Ritter Story* (New York: Chappell & Co., Inc., 1976), 180.

15 Ibid.

16 Full copy on file at the Country Music Foundation.

17 Ernest Tubb, qtd. on *The Ralph Emery Show*.

18 *The Pamper Pamphlet* 3.7 (July 1967): 8.

19 Hal Smith, interview by the author, July 25, 1995.

20 Ibid.

21 Ernest Tubb, interview by Hairl Hensley, *Inside Music City*, October 29, 1977.

22 Hal Smith, interview.

23 Well, in Buddy's case, a hat at least, as he usually kept his head down, facing his steel guitar strings.

24 "Ernest Tubb Stars in New TV Series," *Music City News* 3.3 (September 1965): 4.

25 Hal Smith, interview.

26 Ibid.

27 Ernest Tubb, interview by Hairl Hensley.

27 DECLINE SETS IN

1 "E.T. Answers Our Questions," *Melody Trails* 13.2 (April-June 1957): 11.

2 Douglas Glenn Tubb had resurfaced as a top-notch writer himself by penning Henson Cargill's 1967–1968 smash hit with Jack Moran, "Skip a Rope." The same twosome

wrote Tubb's "Tommy's Doll," which in 1969 was the flip side of "Saturday Satan Sunday Saint."

3 Leon Rhodes, interview by Eddie Stubbs, March 27, 1995.

4 Ibid.

5 Jack Greene, interview by Eddie Stubbs, June, 1993.

6 Cal Smith, qtd. on *The Ralph Emery Show,* March 26, 1973.

7 Jackie Pyke, "I Talked with Ernest Tubb," *The Ernest Tubb Discography: 1936–1969* by Norma Barthel (Privately published, 1970), 20.

8 *Keeping up with Ernest Tubb & the Texas Troubadours* (March 1968): 1.

9 *Keeping up with Ernest Tubb & the Texas Troubadours* (March 1969): 1.

10 Leon Rhodes, interview by Eddie Stubbs.

11 Ibid.

12 Billy Parker, telephone interview by the author, January 27, 1994.

13 Ibid.

14 Billy Parker, qtd. on *Thanks, Troubadour, Thanks,* TV documentary, Hallway Productions, 1987.

15 Billy Parker, telephone interview.

16 Hear him on Tubb records of the 1970–1971 period, particularly "Shenandoah Waltz."

17 See *Melody Trails* (autumn 1970).

18 Jack Leonard, qtd. on *Thanks, Troubadour, Thanks.*

19 Steve Chapman, qtd. on *Thanks, Troubadour, Thanks.*

20 Billy Byrd, interview by the author, May 3, 1994.

21 Ibid.

22 Buddy Charleton, interview by the author, January 2, 1994.

23 Ibid.

24 Ibid.

25 Billy Byrd, interview.

26 Ibid.

27 Don Helms, interview by the author, August 4, 1994.

28 Ibid.

29 Pete Mitchell, qtd. on *Nashville Nights with Carol Lee,* April 29, 1994.

30 Keith Bilbrey, qtd. on *Nashville Nights with Carol Lee,* March 11, 1994.

31 Dave Tianen, "Ageless Ernest Aims at More Than Six Years," *Green Bay Press Gazette,* February 19, 1982, n.p.

32 Jane Sanderson, "The 'New Way' Is Old Hat for Tubb," *Memphis Press-Scimitar,* January 3, 1975, n.p.

33 Pyke, "I Talked With Ernest Tubb," 23.

34 Gene Grey, "Tubb Lights Up Crippled Fan" (Binghamton, New York) *Evening Press,* March 5, 1978, p. 5A.

35 Kenn Murrah, "Audiences Same, Ernest Tubb Says," *Newport News Daily Press,* September 14, 1975, n.p.

36 Bob Claypool, "The Elder Statesman," *Houston Post,* April 22, 1973, p. 23.

37 John Moulder, "Ernest Tubb: Dirty David's Foul Mouth Hurts Country," *Rambler,* December 16, 1976, pp. 13–14.

38 Michael Willard, "Grand Ole Opry Quits Skid Row," *Pittsburgh Press,* October 8, 1972, n.p.

39 Bill Hance, "Opry Move Leaves Void on Broadway," *Nashville Banner,* March 18, 1974, n.p.

40 Bill Anderson, interview by the author, June 2, 1994.

41 Ernest Tubb to Bill French, February 29, 1972. Copy furnished by Mrs. Donna DiVito, daughter of Mr. French.

28 THE END OF LONG-TERM RELATIONSHIPS

1 "Ernest Tubb, 'The Texas Troubadour,' " *Ernest Tubb 1975* (Roland, Okla.: E.T.F.C. Enterprises, 1976), 3.

2 Ibid.

3 Bill Hance, "Ernest Tubb's Long Marriage on the Rocks," *Nashville Banner,* May 8, 1975, n.p.

4 Ibid.

5 Norma Barthel, "Summing Up 1975," *Ernest Tubb 1975,* p. 48.

6 John Moulder, "Ernest Tubb: Dirty David's Foul Mouth Hurts Country," *The Rambler* (December 16, 1976): 14.

7 Ernest Tubb, interview by Hairl Hensley, *Inside Music City,* October 29, 1977.

8 Charles Seabrook, "Tubb Walking Floor Over New Music Row," *Atlanta Journal,* April 29, 1977, p. 8-A.

9 Ernest Tubb, interview by Hairl Hensley.

10 Bradley retired in January, and Kapp died March 1, 1976. Curiously, when I interviewed Tubb in October 1977, he mistakenly thought Kapp was still alive, though in a vegetative condition.

11 Bill Anderson, interview by the author, June 2, 1994.

12 Ernest Tubb, interview by Bob Allen, August 29, 1978. Tape on file at Country Music Foundation.

13 "Ernest Tubb Remembered," *Country Music* 111 (January/February 1985): 49.

14 Ernest Tubb, qtd. on *The Ralph Emery Show,* January 9, 1975.

15 Gene Grey, "Tubb Lights Up Crippled Fan" (Binghamton, New York) *Evening Press,* March 5, 1978, p. 5-A.

16 Dave Tianen, "Ageless Ernest Aims at More Than Six Years," *Green Bay Press Gazette,* February 19, 1982, n.p.

17 "45-Year Veteran Still Going Strong," *Oklahoma City Oklahoman,* February 5, 1978, n.p.

18 Jack Hurst, "New Album Says 'Happy Birthday' to Ernest Tubb," *Chicago Tribune,* March 15, 1979, n.p.

19 Don Rhodes, "Ernest Tubb Ranks as Singing Legend," *Augusta Chronicle,* January 8, 1972, n.p.

20 It was there, on the second floor of a small yellow building, that I interviewed Justin the day Elvis Presley died, August 16, 1977.

21 Justin Tubb, interview by the author, August 16, 1977.

22 Lynn Harvey, "Ernest Tubb Record Shop Open On Row," *Nashville Tennessean,* June 3, 1976, pp. 1 and 18.

23 Photo by Jennifer Bohler with caption, "The Country Column," *Cash Box,* May 19, 1979, p. 36. The story carries the amiable photo of all four partners—Justin Tubb, Ernest Tubb, Charles Mosley, and David McCormick—cutting the ribbon.

24 Stockholders' Agreement, on file at Nashville's Probate Court under the contested Ernest Tubb estate.

25 Justin Tubb, interview by the author, August 8, 1994.

26 Gene Grey, "Tubb Lights Up Crippled Fan" (Binghamton, New York) *Evening Press,* March 5, 1978, p. 5-A.

29   A LEGEND WITH A LEGACY

1 Jack Hurst, "Old Pal, New Label Put Tubb on Top," *Chicago Tribune,* September 7, 1978, n.p.

2 *ETFC Newsletter* (September-October 1977): 1.

3 Ernest Tubb, interview by Hairl Hensley, *Inside Music City,* October 29, 1977.

4 *ETFC Newsletter* (November-December 1977): 2.

5 Ernest Tubb, interview by Bob Allen, August 29, 1978.

6 Hurst, "Old Pal, New Label Put Tubb on Top," n.p.

7 Pete Drake, interview by Bob Allen, August 29, 1978.

8 Laura Eipper, "Opry's Tubb Celebrates Special 65th," *Nashville Tennessean,* February 12, 1979, n.p.

9 David MacKenzie, "Country Pals Go on Record for Legendary Ernest Tubb," *Tulsa Daily World,* April 13, 1979, n.p.

10 Ibid.

11 See discography for details. Tubb mentioned working on this song at the time of my interview with him October 4, 1977.

12 Nashville *Tennessean,* April 11, 1979, p. 25.

13 The author was in attendance that night and writes from personal memory.

14 Jack Greene, interview by the author, April 24, 1995.

15 Tubb played the Lone Star Cafe three times, I know: December 14, 1978; December 16, 1979; and June 28, 1982. He played the Nelson picnic in 1979 and 1980, and on an earlier Fourth of July—the nation's Bicentennial Day, in fact (1976)—was on the bill with Nelson at a Kerrville, Texas, festival, ruined that day by torrential rains.

16 Owsley's recollections on a special *Midnite Jamboree* tribute to Tubb, the Saturday night after his death, September 8, 1984.

17 Ronnie Dale, qtd. on *Nashville Nights with Carol Lee,* April 29, 1994.

18 Hoot Borden, "Hoot's Report," *Keeping up with E.T.,* September 1979, 3–4.

19 Jack Greene, interview.

20 Lynn Owsley, telephone conversation with the author, May 24, 1995.

21 Ronnie Dale, qtd. on *Nashville Nights with Carol Lee.*

22 Ibid.

23 A practical joke Owsley once sprung at the expense of Tubb and Jimmy Day was to put Day's beer cases in the spot normally reserved for Tubb's fruit cocktail. The cans ended up on the bus floor, with Tubb cursing, "That alcoholic son-of-a-bitch. Before this bus leaves Nashville again, I want another cooler just for him."

24 Ernest Tubb to Bill French, letter dated "On Tour, Chelsea, Okla.," August 13, 1981.

25 Buddy Charleton, interview by Eddie Stubbs, January 2, 1994.

26 Lynn Owsley, telephone conversation.

27 Ibid.

28 Buddy Charleton, interview by Eddie Stubbs.

29 Justin Tubb, interview by the author, August 8, 1994.

30 Ernest Tubb, qtd. on *The Ralph Emery Show,* January 10, 1975.

31 Ernest Tubb, interview by Hairl Hensley.

32 Ronnie Dale, qtd. on *Nashville Nights with Carol Lee.*

33 Buddy Charleton, qtd. on *Nashville Nights with Carol Lee,* March 11, 1994.

34 Jack Greene, qtd. on *Nashville Nights with Carol Lee,* March 11, 1994.

35 Lynn Owsley, telephone conversation.

36 Junior Brown, interview by the author, April 20, 1994.

30 THE CURTAIN FALLS

1 "Troubles for the Troubadour?" *Raleigh Times,* October 19, 1982, n.p.

2 "Tubb's Vocal Woes Blamed on Cold," *Omaha World-Herald,* August 9, 1982, n.p.

3 Earl Moseley, "Memphis Shows Admiration For Ernest Tubb," *Amarillo Daily News,* August 30, 1982, n.p.

4 Justin Tubb, interview by the author, August 8, 1994.

5 *Ernest Tubb Fan Club* (winter 1983): 1.

6 *Ernest Tubb Fan Club* (spring 1983): 1.

7 *Ernest Tubb Fan Club* (summer 1983): 1.

8 Justin Tubb, "Ernest Tubb Remembered," *Country Music* 111 (January-February 1985): 49.

9 Ibid.

10 Loretta Lynn, qtd. on *Thanks, Troubadour, Thanks,* TV documentary, Hallway Productions, 1987.

11 Justin Tubb, "Ernest Tubb Remembered," *Country Music* 111, January-February, 1985: 49.

12 Hank Snow, interview by the author, February 1, 1994.

13 "Rumor City," p. 2; "Editorial," p. 3, *Country Music Pioneer Update* 1.1 (April 1984): 2–3.

14 Clyde Moody, "Letter from the President," *Country Music Pioneer Update* 1.3 (June 1984): 1–2.

15 Clyde Moody, "Letter from the President," *Country Music Pioneer Update* 1.4–5 (July-August 1984): 1–2.

16 Ibid., 2.

17 Clyde Moody, "Letter from the President," *Country Music Pioneer Update* 1.6 (September 1984): 1–2.

18 "Now Is the Time to Rally," *Country Music Pioneer Update* 1.6 (September 1984): 3.

19 Justin Tubb, qtd. on *Thanks, Troubadour, Thanks.*

20 Porter Wagoner, qtd. on *Thanks, Troubadour, Thanks.*

21 Cal Smith, qtd. on. *Thanks, Troubadour, Thanks.*

22 Jack Greene, interview by the author, April 24, 1995.

23 "Opry Star Ernest Tubb Dies," *Nashville Banner,* September 6, 1984, pp. 1 and 10.

24 Bob Oermann, "Tubb Dies Surrounded by Family, Stars," Nashville *Tennessean,* September 7, 1984, pp. 1 and 4.

25 Douglas Glenn Tubb, interview by the author, May 3, 1994.

26 "Grand Ole Opry Pays Respect to Ernest Tubb," Nashville *Tennessean,* September 9, 1984.

27 Ibid.

28 Justin Tubb, letter, *The Troubadour* 5 (summer 1986): 2.

29 Justin Tubb, "Q & A," *The Troubadour* (late 1986; no volume, exact date, or page).

30 Quoted from Justin Tubb's Probate Court filing, November 19, 1984.

31 Complete list in the large Davidson County Probate Court Ernest Tubb file.

32 "Tubb Estate Picked Clean by IRS, Debts," *Nashville Banner,* July 29, 1986, n.p.

33 A combined Justin Tubb/Ernest Tubb Fan Club petered out at the end of 1987, after two years and eight months. Norma Barthel then restarted a separate Ernest Tubb Memorial Fan Club; its last newsletter appeared September 3, 1990. She has been made the honorary president of the Texas Troubadours Fan Club, initiated in the spring of 1994 when Jack Leonard, Ronnie Dale, Lynn Owsley, and others hit the road with a revamped group drawn from the lineup late in Tubb's career.

34 Sarah Ellen Baker Tubb Ashton was living with Jewell in a house bought by Ernest in Franklin, Tennessee, when she died at age eighty-four in December 1967. Calvin Robert Tubb Sr. died July 15, 1971, near Kemp, three months shy of age eighty-five.

31 A SUMMING UP: LEGACIES—
LASTING AND OTHERWISE

1 Doug Green, "Ernest Tubb Remembered," *Country Music* 111 (January-February 1985): 48.

2 RCA Victor LSP-3371.

3 Professor Jimmie Rogers of the University of Arkansas in his fine lyrical studies has called it "the sincerity contract," and says that to some degree any successful country artist will establish that with his fans.

4 Justin Tubb, interview by the author, August 8, 1994.

5 Ibid.

6   Danny Dill, interview by the author, January 26, 1994.

7   Ibid.

8   Cal Smith, qtd. on *Thanks, Troubadour, Thanks,* TV documentary, Hallway Productions, 1987.

9   Buddy Charleton, interview by Eddie Stubbs, January 2, 1994.

10 Eddy Arnold, interview by the author, November 23, 1993.

11 Justin Tubb, interview.

12 All recordings made between 1936 and 1975 are now reissued or about to be on four CD boxes by Germany's Bear Family Records. The later (Pete Drake-produced) material is also available in many forms; see discography for release information.

13 Lynn Owsley, telephone interview by the author, May 24, 1995.

THE ERNEST TUBB DISCOGRAPHY

INTRODUCTION

Perhaps the term "sessionography" would more accurately describe this work, although I have used "discography" in the sense of a chronological session listing of all tracks, issued or unissued, ever since I first undertook a study of Ernest Tubb's recording career for the *Journal of Country Music* some fifteen years ago. These pages supersede all Tubb discographies I have previously prepared, either for that journal (in two parts) or for Bear Family Records (three installments so far). The suggestions and advice of Joe Specht, Donna DiVito, Geoff Hayes, and others have greatly aided the task of excising errors, filling in omissions, and reconciling inconsistencies from those former works, though the mistakes then and now are solely my responsibility.

"Master #" lists company master or matrix numbers, with prefixes where applicable. Decca Records for years used both Nashville ("NT," "N," then "NA") and New York matrix numbers for recordings made in Nashville; I list both, giving precedence for sequencing to the Nashville series. For those recordings with both Decca and World master numbers assigned, I have arbitrarily given top listing to Decca. The number of takes on a given recording was known in so few cases (percentage-wise) that only rarely is its existence hinted at, as when alternate takes were issued. It is certainly possible that I have overlooked the existence of some issued alternate takes; collectors, let me know.

Spelling and punctuation on song title and composer names generally follow label usage, however odd or inconsistent those may often be. The exceptions on which I exercised editorial control are noted. Publisher credits on songs—an addition to my earlier Tubb discographies—also follow record label citations or, in the case of unissued tracks, company file information where available. Explanatory notes offer song histories or sources of interest and also point out the occasional editorial correction.

The "Singles" and "LPs" columns list only domestic (U.S.) parent record company releases—original issues and reissues. "Singles" include all 78 rpm issues, all 45 rpm singles and all 45 rpm extended plays. Where a given recording was issued on both 78 and 45 speeds, both numbers are listed, since Decca for many years (even past the demise of the

78) prefixed their 45s with "9-". Under "LPs" (long plays), I have lumped together all ten-inch vinyl releases, all twelve-inch vinyl releases (mono and stereo numbers, the latter almost always differing from the former by the addition of an initial "7"), sixteen-inch World transcription release numbers (often unique to a given track), and compact disc release numbers.

Date, site, time, and producer are known in most cases. Session personnel, a key interest to fans and scholars alike, reflects some educated guesswork, particularly for the period between 1949 and 1957. Careful listening, knowledge of Tubb's band members at a given time, and musicians' recollections become the discographer's sole recourse, because extant company files are not consistently specific for personnel until 1958. Undocumented overdub sessions become a problem after 1977.

I have not included recordings by Tubb's Texas Troubadours, even in cases of shared sessions. These would make an interesting separate study. Nor have I included transcribed performances other than world.

The author welcomes corrections and additions, mailed to his attention at the Country Music Foundation, 4 Music Square East, Nashville, TN 37203.

LIST OF ABBREVIATIONS (in order of occurrence)

BS	RCA Bluebird master number prefix
B-	RCA Bluebird 78 rpm release number prefix
LSP	RCA Victor stereo LP prefix
DLA	Decca Los Angeles master number prefix
9-	Decca 45 rpm release number prefix (dropped 1961)
ED	Decca 45 rpm extended-play release number prefix
DL	"Decca Longplay"—33 rpm album release number prefix
MCAD	MCA compact disc release number prefix
L	Decca and World Los Angeles master number prefix
A	Decca 78 rpm album release number prefix
W-	World release number prefix
C	Decca and World Chicago master number prefix
800-	World hillbilly series release number prefix
-CD	World release number suffix
VL	Vocalion 33 rpm long-play album release number prefix
-F	World release number suffix
-E	World release number suffix
NT	Earliest Decca Nashville master number prefix
N	Next earliest Decca Nashville master number prefix
NA	Most common Decca Nashville master number prefix (1949–1975)
DXB	Mono release number prefix, *The Ernest Tubb Story*
DXSA	Stereo release number prefix, *The Ernest Tubb Story*
2-	MCA Records double-album release number prefix

FG	First Generation 33 rpm and 45 rpm release number prefix
CL	Cachet Records album release number prefix
TV	First Generation Records LP release number prefix
LL	LaserLight Records compact disc release number prefix
SOR	Step One Records compact disc release number prefix
CS	Cachet Records 45 rpm release number prefix
FGS	First Generation Records 45 rpm release number prefix
AW	Award Records 45 rpm release number prefix
SF	Sound Factory Records 45 rpm release number prefix
MG	Mickey Gilley Records 33 rpm release number prefix
SW	Soundwaves Records 45 rpm release number prefix
SWS	Soundwaves Records 33 rpm release number prefix
WB	Warner Brothers Records 45 rpm release number prefix
EL	Elektra Records 33 rpm release number prefix
AHL	RCA Records 33 rpm release number prefix

DISCOGRAPHY

10-27-36 Texas Hotel; San Antonio, Texas. 1:00-2:15 P.M. Producer: Eli Oberstein. Vocal: Ernest Tubb. Rhythm guitar: Ernest Tubb.

Master #	Title-Composers-Publishers	Singles	LPs
BS 02952	THE PASSING OF JIMMIE RODGERS (Elsie McWilliams) Peer-Southern Music, Inc.	B-6693	LSP-4073
BS 02953	THE LAST THOUGHTS OF JIMMIE RODGERS (Elsie McWilliams) Peer-Southern Music, Inc.	B-6693	LSP-4073
BS 02954	MARRIED MAN BLUES (Ernest Tubb) American Music, Inc.	B-8899	
BS 02955	MEAN OLD BEDBUG BLUES (Ernest Tubb)	B-8899*	
BS 02956	MY MOTHER IS LONELY (Ernest Tubb) American Music, Inc.	B-8966	
BS 02957	THE RIGHT TRAIN TO HEAVEN (Ernest Tubb) American Music, Inc.	B-8966	

03-02-37 Texas Hotel; San Antonio, Texas. 2:15-2:30 P.M. Producer: Eli Oberstein. Vocal: Ernest Tubb. Rhythm guitar: Ernest Tubb. Lead guitar: Merwyn J. Buffington (1).

BS 07475	THE T.B. IS WHIPPING ME (Ernest Tubb)	B-7000	RCA 9507
BS 07476	SINCE THAT BLACK CAT CROSSED MY PATH (1) (Elsie McWilliams) Peer-Southern Music, Inc.	B-7000	

*On July 25, 1993, Otto Kitsinger told me that B-8899, by no means the rarest Tubb Bluebird—probably the least rare, in fact—just sold at auction for $111.

04-04-40 Rice Hotel; Houston, Texas. Time: Unknown. Producer: Dave Kapp. Vocal: Ernest Tubb. Rhythm guitar: Ernest Tubb. Lead guitar: Jimmie Short.

92006	BLUE-EYED ELAINE (Ernest Tubb)	5825
	American Music, Inc.	46093
		9-46093
92007	I'LL NEVER CRY OVER YOU (Ernest Tubb)	5846
	American Music, Inc.	46007
92008	I'LL GET ALONG SOMEHOW (Ernest Tubb)	5825
	American Music, Inc.	46092
		9-46092
92009	YOU BROKE A HEART (THAT WAS BREAKING FOR YOU) (Ernest Tubb) American Music, Inc.	5846

10-28-40 Los Angeles, California. Time: Unknown. Producer: Unknown. Vocal: Ernest Tubb. Rhythm guitar: Ernest Tubb. Lead guitar: Dick Ketner.

DLA 2221	I AIN'T GONNA LOVE YOU ANYMORE (Ernest Tubb) American Music, Inc.	5900
DLA 2222	I'M GLAD I MET YOU AFTER ALL (Ernest Tubb) American Music, Inc.	5910
DLA 2223	I CARED FOR YOU MORE THAN I KNEW (Mrs. Jimmie Rodgers) American Music, Inc.	5938
DLA 2224	YOU'LL LOVE ME TOO LATE (Ernest Tubb) American Music, Inc.	5920

10-29-40 Los Angeles, California. Time: Unknown. Producer: Unknown. Vocal: Ernest Tubb. Rhythm guitar: Ernest Tubb. Lead guitar: Dick Ketner.

DLA 2225	I'VE REALLY LEARNED A LOT (Ernest Tubb) American Music, Inc.	6076
DLA 2226	SWELL SAN ANGELO (Ernest Tubb) American Music, Inc.	5938
DLA 2227	I KNOW WHAT IT MEANS TO BE LONELY (Ernest Tubb) American Music, Inc.	6054
DLA 2228	PLEASE REMEMBER ME (Ernest Tubb) American Music, Inc.	5910

10-30-40 Los Angeles, California. Time: Unknown. Producer: Unknown. Vocal: Ernest Tubb. Rhythm guitar: Ernest Tubb. Lead guitar: Dick Ketner.

DLA 2231	MY RAINBOW TRAIL (Elsie McWilliams) American Music, Inc.	5993
DLA 2232	LAST NIGHT I DREAMED (Ernest Tubb) American Music, Inc.	5920
DLA 2233	I'M MISSING YOU (Mrs. Jimmie Rodgers) American Music, Inc.	5958
DLA 2234	MY BABY AND MY WIFE (Ernest Tubb) American Music, Inc.	5900

04-26-41 Biggs Studio; Dallas, Texas. Time: Unknown. Producer: Dave Kapp. Vocal:
Ernest Tubb. Bass: Unknown. Rhythm guitar: Ernest Tubb. Steel guitar: Fay
"Smitty" Smith (1). Lead guitar: Fay "Smitty" Smith.

93673	WALKING THE FLOOR OVER YOU (Ernest Tubb)	5958	DL 5301
	American Music, Inc.	46006	DL 8291
		(A-808)	MCAD-10086
		9-46006	DL 4010
		(9-146)	DL 74010
		ED 2356	
93674	WHEN THE WORLD HAS TURNED YOU DOWN	6023	
	(Ernest Tubb) American Music, Inc.	46092	
		9-46092	
93675	OUR BABY'S BOOK (1) (Ernest Tubb)	6040	MCAD-10086
	American Music, Inc.	46093;	
		9-46093	
		ED 2769	
93676	I'LL ALWAYS BE GLAD TO TAKE YOU BACK	5993	DL 5301
	(Ernest Tubb) American Music, Inc.	46006	DL 8291
		(A-808)	
		9-46006	
		(9-146)	
		ED 2356	
93677	MEAN MAMA BLUES (Ernest Tubb)	5976	
	American Music, Inc.	46162	
		9-46162	
93678	I WONDER WHY YOU SAID GOODBYE	5976	
	(Ernest Tubb) American Music, Inc.	46007	

11-17-41 Chicago, Illinois. Time: Unknown. Producer: Dave Kapp. Vocal: Ernest Tubb.
Bass: Unknown. Rhythm guitar: Ernest Tubb. Lead guitar: Fay "Smitty"
Smith. Steel guitar: Fay "Smitty" Smith (1).

93791	I AIN'T GOIN' HONKY TONKIN' ANYMORE	6007
	(Ernest Tubb) American Music, Inc.	46125
		9-46125
93792	I HATE TO SEE YOU GO (Homer Hargrove-Ernest	6084
	Tubb) American Music, Inc.	46091
		9-46091
93793	TIME AFTER TIME (Jimmie Short-Leon Short)	6023
	American Music, Inc.	46091
		9-46091
93794	FIRST YEAR BLUES (Ernest Tubb)	6007
	American Music, Inc.	
93795	JUST ROLLIN' ON (Ernest Tubb)	
	American Music, Inc.	
93796	THERE'S NOTHING MORE TO SAY (Ernest Tubb)	6076
	American Music, Inc.	

| 93797 | WASTING MY LIFE AWAY (Ernest Tubb) American Music, Inc. | 6054 | |
| 93798 | YOU MAY HAVE YOUR PICTURE (1) (Ernest Tubb) American Music, Inc. | 6040 | |

07-17-42 Los Angeles, California. 11:00 A.M.-1:30 P.M. Producer: Unknown. Vocal: Ernest Tubb. Bass: Wesley Tuttle. Rhythm guitar: Ernest Tubb; Charles Quirk. Lead guitar: Eddie Tudor.

L 3099	THAT SAME OLD STORY (Fleming Allan-Ernest Tubb) American Music, Inc.	6084	
L 3100	TRY ME ONE MORE TIME (Ernest Tubb) American Music, Inc.	6093 46047 (A-808) ED 2357 9-46047 (9-146)	DL 5301 DL 8291
L 3101	YOU NEARLY LOSE YOUR MIND (Ernest Tubb) American Music, Inc.	6067 46125 9-46125	MCAD-10086
L 3102	THAT'S WHEN IT'S COMING HOME TO YOU (Lois Snapp-Ernest Tubb) American Music, Inc.	6093	
L 3103	I DON'T WANT YOU AFTER ALL (Ernest Tubb) American Music, Inc.		
L 3104	I'M WONDERING HOW (Ernest Tubb) American Music, Inc.	6067	

01-13-44 Los Angeles, California. Time: Unknown. Producer: Joe Perry. Vocal: Ernest Tubb. Bass: Herbert M. "Tommy" Paige. Rhythm guitar: Ernest Tubb; Melvin Leon Short. Fiddle: Johnny Sapp. Lead guitar: Erwin Jimmie Short.

L 3279 L 50148	TOMORROW NEVER COMES (Johnny Bond-Ernest Tubb) Cross Music, Inc.	6106 46289 9-46289	W-20 MCAD-10086
L 3280 L 50149	SOLDIER'S LAST LETTER (Henry Stewart-Ernest Tubb) Cross Music, Inc.	6098 46047 (A-808) 9-46047 (9-146) ED 2357	DL 8291 DL 4647 DL 74657 DL 5301 W-22 MCAD-10086
L 3281 L 50150	CARELESS DARLIN' (Lou Wayne-Bob Shelton-Ernest Tubb) Cross Music, Inc.	6110 46048	W-21
L 3282 L 50151	YESTERDAY'S TEARS (Ernest Tubb) American Music, Inc.	6098 46162 9-46162	W-20

01-15-44 Los Angeles, California. Time: Unknown. Producer: Joe Perry. Vocal: Ernest Tubb. Bass: Tommy Paige. Rhythm guitar: Ernest Tubb; Leon Short. Fiddle: Johnny Sapp. Lead guitar: Jimmie Short.

L 3287	THOSE SIMPLE THINGS ARE WORTH A MILLION		W-22
L 50156	NOW (Jewel Mathes–Ernest Tubb)		W-609
	American Music, Inc.		
L 3288	ANSWER TO "WALKING THE FLOOR OVER YOU"	46029	W-21
L 50157	(Ernest Tubb) American Music, Inc.	(A-529)	W-609
L 3289	YOU WON'T EVER FORGET ME	46031	W-23
L 50158	(Lois Snapp-Ernest Tubb) Cross Music Co.	(A-529)	W-609
		9-46031	
L 3290	KEEP MY MEM'RY IN YOUR HEART (Ernest Tubb)	6106	W-20
L 50159	Cross Music, Inc.		
L 3291	I LOST MY ACE OF HEARTS (Jimmie Short)	W-21	
L 50160	Cross Music Co.		
L 3292	THOUGH THE DAYS WERE ONLY SEVEN	46031	W-22
L 50161	(Ernest Tubb-Ruth Smith) American Music, Inc.	(A-529)	
		9-46031	
L 3293	WITH TEARS IN MY EYES (Paul Howard)		W-30
L 50162	Acuff-Rose Publications, Inc.		
L 3294	ARE YOU WAITING JUST FOR ME? (Ernest Tubb)	6110	W-21
L 50163	American Music, Inc.	46289	
		9-46289	

01-17-44 Los Angeles, California. Time: Unknown. Producer: Joe Perry. Vocal: Ernest Tubb. Bass: Herbert M. "Butterball" Paige. Lead electric guitar: James Erwin Short. Rhythm guitar: Ernest Tubb; Melvin Leon Short. Fiddle: Johnny Sapp.

L 50164	I'LL GET ALONG SOMEHOW (Ernest Tubb)	W-23
	American Music, Inc.	
L 50165	BLUE EYED ELAINE (Ernest Tubb)	W-22
	American Music, Inc.	
L 50166	YOU'LL LOVE ME TOO LATE (Ernest Tubb)	W-23
	American Music, Inc.	
L 50167	I'LL NEVER LOSE YOU THOUGH YOU'RE GONE	W-33;
	(Ernest Tubb) American Music, Inc.	609
L 50168	I'M TOO BLUE TO WORRY OVER YOU	W-24;
	(Ernest Tubb) American Music, Inc.	609
L 50169	THERE'S NOTHING MORE TO SAY (Ernest Tubb)	W-24;
	American Music, Inc.	609
L 50170	I HATE TO SEE YOU GO (Homer Hargrove-	W-21
	Ernest Tubb) American Music, Inc.	
L 50171	I'LL ALWAYS BE GLAD TO TAKE YOU BACK	W-23
	(Ernest Tubb) American Music, Inc.	
L 50172	TOO LATE TO WORRY, TOO BLUE TO CRY	W-20
	(Al Dexter) American Music, Inc.	
L 50173	I'M WONDERING HOW (Ernest Tubb)	W-21
	American Music, Inc.	
L 50174	LAST NIGHT I DREAMED (Ernest Tubb)	W-23
	American Music, Inc.	

L 50175	THIS TIME WE'RE REALLY THROUGH	W-30
	(Ernest Tubb-Lew Jenkins) American Music, Inc.	
L 50176	YOU MAY HAVE YOUR PICTURE (Ernest Tubb)	W-24
	American Music, Inc.	
L 50177	I AIN'T GOIN' HONKY TONKIN' ANYMORE	W-24
	(Ernest Tubb) American Music, Inc.	

01-18-44 Los Angeles, California. Time: Unknown. Producer: Joe Perry. Vocal: Ernest Tubb. Bass: Herbert M. "Butterball" Paige. Lead electric guitar: Erwin Jimmie Short. Rhythm guitar: Ernest Tubb; Melvin Leon Short. Fiddle: Johnny Sapp.

L 50178	WALKING THE FLOOR OVER YOU (Ernest Tubb)	W-21
	American Music, Inc.	
L 50179	HAVE YOU CHANGED YOUR MIND? (Ernest Tubb)	W-24
	American Music, Inc.	
L 50180	JUST ROLLIN' ON (Ernest Tubb)	W-24
	American Music, Inc.	
L 50181	YOU NEARLY LOSE YOUR MIND (Ernest Tubb)	W-21
	American Music, Inc.	
L 50182	I'LL NEVER CRY OVER YOU (Ernest Tubb)	W-23
	American Music, Inc.	
L 50183	OUR BABY'S BOOK (Ernest Tubb)	W-22
	American Music, Inc.	
L 50184	WHEN THE WORLD HAS TURNED YOU DOWN	W-22
	(Ernest Tubb) American Music, Inc.	
L 50185	I WONDER WHY YOU SAID GOODBYE	W-22
	(Ernest Tubb) American Music, Inc.	
L 50186	I'M GLAD I MET YOU AFTER ALL (Ernest Tubb)	W-23
	American Music, Inc.	
L 50187	THAT'S ALL SHE WROTE (Ernest Tubb)	W-24
	American Music, Inc.	
L 50188	I AIN'T GONNA LOVE YOU ANYMORE	W-24
	(Ernest Tubb) American Music, Inc.	
L 50189	I DON'T WANT YOU AFTER ALL (Ernest Tubb)	W-23
	American Music, Inc.	
L 50190	JUST CRYING TO MYSELF	W-24
	(Early L. Graham-Ernest Tubb) Cross Music Co.	
L 50191	TRY ME ONE MORE TIME (Ernest Tubb)	W-22
	American Music, Inc.	

05-21-45 Chicago, Illinois. 10:45 A.M.-1:15 P.M. Producer: Unknown. Vocal: Ernest Tubb. Bass: Jack Drake. Lead electric guitar: Leon Short. Rhythm guitar: Ernest Tubb. Fiddle: Johnny Sapp. Steel guitar: Ray "Kemo" Head.

C 25256	I'VE LIVED A LIE (Ernest Tubb-Wallace Fowler)	800-9644
	Cross Music Co.	
C 25257	WONDERING IF YOU'RE WONDERING TOO	800-9645
	(Ernest Tubb) Cross Music Co.	

C 25258	WHEN LOVE TURNS TO HATE (Ernest Tubb- Pete Pyle-Chuck Harding) Cross Music Co.	800-9646
C 25259	THERE'S A NEW MOON OVER MY SHOULDER (Jimmie Davis-Ekko Whelan-Lee Blastic) Peer International	800-9647
C 25260	DAISY MAY (Floyd Tillman) Peer International	800-9648
C 25261	I HUNG MY HEAD AND CRIED (Jimmie Davis-Cliff Bruner) Peer International	9839
C 25262	THERE'S NOTHIN' ON MY MIND (Ernest Tubb) Cross Music Co.	9840
C 25263	TOO LATE TO WORRY, TOO BLUE TO CRY (Al Dexter) Cross Music Co.	9841
C 25264	LOVE GONE COLD (Johnny Bond) Peer International	9842
C 25265	YOU BROUGHT SORROW TO MY HEART (Johnny Bond-H. H. Melka) Peer International	9843

05-21-45 Chicago, Illinois. 3:30 P.M.-6:10 P.M. Producer: Unknown. Vocal: Ernest Tubb. Bass: Jack Drake. Lead electric guitar: Leon Short. Rhythm guitar: Ernest Tubb. Fiddle: Johnny Sapp. Steel guitar: Ray "Kemo" Head.

C 25271	HOME IN SAN ANTONE (Floyd Jenkins) Acuff-Rose Publications	10125
C 25272	DARLING, WHAT MORE CAN I DO? (Gene Autry- Jenny Lou Carson) Western Music Publishing Co.	10124
C 25273	BLUE BONNET LANE (Cindy Walker) American Music, Inc.	10126
C 25274	AT MAIL CALL TODAY (Gene Autry-Fred Rose) Western Music Publishing Co.	
C 25275	I BELIEVE I'M ENTITLED TO YOU (Cliff Carlisle- Chester Rice-Mel Foree) Joe McDaniels Music	10127
C 25276	YOU'RE GOING TO BE SORRY (Ernest Tubb) Cross Music Co.	10444
C 25277	I HANG MY HEAD AND CRY (Gene Autry-Fred Rose- Ray Whitley) Western Music Publishing Co.	
C 25278	EACH NIGHT AT NINE (Floyd Tillman) Peer International	
C 25279	MY CONFESSION (Bob Wills) Bourne, Inc.	10343
C 25280	MY HILLBILLY BABY* (Rex Griffin) Peer International	

05-23-45 Chicago, Illinois. 9:30 A.M.-10:45 A.M. Producer: Unknown. Vocal: Ernest Tubb. Bass: Jack Drake. Rhythm guitar: Ernest Tubb. Lead electric guitar: Leon Short. Steel guitar: Ray "Kemo" Head. Fiddle: Johnny Sapp.

C 25301	THAT'S WHY I'M CRYING OVER YOU (Ernest Tubb-Tommy Covington) Cross Music Co.	800-8029

*Remade May 24; see below.

C 25302	GONE AND LEFT ME BLUES	800-8030
	(Jimmy Wakely-Johnny Bond) Leeds Music Corp.	
C 25303	WHEN THE TUMBLE WEEDS COME TUMBLING	800-8031
	DOWN AGAIN (Gene Autry) M. M. Cole Corp.	
C 25304	I'LL BE TRUE WHILE YOU'RE GONE (Gene Autry)	800-8032
	Western Music Publishing Co.	
C 25305	THE END OF THE WORLD	800-8234
	(Fred Rose-Jimmie Davis) Leeds Music Corp.	

05-23-45   Chicago, Illinois. 2:00 P.M.-6:00 P.M. Producer: Unknown. Vocal: Ernest Tubb. Bass: Jack Drake. Rhythm guitar: Ernest Tubb. Lead electric guitar: Leon Short. Steel guitar: Ray "Kemo" Head. Fiddle: Johnny Sapp.

C 25306	IT JUST DON'T MATTER NOW (Ernest Tubb)	800-8235
	Cross Music Co.	
C 25307	YOU'RE ON MY MIND (Ted Daffan)	800-8236
	Peer International	
C 25308	I'M WASTING MY TEARS ON YOU	800-8237
	(Tex Ritter-Frank Harford) Peer International	
C 25309	TEN YEARS (Johnny Bond) Peer International	800-8238
C 25310	OLD LOVE LETTERS (BRING MEMORIES OF YOU)	10446
	(Jimmie Rodgers-Lou Herscher-Dwight Butcher)	
	Peer International	
C 25311	LOW AND LONELY (Floyd Jenkins)	800-8033
	Acuff-Rose Publications	
C 25312	WHERE THE DEEP WATERS FLOW (Ted Daffan)	800-8725
	Peer International	
C 25313	YOU MAY HAVE YOUR PICTURE (Ernest Tubb)	800-8959
	American Music, Inc.	
C 25314	IT'S COMING BACK TO YOU*	800-8963
	(Lois Snapp-Ernest Tubb) American Music, Inc.	
C 25315	OVER THE RIVER (Rex Griffin) Peer International	800-9110
C 25316	YOU DON'T CARE (Johnny Bond)	800-8960
	Peer International	
C 25317	LET ME SMILE MY LAST SMILE AT YOU (Cliff	800-8726
	Bruner-Jimmie Davis) Southern Music Publishing	
C 25318	I'M TIRED OF YOU (Ted Daffan) Peer International	800-8961
C 25319	YOU TOLD ME A LIE (Jimmie Davis-Buck Nation)	800-9259
	Peer International	
C 25320	FRANKIE AND JOHNNIE (Jimmie Rodgers, arr.)	800-8874
	Peer International	

05-24-45   Chicago, Illinois. 9:00 A.M.-11:50 A.M. Producer: Unknown. Vocal: Ernest Tubb. Bass: Jack Drake. Rhythm guitar: Ernest Tubb. Lead electric guitar: Leon Short. Steel guitar: Ray "Kemo" Head. Fiddle: Johnny Sapp.

*This is, of course, a mistitled remake of Tubb's earlier "That's When It's Coming Home to You."

C 25321	JEALOUS HEART (Jenny Lou Carson) Acuff-Rose Publications		800-9109
C 25322	CRYING MYSELF TO SLEEP (Bob Atcher) Peer International		800-8728
C 25323	FORT WORTH JAIL (Dick Reinhart) Western Music Publishing Co.		800-8962
C 25324	YOU'RE BREAKING MY HEART (H. H. Melka) Peer International		10447
C 25280	MY HILLBILLY BABY (Remake) (Rex Griffin) Peer International		10128
C 25325	FARTHER AND FARTHER APART (Fred Rose) Acuff-Rose Publications		800-8727
C 25326	I LOVED YOU ONCE (Rex Griffin-Jimmie Davis) Peer International		800-8724
C 25327	I'LL STEP ASIDE (Johnny Bond) Cherio Music Publishing	(DECCA 46041)	112-CD VL (7)3684
C 25328	WORRIED MIND (Jimmie Davis-Ted Daffan) Southern Music Publishing		800-9260
C 25329	A YEAR AGO TONIGHT (Gene Autry) Western Music Publishing Co.		800-7904
C 25330	TIME CHANGES EVERYTHING (Bob Wills-Tommy Duncan) Peer International		800-7905
C 25331	WHAT GOOD WILL IT DO? (Tommy Duncan-Duane Howard) Peer International		112-F
C 25332	MY TIME WILL COME SOMEDAY (Cliff Bruner-Jimmie Davis) Southern Music Publishing		800-7907

05-24-45 Chicago, Illinois. 1:25 P.M.-4:00 P.M. Producer: Unknown. Vocal: Ernest Tubb. Bass: Jack Drake. Rhythm guitar: Ernest Tubb. Lead electric guitar: Leon Short. Steel guitar: Ray "Kemo" Head. Fiddle: Johnny Sapp.

C 25333	GREY-EYED DARLING (Ted Daffan) Peer International	800-7908
C 25334	I NEVER CROSS YOUR MIND (Johnny Sapp) Cross Music Co.	800-7906
C 25335	I TOLD YOU SO (Jimmie Davis-Rex Griffin) Peer International	10448
C 25336	I'M BEGINNING TO FORGET YOU (Floy Case-Jimmie Davis) Peer International	800-8875
C 25337	I'M GONNA BE LONG GONE WHEN I GO AWAY (Bob Miller) Bob Miller Inc.	800-9111
C 25338	I WALK ALONE (Herbert W. Wilson) Adams, Vee & Abbott, Inc.	10339

06-05-45 Chicago, Illinois. 1:30 P.M.-4:30 P.M. Producer: Unknown. Vocal: Ernest Tubb. Bass: Jack Drake. Rhythm guitar: Ernest Tubb. Lead electric guitar: Leon Short. Steel guitar: Ray "Kemo" Head. Fiddle: Johnny Sapp.

C 25339 (A,B)	HEART OF STONE (Johnny Bond-Ernest Tubb)	10340
C 25340	YOU'LL WANT ME BACK (BUT I WON'T CARE) (Ernest Tubb) Cross Music Co.	10445
C 25341	OUR BABY BOY (Milton Brown) Southern Music	112-E
C 25342	HANG YOUR HEAD IN SHAME (Fred Rose-Ed G. Nelson-Steve Nelson)	800-7931
C 25343	THE LAST GOODBYE (Sammy Forsmark-Ernest Tubb)	800-8876
C 25344	PINS AND NEEDLES (IN MY HEART) (Floyd Jenkins) Acuff-Rose Publications	800-9113
C 25345	THE LOVE I HAVE FOR YOU (Jimmie Davis) Peer International	800-7932
C 25346	I'LL NEVER TELL YOU I LOVE YOU (Rex Griffin) Peer International	800-9261
C 25347	I KNEW THE MOMENT I LOST YOU (Bob Wills-Tommy Duncan) Peer International	800-9112
C 25349	I WONDER IF YOU FEEL THE WAY I DO (Bob Wills-Tommy Duncan) Peer International	800-7933

06-06-45 Chicago, Illinois. 10:00 A.M.-12:30 P.M. Producer: Unknown. Vocal: Ernest Tubb. Bass: Jack Drake. Rhythm guitar: Ernest Tubb. Lead electric guitar: Leon Short. Steel guitar: Ray "Kemo" Head. Fiddle: Johnny Sapp.

C 25350	I'LL HAVE TO LIVE AND LEARN (Zeke Clements) Adams, Vee & Abbott, Inc.	10342
C 25351	NATIONAL LAMENT (Ernest Tubb-Jimmie Lanson)	
C 25352	TWEEDLE-O-TWILL (Gene Autry-Fred Rose) Western Music Publishing	800-7929
C 25353	THERE'S A RAINBOW ON THE RIO COLORADO (Gene Autry-Fred Rose) Palace Music	800-7930
C 25354	ACTION SPEAKS LOUDER THAN WORDS (Buddy Jones-Jimmie Davis) Peer International	800-8877
C 25355	LEFT ALL ALONE (Ernest Tubb) Cross Music Co.	800-9263
C 25356	TWO MORE YEARS (AND I'LL BE FREE) (Floyd Tillman) Peer International	800-8878
C 25357	TRAILING HOME TO MOTHER (Ray Whitley-A. Arnold)	800-9262

08-14-45 Chicago, Illinois. Time: Unknown. Producer: Unknown. Vocal: Ernest Tubb. Bass: Jack Drake. Rhythm guitar: Ernest Tubb; Leon Short. Fiddle: Johnny Sapp. Steel guitar: Ray Head. Lead guitar: Jimmie Short.

C-25424 73035	IT'S BEEN SO LONG DARLING (Ernest Tubb) American Music, Inc.	6112 46048	MCAD-10086
C-25425 73036	SHOULD I COME BACK HOME TO YOU? (Ernest Tubb) American Music, Inc.	6112	

C-25426	THERE'S A LITTLE BIT OF EVERYTHING IN TEXAS	9002	VL 3684
73042	(Ernest Tubb) American Music, Inc.		VL 73684
C-25427	DARLING, WHAT MORE CAN I DO? (Gene Autry-	9002	
73037	Jenny Lou Carson) Western Music Pub. Co.		

08-15-45 Chicago, Illinois. Time: Unknown. Producer: Unknown. Vocal: Ernest Tubb. Bass: Jack Drake. Rhythm guitar: Ernest Tubb; Leon Short. Fiddle: Johnny Sapp. Steel guitar: Ray Head. Lead guitar: Jimmie Short.

C-25428	IT JUST DON'T MATTER NOW (Ernest Tubb)	
73038	American Music, Inc.	
C-25429	I'M BEGINNING TO FORGET YOU	46013
73039	(Floy Case-Jimmie Davis) Peer-Southern Music, Inc.	
C-25430	WHEN LOVE TURNS TO HATE (Pete Pyle-	
73040	Chuck Harding-Ernest Tubb) Cross Music Co.	
C-25431	YOU'LL WANT ME BACK (BUT I WON'T CARE)	46029
73041	(Ernest Tubb) American Music, Inc.	(A-529)

02-13-46 Chicago, Illinois. Time: Unknown. Producer: Unknown. Vocal: Ernest Tubb. Bass: Jack Drake. Rhythm guitar: Ernest Tubb; Leon Short. Fiddle: Johnny Sapp. Steel guitar: Ray Head. Lead guitar: Jimmie Short.

C-25447	THERE'S GONNA BE SOME CHANGES MADE	46041
73417	AROUND HERE (Ernest Tubb) American Music, Inc.	
C-25448	YOU WERE ONLY TEASING ME (T. Texas Tyler)	46013
73418	American Music, Inc.	
C-25449	I'M FREE AT LAST (Ernest Tubb)	46030
73419	American Music, Inc.	(A-529)
C-25450	HEART OF STONE (Johnny Bond-Ernest Tubb)	
73420		

02-14-46 Chicago, Illinois. Time: Unknown. Producer: Unknown. Vocal: Ernest Tubb. Bass: Jack Drake. Rhythm guitar: Ernest Tubb; Leon Short. Fiddle: Johnny Sapp. Steel guitar: Ray Head. Lead guitar: Jimmie Short.

C-25455	THOSE SIMPLE THINGS ARE WORTH A MILLION	46030
73425	NOW (Jewel Mathes-Ernest Tubb)	(A-529)
	American Music, Inc.	

09-17-46 New York, New York. 11:00 A.M.-2:00 P.M. Producer: Dave Kapp. Vocal: Ernest Tubb. Bass: Jack Drake. Rhythm guitar: Ernest Tubb; Leon Short. Fiddle: Red Herron. Steel guitar: Wayne Fleming. Lead guitar: Jimmie Short.

73678	FILIPINO BABY (Billy Cox-Clarke Van Ness)	46019	DL 8291
	Shapiro, Bernstein & Co. Inc.	ED 2026	
		9-46019	
73679	DRIVIN' NAILS IN MY COFFIN (Jerry Irby)	46019	VL 3684
	Hill & Range, Inc.	9-46019	VL 73684

73680	RAINBOW AT MIDNIGHT (John A. Miller)	46018	DL 8291
	Shapiro, Bernstein & Co. Inc.	(A-808)	DL 5301
		9-46018	DL 4090
		(9-146)	DL 74090
		ED 2356	
73681	I DON'T BLAME YOU (Jim Scott-Ernest Tubb)	46018	DL 5301
	Ernest Tubb Music, Inc.	(A-808)	DL 8291
		9-46018	
		(9-146)	
		ED 2356	

09-18-46 New York, New York. 12:00-3:00 P.M. Producer: Dave Kapp. Vocal: Ernest Tubb. Bass: Jack Drake. Rhythm guitar: Ernest Tubb; Leon Short. Fiddle: Red Herron. Steel guitar: Wayne Fleming. Lead guitar: Jimmie Short.

73682	THE LAST GOODBYE		
	(Sammy Forsmark-Ernest Tubb)		
73683	GET IN OR GET OUT OF MY HEART (Ernest Tubb)		
	Ernest Tubb Music, Inc.		
73684	HOW CAN I BE SURE (Rex Griffin-Ernest Tubb)	46032	
	Hill & Range, Inc.	(A-529)	
73685	THOSE TEARS IN YOUR EYES (WERE NOT FOR ME)	46032	
	(Ernest Tubb)	(A-529)	

02-10-47 Chicago, Illinois. 2:00-7:30 P.M. Producer: Dave Kapp. Vocal: Ernest Tubb. Bass: Jack Drake. Rhythm guitar: Ernest Tubb; Leon Short. Fiddle: Red Herron. Steel guitar: Jerry Byrd. Lead guitar: Jimmie Short.

C-25509	SO ROUND, SO FIRM, SO FULLY PACKED	46040
73800	(Merle Travis-Cliffie Stone-Eddie Kirk)	
	American Music, Inc.	
C-25510	DON'T LOOK NOW (BUT YOUR BROKEN HEART IS	46040
73801	SHOWING) (Ernest Tubb) Ernest Tubb Music, Inc.	
C-25511	A HUNDRED AND SIXTY ACRES (Dave Kapp)	
	Garland Music, Inc.	
C-25512	A W-O-M-A-N HAS WRECKED MANY A GOOD MAN	
	(Mrs. Jimmie Rodgers-Ernest Tubb)	
	Ernest Tubb Music, Inc.	

03-24-47 Los Angeles, California. 2:00-4:45 P.M. Producer: Unknown. Vocal: Ernest Tubb. Bass: Jack Drake. Rhythm guitar: Ernest Tubb; Leon Short. Fiddle: Red Herron. Steel guitar: Jerry Byrd. Lead guitar: Jimmie Short.

L 4383	YOU HIT THE NAIL RIGHT ON THE HEAD	46061
	(Zeb Turner-Ernest Tubb) Ernest Tubb Music, Inc.	
L 4384 `	TWO WRONGS DON'T MAKE A RIGHT (Ernest	46061
	Tubb-Redd Stewart) Ernest Tubb Music, Inc.	

08-11-47 Castle Studios; Nashville, Tennessee. 9:30 A.M.-1:30 P.M. Producer: Paul
Cohen. Vocal: Ernest Tubb. Bass: Jack Drake. Rhythm guitar: Ernest Tubb;
Leon Short; Tommy Paige. Fiddle: Hal Smith. Steel guitar: Jerry Byrd. Lead
guitar: Jimmie Short.

NT 108	THAT WILD AND WICKED LOOK IN YOUR EYE	46134	
74046	(Sam Nichols) Hill & Range Songs, Inc.	9-46134	
NT 109	A LONELY HEART KNOWS (Hank Thompson)	46113	
74047	Hill & Range Songs, Inc.		
NT 110	DON'T YOUR FACE LOOK RED (Ernest Tubb)		
74048	Ernest Tubb Music, Inc.		
NT 111	ANSWER TO RAINBOW AT MIDNIGHT (Lost John	46078	
74049	Miller-Ernest Tubb) Shapiro, Bernstein & Co. Inc.		

08-13-47 Castle Studios; Nashville, Tennessee. 2:30-6:00 P.M. Producer: Paul Cohen.
Vocal: Ernest Tubb. Bass: Jack Drake. Rhythm guitar: Ernest Tubb; Leon
Short; Tommy Paige. Fiddle: Hal Smith. Steel guitar: Jerry Byrd. Lead guitar:
Jimmie Short.

NT 120	WATCHING MY PAST GO BY (Ernest Tubb)		
74058	Ernest Tubb Music, Inc.		
NT 121	A W-O-M-A-N HAS WRECKED MANY A GOOD MAN	46113	
74059	(Mrs. Jimmie Rodgers-Ernest Tubb)		
	Ernest Tubb Music, Inc.		
NT 122	HEADIN' DOWN THE WRONG HIGHWAY	46078	
74060	(Ted Daffan) Hill & Range Songs, Inc.		
NT 123	WHITE CHRISTMAS (Irving Berlin)		
74061	Irving Berlin Music		

12-14-47 Castle Studios; Nashville, Tennessee. 12:00-6:00 P.M. Producer: Paul Cohen.
Vocal: Ernest Tubb. Bass: Jack Drake. Rhythm guitar: Ernest Tubb; Bill Drake.
Fiddle: Hal Smith. Steel guitar: Jerry Byrd. Lead guitar: Tommy Paige.

N 513	LET'S SAY GOODBYE LIKE WE SAID HELLO (IN A	46144	DL 5301
74265	FRIENDLY KIND OF WAY)	A-808	DL 8291
	(Jimmie Skinner-Ernest Tubb)	ED 2357	
	Ernest Tubb Music, Inc.	9-146	
		9-46144	
N 514	TAKIN' IT EASY HERE (Ernie Lee)		
74266	Ernest Tubb Music, Inc.		
N 515	SEAMAN'S BLUES (Billy Talmadge Tubb-Ernest	46119	DL 8291
74267	Tubb) Ernest Tubb Music, Inc.	ED 2026	DL 75252
		9-46119	MCA 84
			MCAD-10086
N 516	HOW CAN I FORGET YOU (Cindy Walker-Ernest		
74268	Tubb) Ernest Tubb Music, Inc.		

N 517   YESTERDAY'S WINNER IS A LOSER TODAY
74269   (Jimmie Skinner-Jesse Rogers-Ernest Tubb)
          Ernest Tubb Music, Inc.
N 518   I'M WITH A CROWD BUT SO ALONE*
74270   (Elaine Tubb-Carl Story) Ernest Tubb Music, Inc.

12-15-47   Castle Studios; Nashville, Tennessee. 9:30 P.M.-12:30 A.M. Producer: Paul
          Cohen. Vocal: Ernest Tubb. Bass: Jack Drake. Rhythm guitar: Ernest Tubb;
          Bill Drake. Electric rhythm guitar: Zeke Turner. Fiddle: Hal Smith. Steel guitar:
          Jerry Byrd. Lead guitar: Tommy Paige.

N 528   IT'S A LONELY WORLD (WHEN YOU'RE ALL
74337   ALONE)** (Redd Stewart-Ernest Tubb)
          Ernest Tubb Music, Inc.
N 529   MISSISSIPPI GAL (Sam Nichols-Taylor McPeters-
74338   Daniel Cypert) Hill & Range Songs, Inc.
N 530   THE TROUBLE WITH ME IS TROUBLE
74339   (Ernest Tubb) Ernest Tubb Music, Inc.
N 531   HEART, PLEASE BE STILL*** (Tommy Paige-Baby
74340   Stewart-Ernest Tubb) Ernest Tubb Music, Inc.

12-16-47   Castle Studios; Nashville, Tennessee. 5:00 P.M.-8:00 P.M. Producer: Paul
          Cohen. Vocal: Ernest Tubb. Bass: Jack Drake. Electric rhythm guitar: Zeke
          Turner. Rhythm guitar: Ernest Tubb; Bill Drake. Fiddle: Hal Smith? (may not
          be a fiddle). Steel guitar: Jerry Byrd. Lead guitar: Tommy Paige.

N 538	WAITING FOR A TRAIN (Jimmie Rodgers)	46119	
74347	Peer-Southern Music, Inc.	9-46119	
N 539	I HOPE I'M WRONG (Betty Wade)		
74348	Ernest Tubb Music, Inc.		
N 540	FOREVER IS ENDING TODAY	46134	MCAD-10086
74349	(Johnny Bond-Ike Cargill-Ernest Tubb)	9-46134	
N 541	HAVE YOU EVER BEEN LONELY (HAVE YOU EVER	46144	DL 5301
74350	BEEN BLUE)? (Peter DeRose-George Brown)	(A-808;	DL 8291
	Shapiro, Bernstein & Co., Inc.	9-146)	
		ED 2357	
		9-46144	

*Carl W. Story Jr. copyrighted "I'm With a Crowd but So Alone" in his own name July 30, 1947; Elaine
Tubb was added to the copyright May 25, 1948, though Tubb would not record a released version until
1951. Story joined forces with former Tubb co-writer Lois Snapp in Fort Worth in the late 1940s, with
their copyrighted "I'm Walking Out on You" (January 28, 1948).

**"It's a Lonely World" seems to have been first recorded at a Cowboy Copas session, prior to March 8,
1947, a version only released in 1961! Redd Stewart and Copas are listed as composers on the eventual
release.

***"Heart Please Be Still" was copyrighted by Paige and Stewart on June 14, 1947, when Paige was in
Dunn, North Carolina, and Stewart in Blytheville, Arkansas. Tubb joined the copyright and secured the
publishing on May 25, 1948. Paige's Bullet Record of this was the only release: Tubb's never came out.

01-23-49   Castle Studios; Nashville, Tennessee. 6:15-8:15 P.M.; 7:15 A.M.-10:15 A.M.
01-24-49   Producer: Paul Cohen. Vocal: Ernest Tubb. Bass: Jack Drake. Rhythm guitar:
Bill Drake. Fiddle: Hal Smith. Steel guitar: Don Davis or Dickie Harris. Lead
guitar: Tommy Paige. Banjo: Possibly Banjo Murphy.

NA 1002	TILL THE END OF THE WORLD (Vaughn Horton)	46150	DL 8291
74716	Southern Music Publishing, Inc.	ED 2026	
		9-46150	
NA 1003	DADDY, WHEN IS MOMMY COMING HOME (Troy L.	46150	
74715	Martin-Ernest Tubb) Hill & Range Songs, Inc.	9-46150	
		ED 2769	

02-15-49   Los Angeles, California. 1:00-4:00 P.M. Producer: Victor Schoen. Vocal: Ernest
Tubb; LaVerne Andrews; Maxine Andrews; Patty Andrews. Lead guitar:
Herbert M. "Tommy" Paige. Steel guitar: Wesley Webb "Speedy" West (1).
Rhythm guitar: Eddie Kirk. Bass: Alfred Caldwell. Drums: Irv Cottler (2).
Piano: Melvin W. "Wally" Weschler (2).

L 4897	DON'T ROB ANOTHER MAN'S CASTLE (1)	24592
	(Jenny Lou Carson) Hill & Range Songs, Inc.	9-24592
L 4898	I'M BITING MY FINGERNAILS AND THINKING OF	24592
	YOU (2) (Roy West-Ernest Benedict-Lenny Sanders-	9-24592
	Ernest Tubb) Hill & Range Songs, Inc.	

06-12-49   Castle Studios; Nashville, Tennessee. 3:00-6:00 P.M.; 7:00-10:00 P.M. Producer:
Paul Cohen. Vocal: Ernest Tubb. Bass: Jack Drake. Rhythm guitar: Bill Drake
or Velma Williams Smith. Fiddle: Hal Smith. Steel guitar: Dickie Harris. Lead
guitar: Tommy Paige. Mandolin: Mack McGarr. Electric chunk rhythm guitar:
Zeke Turner.

NA 175	MY FILIPINO ROSE (Clarence E. Snow)	46175	
74977	Hill & Range Songs, Inc.	9-46175	
NA 176	MY TENNESSEE BABY (Ernest Tubb)	46173	
74978	Ernest Tubb Music, Inc.	9-46173	
NA 177	SLIPPING AROUND (Floyd Tillman)	46173	DL 8291
74979	Peer International	ED 2026	
		9-46173	
NA 178	WARM RED WINE (Cindy Walker)	46175	DL 75252
74980	Hill & Range Songs, Inc.	9-46175	MCA 84
NA 179	DRIFTWOOD ON THE RIVER	46377	
74981	(Bob Miller-John Klenner) Bob Miller, Inc.	9-46377	

08-26-49   Castle Studios; Nashville, Tennessee. 2:30-5:30 P.M. Producer: Paul Cohen.
Vocal: Ernest Tubb; The Three Troubadettes. Bass: Jack Drake. Rhythm
electric guitar: Zeke Turner. Acoustic rhythm guitar: Unknown. Steel guitar:
Don Davis. Lead guitar: Billy Byrd. Organ: Owen Bradley.

NA 2028	WHITE CHRISTMAS* (Irving Berlin)	46186	DL 4518
75219	Irving Berlin Music Corp.	(A-791)	DL 5497
		ED 2089	DL 74518
		(9-98)	
		25758	
		9-46186	
NA 2029	BLUE CHRISTMAS* (Billy Hayes-Jay Johnson)	46186	DL 5497
75220	Choice Music, Inc.	ED 2089	
		(A-791)	
		25758	
		(9-98)	
		9-46186	

11-08-49 Castle Studios; Nashville, Tennessee. 11:00-12:00 P.M. Producer: Paul Cohen. Vocal: Ernest Tubb; Red Foley. Bass: Ernie Newton. Rhythm guitar: Jack Shook. Steel guitar: Don Helms. Drums: Farris Coursey. Lead guitar: Billy Byrd (2); Grady Martin (1, 2). Organ: Owen Bradley (1).

NA 2041	TENNESSEE BORDER NO. 2 (1)	46200	DL 8298
75497	(Jimmy Work-Kenneth Burns-Henry Haynes)	ED 2368	
	Hill & Range Songs, Inc.		
NA 2045	DON'T BE ASHAMED OF YOUR AGE (2)	46200	DL 8298
75496	(Cindy Walker-Bob Wills) Hill & Range Songs, Inc.	ED 2024	MCAD-10084

11-09-49 Castle Studios; Nashville, Tennessee. 4:45-8:15 P.M. Producer: Paul Cohen. Vocal: Ernest Tubb. Bass: Jack Drake. Rhythm guitar: Jack Shook. Steel guitar: Don Helms. Lead guitar: Billy Byrd. Mandolin: Mack McGarr.

NA 2042	LETTERS HAVE NO ARMS (Arbie Gibson-Ernest	46207	MCAD-10086
75540	Tubb) Ernest Tubb Music, Inc.	9-46207	
NA 2043	I'LL TAKE A BACK SEAT FOR YOU (Ernest Tubb)	46207	
75541	Ernest Tubb Music, Inc.	9-46207	
NA 2044	THROW YOUR LOVE MY WAY (Loys Southerland-	46243	MCAD-10086
75542	Ernest Tubb) Ernest Tubb Music, Inc.**	9-46243	

11-10-49 Castle Studios; Nashville, Tennessee. 8:30-11:30 P.M. Producer: Paul Cohen. Vocal: Ernest Tubb. Bass: Jack Drake. Rhythm guitar: Jack Shook. Lead guitar: Billy Byrd. Organ: Owen Bradley.

NA 2050	STAND BY ME (C. A. Tindley-F. A. Clark)	14506	DL 5334
75532		A-856/	VL 3765
		9-236	VL 73765

*The takes are different between the single (46186) and the EP (2089) on both of these cuts.
**Loys Southerland is the maiden name of Mrs. Wayne Raney. Wayne wrote the song, but had an exclusive contract with Syd Nathan's Lois Music Company, so when Ernest accepted it for recording on condition that he publish it and be co-writer, Raney put it in his wife's name.

NA 2051	THE OLD RUGGED CROSS (George Bennard)	14532	DL 5334
75533		A-856/	VL 3765
		9-236	VL 73765
NA 2052	WHAT A FRIEND WE HAVE IN JESUS (Charles C.	14515	DL 5334
75534	Converse-Joseph Scriven–Horatius Bonar)	A-856/	VL 3765
		9-236	VL 73765
NA 2053	THE WONDERFUL CITY	14515	DL 5334
75535	(Elsie McWilliams-Jimmie Rodgers)	A-856/	VL 3765
	Peer International	9-236	VL 73765
NA 2054	WHEN I TAKE MY VACATION IN HEAVEN	14506	DL 5334
75536	(Herbert Buffum) Leeds Music Corp.	A-856/	VL 3765
		9-236	VL 73765
NA 2055	FARTHER ALONG (W. B. Stevens)	14532	DL 5334
75537		A-856/	VL 3765
		9-236	VL 73765

12-29-49   Castle Studios; Nashville, Tennessee. 8:30-11:30 P.M. Producer: Paul Cohen. Vocal: Ernest Tubb. Bass: Jack Drake. Rhythm guitar: Ernest Tubb. Fiddle: Dale Potter. Steel guitar: Don Helms. Lead guitar: Billy Byrd.

NA 2067	I LOVE YOU BECAUSE (Leon Payne)	46213
75651	Acuff-Rose Publications, Inc.	9-46213
NA 2068	GIVE ME A LITTLE OLD-FASHIONED LOVE	46243
75652	(Ernest Tubb) Ernest Tubb Music, Inc.	9-46243
NA 2069	UNFAITHFUL ONE (A. Lyles-Cliff Bruner)	46213
75653	Peer International	9-46213

06-23-50   Castle Studios; Nashville, Tennessee. 2:30-5:30 P.M. Producer: Paul Cohen. Vocal: Ernest Tubb; Red Foley. Bass: Ernie Newton. Rhythm guitar: Jack Shook. Steel guitar: Billy Robinson. Drums: Farris Coursey. Lead guitar: Billy Byrd. Second lead guitar: Grady Martin. Piano: Owen Bradley.

NA 2148	HILLBILLY FEVER #2 (George Vaughn)*	46255	DL 8298
76536	Charter Music Co.	ED 2367	
NA 2149	TEXAS VS. KENTUCKY (Cindy Walker)	46278	
76537	Music City Songs	9-46278	

06-29-50   Castle Studios; Nashville, Tennessee. 2:00-5:00 P.M. Producer: Paul Cohen. Vocal: Ernest Tubb. Bass: Jack Drake. Rhythm guitar: Ernest Tubb. Steel guitar: Dickie Harris. Drums: Farris Coursey. Lead guitar: Billy Byrd.

NA 2162	G-I-R-L SPELLS TROUBLE	46257	
76562	(Arbie Gibson-Ernest Tubb)	9-46257	
	Jenny Lou Carson Music, Inc.		
NA 2163	YOU DON'T HAVE TO BE A BABY TO CRY	46257	VL 3684
76563	(Terry Shand-Bob Merrill)	9-46257	VL 73684
	R.F.D. Music Publishing Co., Inc.		

*"George Vaughn" is a pseudonym for Vaughn Horton.

NA 2164	MOTHER, THE QUEEN OF MY HEART (Hoyt Bryant-	46306	DL 5336
76564	Jimmie Rodgers) Peer International	(A-858)	
		9-46306	
		(9-238)	
		91080	
		(ED 588)	

06-30-50 Castle Studios; Nashville, Tennessee. 11:30 P.M.-1:30 A.M. Producer: Paul
Cohen. Vocal: Ernest Tubb; Red Foley; Sunshine Trio. Bass: Ernie Newton.
Rhythm guitar: Jack Shook. Steel guitar: Billy Robinson. Drums: Farris
Coursey. Lead guitar: Billy Byrd. Second lead guitar: Grady Martin. Piano:
Owen Bradley.

NA 2169	GOODNIGHT IRENE (Hudie Ledbetter-John Lomax)	46255	DL 8298
76569	Ludlow Music, Inc.	ED 2024	

09-09-50 Castle Studios; Nashville, Tennessee. 1:30-5:30 P.M. Producer: Paul Cohen.
Vocal: Ernest Tubb; Beasley Sisters (1,2). Bass: Jack Drake. Rhythm guitar:
Jack Shook. Steel guitar: Dickie Harris. Drums: Farris Coursey. Lead guitar:
Billy Byrd. Organ: Owen Bradley (1,2). Piano: Owen Bradley (3).

NA 2208	CHRISTMAS ISLAND (1) (Lyle Moraine)	46268	DL 5497
76818	Northern Music Corp., Inc.	(A-791)	DL 4518
		9-46268	DL 74518
		(9-98)	
		ED 2089	
NA 2209	C-H-R-I-S-T-M-A-S (2) (Jenny Lou Carson-Eddy	46268	DL 5497
76819	Arnold) Hill & Range Songs, Inc.	(A-791)	DL 4518
		9-46268	DL 74518
		(9-98)	
		ED 2089	
NA 2210	(REMEMBER ME) I'M THE ONE WHO LOVES YOU	46269	
76820	(Stuart Hamblen) Stuart Hamblen Music Co.	9-46269	
NA 2211	I NEED ATTENTION BAD (3)* (Baby Stewart-Ernest	46269	
76821	Tubb) Hill & Range Songs, Inc.	9-46269	

10-11-50 Castle Studios; Nashville, Tennessee. 3:00-6:00 P.M. Producer: Paul Cohen.
Vocal: Ernest Tubb. Bass: Jack Drake. Rhythm guitar: Jack Shook. Steel
guitar: Dickie Harris. Lead guitar: Billy Byrd.

NA 2238	I'M LONELY AND BLUE (Elsie McWilliams-Jimmie	46306	DL 5336
80022	Rodgers) Peer International, Inc.	(A-858)	
		9-46306	
		(9-238)	
		ED 588	

*"I Need Attention Bad" was copyrighted 9-15-50, six days later. Baby Stewart wrote "I'm Gonna Even up
the Score," copyrighted July 17, 1947, and Tubb sang it in live performance but never on records.

NA 2239	WHY DID YOU GIVE ME YOUR LOVE?	46307	DL 5336
80023	(Jimmie Rodgers) Peer International, Inc.	(A-858)	
		9-46307	
		(9-238)	
		ED 588	
NA 2240	I'M FREE FROM THE CHAIN GANG NOW	46307	DL 5336
80024	(Lou Herscher-Saul Klein) Peer International, Inc.	(A-858)	
		9-46307	
		(9-238)	
		ED 588	
NA 2241	WHY SHOULD I BE LONELY?	46308	DL 5336
80025	(Jimmie Rodgers-Estelle Lovell)	(A-858)	
	Peer International, Inc.	9-46308	
		(9-238)	
		ED 588	
NA 2242	HOBO'S MEDITATION (Jimmie Rodgers)*	46308	DL 5336
80026	Peer International, Inc.	(A-858)	
		9-46308	
		(9-238)	
		ED 588	

10-13-50 Castle Studios; Nashville, Tennessee. 9:30 P.M.-12:30 A.M. Producer: Paul Cohen. Vocal: Ernest Tubb; Red Foley; Minnie Pearl; Sunshine Trio. Bass: Ernie Newton. Rhythm guitar: Jack Shook. Steel guitar: Billy Robinson. Drums: Farris Coursey. Lead guitar: Billy Byrd. Second lead guitar: Hank Garland or Grady Martin. Piano: Owen Bradley.

NA 2252	GOOD MORNING IRENE (George Vaughn)		
80035			
NA 2253	THE LOVEBUG ITCH (Jenny Lou Carson-Roy	46278	
80036	Botkin) Jenny Lou Carson Music, Inc.	9-46278	

01-11-51 Castle Studios; Nashville, Tennessee. 2:00-5:30 P.M. Producer: Paul Cohen. Vocal: Ernest Tubb. Bass: Jack Drake. Rhythm guitar: Unknown. Steel guitar: Dickie Harris. Lead guitar: Billy Byrd. Piano: Owen Bradley (1,2). Organ: Owen Bradley (3). Vibraphone: Grady Martin (3).

NA 2292	DON'T STAY TOO LONG (1) (Don Whitney-	46296	
80339	Ernest Tubb) Ernest Tubb Music, Inc.	9-46296	
NA 2293	I'M STEPPING OUT OF THE PICTURE (2)	46377	
80340	(Jenny Lou Carson) Jenny Lou Carson Music, Inc.	9-46377	
NA 2294	MAY THE GOOD LORD BLESS AND KEEP YOU (3)	46295	DL 5334
80341	(Meredith Willson) Pickwick Music Corp.	14561	VL 3765
		A-856/	VL 73765
		9-236;	
		9-46295	

*From lyrics by Floyd D. Henderson.

01-15-51 Castle Studios; Nashville, Tennessee. 5:30-9:30 P.M. Producer: Paul Cohen. Vocal: Ernest Tubb. Bass: Jack Drake. Rhythm guitar: Jack Shook. Steel guitar: Dickie Harris. Lead guitar: Billy Byrd. Organ: Owen Bradley (1). Piano: Owen Bradley (2,3,4).

NA 2305	WHEN IT'S PRAYER MEETIN' TIME IN THE	46295	DL 5334
80403	HOLLOW (1) (Fleming Allan-Al Rice)	14561	VL 3765
	M. M. Cole Pub., Inc.	A-856/	VL 73765
		9-236	
		9-46295	
NA 2306	A DRUNKARD'S CHILD (2)	46309	DL 5336
80404	(Andrew Jenkins-Jimmie Rodgers)	A-858/	
	Peer International, Inc.	9-238	
		ED 91181	
		ED 588	
NA 2307	ANY OLD TIME (3) (Jimmie Rodgers)	46309	DL 5336
80401	Peer International, Inc.	A-858/	
		9-238	
		ED 91181	
		ED 588	
NA 2308	IF YOU WANT SOME LOVIN' (4)	46296	
80402	(Ted Johnson-Dude Martin-Joe Bruhl)	9-46296	
	Acuff-Rose Publications, Inc.		

01-17-51 Castle Studios; Nashville, Tennessee. 1:30-5:30 P.M. Producer: Paul Cohen. Vocal: Ernest Tubb; Red Foley; Anita Kerr Singers (1). Bass: Jack Drake. Rhythm guitar: Jack Shook. Steel guitar: Billy Robinson. Drums: Farris Coursey. Lead guitar: Hank Garland. Piano: Owen Bradley (2). Organ: Owen Bradley (1).

NA 2309	SO LONG (IT'S BEEN GOOD TO KNOW YUH) (1)	46297
80407	(Woody Guthrie) Folkways Music Publishing, Inc.	9-46297
NA 2310	THE CHICKEN SONG (2) (Terry Shand-Bob Merrill)	46297
80408	Leeds Music Corp.	9-46297

03-09-51 Castle Studios; Nashville, Tennessee. 1:45-4:45 P.M. Producer: Paul Cohen. Vocal: Ernest Tubb; Red Foley; Anita Kerr Singers. Bass: Jack Drake. Rhythm guitar: Jack Shook. Drums: Farris Coursey. Lead guitar: Grady Martin. Second lead guitar: Hank Garland. Organ: Owen Bradley. Violins: Unknown. Cello: Unknown. Clarinet: Unknown.

NA 2337	THE STRANGE LITTLE GIRL	46311	DL 8298
80687	(Jerry Ross-Richard Adler) Frank Music Corp.	ED 2367	
		9-46311	
NA 2338	KENTUCKY WALTZ (Bill Monroe) Peer International	46311	DL 8298
80688		9-46311	
		ED 2024	

06-15-51 Castle Studios; Nashville, Tennessee. 7:30 P.M.-2:00 A.M. Producer: Paul
Cohen. Vocal: Ernest Tubb; Anita Kerr Singers (1,2). Bass: Jack Drake.
Rhythm guitar: Rusty Gabbard. Steel guitar: Dickie Harris. Drums: Farris
Coursey. Lead guitar: Billy Byrd. Second lead guitar: Grady Martin. Piano:
Owen Bradley.

NA 2411	HEY LA LA (1) (Ray Price-Leonard McRight)	46338	DL 75252
81174	Jim Beck Music Co.	9-46338	MCA 84
NA2412	ROSE OF THE MOUNTAIN (2) (Hans Lang-Jack	46343	
81175	Rollins-Frances Kane) Hill & Range Songs, Inc.	9-46343	
NA 2413	PRECIOUS LITTLE BABY (Lee Roberts)	46338	
81176	Tannen Music Corp.	9-46338	
NA 2414	I'M WITH A CROWD BUT SO ALONE	46343	
81177	(Elaine Tubb-Carl Story) Ernest Tubb Music, Inc.	9-46343	

11-13-51 Castle Studios; Nashville, Tennessee. 2:15-6:15 P.M. Producer: Paul Cohen.
Vocal: Ernest Tubb. Bass: Jack Drake. Rhythm guitar: Rusty Gabbard. Steel
guitar: Dickie Harris. Drums: Farris Coursey. Lead guitar: Billy Byrd. Second
lead guitar: Grady Martin. Piano: Owen Bradley.

NA 2540	SO MANY TIMES (Cindy Walker)	28310
81878	Ernest Tubb Music, Inc.	9-28310
NA 2541	MY MOTHER MUST HAVE BEEN A GIRL LIKE YOU	28067
81879	(Justin Tubb) Ernest Tubb Music, Inc.	9-28067
NA 2542	SOMEBODY'S STOLEN MY HONEY	28067
81880	(Boudleaux Bryant) Tannen Music, Inc.	9-28067
NA 2543	A HEARTSICK SOLDIER ON HEARTBREAK RIDGE	46389
81881	(Max Fidler-Nellie Kane-Ernest Tubb)	9-46389
	Comet Music Co.	

11-14-51 Castle Studios; Nashville, Tennessee. 7:10-11:10 P.M. Producer: Paul Cohen.
Vocal: Ernest Tubb; Red Foley. Bass: Ernie Newton. Rhythm guitar: Jack
Shook. Fiddle: Tommy Jackson. Steel guitar: Billy Robinson. Drums: Farris
Coursey. Lead guitar: Billy Byrd. Second lead guitar: Grady Martin. Piano:
Owen Bradley.

NA 2544	I'M IN LOVE WITH MOLLY (Cy Coben)	46387	DL 8298
81882	Leo Talent Music, Inc.	ED 2367	
		9-46387	
NA 2545	TOO OLD TO CUT THE MUSTARD (Bill Carlisle)	46387	DL 8298
81883	Acuff-Rose Publications	ED 2024	
		9-46387	

11-30-51 Castle Studios; Nashville, Tennessee. 1:30-4:30 P.M. Producer: Paul Cohen.
Vocal: Ernest Tubb. Bass: Jack Drake. Rhythm guitar: Rusty Gabbard. Steel
guitar: Dickie Harris. Drums: Farris Coursey. Lead guitar: Billy Byrd. Piano:
Owen Bradley.

NA 2550	MISSING IN ACTION (Helen Kays-Arthur Q. Smith)	46389	DL 75252
81922	Peer International Corp.	9-46389	MCA 20427
NA 2551	I WILL MISS YOU WHEN YOU GO	28550	
81923	(Baby Stewart-Ernest Tubb)	ED 2769	
	Ernest Tubb Music, Inc.	9-28550	

06-16-52 Castle Studios; Nashville, Tennessee. 2:30-6:00 P.M. Producer: Paul Cohen. Vocal: Ernest Tubb. Bass: Jack Drake. Rhythm guitar: Danny Dill. Steel guitar: Dickie Harris. Lead guitar: Billy Byrd. Piano: Owen "Half Moon" Bradley.

NA 2734	FORTUNES IN MEMORIES (Charlie Walker-	28310	DL 5451
82985	Lou Wayne) Acuff-Rose Publications, Inc.	9-28310	DL 75252
			MCA 84
			MCAD-10086
NA 2735	DEAR JUDGE (Billy Hughes)	28550	
82986	Ernest Tubb Music, Inc.	9-28550	
NA 2736	DON'T BRUSH THEM ON ME (Ernest Tubb)	28777	
82987	Ernest Tubb Music, Inc.	9-28777	
NA 2737	I LOVE EVERYTHING YOU DO		
82988	(Jack Davis-Jimmie Davis) Peer International		

09-28-52 Castle Studios; Nashville, Tennessee. 2:15-5:15 P.M. Producer: Paul Cohen. Vocal: Ernest Tubb. Bass: Jack Drake. Rhythm guitar: Danny Dill. Steel guitar: Dickie Harris. Lead guitar: Billy Byrd. Piano: Owen Bradley.

NA 2833	SOMEBODY LOVES YOU (Peter DeRose-	28448	DL 5451
83463	Charles Tobias) Edwin H. Morris & Co. Inc.	9-28448	
NA 2834	DON'T TRIFLE ON YOUR SWEETHEART	28448	
83464	(Leon Payne) Hill & Range Songs, Inc.	9-28448	
NA 2835	WE NEED GOD FOR CHRISTMAS (Alma F.	28946	DL 4518
83465	Donaldson-Ernest Tubb) Ernest Tubb Music, Inc.	9-28946	DL 74518

09-29-52 Castle Studios; Nashville, Tennessee. 2:30-5:30 P.M. Producer: Paul Cohen. Vocal: Ernest Tubb; Beasley Sisters. Bass: Jack Drake. Rhythm guitar: Danny Dill. Steel guitar: Dickie Harris. Drums: Farris Coursey. Lead guitar: Billy Byrd. Piano: Owen Bradley.

NA 2836	MERRY TEXAS CHRISTMAS, YOU ALL!	28453	DL 4518
83466	(Leon A. Harris, Jr.-Bob Miller) Bob Miller Music	9-28453	DL 74518
NA 2837	BLUE SNOWFLAKES (Billy Hayes)	28453	DL 4518
83467	R.F.D. Music Publishing Co., Inc.	9-28453	DL 74518

02-24-53 Castle Studios; Nashville, Tennessee. 4:15-10:15 P.M. Producer: Paul Cohen. Vocal: Ernest Tubb. Bass: Jack Drake. Rhythm guitar: Danny Dill. Steel guitar: Dickie Harris. Drums: Farris Coursey. Lead guitar: Billy Byrd. Second lead guitar: Grady Martin. Piano: Owen Bradley.

NA 2937	HANK, IT WILL NEVER BE THE SAME WITHOUT	28630	
84014	YOU (Justin Tubb-Ernest Tubb)	9-28630	
	Ernest Tubb Music, Inc.		

NA 2938	BEYOND THE SUNSET (Virgil P. Brock-Blanche Kerr	28630	
84015	Brock) Rodeheaver Co./Robbins Music Corp.	9-28630	
		ED 2769	
NA 2939	WHEN JIMMIE RODGERS SAID GOODBYE	28696	
84016	(Dwight Butcher-Lou Herscher) Jerry Vogel Music	ED 2059	
		9-28696	
NA 2940	JIMMIE RODGERS' LAST THOUGHTS (Elsie	28696	
84017	McWilliams-Ernest Tubb) Peer International	ED 2059	
		9-28696	
NA 2941	MY WASTED PAST (Roy Duke-Ernest Tubb)	28777	
84018	Ernest Tubb Music, Inc.	9-28777	
NA 2942	COUNTERFEIT KISSES (Carrie Fraley-Evelyn	28869	
84019	Fielding-Gene MacGregor) Ernest Tubb Music, Inc.	9-28869	
NA 2943	THE HONEYMOON IS OVER (Floyd Tillman-		
84020	Ralph C. Smith) Hill & Range Songs, Inc.		

02-27-53　Castle Studios; Nashville, Tennessee. 2:30-6:30 P.M. Producer: Paul Cohen. Vocal: Ernest Tubb; Red Foley. Bass: Jack Drake. Rhythm guitar: Jack Shook. Steel guitar: Dickie Harris. Drums: Farris Coursey. Lead guitar: Grady Martin. Second lead guitar: Hank Garland. Piano: Owen Bradley.

NA 2944	NO HELP WANTED #2 (Bill Carlisle)	28634	DL 8298
84036	Acuff-Rose Publications	ED 2367	
		9-28634	
NA 2945	YOU'RE A REAL GOOD FRIEND	28634	DL 8298
84037	(Cy Coben-Charles Grean) Alamo Music, Inc.	ED 2368	
		9-28634	

08-05-53　Castle Studios; Nashville, Tennessee. 2:45-5:45 P.M. Producer: Paul Cohen. Vocal: Ernest Tubb (1); Violet Elaine "Scooter Bill" Tubb. Bass: Jack Drake. Rhythm guitar: Danny Dill. Steel guitar: Dickie Harris. Drums: Farris Coursey. Lead guitar: Billy Byrd. Second lead guitar: Grady Martin. Piano: Owen Bradley.

NA 3098	A DEAR JOHN LETTER (1) (Billy Barton-Lewis	28837	
84980	Talley-Charles "Fuzzy" Owen) Central Songs, Inc.	9-28837	
NA 3099	MEAN AGE, IN BETWEEN AGE BLUES	28837	
84981	(Jack Rollins-Dave Coleman) Aberbach, Inc.	9-28837	

08-06-53　Castle Studios; Nashville, Tennessee. 3:00-6:00 P.M. Producer: Paul Cohen. Vocal: Ernest Tubb; Red Foley. Bass: Jack Drake or Ernie Newton. Rhythm guitar: Jack Shook. Steel guitar: Dickie Harris (2). Drums: Farris Coursey. Lead guitar: Hank Garland. Second lead guitar: Grady Martin. Piano: Owen Bradley. Blocks: Farris Coursey (1).

NA 3104	DOUBLE DATIN' (1) (Kay Twomey-Fred Wise-	29195	DL 8298
85113	Ben Weisman) Alamo Music, Inc.	ED 2368	
		9-29195	

NA 3105	IT'S THE MILEAGE THAT'S SLOWIN' US DOWN (2)	29195	DL 8298
85114	(Vic McAlpin) Acuff-Rose Publications, Inc.	ED 2368	
		9-29195	

08-14-53 Castle Studios; Nashville, Tennessee. 2:30-5:30 Producer: Paul Cohen. Vocal: Ernest Tubb. Bass: Jack Drake. Rhythm guitar: Danny Dill. Steel guitar: Dickie Harris. Drums: Farris Coursey. Lead guitar: Billy Byrd. Second lead guitar: Grady Martin. Piano: Owen Bradley.

NA 3116	DIVORCE GRANTED (Charles Eastman Tebbetts-	28869
85110	Dave Washington) Forrest Music Corp.	9-28869
NA 3117	HONKY TONK HEART (Ralph C. Smith)	29011
85111	Hill & Range Songs, Inc.	9-29011
NA 3118	I'M NOT LOOKING FOR AN ANGEL (Billy Hughes)	29011
85112	Hill & Range Songs, Inc.	9-29011

09-02-53 Castle Studios; Nashville, Tennessee. 1:45-4:45 P.M. Producer: Paul Cohen. Vocal: Ernest Tubb. Bass: Jack Drake. Rhythm guitar: Danny Dill. Steel guitar: Dickie Harris. Drums: Farris Coursey. Lead guitar: Billy Byrd. Second lead guitar: Grady Martin.

NA 3121	I MET A FRIEND (Charles Fay Smith)	29624	VL 3765
85314	Ernest Tubb Music, Inc.	9-29624	VL 73765
NA 3122	WHEN JESUS CALLS (Willie Phelps)	29624	VL 3765
85315	Ernest Tubb Music, Inc.	9-29624	VL 73765

10-06-53 Castle Studios; Nashville, Tennessee. Time: Unknown. Producer: Paul Cohen. Vocal: Ernest Tubb; Red Foley. Bass: Jack Drake. Rhythm guitar: Jack Shook. Fiddle: Tommy Jackson. Steel guitar: Dickie Harris. Drums: Farris Coursey. Lead guitar: Billy Byrd. Second lead guitar: Grady Martin. Piano: Owen Bradley.

NA 3144	TOO OLD TO TANGO* (Sheb Wooley)	28911
85255	Aberbach-Brenner Music	9-28911
NA 3145	DR. KETCHUM* (Sheb Wooley) Aberbach, Inc.	28911
85256		9-28911

10-23-53 Castle Studios; Nashville, Tennessee. 2:30-5:30 P.M. Producer: Paul Cohen. Vocal: Ernest Tubb. Bass: Jack Drake. Rhythm guitar: Unknown. Steel guitar: Dickie Harris. Drums: Farris Coursey. Lead guitar: Billy Byrd. Piano: Owen Bradley.

NA 3160	I'M TRIMMING MY CHRISTMAS TREE WITH	28946	DL 4518
85434	TEARDROPS (Frank Team-Ernest Tubb)**	9-28946	DL 74518
	Hill & Range Songs, Inc.		

*"Too Young to Tango," also Sheb's composition, a record for Sunshine Ruby on RCA Victor, spring 1953 (*Billboard* 5-30-53). "Dr. Ketchum" is Sheb's nonsense takeoff on the Kinsey report on human sexuality.
**"Frank Team" is a pseudonym for H&R staff writer Ben Weisman.

NA 3161   LOVE LIFTED ME (James Rowe-Howard Smith)   MCAD-10086
85435

01-11-54   Bradley Studios; Nashville, Tennessee. 2:45-5:45 P.M. Producer: Paul Cohen.
Vocal: Ernest Tubb. Bass: Jack Drake. Rhythm guitar: Unknown. Steel guitar:
Dickie Harris. Drums: Farris Coursey. Lead guitar: Billy Byrd. Second lead
guitar: Grady Martin (1). Piano: Owen Bradley.

NA 3220	TILL WE TWO ARE ONE (1) (Tom Glazer-Billy	29020	VL 3684
85691	Martin-Larry Martin) Shapiro, Bernstein & Co.	9-29020	VL 73684
NA 3221	YOUR MOTHER, YOUR DARLING, YOUR FRIEND	29103	
85692	(Jack Henley-Ernest Tubb) Ernest Tubb Music, Inc.	9-29103	
NA 3222	BABY YOUR MOTHER (LIKE SHE BABIED YOU) (1)	29103	
85693	(Joe Burke-Dolly Morse-Andrew Donnelly)	9-29103	
	Leo Feist, Inc.		
NA 3223	JEALOUS LOVING HEART (Billy Talmadge Tubb-	29020	VL 3684
85694	Ernest Tubb) Ernest Tubb Music, Inc.	9-29020	

06-22-54   Bradley Studios; Nashville, Tennessee. 1:35-3:35 P.M. Producer: Paul Cohen.
Vocal: Ernest Tubb. Bass: Jack Drake. Rhythm guitar: Unknown. Fiddle:
Tommy Jackson. Steel guitar: Dickie Harris. Drums: Farris Coursey. Lead
guitar: Billy Byrd. Piano: Owen Bradley.

NA 3325	TWO GLASSES, JOE (Cindy Walker)	29220	VL 3684
86485	Ernest Tubb Music, Inc.	9-29220	DL 4881
			VL 73684
			MCAD-10086
			DL 74881
NA 3326	THE WOMAN'S TOUCH (Cindy Walker)	29415	
86486	Ernest Tubb Music, Inc.	9-29415	
NA 3327	JOURNEY'S END (Virgil "Pappy" Stewart-Ernest	29220	VL 3684
86487	Tubb) Ernest Tubb Music, Inc.	9-29220	VL 73684
NA 3328	KANSAS CITY BLUES (Ernest Tubb)	29415	VL 3684
86488	Ernest Tubb Music, Inc.	9-29415	VL 73684

10-29-54   Bradley Studios; Nashville, Tennessee. 10:30 P.M.-1:30 A.M. Producer: Paul
Cohen. Vocal: Ernest Tubb. Bass: Jack Drake. Rhythm guitar: Unknown. Steel
guitar: Dickie Harris. Drums: Farris Coursey. Lead guitar: Billy Byrd. Piano:
Owen Bradley (1).

NA 3390	LONELY CHRISTMAS EVE (1) (Buddy Thornton)	29350	DL 4518
86988	Four Star Sales Co., Inc.	9-29350	DL 74518
NA 3391	I'LL BE WALKING THE FLOOR THIS CHRISTMAS	29350	DL 4518
86989	(Justin Tubb-Doug Tubb) Ernest Tubb Music, Inc.	9-29350	DL 74518

04-06-55   Bradley Studios; Nashville, Tennessee. 6:00-9:00 P.M. Producer: Paul Cohen.
Vocal: Ernest Tubb. Bass: Jack Drake. Rhythm guitar: Rusty Gabbard. Fiddle:
Dale Potter. Steel guitar: Dickie Harris. Drums: Farris Coursey or Murrey
Harman. Lead guitar: Billy Byrd. Piano: Owen Bradley.

BR 9088	HAVE YOU SEEN MY BOOGIE WOOGIE BABY	29520	
87748	(Vern Adams) Hudson-Dart Music Co.	9-29520	
BR 9089	IT'S A LONELY WORLD (Redd Stewart-Ernest Tubb)	29520	VL 3684
87749	Ernest Tubb Music, Inc.	9-29520	VL 73684
BR 9090	I'VE GOT THE BLUES FOR MAMMY (Hy Heath-		
87750	William Daugherty) Acuff-Rose Publishing		

07-14-55 Bradley Studios; Nashville, Tennessee. Time: Unknown. Producer: Paul Cohen. Vocal: Ernest Tubb. Bass: Jack Drake. Rhythm guitar: Rusty Gabbard. Fiddle: Tommy Jackson; Dale Potter (1). Steel guitar: Dickie Harris. Drums: Farris Coursey. Lead guitar: Billy Byrd. Second lead guitar: Unknown. Piano: Owen Bradley.

NA 9161	(I'M GONNA MAKE MY HOME) A MILLION MILES	29633	
88395	FROM HERE (Talmadge Tubb-Ernest Tubb)	9-29633	
	Ernest Tubb Music, Inc.		
NA 9162	THE YELLOW ROSE OF TEXAS (1) (Don George)	29633	VL 3684
88396	Planetary Music Publishing	9-29633	VL 73684

10-12-55 Bradley Studios, Nashville, Tennessee. Time: Unknown. Producer: Paul Cohen. Vocal: Ernest Tubb. Bass: Jack Drake. Rhythm guitar: Rusty Gabbard. Fiddle: Dale Potter. Steel guitar: Dickie Harris. Drums: Farris Coursey. Lead guitar: Billy Byrd. Piano: Owen Bradley.

NA 9186	ANSWER THE PHONE (Cindy Walker)	29731	DL 75252
88780	Ernest Tubb Music, Inc.	9-29731	MCA 84
NA 9187	THE HONEYMOON IS OVER (Floyd Tillman-		
88781	Ralph C. Smith) Hill & Range Songs, Inc.		

10-26-55 Bradley Studios; Nashville, Tennessee. 7:30-11:30 P.M. Producer: Paul Cohen. Vocal: Ernest Tubb. Bass: Jack Drake. Rhythm guitar: Rusty Gabbard. Fiddle: Tommy Jackson. Steel guitar: Dickie Harris. Drums: Farris Coursey or Murrey Harman. Lead guitar: Billy Byrd. Piano: Owen Bradley.

NA 9196	THIRTY DAYS (TO COME BACK HOME)	29731	
88812	(Chuck Berry) Arc Music Corp.	9-29731	
NA 9197	DOORSTEP TO HEAVEN (Leon Payne)		
88813	Rumblero Music		
NA 9198	WILL YOU BE SATISFIED THAT WAY	29934	
88814	(Jimmie Skinner) Ernest Tubb Music, Inc.	9-29934	
NA 9199	STEPPIN' OUT (Billy Starr) Forrest Music		
88815	Publishing-Campbell Music, Inc.		

01-24-56 Bradley Studios; Nashville, Tennessee. Time: Unknown. Producer: Paul Cohen. Vocal: Ernest Tubb. Bass: Jack Drake. Rhythm guitar: Rusty Gabbard. Fiddle: Tommy Jackson (1). Steel guitar: Dickie Harris. Drums: Farris Coursey or Murrey Harman. Lead guitar: Billy Byrd. Piano: Owen Bradley or Floyd Cramer.

NA 9278	IF I NEVER HAVE ANYTHING ELSE (1)	29836
89268	(Lilly C. McAlpin-Joachim Millien-Ernest Tubb)	9-29836
	Ernest Tubb Music, Inc.	
NA 9279	SO DOGGONE LONESOME (Johnny Cash)	29836
89269	Hi-Lo Music, Inc.	9-29836

04-12-56   Bradley Studios; Nashville, Tennessee. Time: Unknown. Producer: Paul Cohen. Vocal: Ernest Tubb. Bass: Jack Drake. Rhythm guitar: Rusty Gabbard. Fiddle: Tommy Jackson. Steel guitar: Dickie Harris. Drums: Farris Coursey or Murrey Harman. Lead guitar: Billy Byrd. Piano: Owen Bradley or Floyd Cramer.

NA 9325	OLD LOVE LETTERS (BRING MEMORIES OF YOU)	ED 2422
89786	(Jimmie Rodgers-Dwight Butcher-Lou Herscher)	
	Southern Music Publishing Co., Inc.	
NA 9326	JIMMIE RODGERS' LAST BLUE YODEL (THE	29934
89787	WOMEN MAKE A FOOL OUT OF ME)	9-29934
	(Jimmie Rodgers) Peer International	
NA 9327	TRAVELIN' BLUES (Shelley Lee Alley-	ED 2422
89788	Jimmie Rodgers) Peer International	

06-12-56   Bradley Studio; Nashville, Tennessee. Time: Unknown. Producer: Paul Cohen. Vocal: Ernest Tubb. Bass: Jack Drake. Rhythm guitar: Rusty Gabbard. Fiddle: Tommy Jackson. Steel guitar: Dickie Harris. Drums: Farris Coursey or Murrey Harman. Lead guitar: Billy Byrd. Piano: Owen Bradley or Floyd Cramer.

NA 9409	YOU'RE THE ONLY GOOD THING (Jack Toombs)	ED 2523	DL 8553
100218	Golden West Melodies		VL 3877
			VL 73877
NA 9410	I'VE GOT THE BLUES FOR MAMMY (Hy Heath-	ED 2521	DL 8553
100219	William Daughtery) Acuff-Rose Publishing		VL 3877
			VL 73877
NA 9411	I DREAMED OF AN OLD LOVE AFFAIR	ED 2522	DL 8553
10220	(Bonnie Dodd-Jimmie Davis-Charles Mitchell)		VL 3877
	Peer International		VL 73877
NA 9412	(I KNOW MY BABY LOVES ME) IN HER OWN	ED 2521	DL 8553
10221	PECULIAR WAY (Riley Shepard-Don Canton)		VL 3877
	American Music, Inc.		VL 73877

06-13-56   Bradley Studios; Nashville, Tennessee. 7:15-10:15 P.M. Producer: Paul Cohen. Vocal: Ernest Tubb. Bass: Jack Drake. Rhythm guitar: Rusty Gabbard. Fiddle: Tommy Jackson. Steel guitar: Dickie Harris. Drums: Farris Coursey or Murrey Harman. Lead guitar: Billy Byrd. Piano: Owen Bradley.

NA 9413	MISSISSIPPI GAL (Sam Nichols-Taylor McPeters-	ED 2522	DL 8553
100222	Daniel Cypert) Hill & Range Songs, Inc.		VL 3877
			VL 73877
NA 9414	THERE'S NO FOOL LIKE A YOUNG FOOL	ED 2523	DL 8553
100223	(Bette Thomasson) Tree Publishing Co., Inc.		VL 3877
			VL 73877

NA 9415	I KNEW THE MOMENT I LOST YOU	ED 2523	DL 8553
100224	(Tommy Duncan-Bob Wills) Bourne Inc.		VL 3877
			VL 73877
NA 9416	YOU'RE BREAKING MY HEART (H. H. Melka)	ED 2521	DL 8553
100225	Peer International		

06-14-56 Bradley Studios; Nashville, Tennessee. 7:15-10:15 P.M. Producer: Paul Cohen. Vocal: Ernest Tubb. Bass: Jack Drake. Rhythm guitar: Rusty Gabbard. Fiddle: Tommy Jackson. Steel guitar: Dickie Harris. Drums: Farris Coursey or Murrey Harman. Lead guitar: Billy Byrd. Piano: Owen Bradley.

NA 9417	WHEN A SOLDIER KNOCKS AND FINDS NOBODY	ED 2522	DL 8553
100226	HOME (Moon Mullican-Lou Wayne-Ernest Tubb)		VL 3877
	Cross Music, Inc.		VL 73877
NA 9418	THIS TROUBLED MIND O' MINE (Billy Hughes-	ED 2521	DL 8553
100227	Johnny Tyler) Hill & Range Songs, Inc.		VL 3877
			VL 73877
NA 9419	MY HILLBILLY BABY (Rex Griffin)	ED 2523	DL 8553
100228	Peer International		VL 3877
			VL 73877
NA 9420	DAISY MAY (Floyd Tillman) Peer International	ED 2522	DL 8553
100229			VL 3877
			VL 73877

09-13-56 Bradley Studios; Nashville, Tennessee. 7:15-10:15 P.M. Producer: Paul Cohen. Vocal: Ernest Tubb. Bass: Jack Drake. Rhythm guitar: Rusty Gabbard. Fiddle: Tommy Jackson. Steel guitar: Dickie Harris. Drums: Farris Coursey or Murrey Harman. Lead guitar: Billy Byrd. Piano: Owen Bradley or Floyd Cramer.

NA 9524	LOVING YOU MY WEAKNESS (Roy Duke)	30098
100625	Ernest Tubb Music, Inc.	9-30098
NA 9525	TREAT HER RIGHT (Buck Bryant)	30098
100626	Golden West Melodies	9-30098
		ED 2626
NA 9526	I WANT YOU TO KNOW I LOVE YOU (Cindy Walker)	
100627	Ernest Tubb Music, Inc.	

01-16-57 (Scratched out in logs; they have 1–17, though.)
Bradley Studios; Nashville, Tennessee. Time: Unknown. Producer: Paul Cohen. Vocal: Ernest Tubb. Bass: Jack Drake. Rhythm guitar: Rusty Gabbard. Fiddle: Dale Potter (2). Drums: Farris Coursey or Murrey Harman. Steel guitar: Unknown (1). Lead guitar: Billy Byrd (electric-1; acoustic-2). Second lead guitar: Grady Martin (1). Piano: Floyd Cramer.

NA 9631	DON'T FORBID ME (1) (Charles Singleton)	30219	VL 3684
101398`	Roosevelt Music Co., Inc.	9-30219	VL 73684
		ED 2626	
NA 9632	GOD'S EYES (2) (Eddie Noack)	30219	
101399	Ernest Tubb Music, Inc.	9-30219	

01-17-57   Bradley Studios; Nashville, Tennessee. 10:15 P.M.-1:15 A.M. (Bradley logs list
"9-10"). Producer: Paul Cohen. Vocal: Ernest Tubb. Bass: Jack Drake. Rhythm
guitar: Rusty Gabbard. Fiddle: Tommy Jackson; Dale Potter, second fiddle (1).
Steel guitar: Ray "Kemo" Head. Drums: Farris Coursey or Murrey Harman.
Lead guitar: Billy Byrd. Second lead guitar: Grady Martin (1). Piano: Floyd
Cramer.

NA 9633	MY TREASURE (1) (Johnny Cash) Hi Lo Music	30422
101942		9-30422
		ED 2626
NA 9634	THE GALS DON'T MEAN A THING (IN MY YOUNG	
101943	LIFE) (Arbie Gibson-Curt Massey)	

02-02-57   Bradley Studios; Nashville, Tennessee. 4:30-7:30 P.M. (Bradley logs: "4-7," so
they were close.) Producer: Paul Cohen. Vocal: Ernest Tubb; Teddy and
Doyle Wilburn. Bass: Jack Drake. Rhythm guitar: Rusty Gabbard. Steel guitar:
Unknown. Drums: Farris Coursey or Murrey Harman. Lead guitar: Billy Byrd.
Second lead guitar: Grady Martin. Piano: Floyd Cramer.

NA 9649	LEAVE ME (Ruby Glasgow) Sure Fire Music Co.	30305
101927		9-30305
		ED 2627
NA 9650	MISTER LOVE (Rusty Kershaw-Doug Kershaw)	30305
101928	Acuff-Rose Publications	9-30305
		ED 2627

07-18-57   Bradley Studios; Nashville, Tennessee. 6:00-9:00 P.M. (Only source: Bradley
logs.) Producer: Paul Cohen (Engineer: Mort Thomasson). Vocal: Ernest
Tubb. Bass: Jack Drake. Rhythm guitar: Rusty Gabbard. Fiddle: Grady Martin
(2) (Bradley logs). Drums: Farris Coursey (in Bradley logs!). Lead guitar: Billy
Byrd. Second lead guitar: Grady Martin (1). Piano: Floyd Cramer.

NA 9913	I ALWAYS WENT THROUGH (1) (Cindy Walker)	
102987	Ernest Tubb Music, Inc.	
NA 9914	GO HOME (2) (Johnny Rion)	30422
102988	Ernest Tubb Music, Inc.	9-30422

11-11-57   Bradley Studios; Nashville, Tennessee. 7:00 P.M. Start. Producer: Paul Cohen.
Vocal: Ernest Tubb; Teddy and Doyle Wilburn; Anita Kerr Singers. Bass: Jack
Drake. Rhythm guitar: Rusty Gabbard. Drums: Farris Coursey or Murrey
Harman. Lead guitar: Billy Byrd (1), Grady Martin (2). Piano: Floyd Cramer.
Hand Clapping: Anita Kerr Singers (1).

NA 9974	HEY MR. BLUEBIRD (1) (Cindy Walker)	30610
103760	Ernest Tubb Music, Inc.	9-30610
		ED 2627
NA 9975	HOW DO WE KNOW (2) (Cindy Walker)	30610
103761	Ernest Tubb Music, Inc.	9-30610
		ED 2627

11-12-57   Bradley Studios; Nashville, Tennessee. 7:00 P.M. Start. Producer: Paul Cohen. Vocal: Ernest Tubb; Anita Kerr Singers. Bass: Jack Drake. Rhythm guitar: Rusty Gabbard. Drums: Murrey Harman. Lead guitar: Grady Martin (1,2). Second lead guitar: Hank Garland (1). Piano: Owen Bradley (1); Floyd Cramer (2).

NA 9976	HOUSE OF GLASS (1) (Jimmy Duncan)	30549	
103762	Blue Grass Music, Inc.	9-30549	
		ED 2626	
NA 9977	HEAVEN HELP ME (2) (Cindy Walker)	30549	
103763	Ernest Tubb Music, Inc.	9-30549	

11-13-57   Bradley Studios (Quonset Hut: logs); Nashville, Tennessee. 7:00 P.M. Start. Producer: Paul Cohen. Vocal: Ernest Tubb; Anita Kerr Singers (1,2). Bass: Jack Drake. Rhythm guitar: Rusty Gabbard. Fiddle: Tommy Jackson (1,3,4). Drums: Murrey Harman. Lead guitar: Billy Byrd. Second lead guitar: Grady Martin (1,2,4). Electric bass: Grady Martin (1,2). Piano: Floyd Cramer (1,2,4).

NA 9978	TANGLED MIND (1) (Ted Daffan-Herman Shoss)	ED 2563	
103685	Hill & Range Songs, Inc.		
NA 9979	HOME OF THE BLUES (2) (Johnny Cash-Lilly	ED 2563	
103686	McAlpin-Glenn Douglas) Hi Lo Music, Inc.		
NA 9980	I FOUND MY GIRL IN THE U.S.A. (3)	30526	DL 8733
103687	(Jimmie Skinner) Starrite Music Co.	9-30526	
		ED 2563	
NA 9981	GEISHA GIRL (4) (Lawton Williams) Fairway Music	30526	DL 8733
103688		9-30526	
		ED 2563	

11-14-57   Bradley Studios; Nashville, Tennessee. Time: Unknown. Producer: Paul Cohen. Vocal: Ernest Tubb. Bass: Jack Drake. Rhythm guitar: Rusty Gabbard. Steel guitar: Ray Kemo Head (1,3). Drums: Farris Coursey or Murrey Harman. Lead guitar: Billy Byrd (1); Grady Martin (2,3). Second lead guitar: Grady Martin (1). Piano: Floyd Cramer (2,3). Electric bass: Harold Bradley (2).

NA 9982	I WONDER WHY I WORRY OVER YOU (1)
103698	(Dave Denney-Steve Nelson-Ernest Tubb)
	Ernest Tubb Music, Inc.
NA 9983	DEEP PURPLE BLUES (2) (Cindy Walker) Ernest
103699	Tubb Music, Inc.
NA 9984	PLEASE KEEP ME IN MIND (3) (Hillman Baker)
103700	Merge Music

05-16-58   Bradley Film & Recording Studio; Nashville, Tennessee. 8:15-11:15 P.M. Producer: Owen Bradley. Vocal: Ernest Tubb. Bass: Jack Drake. Rhythm guitar: Johnny Johnson. Steel guitar: Buddy Emmons. Drums: Farris Coursey. Lead guitar: Billy Byrd. Electric bass: Grady Martin. Piano: Floyd Cramer.

NA 10272	DEEP PURPLE BLUES (Cindy Walker)	9-30685	
105021	Ernest Tubb Music, Inc.		
NA 10273	PLEASE KEEP ME IN MIND (Hillman Baker)		DL 4393
105022	Merge Music		DL 74393

THE GALS DON'T MEAN A THING
(Arbie Gibson-Curt Massey)

NA 10274   I WONDER WHY I WORRY OVER YOU   DL 8834
105023   (Dave Denney-Steve Nelson-Ernest Tubb)   DL 78834
             Ernest Tubb Music, Inc.

05-19-58   Bradley Film & Recording Studio; Nashville, Tennessee. 8:00-11:00 P.M.
Producer: Owen Bradley. Vocal: Ernest Tubb. Bass: Jack Drake. Rhythm guitar:
Johnny Johnson. Steel guitar: Buddy Emmons. Drums: Farris Coursey. Lead
guitar: Billy Byrd. Second lead guitar: Grady Martin. Piano: Floyd Cramer.

NA 10275	I'M A LONG GONE DADDY (Hank Williams)	ED 2643	DL 8834
105024	Acuff-Rose Publications, Inc.		DL 78834
NA 10276	YOUR CHEATIN' HEART (Hank Williams)	ED 2643	DL 8834
105025	Acuff-Rose Publications, Inc.		DL 78834
NA 10277	DON'T TRADE YOUR OLD-FASHIONED		DL 8834
105026	SWEETHEART (FOR A HONKY-TONK QUEEN)		DL 78834
	(Eddie Noack) Starrite Music Co.		
NA 10278	IT MAKES NO DIFFERENCE NOW	ED 2643	DL 8834
105027	(Floyd Tillman-Jimmie Davis) Peer International		DL 78834

05-20-58   Bradley Film & Recording Studio; Nashville, Tennessee. 8:15-11:15 P.M.
Producer: Owen Bradley. Engineers: Jim Lockert, Selby Coffeen. Vocal: Ernest
Tubb. Bass: Jack Drake. Rhythm guitar: Johnny Johnson. Fiddle: Tommy
Jackson. Steel guitar: Buddy Emmons. Drums: Farris Coursey. Lead guitar:
Billy Byrd. Second lead guitar: Grady Martin. Piano: Floyd Cramer.

NA 10281	SAN ANTONIO ROSE (Bob Wills-Tommy Duncan)	ED 2643	DL 8834
105028	Bourne, Inc.		DL 78834
NA 10282	I ALWAYS WENT THROUGH (Cindy Walker)		
105029	Ernest Tubb Music, Inc.		

05-22-58   Bradley Film & Recording Studios; Nashville, Tennessee. 8:15-11:15 P.M.
Producer: Owen Bradley. Vocal: Ernest Tubb. Bass: Jack Drake. Rhythm
guitar: Johnny Johnson. Fiddle: Tommy Jackson. Steel guitar: Buddy Emmons.
Drums: Farris Coursey. Lead guitar: Billy Byrd. Piano: Floyd Cramer.

NA 10287	I WANT YOU TO KNOW I LOVE YOU (Cindy Walker)	DL 4045
105030	Ernest Tubb Music, Inc.	DL 74045
NA 10288	THAT, MY DARLIN', IS ME (Justin Tubb)	DL 8834
105031	Ernest Tubb Music, Inc.	DL 7834
NA 10289	I'LL GET ALONG SOMEHOW (Ernest Tubb)	DL 8871;
105032	American Music, Inc.	DL 4118
		DX 159;
		DX 7159
		DL 5006;
		DL 75006
		MCA 2-4040;
		DL 74118
		MCA 16

06-09-58   Bradley Film & Recording Studio; Nashville, Tennessee. 8:00-11:00 P.M.
Producer: Owen Bradley. Vocal: Ernest Tubb. Bass: Jack Drake. Rhythm guitar:
Johnny Johnson. Steel guitar: Buddy Emmons. Drums: Farris Coursey. Lead
guitar: Billy Byrd. Second lead guitar: Grady Martin. Piano: Floyd Cramer.

NA 10290	EDUCATED MAMA (Hal Willis-Ginger Willis)		DL 8834
105136	Tree Publishing Co.		DL 78834
NA 10291	I'M WAITING FOR SHIP THAT NEVER COME IN		DL 8834
105137	(Abe Ulman-Jack Yellen-William Raskin)		DL 78834
	Forster Music Publishing, Inc.		

06-11-58   Bradley Film & Recording Studio; Nashville, Tennessee. 8:50 P.M.-12:50 A.M.
Producer: Owen Bradley. Vocal: Ernest Tubb. Bass: Jack Drake. Rhythm guitar:
Johnny Johnson. Steel guitar: Buddy Emmons. Drums: Farris Coursey. Lead
guitar: Billy Byrd. Second lead guitar: Grady Martin. Piano: Floyd Cramer.

NA 10292	HALF A MIND (Roger Miller)	9-30685	DL 5006
105138	Tree Publishing Co., Inc.		DL 75006
			MCA 16
NA 10293	NEXT TIME (Glenn Douglas) Be Are Music	9-30952	
105139		ED 2091	
NA 10294	GOODBYE SUNSHINE HELLO BLUES	9-30759	
105140	(Billy Talmadge Tubb) Ernest Tubb Music, Inc.		

09-24-58   Bradley Film & Recording Studio; Nashville, Tennessee. 7:30-10:30 P.M.
Producer: Owen Bradley. Vocal: Ernest Tubb. Bass: Jack Drake. Rhythm guitar:
Johnny Johnson. Steel guitar: Buddy Emmons. Drums: Murrey Harman. Lead
guitar: Billy Byrd. Second lead guitar: Grady Martin. Piano: Floyd Cramer.

NA 10383	IT'S THE AGE THAT MAKES THE DIFFERENCE		DL 8834
105736	(Vernon Claude-George Sherry) Peer International		DL 78834
NA 10384	WHAT AM I LIVING FOR (Fred Jay-Al Harris)	9-30759	
105737	Progressive Music Pub. Co./Rush Music Corp.		

10-06-58   Bradley Film & Recording Studio; Nashville, Tennessee. 8:15-11:15 P.M.
Producer: Owen Bradley. Vocal: Ernest Tubb. Bass: Jack Drake. Rhythm guitar:
Johnny Johnson. Steel guitar: Buddy Emmons. Drums: Murrey Harman. Lead
guitar: Billy Byrd. Second lead guitar: Grady Martin. Piano: Floyd Cramer.

NA 10395	THE NEXT VOICE YOU HEAR (Cindy Walker)		DL 8334
105794	Hill & Range/Brenner Music		DL 78834
NA 10396	ALL THOSE YESTERDAYS (Ernest Tubb)		DL 8334
105795	Ernest Tubb Music, Inc.		DL 78834
NA 10397	WALKING THE FLOOR OVER YOU (Ernest Tubb)		DXB 159;
105796	American Music, Inc.		DXSA 7159;
			DL 4118;
			MCA 24;
			MCA 2-4040;
			DL 8871
			DL 5006;
			DL 75006
			DL 74118

NA 10398   WHEN THE WORLD HAS TURNED YOU DOWN   DL 8871;
105797   (Ernest Tubb) American Music, Inc.   DL 4118;

DXB 159/

DXSA 7159;

MCA 2-4040;

DL 74118

10-08-58 Bradley Film & Recording Studio; Nashville, Tennessee. 8:15-11:15 P.M. Producer: Owen Bradley. Vocal: Ernest Tubb. Bass: Jack Drake. Rhythm guitar: H. K. "Smiley" Wilson; Grady Martin. Steel guitar: Buddy Emmons. Drums: Murrey Harman. Lead guitar: Billy Byrd. Piano: Floyd Cramer.

NA 10399   I'LL ALWAYS BE GLAD TO TAKE YOU BACK   DXB 159/
105798   (Ernest Tubb) American Music, Inc.   DXSA 7159;

DL 8871;

DL 4118;

MCA 24;

MCA 2-4040

DL 74118

NA 10400   IT'S BEEN SO LONG DARLIN' (Ernest Tubb)   DXB 159/
105799   American Music, Inc.   DXSA 7159;

DL 8872;

MCA 2-4040

NA 10401   CARELESS DARLIN' (Lou Wayne-Bob Shelton-   ED 2655 DL 8872;
105800   Ernest Tubb) American Music, Inc.   MCA 2-4040;

DXB 159/

DXSA 7159

NA 10402   THOUGH THE DAYS WERE ONLY SEVEN   DXB 159/
105801   (Ruth Smith-Ernest Tubb) American Music, Inc.   DXSA 7159;

DL 8872;

MCA 2-4040

10-09-58 Bradley Film & Recording Studio; Nashville, Tennessee. 8:15-11:15 P.M. Producer: Owen Bradley. Vocal: Ernest Tubb. Bass: Jack Drake. Rhythm guitar: Johnny Johnson. Steel guitar: Buddy Emmons. Drums: Murrey Harman. Lead guitar: Billy Byrd. Second lead guitar: Grady Martin. Piano: Floyd Cramer.

NA 10405   LAST NIGHT I DREAMED (Ernest Tubb)   DXB 159/
105856   American Music, Inc.   DXSA 7159;

DL 8872;

MCA 2-4040

NA 10406   SLIPPING AROUND* (Floyd Tillman)   DXB 159/
105857   Peer International   DXSA 7159;

DL 8871;

DL 4118;

MCA 24;

MCA 2-4040

*First instance on an Ernest Tubb record of the soon-to-be-popular "shuffle beat."

NA 10407	I LOVE YOU BECAUSE (Leon Payne)		DXB 159/
105858	Acuff-Rose Publications, Inc.		DXSA 7159;
			DL 8872;
			MCA 2-4040

NA 10408	THERE'S NOTHING MORE TO SAY (Ernest Tubb)		DXB 159/
105859	American Music, Inc.		DXSA 7159;
			DL 8871;
			DL 4118;
			MCA 24;
			MCA 2-4040
			DL 74118

10-10-58 Bradley Film & Recording Studio; Nashville, Tennessee. 8:15-11:15 P.M. Producer: Owen Bradley. Vocal: Ernest Tubb. Bass: Jack Drake. Rhythm guitar: Johnny Johnson. Fiddle: Tommy Jackson. Steel guitar: Buddy Emmons. Drums: Murrey Harman. Lead guitar: Billy Byrd. Second lead guitar: Grady Martin. Piano: Floyd Cramer.

NA 10412	THERE'S A LITTLE BIT OF EVERYTHING IN TEXAS		DXB 159/
105860	(Ernest Tubb) American Music, Inc.		DXSA 7159;
			DL 4118;
			DL 8871;
			MCA 2-4040;
			MCA 24
			DL 74118

NA 10413	YOU NEARLY LOSE YOUR MIND (Ernest Tubb)	ED 2625	DXB 159/
105861	American Music, Inc.		DXSA 7159;
			DL 8872;
			MCA 2-4040

NA 10414	BLUE CHRISTMAS (Billy Hayes-Jay Johnson) MCA		DXB 159/
105862	65024 R.F.D. Music Corp.		DXSA 7159;
			DL 4518;
			DL 74518;
			DL 8872;
			MCA 2-4040

NA 10415	DON'T ROB ANOTHER MAN'S CASTLE		DXB 159/
105863	(Jenny Lou Carson) Hill & Range Songs, Inc.		DXSA 7159;
			DL 8872;
			MCA 2-4040

02-23-59 Bradley Film & Recording Studio; Nashville, Tennessee. 9:00-12:00 P.M. Producer: Owen Bradley. Vocal: Ernest Tubb. Bass: Jack Drake. Rhythm guitar: Johnny Johnson. Fiddle: Tommy Jackson. Steel guitar: Buddy Emmons. Drums: Murrey Harman. Lead guitar: Billy Byrd. Piano: Floyd Cramer.

NA 10625	WHAT I KNOW ABOUT HER (Jimmy Walton-	9-30952
106729	Wynn Stewart-Mack McKeel) Central Songs, Inc.	
NA 10626	I CRIED A TEAR (Al Julia-Fred Jay)	9-30872
106730	Progressive Music, Inc.	

02-24-59 Bradley Film & Recording Studio; Nashville, Tennessee. 9:00 P.M.-12:30 A.M.
Producer: Owen Bradley. Vocal: Ernest Tubb; Jordanaires. Bass: Jack Drake.
Rhythm guitar: Johnny Johnson; Grady Martin. Steel guitar: Buddy Emmons.
Drums: Murrey Harman. Lead guitar: Billy Byrd. Piano: Floyd Cramer.

NA 10627	LET'S SAY GOODBYE LIKE WE SAID HELLO (IN A	DXB 159/
106731	FRIENDLY KIND OF WAY)	DXSA 7159;
	(Jimmie Skinner-Ernest Tubb)	DL 4118;
	Ernest Tubb Music, Inc.	DL 75006;
		MCA 2-4040;
		MCA 16;
		MCA 24;
		DL 74118;
		DL 5006
NA 10628	DRIFTWOOD ON THE RIVER	DXB 159/
106732	(Bob Miller-John Klenner) Bob Miller Publishing	DXSA 7159
		DL 4118;
		MCA 2-4040;
		MCA 24;
		DL 74118
NA 10629	I WONDER WHY YOU SAID GOODBYE	
106733	(Ernest Tubb) American Music, Inc.	

02-26-59 Bradley Film & Recording Studio; Nashville, Tennessee. 7:15-11:15 P.M.
Producer: Owen Bradley. Vocal: Ernest Tubb; Jordanaires. Bass: Jack Drake.
Rhythm guitar: Johnny Johnson. Steel guitar: Buddy Emmons. Drums:
Murrey Harman. Lead guitar: Billy Byrd. Piano: Floyd Cramer.

NA 10629	I WONDER WHY YOU SAID GOODBYE	DXB 159/
106734	(Ernest Tubb) American Music, Inc.	DXSA 7159;
		DL 8872;
		DL 75006;
		MCA 16;
		MCA 2-4040
		DL 5006
NA 10630	TOMORROW NEVER COMES	DXB 159/
106735	(Johnny Bond-Ernest Tubb) American Music, Inc.	DXSA 7159
		DL 8872;
		DL 75252;
		MCA 84;
		MCA 2-4040
NA 10631	FILIPINO BABY (Billy Cox-Clarke Van Ness)	DXB 159/
106736	Shapiro Bernstein & Co.	DXSA 7159;
		DL 8871;
		DL 4118;
		DL 75252;
		MCA 24;
		MCA 84;
		MCA 2-4040
		DL 74118

NA 10632	I'D RATHER BE (Cindy Walker)		DL 4134;
106737	Ernest Tubb Music, Inc.		DL 74134

03-02-59 Bradley Film & Recording Studio; Nashville, Tennessee. 8:00-11:30 P.M. Producer: Owen Bradley. Vocal: Ernest Tubb; Anita Kerr Singers (except on NA 10637). Bass: Jack Drake. Rhythm guitar: Johnny Johnson. Steel guitar: Buddy Emmons. Drums: Murrey Harman. Lead guitar: Billy Byrd. Piano: Floyd Cramer.

NA 10633	LETTERS HAVE NO ARMS		DXB 159/
106753	(Arbie Gibson-Ernest Tubb)		DXSA 7159;
	Ernest Tubb Music, Inc.		DL 8872;
			MCA 2-4040
NA 10634	RAINBOW AT MIDNIGHT (Lost John Miller)	ED 2655	DXB 159/
106754	Shapiro Bernstein & Co., Inc.		DXSA 7159;
			DL 4118;
			DL 8871;
			DL 5006;
			MCA 16;
			MCA 24;
			MCA 2-4040;
			DL 74118;
			DL 75006
NA 10635	HAVE YOU EVER BEEN LONELY (HAVE YOU EVER	ED 2655	DL 8871-
106755	BEEN BLUE) (George Brown-Peter DeRose)		DXB 159/
	Shapiro Bernstein & Co., Inc.		DXSA 7159;
			DL 4118;
			MCA 24;
			MCA 2-4040
			DL 74118
NA 10636	I WILL MISS YOU WHEN YOU GO (Baby Stewart-		DL 8872
106756	Ernest Tubb) Ernest Tubb Music, Inc.		DXB 159
			MCA 2-4040
			DXSA 7159
NA 10637	I'D RATHER BE (Cindy Walker)	9-30872	
106757	Ernest Tubb Music, Inc.		

03-20-60 Bradley Film & Recording Studio; Nashville, Tennessee. 8:00-11:30 P.M. Producer: Owen Bradley. Vocal: Ernest Tubb. Bass: Jack Drake. Rhythm guitar: Johnny Johnson. Steel guitar: Bobby Garrett. Drums: Farris Coursey. Lead guitar: Buddy Emmons. Second lead guitar: Grady Martin. Piano: Owen Bradley.

NA 11021	LIVE IT UP (Cindy Walker) Ernest Tubb Music, Inc.	9-31082
108881		ED 2691
NA 11022	(I'VE LOST YOU) SO WHY SHOULD I CARE	
108882	(Richard Howard) Shapiro Bernstein & Co., Inc.	

NA 11023   ACCIDENTLY ON PURPOSE (George Jones-Darrell   9-31082
108883   Edwards) Glad Music Co./Starday Music   ED 2691

03-29-60   Bradley Film & Recording Studio; Nashville, Tennessee. 8:30-11:30 P.M.
Producer: Owen Bradley. Vocal: Ernest Tubb. Bass: Jack Drake. Rhythm
guitar: Johnny Johnson. Steel guitar: Bobby Garrett. Drums: Murrey Harman.
Lead guitar: Buddy Emmons. Second lead guitar: Grady Martin. Piano: Floyd
Cramer.

NA 11064	DO IT NOW (Jimmy Dallas)		DL 74042;
109005	Bee Gee Music Publishing Inc.		DL 4042
NA 11065	HE'LL HAVE TO GO (Joe Allison-Audrey Allison)	ED 2680	DL 74042;
109006	Central Songs, Inc.		DL 4042
NA 11066	MISTER BLUES (Jack Toombs) Exellorec, Inc.		DL 4042;
109007			DL 74042
NA 11067	THE KIND OF LOVE SHE GAVE TO ME		DL 74042;
109008	(Jimmie Skinner) Jimmie Skinner Music, Inc.		DL 4042

03-30-60   Bradley Film & Recording Studio; Nashville, Tennessee. 12:00-3:00 P.M.
Producer: Owen Bradley. Vocal: Ernest Tubb. Bass: Jack Drake. Rhythm
guitar: Johnny Johnson. Steel guitar: Bobby Garrett. Drums: Murrey Harman.
Lead guitar: Buddy Emmons. Second lead guitar: Grady Martin.

NA 11072	PICK ME UP ON YOUR WAY DOWN	DL 74042
109013	(Harlan Howard) Pamper Music Co.	DL 4042
NA 11073	THIS AIN'T THE BLUES (Instrumental)	
109014	(Speedy West) Central Songs, Inc.	

04-06-60   Bradley Film & Recording Studio; Nashville, Tennessee. 7:00-10:00 P.M.
Producer: Owen Bradley. Vocal: Ernest Tubb. Bass: Jack Drake. Rhythm
guitar: Johnny Johnson; Grady Martin. Steel guitar: Bobby Garrett. Drums:
Murrey Harman. Lead guitar: Buddy Emmons. Piano: Floyd Cramer.

NA 11078	YOU WIN AGAIN (Hank Williams)		DL 74042
109037	Acuff-Rose Publishing, Inc.		DL 4042
NA 11079	I BELIEVE I'M ENTITLED TO YOU (Chester Rice-		DL 74042
109038	Mel Foree-Cliff Carlisle) Hill & Range Songs, Inc.		DL 4042
NA 11080	A GUY NAMED JOE (Harlan Howard)	9-31161	DL 74042
109039	Lu-Tal Publishing Co Pamper Music Co.	ED 2680	DL 4042
NA 11081	WHO'LL BUY THE WINE (Billy Mize)		DL 74042
109040	Penny Music Co./Kentucky Music Inc.		DL 4042

04-07-60   Bradley Film & Recording Studio; Nashville, Tennessee. 7:30-11:00 P.M.
Producer: Owen Bradley. Vocal: Ernest Tubb. Bass: Jack Drake. Rhythm guitar:
Johnny Johnson. Steel guitar: Bobby Garrett. Drums: Murrey Harman. Lead
guitar: Buddy Emmons. Second lead guitar: Grady Martin. Piano: Floyd Cramer.

NA 11082	WHY I'M WALKIN' (Melvin Endsley-Stonewall	DL 74042
109041	Jackson) Ernest Tubb Music, Inc.	DL 4042

NA 11083	WHITE SILVER SANDS (Charles G. Matthews-	9-31161	DL 74042
109042	G. Hart) Sharina Music Co., Inc.	ED 2680	DL 4042
NA 11084	AM I THAT EASY TO FORGET?	ED 2680	DL 74042
109043	(Carl Belew-W. S. Stevenson) Four Star Music		DL 4042

06-06-60 Bradley Film & Recording Studio; Nashville, Tennessee. 2:30-5:30 P.M.
Producer: Owen Bradley. Vocal: Ernest Tubb; Anita Kerr Singers. Bass: Jack
Drake. Rhythm guitar: Johnny Johnson. Steel guitar: Bobby Garrett. Drums:
Farris Coursey. Lead guitar: Billy Byrd. Piano: Hargus Robbins.

NA 11164	EVERYBODY'S SOMEBODY'S FOOL (Howard	9-31119
109217	Greenfield-Jack Keller) Aldon Music Co., Inc.	ED 2691
NA 11165	LET THE LITTLE GIRL DANCE (Carl Spencer*-	9-31119
109218	Bert Lawrence) Hi-Hoss Music Publishing Corp.	ED 2691

09-21-60 Bradley Film & Recording Studio; Nashville, Tennessee. 8:00-11:00 P.M.
Producer: Owen Bradley. Vocal: Ernest Tubb. Bass: Jack Drake. Rhythm
guitar: Johnny Johnson. Steel guitar: Buddy Emmons. Drums: Billy Bun
Wilson. Lead guitar: Leon Rhodes. Piano: Floyd Cramer.

NA 11267	CANDY KISSES (George Morgan)	DL 74046
109688	Hill & Range Songs, Inc.	DL 4046
NA 11268	IT HAPPENED WHEN I REALLY NEEDED YOU (Carl	DL 74046
109689	Belew-W. S. Stevenson) Wallace Fowler Music Co.	DL 4046
NA 11269	WONDERING (Joe Werner) Hill & Range Songs, Inc.	DL 74046
109690		DL 4046
NA 11270	COLD COLD HEART (Hank Williams)	DL 74046
109691	Acuff-Rose Publishing Co., Inc.	DL 4046

09-28-60 Bradley Film & Recording Studio; Nashville, Tennessee. 11:30 P.M.-2:30 A.M.
Producer: Owen Bradley. Vocal: Ernest Tubb; Anita Kerr Singers. Bass: Jack
Drake. Rhythm guitar: Johnny Johnson. Steel guitar: Ben Schaenfele. Drums:
Billy Bun Wilson. Lead guitar: Leon Rhodes. Six-string bass guitar: Grady
Martin. Piano: Floyd Cramer.

NA 11271	FOUR WALLS (Marvin Moore-George Campbell)		DL 74046
109712	Unart Music Corporation		DL 4046
NA 11272	BOUQUET OF ROSES (Steve Nelson-Bob Hilliard)		DL 74046
109713	Hill & Range Songs, Inc.		DL 4046
NA 11273	CRAZY ARMS (Chuck Seals-Ralph Mooney)	ED 2728	DL 74046
109714	Tree Publishing Inc./Champion Music Corp.		DL 4046

09-29-60 Bradley Film & Recording Studio; Nashville, Tennessee. 11:30 P.M.-3:30 A.M.
Producer: Owen Bradley. Vocal: Ernest Tubb. Bass: Jack Drake. Rhythm
guitar: Johnny Johnson. Steel guitar: Buddy Emmons. Drums: Billy Bun
Wilson. Lead guitar: Leon Rhodes. Six-string bass guitar: Grady Martin (1,2).
Piano: Floyd Cramer.

*Some sources say "Henry Glover" as co-writer with Spencer.

NA 11274	I LOVE YOU SO MUCH IT HURTS (Floyd Tillman)		DL 74046
109712	Melody Lane		DL 4046
NA 11275	I WALK THE LINE (1) (Johnny Cash) Hi Lo Music	ED 2728	DL 74046
109713			DL 4046
NA 11276	LITTLE OLE BAND OF GOLD (2) (Harlan Howard)	9-31196	DL 75252
109714	Pamper Music	ED 2706	

10-25-60   Bradley Film & Recording Studio; Nashville, Tennessee. 7:15-10:15 P.M.
Producer: Owen Bradley. Vocal: Ernest Tubb. Bass: Jack Drake. Rhythm
guitar: Johnny Johnson. Steel guitar: Buddy Emmons. Drums: Billy Bun
Wilson. Lead guitar: Leon Rhodes. Six-string bass guitar: Grady Martin (1).
Piano: Floyd Cramer. Second electric lead guitar: Grady Martin (2).

NA 11281	WABASH CANNONBALL (1) (A. P. Carter)	DL 74046
109779	Peer International	DL 4046
NA 11282	I'M MOVIN' ON (2) (Clarence E. Snow)	DL 74046
109780	Hill & Range Songs, Inc.	DL 4046

11-27-60   Bradley Film & Recording Studio; Nashville, Tennessee. 7:30-10:30 P.M.
Producer: Owen Bradley. Vocal: Ernest Tubb. Bass: Jack Drake. Rhythm guitar:
Johnny Johnson. Steel guitar: Pete Drake. Drums: Farris Coursey. Lead guitar:
Leon Rhodes. Six-string bass guitar: Grady Martin. Piano: Floyd Cramer.

NA 11329	TENNESSEE SATURDAY NIGHT (Billy Hughes)	DL 74046
109890	Hill & Range Songs, Inc.	DL 4046
NA 11330	SIGNED, SEALED AND DELIVERED	DL 74046
109891	(Lloyd Copas-Lois Mann) Lois Music	DL 4046

12-04-60   Bradley Film & Recording Studio; Nashville, Tennessee. 7:30-10:30 P.M.
Producer: Owen Bradley. Vocal: Ernest Tubb. Bass: Jack Drake. Rhythm
guitar: Johnny Johnson. Steel guitar: Buddy Emmons. Drums: Billy Bun
Wilson. Lead guitar: Leon Rhodes. Piano: Floyd Cramer.

NA 11352	THOUGHTS OF A FOOL (Wayne Walker-Mel Tillis)	31241	DL 75252
109963	Cedarwood Publishing	ED 2718	MCA 84
NA 11353	GIRL FROM ABILENE (Jan Crutchfield-Jerry	31196	
109913	Crutchfield) Tree Publishing Co.	ED 2706	

12-05-60   Bradley Film & Recording Studios; Nashville, Tennessee. 7:15-10:15 P.M.
Producer: Owen Bradley. Vocal: Ernest Tubb. Bass: Jack Drake. Rhythm
guitar: Johnny Johnson. Steel guitar: Buddy Emmons. Drums: Billy Bun
Wilson. Lead guitar: Leon Rhodes. Six-string bass guitar: Grady Martin (1).
Second lead guitar: Grady Martin (2). Piano: Floyd Cramer.

NA 11354	THE SAME THING AS ME (1) (Justin Tubb)		DL 74045
109965	Tenn-Tex Music Co.		DL 4045
NA 11355	CHRISTMAS IS JUST ANOTHER DAY FOR ME (2)	31334	DL 4518
109966	(Harlan Howard) Pamper Music, Inc.		DL 4343
			DL 74343
			DL 74518

NA 11356	I HATE TO SEE YOU GO (1) (Homer Hargrove-		DL 4045
109967	Ernest Tubb) American Music, Inc.		DL 74045
NA 11357	I'M SORRY NOW (1) (Cliff Johnson)		DL 4045
109968			DL 74045

12-20-60   Bradley Recording Studios; Nashville, Tennessee. 7:30-10:30 P.M. Producer: Owen Bradley. Vocal: Ernest Tubb. Bass: Jack Drake. Rhythm guitar: Johnny Johnson. Steel guitar: Pete Drake. Drums: Billy Bun Wilson. Lead guitar: Leon Rhodes. Six-string bass guitar: Grady Martin. Piano: Floyd Cramer.

NA 11372	WHAT WILL YOU TELL THEM? (Justin Tubb)	31300	
109992	Tenn-Tex Music Co., Inc.	ED 2718	
NA 11373	IT IS NO SECRET (Stuart Hamblen)		DL 4045
109993	Stuart Hamblen Music		DL 74045
NA 11374	DON'T JUST STAND THERE (WHEN YOU FEEL LIKE	31241	
109994	YOU'RE IN LOVE) (Cherokee Jack Henley-Ernest	ED 2706	
	Tubb) Ernest Tubb Music, Inc.		

12-21-60   Bradley Recording Studios; Nashville, Tennessee. 7:30-11:00 P.M. Producer: Owen Bradley. Vocal: Ernest Tubb. Bass: Jack Drake. Rhythm guitar: Johnny Johnson. Steel guitar: Pete Drake. Drums: Billy Bun Wilson. Lead guitar: Leon Rhodes. Six-string bass guitar: Grady Martin. Piano: Floyd Cramer.

NA 11379	BIG BLUE DIAMOND (Earl "Kit" Carson)
109995	Fort Knox Music Co.
NA 11380	I'LL JUST HAVE A CUP OF COFFEE (THEN I'LL GO)
109996	(Bill Brock) Mixer Music/Tree Publishing Co. Inc.

05-28-61   Bradley Recording Studios; Nashville, Tennessee. 8:15-11:15 P.M. Producer: Owen Bradley. Vocal: Ernest Tubb. Bass: Jack Drake. Rhythm guitar: Johnny Johnson. Steel guitar: Buddy Emmons. Drums: Jan Kurtis. Lead guitar: Leon Rhodes. Second lead guitar: Grady Martin. Piano: Hargus Robbins.

NA 11562	GO TO SLEEP CONSCIENCE (DON'T HURT ME THIS	31357
110700	TIME) (Carl Story-Ernest Tubb)	ED 2718
	Ernest Tubb Music, Inc.	
NA 11565	THROUGH THAT DOOR (Hank Cochran)	31300
110703	Pamper Music	ED 2706

06-29-61   Bradley Recording Studios; Nashville, Tennessee. 8:30-11:30 P.M. Producer: Owen Bradley. Vocal: Ernest Tubb. Bass: Jack Drake. Rhythm guitar: Johnny Johnson. Fiddle: Dale Potter. Steel guitar: Buddy Emmons. Drums: Jan Kurtis. Lead guitar: Leon Rhodes. Second lead guitar: Hank Garland.

NA 11604	WHAT KIND OF GOD DO YOU THINK YOU ARE
110801	(Jimmie John)* Copar Music, Inc.

*Jimmie John is Jim Fullen, who first recorded this song, though bigger versions were done by Wayne Walker on Brunswick and Slim Whitman on Imperial, each of which closely copied the original.

08-04-61   Bradley Studios; Nashville, Tennessee. Time: Unknown. Producer: Owen
Bradley. Vocal: Ernest Tubb. Bass: Jack Drake. Rhythm guitar: Johnny Johnson.
Steel guitar: Buddy Emmons. Drums: Jan Kurtis. Lead guitar: Leon Rhodes.

NA 11843	WALKING THE FLOOR OVER YOU* (Ernest Tubb)	ED 2791	DL 4045
110931	American Music, Inc.		DL 74045

09-14-61   Bradley Recording Studios; Nashville, Tennessee. 7:45-10:45 P.M. Producer:
Owen Bradley. Vocal: Ernest Tubb. Bass: Jack Drake. Rhythm guitar: Johnny
Johnson. Steel guitar: Buddy Emmons. Drums: Jan Kurtis. Lead guitar: Leon
Rhodes. Second lead guitar: Grady Martin. Piano: Floyd Cramer.

NA 11711	RUDOLPH THE RED-NOSED REINDEER	31334	DL 4518
111086	(Johnny Marks) St. Nicholas Music, Inc.		DL 74518
			MCA 20629
			VL 3812
			VL 73812
NA 11712	I NEVER COULD SAY NO (Harlan Howard)	31357	
111087	Pamper Music	ED 2718	
NA 11713	IN AND OUT (OF EVERY HEART IN TOWN)		DL 4321
111088	(Hugh Ashley) Earl Barton Music		DL 74321

03-02-62   Bradley Recording Studios; Nashville, Tennessee. 9:30 P.M.-12:30 A.M.
Producer: Owen Bradley. Vocal: Ernest Tubb. Bass: Jack Drake. Steel guitar:
Buddy Charleton. Lead guitar: Leon Rhodes. Electric bass or second lead
guitar: Grady Martin. Rhythm guitar: Johnny Johnson. Drums: Jan Kurtis.
Piano: Floyd Cramer.

NA 11940	WOMEN MAKE A FOOL OUT OF ME**	ED 2739	DL 4321
111901	(Jimmie Rodgers) Peer International, Inc.		DL 74321
NA 11941	DRIVIN' NAILS IN MY COFFIN (Jerry Irby)		DL 4321
111902	Hill & Range Songs, Inc.		DL 74321
NA 11942	INTRODUCTION TO ERNEST TUBB ("WALKING THE		DL 4321
111903	FLOOR OVER YOU") (Ernest Tubb) (Instrumental)		DL 74321
	American Music, Inc.		

03-04-62   Bradley Recording Studios; Nashville, Tennessee. 7:15-10:15 P.M. Producer:
Owen Bradley. Vocal: Ernest Tubb. Bass: Jack Drake. Rhythm guitar: Johnny
Johnson. Lead guitar: Leon Rhodes. Steel guitar: Buddy Charleton. Drums: Jan
Kurtis. Piano: Floyd Cramer. Electric bass or second lead guitar: Grady Martin.

NA 11943	PICK ME UP ON YOUR WAY DOWN
111904	(Harlan Howard) Pamper Music
NA 11944	TRY ME ONE MORE TIME (Ernest Tubb)
111905	American Music, Inc.

*"Short version: Use beginning and end of album," according to Decca's master sheet. Note break in
"NA" master sequence, probably due to an unsuccessful attempt at a later remake.
**The title, as used here on the release, is a variant of "Jimmie Rodgers' Last Blue Yodel (The Women
Make a Fool out of Me)," which Decca used for Tubb's 1956 recording.

NA 11945 LOVER'S WALTZ (Leon Rhodes-Clay Allen)   DL 4321
111906   DL 74321
NA 11946 SHOW HER LOTS OF GOLD (Tommy Hill-Ray King)
111907   Fort Knox Music/Trio Music Co. Inc.

03-19-62 Bradley Recording Studios; Nashville, Tennessee. 7:15-10:15 P.M. Producer: Owen Bradley. Vocal: Ernest Tubb. Bass: Jack Drake. Rhythm guitar: Johnny Johnson. Lead guitar: Leon Rhodes. Steel guitar: Buddy Charleton. Drums: Jan Kurtis. Piano: Hargus Robbins. Electric bass or second lead guitar: Billy Grammer.

NA 11956 I'M LOOKING HIGH AND LOW FOR MY BABY   31399 DL 4539
111970   (Art Gibson) Cherio Music Publishing, Inc.   ED 2728 DL 74539
NA 11957 GO ON HOME (Hank Cochran) Pamper Music   ED 2739 DL 4321
111971   DL 74321
NA 11958 TRY ME ONE MORE TIME (Ernest Tubb)   DL 4321
111972   American Music, Inc.   DL 74321

04-04-62 Bradley Recording Studios; Nashville, Tennessee. 11:00 P.M.-2:00 A.M. Producer: Owen Bradley. Vocal: Ernest Tubb. Bass: Jack Drake. Rhythm guitar: Johnny Johnson. Lead guitar: Leon Rhodes. Steel guitar: Buddy Charleton. Drums: Jan Kurtis. Piano: Floyd Cramer. Electric bass or second lead guitar: Grady Martin.

NA 12011 WATCHING MY PAST GO BY (Ernest Tubb)   DL 4321
112115   Ernest Tubb Music, Inc.   DL 74321
NA 12012 SHOW HER LOTS OF GOLD (Tommy Hill-Ray King)   31399
112116   Fort Knox Music/Trio Music Co., Inc.   ED 2728
NA 12013 BANDERA WALTZ (O. B. "Easy" Adams)   DL 4321
112117   Main Street Music   DL 74321

04-17-62 Bradley Recording Studios; Nashville, Tennessee. 8:00-11:00 P.M. Producer: Owen Bradley. Vocal: Ernest Tubb. Bass: Jack Drake. Rhythm guitar: Johnny Johnson. Lead guitar: Leon Rhodes. Steel guitar: Buddy Charleton. Drums: Jan Kurtis. Piano: Bill Pursell. Electric bass or second lead guitar: Grady Martin.

NA 12020 I TOLD YOU SO (Rex Griffin-Jimmie Davis)   DL 4385
112101   Peer International   DL 74385
NA 12021 I LOVED YOU ONCE (Rex Griffin-Jimmie Davis)   DL 4385
112102   Peer International   DL 74385

04-19-62 Bradley Studios; Nashville, Tennessee. 7:00-10:00 P.M. Producer: Owen Bradley. Vocal: Ernest Tubb. Bass: Jack Drake. Rhythm guitar: Johnny Johnson. Lead guitar: Leon Rhodes. Steel guitar: Buddy Charleton. Drums: Jan Kurtis. Piano: Hargus Robbins. Electric bass or second lead guitar: Grady Martin.

NA 12022 AN OLD FADED PHOTOGRAPH (Rex Griffin)   DL 4385
112130   M. M. Cole   DL 74385

| NA 12023
112131 | THE LAST LETTER (Rex Griffin) M. M. Cole | ED 2774 | DL 4385
DL 74385 |

06-11-62 Bradley Studios; Nashville, Tennessee. 7:00-11:00 P.M. Producer: Owen
Bradley. Vocal: Ernest Tubb. Bass: Jack Drake. Rhythm guitar: Johnny
Johnson. Lead guitar: Leon Rhodes. Steel guitar: Buddy Charleton. Drums:
Bob Steele. Piano: Floyd Cramer. Fiddle: Tommy Jackson.

NA 12109 112343	BEYOND THE LAST MILE (Rex Griffin) Peer International		DL 4385 DL 74385
NA 12110 112344	JUST CALL ME LONESOME (Rex Griffin) Copar Music		
NA 12111 112345	JUST PARDNERS (Rex Griffin) Peer International		DL 4385 DL 74385

06-12-62 Bradley Studios; Nashville, Tennessee. 7:00-10:30 P.M. Producer: Owen
Bradley. Vocal: Ernest Tubb. Bass: Jack Drake. Rhythm guitar: Johnny
Johnson. Lead guitar: Leon Rhodes. Steel guitar: Buddy Charleton. Drums:
Bob Steele. Piano: Floyd Cramer. Fiddle: Tommy Jackson.

NA 12112 112346	IF YOU CALL THAT GONE, GOODBYE (Rex Griffin) Peer International		DL 4385 DL 74385
NA 12113 112347	HOW CAN I BE SURE (Rex Griffin-Ernest Tubb) Ernest Tubb Music, Inc.		
NA 12114 112348	I'LL NEVER TELL YOU I LOVE YOU (Rex Griffin) Peer International		DL 4385 DL 74385

06-13-62 Bradley Studios; Nashville, Tennessee. 7:00-10:00 P.M. Producer: Owen
Bradley. Vocal: Ernest Tubb. Bass: Jack Drake. Rhythm guitar: Johnny
Johnson. Lead guitar: Leon Rhodes. Steel guitar: Buddy Charleton. Drums:
Bob Steele. Piano: Floyd Cramer. Fiddle: Tommy Jackson.

NA 12115 112349	I THINK I'LL GIVE UP (Rex Griffin) Peer International		DL 4385 DL 74385
NA 12116 112350	HOW CAN I BE SURE (Rex Griffin-Ernest Tubb) Ernest Tubb Music, Inc.		DL 4385 DL 74385
NA 12117 112351	JUST CALL ME LONESOME (Rex Griffin) Copar Music	ED 2774	DL 4385 DL 74385

08-30-62 Bradley Studios; Nashville, Tennessee. 7:00-10:00 P.M. Producer: Owen
Bradley. Vocal: Ernest Tubb. Bass: Jack Drake. Rhythm guitar: Johnny
Johnson. Lead guitar: Leon Rhodes. Steel guitar: Buddy Charleton. Drums:
Jack Greene. Electric bass or second lead guitar: Grady Martin.

| NA 12178
112589 | HOUSE OF SORROW (Ernest Tubb)
Ernest Tubb Music, Inc. | 31428
ED 2739 |
| NA 12179
112590 | NO LETTER TODAY (Frankie Brown)
Southern Music | 31428
ED 2739 |

01-10-63 Bradley Studios; Nashville, Tennessee. 7:00-10:00 P.M. Producer: Owen Bradley. Vocal: Ernest Tubb. Bass: Jack Drake. Rhythm guitar: Grant C. Shofner. Lead guitar: Leon Rhodes. Steel guitar: Buddy Charleton. Drums: Jack Greene. Piano: Floyd Cramer. Electric bass or second lead guitar: Grady Martin.

NA 12323	THE GREAT SPECKLED BIRD (Guy Smith)	DL 4397
112987	M. M. Cole	DL 74397
NA 12324	FAMILY BIBLE (Claude Gray-Paul Buskirk-Walt	DL 4397
112988	Breeland) Glad Music	DL 74397
NA 12325	HE'LL UNDERSTAND AND SAY WELL DONE (J. R.	DL 4397
112989	Baxter-Lucie E. Campbell) Stamps Baxter Music	DL 74397

01-28-63 Bradley Studios; Nashville, Tennessee. 7:00-10:00 P.M. Producer: Owen Bradley. Vocal: Ernest Tubb. Bass: Jack Drake. Rhythm guitar: Grant Shofner. Lead guitar: Leon Rhodes. Steel guitar: Buddy Charleton. Drums: Jack Greene.

NA 12333	MR. JUKE BOX (W. E. Davis-Ralph Davis)
113032	Window Music

01-29-63 Bradley Studios; Nashville, Tennessee. 7:30-10:30 P.M. Producer: Owen Bradley. Vocal: Ernest Tubb. Bass: Jack Drake. Rhythm guitar: Grant Shofner. Lead guitar: Leon Rhodes. Steel guitar: Buddy Charleton. Drums: Jack Greene. Piano: Hargus Robbins. Electric bass or second lead guitar: Grady Martin.

NA 12334	MR. JUKE BOX (W. E. Davis-Ralph Davis)	31476	DL 5006
113033	Window Music	ED 2774	DL 75006
			MCA 16
NA 12335	WALKING THE FLOOR OVER YOU (Ernest Tubb)	31476	
113034	Noma Music, Inc.	MCA	
		60078	
NA 12336	THAT'S ALL SHE WROTE (Ernest Tubb)		DL 4514
113035	Ernest Tubb Music, Inc.		DL 74514
NA 12337	JUST ONE MORE (George Jones) Glad Music		
113036			

02-11-63 Bradley Studios; Nashville, Tennessee. 7:00-10:30 P.M. Producer: Owen Bradley. Vocal: Ernest Tubb; Jordanaires. Bass: Jack Drake. Rhythm guitar: Grant Shofner. Lead guitar: Leon Rhodes. Steel guitar: Buddy Charleton. Drums: Jack Greene. Piano: Floyd Cramer. Electric bass or second lead guitar: Grady Martin.

NA 12383	WINGS OF A DOVE (Bob Ferguson)	DL 4397
113172	Bee-Gee Music Publishing	DL 74397
NA 12384	I SAW THE LIGHT (Hank Williams)	DL 4397
113173	Acuff-Rose Publishing, Inc.	DL 74397
NA 12385	STAND BY ME (C. A. Tindley-F. A. Clark)	DL 4397
113174	(Arr. Ernest Tubb) Ernest Tubb Music, Inc.	DL 74397

NA 12386	WHAT A FRIEND WE HAVE IN JESUS (Charles C.	DL 4397
113175	Converse-Joseph Scriven-Horatius Bonar)	DL 74397
NA 12387	WHEN IT'S PRAYER MEETIN' TIME IN THE HOLLOW	DL 4397
113176	(Fleming Allan-Al Rice) M. M. Cole Pub. Inc.	DL 74397

02-12-63 Bradley Studios; Nashville, Tennessee. 7:00-10:00 P.M. Producer: Owen Bradley. Vocal: Ernest Tubb. Bass: Jack Drake. Rhythm guitar: Grant Shofner. Lead guitar: Leon Rhodes. Steel guitar: Buddy Charleton. Drums: Jack Greene. Piano: Hargus Robbins. Electric bass or second lead guitar: Harold Bradley.

NA 12388	PRECIOUS MEMORIES (P.D.)	DL 4397
113201		DL 74397
NA 12389	IF WE NEVER MEET AGAIN (Albert E. Brumley)	DL 4397
113202	Albert E. Brumley Music	DL 74397
NA 12390	LONESOME VALLEY (P.D.)	DL 4397
113203		DL 74397

03-11-63 Bradley Studios; Nashville, Tennessee. 7:00-10:00 P.M. Producer: Owen Bradley. Vocal: Ernest Tubb. Bass: Jack Drake. Rhythm guitar: Grant Shofner. Lead guitar: Leon Rhodes. Steel guitar: Buddy Charleton. Drums: Jack Greene. Piano: Floyd Cramer. Electric bass or second lead guitar: Grady Martin.

NA 12420	FOLLOW ME (Sandra Adlon-Virginia Balmer-Leon	DL 4397
113261	Rhodes) Ernest Tubb Music, Inc.	DL 74397
NA 12421	YOUR SIDE OF THE STORY (Justin Tubb) Starday	
113262		

07-08-63 Bradley Studios; Nashville, Tennessee. 7:00-11:00 P.M. Producer: Owen Bradley. Vocal: Ernest Tubb. Bass: Jack Drake. Rhythm guitar: Grant Shofner. Lead guitar: Leon Rhodes. Steel guitar: Buddy Charleton. Drums: Harold Weakley. Piano: Hargus Robbins. Electric bass or second lead guitar: Harold Bradley.

NA 12561	BE BETTER TO YOUR BABY (Justin Tubb)	31614	DL 4622
113780	Tree Publishing	ED 2787	DL 74622
NA 12562	THE WAY THAT YOU'RE LIVING (IS BREAKING MY	31526	DL 4514
113781	HEART) (Jimmy Swann)		DL 74514
	Acuff-Rose Publications, Inc.		
NA 12563	YOUR SIDE OF THE STORY (Justin Tubb) Starday		DL 4514
113782			DL 74514

07-09-63 Bradley Studios; Nashville, Tennessee. 7:00-11:00 P.M. Producer: Owen Bradley. Vocal: Ernest Tubb. Bass: Jack Drake. Rhythm guitar: Grant Shofner. Lead guitar: Leon Rhodes. Steel guitar: Buddy Charleton. Drums: Jack Greene. Piano: Hargus Robbins. Electric bass or second lead guitar: Harold Bradley.

NA 12564	BEYOND THE LAST MILE (Rex Griffin)
113778	Peer International

| NA 12565 | THANKS A LOT (Eddie Miller-Don Sessions) | | DL 4622 |
| 113779 | Hotpoint Music | | DL 74622 |

07-10-63 Bradley Studios; Nashville, Tennessee. 7:00-10:00 P.M. Producer: Owen Bradley. Vocal: Ernest Tubb. Bass: Jack Drake. Rhythm guitar: Grant Shofner. Lead guitar: Leon Rhodes. Steel guitar: Buddy Charleton. Drums: Jack Greene. Piano: Hargus Robbins. Electric bass: Harold Bradley.

NA 12566	THANKS A LOT (Eddie Miller-Don Sessions)	31526	DL 4514
113795	Hotpoint Music	ED 2797	DL 74514
		ED 2774	DL 5006
			DL 75006
			MCA 16
			MCAD-10086
NA 12567	LONESOME 7-7203 (Justin Tubb)		
113796	Cedarwood Publishing Co.		

08-08-63 Bradley Studios; Nashville, Tennessee. 7:00-10:00 P.M. Producer: Owen Bradley. Vocal: Ernest Tubb. Bass: Jack Drake. Rhythm guitar: Grant Shofner. Lead guitar: Leon Rhodes. Steel guitar: Buddy Charleton. Drums: Jack Greene. Piano: Floyd Cramer. Electric bass or second lead guitar: Grady Martin.

NA 12602	STOP ME (IF YOU'VE HEARD THIS ONE BEFORE)	ED 2797	DL 4514
113912	(Justin Tubb) Tree Publishing		DL 74514
NA 12603	BIG FOOL OF THE YEAR (Justin Tubb) Jat Music		DL 4514
113913			DL 74514

08-12-63 Bradley Studios; Nashville, Tennessee. 7:00-10:00 P.M. Producer: Owen Bradley. Vocal: Ernest Tubb. Bass: Jack Drake. Rhythm guitar: Grant Shofner. Lead guitar: Leon Rhodes. Steel guitar: Buddy Charleton. Drums: Jack Greene. Piano: Floyd Cramer. Electric bass or second lead guitar: Grady Martin.

NA 12604	TAKE A LETTER, MISS GRAY (Justin Tubb)	ED 2787	DL 4514
113932	Tree Publishing		DL 74514
NA 12605	LONESOME 7-7203 (Justin Tubb)		DL 4514
113933	Cedarwood Publishing		DL 74514

01-09-64 Bradley Studios; Nashville, Tennessee. 9:30-11:30 P.M. Producer: Owen Bradley. Vocal: Ernest Tubb. Bass: Jack Drake. Rhythm guitar: Grant Shofner. Lead guitar: Leon Rhodes. Steel guitar: Buddy Charleton. Drums: Jack Greene. Piano: Floyd Cramer. Electric bass or second lead guitar: Grady Martin.

NA 12780	THINK OF ME, THINKING OF YOU	31614	
114365	(Charlie Abbott-Dale Winbrow-Johnny Marvin) Edwin H. Morris Co. Inc.		
NA 12781	THE GREEN LIGHT (Hank Thompson) Brazos Valley	ED 2797	DL 4514
114366			DL 74514

01-20-64 Bradley Studios; Nashville, Tennessee. 6:00-9:00 P.M. Producer: Owen Bradley. Vocal: Ernest Tubb. Bass: Jack Drake. Rhythm guitar: Grant Shofner. Lead guitar: Leon Rhodes. Steel guitar: Buddy Charleton. Drums: Jack Greene. Piano: Hargus Robbins. Electric bass or second lead guitar: Grady Martin.

NA 12787	THERE SHE GOES (Eddie Miller-W. S. Stevenson)		DL 4514
114382	Four Star Sales		DL 74514
NA 12788	I ALMOST LOST MY MIND (Ivory Joe Hunter)	ED 2787	DL 4514
114383			DL 74514
NA 12789	STEPPIN' OUT (Billy Starr)	ED 2787	DL 4514
114384	Forrest Music Publishing/Campbell Music, Inc.		DL 74514

03-10-64 Bradley Studios; Nashville, Tennessee. 6:00-10:00 P.M. Producer: Owen Bradley. Vocal: Ernest Tubb; Loretta Lynn. Bass: Jack Drake. Rhythm guitar: Grant Shofner. Lead guitar: Leon Rhodes. Steel guitar: Buddy Charleton. Drums: Jack Greene. Piano: Bill Pursell. Electric bass or second lead guitar: Jerry Shook.

NA 12884	LOVE WAS RIGHT HERE ALL THE TIME	31643	DL 4639
114663	(Billy Henson-Charles Snoddy) Window Music Co.		DL 74639
NA 12885	I'LL JUST CALL YOU DARLIN' (Johnny Colmus)		DL 4639
114664	Careers BMG Music Publishing		DL 74639
NA 12886	TWO IN THE COLD (Ellen Reeves)		DL 4639
114665	Sure-Fire Music Company, Inc.		DL 74639
NA 12887	MR. & MRS. USED TO BE (Joe Deaton)	31643	DL 4639
114666	Sure-Fire Music Co., Inc.		DL 74639

07-23-64 Bradley Studios; Nashville, Tennessee. 9:30-1:00 P.M. Producer: Owen Bradley. Vocal: Ernest Tubb. Bass: Jack Drake. Rhythm guitar: Grant Shofner. Lead guitar: Leon Rhodes. Steel guitar: Buddy Charleton. Drums: Jack Greene. Piano: Floyd Cramer. Electric bass or second lead guitar: Grady Martin.

NA 13014	PASS THE BOOZE (Gene Northington-Ray Butts)	31706	DL 75252
115096	Lonzo and Oscar Music Publishing Co., Inc.	ED 2797	MCA 84

10-14-64 Bradley Studios; Nashville, Tennessee. 10:00 P.M.-1:00 A.M. Producer: Owen Bradley. Vocal: Ernest Tubb. Bass: Jack Drake. Rhythm guitar: Grant Shofner. Lead guitar: Leon Rhodes. Steel guitar: Buddy Charleton. Drums: Jack Greene. Piano: Jerry Smith. Electric bass: Harold Bradley.

NA 13113	(A MEMORY) THAT'S ALL YOU'LL EVER BE TO ME	31706
115305	(Norman Owens-Lance Guynes)	
	Ernest Tubb Music, Inc.	
NA 13114	TURN AROUND WALK AWAY (Donnie Abercrombie-	31742
115306	Ernest Tubb) Ernest Tubb Music, Inc.	
NA 13115	RED TOP (Instrumental) (Hampton Kynaral)	
115307	Cherio Music Publishing	

10-19-64 Bradley Studios; Nashville, Tennessee. 2:00-5:00 P.M. Producer: Owen
Bradley. Vocal: Ernest Tubb. Bass: Jack Drake. Rhythm guitar: Grant Shofner.
Lead guitar: Leon Rhodes. Steel guitar: Buddy Charleton. Drums: Jack
Greene. Piano: Hargus Robbins. Electric bass or second lead guitar: Jerry
Shook.

NA 13128	HELLO WORLD (Norman Owens-Wynn Stewart)		
115324	Ernest Tubb Music, Inc.		
NA 13129	THE LAST GOODBYE		DL 4746
115325	(Sammy Forsmark-Ernest Tubb)		DL 74746
NA 13130	THAT'S WHEN IT'S COMING HOME TO YOU		DL 4681
115326	(Lois Snapp-Ernest Tubb) American Music, Inc.		DL 74681

01-12-65 Columbia Studios; Nashville, Tennessee. 6:00-9:00 P.M. Producer: Owen
Bradley. Vocal: Ernest Tubb; Loretta Lynn. Bass: Jack Drake. Rhythm guitar:
Grant Shofner. Lead guitar: Leon Rhodes. Steel guitar: Buddy Charleton.
Drums: Jack Greene. Piano: Bill Pursell. Electric bass or second lead guitar:
Jerry Shook.

NA 13219	ARE YOU MINE (Don Grashey-Jim Amadeo-Myrna		DL 4639
115585	Petrunka) Jamie Music Publishing Co.		DL 74639
			2-4000
NA 13220	JUST BETWEEN THE TWO OF US (Liz Anderson)		DL 4639
115586	Wilderness Music Publishing		DL 74639

01-13-65 Columbia Studios; Nashville, Tennessee. 6:00-9:00 P.M. Producer: Owen
Bradley. Vocal: Ernest Tubb. Bass: Jack Drake. Rhythm guitar: Grant Shofner.
Lead guitar: Leon Rhodes. Steel guitar: Buddy Charleton. Drums: Jack
Greene. Piano: Jerry Smith. Electric bass or second lead guitar: Jerry Shook.

NA 13221	LOTS OF LUCK (Eddie Miller)	31824	DL 4867
115587	Tree Publishing Co., Inc.		DL 74867
NA 13222	(MY FRIENDS ARE GONNA BE) STRANGERS		DL 4681
115588	(Liz Anderson-Casey Anderson)		DL 74681
	Wilderness Music Publishing		

01-14-65 Columbia Studios; Nashville, Tennessee. 6:00-9:00 P.M. Producer: Owen
Bradley. Vocal: Ernest Tubb. Bass: Jack Drake. Rhythm guitar: Grant Shofner.
Lead guitar: Leon Rhodes. Steel guitar: Buddy Charleton. Drums: Jack
Greene. Piano: Jerry Smith. Electric bass or second lead guitar: Jerry
Shook.

NA 13223	DO WHAT YOU DO DO WELL (Ned Miller)	31742	DL 4671
115589	Central Songs, Inc.		DL 74671
NA 13224	THROW YOUR LOVE MY WAY (Loys Southerland-		DL 4681
115590	Ernest Tubb) Ernest Tubb Music, Inc.		DL 74681
NA 13225	THE WILD SIDE OF LIFE (W. Warren-A. A. Carter)		DL 4640
115591	EMI/Unart Catalog Inc.		DL 74640

01-15-65 Columbia Studios; Nashville, Tennessee. 6:00-9:00 P.M. Producer: Owen
Bradley. Vocal: Ernest Tubb. Bass: Jack Drake. Rhythm guitar: Grant Shofner.
Lead guitar: Leon Rhodes. Steel guitar: Buddy Charleton. Drums: Jack
Greene. Piano: Jerry Smith. Electric bass or second lead guitar: Jerry Shook.

NA 13230	I'M WITH A CROWD BUT SO ALONE	DL 4681
115596	(Elaine Tubb-Carl Story) Ernest Tubb Music, Inc.	DL 74681
NA 13231	GIVE ME A LITTLE OLD FASHIONED LOVE	DL 4681
115597	(Ernest Tubb) Ernest Tubb Music, Inc.	DL 74681
NA 13232	PRECIOUS LITTLE BABY (Lee Roberts)	DL 4681
115598	Tannen Music	DL 74681
NA 13233	I WONDER WHERE YOU ARE TONIGHT	DL 4640
115599	(Johnny Bond) Red River Songs, Inc.	DL 74640

01-18-65 Columbia Recording Studios; Nashville, Tennessee. 6:00-9:30 P.M. Producer:
Owen Bradley. Vocal: Ernest Tubb; Loretta Lynn. Bass: Jack Drake. Rhythm
guitar: Grant Shofner. Lead guitar: Leon Rhodes. Steel guitar: Buddy
Charleton. Drums: Jack Greene. Piano: Jerry Smith. Electric bass or second
lead guitar: Jerry Shook.

NA 13238	I REACHED FOR THE WINE (Joyce Ann Allsup)	DL 4639
115606	Joyall Music Publishing Co.	DL 74639
NA 13239	MY PAST BROUGHT ME TO YOU (YOUR PAST	DL 4639
115607	BROUGHT YOU TO ME) (Bill Brock) Vanjo Music	DL 74639
NA 13240	A DEAR JOHN LETTER (Billy Barton-Lewis Talley-	DL 4639
115608	Fuzzy Owen) Central Songs, Inc.	DL 74639

01-19-65 Columbia Recording Studios; Nashville, Tennessee. 6:00-9:30 P.M. Producer:
Owen Bradley. Vocal: Ernest Tubb; Loretta Lynn. Bass: Jack Drake. Rhythm
guitar: Grant Shofner. Lead guitar: Leon Rhodes. Steel guitar: Buddy
Charleton. Drums: Jack Greene. Piano: Jerry Smith. Electric bass or second
lead guitar: Jerry Shook.

NA 13241	WE'RE NOT KIDS ANYMORE (Loretta Lynn)	31793	DL 4639
115613	Sure-Fire Music Co., Inc.		DL 74639
NA 13242	KEEP THOSE CARDS AND LETTERS COMING IN		DL 4639
115614	(Harlan Howard) Tree Publishing Co., Inc.		DL 74639
NA 13243	OUR HEARTS ARE HOLDING HANDS	31793	DL 4639
115615	(Bill Anderson) Moss Rose Publications, Inc.		DL 74639

02-08-65 Columbia Recording Studios; Nashville, Tennessee. 6:00-9:00 P.M. Producer:
Owen Bradley. Vocal: Ernest Tubb. Bass: Jack Drake. Rhythm guitar: Grant
Shofner. Lead guitar: Leon Rhodes. Steel guitar: Buddy Charleton. Drums:
Jack Greene. Piano: Hargus Robbins. Electric bass or second lead guitar:
Jerry Shook.

NA 13270	EACH NIGHT AT NINE (Floyd Tillman)	DL 4640
115679	Peer International	DL 74640

NA 13271	BIG CITY (Paul Williams-Sam Humphrey)	DL 4640
115680	Sure-Fire Music Co., Inc.	DL 74640
NA 13272	BEFORE I'M OVER YOU (Betty Sue Perry)	DL 4640
115681	Sure-Fire Music Co., Inc.	DL 74640

02-15-65 RCA Victor Recording Studio; Nashville, Tennessee. 10:00 P.M.-1:00 A.M. Producer: Owen Bradley. Vocal: Ernest Tubb. Bass: Jack Drake. Rhythm guitar: Grant Shofner. Lead guitar: Leon Rhodes. Steel guitar: Buddy Charleton. Drums: Jack Greene. Piano: Jerry Smith. Electric bass or second lead guitar: Jerry Shook.

NA 13291	BEGGAR TO A KING (J. P. Richardson)	DL 4640
115704	Starrite Music Co.	DL 74640
NA 13292	WHEN TWO WORLDS COLLIDE	DL 4640
115705	(Roger Miller-Bill Anderson) Tree Music Publishing	DL 74640
NA 13293	FRAULEIN (Lawton Williams) Travis Music Co.	DL 4640
115706		DL 74640

02-16-65 Columbia Recording Studio; Nashville, Tennessee. 6:00-9:30 P.M. Producer: Owen Bradley. Vocal: Ernest Tubb. Bass: Jack Drake. Rhythm guitar: Grant Shofner. Lead guitar: Leon Rhodes. Steel guitar: Buddy Charleton. Drums: Jack Greene. Piano: Hargus Robbins. Electric bass or second lead guitar: Jerry Shook.

NA 13299	SHE CALLED ME BABY (Harlan Howard)	DL 4640
115714	Central Songs, Inc.	DL 74640
NA 13300	TELL HER SO (Glenn Douglas Tubb)	DL 4640
115715	Combine Music	DL 74640
NA 13301	DON'T BE ANGRY (Stonewall Jackson)	DL 4640
115716	Cedarwood Music	DL 74640
NA 13302	I'VE GOT A TIGER BY THE TAIL (Harlan Howard-	DL 4640
115717	Buck Owens) Blue Book Music, Inc.	DL 74640

04-19-65 RCA Victor Recording Studio; Nashville, Tennessee. 6:00-9:00 P.M. Producer: Owen Bradley. Vocal: Ernest Tubb. Bass: Jack Drake. Rhythm guitar: Grant Shofner; Jerry Shook. Lead guitar: Leon Rhodes—acoustic. Steel guitar: Buddy Charleton. Drums: Jack Greene. Piano: Jerry Smith.

NA 13394	WALTZ ACROSS TEXAS (Billy Talmadge Tubb)	31824	DL 4867
115968	Ernest Tubb Music, Inc.*	MCA	DL 5006
		60078	MCA 16
			MCAD 10086
			DL 74867
			DL 75006
			MCA 2-6892

*Remainder of this session was devoted to the Texas Troubadours.

04-20-65   RCA Victor Studios; Nashville, Tennessee. 6:00-9:00 P.M. Producer: Owen
Bradley. Vocal: Ernest Tubb. Bass: Jack Drake. Rhythm guitar: Grant Shofner.
Lead guitar: Leon Rhodes. Steel guitar: Buddy Charleton. Drums: Jack
Greene. Piano: Jerry Smith. Electric bass or second lead guitar: Jerry
Shook.

NA 13404	LOST HIGHWAY (Leon Payne)		DL 4746
115978	Acuff-Rose Publications		DL 74746
NA 13405	AFTER THE BOY GETS THE GIRL (Wayne Walker)	31861	
115979	Cedarwood Publishing*		

04-21-65   RCA Victor Recording Studio; Nashville, Tennessee. 6:00-9:00 P.M. Producer:
Owen Bradley. Vocal: Ernest Tubb. Bass: Jack Drake. Rhythm guitar: Grant
Shofner. Lead guitar: Leon Rhodes. Steel guitar: Buddy Charleton. Drums:
Jack Greene. Piano: Jerry Smith. Electric bass or second lead guitar: Jerry
Shook.

NA 13411	I'LL BE THERE (Rusty Gabbard-Ray Price)	DL 4746
115981	Ernest Tubb Music, Inc.	DL 74746
NA 13412	HOLDIN' HANDS (George Henkel-Tex Fletcher)	DL 4772
115982	Tex Fletcher Music	DL 74772
NA 13413	WITH TEARS IN MY EYES (Paul Howard)	DL 4746
115983	Acuff-Rose Publications, Inc.	DL 74746

06-21-65   RCA Victor Studio; Nashville, Tennessee. 10:00 A.M.-1:00 P.M. Producer: Owen
Bradley. Vocal: Ernest Tubb. Bass: Jack Drake. Rhythm guitar: Grant Shofner.
Lead guitar: Leon Rhodes. Steel guitar: Buddy Charleton. Drums: Jack
Greene. Piano: Jerry Smith.

NA 13638	BLUE CHRISTMAS TREE (Eddie Miller-Bob Morris)	31866
116280	Blue Book Music, Inc.	
NA 13639	WHO'S GONNA BE YOUR SANTA CLAUS THIS YEAR	31866
116281	(Byron Baker) Window Music Co., Inc.	

09-28-65   RCA Victor Studio; Nashville, Tennessee. 10:00 P.M.-1:00 A.M. Producer: Owen
Bradley. Vocal: Ernest Tubb. Bass: Jack Drake. Rhythm guitar: Grant Shofner.
Lead guitar: Leon Rhodes. Steel guitar: Buddy Charleton. Drums: Jack
Greene. Piano: Jerry Smith. Electric bass or second lead guitar: Jerry
Shook.

NA 13731	IT'S FOR GOD, AND COUNTRY, AND YOU, MOM	31861	
116585	(THAT'S WHY I'M FIGHTING IN VIET NAM)		
	(Dave McEnery) Medallion Songs, Inc.		
NA 13732	YOU'LL STILL BE IN MY HEART		DL 4746
116586	(Ted West-Buddy Starcher)		DL 74746
NA 13733	FORGIVE ME (Wiley Walker-Gene Sullivan)		DL 4746
116587	Peer International		DL 74746

*Two previous cuts on this session were by the Texas Troubadours.

12-17-65 Bradley's Barn; Mt. Juliet, Tennessee. Unknown (Total session for several artists was 41.5 minutes). Producer: Owen Bradley. Vocal: Ernest Tubb; Wilburn Brothers (1). Bass: Jack Drake. Rhythm guitar: Grant Shofner. Lead guitar: Leon Rhodes. Steel guitar: Buddy Charleton. Drums: Jack Greene. Electric bass: Harold Bradley.

NA 13834	THERE'S GONNA BE SOME CHANGES MADE	DL 4721
116850	AROUND HERE (Ernest Tubb) American Music, Inc.	DL 74721
NA 13839	YOU'LL NEVER GET A BETTER CHANCE THAN	DL 4721
116855	THIS (Justin Tubb) Tree Publishing Co.	DL 74721
NA 13840	HEY MR. BLUEBIRD (Cindy Walker) (1)	DL 4721
116856	Ernest Tubb Music, Inc.*	DL 74721

12-20-65 RCA Victor Recording Studio; Nashville, Tennessee. 6:00-9:00 P.M. Producer: Owen Bradley. Vocal: Ernest Tubb. Bass: Jack Drake. Rhythm guitar: Grant Shofner. Lead guitar: Leon Rhodes. Steel guitar: Buddy Charleton. Drums: Jack Greene. Piano: Jerry Smith. Electric bass or second lead guitar: Jerry Shook.

NA 13842	TOO MANY RIVERS (Harlan Howard)	DL 4746
116858	Combine Music Corp.	DL 74746
NA 13843	MY SHOES KEEP WALKING BACK TO YOU	DL 4746
116859	(Lee Ross-Bob Wills) Copar Music	DL 74746

12-21-65 RCA Victor Recording Studio; Nashville, Tennessee. 6:00-9:00 P.M. Producer: Owen Bradley. Vocal: Ernest Tubb. Bass: Jack Drake. Rhythm guitar: Grant Shofner. Lead guitar: Leon Rhodes. Steel guitar: Buddy Charleton. Drums: Jack Greene. Piano: Jerry Smith. Electric bass or second lead guitar: Jerry Shook.

NA 13844	TILL MY GETUP HAS GOT UP AND GONE	31908
116860	(Bud Logan-Charles Snoddy) Tuckahoe Music, Inc.	
NA 13845	RELEASE ME (Eddie Miller-W. S. Stevenson)	DL 4746
116861	Four Star Music	DL 74746
NA 13846	MOM AND DAD'S WALTZ (Lefty Frizzell)	DL 4746
116862	Hill & Range Songs, Inc.	DL 74746
NA 13847	BORN TO LOSE (Frankie Brown)**	
116863	Peer International	

12-22-65 RCA Victor Recording Studio; Nashville, Tennessee. 6:00-9:00 P.M. Producer: Owen Bradley. Vocal: Ernest Tubb. Bass: Jack Drake. Rhythm guitar: Grant Shofner. Lead guitar: Leon Rhodes. Steel guitar: Buddy Charleton. Drums: Jack Greene. Piano: Jerry Smith. Electric bass or second lead guitar: Jerry Shook.

NA 13851	HELLO TROUBLE (COME ON IN)	DL 4746
116864	(Eddie McDuff-Orville Couch)	DL 74746
	Tree Publishing Co., Inc./Tyler Publishing Co.	

*These are Tubb's songs for the album *The Wilburn Brothers Show.*
**"Frankie Brown" is a pseudonym for Ted Daffan.

NA 13852   JUST ONE MORE (George Jones)   31908
116865   Starrite Publishing Co.
NA 13853   BORN TO LOSE (Frankie Brown) Peer International   DL 4746
116866   DL 74746
NA 13854   I'LL KEEP ON LOVING YOU (Floyd Tillman)
116867   Peer International

02-28-66   Columbia Recording Studio; Nashville, Tennessee. 6:00-9:00 P.M. Producer: Owen Bradley. Vocal: Ernest Tubb. Bass: Jack Drake. Rhythm guitar: Grant Shofner. Lead guitar: Leon Rhodes. Steel guitar: Buddy Charleton. Drums: Willie Ackerman. Piano: Moon Mullican. Electric bass or second lead guitar: Jerry Shook.

NA 13950   UNDER YOUR SPELL AGAIN   DL 4772
117076   (Buck Owens-Dusty Rhodes) Central Songs   DL 74772
NA 13951   THEY'LL NEVER TAKE HER LOVE FROM ME
117077   (Leon Payne) Acuff-Rose Publications, Inc.

03-01-66   Columbia Recording Studio; Nashville, Tennessee. 6:00-9:00 P.M. Producer: Owen Bradley. Vocal: Ernest Tubb. Bass: Jack Drake. Rhythm guitar: Grant Shofner. Lead guitar: Leon Rhodes. Steel guitar: Buddy Charleton. Drums: Jack Greene. Piano: Moon Mullican. Electric bass or second lead guitar: Jerry Shook.

NA 13958   REMEMBER ME (WHEN THE CANDLELIGHTS ARE   DL 4772
117095   GLEAMING) (Scott Wiseman) Duchess Music Corp.   DL 74772
NA 13959   TENNESSEE WALTZ (Pee Wee King-Redd Stewart)   DL 4772
117096   Acuff-Rose Publications   DL 74772
NA 13960   FIREBALL MAIL (Floyd Jenkins)* Milene Music, Inc. DL 4772
117097   DL 74772
NA 13961   I HUNG MY HEAD AND CRIED   DL 4772
117098   (Cliff Bruner-Jimmie Davis) Peer International   DL 74772

03-02-66   RCA Victor Studio; Nashville, Tennessee. 6:00-9:00 P.M. Producer: Owen Bradley. Vocal: Ernest Tubb. Bass: Jack Drake. Rhythm guitar: Grant Shofner. Lead guitar: Leon Rhodes. Steel guitar: Buddy Charleton. Drums: Jack Greene. Piano: Moon Mullican. Electric bass or second lead guitar: Jerry Shook.

NA 13966   BEFORE I MET YOU (Charles Seitz-Cannonball   DL 4772
117099   Lewis-Elmer Rader) Peer International   DL 74772
NA 13967   MEMPHIS (Chuck Berry) Arc Music   DL 4772
117100   DL 74772
NA 13968   I'M GONNA TIE ONE ON TONIGHT (Lee Nichols)   DL 4772
117101   Sure-Fire Music   DL 74772

*"Floyd Jenkins" is a pseudonym for Fred Rose.

04-01-66   RCA Victor Studio; Nashville, Tennessee. 6:00-9:00 P.M. Producer: Owen
Bradley. Vocal: Ernest Tubb. Bass: Jack Drake. Rhythm guitar: Grant Shofner.
Lead guitar: Leon Rhodes. Steel guitar: Buddy Charleton. Drums: Jack
Greene. Piano: Jerry Smith. Electric bass or second lead guitar: Jerry Shook.

NA 14004	MAY THE BIRD OF PARADISE FLY UP YOUR NOSE		DL 4772
117208	(Neal Merritt) Central Songs		DL 74772
NA 14005	WAITIN' IN YOUR WELFARE LINE		DL 4772
117209	(Nat Stuckey-Don Rich-Buck Owens) Central Songs		DL 74772
NA 14006	NO MATTER WHAT HAPPENS MY DARLING		DL 4772
117210	(Johnny Lange-Lew Porter) Leeds Music Corporation		DL 74772

08-11-66   RCA Victor Studio; Nashville, Tennessee. 6:00-9:00 P.M. Producer: Owen
Bradley. Vocal: Ernest Tubb. Bass: Jack Drake. Rhythm guitar: Grant Shofner.
Lead guitar: Leon Rhodes. Steel guitar: Buddy Charleton. Drums: Jack Greene.
Piano: Hargus Robbins. Electric bass or second lead guitar: Jerry Shook.

NA 14194	ANOTHER STORY, ANOTHER TIME, ANOTHER	32022	DL 4867
117815	PLACE (Arleigh Duff) Marson Music		DL 74867
			DL 5006
			DL 75006
			MCA 16
NA 14195	THERE'S NO ROOM IN MY HEART (FOR THE	32022	DL 4867
117816	BLUES) (William E. Grishaw-Fred Rose) Milene Music		DL 74867

12-21-66   Columbia Recording Studio; Nashville, Tennessee. 6:00-10:00 P.M. Producer:
Owen Bradley. Vocal: Ernest Tubb; Loretta Lynn. Bass: Jack Drake. Rhythm
guitar: Grant Shofner. Lead guitar: Pete Wade. Steel guitar: Buddy Charleton.
Drums: Jack Greene. Piano: Hargus Robbins. Electric bass: Kelso Herston.

NA 14434	YEARNING (George Jones-Eddie Edding)		DL 4872
118360	Starrite Publishing Co.		DL 74872
NA 14435	SWEET THANG (Nat Stuckey)	32091	DL 4872
118361	Su-Ma Music/Nat Stuckey Publishing	60155	DL 74872
			2-4000
NA 14436	LET'S STOP RIGHT WHERE WE ARE (Loretta Lynn)		DL 4872
118362	Sure-Fire Music, Inc.		DL 74872
			2-4000
NA 14437	BEAUTIFUL, UNHAPPY HOME (Teddy Wilburn-	32091	DL 4872
118363	Johnny Russell) Sure-Fire Music, Inc.	60155	DL 74872
			2-4000

12-30-66   Columbia Recording Studio; Nashville, Tennessee. 6:00-9:00 P.M. Producer:
Owen Bradley. Vocal: Ernest Tubb; Loretta Lynn. Bass: Jack Drake. Rhythm
guitar: Grant Shofner. Lead guitar: Wayne Moss. Steel guitar: Buddy
Charleton. Drums: Jack Greene. Piano: Hargus Robbins. Electric bass: Harold
Bradley.

NA 14438	I'M BITING MY FINGERNAILS AND THINKING OF		DL 4872
118389	YOU (Lenny Sanders-Roy West-Ernest Benedict-		DL 74872
	Ernest Tubb) Hill & Range Songs, Inc.		2-4000
NA 14439	LOVE IS NO EXCUSE (Justin Tubb)		DL 4872
118390	Tree Publishing Co., Inc.		DL 74872
			2-4000
NA 14440	ONE TO TEN (Mildred Burk) Sure Fire Music Co., Inc.		DL 4872
118391			74872
			2-4000
NA 14441	THE THIN GREY LINE (Betty Sue Perry)		DL 4872
118392	Sure-Fire Music, Inc.		DL 74872
			2-4000

01-04-67   Columbia Recording Studio; Nashville, Tennessee. 6:00-9:00 P.M. Producer: Owen Bradley. Vocal: Ernest Tubb; Loretta Lynn. Bass: Jack Drake. Rhythm guitar: Grant Shofner. Lead guitar: Steve Chapman. Steel guitar: Buddy Charleton. Drums: Murrey Harman. Piano: Hargus Robbins. Electric bass: Harold Bradley.

NA 14446	BEAUTIFUL FRIENDSHIPS (Jack Rhodes-Faye Keys-		DL 4872
118449	Larry Ground) Careers BMG Music Publishing		DL 74872
			2-4000
NA 14447	WE'LL NEVER CHANGE (John Earl Clift)		DL 4872
118450			DL 74872
			2-4000
NA 14448	BARTENDER (Loretta Lynn-Margaret Britton		DL 4872
118451	Vaughn) Sure Fire Music Co., Inc.		DL 74872
			2-4000
NA 14449	I'M NOT LEAVIN' YOU (IT'S ALL IN YOUR MIND)		DL 4872
118452	(Johnny Tillotson-Lucille Cosenza)		DL 74872
	Ridge Music Corporation		2-4000

01-09-67   Columbia Recording Studio; Nashville, Tennessee. 6:00-9:00 P.M. Producer: Owen Bradley. Vocal: Ernest Tubb. Bass: Jack Drake. Rhythm guitar: Grant Shofner. Lead guitar: Steve Chapman. Steel guitar: Buddy Charleton. Drums: Jack Greene. Piano: Hargus Robbins. Electric bass or second lead guitar: Jerry Shook.

NA 14450	YESTERDAY'S WINNER IS A LOSER TODAY	32131	DL 4867
118461	(Jimmie Skinner-Jesse Rogers-Ernest Tubb)		DL 74867
	Ernest Tubb Music, Inc.		
NA 14451	IN THE JAILHOUSE NOW (Jimmie Rodgers)	32131	DL 4867
118462	Peer International		DL 74867
NA 14452	APARTMENT #9 (Johnny Paycheck-Fern Foley-		
118463	Charles Owen) Owen Publishing Company		

01-11-67   RCA Victor Recording Studio; Nashville, Tennessee. 6:00-9:00 P.M. Producer: Owen Bradley. Vocal: Ernest Tubb. Bass: Jack Drake. Rhythm guitar: Grant

Shofner. Lead guitar: Steve Chapman. Steel guitar: Buddy Charleton. Drums: Jack Greene. Piano: Bill Pursell. Electric bass or second lead guitar: Jerry Shook.

NA 14456	BRING YOUR HEART HOME (Tom T. Hall)	DL 4867
118466	New Keys Music, Inc.	DL 74867
NA 14457	THE COLD HARD FACTS OF LIFE (Bill Anderson)	
118467	Stallion Music	

01-13-67 RCA Victor Recording Studio; Nashville, Tennessee. 6:00-9:30 P.M. Producer: Owen Bradley. Vocal: Ernest Tubb. Bass: Jack Drake. Rhythm guitar: Grant Shofner. Lead guitar: Steve Chapman. Steel guitar: Buddy Charleton. Drums: Len Miller. Piano: Bill Pursell. Electric bass or second lead guitar: Jerry Shook.

NA 14458	TAKIN' IT EASY HERE (Ernie Lee)	DL 4867
118479	Ernest Tubb Music	DL 74867
NA 14459	LOOSE TALK (Freddie Hart-Ann Lucas)	DL 4867
118480	Central Songs	DL 74867
NA 14460	YOU BEAT ALL I EVER SAW (Johnny Cash)	DL 4867
118481	South Wind Music	DL 74867
NA 14461	APARTMENT #9 (Johnny Paycheck-Fern Foley-	DL 4867
118482	Charles Owen) Owen Publishing Company	DL 74867
NA 14462	I NEVER HAD THE ONE I WANTED (Jimmy Louis-	DL 4867
118483	Claude Gray-Sheb Wooley) Vanjo Music	DL 74867

10-31-67 Bradley's Barn; Mt. Juliet, Tennessee. 2:00-5:00 P.M. Producer: Owen Bradley. Vocal: Ernest Tubb. Bass: Jack Drake. Rhythm guitar: Grant Shofner. Lead guitar: Steve Chapman. Steel guitar: Buddy Charleton. Drums: Bill Pfender. Piano: Hargus Robbins. Electric bass or second lead guitar: Grady Martin.

NA 14826	TOO MUCH OF NOT ENOUGH (Jack Ripley)	
119543	Ernest Tubb Music, Inc.	
NA 14827	NOTHING IS BETTER THAN YOU (Hap E. Howell)	32237
119544	Ernest Tubb Music, Inc.	
NA 14828	IT SURE HELPS A LOT (Buckley Maxwell-Jerry	32377
119545	Crutchfield) Champion Music	

11-01-67 Bradley's Barn; Mt. Juliet, Tennessee. 6:00-9:00 P.M. Producer: Owen Bradley. Vocal: Ernest Tubb. Bass: Jack Drake. Rhythm guitar: Grant Shofner. Lead guitar: Steve Chapman. Steel guitar: Buddy Charleton. Drums: Bill Pfender. Piano: Hargus Robbins. Electric bass or second lead guitar: Grady Martin.

NA 14829	TOO MUCH OF NOT ENOUGH (Jack Ripley)	32237
119548	Ernest Tubb Music, Inc.	
NA 14830	TAKE THESE CHAINS FROM MY HEART	DL 4957
119549	(Fred Rose-Hy Heath) Milene Music, Inc.	DL 74957
NA 14831	I CAN'T HELP IT (IF I'M STILL IN LOVE WITH YOU)	DL 4957
119550	(Hank Williams) Fred Rose Publishing Co.	DL 74957

| NA 14832 | HEY GOOD LOOKIN' (Hank Williams) | DL 4957 |
| 119551 | Fred Rose Publishing Co. | DL 74957 |

11-01-67 Bradley's Barn; Mt. Juliet, Tennessee. 10:00 P.M.-1:00 A.M. Producer: Owen Bradley. Vocal: Ernest Tubb. Bass: Jack Drake. Rhythm guitar: Grant Shofner. Lead guitar: Steve Chapman. Steel guitar: Buddy Charleton. Drums: Bill Pfender. Piano: Hargus Robbins. Electric bass or second lead guitar: Grady Martin.

NA 14833	I'M SO LONESOME I COULD CRY (Hank Williams)	DL 4957
119552	Acuff-Rose Publishing Co.	DL 74957
NA 14834	WINDOW SHOPPING (Marcel Joseph)	DL 4957
119553	Fred Rose Publishing Co.	DL 74957
NA 14835	SOMEDAY YOU'LL CALL MY NAME	DL 4957
119554	(Jean Branch-Eddie Hill) Acuff-Rose Publishing Co.	DL 74957
NA 14836	I COULD NEVER BE ASHAMED OF YOU	DL 4957
119555	(Hank Williams) Acuff-Rose Publishing Co.	DL 74957

12-19-67 Bradley's Barn; Mt. Juliet, Tennessee. 2:00-5:00 P.M. Producer: Owen Bradley. Vocal: Ernest Tubb. Bass: Jack Drake. Rhythm guitar: Grant Shofner. Lead guitar: Steve Chapman. Steel guitar: Buddy Charleton. Drums: Bill Pfender. Piano: Hargus Robbins. Electric bass or second lead guitar: Jerry Shook.

NA 14891	MANSION ON THE HILL (Hank Williams-Fred Rose)	DL 4957
119718	Milene Music, Inc.	DL 74957
NA 14892	MIND YOUR OWN BUSINESS (Hank Williams)	DL 4957
119719	Acuff-Rose Publishing	DL 74957
NA 14893	YOUR CHEATIN' HEART (Hank Williams)	DL 4957
119720	Acuff-Rose Publishing	DL 74957
NA 14894	COLD COLD HEART (Hank Williams)	DL 4957
119721	Acuff-Rose Publishing	DL 74957

02-26-68 Bradley's Barn; Mt. Juliet, Tennessee. 6:00-9:00 P.M. Producer: Owen Bradley. Vocal: Ernest Tubb. Bass: Jack Drake. Rhythm guitar: Grant Shofner. Lead guitar: Steve Chapman. Steel guitar: Buddy Charleton. Drums: Bill Pfender. Piano: Bill Pursell. Electric bass or second lead guitar: Buck Evans.

NA 15026	IF MY HEART HAD WINDOWS (Dallas Frazier)		DL 75072
119990	Blue Crest Music/Glad Music		
NA 15027	I'M GONNA MAKE LIKE A SNAKE (Loretta Lynn)	32315	
119991	Sure-Fire Music Co., Inc.		
NA 15028	LIFE TURNED HER THAT WAY (Mel Tillis)		DL 75072
119992	Cedarwood Publishing		

02-27-68 Bradley's Barn; Mt. Juliet, Tennessee. 6:00-9:00 P.M. (first two); 10:00 P.M.-1:00 A.M. (last four). Producer: Owen Bradley. Vocal: Ernest Tubb. Bass: Jack Drake. Rhythm guitar: Grant Shofner. Lead guitar: Steve Chapman. Steel guitar: Buddy Charleton. Drums: Bill Pfender. Piano: Bob Wilson. Electric bass: Buck Evans.

NA 15029 119993	CRYING TIME (Buck Owens) Blue Book Music		DL 75072
NA 15030 119994	ONE MORE MEMORY (Vern Stovall-Bobby George) Four Star Music Co.		
NA 15031 119995	IF I EVER STOP HURTIN' (Billy Hughes) Ernest Tubb Music, Inc.		DL 75122
NA 15032 119996	JUST PACK UP AND GO (Billy Hughes) Ernest Tubb Music, Inc.	32377	
NA 15033 119997	I THREW AWAY THE ROSE (Merle Haggard) Blue Book Music		
NA 15034 119998	SEND ME THE PILLOW YOU DREAM ON (Hank Locklin) Four Star Music Co.		DL 75114

03-06-68   Bradley's Barn; Mt. Juliet, Tennessee. 6:00-9:30 P.M. Producer: Owen Bradley. Vocal: Ernest Tubb. Bass: Jack Drake. Rhythm guitar: Grant Shofner. Lead guitar: Steve Chapman. Steel guitar: Buddy Charleton. Drums: Bill Pfender. Piano: Jerry Smith. Electric bass: Buck Evans.

NA 15047 120070	MAMA, WHO WAS THAT MAN? (Billy Hughes) Ernest Tubb Music, Inc.	32315	
NA 15048 120071	DON'T SQUEEZE MY SHARMON (Carl Belew- Van Givens) Acuff-Rose Music, Inc./A.R. Songs		DL 75072
NA 15049 120072	SING ME BACK HOME (Merle Haggard) Bluebook Music		DL 75072
NA 15050 120073	A DIME AT A TIME (Jerry Chesnut-D. Bruce) Pass Key Music Co.		DL 75072

03-11-68   Bradley's Barn; Mt. Juliet, Tennessee. 6:00-9:30 P.M. Producer: Owen Bradley. Vocal: Ernest Tubb. Bass: Jack Drake. Rhythm guitar: Grant Shofner. Lead guitar: Steve Chapman. Steel guitar: Buddy Charleton. Drums: Bill Pfender. Piano: Jerry Smith. Electric bass: Buck Evans.

NA 15051 120074	THE BOTTLE LET ME DOWN (Merle Haggard) Blue Book Music	DL 75072
NA 15052 120075	DESTINATION ATLANTA G.A. (Bill Hayes-Bill Howard) Forrest Hills Music	DL 75072
NA 15053 120076	THE IMAGE OF ME (Wayne Kemp) Tree Publishing	DL 75072

04-16-68   Bradley's Barn; Mt. Juliet, Tennessee. 6:00-9:00 P.M. Producer: Owen Bradley. Vocal: Ernest Tubb. Bass: Jack Drake. Rhythm guitar: Grant Shofner. Lead guitar: Steve Chapman. Steel guitar: Buddy Charleton. Drums: D. J. Fontana. Piano: Jerry Smith. Electric bass: Buck Evans.

| NA 15121 120208 | THAT'S THE CHANCE I'LL HAVE TO TAKE (Jackson King) Wilderness Music | DL 75072 |
| NA 15122 120209 | TODAY (Hank Thompson) Brazos Valley Music Co. | DL 75114 |

| NA 15123 | SHE WENT A LITTLE BIT FARTHER | | DL 75072 |
| 120210 | (Merle Kilgore-Mack Vickery) Al Gallico Music | | |

12-20-68 Bradley's Barn; Mt. Juliet, Tennessee. 6:00-9:30 P.M. Producer: Owen Bradley. Vocal: Ernest Tubb; Jordanaires. Bass: Eugene Stanley. Rhythm guitar: Grant Shofner. Lead guitar: Steve Chapman. Steel guitar: Buddy Charleton. Drums: Wayne Jernigan. Piano: Hargus Robbins. Electric bass: Harold Bradley.

NA 15388	SATURDAY SATAN SUNDAY SAINT (Wayne Walker)	32448	DL 75122
121025	Cedarwood Publishing		
NA 15389	TOMMY'S DOLL (Glenn Tubb-Jack Moran)	32448	DL 75122
121026	Tree Publishing		
NA 15390	ONE MORE MEMORY (Vern Stovall-Bobby George)	32532	DL 75122
121027	Four Star Music Co., Inc.		

02-18-69 Bradley's Barn; Mt. Juliet, Tennessee. 6:00-10:00 P.M. Producer: Owen Bradley. Vocal: Ernest Tubb; Loretta Lynn. Bass: Noel Eugene Stanley. Rhythm guitar: Billy Parker. Lead guitar: Steve Chapman. Steel guitar: Buddy Charleton. Drums: Wayne Jernigan. Piano: Floyd Cramer. Electric bass: James Wilkerson.

NA 15445	IF WE PUT OUR HEADS TOGETHER (OUR HEARTS	32570	DL 75115
121237	WILL TELL US WHAT TO DO)		2-4000
	(Loretta Lynn-Lorne Allen) Sure-Fire Music Co.		
NA 15446	I CHASED YOU TILL YOU CAUGHT ME	32570	DL 75115
121238	(Wayne Walker) Ernest Tubb Music, Inc.		2-4000
NA 15447	I WON'T CHEAT AGAIN ON YOU (IF YOU WON'T		DL 75115
121239	CHEAT ON ME) (Milton L. Brown)		2-4000
	Ernest Tubb Music, Inc.		
NA 15448	WHO'S GONNA TAKE THE GARBAGE OUT	32496	DL 75115
121240	(Teddy Wilburn-Johnny Tillotson-Lucille Cosenza)		2-4000
	Ridge Music Corp.		

03-03-69 Columbia Studios; Nashville, Tennessee. 2:00-5:30 P.M. Producer: Owen Bradley. Vocal: Ernest Tubb. Lead guitar: Steve Chapman. Steel guitar: Buddy Charleton. Bass: Noel Stanley. Rhythm guitar: Billy Parker. Drums: Wayne Jernigan. Piano: Hargus Robbins. Electric bass: Jimmy Wilkerson.

NA 15458	LET'S TURN BACK THE YEARS (Hank Williams)		DL 75114
121244	Acuff-Rose Publishing		
NA 15459	FOLSOM PRISON BLUES (Johnny Cash)		DL 75122
121245	Hi Lo Music		
NA 15460	MAKING BELIEVE (Jimmy Work)		DL 75122
121246	Acuff-Rose Publications, Inc.		

03-11-69 Columbia Recording Studios; Nashville, Tennessee. 6:00-10:00 P.M. Producer: Owen Bradley. Vocal: Ernest Tubb; Loretta Lynn. Lead guitar: Steve Chapman. Steel guitar: Buddy Charleton. Bass: Noel Stanley. Rhythm guitar: Billy Parker. Drums: Wayne Jernigan. Piano: Floyd Cramer. Electric bass: Harold Bradley.

NA 15468	HOLDING ON TO NOTHING (Jerry Chesnut)		DL 75115
121291	Tree Publishing Co., Inc.		2-4000
NA 15469	SOMEWHERE BETWEEN (Merle Haggard)	32496	DL 75115
121292	Blue Book Music		
NA 15470	LET'S WAIT A LITTLE LONGER (Curly Putman-		DL 75115
121293	Billy Sherrill) Tree Publishing Co., Inc.		2-4000

03-17-69　Columbia Recording Studios; Nashville, Tennessee. 10:00 P.M.-1:30 A.M. Producer: Owen Bradley. Vocal: Ernest Tubb. Lead guitar: Steve Chapman. Steel guitar: Buddy Charleton. Bass: Noel Stanley. Rhythm guitar: Billy Parker; Jerry Shook. Drums: Wayne Jernigan. Piano: Jerry Smith.

NA 15474	THE CARROLL COUNTY ACCIDENT (Bob Ferguson)	DL 75122
121306	Warden Music Company	
NA 15475	I STARTED LOVING YOU AGAIN	DL 75122
121307	(Merle Haggard-Bonnie Owens) Blue Book Music	
NA 15476	GAMES PEOPLE PLAY (Joe South)	DL 75122
121308	Lowery Music Co., Inc.	

03-19-69　Columbia Recording Studios; Nashville, Tennessee. 10:00 P.M.-1:00 A.M. Producer: Owen Bradley. Vocal: Ernest Tubb. Lead guitar: Steve Chapman. Steel guitar: Buddy Charleton. Bass: Noel Stanley. Rhythm guitar: Billy Parker. Drums: Wayne Jernigan. Piano: Jerry Smith. Electric bass: Harold Bradley.

NA 15477	SHE'S LOOKING BETTER BY THE MINUTE		DL 75122
121309	(Jimmie Helms-Grant Townsley) Sure-Fire Music Co.		
NA 15478	JUST A DRINK AWAY (Bobby Lewis-Billy Parker)	32532	DL 75122
121310	Tree Publishing Co. Inc.		
NA 15479	SOMEBODY BETTER THAN ME	32632	DL 75222
121311	(Billy Hughes-Ernest Tubb) Ernest Tubb Music, Inc.		

03-31-69　Bradley's Barn; Mt. Juliet, Tennessee. 10:00 P.M.-1:00 A.M. Producer: Owen Bradley. Vocal: Ernest Tubb. Lead guitar: Steve Chapman. Steel guitar: Buddy Charleton. Bass: Noel Stanley. Rhythm guitar: Billy Parker. Drums: Wayne Jernigan. Piano: Larry Butler. Electric bass: Jimmy Wilkerson.

NA 15512	GIVE MY LOVE TO ROSE (Johnny Cash)	DL 75114
121391	Knox Music	
NA 15513	I'LL GO ON ALONE (Marty Robbins)	DL 75114
121392	Acuff-Rose Publishing	
NA 15514	I NEED ATTENTION BAD	DL 75114
121393	(Baby Stewart-Ernest Tubb) Ernest Tubb Music, Inc.	
NA 15515	YESTERDAY'S TEARS (Ernest Tubb)	DL 75114
121394	American Music	

04-01-69　Bradley's Barn; Mt. Juliet, Tennessee. 6:00-9:30 P.M. Producer: Owen Bradley. Vocal: Ernest Tubb; Loretta Lynn. Lead guitar: Steve Chapman. Steel guitar: Buddy Charleton. Bass: Noel Stanley. Rhythm guitar: Billy Parker. Drums: Wayne Jernigan. Piano: Hargus Robbins. Electric bass: Harold Bradley.

NA 15516	WON'T YOU COME HOME (AND TALK TO A	DL 75115
121396	STRANGER) (Wayne Kemp) Tree Publishing Co., Inc.	2-4000
NA 15517	THAT ODD COUPLE (Betty Amos)	DL 75115
121397	Careers BMG Music Publishing	2-4000
NA 15518	TOUCH AND GO (Darrell Statler)	DL 75115
121398	Bronze Music, Inc.	2-4000
NA 15519	LET THE WORLD KEEP ON A TURNIN'	DL 75115
121399	(Buck Owens) Tree Publishing Co., Inc.	

04-03-69 Bradley's Barn; Mt. Juliet, Tennessee. 6:00-9:00 P.M. Producer: Owen Bradley. Vocal: Ernest Tubb. Lead guitar: Steve Chapman. Steel guitar: Buddy Charleton. Bass: Noel Stanley. Rhythm guitar: Billy Parker. Drums: Wayne Jernigan. Piano: Hargus Robbins. Electric bass: Harold Bradley.

NA 15525	BLUE EYED ELAINE (Ernest Tubb) American Music	DL 75114
121413		
NA 15526	OUR BABY'S BOOK (Ernest Tubb) American Music	DL 75114
121414		
NA 15527	I'M FREE AT LAST (Ernest Tubb) American Music	DL 75114
121415		
NA 15528	YOU WON'T EVER FORGET ME	DL 75114
121416	(Lois Snapp-Ernest Tubb) American Music	

01-05-70 Bradley's Barn; Mt. Juliet, Tennessee. 6:00-9:00 P.M. Producer: Owen Bradley. Vocal: Ernest Tubb; Jordanaires. Lead guitar: Billy Byrd. Steel guitar: Buddy Charleton. Bass: Joe Pruneda. Rhythm guitar: Billy Parker. Drums: Wayne Jernigan. Piano: Hargus Robbins. Electric bass: James Wilkerson.

NA 15883	IT'S AMERICA (LOVE IT OR LEAVE IT)	32632	DL 75222
122375	(Jimmie Helms) Sure-Fire Music		
NA 15884	A GOOD YEAR FOR THE WINE	32690	
122376	(Fred Burch-Tandy Rice) Show Biz Music		

04-06-70 Bradley's Barn. 6:00-9:30 P.M. Producer: Owen Bradley. Vocal: Ernest Tubb. Lead guitar: Billy Byrd. Steel guitar: Buddy Charleton. Bass: Joe Pruneda. Rhythm guitar: Billy Parker. Drums: Wayne Jernigan. Piano: Jerry Smith. Electric bass: James Wilkerson. Fiddle: Leon Boulanger.

NA 15995	WHEN THE GRASS GROWS OVER ME (Don Chapel)	DL 75222
122636	Glad Music	
NA 15996	WINE ME UP (Faron Young-E. Crandell)	DL 75222
122637	Passport Music	
NA 15997	I'M SO AFRAID OF LOSING YOU AGAIN	DL 75222
122638	(A. L. Owens-Dallas Frazier)	
	Blue Crest Music/Hill & Range Songs, Inc.	

04-21-70 Bradley's Barn; Mt. Juliet, Tennessee. 6:00-9:00 P.M. Producer: Owen Bradley. Vocal: Ernest Tubb. Lead guitar: Billy Byrd. Steel guitar: Buddy Charleton. Bass: Joe Pruneda. Rhythm guitar: Billy Parker. Drums: Wayne Jernigan. Piano: Hargus Robbins. Electric bass: James Wilkerson. Fiddle: Leon Boulanger.

NA 16046	ONE MINUTE PAST ETERNITY (William E. Taylor-		DL 75222
122754	Stanley Kesler) Hilo Music/Hill & Range Songs, Inc.		
NA 16047	BE GLAD (Justin Tubb-Kent Westberry)		DL 75222
122755	Tree International		
NA 16048	DEAR JUDGE (Billy Hughes)	32690	DL 75222
122756	Hill & Range Songs, Inc.		

04-28-70 Bradley's Barn; Mt. Juliet, Tennessee. 6:00-10:00 P.M. Producer: Owen Bradley. Vocal: Ernest Tubb. Lead guitar: Billy Byrd. Steel guitar: Buddy Charleton. Bass: Joe Pruneda. Rhythm guitar: Billy Parker. Drums: Wayne Jernigan. Piano: Hargus Robbins. Electric bass: Harold Bradley. Fiddle: Leon Boulanger.

NA 16062	A GOOD YEAR FOR THE WINE		DL 75222
122818	(Fred Burch-Tandy Rice) Show Biz Music		
NA 16063	EVEN THE BAD TIMES ARE GOOD		DL 75222
122819	(Carl Belew-Clyde Pitts) Four Star Music		
NA 16064	SHE'S A LITTLE BIT COUNTRY (Harlan Howard)		DL 75222
122820	Wilderness Music Publishing Co. Inc.		
NA 16065	PEARLIE MAE'S PLACE (jacket) PEARLY MAY'S		DL 75222
122821	PLACE (label) (Jim Anglin) Fred Rose Music		

12-21-70 Bradley's Barn; Mt. Juliet, Tennessee. 6:00-9:00 P.M. Producer: Owen Bradley. Vocal: Ernest Tubb. Lead guitar: Jack Mollette. Steel guitar: Buddy Charleton. Bass: Joe Pruneda. Rhythm guitar: Ray Edenton. Drums: Sonny Lonas. Piano: Hargus Robbins. Electric bass: Harold Bradley. Fiddle: Leon Boulanger.

NA 16289	WHEN OLE GOIN' GETS A GOIN' (Eddie Miller)	32800	DL 75301
123316	Tree Publishing		
NA 16290	TEACH MY DADDY HOW TO PRAY	32943	DL 75345
123317	(Jim Owen-Jim Baker) Sawgrass Music		
NA 16291	ONE SWEET HELLO (Merle Haggard)	32800	DL 75301
123318	Blue Book Music		

12-22-70 Bradley's Barn; Mt. Juliet, Tennessee. 6:00-9:00 P.M. Producer: Owen Bradley. Vocal: Ernest Tubb. Lead guitar: Jack Mollette. Steel guitar: Buddy Charleton. Bass: Joe Pruneda. Rhythm guitar: Ray Edenton. Drums: Sonny Lonas. Piano: Hargus Robbins. Electric bass: Harold Bradley. Fiddle: Leon Boulanger.

NA 16292	DON'T BACK A MAN UP IN A CORNER	32849	DL 75301
123319	(Harlan Howard) Wilderness Music Publishing		
NA 16293	COMMERCIAL AFFECTION (Mel Tillis)		DL 75301
123320	Cedarwood Publishing/Sawgrass Music		
NA 16294	THE KEY'S IN THE MAILBOX (Harlan Howard)		DL 75301
123321	Wilderness Music Publishing		

12-30-70 Bradley's Barn; Mt. Juliet, Tennessee. 6:00-9:30 P.M. Producer: Owen Bradley. Vocal: Ernest Tubb. Lead guitar: Jack Mollette. Steel guitar: Buddy Charleton. Bass: Joe Pruneda. Rhythm guitar: Ray Edenton. Drums: Sonny Lonas. Piano: Hargus Robbins. Electric bass: Harold Bradley. Fiddle: Leon Boulanger.

NA 16295	SHE GOES WALKING THROUGH MY MIND		DL 75301
123337	(Bill Eldridge-Gary Stewart-Walter Haynes)		
	Forrest Hills Music, Inc.		
NA 16296	HELP ME MAKE IT THROUGH THE NIGHT		DL 75301
123338	(Kris Kristofferson) Combine Music Corp.		
NA 16297	SHENANDOAH WALTZ (Clyde Moody-Chubby Wise)	32849	DL 75301
123339	Acuff-Rose Publications		

05-14-71 Bradley's Barn; Mt. Juliet, Tennessee. 10:00 P.M.-1:00 A.M. Producer: Owen Bradley. Vocal: Ernest Tubb. Lead guitar: Jack Mollette. Steel guitar: Buddy Charleton. Bass: Joe Pruneda. Rhythm guitar: Ray Edenton. Drums: Sonny Lonas. Piano: Jerry Smith. Electric bass: Harold Bradley. Fiddle: Leon Boulanger.

NA 16453	AS LONG AS THERE'S A SUNDAY (Justin Tubb)	DL 75301
123534	Tree Publishing Company, Inc.	
NA 16454	SOMETIMES YOU JUST CAN'T WIN	DL 75301
123535	(Smokey Stover) Glad Music	
NA 16455	TOUCHING HOME (Dallas Frazier-A. L. "Doodle"	DL 75301
123536	Owens) Blue Crest Music	
NA 16456	LOOK TWICE BEFORE YOU GO (Jimmie Skinner)	DL 75301
123537	Ernest Tubb Music, Inc.	

01-26-72 Bradley's Barn; Mt. Juliet, Tennessee. 6:00-9:00 P.M. Producer: Owen Bradley. Vocal: Ernest Tubb. Lead guitar: Jack Mollette. Steel guitar: Buddy Charleton. Bass: Joe Pruneda. Rhythm guitar: Ray Edenton. Drums: Bill Pfender. Piano: Hargus Robbins. Electric bass: Harold Bradley. Fiddle: Leon Boulanger.

NA 16689	I'VE BEEN WALKIN' (G Flatt-E. Graves)		DL 75345
123862	Flatland Music		
NA 16690	SAY SOMETHING NICE TO SARAH (Johnny Cash-	32943	DL 75345
123863	Winnafred Rushing Kelly) House of Cash		
NA 16691	THE ROAD IS CLOSED (Hank Cochran)		DL 75388
123864	Tree International		

02-15-72 Bradley's Barn; Mt. Juliet, Tennessee. 6:00-9:00 P.M. Producer: Owen Bradley. Vocal: Ernest Tubb. Lead guitar: Jack Mollette. Steel guitar: Buddy Charleton. Bass: Joe Pruneda. Rhythm guitar: Ray Edenton. Drums: Bill Pfender. Piano: Hargus Robbins. Electric bass: Jerry Shook.

NA 16714	HONKY TONKS & YOU (Billy Hughes)	DL 75345
123892	Ernest Tubb Music, Inc.	
NA 16715	NINETY-NINE YEARS (Glen Johnson)	DL 75345
123893	Sure-Fire Music	
NA 16716	IT'S FOUR IN THE MORNING (Jerry Chesnut)	DL 75345
123894	Pass Key Publishing Co.	
NA 16717	HEARTACHES BY THE NUMBER (Harlan Howard)	DL 75345
123895	Pamper Music Co.	

02-16-72   Bradley's Barn; Mt. Juliet, Tennessee. 6:00-9:00 P.M. Producer: Owen Bradley. Vocal: Ernest Tubb. Lead guitar: Jack Mollette. Steel guitar: Buddy Charleton. Bass: Joe Pruneda. Rhythm guitar: Ray Edenton. Drums: Bill Pfender. Piano: Hargus Robbins. Electric bass: Harold Bradley. Fiddle: Leon Boulanger.

NA 16720	I CARE NO MORE (Jesse Ashlock)		DL 75345
123889	Hill & Range Music, Inc.		
NA 16721	IN THIS CORNER (Marty Robbins) Mariposa Music	33014	DL 75388
123890			
NA 16722	GOOD HEARTED WOMAN (Waylon Jennings-Willie		DL 75345
123891	Nelson) Baron Music Publishing Co.		

09-12-72   Bradley's Barn; Mt. Juliet, Tennessee. 6:00-9:00 P.M. Producer: Owen Bradley. Vocal: Ernest Tubb. Lead guitar: Jack Mollette. Steel guitar: Buddy Charleton. Bass: Joe Pruneda. Rhythm guitar: Jerry Shook. Drums: Bill Pfender. Piano: Hargus Robbins. Electric bass: Harold Bradley.

NA 16905	BABY IT'S SO HARD TO BE GOOD (Harlan Howard)	33014	DL 75388
124090	Wilderness Music Co. Inc.		
NA 16906	IT'S NOT LOVE (BUT IT'S NOT BAD) (Hank		DL 75388
124091	Cochran-Glenn Martin) Tree Publishing Co. Inc.		
NA 16907	I DON'T BELIEVE I'LL FALL IN LOVE TODAY		DL 75388
124092	(Harlan Howard) Central Songs		

09-12-72   Bradley's Barn; Mt. Juliet, Tennessee. 9:00-12:00 P.M. Producer: Owen Bradley. Vocal: Ernest Tubb. Lead guitar: Jack Mollette. Steel guitar: Buddy Charleton. Bass: Joe Pruneda. Rhythm guitar: Jerry Shook. Drums: Bill Pfender. Piano: Hargus Robbins. Electric bass: Harold Bradley.

NA 16908	BUBBLES IN MY BEER (Bob Wills-Tommy Duncan-	DL 75388
124086	Cindy Walker) Hill & Range Songs, Inc.	
NA 16909	HILLBILLY WALTZ (G. Russell-R. Russell)	DL 75388
124087	Adventure Music Co. Inc.	
NA 16910	BIG BLUE DIAMOND (Earl Kit Carson)	DL 75388
124088	Fort Knox Music Co.	
NA 16911	I'VE GOT A NEW HEARTACHE	DL 75388
124089	(Wayne Walker-Ray Price) Cedarwood Publishing	

09-13-72   Bradley's Barn; Mt. Juliet, Tennessee. 6:00-9:00 P.M. Producer: Owen Bradley. Vocal: Ernest Tubb. Lead guitar: Jack Mollette. Steel guitar: Buddy Charleton. Bass: Joe Pruneda. Rhythm guitar: Herman Wade. Drums: Bill Pfender. Piano: Hargus Robbins. Electric bass: Harold Bradley.

NA 16912	EVERYBODY'S REACHING OUT FOR SOMEONE	
124093	(Dickey Lee-Allen Reynolds) Jack Music Co. Inc.	
NA 16913	TRUCK DRIVING MAN (Terry Fell)	DL 75388
124094	American Music Inc.	
NA 16914	THAT CERTAIN ONE (Don Reid) House of Cash Inc.	DL 75388
124095		

03-13-73   Bradley's Barn; Mt. Juliet, Tennessee. 6:00-9:00 P.M. Producer: Owen Bradley.
Vocal: Ernest Tubb. Rhythm guitar: Steve Chapman. Steel guitar: Buddy
Charleton. Bass: Joe Pruneda. Lead guitar: Bobby Davis. Drums: Don Mills.
Piano: Jerry Smith. Electric bass: Harold Bradley.

NA 17090	MISSING IN ACTION (Helen Kays-Arthur Q. Smith)		MCA 341
MC 1433	Peer International		
NA 17091	THE TEXAS TROUBADOUR (Porter Wagoner)	40056	MCA 341
MC 1434	Owepar Music		

03-16-73   Bradley's Barn; Mt. Juliet, Tennessee. 6:00-9:00 P.M. Producer: Owen Bradley.
Vocal: Ernest Tubb. Rhythm guitar: Steve Chapman. Steel guitar: Buddy
Charleton. Bass: Joe Pruneda. Lead guitar: Bobby Davis. Drums: Don Mills.
Piano: Jerry Smith. Electric bass: Jerry Shook.

NA 17096	DON'T SHE LOOK GOOD (Jerry Chesnut)	MCA 341
MC 1435	Passkey Music Co., Inc.	
NA 17097	A DAISY A DAY (Jud Strunk)	MCA 341
MC 1436	Pierre Cossette Music Co./Every Little Tune, Inc.	
NA 17098	MILES IN MEMORIES (Carl Story-Ernest Tubb)	MCA 341
MC 1437	Ernest Tubb Music, Inc.	

03-19-73   Bradley's Barn; Mt. Juliet, Tennessee. 6:00-9:00 P.M. Producer: Owen Bradley.
Vocal: Ernest Tubb. Lead guitar: Bobby Davis. Steel guitar: Buddy Charleton.
Bass: Joe Pruneda. Rhythm guitar: Ray Edenton. Drums: Don Mills. Piano:
Hargus Robbins. Electric bass: Harold Bradley.

NA 17102	TEXAS DANCE HALL GIRL (Justin Tubb)		MCA 341
MC 1459	Sure-Fire Music Co., Inc.		
NA 17103	THE LORD KNOWS I'M DRINKING (Bill Anderson)		MCA 341
MC 1460	Stallion Music, Inc.		
NA 17104	I'VE GOT ALL THE HEARTACHES I CAN HANDLE	40056	MCA 341
MC 1461	(Shel Silverstein) Evil Eye Music, Inc.		

03-19-73   Bradley's Barn; Mt. Juliet, Tennessee. 9:00-12:00 P.M. Producer: Owen Bradley.
Vocal: Ernest Tubb. Lead guitar: Bobby Davis. Steel guitar: Buddy Charleton.
Bass: Joe Pruneda. Rhythm guitar: Ray Edenton. Drums: Don Mills. Piano:
Hargus Robbins. Electric bass: Harold Bradley.

NA 17105	PASS ME BY (IF YOU'RE ONLY PASSING THROUGH)	MCA 341
MC 1438	(Hillman Hall) Hallnote Music	
NA 17106	WHAT MY WOMAN CAN'T DO (Earl Montgomery-	MCA 341
MC 1439	Billy Sherrill-George Jones) Algee Music	
	Corp./Altam Music Corp.	
NA 17107	THE LAST LETTER (Rex Griffin) Hill & Range Songs,	MCA 341
MC 1440	Inc.	

02-20-74   Bradley's Barn; Mt. Juliet, Tennessee. 6:00-9:00 P.M. Producer: Walter Haynes.
Vocal: Ernest Tubb. Lead guitar: Billy Byrd. Steel guitar: Don Helms. Bass: Joe
Pruneda. Rhythm guitar: Steve Chapman. Drums: Don Mills. Piano: Jerry
Whitehurst.

NA 17380	ANYTHING BUT THIS (Shel Silverstein)	40222
MC 2703	Evil Eye Music	
NA 17381	DON'T WATER DOWN THE BAD NEWS (Don Wayne)	40222
MC 2704	Tree Publishing Co., Inc.	

05-28-75 Bradley's Barn; Mt. Juliet, Tennessee. 6:00-9:00 P.M. Producer: Owen Bradley. Vocal: Ernest Tubb. Lead guitar: Pete Mitchell. Steel guitar: Lynn Owsley. Bass: David Evans. Rhythm guitar: Wayne Hammond. Drums: Don Mills. Piano: Henry Gene Dunlap.

NA 17707	THE BUSIEST MEMORY IN TOWN		MCA 496
MC 4171	(Geoffrey Morgan) Pi-Gem Music Inc.		
NA 17708	I'D LIKE TO LIVE IT AGAIN (Smokey Stover)	40436	MCA 496
MC 4172	Cary & Mr. Wilson Music		
NA 17709	IF YOU DON'T QUIT CHECKIN' ON ME (I'M	40436	MCA 496
MC 4173	CHECKIN' OUT ON YOU) (Larry Cheshire-Murry Kellum) Cary & Mr. Wilson Music/Rodeo Cowboy Music		

05-29-75 Bradley's Barn; Mt. Juliet, Tennessee. 6:00-9:00 P.M. Producer: Owen Bradley. Vocal: Ernest Tubb. Lead guitar: Pete Mitchell. Steel guitar: Lynn Owsley. Bass: David Evans. Rhythm guitar: Wayne Hammond. Drums: Don Mills. Piano: Hargus Robbins. Electric bass: Harold Bradley.

NA 17710	SOMEWHERE COUNTRY—SOMEWHERE CITY U.S.A.	MCA 496
MC 4187	(Chris Stevenson) Ernest Tubb Music Inc.	
NA 17711	HOLDING THINGS TOGETHER (Merle Haggard)	MCA 496
MC 4188	Shade Tree Music, Inc.	
NA 17712	I'M LIVING IN SUNSHINE (Joe Rogers)	MCA 496
MC 4189	Cary & Mr. Wilson Music	

06-17-75 Bradley's Barn; Mt. Juliet, Tennessee. 6:00-9:30 P.M. Producer: Owen Bradley. Vocal: Ernest Tubb. Lead guitar: Pete Mitchell. Steel guitar: Lynn Owsley. Bass: David Evans. Rhythm guitar: Wayne Hammond. Drums: Don Mills. Piano: Owen Bradley.

NA 17719	YOU'RE MY BEST FRIEND (Wayland Holyfield)	MCA 496
MC 4223	Don Williams Music, Inc.	
NA 17720	SHE'S ALREADY GONE (Jim Mundy)	MCA 496
MC 4224	Chappell & Co., Inc.	

06-18-75 Bradley's Barn; Mt. Juliet, Tennessee. 6:00-10:00 P.M. Producer: Owen Bradley. Vocal: Ernest Tubb. Lead guitar: Pete Mitchell. Steel guitar: Lynn Owsley. Bass: David Evans. Rhythm guitar: Wayne Hammond. Drums: Don Mills. Piano: Owen Bradley. Electric bass: Harold Bradley. Fiddle: Johnny Gimble (1).

NA 17721	IT'S TIME TO PAY THE FIDDLER (1)	MCA 496
MC 4225	(Don Wayne-Walter Haynes) Coal Miners Music Inc.	
NA 17722	THE DOOR'S ALWAYS OPEN	MCA 496
MC 4226	(Dickey Lee-Bob McDill) Jack Music, Inc.	

02-28-77 Fireside Studio; Nashville, Tennessee. 6:00-9:00 P.M.; 9:00 P.M.-12:00 Midnight. Producer: Fuzzy Owen. Vocal: Merle Haggard; Ernest Tubb (1). Bass: Dave Kirby. Rhythm guitar: Hollis Delaughter (Red Lane). Lead electric guitar: Grady Martin. Steel guitar: Joe Allen.

TROUBADOUR (Cindy Walker) House of Cash/
Southwind Music/Unichappell Music, Inc.
TRY ME ONE MORE TIME (Ernest Tubb)
Rightsong Music, Inc.
I'LL ALWAYS BE GLAD TO TAKE YOU BACK
(Ernest Tubb) Rightsong Music, Inc.
IT'S BEEN SO LONG DARLING (Ernest Tubb)
Rightsong Music, Inc.
DON'T YOU EVER GET TIRED (OF HURTING ME)
(Hank Cochran) Tree Publishing Co., Inc.
I STARTED LOVING YOU AGAIN (1)
(Merle Haggard) Blue Book Music
IT MAKES NO DIFFERENCE NOW (Floyd Tillman)
Peer International

03-23-77 Pete's Place; Nashville, Tennessee. 6:00-9:00 P.M. Producer: Pete Drake. Vocal: Ernest Tubb. Bass: Joe Pruneda Jr.; Harold Bradley. Rhythm guitar: Wayne Hammond. Guitar: Jack Solomon. Lead electric guitar: Pete Michaud. Steel guitar: Lynn Owsley. Drums: Bobby Rector. Piano: Owen Bradley.

A MONTH OF SUNDAYS (Justin Tubb)	FGS 002	FG LP 001
Window Music Pub. Cary & Mr. Wilson Music, Inc.		LL 12116
SOMETIMES I DO (Jeannie Seely)	FGS 001	FG LP 001
Tree Publishing Co.		LL 12115
A GOOD MIND TO LOVE HER ANYWAY		FG LP 001
(Murry Kellum-Larry Cheshire-Craig Chambers)		LL 12119
Cary & Mr. Wilson Music Inc.		
HALF MY HEART'S IN TEXAS (Linda Hargrove)	FGS 001	FG LP 001
Window Music Pub. Co. Beechwood Music Corp.		LL 12115

03-24-77 Pete's Place; Nashville, Tennessee. 6:00-9:00 P.M. Producer: Pete Drake. Vocal: Ernest Tubb. Bass: Joe Pruneda Jr.; Harold Bradley. Rhythm guitar: Wayne Hammond. Lead electric guitar: Pete Michaud. Steel guitar: Lynn Owsley. Drums: Bobby Rector. Guitar: Jack Solomon. Piano: Owen Bradley.

WALKIN' THE FLOOR OVER YOU* (Ernest Tubb)	CS 4-4507	FG LP 0002
Rightsong Music, Inc.		TV 1033
		LL 12116
		CL3-3001
		SOR 0049

*Trio: Merle Haggard part overdubbed 7-20-78; Charlie Daniels part overdubbed 9-12-78; Chet Atkins instrumental part overdubbed 11-10-78 and 1-15-79. Other vocals later added: Tim Boone, Pam Rose, Mary Ann Kennedy, Linda Hargrove, the Wilburn Brothers, Norro Wilson, Stan Byrd, Carmol Taylor, and Wayland Stubblefield.

03-25-77   Pete's Place; Nashville, Tennessee. 6:00-9:00 P.M. Producer: Pete Drake. Vocal: Ernest Tubb. Bass: Joe Pruneda Jr.; Harold Bradley. Rhythm guitar: Jack Solomon; Wayne Hammond. Lead electric guitar: Pete Michaud. Steel guitar: Lynn Owsley. Drums: Bobby Rector. Piano: Owen Bradley.

JEALOUS LOVING HEART* (Talmadge Tubb-Ernest Tubb) Ernest Tubb Music, Inc.	CS 4-4501	FG LP 0002
		TV 1033
		FG LP 001
		CL3-3001
		LL 12116
		SOR 0049
YOU'RE THE ONLY GOOD THING** (Jack Toombs) Golden West Melodies, Inc.		FG LP 0002
		TV 1033
		LL 12117
		CL3-3001
		SOR 0049
PAPERS AND PENS (Judy Mehaffey-Wayne Walker) Cary & Mr. Wilson Music, Inc.		FG LP 001
		LL 12116

04-04-77   Pete's Place; Nashville, Tennessee. 6:00-9:00 P.M. Producer: Pete Drake. Vocal: Ernest Tubb. Bass: Joe Pruneda Jr.; Harold Bradley. Rhythm guitar: Jack Solomon; Wayne Hammond. Lead electric guitar: Pete Michaud. Steel guitar: Lynn Owsley. Drums: Bobby Rector. Piano: Jeffrey Tweel.

WALTZ ACROSS TEXAS*** (Talmadge Tubb-Ernest Tubb) Ernest Tubb Music, Inc.	CS 4-4501	FG LP 0002
		TV 1033
		LL 12115
		CL3-3001
		SOR 0049
SET UP TWO GLASSES JOE† (Cindy Walker) Ernest Tubb Music, Inc.		FG LP 0002
		TV 1033
		LL 12117
		CL3-3001
		SOR 0049

*Johnny Cash duet part added 8-8-78. Ernest Tubb Jr., "Tinker," overdubbed lead guitar part on 10-16-78 or 10-30-78. Henry Strezlecki overdubbed on bass.

**Charlie Rich duet part added at Rich's sessions of July 24–26 or August 9, 1978. Pete Drake overdubbed steel part; as did Jerry Kennedy guitar.

***Duet: Willie Nelson overdubbed 7-11-78 or 9-22-78; Charlie Daniels overdubbed lead electric guitar part on 9-12-78 or 12-4-78. Other overdub musicians: Gary Paxton, vocal; Jerry Shook, electric guitar; Billy Sanford, electric guitar; Johnny Cox, steel guitar; Charlie McCoy, harmonica.

†Duet: Ferlin Husky overdubbed 10-11-78; Simon Crum 10-13-78. Overdub musicians: Shorty Lavender, fiddle; Jerry Carrigan, drums; Jimmy Crawford, steel guitar; Phil Baugh, lead guitar.

Title is obviously a variant of the correct one, "Two Glasses, Joe."

YOU NEARLY LOSE YOUR MIND* (Ernest Tubb)	FG LP 0002
Rightsong Music, Inc.	TV 1033
	LL 12118
	SOR 0049

04-05-77 Pete's Place; Nashville, Tennessee. 6:00-9:00 P.M. Producer: Pete Drake. Vocal: Ernest Tubb. Bass: Joe Pruneda Jr.; Harold Bradley. Rhythm guitar: Wayne Hammond; Jack Solomon. Lead electric guitar: Pete Michaud. Steel guitar: Lynn Owsley. Drums: Bobby Rector. Piano: Jeff Tweel.

OUR BABY'S BOOK (Ernest Tubb)		FG LP 001
Noma Music, Inc.		FG LP 0002**
		TV 1033**
		LL 12119**
		CL3-3001**
		SOR 0049**
ANSWER THE PHONE (Cindy Walker)		FG LP 001
Ernest Tubb Music, Inc.		FG LP 0002***
		TV 1033***
		LL 12115***
		SOR 0049***
SOLDIER'S LAST LETTER (Henry Stewart-Ernest		FG LP 001
Tubb) Ernest Tubb Music, Inc.		FG LP 0002†
		TV 1033†
		LL 12119†
		SOR 0049†
JOURNEY'S END (Ernest Tubb-Virgil F. "Pappy"	FGS 002	FG LP 001
Stewart) Ernest Tubb Music, Inc.		FG LP 0002††
		TV 1033††
		LL 12118††
		CL3-3001††
		SOR 0049††

10-17-77 Pete's Place; Nashville, Tennessee. 6:00-9:00 P.M. Producer: Pete Drake. Vocal: Ernest Tubb. Bass: Joe Pruneda Jr. Rhythm guitar: Jack Solomon; Lawrence "Ronnie" Blackwell. Lead electric guitar: Pete Michaud. Steel guitar: Lynn Owsley. Drums: Charles Browning. Piano: Jeffrey Tweel.

*Trio: Waylon Jennings and Willie Nelson overdubbed 7-11-78 and/or 9-22-78. Nelson only appears on the recent LL 12118. Speedy West overdubbed steel part on 10-21-78 or 12-6-78. Other musicians over-dubbed later were Shorty Lavender, fiddle, and Hayward Bishop, drums.
**Vocal overdubbed by Cal Smith 7-18-78.
***Vocal overdubbed by Loretta Lynn 8-3-78. Billy Grammer overdubbed electric guitar break 10-9-78.
†Vocal overdubbed by Johnny Cash 8-8-78 or 9-12-78. Piano part overdubbed by Owen Bradley.
††Overdubbed by Marty Robbins 8-20-78 and Wilburn Brothers 10-11-78. Billy Byrd's lead guitar break is also a later overdub. Robbins at one point sings harmony with himself.

WHEN THE WORLD HAS TURNED YOU DOWN (Ernest Tubb) Rightsong Music		FG LP 0002*
		TV 1033*
		LL 12118
		SOR 0049*
LET'S SAY GOODBYE LIKE WE SAID HELLO** (Jimmie Skinner-Ernest Tubb) Ernest Tubb Music, Inc.	CS 4-4507	FG LP 0002
		TV 1033
		LL 12115
		CL3-3001
		SOR 0049
SEAMAN'S BLUES (Billy Talmadge Tubb-Ernest Tubb) Ernest Tubb Music, Inc.		FG LP 0002
		TV 1033
		LL 12118
		SOR 0049***
THANKS A LOT (Eddie Miller-Don Sessions) Regent Music		FG LP 0002
		TV 1033
		LL 12117
		CL3-3001
		SOR 0049†
BLUE EYED ELAINE (Ernest Tubb) Noma Music, Inc.		FG LP 001
		FG LP 0002††
		TV 1033††
		LL 12118††
		CL3-3001††
		SOR 0049††

08-14-78   Pete's Place; Nashville, Tennessee. 6:00-9:00 P.M. Producer: Pete Drake. Vocal: Ernest Tubb. Bass: Larry D. Emmons; Tommy D. Allsup. Rhythm guitar: Walter "Rusty" Adams. Lead electric guitar: Pete Michaud. Acoustic guitar: James D. Capps. Steel guitar: Lynn Owsley. Piano: Owen Bradley. Drums: Randy M. "Panda" Woolery.

*Vocal overdubs by Vern Gosdin 7-18-78 and 9-29-78 and by Waylon Jennings 10-3-78 and 10-12-78. Jennings appears only on those issues marked with an asterisk, playing a guitar break and singing the third verse. George Richey on piano was also a later overdub.

**Overdubbed by Johnny Paycheck 7-11-78 and 9-22-78. Grady Martin instrumental break overdubbed 11-10-78. "Guest Mixer" listed as Lou Bradley on this cut.

***Vocal and lead guitar dubbed by Merle Haggard 7-20-78. Shorty Lavender fiddle part and Jerry Carrigan on drums overdubbed 9-28-78. "Guest Mixer" here was rockabilly legend Scotty Moore.

†Vocal overdub by Loretta Lynn 8-3-78. Johnny Cox overdubbed a later steel part, and Scotty Moore again served as "Guest Mixer."

††Overdubbed by Justin Tubb 8-18-78 and 9-27-78; Phil Baugh and Jimmy Crawford overdubbed their instrumental break on 10-27-78. Billy Linneman overdubbed bass part, and Selby Coffeen was later the "Guest Mixer."

HALF A MIND* (Roger Miller) Tree Publishing   FGS 006   FG LP 0002

TV 1033

LL 12116

CL3-3001

SOR 0049

RAINBOW AT MIDNIGHT** (Lost John Miller)   FG LP 0002
Shapiro, Bernstein & Co.

TV 1033

LL 12118

LL 12119

SOR 0049

FILIPINO BABY*** (Billy Cox-Clark Van Ness)   FG LP 0002
Shapiro, Bernstein & Co.

TV 1033

LL 12118

SOR 0049

JIMMIE RODGERS'S LAST BLUE YODEL (THE   FG LP 0002
WOMEN MAKE A FOOL OUT OF ME)†   TV 1033
(Jimmie Rodgers) Peer International   LL 12117

CL3-3001

SOR 0049

IT'S BEEN SO LONG DARLING†† (Ernest Tubb)   FG LP 0002
Rightsong Music

TV 1033

LL 12117

SOR 0049

LL 12119

01-22-79   Pete's Place; Nashville. 6:00-9:00 P.M. Producer: Pete Drake. Vocal: Ernest Tubb. Bass: Larry D. Emmons. Rhythm guitar: Jack Solomon; Walter "Rusty" Adams; Tommy Hill. Lead electric guitar: Pete Michaud. Steel guitar: Lynn Owsley. Drums: Jimmy Joe Heap. Piano: Jeff Tweel.

ONE MORE DAY (Ernest Tubb) Pete Drake Music   LL 12117
I AIN'T BEEN RIGHT SINCE YOU WENT WRONG   LL 12118
(Ernest Tubb) Pete Drake Music
SAD SONGS AND WALTZES††† (Willie Nelson)   LL 12115
Tree Publishing Co.

*Overdubbed by George Jones 8-21-78 and 9-25-78. Buddy Emmons overdubbed steel guitar break on the latter date also. Two "Guest Mixers" for this cut: Glenn Snoddy and Lynn Snider.

**Overdubbed by Marty Robbins 8-20-78, who appears on all versions except LL 12119, the only Tubb solo release. Reggie Young overdubbed electric guitar break on 11-28-78. Henry Strezlecki also overdubbed a bass part.

***Duet overdubbed by George Jones 8-21-78 or 9-25-78. Guest mixer was Jerry Bradley, the pianist's son.

†Vocal overdubbed by Conway Twitty 8-17-78. The two parts of the song title are reversed on CD issue to read "The Women Make a Fool out of Me (Jimmie Rodgers' Last Blue Yodel)." Overdub musicians were Bob Moore on bass and Jerry Kennedy on lead guitar.

††Overdubbed by Conway Twitty 8-17-78. The only nonoverdubbed, solo Tubb release is LL-12117. Pete Wade overdubbed lead guitar part on 11-10-78. The other overdubbed musician was Ed Labunski, electric piano.

†††Vocal overdub by Gene Watson, date unknown.

| 1979 | Music City Recorders; Nashville, Tennessee. Producer: Biff Collie. Vocal: Ernest Tubb (as part of Atlas Artists Cowboy Rhythm Band)* | |

HOUSTON IS A HONKY TONK TOWN	AW 1040A
(Gail R. Redd-Mitchell Torok)	
Cedarwood Publishing/Parjo Enterprises	
WELCOME BACK AGAIN (Biff Collie) Unknown	AW 1040B
(WHAT THIS COUNTRY NEEDS IS) A GOOD OLD	AW 1046A
COUNTRY SONG (Vaughn Horton) Unknown	

05-19-80   Pete's Place; Nashville, Tennessee. 6:00-9:00 P.M. Producer: Pete Drake. Vocal: Ernest Tubb. Bass guitar: Harold Bradley. Rhythm guitar: Ronnie Dale Rotroff. Lead electric guitar: Pete Michaud. Steel guitar: John R. "Dumplin'" Cox. Drums: Jerry Don Borden. Piano: Owen Bradley.

DRIFTWOOD ON THE RIVER**	LL 12116
(John Klenner-Bob Miller) MCA Music, Inc.	SOR 0049
I'M GONNA MAKE MY HOME (A MILLION MILES	LL 12116
FROM HERE)*** (Ernest Tubb-Talmadge Tubb)	
Ernest Tubb Music, Inc.	
I'LL ALWAYS BE GLAD TO TAKE YOU HOME****	LL 12116
(Ernest Tubb) Rightsong Music, Inc.	
LETTERS HAVE NO ARMS† (Arbie Gibson-Ernest	LL 12116
Tubb) Unichappell Music, Inc.	
GIVE ME AN OLD FASHION LOVE†† (Ernest Tubb)	LL 12118
Ernest Tubb Music, Inc.	
TRY ME ONE MORE TIME††† (Ernest Tubb)	LL 12115
Noma Music	

05-20-80   Pete's Place; Nashville, Tennessee. 6:00-9:00 P.M. Producer: Pete Drake. Vocal: Ernest Tubb. Bass: Harold Bradley. Rhythm guitar: Ronnie Dale Rotroff. Lead electric guitar: Peter Michaud. Steel guitar: Johnny R. "Dumplin'" Cox. Drums: Jerry Don Borden. Piano: Owen Bradley.

*The Atlas Artists Cowboy Rhythm Band was an agglomeration of those artists Haze Jones was then booking through Atlas Artists. The artists—Ernest Tubb, Justin Tubb, Little David Wilkins, Dick Shuey, Ted Barton, Wyatt Webb, Charlie Louvin, Ernie Ashworth, Barbi Green, Little Roy Wiggins, Marty Martel, Charlie Walker, and Connie Eaton—were recorded separately. Musicians' tracks were laid down at two studios: Pete's Place on "Houston Is a Honky Tonk Town," and the Music Mill for the others.

**Vocal overdub by Billy Walker, date unknown.

***Note that parentheses are reversed from their position on all earlier Tubb recordings of the song. David Rodgers provided overdubbed duet part at unknown date.

****Obvious mistake: should be "BACK." Overdubbed by Chip Taylor at unknown date.

†Vocal overdub by Kris Kristofferson at unknown date. Tom Brumley plays overdubbed steel break, also of unknown date.

††Session logs tend to be cavalier about accuracy; here, no one bothered to render the correct title, "Give Me a Little Old-Fashioned Love."

†††Label only credits Jeannie Seely with overdubbed duet, but Jack Greene is here too; both artists added at unknown date.

I'LL STEP ASIDE* (Johnny Bond)	LL 12115
Unichappell Music, Inc.	SOR 0049
(WHEN YOU FEEL LIKE YOU'RE IN LOVE) DON'T	LL 12119
JUST STAND THERE** (Cherokee Jack Henley-	SOR 0049
Ernest Tubb) Ernest Tubb Music, Inc.	
I WONDER WHY YOU SAID GOODBYE***	LL 12117
(Ernest Tubb) Unichappell Music, Inc.	
I'M WITH A CROWD BUT SO ALONE†	LL 12119
(Elaine Tubb-Carl Story) Ernest Tubb Music, Inc.	SOR 0049
HAVE YOU EVER BEEN LONELY (HAVE YOU EVER	LL 12119
BEEN BLUE)†† (George Brown-Peter DeRose)	SOR 0049
Shapiro, Bernstein & Co.	

11-12-80 Pete's Place; Nashville, Tennessee. 10:00 A.M.-1:00 P.M. (first two songs); 2:00-5:00 P.M. Producer: Pete Drake. Vocal: Ernest Tubb. Bass guitar: Harold Bradley. Rhythm guitar: Ronnie Dale Rotroff; Ernest Tubb Jr.; Jack Solomon. Lead electric guitar: Peter Michaud. Steel guitar: Johnny R. "Dumplin'" Cox. Drums: Jimmy Joe Heap. Piano: Jeffrey Tweel.

MR. JUKE BOX††† (Eddie Davis-Ralph Davis)	LL 12115
Careers BMG Music Inc.	
TOMORROW NEVER COMES‡	LL 12115
(Ernest Tubb-Johnny Bond)	SOR 0049
Unichappell Music/Elvis Presley Music	
THERE'S A LITTLE BIT OF EVERYTHING IN	LL 12116
TEXAS‡‡ (Ernest Tubb)	SOR 0049
Unichappell Music/Elvis Presley Music	
SWEET THANG‡‡‡ (Nat Stuckey)	LL 12119
Tree Publishing/Su-Ma Publishing	SOR 0049

01-15-81 LSI Recording Studios; Nashville, Tennessee. 2:00-5:00 P.M. Producers: Phil Baugh, Buddy Emmons. Vocal: Ernest Tubb (1), Sammi Smith. Bass: Walter David Smith. Rhythm guitar: Leon Rhodes. Lead electric guitar: Phil Baugh. Steel guitar: Buddy Emmons. Drums: Terry L. McMillan, Murrey Harman. Piano: William Rainsford. Banjo: Victor Jordan.

I'LL BE YOUR SAN ANTONE ROSE (Susanna Clark)
Sunbury Music, Inc.

*Vocal overdubs at unknown date by Jack Greene, Jeannie Seely, and King Edward Smith.
**Overdubbed at unknown date by rock star Leon Russell and his country alter ego, Hank Wilson, playing the piano break.
***Vocal overdub by Crazy Joe, who is Joe Rhenda, pianist and comic, and at that time Carmol Taylor's manager.
†Vocal and lead guitar overdub by Roy Clark at unknown date.
††Vocal overdub by Mel Tillis, date unknown.
†††Jack Greene duet overdubbed at later date.
‡B. J. Thomas overdubbed harmony at later date.
‡‡Roy Clark overdubbed as lead guitarist at a later date.
‡‡‡Melba Montgomery part overdubbed at later date.

WALTZ ACROSS TEXAS (1) (Talmadge Tubb-Ernest   SF 432-FL
Tubb) Ernest Tubb Music, Inc.
CODE OF THE WEST (Marcia Lynn Beverly)

03-11-81   Pete's Place; Nashville, Tennessee. 6:00-9:00 P.M. Producer: Pete Drake. Vocal: Ernest Tubb. Bass guitar: Harold Bradley (acoustic on "Dear Judge"). Rhythm guitar: Ronnie Dale Rotroff; William Hullett. Lead electric guitar: Pete Michaud. Steel guitar: Lynn Owsley. Drums: Jerry Don Borden. Piano: Owen Bradley.

DEAR JUDGE* (Billy Hughes)	LL 12117
Unichappell Music, Inc.	
DRIVIN' NAILS IN MY COFFIN** (Jerry Irby)	LL 12119
Unichappell Music, Inc.	SOR 0049
YESTERDAY'S WINNER IS A LOSER TODAY***	LL 12117
(Ernest Tubb-Jimmie Skinner-Jesse Rodgers)	SOR 0049
Ernest Tubb Music, Inc.	
THAT WILD AND WICKED LOOK IN YOUR EYES	LL 12117
(Sam Nicholas)† Unichappell Music, Inc.	

Early 1981   Pete's Place; Nashville, Tennessee. Time: Unknown. Producer: Pete Drake. Vocal: Ernest Tubb.

ONE WAY LOVE (Floyd Tillman)	MG 5004
Points West Publishing Co.	

Unknown   (Texas Session) Gilley's Studio; Pasadena, Texas. Time: Unknown. Producer: Johnny Gimble. Vocal: Floyd Tillman. Fiddle: Johnny Gimble. Steel guitar: Herb Remington. Piano: Clyde Brewer. Acoustic guitar: Dick Gimble. Drums: Leo Dolan.

07-26-82   Creative Workshop; Nashville, Tennessee. 6:00-9:00 P.M. Producer: Joe Gibson. Vocal: Ernest Tubb (1); Billy Parker. Bass: Walter David Smith. Rhythm guitar: Leon Rhodes. Lead electric guitar: James D. Capps. Steel guitar: Doyle Lawton Grisham. Fiddle: Hubert D. "Hoot" Hester, Tommy Williams. Piano: Cecil Ray Cobb.

TOO MANY IRONS IN THE FIRE (James H. Forst)		SWS 3310
Hitkit Music		
TOMORROW NEVER COMES (1)	SW 4729	SWS 3310
(Ernest Tubb-Johnny Bond)		
Unichappell Music/Elvis Presley Music		

*Overdubbed vocal by Billy Parker, date unknown.

**Overdubbed guest vocalist Boxcar Willie also sings a tenor part in places. Date of his recording unknown.

***Overdubbed vocal by Gene Watson, date unknown.

†Title and author are misspelled on CD issue: last word should be "Eye," and the writer should be "Sam Nichols." Harmony duet by Razzy Bailey was added at later, unknown date.

LOVE DON'T KNOW A LADY (Merrill Lynn Lane)   SWS 3310
Hitkit Music/Merlane Music

08-05-82 Sound Stage Studio; Nashville, Tennessee. Time: Unknown. Producers: Jimmy
Bowen, Hank Williams Jr. Vocal: Ernest Tubb, Waylon Jennings, Hank
Williams Jr. Bass: David Hungate. Rhythm guitar: Kenny Mims. Lead electric
guitar: Billy Joe Walker; Reggie Young. Drums: Matt Betton Jr. Piano: Larry
Muhoberac. Keyboards: David Briggs. Clarinet: Dennis Solee. Mandolin:
Kieran Kane.

LEAVE THEM BOYS ALONE* (Dean Dillon-Hank   WB 7-29633 EL 60233
Williams Jr.-Gary Stewart-Tanya Tucker)   AHL 1-4826
Forrest Hills Music Inc./Tanya Tucker Music/
Tree Publishing Co.

*Johnnie Walker, Tubb's Nashville pianist, recalled that like his idol Jimmie Rodgers, Tubb had to rest at
this session on a studio cot.

INDEX

DISCOGRAPHY SONG TITLE INDEX

Ronnie Pugh is the Head of Reference at the Country Music
Foundation in Nashville.

Library of Congress Cataloging-in-Publication Data
Pugh, Ronnie.
Ernest Tubb : the Texas troubadour / Ronnie Pugh.
Discography: p.
Includes index.
isbn 0-8223-1859-8 (alk. paper)
1. Tubb, Ernest, 1914-   . 2. Country musicians—United States—
Biography.   I. Title.
ML420.T87P84   1996
782.42′1642′092—dc20
[B]   96-7918CIP